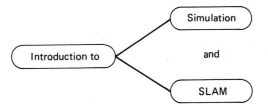

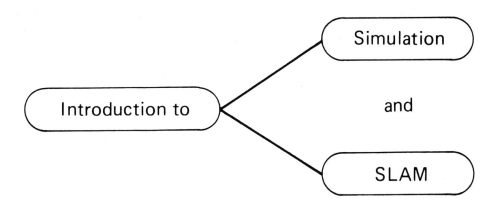

A. ALAN B. PRITSKER
Professor, *Purdue University*
President, *Pritsker & Associates, Inc.*

CLAUDE DENNIS PEGDEN
Associate Professor, *The Pennsylvania State University*
Consultant, *Pritsker & Associates, Inc.*

A HALSTED PRESS BOOK
JOHN WILEY & SONS
New York • Chichester • Brisbane

SYSTEMS PUBLISHING CORPORATION
West Lafayette, Indiana

Distributed by:

Halsted Press, a Division of
John Wiley & Sons, Inc., New York

and

Systems Publishing Corporation
P.O. Box 2161
West Lafayette, Indiana 47906

Library of Congress Cataloging in Publication Data
Pritsker, A   Alan B   1933–
    Introduction to simulation and SLAM.

    1. Digital computer simulation.   2. SLAM (Computer
program language)   I. Pegden, Claude Dennis, joint
author.   II. Title.
QA76.9.C65P74   001.4'24   78-23385
ISBN 0–470–26588–4

Printed in the United States of America
10 9 8 7 6 5 4 3 2

To Loring G. Mitten, a professor's professor; and
    C. B. Gambrell, Jr., a leader of men   ——AABP

To my parents,
    Claude H. and Phyllis I. Pegden   ——CDP

Preface

This textbook combines the presentation of a simulation language and the background material required for performing simulation projects. Thus, for the first time, a complete simulation methodology is available in textbook form.

SLAM, a new *s*imulation *l*anguage for *a*lternative *m*odeling, is described in detail. SLAM is an advanced FORTRAN based language that allows simulation models to be built based on three different world views. It provides network symbols for building graphical models that are easily translated into input statements for direct computer processing. It contains subprograms that support both discrete event and continuous model developments, and specifies the organizational structure for building such models. By combining network, discrete event, and continuous modeling capabilities, SLAM allows the systems analyst to develop models from a process-interaction, next-event, or activity-scanning perspective. The interfaces between the modeling approaches are explicitly defined to allow new conceptual views of systems to be explored.

In the text, Chapters 4 through 11 provide a detailed description of SLAM. Eighteen complete examples and numerous illustrations are provided. Input procedures and output reports are described. The organizational structure provided by SLAM for helping the analyst to build models is explained, illustrated, and applied.

The text supplies information on simulation techniques in general and the specific procedures for using simulation in industry and government. Chapters on the simulation approach to problem resolution (Chapter 1), simulation model building (Chapter 3), and applications of simulation (Chapter 14) are included. Chapter 2 provides the basic information on probability and statistics required by the simulation analyst when collecting and summarizing data, identifying system parameters, and generating sample values randomly. Chapter 13 presents the methods for estimating performance measures from simulation outputs. Procedures for obtaining simulation outputs efficiently are presented. A comparison of simulation languages is made in Chapter 12, and emphasis is given to the important factors that should be considered when choosing and using a simulation language.

Appendices are included to provide ready reference to the SLAM language elements and subprograms, inputs, and diagnostics. At the end of each chapter, exercises are given which require the application of the material presented.

This book can be used in courses in business, engineering, or computer science at the senior or first year graduate level depending on the goal of the course. Emphasis is placed on developing problem solving skills and the SLAM simulation language capabilities. Thus, many examples are provided that illustrate procedures for modeling systems. The probability and statistics chapters are written to support the material on simulation modeling and analysis. The book has been designed with the following chapter dependencies in mind.

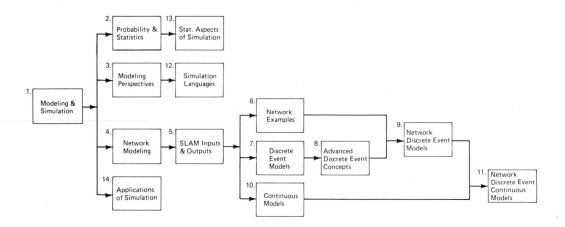

The SLAM program is maintained and distributed by Pritsker & Associates, Inc., P. O. Box 2413, West Lafayette, Indiana 47906, from whom copies of the source tape may be purchased.

Throughout the development of SLAM and the preparation of this textbook, we have received support and encouragement from many sources. We want to thank the faculty of the Industrial and Systems Engineering Department at the University of Alabama in Huntsville and the staff of Pritsker & Associates for their encouragement during this period. In particular, we gratefully acknowledge the unselfish aid and encouragement given by Professor Robert E. Shannon. In addition, we thank Professor Jafar Hoomani, Dean of Science and Engineering at the University of Alabama in Huntsville, and David B. Wortman, Vice President of Pritsker & Associates, for their support throughout this project.

Material contained in this book is based on information contained in books by Thomas Schriber, George S. Fishman, and Robert E. Shannon. We thank these friends for granting us permission to use materials from their books.

In the development, running, and debugging of SLAM, we received assistance from Steve Roberts, Mike Fague, and Srirup Gangopadhyay, graduate students at the University of Alabama in Huntsville, and Anne Spinosa and Jerome Sabuda of Pritsker & Associates. We gratefully acknowledge their help and their suggestions for improving the language. Throughout the years, we have received language design and development assistance from many individuals. In particular, the contributions of Nicholas R. Hurst, Ware Washam, and C. Elliott Sigal have been significant and we extend our appreciation for their efforts.

Our thanks go to Neal Bengtson, Steven Duket, Gordon Hazen, C. Elliott Sigal, and James R. Wilson for reviewing the manuscript and making suggestions that helped clarify important aspects of simulation and the SLAM language. In particular, we acknowledge the contributions of James R. Wilson in Chapter 13 on statistical aspects of simulation. We also want to thank Nicholas J. Crnich of R. R. Donnelley and Company and Andrée Coers of SSPA Typesetting, Inc., for their assistance in the design and manufacture of the book; Judy Duvall, Virginia Cunningham, Barbara Ford, and Laura Stevens for their efforts in typing, preparation of figures, and copying numerous drafts of the book; and Anne Pritsker for reviewing and editing the manuscript.

A. ALAN B. PRITSKER
CLAUDE DENNIS PEGDEN

West Lafayette, Indiana
August 1978

Table of Contents

Examples

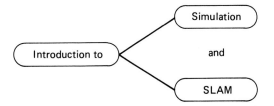

CHAPTER 1

Introduction to Modeling and Simulation

1.1   PROBLEM SOLVING

The problems facing industry, commerce, government, and society in general continue to grow in size and complexity. The need for procedures and techniques for resolving such problems is apparent. This book advocates the use of modeling and, in particular, simulation modeling for the resolution of problems. Simulation models can be employed at four levels:

- As explanatory devices to define a system or problem;
- As analysis vehicles to determine critical elements, components and issues;
- As design assessors to synthesize and evaluate proposed solutions;
- As predictors to forecast and aid in planning future developments.

1

In order to resolve problems using simulation models, it is necessary to understand the systems and to define problems relating to those systems. In our judgment, models should be developed to resolve specific problems. The form of the model, although dependent on the problem solver's background, requires an organized structure for viewing systems. A simulation language provides such a vehicle. It also translates a model description into a form acceptable by a computing system. The computer is used to exercise the model to provide outputs that can be analyzed in order that decisions relating to problem resolution can be made.

The primary emphasis of this book is on the presentation, documentation, and use of a new *s*imulation *l*anguage for *a*lternative *m*odeling, SLAM. SLAM supports the modeling of systems from diverse points of view. In this book, we model systems using these points of view and thus the book contains information on different methods of structuring models of systems.

SLAM has been designed to support engineers, managers, and researchers. To do this it provides, in addition to modeling views, extensive input and output capabilities. Since many of today's problems are statistical in nature, the input and output capabilities require a background in probability and statistics. Thus, parts of this book are devoted to presenting probabilistic and statistical concepts related to problem solving using simulation models.

The goal of this book is to provide useful information for problem solving. The book is both an introduction to simulation methodology and an introduction to SLAM. In this chapter, we present general discussions and definitions of simulation-related topics and our suggested procedure for conducting projects that resolve problems by employing simulation models.

1.2 MODELS

Models are *descriptions* of systems. In the physical sciences, models are usually developed based on theoretical laws and principles. The models may be scaled physical objects (iconic models), mathematical equations and relations (abstract models), or graphical representations (visual models). The usefulness of models has been demonstrated in describing, designing, and analyzing systems. Many students are educated in their discipline by learning how to build and use models. Model building is a complex process and in most fields is an art. The modeling of a system is made easier if: 1) physical laws are available that pertain to the system;

2) a pictorial or graphical representation can be made of the system; and 3) the variability of system inputs, elements, and outputs is manageable (7).

The modeling of complex, large-scale systems is often more difficult than the modeling of physical systems for the following reasons: 1) few fundamental laws are available; 2) many procedural elements are involved which are difficult to describe and represent; 3) policy inputs are required which are hard to quantify; 4) random components are significant elements; and 5) human decision making is an integral part of such systems. Through the use of a simulation approach, we will illustrate methods for alleviating these difficulties.

1.3   MODEL BUILDING

Since a model is a description of a system, it is also an *abstraction* of a system. To develop an abstraction, a model builder must decide on the elements of the system to include in his model. To make such decisions, a purpose for model building should be established. Reference to this purpose should be made when deciding if an element of a system is significant and, hence, should be modeled. The success of a modeler depends on how well he can define significant elements and the relationships between elements.

A pictorial view of our proposed model building approach is shown in Figure 1-1. A system is considered as a set of interdependent objects united to perform a specified function. The concept of a system is not well-defined. A particular definition of a system's objects, and their function is subjective and depends on the individual who is defining the system. Because of this, the first step of our approach is the development of a purpose for modeling that is based on a stated problem or project goal. Based on this purpose, the boundaries of the system and a level of modeling detail are established. This abstraction results in a model that smooths out many of the rough ill-defined edges of the actual system. We also include in the model the desired performance measures and design alternatives to be evaluated. These can be considered as part of the model or as inputs to the model. Assessments of design alternatives in terms of the specified performance measures are considered as model outputs. Typically, the assessment process requires redefinitions and redesigns. In fact, the entire model building approach is performed iteratively. When recommendations can be made based on the assessment of alternatives, an implementation phase is initiated. Implementation should be carried out in a well-defined environment with an explicit set of recommendations. Major decisions should have been made before implementation is attempted.

Simulation models are ideally suited for carrying out the problem-solving approach illustrated in Figure 1-1. Simulation provides the flexibility to build either aggregate or detailed models. It also supports the concepts of iterative model building by allowing models to be embellished through simple and direct additions. These aspects of simulation models are described in the next section.

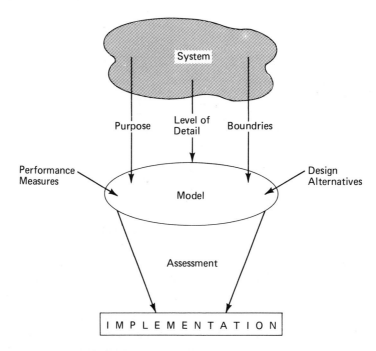

Figure 1-1.   A model building approach for problem solving.

1.4   SIMULATION MODELS

In this book, we restrict our attention to simulation models that are built for use on digital computers. Within this context, a simulation model is a mathematical-logical representation of a system which can be exercised in an experimental fashion on a digital computer. Thus, a simulation model can be considered as a laboratory version of a system. Once a simulation model is developed, experiments can be performed. These experiments, or simulations, permit inferences to be drawn about systems

- Without building them, if they are only proposed systems;
- Without disturbing them, if they are operating systems that are costly or unsafe to experiment with;
- Without destroying them, if the object of an experiment is to determine their limits of stress.

In this way, simulation models can be used for design, procedural analysis, and performance assessment (6).

Simulation has been used to study such wide ranging topics as urban systems, economic systems, business systems, production systems, biological systems, social systems, transportation sytems, health care delivery systems, and many more. Table 1-1 presents areas in which simulation methods are currently being used (2). Surveys by Shannon and Biles (8), Turban (10), and Weston as reported by Shannon (9) all indicate that simulation and statistical methods are the most widely-used management science and operations research techniques employed by industry and government.

Table 1-1   Areas in which simulation methods are currently being used†.

Air traffic control queuing	Industry models
Aircraft maintenance scheduling	Textile
Airport design	Petroleum (financial aspects)
Ambulance location and dispatching	Information system design
Assembly line scheduling	Intergroup communication (sociological studies)
Bank teller scheduling	Inventory reorder rule design
Bus (city) scheduling	Aerospace
Circuit design	Manufacturing
Clerical processing system design	Military logistics
Communication system design	Hospitals
Computer time sharing	Job shop scheduling
Telephone traffic routing	Aircraft parts
Message system	Metals forming
Mobile communications	Work-in-process control
Computer memory-fabrication test-facility design	Shipyard
Consumer behavior prediction	Library operations design
Brand selection	Maintenance scheduling
Promotion decisions	Airlines
Advertising allocation	Glass furnaces
Court system resource allocation	Steel furnaces
Distribution system design	Computer field service
Warehouse location	National manpower adjustment system
Mail (post office)	Natural resource (mine) scheduling
Soft drink bottling	Iron ore
Bank courier	Strip mining
Intrahospital material flow	Parking facility design

Table 1-1   (*continued*)

Enterprise models	Numerically controlled production facility design
Steel production	Personnel scheduling
Hospital	Inspection department
Shipping line	Spacecraft trips
Railroad operations	Petrochemical process design
School district	Solvent recovery
Equipment scheduling	Police response system design
Aircraft	Political voting prediction
Facility layout	Rail freight car dispatching
Pharmaceutical center	Railroad traffic scheduling
Financial forecasting	Steel mill scheduling
Insurance	Taxi dispatching
Schools	Traffic light timing
Computer leasing	Truck dispatching and loading
Insurance manpower hiring decisions	University financial and operational forecasting
Grain terminal operation	Urban traffic system design
Harbor design	Water resources development

†Source: Emshoff, J. R. and R. L. Sisson, *Design and Use of Computer Simulation Models,* ©1970, p. 264. Reprinted by permission of The Macmillan Company, New York, N.Y.

Simulation modeling assumes that we can describe a system in terms acceptable to a computing system. In this regard, a key concept is that of a *system state description*. If a system can be characterized by a set of variables, with each combination of variable values representing a unique state or condition of the system, then manipulation of the variable values simulates movement of the system from state to state. This is precisely what simulation is: *the representation of the dynamic behavior of the system by moving it from state to state in accordance with well-defined operating rules.*

Changes in the state of a system can occur continuously over time or at discrete instants in time. Although the procedures for describing the dynamic behavior of discrete and continuous change models differ, the basic concept of simulating a system by portraying the changes in the state of the system over time remains the same. In the next section, we will illustrate this fundamental concept with a simple discrete change system.

1.5   SIMULATION OF A BANK TELLER

As an example of the concept of simulation, we will examine the processing of customers by a teller at a bank. Customers arrive to the bank, wait for service by the teller if the teller is busy, are served, and then depart the system. Customers arriving to the system when the teller is busy wait in a single queue in front of the teller. For simplicity, we assume that the time of arrival of a customer and the service time by the teller for each customer are known. These values are given in Table 1-2. Our objective is to manually simulate the above system to determine the percent of time the teller is idle and the average time a customer spends at the bank.

Since a simulation is the dynamic portrayal of the changes in the state of a system over time, the states of the system must be defined. For this example, they can be defined by the status of the teller (busy or idle) and by the number of customers at the bank. The state of the system is changed by: 1) a customer arriving to the bank; and 2) the completion of service by the teller and subsequent departure of the customer. To illustrate a simulation, we will determine the state of the system over time by processing the events corresponding to the arrival and departure of customers in a time-ordered sequence.

The manual simulation of this example corresponding to the values in Table 1-2 is summarized in Table 1-3 by customer number. It is assumed that there are initially no customers in the system, the teller is idle, and the first customer is to arrive at time 3.2.

In Table 1-3, columns (1) and (2) are taken from Table 1-2. The start of service time given in column (3) depends on whether the preceding customer has departed the bank. It is taken as the larger value of the arrival time of the customer and the departure time of the preceding customer. Column (4), the departure time, is the sum of the column (3) and the service time for the customer given in Table 1-2. Values for time in queue and time in bank for each customer are computed as shown in Table 1-3. Average values per customer for these variables are 2.61 minutes and 5.81 minutes, respectively.

Table 1-2 Customer arrival and service times.

Customer Number	Time of Arrival (Minutes)	Service Time (Minutes)
1	3.2	3.8
2	10.9	3.5
3	13.2	4.2
4	14.8	3.1
5	17.7	2.4
6	19.8	4.3
7	21.5	2.7
8	26.3	2.1
9	32.1	2.5
10	36.6	3.4

Table 1-3 presents a good summary of information concerning the customer but does not provide information about the teller and the queue size for the teller. To portray such information, it is convenient to examine the events associated with the situation.

Table 1-3   Manual simulation of bank teller.

Customer Number (1)	Arrival Time (2)	Start Service Time (3)	Departure Time (4)	Time in Queue (5)=(3)−(2)	Time in Bank (6)=(4)−(2)
1	3.2	3.2	7.0	0.0	3.8
2	10.9	10.9	14.4	0.0	3.5
3	13.2	14.4	18.6	1.2	5.4
4	14.8	18.6	21.7	3.8	6.9
5	17.7	21.7	24.1	4.0	6.4
6	19.8	24.1	28.4	4.3	8.6
7	21.5	28.4	31.1	6.9	9.6
8	26.3	31.1	33.2	4.8	6.9
9	32.1	33.2	35.7	1.1	3.6
10	36.6	36.6	40.0	0.0	3.4

The logic associated with processing the arrival and departure events depends on the state of the system at the time of the event. In the case of the arrival event, the disposition of the arriving customer is based on the status of the teller. If the teller is idle, the status of the teller is changed to busy and the departure event is scheduled for the customer by adding his service time to the current time. However, if the teller is busy at the time of an arrival, the customer cannot begin service at the current time and, therefore, he enters the queue (the queue length is increased by 1). For the departure event, the logic associated with processing the event is based on queue length. If a customer is waiting in the queue, the teller status remains busy, the queue length is reduced by 1, and the departure event for the first waiting customer is scheduled. However, if the queue is empty, the status of the teller is set to idle.

An event-oriented description of the bank teller status and the number of customers at the bank is given in Table 1-4. In Table 1-4, the events are listed in chronological order. A graphic portrayal of the status variables over time is shown in Figure 1-2. These results indicate that the average number of customers at the bank in the first 40 minutes is 1.4525 and that the teller is idle 20 percent of the time.

In order to place the arrival and departure events in their proper chronological order, it is necessary to maintain a record or calendar of future events to be processed. This is done by maintaining the times of the next arrival event and next

Table 1-4 Event-oriented description of bank teller simulation.

Event Time	Customer Number	Event Type	Number in Queue	Number in Bank	Teller Status	Teller Idle Time
0.0	—	Start	0	0	Idle	—
3.2	1	Arrival	0	1	Busy	3.2
7.0	1	Departure	0	0	Idle	
10.9	2	Arrival	0	1	Busy	3.9
13.2	3	Arrival	1	2	Busy	
14.4	2	Departure	0	1	Busy	
14.8	4	Arrival	1	2	Busy	
17.7	5	Arrival	2	3	Busy	
18.6	3	Departure	1	2	Busy	
19.8	6	Arrival	2	3	Busy	
21.5	7	Arrival	3	4	Busy	
21.7	4	Departure	2	3	Busy	
24.1	5	Departure	1	2	Busy	
26.3	8	Arrival	2	3	Busy	
28.4	6	Departure	1	2	Busy	
31.1	7	Departure	0	1	Busy	
32.1	9	Arrival	1	2	Busy	
33.2	8	Departure	0	1	Busy	
35.7	9	Departure	0	0	Idle	
36.6	10	Arrival	0	1	Busy	0.9
40.0	10	Departure	0	0	Idle	

departure event. The next event to be processed is then selected by comparing these event times. For situations with many events, an ordered list of events would be maintained which is referred to as an event file or event calendar.

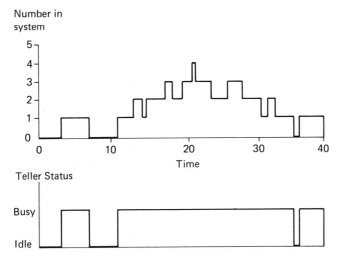

Figure 1-2 Graphic portrayal of bank teller simulation.

There are several important concepts illustrated by this example. We observe that at any instant in simulated time, the model is in a particular *state*. As *events* occur, the state of the system may change as prescribed by the logical-mathematical relationships associated with the events. Thus, the events define the dynamic structure of the system. Given the starting state, the logic for processing each event, and a method for specifying sample values, our problem is largely one of bookkeeping. An essential element in our bookkeeping scheme is an event calendar which provides a mechanism for recording and sequencing future events. Another point to observe is that we can view the state changes from two perspectives: 1. the *process* that the customer encounters as he seeks service (the customer's view); or 2. the *events* that cause the state of the teller to change (the teller's or bank's view). These so called world views are described in detail in Chapter 3.

1.6   THE SIMULATION PROCESS

As we alluded to earlier, the process for the successful development of a simulation model consists of beginning with a simple model which is embellished in an evolutionary fashion to meet problem-solving requirements. Within this process, the following stages of development can be identified.†

1. Problem Formulation	The definition of the problem to be studied including a statement of the problem-solving objective.
2. Model Building	The abstraction of the system into mathematical-logical relationships in accordance with the problem formulation.
3. Data Acquisition	The identification, specification, and collection of data.
4. Model Translation	The preparing of the model for computer processing.
5. Verification	The process of establishing that the computer program executes as intended.
6. Validation	The process of establishing that a desired accuracy or correspondence exists between the simulation model and the real system.

---

† The stages listed are a slightly modified version of those presented by Shannon (9).

7. Strategic and Tactical Planning	The process of establishing the experimental conditions for using the model.
8. Experimentation	The execution of the simulation model to obtain output values.
9. Analysis of Results	The process of analyzing the simulation outputs to draw inferences and make recommendations for problem resolution.
10. Implementation and Documentation	The process of implementing decisions resulting from the simulation and documenting the model and its use.

Although some of these steps were discussed in conjunction with model building, we prefer to restate them here due to the importance of the concepts.

The first task in a simulation project is the construction of a clear definition of the problem and an explicit statement of the objectives of the analysis. Because of the evolutionary nature of simulation, problem definition is a continuing process which typically occurs throughout the duration of the study. As additional insights into the problem are gained and additional questions become of interest, the problem definition is revised accordingly.

Once an initial problem statement is formulated, the task of formulating a model of the system begins. The model of a system consists of both a static and dynamic description. The static description defines the elements of the system and the characteristics of the elements. The dynamic description defines the way in which the elements of the system interact to cause changes to the state of the system over time.

The actual process of formulating the model is one which is largely an art. The modeler must understand the structure and operating rules of the system and be able to extract the essence of the system without including unnecessary detail. The model should be easily understood, yet sufficiently complex to realistically reflect the important characteristics of the real system. The crucial decisions concern what simplifying assumptions are valid, what elements should be included in the model, and what interactions occur between the elements. The amount of detail included in the model should be based on the purpose for which the model is being built. Only those elements that could cause significant differences in decision-making need be considered.

Both the problem formulation and modeling phases require close interaction among project personnel. "First cut" models should be built, analyzed, and discussed. In many cases, this will require heroic assumptions and a willingness on the part of the modeler to expose his potential ignorance of the system under study. However, an evolutionary modeling process allows inaccuracies to be discovered more quickly and corrected more efficiently than would otherwise be possible. Furthermore, the close interaction in the problem definition and model formulation phases creates confidence in the model on the part of the model user and therefore helps to ensure a successful implementation of simulation results.

The model formulation phase will generate data input requirements for the model. Some of the data required may be readily available while other data requirements may involve considerable time and cost for collection. Typically, such data input values are initially hypothesized or based on a preliminary analysis. In some cases, the exact values for one or more of the input parameters may have little effect on the simulation results. The sensitivity of the simulation results to changes in the input data to the model can be evaluated by making a series of simulation runs while varying the input parameter values. In this way, the simulation model can be used to determine how best to allocate money and time in refining the input data to the model.

Once a model has been developed and initial estimates have been established for the input data, the next task is to translate the model into a computer acceptable form. Although a simulation model can be programmed using a general purpose language, there are distinct advantages to using a simulation language. In addition to the savings in programming time, a simulation language also assists in model formulation by providing a set of concepts for articulating the system description. In this text, we describe in detail the use of the SLAM simulation language which provides a graphical vehicle that combines the model formulation and translation task into a single activity. SLAM also includes a programming capability to allow models to be embellished in an evolutionary fashion to any level of detail required to reflect the complexities of the system being studied.

The verification and validation stages are concerned with evaluating the performance of the simulation model. The verification task consists of determining that the translated model executes on the computer as the modeler intended. This is typically done by manual checking of calculations. Fishman and Kiviat (3) describe statistical methods which can aid in the verification process. The validation task consists of determining that the simulation model is a reasonable representation of the system (11). Validation is normally performed in levels. We recommend that a validation be performed on data inputs, model elements, subsystems, and interface points. Validation of simulation models, although difficult, is a significantly easier task than validating other types of models, for example, validating a linear programming formulation. In simulation models, there is a correspondence between the model elements and system elements. Hence, testing for reasonableness involves a comparison of model and system structure and comparisons of the number of times elemental decisions or subsystem tasks are performed.

Specific types of validation involve evaluating reasonableness using all constant values in the simulation model or assessing the sensitivity of outputs to parametric variation of data inputs. In making validation studies, the comparison yardstick should be both past system outputs and experiential knowledge of system performance behavior. A point to remember is that past system outputs are but one sample record of what could have happened.

Strategic and tactical planning refer to the task of establishing the experimental conditions for the simulation runs (1). The strategic planning task consists of developing an efficient experimental design to either explain the relationship between the simulation response and the controllable variables, or to find the combination of values for the controllable variables which either minimize or maximize the simulation response. In contrast, tactical planning is concerned with how each simulation within the experimental design is to be made to glean the most information from the data. Two specific issues in tactical planning are the starting conditions for simulation runs and methods for reducing the variance of the mean response.

The next stages in the simulation development process are experimentation and analysis of results. These phases of simulation development involve the exercising of the simulation model and the interpretation of the outputs. When simulation results are used to draw inferences or to test hypotheses, statistical methods should be employed.

The final stages in the simulation development process are the implementation of results and the documentation of the simulation model and its use. No simulation project should be considered complete until its results are used in the decision-making process. The success of the implementation task is largely dependent upon the degree to which the modeler has successfully performed the other activities in the simulation development process. If the model builder and model user have worked closely together and they both understand the model and its outputs, then it is likely that the results of the project will be implemented with vigor. On the other hand, if the model formulation and underlying assumptions are not effectively communicated, then it is more difficult to have recommendations implemented, regardless of the elegance and validity of the simulation model.

The stages of simulation development outlined above are rarely performed in a structured sequence beginning with problem definition and ending with documentation. A simulation project may involve false starts, erroneous assumptions which must later be abandoned, reformulation of the problem objectives, and repeated evaluation and redesign of the model. If properly done, however, this iterative process should result in a simulation model which properly assesses alternatives and enhances the decision-making process (4, 5).

1.7   CHAPTER SUMMARY

Simulation is a technique that has been employed extensively to solve problems. Simulation models are abstractions of systems. They should be built quickly, explained to all project personnel, and changed when necessary. The implementation of recommendations to improve system performance is an integral part of the simulation methodology.

1.8   EXERCISES

1-1. Define the elements shown in Figure 1-1 for a specific problem related to your organization. Include proposed design alternatives, assessment procedures, and one possible implementation outcome. Repeat this exercise from your supervisor's (instructor's) perspective.

1-2. Categorize the areas listed in Table 1-1 according to the courses you have taken during your academic studies.

1-3. Explain how a simulation language supports modeling from a problem organization standpoint.

1-4. In the simulation of the bank teller, hypothesize a relation between the average time in bank per customer and average number of customers in the bank. Determine if your hypothesis holds for average time in queue and average number in queue.

1-5. Discuss how a simulation language impacts on each of the stages of the simulation process.

1-6. Describe the operation of a machine tool.

1-7. Describe the events associated with maintaining accounting records.

1-8. Reduce the number of stages in the simulation process from ten to seven by combining the most similar activities. Provide a rationale for your decisions.

1-9. Discuss how a data base system could support your simulation modeling and analysis activities.

1.9 REFERENCES

1. Conway, R. W., B. M. Johnson, and W. L. Maxwell, "Some Problems of Digital Systems Simulation," *Management Science,* Vol. 6, 1959, pp. 92-110.
2. Emshoff, J. R. and R. L. Sisson, *Design and Use of Computer Simulation Models,* Macmillan, 1970.
3. Fishman, G. S. and P. J. Kiviat, "Analysis of Simulated Generated Time Series," *Management Science,* Vol. 13, 1967, pp. 525-557.
4. Mihram, G. A., "The Modeling Process," *IEEE Transactions on Systems, Man and Cybernetics,* Vol. SMC-2, 1972, pp. 621-629.
5. Mihram, G. A., *Simulation: Statistical Foundations and Methodology,* Academic Press, 1972.
6. Pritsker, A. A. B., *The GASP IV Simulation Language,* John Wiley, 1974.
7. Pritsker, A. A. B., *Modeling and Analysis Using Q-GERT Networks,* Halsted Press and Pritsker & Associates, Inc., 1977.
8. Shannon, R. E. and W. E. Biles, "The Utility of Certain Curriculum Topics to Operations Research Practitioners," *Operations Research,* Vol. 18, 1970, pp. 741-745.
9. Shannon, R. E., *Systems Simulation: The Art and Science,* Prentice-Hall, 1975.
10. Turban, E., "A Sample Survey of Operations Research Activities at the Corporate Level," *Operations Research,* Vol. 20, 1972, pp. 708-721.
11. Van Horn, R. L., "Validation of Simulation Results," *Management Science,* Vol. 17, 1971, pp. 247-258.

CHAPTER 2

Probability and Statistics

2.1   INTRODUCTION

Systems to be simulated are generally composed of one or more elements that have uncertainty associated with them. Such systems evolve through time in a manner that is not completely predictable and are referred to as stochastic systems. The simulation of stochastic systems requires that the variability of the elements in the system be characterized using probability concepts. The outputs from a simulation model are also probabilistic, and therefore statistical interpretations about them are usually required. Although the reader will likely have some familiarity with probability and statistics, this chapter is included to provide a review of important probability and statistics concepts related to simulation modeling and analysis.†
We presume the reader has had previous exposure to probability and statistics at the level of one of the introductory books listed at the end of the chapter (7, 12, 14, 19).

2.2   EXPERIMENT, SAMPLE SPACE, AND OUTCOMES

An experiment is a well defined procedure or process whose outcome is observable but is not known with certainty in advance. The set of all possible outcomes

---

† Readers only interested in the statistical problems related to simulation should go directly to Section 2.15.

is called the sample space. If the sample space is finite or countably infinite, it is said to be discrete; otherwise it is continuous.

Outcomes can be combined to form new outcomes† by the set theory operations of union ($\cup$) and intersection ($\cap$). If the outcome C is defined as the union of a set of outcomes A and a set of outcomes B, denoted $C = A \cup B$, then C consists of the set of all outcomes within A or B. If the outcome D consists of the intersection of A and B, denoted $D = A \cap B$, then D consists of the set of outcomes that are in both A and B.

As an example of the concepts discussed above, consider the operation of a single teller bank system. Customers arrive to the bank, possibly wait, and are processed by the teller. Both the time between arrivals of customers to the bank and the service time by the teller will be assumed to exhibit variability. Let us define our first experiment as observing the time between customer arrivals to the bank. The sample space for the experiment consists of all possible observations for the time between arrivals. Since the time between customer arrivals can be any nonnegative real value, the sample space is continuous. An outcome is defined as any subset of the sample space, and therefore one possible outcome could be defined as the occurrence of an interarrival time between 8 and 9 minutes.

As a second example, consider the experiment of observing the number of customers processed during the first hour of operation. The number of customers processed during the first hour can be any of the values 0, 1, 2, 3, . . . , that is, the set of nonnegative integers. In this case, the sample space is discrete. One possible outcome could be defined as the processing of five customers during the one hour period.

2.3 PROBABILITY

The probability of an outcome is a measure of the degree of likelihood that the outcome will occur. More formally, a probability measure is a function $\mathbf{P}(\ )$ which maps outcomes into real numbers and satisfies the following axioms of probability:

1. $0 \leqslant \mathbf{P}(E) \leqslant 1$ for any outcome E
2. $\mathbf{P}(S) = 1$ where S is the sample space or "certain outcome"

---

† Typically, the term "event" is used to describe combinations of outcomes. In simulation terminology, an event is defined differently so we avoid its use here.

3.   If E_1, E_2, E_3, . . . are mutually exclusive outcomes, then

$$\mathbf{P}(E_1 \cup E_2 \cup E_3 \ldots) = \mathbf{P}(E_1) + \mathbf{P}(E_2) + \mathbf{P}(E_3) + \ldots$$

From these three axioms and the rules of set theory, the basic laws of probability can be derived. However, these axioms are not sufficient to compute the probability of an outcome. Numerical values for probabilities are usually difficult to obtain; nevertheless it is useful to postulate their existence.

In some simple cases, the exact probability of an outcome can be calculated using combinatorial analysis. Examples of this include determining the probability of h heads in n tosses of a fair coin and computing the probability of three aces in a five card hand. However, in most cases the exact probability of an outcome cannot be calculated. In such cases, an approximate value for the probability of an outcome can sometimes be obtained using the frequency interpretation of probability. If we repeat an experiment n times and outcome E occurs k times, then $\frac{k}{n}$ is the proportion of times that E occurs. The probability of E can be interpreted as

$$\mathbf{P}(E) = \lim_{n \to \infty} \frac{k}{n},$$

assuming the limit exists. By selecting a sufficiently large value of n, the proportion of occurrences, $\frac{k}{n}$, approximates the probability of E. The approximate values for probabilities obtained in this way can be shown to satisfy the axioms of probability stated earlier. The practical limitation of this approach is that it is sometimes not possible or economical to perform the required experimentation.

2.4   RANDOM VARIABLES AND PROBABILITY DISTRIBUTIONS

A function which assigns a real number to each outcome in the sample space is called a random variable. Discrete random variables are those that take on a finite or a countably infinite set of values. Continuous random variables can take on a continuum of values. In our example of the bank teller system, the inter-arrival time is a continuous random variable and the number of customers processed during the first hour is a discrete random variable.

A probability distribution is any rule which assigns a probability to each possible value of a random variable. The rule for assigning probabilities takes on two distinct forms depending upon whether the random variable is discrete or continuous.

For discrete random variables, the probability associated with each value of the random variable is commonly specified using a probability mass function, p(x), defined as†

$$p(x_i) = \mathbf{P}(X = x_i)$$

For each possible value x_i, the function assigns a specific probability that the random variable X assumes the value x_i. The axioms of probability impose the following restrictions on $p(x_i)$.

$$0 \leqslant p(x_i) \leqslant 1 \qquad \text{for all i}$$

$$\sum_{\text{all i}} p(x_i) = 1$$

An alternate representation for the probability distribution is the cumulative distribution function, F(x), defined as follows:

$$F(x) = \mathbf{P}(X \leqslant x)$$

In this case, the function F(x) specifies the probability that the random variable X assumes a value less than or equal to x. From the axioms of probability, F(x) must have the following properties:

$$0 \leqslant F(x) \leqslant 1 \qquad \text{for all x,}$$
$$F(-\infty) = 0,$$
and
$$F(\infty) = 1.$$

The distribution function is related to the probability mass function by

$$F(x) = \sum_{x_i \leqslant x} p(x_i)$$

As an example of a discrete probability distribution, consider an experiment consisting of three tosses of a fair coin. Let the random variable X denote the number of heads obtained from the three tosses. The random variable X can assume the discrete value of 0, 1, 2, or 3. There are eight possible outcomes of which 1 has 0 heads, 3 have 1 head, 3 have 2 heads and 1 has 3 heads. The probability mass function for the random variable X is depicted in Figure 2-1 and the cumulative distribution function is depicted in Figure 2-2.

---

† When presenting probability and statistics concepts, we will attempt to use a capital letter to indicate a random variable and a lower case letter to indicate an observed potential numerical value. Sometimes this is not feasible; however, the context of the discussion should clarify the situation.

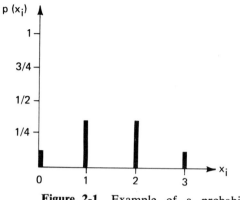

Figure 2-1 Example of a probability mass function.

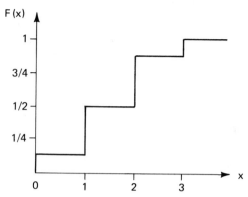

Figure 2-2 Example of a cumulative distribution function.

For continuous random variables, a different form for the probability distribution is required. Since the random variable can assume any of an uncountably infinite number of values, the probability of a specific value is zero. This does not say that the value is impossible, but that the value is extremely unlikely given the infinite number of alternative values. However, the probability that the variable assumes a value in the interval between two distinct points a and b will generally not be zero. Therefore, the probability mass function as defined for the discrete case is replaced in the continuous case by the probability density function, $f(x)$, defined according to the following relationship

$$P(a \leqslant X \leqslant b) = \int_a^b f(x)dx$$

Thus the probability density function, when integrated between a and b, gives the probability that the random variable will assume a value in the interval between a and b. To be consistent with the axioms of probability, the probability density function must satisfy the following conditions

$$f(x) \geqslant 0$$

$$\int_{-\infty}^{\infty} f(x)dx = 1$$

The cumulative distribution function, $F(x)$, defined for the continuous case is

$$F(x) = \int_{-\infty}^{x} f(y)dy = P(X \leqslant x)$$

The function $F(x)$ defines the probability that the continuous random variable X assumes a value less than or equal to x.

As an example of a continuous probability distribution, consider a random variable X which can assume any value in the range between 0 and 1. Assuming that each of the uncountably infinite number of possible values are equally likely, the corresponding probability density function and cumulative distribution function are shown in Figures 2-3 and 2-4, respectively. The probability that the random variable X assumes a value in the interval between .50 and .75 is the area under the probability density function between .50 and .75. For the random variable depicted in Figure 2-3, this probability is equal to .25.

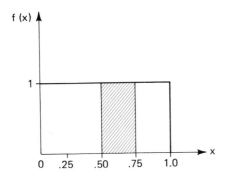

Figure 2-3 Example of a probability density function.

Figure 2-4 Example of a cumulative distribution function.

A random variable can also be both continuous and discrete. Random variables of this type are referred to as having "mixed" distributions. A random variable having a mixed distribution can assume either discrete values with finite probabilities or a continuum of values as prescribed by a probability density function. Figure 2-5 depicts such a distribution where the discrete values 1 and 2 each occur with a probability of 1/3 as denoted by the spikes on the graph. The values between 1 and 2 are governed by the density function $f(x) = 1/3$.

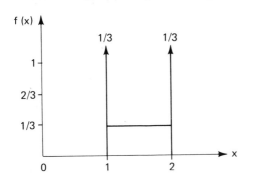
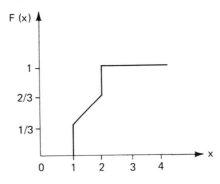

Figure 2-5 Example of a mixed distribution.

Such a distribution would result if samples were drawn from a continuous distribution with equally likely values in the range from 0 to 3, with values greater than 2 set to 2, and values less than 1 set to 1. The equation for the cumulative distribution function for this random variable is

$$F(x) = \begin{cases} 0 & x < 1 \\ \dfrac{1}{3} + \dfrac{x-1}{3} & 1 \leqslant x < 2 \\ 1 & x \geqslant 2 \end{cases}$$

From this equation and Figure 2-5, we see that $F(x)$ has discontinuities at $x = 1$ and $x = 2$. At points of discontinuity, $P(X=x)$ is equal to the jump which $F(x)$ makes at the point x. For example, $P[X=1] = 1/3$. However, for $1 < x < 2$, $F(x)$ is continuous at x and $P(X=x) = 0$.

2.5 EXPECTATION AND MOMENTS

It is sometimes desirable to characterize a random variable by one or more values which summarize information contained in its probability distribution function. The expectation or expected value of a random variable X, denoted E[X], is such a value and is defined as follows:

$$E[X] = \sum_{\text{all } i} x_i\, p(x_i) \qquad \text{when X is discrete}$$

$$E[X] = \int_{\text{all } x} x\, f(x)\, dx \qquad \text{when X is continuous}$$

The expectation is a probability weighted average of all possible values of X and therefore a measure of centrality for the distribution. For this reason, it is called the mean value.

Expectations can be taken of functions of random variables. In particular, the expectation of X^n is defined as the nth moment of a random variable and can be expressed as follows

$$E[X^n] = \sum_{\text{all } i} x_i{}^n p(x_i) \qquad \text{when X is discrete}$$

$$E[X^n] = \int_{\text{all } x} x^n\, f(x)\, dx \qquad \text{when X is continuous}$$

The expected value is a special case of the above when n=1, and, hence, is called the first moment.

A variant of the nth moment is the nth moment about the mean which is defined as

$$E[(X - E[X])^n]$$

In this case, the expected value of X is subtracted from X before computing the nth moment.

A moment of particular importance in probability theory is the second moment about the mean, commonly referred to as the variance of X, and is denoted as σ^2 or Var[X]. The variance of a random variable is a measure of the spread of the probability distribution. If a random variable has a small variance, then samples tend to occur near the expected value. The square root of the variance is referred to as the standard deviation of the random variable.

If X and Y are random variables, then the covariance of X and Y, denoted Cov[X,Y], is defined as

$$Cov[X,Y] = E[(X - E[X])(Y - E[Y])]$$

The covariance is important because it measures the linear association, if any, between X and Y. If the outcome of X has no influence on the outcome of Y, then X and Y are said to be independent and the Cov[X,Y] will be zero. More formally, X and Y are independent if and only if:

$$p(y|x) = p(y)$$ in the discrete case where $p(y|x)$ is the probability that Y=y given X=x

$$f(y|x) = f(y)$$ in the continuous case where $f(y|x)$ is the conditional density function of Y for X=x.

These statements specify that the probability distribution of Y given knowledge of X is the same as the probability distribution of Y without knowledge of X.

A measure of dependence which is related to the covariance is the correlation coefficient, ρ, defined as

$$\rho = \frac{Cov[X,Y]}{\sqrt{Var[X] \cdot Var[Y]}}$$

The correlation coefficient has a range from -1 to 1 with a value of zero indicating no correlation between X and Y. A positive sign indicates that Y tends to be high when X is high, and a negative sign indicates that Y tends to be low when X is high. The magnitude of ρ indicates the degree of linearity of Y plotted against X. If a plot of Y versus X is a straight line, then $\rho = \pm 1$. If X and Y are independent, then a plot of Y versus X will produce random points and ρ will equal zero. Typical scatter diagrams of Y versus X for different values of ρ are depicted in Figure 2-6.

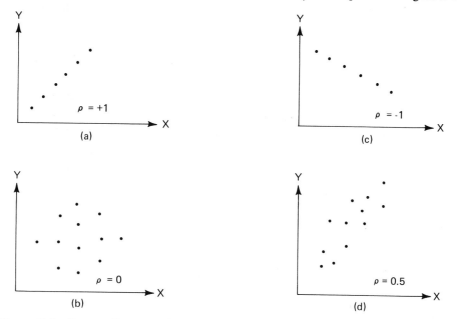

Figure 2-6   Scatter diagrams of Y versus X for various values of ρ.

2.6   FUNCTIONS OF RANDOM VARIABLES

A function of a random variable is itself a random variable. In this section, we summarize several important properties of functions of random variables.

If X and Y are random variables and k is any arbitrary constant, then the following properties for expectation can be derived:

$$E[X + Y] = E[X] + E[Y]$$
$$E[kX] = kE[X]$$
$$E[X + k] = E[X] + k$$

The similar properties for variances are less obvious than those for expectation and are

$$Var[X + Y] = Var[X] + Var[Y] + 2\,Cov[X,Y]$$
$$Var[kX] = k^2\,Var[X]$$
$$Var[X + k] = Var[X]$$
$$Var[kX + nY] = k^2\,Var[X] + n^2\,Var[Y] + 2kn\,Cov[X,Y]$$

Note that if X and Y are independent random variables, then the $Cov[X,Y]$ is zero, and

$$Var[X + Y] = Var[X] + Var[Y] \qquad \text{for X and Y independent}$$

A random variable of considerable importance in statistics is the sample mean, $\overline{X}_I$, of I samples from a probability distribution. The sample mean is defined as the sum of the samples divided by the number of samples and can be notationally expressed as

$$\overline{X}_I = \frac{1}{I} \sum_{i=1}^{I} X_i$$

Assuming that the X_i are independent and identically distributed (iid) random variables and using the properties of expectation and variance, we can derive the following results:

$$E[\overline{X}_I] = E[X]$$

and
$$Var[\overline{X}_I] = \frac{Var[X]}{I}$$

The variance of the sample mean of I independent samples is a factor $1/I$ smaller than the variance of the random variable from which the samples are drawn. Hence, by selecting a sufficiently large I, the variance of the sample mean can be reduced to an arbitrarily small value.

Note that the relationship given above for the variance of $\overline{X}_I$ applies only if the samples are independent. If the samples are not independent, the calculation of $Var[\overline{X}_I]$ requires the consideration of the covariances between samples. For example, in the bank teller problem, the waiting times for successive customers will be correlated because there is a greater likelihood that the $(i+1)$st customer will be delayed if the ith customer waits than if the ith customer begins service immediately. Hence the variance of the average waiting time cannot be estimated by simply dividing the variance of the waiting time by the number of samples. Such a sequence of correlated samples is referred to as an autocorrelated series. In Section 2.15 and in Chapter 13, we will address the problem of estimating the variance of a sample mean for an autocorrelated series.

2.7   GENERATING FUNCTIONS

A commonly referred to function of a random variable is the generating function. Several types of generating functions have been defined and we will discuss only the probability generating function and the moment generating function. The probability generating function for a discrete random variable is defined as

$$A(s) = \sum_i p(x_i)s^i$$

If $A(s)$ is known in a closed form then the probabilities, $p(x_i)$, can be obtained by taking the ith derivative with respect to s and setting s equal to zero. (If $A(s)$ is in a polynomial form, $p(x_i)$ can be seen by inspection.) The expectation of X can be obtained from $A(s)$ by taking the first derivative with respect to s and setting s=1. Higher order moments can be obtained in a similar fashion but require combinations of derivatives. A function related to the probability generating function is the Z-transform.

The moment generating function, MGF, of a random variable X, is defined as

$$M(s) = E[e^{sX}]$$

The nth moment about the origin is obtained by taking the nth derivative with respect to s, that is,

$$\frac{d^n M(s)}{ds^n} = E[X^n e^{sX}]$$

By setting s=0, we have $E[X^n]$. A function related to the moment generating function is the characteristic function.

In addition to obtaining moments of a random variable from generating functions, they are useful for obtaining moments of sums of independent random variables. For example, if $W = X + Y$ and X and Y are independent then

$$E[e^{sW}] = E[e^{s(X+Y)}] = E[e^{sX}]E[e^{sY}]$$

Thus, the MGF of W is the product of the MGFs of X and Y. The moments for W can then be obtained from its MGF. Tables of probability generating functions and moment generating functions for the commonly used random variables are available (4,10).

2.8   LAW OF LARGE NUMBERS AND
CENTRAL LIMIT THEOREM

There are two important theorems which characterize the behavior of $\overline{X}_I$ as the number of samples increases to infinity. The first theorem is the strong law of large numbers and states the intuitive result that as the sample size, I, increases, that with probability one, $\overline{X}_I$ approaches E[X]. An associated result referred to as the weak law of large number is:

$$\lim_{I \to \infty} \mathbf{P}\{|\overline{X}_I - E[X]| > \epsilon\} = 0 \qquad \text{for any positive } \epsilon$$

This simply says that for any positive value of ϵ, however small, the probability that the difference between $\overline{X}_I$ and E[X] exceeds ϵ approaches zero as I approaches infinity.

The second important theorem which characterizes the behavior of $\overline{X}_I$ is the Central Limit Theorem. This theorem states that under certain mild conditions, the distribution of the sum of I independent samples of X approaches the normal distribution† as I approaches infinity, regardless of the distribution of X. Hence, sample means are approximately normally distributed for sufficiently large I. It is difficult to say what sample size is sufficient for assuring normality. However, relatively small sample sizes, like 10 to 15, are often sufficient. Many variations of the central limit theorem exist. In particular, one variation involves the conditions under which the central limit theorem is applicable for sequences of dependent random variables. These conditions are described in the Appendix to Chapter 13.

2.9   DISTRIBUTIONS

In the previous sections, we described properties of random variables and their distributions in general. We now describe several specific distributions which are important in modeling random processes. The characteristics of the distributions that would lead a modeler to select a particular random variable type to represent

---

† The normal distribution is described in the next section.

a random process or activity are described. For a more formal discussion and graphical descriptions of distributions, the books "Statistical Methods in Engineering" by Hahn and Shapiro (11) and "Statistical Distributions" by Hastings and Peacock (13) are recommended.

Throughout the discussion, the following variable definitions will be used:

$$X = \text{the random variable}$$
$$f(x) = \text{the density function of X}$$
$$p(x) = \text{probability mass function of X.}$$
$$a = \text{minimum;}$$
$$b = \text{maximum;}$$
$$m = \text{mode;}$$
$$\mu = \text{mean} = E[X]$$
$$\sigma^2 = \text{variance} = E[(X-\mu)^2]$$
$$\sigma = \text{standard deviation}$$
$$\alpha = \text{a parameter of the density function}$$
$$\beta = \text{a parameter of the density function}$$

For those density functions which are not expressed in terms of μ and σ, formulas for μ and σ will be given.

2.9.1   Uniform Distribution

The uniform density function specifies that every value between a minimum and maximum value is equally likely. The use of the uniform distribution often implies a complete lack of knowledge concerning the random variable other than that it is

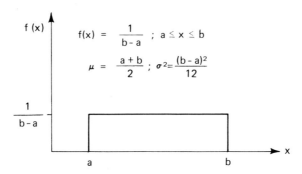

$$f(x) = \frac{1}{b-a} \; ; \; a \leq x \leq b$$

$$\mu = \frac{a+b}{2} \; ; \; \sigma^2 = \frac{(b-a)^2}{12}$$

Figure 2-7   Uniform density function and illustration.

between a minimum value and a maximum value. Another way of saying this is that the probability that a value is in a specified interval is proportional to the length of the interval. Another name for the uniform distribution is the rectangular distribution. Figure 2-7 gives the density function for the uniform distribution and its graph.

2.9.2   Triangular Distribution

The triangular distribution is one step up from the uniform distribution. For this distribution, three values are specified: a minimum, a mode, and a maximum. The density function consists of two linear parts: one part increases from the minimum to the mode value; and the other part decreases from the mode value to the maximum. The average associated with a triangular density is the sum of the minimum, mode and maximum divided by 3. The triangular distribution is used when a most likely value can be ascertained along with minimum and maximum values, and a piecewise linear density function seems appropriate. Figure 2-8 gives the density function for the triangular distribution and its graph.

The triangular distribution is easy to use and explain, and should be given serious consideration when hypothesizing a form for a random variable.

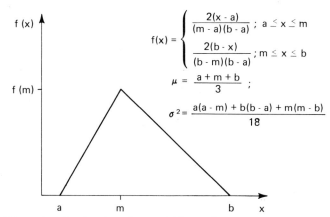

$$f(x) = \begin{cases} \dfrac{2(x-a)}{(m-a)(b-a)} & ; \ a \le x \le m \\[2mm] \dfrac{2(b-x)}{(b-m)(b-a)} & ; \ m \le x \le b \end{cases}$$

$$\mu = \frac{a+m+b}{3} \ ;$$

$$\sigma^2 = \frac{a(a-m)+b(b-a)+m(m-b)}{18}$$

Figure 2-8   Triangular density function and illustration.

2.9.3   Exponential Distribution

If the probability that one and only one outcome will occur during a small time interval Δt is proportional to Δt and if the occurrence of the outcome is independent of the occurrence of other outcomes then the time interval between occurrences of outcomes is exponentially distributed. Another way of saying the above is that the activity characterized by an exponential distribution has the same probability of being completed in any subsequent period of time Δt. Thus, if the activity has been ongoing for t time units, the probability that it will end in the next Δt time units is the same as if it had just been started. This lack of conditioning of remaining time on past time expended is called the Markov or forgetfulness property. There is direct association between the assumption of an exponential activity duration and Markovian assumptions. The use of an exponential distribution assumes a large variability. If the expected duration of an activity is μ, then the variance is μ^2. The exponential distribution has one of the largest variances associated with it of the common distribution types. The exponential distribution can be manipulated mathematically with ease and is assumed for many studies because of this property.

Figure 2-9 gives the density function for the exponential distribution and its graph.

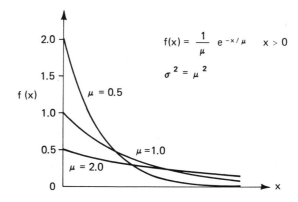

Figure 2-9   Exponential density function and illustrations.

2.9.4   Poisson Distribution

The Poisson distribution is a discrete distribution and usually pertains to the number of outcomes occurring in a specified time period. If the duration of time between outcomes is exponentially distributed and they occur one at a time, then the number that occur in a fixed time interval can be shown to be Poisson distributed. Thus, if the interarrival distribution is exponential, the number of arrivals will be Poisson distributed. The Poisson distribution is frequently used as a limiting case approximation to the binomial distribution where the binomial distribution is used to represent a series of independent Bernoulli trials (an outcome of a trial is go-no go, success-failure, yes-no). For large mean, the normal distribution is used to approximate the Poisson distribution.

Figure 2-10 gives the Poisson probability mass function and illustrates its form.

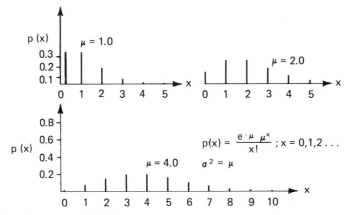

Figure 2-10   Poisson probability mass function and illustrations.

2.9.5   Normal Distribution

The normal or Gaussian distribution is the most prominent distribution in probability and statistics. Justification for the use of the normal distribution comes from the Central Limit Theorem which, as discussed previously, specifies that under very broad conditions the distribution of the average or sum of I independent observations from any distribution approaches a normal distribution as I becomes large. Thus, when dealing with phenomena that are related to sums of random variables, approximation by a normal distribution should be considered.

Because of the Central Limit Theorem, it is easy to see why the normal distribution has received a great amount of attention and use in applications of probability and statistics. There is another reason for the heavy use of the normal distribution. The normal distribution also has the advantage of being mathematically tractable and consequently many techniques of statistical inference such as regression analysis and analysis of variance have been derived under the assumption of an underlying normal density function.

As discussed above, for large mean, the normal distribution is a good approximation to the Poisson distribution, which in turn is a limiting distribution for the binomial distribution.

Figure 2-11 gives the density function for the normal distribution and illustrates the distribution for selected values of the mean and standard deviation.

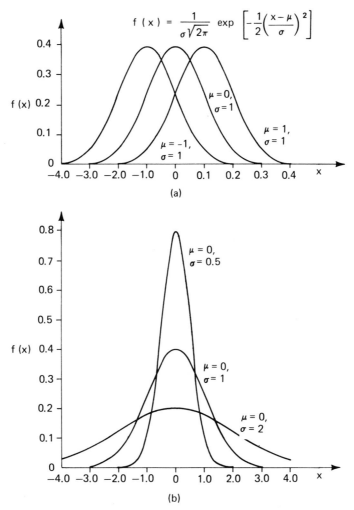

Figure 2-11 Normal density function and illustrations.

2.9.6 Lognormal Distribution

The lognormal distribution is the distribution of a random variable whose natural logarithm follows the normal distribution (11). The lognormal distribution is appropriate for a multiplicative type process in the same manner that the normal distribution is applicable for additive type processes. By use of the Central Limit Theorem, it can be shown that the distribution of the product of independent positive random variables approaches a lognormal distribution.

If a set of data is transformed by taking the logarithm of each data point, and if the transformed data points are normally distributed, then the original data is said to be lognormally distributed. The lognormal distribution has been used as an appropriate model in a wide variety of situations from biology to economics. It is an appropriate model for processes where the value of an observed variable is a random proportion of the previous observed value. Examples of such processes include the distribution of personal incomes, inheritances and bank deposits, and the distribution of particle sizes.

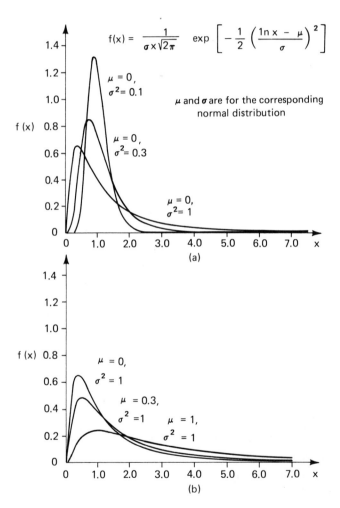

Figure 2-12   Lognormal density function and illustrations.

Figure 2-12 gives the density function for the lognormal distribution and illustrates the distribution for selected values of the mean and variance.

2.9.7   Erlang Distribution

The Erlang distribution is derived as the sum of independent and identically distributed exponential random variables. It is a special case of the gamma distribution, and the density function, illustrations and remarks concerning the gamma distribution apply to the Erlang distribution. The Erlang distribution is used extensively in queueing theory when an activity or service time is considered to occur in phases with each phase being exponentially distributed.

2.9.8   Gamma Distribution

The gamma distribution is a generalization of the Erlang distribution where conceptually the number of sums of exponentials included need not be integer valued. Gamma distributed times can take on values between 0 and infinity. By different parameter settings, the gamma distribution can be made to take on a variety of shapes and, hence, can represent many different physical processes.

The gamma distribution is related to the normal distribution as the sum of squares of normal random variables, which is the chi-squared distribution, is a special case of the gamma distribution. Thus, special cases of the gamma are the chi-squared distribution, the Erlang distribution, and, hence, the exponential distribution.

Figure 2-13 gives the density function for the gamma distribution and illustrates the density function for selected values of its parameters.

2.9.9   Beta Distribution

The beta distribution is defined over a finite range and can take on a wide variety of shapes for different values of its parameters. It can be bell shaped, symmetric or asymmetric, or it can be U-shaped within the finite range. For U-shaped beta functions, the value of the density function goes to infinity as the ends of the range are approached. A simple variant of the beta distribution is referred to as the Pareto distribution which is used to characterize income distributions. Due to the wide

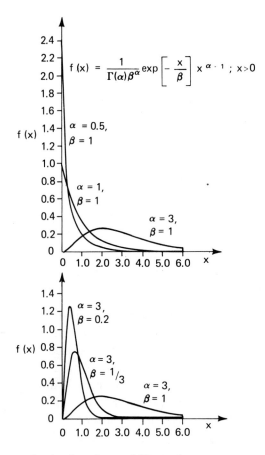

Figure 2-13   Gamma density function and illustrations.

variety of shapes obtainable for the beta distribution, it has been used to fit many different types of data.†

Since the beta distribution is defined over a finite interval, it has been used to describe situations which have a finite range. Examples of this are density functions related to percentages and probability estimates. Frequently, the beta distribution is used as the a priori distribution of the parameter of a binomial process by

---

† In this regard, the warning given by Feller (9) with regard to the law of logistic growth should be mentioned: ".. the only trouble with the theory is that not only the logistic distribution but also the normal, the Cauchy and other distributions can be fitted to the same material with the same or better goodness-of-fit ... Most contradictory theoretical models can be supported by the same observational material."

Bayesian statisticians. Another use of the beta distribution is as the descriptive density function associated with an activity duration in PERT. Subjective estimates of the activity duration based on optimistic (a), pessimistic (b), and most likely (m) values are combined to estimate the mean and variance of the beta distribution as $(a+4m+b)/6$ and $(b-a)^2/36$ respectively.

Figure 2-14 gives the density function for the beta distribution and illustrates the density function for selected values of its parameters.

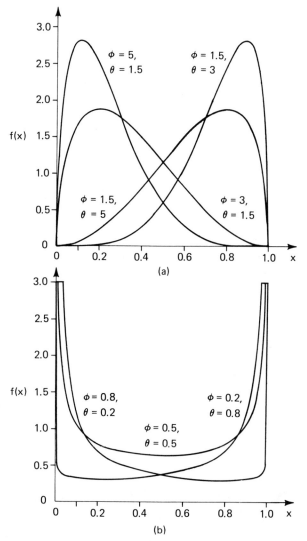

Figure 2-14   Beta density function and illustrations.

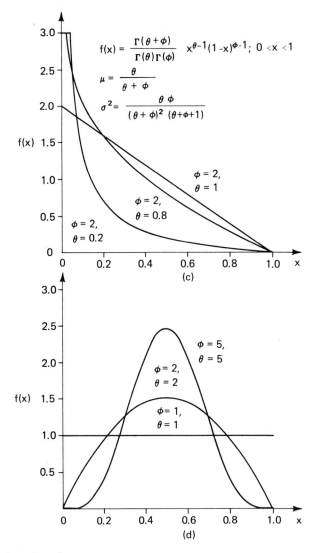

Figure 2-14   (*continued*).

2.10   GENERATING PSEUDORANDOM NUMBERS

Simulation models normally require a method for obtaining random samples from one or more of the distributions described in the last section. The most practical method for generating random samples from a prescribed distribution on a digital computer is to first generate one or more uniform random samples between 0 and 1 and then to transform the uniform sample (or samples) into a new sample with the desired distribution. Independent samples that are uniformly distributed in the interval 0 to 1 are called random numbers and provide the basis for generating samples from all other distributions. We therefore focus first upon the problem of obtaining random numbers and then address the procedures for their transformation into samples from other distributions.

There are at least three methods for obtaining random numbers for digital simulation. The first method is to read a table of random numbers (23) into the computer and then treat the random numbers as data for the simulation problem. The major shortcomings of this method are related to the relative slowness of computers in reading data from an external device and the need to store large tables. A second method is to employ a physical device such as a vacuum tube which generates random noise. A major objection to this method is that the simulation results are not reproducible, thereby complicating model verification and controlled experimentation with model parameters. The third and preferred method is to employ a recursive equation which generates the $(i+1)$st random number from the ith random number. Since the sequence of numbers is produced deterministically by an equation, they are not truly random, and therefore are referred to as "pseudorandom" numbers. However, throughout the text, we will commonly shorten the phrase and refer to such numbers as simply random numbers, with the understanding that they are actually pseudorandom.†

The above discussion indicates the properties that are desirable in a pseudorandom number generator. These are:

1. The numbers should be uniformly distributed in the interval (0,1);
2. The numbers should be independent and, hence, no correlation should exist in a sequence of random numbers;
3. Many numbers should be generated before the same number is obtained. This is referred to as the period or cycle length of the generator;
4. A random number sequence should be reproducible. This implies that different starting values or seeds should be permitted to allow different sequences to be generated;

---

† Because they are generated on digital computers by deterministic methods, there is a great deal of controversy over the definition of pseudorandom numbers. From our perspective and approach to simulation, Lehmer's definition is appealing, " . . . a vague notion embodying the idea of a sequence in which every term is unpredictable to the uninitiated and whose digits pass a certain number of tests . . . depending somewhat on the uses to which the sequence is to be put." (16)

5. The generator should be fast, as many numbers may be required in a simulation; and

6. A low storage requirement is preferred.

The technique which best satisfies these properties and which is in common use today is referred to the congruential method.

The congruential method employs the following recursive equation:

$$z_{i+1} = (az_i + b)(\mathrm{mod}\ c) \qquad i = 0,1,2,\ldots$$
$$r_{i+1} = z_{i+1}/c$$

where z_o is the seed value and r_i is the ith pseudorandom number. This equation denotes that the unnormalized random number, z_{i+1}, is equal to the remainder of $(az_i + b)$ divided by c where z_i is the previous unnormalized random number, z_o is an initial value or seed, and a, b, and c are constants. The assignment of values to the constants a, b, and c has been the subject of intensive research. Fishman (9) presents an excellent review of how to set the constants and the procedures for testing random number generators. In an appendix to this chapter, we summarize the suggested rules for setting a, b, and c for congruential random number generators. Although the rules given in the appendix provide general guidelines for selecting the constants a, b, and c, the overall best values are computer dependent. *We, therefore, recommend that the modeler employ a random number generator that has been specifically designed for the computer on which the simulation model is to be run.*

In simulation modeling, it is frequently desirable to employ several random number streams within the same model. For example, separate random number streams could be employed in a queueing system to model the arrival and service process. In this manner, the same sequence of arrival times can be generated without regard to the order in which service is performed. Thus, different service procedures could be evaluated for the same sequence of arrivals. Random number generators provide for parallel streams by allowing the modeler to provide a different seed value for each stream to be employed.

2.10.1   The Inverse Transformation Method

Random numbers are used as the basis for obtaining samples from a prescribed distribution. The simplest and most fundamental technique which forms the basis for generating such samples is the *inverse transformation method* (1,9). This method uses the information that the random variable $R = F(X)$ is uniformly distributed on the unit interval [0,1]. Thus, to generate a random sample from the distribution of X, we generate a random number r and solve the equation

$$r = F(x)$$

for the corresponding value of $x = F^{-1}(r)$. The proof for the validity of the method is straightforward (20,22) and is based on the following reasoning. Let $R = F(X)$ have distribution function $G(\cdot)$. Then, for $0 \leqslant r \leqslant 1$, we have

$$G(r) = \mathbf{P}[F(X) \leqslant r] = \mathbf{P}[X \leqslant F^{-1}(r)] = F(F^{-1}(r)) = r.$$

Thus, R is uniformly distributed on [0,1].

To illustrate the method for a continuous distribution, consider the problem of generating a sample from the exponential distribution. The cumulative distribution for the exponential is $F(x) = 1 - e^{-\lambda x}$ where $1/\lambda$ is the mean of the exponential. Setting $F(x)$ equal to r and then solving for x yields

$$x = -(1/\lambda) \, ln(r)$$

Hence, if r is uniformly distributed in the range 0 to 1, then x given by the above equation is exponentially distributed with a mean value of $1/\lambda$.

The method is also applicable to discrete distributions. For example, consider the following probability mass function

$$p(0) = .25$$
$$p(1) = .50$$
$$p(2) = .25$$

The cumulative distribution function, $F(x)$, is depicted in Figure 2-15. To obtain a sample from the above distribution, a random number is generated in the range

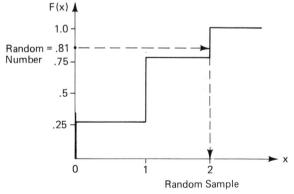

Figure 2-15   Illustration of the inverse transform method for obtaining a sample from a given distribution.

0 to 1, and the graph is entered at this ordinate value. The resulting random sample is then obtained by tracing across the graph to the cumulative curve, and then down to the x-axis. For example, the random number 0.81 yields a random sample of 2 as shown. The intuitive justification for this procedure is that 25 percent of the random numbers are in the range [0,.25], 50 percent in [.25,.75] and 25 percent in [.75,1.00] which is the desired distribution function. An arbitrary but consistent decision should be made at the break points.

The difficulty with the inverse transformation method lies in finding the inverse transformation $F^{-1}(r)$. In some cases, the method leads to a simple explicit transformation as was illustrated for the exponential distribution. However, there are continuous distributions that do not have closed-form inverse functions. Fortunately, for each of the important distributions for which this is the case, special techniques have been developed for generating random samples. The methods employed in SLAM for obtaining random samples are described in Appendix G.

2.11   TESTS FOR RANDOMNESS

The statistical validity of the results of a simulation model are dependent upon the degree of randomness of the random number generator employed. Because of this, many statistical procedures have been developed for testing random number generators. However as noted by Hull and Dobell (15) ". . . no finite class of tests can guarantee the general suitability of a finite sequence of numbers. Given a set of tests, there will always exist a sequence of numbers which passes these tests but which is completely unacceptable for some particular application." This reservation does not present a serious problem as a simulation analyst only desires the properties of randomness that were previously described.

Both analytical and empirical tests have been used to investigate the randomness properties of random number generators. These include the Frequency Test, Serial Test, Gap Test, Sum-of-Digits Tests, Runs Test, as well as many others. Empirical results from the use of the tests are contained in Lewis (16) and Fishman (9). Fishman also describes the spectral (6) and latticed (5,17) procedures for measuring the performance of congruential random number generators with regard to their departure from the desired randomness properties.

2.12   DATA COLLECTION AND ANALYSIS

An essential function in simulation modeling is the collection and analysis of data. This function is required in both defining inputs for the model and in obtaining performance measures from experimentation with the model. In this section, we will review some of the important statistical concepts applicable to data collection and analysis.

2.12.1   Data Acquisition

Data acquisition is the process of obtaining data on a phenomenon of interest. There are a variety of methods by which the data can be acquired. In some cases, the data are available in existing documents, and the problem is that of locating and accessing the data. In other cases, data acquisition may involve the use of questionnaires, field surveys, and physical experimentation.

In aggregate models such as those of urban or economic systems, the required data can frequently be obtained from existing documentation. Common sources of data for these models include census reports, the Statistical Abstract of the United States, United Nations publications, and other publications of governmental and international organizations. Sometimes such data are available in both report form and on computer tape.

In models of business systems, a valuable source of data is the accounting and engineering records of the company. These records are rarely sufficient to form the complete basis for estimating product demand, production cost, and other relevant data. However, they represent a starting point. Questionnaires and field surveys are also potential methods for obtaining data for industrial models.

Physical experimentation is commonly the most expensive and time consuming method for obtaining data. This process includes measurement, recording, and editing of the data. Considerable care must be taken in planning the experiment to assure that the experimental conditions are representative and that the data are recorded correctly. For a discussion of experimental design considerations in data collection, the reader is referred to the text by Bartee (3).

In some cases, there may be no existing data and the available budget or nature of the system may preclude experimentation. An example of such a case would be the use of simulation modeling to compare several proposed assembly line lay-outs. A possible approach to data acquisition in such cases is the use of synthetic or predetermined data (2,18). In this method, estimates of activity durations are synthesized by using tables of standard data. Thus, this method permits activity times to be estimated before the process is actually in operation.

2.12.2   Descriptive Statistics

In both collecting data for defining inputs to the model and collecting data on system performance from the model, we encounter the problem of how to convert the raw data to a usable form. Hence, we are interested in treatments designed to summarize or describe important features of a set of data. These treatments nor-mally summarize the data at the expense of a loss of certain information contained within the data.

Grouping Data.   One method for transforming data into a more manageable form is to group the data into classes or cells. The data is then summarized by tabulating the number of data points which fall within each class. This kind of table is called a frequency distribution table and normally gives a good overall picture of the data. An example of a frequency distribution table for data collected on customer waiting times is depicted below.

Waiting Time (Seconds)	Number of Customers
0 → 20	21
20 → 40	35
40 → 60	42
60 → 80	35
80 → 100	19
100 → 120	10
> 120	10

The numbers in the right-hand column denote the number of customers falling into each class and are called the class frequencies. The numbers in the left-hand column define the range of values in each class and are referred to as the class limits. The difference between the upper class limit and lower class limit in each case is called the class width. Classes with an unbounded upper or lower class limit are referred to as open. If a class has bounded limits, it is denoted as closed. Frequently, the first and/or last class in a frequency distribution will be open.

There are several variations of the class frequency tables which are useful for displaying grouped data. One variation is the cumulative frequency which is obtained by successively adding the frequencies in the frequency table. The cumulative frequency table for the customer waiting time data is depicted below.

Waiting Time Less Than	Cumulative Number of Customers
20	21
40	56
60	98
80	133
100	152
120	162
∞	172

The values in the right hand column represent the cumulative or total number of customers whose waiting time was less than the upper class limit specified in the left hand column. Another variation is obtained by converting the class frequency table (or cumulative table) into a corresponding frequency distribution by dividing each class frequency (cumulative frequency) by the total number of data points. Frequency distributions are particularly useful when comparing two or more distributions.

The frequency and cumulative distribution are sometimes presented graphically in order to enhance the interpretability of the data. The most common among graphical presentations is the histogram which displays the class frequencies as rectangles whose lengths are proportional to the class frequency. Figure 2-16 depicts a histogram for the customer waiting time data.

The primary consideration in the construction of frequency distributions is the specification of the number of classes and the upper and lower class limits for each class. These choices depend upon the nature and ultimate use of the data; however, the following guidelines are offered.

1. Whenever possible, the class widths should be of equal length. Exceptions to this are the first and last classes which are frequently open.

2. Class intervals should not overlap and all data points should fall within a class. In other words, each data point should be assignable to one and only one class.

3. Normally at least five but no more than twenty classes are used.

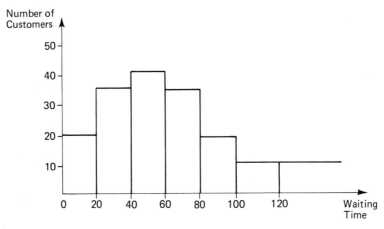

Figure 2-16   Histogram for customer waiting time data.

Parameter Estimation.   If a set of data points consists of all possible observations of a random variable, we refer to it as a *population;* if it contains only part of these observations, we refer to it as a *sample*. Another method for summarizing a set of data is to view the data as a sample which is then used to estimate the parameters of the parent or underlying population. The population parameters of most frequent interest are the mean which provides a measure of centrality, and the variance which provides a measure of dispersion.

To illustrate, consider again the data on customer waiting times. This data can be viewed as a sample from the population which consists of all possible customer waiting times. We can use this sample data to estimate the mean customer waiting time and the variance of the customer waiting time for the population of all possible customers.

Different symbols are used to distinguish between population parameters and estimates of these parameters based upon a sample. The greek letters μ and σ^2 are often used to denote the population mean and variance, respectively. The corresponding estimates of these parameters based upon the sample record $x_1, x_2, \ldots,$ x_I are the average, denoted as $\bar{x}_I$, and the variance estimate, denoted as s_x^2. In order to further distinguish between descriptions of populations and descriptions of samples, the first are referred to as parameters and the second are referred to as statistics.

Before proceeding with this discussion of descriptive statistics, a clarifying point regarding the notation used to describe random samples and experimental values of a random variable or stochastic sequence is necessary. Before an experimental value is observed, it is a random variable denoted by X_i. After a value is observed, it is denoted by x_i. By the sample mean, $\bar{X}_I$, we refer to a random variable that is the sum of I random samples before they are observed divided by I. The average, $\bar{x}_I$, however, is the sum of I observed values x_i divided by I. In an analogous fashion, S_x^2 is the random variable describing an estimate of the sample variance before experimental values are observed and s_x^2 is the estimate of the variance of observed values. This notation conforms to our policy of using capital letters for random variables where possible and lower case letters for numerical quantities.

In constructing estimates of the population parameters from sample data, there are two distinct cases to consider. In the first case, we consider a sample record where we are concerned only with the value of each observation and not the times at which the observations were recorded. The data on customer waiting times is an example of such a record. Statistics derived from a time independent sample record are referred to as *statistics based upon observations*.

The second case to be considered is for variables which have values defined over time. For example, the number of busy tellers in a bank is a random variable that has a value which is defined over time. In this case, we require knowledge of both the values assumed by the random variable and the time periods for which each value persisted. Statistics derived from time dependent records are referred to as *statistics on time-persistent variables*.

The formulas for calculating $\bar{x}_i$ and s_x^2 for both statistics based upon observations and statistics on time-persistent variables are summarized in Table 2-1. For the time-persistent case the sample mean is designated by $\bar{x}_T$ where T is the total time interval observed. Sometimes the formulas for s_x^2 are given in a slightly different form, however the form shown is the most convenient for computational purposes. Note that for statistics based upon observations, the $\sum_{i=1}^{I} x_i$, the $\sum_{i=1}^{I} x_i^2$, and the number of samples I, are sufficient to compute both $\bar{x}_I$ and s_x^2. Similarly, for statistics on time-persistent variables, $\int_0^T x \, dt$, $\int_0^T x^2 \, dt$, and T are required.

Another statistic which is commonly employed in summarizing a set of data is the coefficient of variation, $s_X/\bar{x}_I$. The coefficient of variation expresses the sample

Table 2-1   Formulas for calculating the average and variance of a sample record.

Statistic	Formula	
	Statistics based upon Observations	Statistics for Time Persistent Variables
Sample Mean	$$\bar{x}_I = \frac{\sum\limits_{i=1}^{I} x_i}{I}$$	$$\bar{x}_T = \frac{\int_0^T x(t)\,dt}{T}$$
Sample Variance	$$s_X^2 = \frac{\sum\limits_{i=1}^{I} x_i^2 - I\bar{x}_I^2}{I-1}$$	$$s_X^2 = \frac{\int_0^T x^2(t)\,dt}{T} - \bar{x}_T^2$$

standard deviation relative to the sample mean. The use of the coefficient of variation is advantageous when comparing the variation between two or more sets of data.

2.12.3   Fitting Distributions

In the previous section, we addressed the problem of estimating parameters of the underlying population based upon a sample record. A related but more difficult problem is the use of the sample record to identify the distribution of the population. This problem frequently arises in modeling because of the need to characterize random elements of a system by particular distributions. Although an understanding of the properties of the theoretical distributions described in Section 2.9 will aid the modeler in hypothesizing an appropriate distribution, it is frequently desired to test the hypothesis by applying one or more goodness-of-fit tests to the sample record. The chi-square and Kolmogorov-Smirnov are probably the best known tests, and descriptions and examples of these can be found in most statistics textbooks. In addition, the monograph by Phillips (21) presents an easy to use FORTRAN program for employing goodness-of-fit tests to evaluate a sample record against the common theoretical distributions.

2.13   STATISTICAL INFERENCE

In simulation studies, inferences or predictions concerning the behavior of the system under study are to be made based on experimental results obtained from the simulation. Because a simulation model contains random elements, the outputs from the simulation are observed samples of random variables. As a consequence, any assertions which are made concerning the operation of the system based on simulation results should consider the inherent variability of the simulation outputs. This variability is summarized or taken into account by the use of confidence intervals or through hypothesis testing.

2.13.1   Confidence Intervals

In Section 2.12.2, we discussed methods for estimating the mean and variance parameters of a population based on a sample record. The estimates were calculated as a single number from the sample record and are referred to as *point estimates*. In general, an estimate will differ from the true but unknown parameter as the result of chance variations. The use of a point estimate has the disadvantage that it does not provide the decision maker with a measure of the accuracy of the estimate. A probability statement which specifies the likelihood that the parameter being estimated falls within prescribed bounds provides such a measure and is referred to as confidence interval or an interval estimate.

The parameter of primary interest in simulation analysis is the population mean. In the classical development of the confidence interval for the mean, it is assumed that the samples are independent and identically distributed (iid). Hence, by the Central Limit Theorem, the sample mean, $\bar{X}_I$, is approximately normally distributed for sufficiently large I. As stated previously, the assumption of independence is not a necessary condition for the application of the Central Limit Theorem.

If we assume that $\bar{X}_I$ is normally distributed, then the statistic

$$Z = \frac{\bar{X}_I - \mu}{\sigma_{\bar{x}}}$$

is a random variable which is normally distributed with a mean of zero and standard deviation of one. Furthermore,

$$P[-Z_{a/2} < Z < Z_{a/2}] = 1-\alpha$$

where $Z_{a/2}$ is the value for Z such that the area to its right on the standard normal curve equals $\alpha/2$. Hence, we can assert with probability $1-\alpha$ that

$$\bar{X}_I - Z_{a/2} \cdot \sigma_{\bar{x}} < \mu < \bar{X}_I + Z_{a/2} \cdot \sigma_{\bar{x}} \qquad (2\text{-}1)$$

The above formula assumes knowledge of the standard deviation of the mean, $\sigma_{\bar{x}}$, which is usually unknown. If we use the sample standard deviation of the mean, $S_{\bar{x}}$, to estimate $\sigma_{\bar{x}}$, we can develop a similar relationship by noting that the statistic

$$t = \frac{\bar{X}_I - \mu}{S_{\bar{x}}}$$

is a random variable having a student t-distribution with $I-1$ degrees of freedom. Hence, a $1-\alpha$ confidence interval for μ using the estimate $S_{\bar{x}}$ is given by

$$\bar{X}_I - t_{a/2, I-1} S_{\bar{x}} < \mu < \bar{X}_I + t_{a/2, I-1} S_{\bar{x}} \qquad (2\text{-}2)$$

where $t_{a/2, I-1}$ is a critical value of the t-statistic with $(I-1)$ degrees of freedom.

If the samples X_i are iid, the confidence intervals given by 2-1 and 2-2 are modified by the substitutions

$$\sigma_{\bar{x}} = \frac{\sigma_x}{\sqrt{I}} \qquad (2\text{-}3)$$

and

$$S_{\bar{x}} = \frac{S_x}{\sqrt{I}} \qquad (2\text{-}4)$$

respectively. This substitution provides an expression for the confidence interval based on samples. However, this simple relationship between the variance of the samples and the variance of the mean of the samples is valid only if the samples are independent.

Methods for defining $S_{\bar{x}}$ for use in Expression 2-2 in the case of autocorrelated samples are described in Section 13.3. The most direct approach is to organize the experiment to obtain independent observations which can be accomplished through replicating the simulation or organizing the data into batches.

2.14   HYPOTHESIS TESTING

In some applications of simulation, the objective is to decide if a statement concerning a parameter is true or false. For example, we might want to decide whether a change in a dispatching rule for a job shop reduces the average late time for the jobs processed. Due to the experimental nature of simulation, we must account for the chance variation in the estimates of the parameters being compared. This is done using hypothesis testing.

The general procedure of hypothesis testing calls for defining a *null hypothesis* (denoted H_0) and an *alternate hypothesis* (denoted H_1). The null hypothesis is usually set up with the objective of determining whether or not it can be rejected. For example, if we wish to establish that job loading rule A reduces average late time relative to job loading rule B, we would define the null and alternate hypotheses as

H_0: average waiting time for rule A equals average waiting time for rule B
H_1: average waiting time for rule A is less than the average waiting time for rule B

We would then use the experimental results from simulations with rules A and B to attempt to reject H_0 in favor of H_1.

Testing the null hypothesis against the alternate hypothesis involves selecting a decision rule based on the sample data which leads to the acceptance or rejection of the null hypothesis. Acceptance of the null hypothesis does not infer that the null hypothesis is true, but that there is insufficient evidence based on the sample data to reject the hypothesis.

There are two types of errors that can be made in applying the decision criterion. The *Type I* error is to reject the null hypothesis when the hypothesis is true. The *Type II* error is to accept the null hypothesis when it is false. A decision rule can be judged by the probabilities associated with Type I and Type II errors. These probabilities are typically denoted as α and β probabilities, respectively. The probability α of a Type I error is referred to as the *level of significance* of the test.

The decision criterion is established by constructing a *test statistic* which has a known distribution. The test statistic is calculated from the sample data and is compared using a rejection rule. If the test statistic falls within the critical region, then the null hypothesis is rejected.

The test statistic and rejection rule for hypothesis tests concerning means are summarized in Table 2-2. Tests 1 and 2 are for a mean being equal to a given value μ_0. Tests 3 and 4 concern the comparison of two means. The equations for the test statistics are expressed in terms of $\sigma_{\bar{x}}$ and $S_{\bar{x}}$ since assumptions of independence cannot be prescribed.

Table 2-2 Hypothesis Tests for Means

Null Hypothesis	Condition	Test Statistic†	Test Statistic Distribution	Degrees of Freedom	Alternative Hypothesis	Null Hypothesis Rejection Rule
1. $\mu = \mu_0$	Known $\sigma_{\bar{X}}$	$Z = \dfrac{\bar{X} - \mu}{\sigma_{\bar{X}}}$	Standard Normal	—	$\mu > \mu_0$ $\mu < \mu_0$ $\mu \neq \mu_0$	$Z > Z_\alpha$ $Z < -Z_\alpha$ $\lvert Z \rvert > Z_{\alpha/2}$
2. $\mu = \mu_0$	Unknown $\sigma_{\bar{X}}$	$t = \dfrac{\bar{X} - \mu}{S_{\bar{X}}}$	Student t	$I - 1$	$\mu > \mu_0$ $\mu < \mu_0$ $\mu \neq \mu_0$	$t > t_\alpha$ $t < -t_\alpha$ $\lvert t \rvert > t_{\alpha/2}$
3. $\mu_X = \mu_Y$	Known $\sigma_{\bar{X}}$ and $\sigma_{\bar{Y}}$	$Z = \dfrac{\bar{X} - \bar{Y}}{\sqrt{\sigma_{\bar{X}}^2 + \sigma_{\bar{Y}}^2}}$	Standard Normal	—	$\mu_X > \mu_Y$ $\mu_X < \mu_Y$ $\mu_X \neq \mu_Y$	$Z > Z_\alpha$ $Z < Z_\alpha$ $\lvert Z \rvert > Z_{\alpha/2}$
4. $\mu_X = \mu_Y$	Unknown $\sigma_{\bar{X}}$ and $\sigma_{\bar{Y}}$	$t = \dfrac{\bar{X} - \bar{Y}}{\sqrt{S_{\bar{X}}^2 + S_{\bar{Y}}^2}}$	Student t	Nearest integer to: $\dfrac{(S_{\bar{X}}^2 + S_{\bar{Y}}^2)^2}{\dfrac{S_{\bar{X}}^4}{I_X + 1} + \dfrac{S_{\bar{Y}}^4}{I_Y + 1}} - 2$	$\mu_X > \mu_Y$ $\mu_X < \mu_Y$ $\mu_X \neq \mu_Y$	$t > t_\alpha$ $t < -t_\alpha$ $\lvert t \rvert > t_{\alpha/2}$

Legend:
I = sample size
I_X = sample size for X
I_Y = sample size for Y
μ_0 = hypothesized mean
α = level of significance

†The subscript I has been dropped from $\bar{X}$ and $\bar{Y}$ for convenience.

2.15 STATISTICAL PROBLEMS RELATED TO SIMULATION

Decision analysis based on the results of a simulation model normally requires an estimate of the average simulation response and an estimate of its variance. Both of these estimators are affected by experimental conditions. The experimental conditions which the modeler must establish include the initial or starting states for the simulation, the time at which statistics collection is to begin, and the run length and number of replications. In this section, we will introduce some of the considerations and problems associated with establishing these conditions. In Chapter 13, we discuss these problems in detail.

2.15.1 Initial Conditions

Implicit in every simulation model is an initial condition or starting state for the simulation. The simplest and probably most commonly used initial state is "empty and idle," in which the simulation begins with no entities in the system and all servers idle. The appropriateness of this starting condition depends on the nature of the system being modeled and whether we are interested in the transient or steady-state behavior† of the system.

When the purpose of our analysis is to study the steady-state behavior of a system, we can frequently improve our estimate of the mean by beginning the simulation in a state other than empty and idle. The starting condition can be established by estimating an initial state which is representative of the long term behavior of the system, perhaps by observing the plotted output from a pilot simulation run. For a transient analysis, the starting condition should reflect the initial status of the system.

2.15.2 Data Truncation

A method which is frequently used to reduce any bias in estimating the steady-state mean resulting from the initial conditions is to delay the collection of statistics

---

† Steady-state behavior does not denote a lack of variability in the simulation response, but specifies that the probability mechanism describing this variability is unchanging and is no longer affected by the starting condition.

until after a "warm up" period. This is normally done by specifying a truncation point before which data values are not included in the statistical estimates. The intent is to reduce the initial condition bias in the estimates by eliminating values recorded during the transient period of the simulation. However, by discarding a portion of the data, we are not using observations and, hence, may be increasing the estimated variance of the mean. Thus, by truncation we improve the quality of the estimate of the mean at the possible expense of increased variability in the simulation outputs.

The most common method for determining the truncation point is to examine a plot of the response from a pilot simulation run. The truncation point is selected as the time at which the response "appears" to have reached steady state. There are also methods which attempt to formalize this procedure in the form of a rule which can be incorporated into the simulation program to automatically determine the truncation point during the execution of the simulation. These rules are discussed in Chapter 13.

2.15.3   Run Length and Number of Replications

An important experimental design decision which the analyst must make is the tradeoff between run length and number of replications of the simulation. The use of a few long runs as opposed to many short runs generally produces a better estimate of the steady state mean because the initial bias is introduced fewer times and less data is truncated. However, the reduced number of samples corresponding to fewer replications may increase our estimate of the variance of the mean. The use of many short runs, on the other hand, may introduce a bias due to the starting conditions. The larger the initial bias, the more important it is to use longer runs to reduce the effects of the starting conditions.

There are several alternate methods for specifying the duration of a simulation. Perhaps the most common method is to specify a time at which the simulation is to end. A disadvantage of this method is that the number of samples collected is a random variable and may differ in each replication. A method which allows us to control the sample size is to specify the number of entities which are to be entered into the model. In this case the simulation executes until the prescribed number of entities which are entered into the model are completely processed through the system. Thus, the simulation stops in the empty and idle state. A similar but different method is to specify the number of entities which are processed through the system. Note that in this case the system is not necessarily empty and idle at the time it is stopped. When using this approach, it is necessary to ensure that the entities remaining to be processed are representative. An example where this stopping method may be inappropriate is when a shortest processing time dispatching rule is employed and, hence, jobs with long processing times may be the ones still remaining in the queues.

Another approach for controlling the duration of a simulation is the use of automatic stopping rules. These methods automatically monitor the simulation results at selected intervals during the execution of the simulation. The simulation is stopped when the estimate of the variance of the mean is within a prescribed tolerance. The use of automatic stopping rules is discussed in more detail in Chapter 13.

If we are estimating the variance of an output variable X by replication and if we assume that X is normally distributed (which if X is a mean value is a good assumption) then the number of independent replications of the simulation required to attain a specified confidence interval for X is given by

$$I = \left(\frac{t_{a/2, I-1} S_X}{g} \right)^2$$

where

$t_{a/2, I-1}$ is a value from the table of critical values of the t-statistic with $I-1$ degrees of freedom

g is the half-width of the desired confidence interval

Unfortunately, the use of this formula for I requires knowledge of the t-statistic with $I-1$ degrees of freedom and S_X. Typically, we must assume a value for I, make the I replications of the simulation, obtain values of t and s_X based on these runs, and then use the above formula with these values inserted to test the sufficiency of our initial assumption or to determine the number of additional replications which are required.

2.16   CHAPTER SUMMARY

This chapter has provided the probability and statistics background required for simulation analysis. Detailed developments have not been presented as the intent was to cover a wide range of simulation related topics. The material introduces sufficient simulation subject matter to permit the understanding of simulation modeling concepts and the experimental nature of simulation analysis. It also provides a basis for understanding the detailed aspects associated with the statistical analysis of simulation results to be presented in Chapter 13.

2.17 EXERCISES

2-1.   Given the following simulation results for customer time-in-system for 20 simulation runs, compute an estimate of the mean, variance, and coefficient of variation. Construct a histogram that has 5 cells, a cell width of 1, and the lower
limit of the first cell equal to 0.

    1.1, 2.8, 3.7, 1.9, 4.9, 1.6, .4, 3.8, 1.5, 3.4, 1.9,
    2.1, 3.8, 1.6, 3.2, 2.9, 3.7, 2.0, 4.2, 3.3

2-2.   The following figure depicts the number of customers in a waiting line over a
fifteen minute time interval. Calculate the average and standard deviation of
the number of customers waiting.

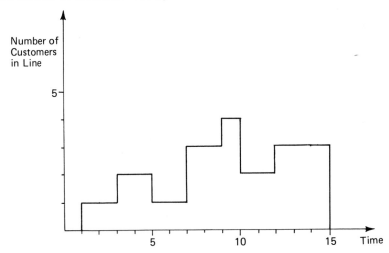

2-3.   A simulation model was employed to study the design of a proposed subway
system. The following are average passenger waiting times in minutes based on
20 independent replications of the simulation model. Construct a 99% confidence
interval for the average passenger waiting time.

    15, 17, 14, 15, 16, 14, 15, 18, 15, 14,
    15, 20, 17, 14, 16, 16, 15, 18, 14, 15

2-4.   The following are average weekly inventory costs in thousands of dollars for two
proposed inventory control policies. The values were obtained from independent
replications of a simulation model of the system. Test the hypothesis that the
average weekly cost for policy A is less than that for policy B at a 5% significance
level.

Policy A
    1.2, 1.3, 1.1, 1.4, 0.9, 1.1, 1.5, 1.2,
    1.3, 1.2, 1.3, 1.4, 1.1, 1.2, 1.0

Policy B
1.1, 1.5, 1.4, 1.3, 1.6, 1.5, 1.4, 1.5,
1.7, 1.3, 1.6, 1.5, 1.8, 1.7, 1.6

2-5.   In a simulation study of a proposed assembly line layout, ten independent replications were made to estimate the average hourly production for the line. Based on this data, estimate the number of runs required to determine the average production rate within 2 units at a one percent significance level.

157, 162, 151, 170, 162, 157, 166, 165, 152, 160

2-6.   Show that the sum of two independent Poisson random variables with mean μ_1 and μ_2 is a random variable which is Poisson distributed with mean $\mu_1 + \mu_2$ (Hint: The moment generating function for the Poisson distribution with mean μ is $e^{\mu(e^s - 1)}$.) What is the distribution of the sum of two independent normal random variables?

2-7.   The thief of Baghdad has been placed in a dungeon with three doors. One door leads to freedom, one door leads to a long tunnel, and a third door leads to a short tunnel. The tunnels return the thief to the dungeon. If the thief returns to the dungeon, he attempts to gain his freedom again but his past experiences do not help him in selecting the door that leads to freedom, that is, we assume a Markov thief. The thief's probabilities of selecting the doors are: 0.30 to freedom; 0.20 to the short tunnel; and 0.50 to the long tunnel. Assuming that the travel times through the long and short tunnels are 6 and 3, respectively, determine the expected time until the thief selects the door which leads to freedom.

2-8.   Use the multiplicative congruential method to generate a sequence of ten random numbers with $c = 256$, $a = 13$, $b = 0$, and $z_0 = 51$.

2-9.   Given that $z_{i+1} = (az_i + b)(\bmod c)$, show that z_{i+1} is only a function of z_0, a, b and c, that is, $z_{i+1} = (a^{i+1}z_0 + b(a^{i+1}-1)/(a-1))(\bmod c)$. Compute z_9 for the values given in Exercise 2-8 using this formula.

2-10. Use the inverse transform method to transform the uniform random numbers from Exercise 2-8 into samples from the continuous distribution whose probability density function is:

$$f(x) = \begin{cases} \dfrac{3x^2}{8}, \text{ if } 0 \leqslant x \leqslant 2 \\ 0 \text{ , otherwise} \end{cases}$$

2-11. Use the inverse transformation method to transform the random samples from Exercise 2-8 into samples from the discrete distribution defined by the following probability mass function:

$P(0) = 1/5$; $P(1) = 1/5$; $P(2) = 2/5$; and $P(3) = 1/5$.

2.18   REFERENCES

1. Abramowitz, M. and I. A. Stegun, Eds., *Handbook of Mathematical Functions,* Applied Mathematics Series 55, Washington, D.C.: National Bureau of Standards, 1964.

2. Barnes, R. M., *Motion and Time Study: Design and Measurement of Work,* Sixth Edition, John Wiley, 1968.

3. Bartee, E. M., *Engineering Experimental Design Fundamentals,* Prentice-Hall, 1968.

4. Beightler, C. S., L. G. Mitten, and G. L. Nemhauser, "A Short Table of Z-Transforms and Generating Functions," *Operations Research,* Vol. 9, 1961, pp. 576-577.

5. Beyer, W. A., R. B. Roof and D. Williamson, "The Lattice Structure of Multiplicative Congruential Pseudo-Random Vectors," *Math. Comp.,* Vol. 25, 1971, pp. 345-363.

6. Conveyou, R. R. and R. D. MacPherson, "Fourier Analysis of Uniform Random Number Generators," *J.ACM,* Vol. 14, 1967, pp. 100-119.

7. Feller, W., *An Introduction to Probability Theory and Its Applications,* John Wiley, 1950.

8. Feller, W., *An Introduction to Probability Theory and Its Applications,* John Wiley, Vol. II, 1972.

9. Fishman, G. S., *Principles of Discrete Event Simulation,* John Wiley, 1978.

10. Giffin, W., *Transform Techniques for Probability Modeling,* Academic Press, 1975.

11. Hahn, G. J. and S. S. Shapiro, *Statistical Methods in Engineering,* John Wiley, 1967.

12. Hald, A., *Statistical Theory with Engineering Applications,* John Wiley, 1952.

13. Hastings, N. A. J. and J. B. Peacock, *Statistical Distributions,* Butterworth, 1975.

14. Hogg, R. V. and A. T. Craig, *Introduction to Mathematical Statistics,* Macmillan, 1970.

15. Hull, T. E. and A. R. Dobell, "Random Number Generators," *SIAM Review,* Vol. 4, 1962, pp. 230-254.

16. Lewis, T. G., *Distribution Sampling for Computer Simulation,* Lexington Books, 1975.

17. Marsaglia, G., "The Structure of Linear Congruential Sequences," in *Applications of Number Theory to Numerical Analysis,* S. K. Zaremba, ed., Academic Press, 1972.

18. Niebel, B. W., *Motion and Time Study,* Fourth Edition, Richard D. Irwin, 1967.

19. Papoulis, A., *Probability, Random Variables, and Stochastic Processes,* McGraw-Hill, 1965.

20. Parzen, E., *Modern Probability Theory and Its Applications,* John Wiley, 1960.

21. Phillips, D. T., Applied Goodness of Fit Testing, AIIE Monograph Series, AIIE-OR-72-1, Atlanta, Georgia, 1972.

22. Pritsker, A. A. B., *The GASP IV Simulation Language,* John Wiley, 1974.

23. RAND Corporation, *A Million Random Digits with 1,000,000 Normal Deviates,* Free Press, 1955.

2.19   APPENDIX: CONGRUENTIAL GENERATORS†

Mixed Congruential Generators

A full period of 2^B before recycling will be obtained on a computer that has B bits/word for the generator

$$z_{i+1} = (az_i + b)(\mathrm{mod}\ c)$$

when
  $c = 2^B$;
  b is relatively prime to c; that is, the greatest common factor of b and c is 1;
and
  $a \equiv 1(\mathrm{mod}\ 4)$ or $a = 1 + 4k$ where k is an integer.

Multiplicative Congruential Generators

A maximal period of 2^{B-2} before recycling will be obtained on a computer that has B bits/word for the generator

$$z_{i+1} = az_i(\mathrm{mod}\ c)$$

when
  $c = 2^B$;
  $a = \pm 3 + 8k$ or $a = 1 + 4k$ for k integer;
and
  z_0 is odd.

Fishman refers to these generators as maximal period multiplicative generators.

For multiplicative congruential generators, a period of $c-1$ can be obtained by setting c equal to the largest prime in 2^B and making the coefficient a, a primitive root of c. In some instances $2^B - 1$ is the largest prime in 2^B. For a to be a primitive root of c, the following equation must be satisfied

$$a^{c-1} = 1 + ck$$

where k is an integer and for any integer $q < c-1$, $(a^q - 1)/c$ is nonintegral. These generators are referred to as prime modulus multiplicative congruential generators.

---

† The material contained in this appendix is based on Fishman which should be read to obtain a detailed discussion (9).

CHAPTER 3

Simulation Modeling Perspectives

3.1   INTRODUCTION

In developing a simulation model, an analyst needs to select a conceptual framework for describing the system to be modeled. The framework or perspective contains a "world view" within which the system functional relationships are perceived and described. If the modeler is employing a simulation language, then the world view will normally be implicit within the language. However, if the modeler elects to employ a general purpose language such as FORTRAN, PL/I, or BASIC, then the perspective for organizing the system description is the responsibility of the modeler. In either case, the world view employed by the modeler provides a conceptual mechanism for articulating the system description. In this chapter, we sum-

60

marize the alternative world views for simulation modeling and introduce the unified modeling framework of SLAM.

3.2 SYSTEMS AND MODELS

A system is a collection of items from a circumscribed sector of reality that is the object of study or interest. Therefore, a system is a relative thing. In one situation, a particular collection of objects may be only a small part of a larger system —a subsystem; in another situation that same collection of objects may be the primary focus of interest and would be considered as the system. The scope of every system, and of every model of a system, is determined solely by its reason for being identified and isolated. The scope of every simulation model is determined by the particular problems the model is designed to solve.

To consider the scope of a system, one must contemplate its boundaries and contents. The boundary of a system may be physical; however, it is better to think of a boundary in terms of cause and effect. Given a tentative system definition, some external factors may affect the system. If they completely govern its behavior, there is no merit in experimenting with the defined system. If they partially influence the system, there are several possibilities:

The system definition may be enlarged to include them.
They may be ignored.
They may be treated as inputs to the system.

If treated as inputs, it is assumed that the factors are functionally specified by prescribed values, tables, or equations. For example, when defining the model of a company's manufacturing system, if the sales of the company's product are considered as inputs to the manufacturing system, the model will not contain a cause and effect sales relation; it only includes a statistical description of historical or predicted sales, which is used as an input. In such a model of the manufacturing system, the sales organization is outside the boundaries of the "defined" system. In systems terminology, objects that are outside the boundaries of the system, but can influence it, constitute the environment of the system. Thus, systems are collections of mutually interacting objects that are affected by outside forces. Figure 3-1 shows such a system.

Models of systems can be classified as either discrete change or continuous change. Note that these terms describe the model and not the real system. In fact,

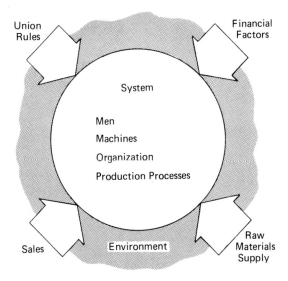

Figure 3-1   Manufacturing system model showing external influences.

it may be possible to model the same system with either a discrete change (hereafter referred to simply as discrete) or a continuous change (continuous) model. In most simulations, time is the major independent variable. Other variables included in the simulation are functions of time and are the dependent variables. The adjectives discrete and continuous when modifying simulation refer to the behavior of the dependent variables.

Discrete simulation occurs when the dependent variables change discretely at specified points in simulated time referred to as event times. The time variable may be either continuous or discrete in such a model, depending on whether the discrete changes in the dependent variable can occur at any point in time or only at specified points.

The bank teller problem discussed in Chapter 1 is an example of a discrete simulation. The dependent variables in that example were the teller status and the number of waiting customers. The event times corresponded to the times at which customers arrived to the system and departed from the system following completion of service by the teller. In general, the values of the dependent variables for discrete models do not change between event times. An example response for a dependent variable in a discrete simulation is shown in Figure 3-2.

In *continuous simulation* the dependent variables of the model may change continuously over simulated time. A continuous model may be either continuous or discrete in time, depending on whether the values of the dependent variables are available at any point in simulated time or only at specified points in simulated

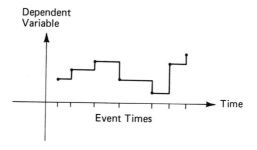

Figure 3-2   Response measurement from a discrete event simulator.

time. Examples of response measurements for continuous simulations are shown in Figure 3-3 and Figure 3-4.

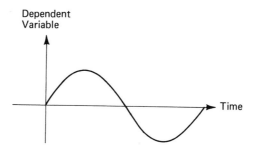

Figure 3-3   Response measurement from a continuous simulator.

The modeling of the concentration of a reactant in a chemical process or the position and velocity of a spacecraft are illustrations of situations where a continu-

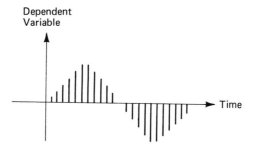

Figure 3-4   Response measurement from a continuous simulator using discrete time steps.

ous representation is appropriate. However, in some cases, it is also useful to model a discrete system with a continuous representation by considering the entities in the system in the aggregate rather than as individual entities. For example, we would probably prefer to model the population of a particular species in a lake using a continuous representation, even though in reality the population changes discretely.

In *combined simulation* the dependent variables of a model may change discretely, continuously, or continuously with discrete jumps superimposed. The time variable may be continuous or discrete. The most important aspect of combined simulation arises from the interaction between discretely and continuously changing variables. For example, when the concentration level of a reactant in a chemical process reaches a prescribed level, the process may be shut down. A combined simulation language must contain provisions for detecting the occurrence of such conditions and for modeling their consequences. An example of a response from a combined simulation model is shown in Figure 3-5.

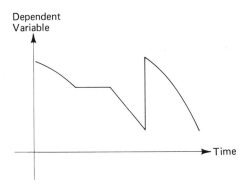

Figure 3-5   Response measurement from a combined simulator.

3.3   DISCRETE SIMULATION MODELING

The objects within the boundaries of a discrete system, such as people, equipment, orders, and raw materials, are called entities. There are many types of entities and each has various characteristics or attributes. Although they engage in different types of activities, entities may have a common attribute requiring that

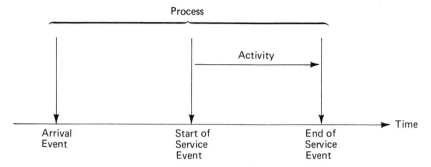

Figure 3-6   Relationship of events, activities, and processes.

they be grouped together. Groupings of entities are called files.† Inserting an entity into a file implies that it has some relation with other entities in the file.

The aim of a discrete simulation model is to reproduce the activities that the entities engage in and thereby learn something about the behavior and performance potential of the system. This is done by defining the states of the system and constructing activities that move it from state to state. The state of a system is defined in terms of the numeric values assigned to the attributes of the entities. A system is said to be in a particular state when all of its entities are in states consonant with the range of attribute values that define that state. Thus, simulation is the dynamic portrayal of the states of a system over time.

In discrete simulation, the state of the system can change only at event times. Since the state of the system remains constant between event times, a complete dynamic portrayal of the state of the system can be obtained by advancing simulated time from one event to the next. This timing mechanism is referred to as the next event approach and is used in most discrete simulation languages.

A discrete simulation model can be formulated by: 1) defining the changes in state that occur at each event time; 2) describing the activities in which the entities in the system engage; or 3) describing the process through which the entities in the system flow. The relationship between the concept of an *event, activity,* and a *process* is depicted in Figure 3-6. An event takes place at an isolated point in time at which decisions are made to start or end activities. A process is a time-ordered sequence of events and may encompass several activities. These concepts lead naturally to three alternative world views for discrete simulation modeling. These world views are commonly referred to as the event, activity scanning, and process orientations, and are described in the following sections. For additional discussions of

---

† The word file is used in SLAM to mean a set of entities or events. The description of systems in terms of entities, attributes and files (sets) was first employed by Markowitz (10).

discrete simulation modeling orientations, the reader is referred to the excellent reviews by Kiviat (7,8).

3.3.1   Event Orientation

In the event-oriented world view, a system is modeled by defining the changes that occur at event times. The task of the modeler is to determine the events that can change the state of the system and then to develop the logic associated with each event type. A simulation of the system is produced by executing the logic associated with each event in a time-ordered sequence.

To illustrate the event orientation, consider again the bank teller problem discussed in Chapter 1. Customers arrive to the system, possibly wait, undergo service by the teller, and then exit the system. The state of the system is defined by the status of the teller and the number of waiting customers. The state of the system remains constant except when a customer arrives to the system or departs from it. Therefore, the event model for this system consists of describing what happens at a customer arrival time and an end-of-service time. Since a change in the state of the system can occur only at these event times, the customer arrival and end-of-service events can be used to completely describe the dynamic structure of the system.

Consider first the logic associated with the customer arrival event. A statement outline for the logical steps in processing this event is as follows:

SCHEDULE NEXT ARRIVAL.
IF THE TELLER IS BUSY: NUMBER WAITING = NUMBER
    WAITING + 1; RETURN.
IF THE TELLER IS IDLE: MAKE THE TELLER BUSY; SCHED-
    ULE AN END OF SERVICE EVENT AT CURRENT TIME +
    SERVICE TIME; RETURN.
END

The first action taken is to schedule the next arrival. This is done to provide a sequence of arrivals. Hence, once the first arrival is scheduled, a continuing stream of arrivals will occur. The disposition of the current customer arrival depends upon the state of the system at the customer arrival time. If the teller is busy, the arriving cutomer must wait, and therefore the state of the system is changed by increasing the number of waiting customers by one. Otherwise, the arriving customer can be placed immediately into service. In this case, the state of the system is changed by setting the status of the teller to busy. In addition, the end-of-service event for the customer must be scheduled to occur at the current simulated time plus the time it takes the teller to serve the customer.

Next, consider the logic associated with processing the end-of-service event. A statement outline summarizing the logical steps for the event is shown below:

> IF THE NUMBER WAITING IS GREATER THAN 0: NUMBER WAITING
>   = NUMBER WAITING −1; SCHEDULE END OF SERVICE EVENT
>   AT CURRENT TIME + SERVICE TIME; RETURN.
> IF THE NUMBER WAITING IS 0: MAKE THE TELLER IDLE; RETURN.
> END

Since the teller is completing service on the current customer, we first test to see if additional customers are waiting for service by the teller. If customers are waiting, we reduce the number waiting by 1 and schedule the end-of-service event for the first waiting customer. Otherwise, we set the teller to idle status.

To create a simulation of the bank teller problem using the event orientation, we would maintain a calendar of events and cause their execution to occur at the proper points in simulated time. The event calendar would initially contain an event notice corresponding to the first arrival event. As the simulation proceeds, additional arrival events and end of service events would be scheduled onto the calendar as prescribed by the logic associated with the events. Each event would be executed in a time-ordered sequence, with simulated time being advanced from one event to the next.

If the modeler employs a general purpose language such as FORTRAN to code a discrete event model, then a considerable amount of programming effort will be directed at developing the event calendar and a timing mechanism for processing the events in their proper chronological order. Since this function is common to all discrete event models, a number of simulation languages have been developed which provide special features for event scheduling, as well as other functions which are commonly encountered in discrete event models. Two of the more commonly used discrete event languages are GASP (12,13) and SIMSCRIPT (9,10). A discussion of these languages and a comparison with SLAM are presented in Chapter 12.

3.3.2   Activity Scanning Orientation

In the activity scanning orientation, the modeler describes the activities in which the entities in the system engage and prescribes the conditions which cause an activity to start or end. The events which start or end the activity are not scheduled by the modeler, but are initiated from the conditions specified for the activity. As simulated time is advanced, the conditions for either starting or ending an activity are scanned. If the prescribed conditions are satisfied, then the appropriate action for the activity is taken. To insure that each activity is accounted for, it is necessary to scan the entire set of activities at each time advance.

For certain types of problems, the activity scanning approach can provide a concise modeling framework. The approach is particularly well suited for situations where an activity duration is indefinite and is determined by the state of the system satisfying a prescribed condition. However, because of the need to scan each activity at each time advance, the approach is relatively inefficient when compared to the discrete event orientation. As a result, the activity scanning orientation has not been widely adopted as a modeling framework for discrete simulations.† However, a number of languages employ specific features which are based on the concept of activity scanning. SLAM includes two methods for incorporating activities whose start and end times are based on system status (see Chapters 4 and 9).

3.3.3   Process Orientation

Many simulation models include sequences of elements which occur in defined patterns, for example, a queue where entities wait for processing by a server. The logic associated with such a sequence of events can be generalized and defined by a single statement. A simulation language could then translate such statements into the appropriate sequence of events. A process oriented language employs such statements to model the flow of entities through a system. These statements define a sequence of events which are automatically executed by the simulation language as the entities move through the process. For example, the following set of statements could have been used to describe the process for the bank teller problem.

```
CREATE ARRIVAL ENTITIES EVERY T TIME UNITS;
AWAIT THE TELLER;
ADVANCE TIME BY THE SERVICE TIME;
FREE THE TELLER;
TERMINATE THE ENTITY;
```

---

† One example of a language which employs the activity scanning approach is CSL (2).

The first statement creates the arrivals of customers to the system with a time between arrivals of T time units. T could be specified to be a constant or to be a sampled value. The "await" statement which follows specifies that the entity is to wait until the teller is idle. This type of statement is analogous to the conditional activity concept employed in the activity scanning orientation. The "advance time" statement models the elapsed time during which the customer is served by the teller. This statement is analogous to the schedule statement in the event orientation as it places an event notice on the calendar that the entity is to complete service at the current simulated time plus the service time. Following completion of service, the entity frees the teller, and then is terminated from the system. The freeing of the teller automatically allows him to process any waiting entities at the await statement.

From the above example, we see that the process orientation combines features of both the event orientation and activity scanning orientation. It provides a description of the flow of the entities through a process consisting of resources. Its simplicity is derived from the fact that the event logic associated with the statements is contained within the simulation language. However, since we are normally restricted to a set of standardized statements provided by the simulation language, our modeling flexibility is not as great as with the event orientation. Also, the disposition of resources after they are used requires careful analysis.

GPSS(6,15), SIMULA(1,5), and Q-GERT(14) are the most commonly used process oriented languages. These languages differ in the types and syntax of the statements provided and in the way in which the statements are combined. GPSS employs a block diagram approach in which a block corresponds to a statement type and the blocks are combined in a manner similar to computer flow charting. In contrast, SIMULA employs a statement orientation which is a superset of ALGOL. Q-GERT employs nodes and branches which are interconnected into a network which models the system of interest. In Chapter 12, we will compare the process features of these languages with the process capabilities employed in SLAM.

3.4   CONTINUOUS SIMULATION MODELING

In a continuous simulation model, the state of the system is represented by dependent variables which change continuously over time. To distinguish continuous change variables from discrete change variables, the former are referred to as *state variables.* A continuous simulation model is constructed by defining equations for a set of state variables whose dynamic behavior simulates the real system.

Models of continuous systems are frequently written in terms of the derivatives of the state variables. The reason for this is that it is often easier to construct a relationship for the rate of change of the state variable than to devise a relationship for the state variable directly. Equations of this form involving derivatives of the state variables are referred to as differential equations. For example, our modeling effort might produce the following differential equation for the state variable s over time t.

$$\frac{ds(t)}{dt} = s^2(t) + t^2$$

$$s(o) = k$$

The first equation specifies the rate of change of s as a function of s and t and the second equation specifies the initial condition for the state variable. The simulation analyst's objective is to determine the response of the state variable over simulated time.

In some cases, it is possible to determine an analytical expression for the state variable, s, given an equation for ds/dt. However in many cases of practical importance, an analytical solution for s will not be known. As a result we must obtain the response, s, by integrating ds/dt over time using an equation of the following type:

$$s(t_2) = s(t_1) + \int_{t_1}^{t_2} \left(\frac{ds}{dt}\right) dt$$

How this integration is performed depends upon whether the modeler employs an analog or digital computer.

During the 1950's and 1960's, analog computers were the primary means for performing continuous simulations. An analog computer represents the state variables in the model by electrical charges. The dynamic structure of the system is modeled using circuit components such as resistors, capacitors, and amplifiers. The principal shortcoming of an analog computer is that the quality of these components limits the accuracy of the results. In addition, the analog computer lacks the logical control functions and data storage capability of the digital computer.

A number of continuous simulation languages have been developed for use on digital computers. It is necessary to recognize that a digital computer is technically discrete in its operation. As a practical matter, however, any variable whose possible values are limited only by the word size of the computer is considered continuous.

Although the digital computer can perform the common mathematical operations such as addition, multiplication, and logical testing with great speed and accuracy, the integration operation requires the use of numerical integration methods. These methods divide the independent variable (normally time) into small slices referred to as *steps*. The values for the state variables requiring integration are obtained by employing an approximation to the derivative of the state variable over time. The accuracy of these methods depends upon the order of the approximation method and the size of the step, with greater accuracy resulting from higher-order approximations and smaller step sizes. Since higher-order approximations and smaller step sizes result in more computations, a trade-off between accuracy of state variable calculations and computer run time exists. A description of the various numerical integration algorithms can be found in any of the introductory texts for numerical analysis (3,17). The numerical integration scheme employed by SLAM for simulating continuous models involving differential equations is described in Appendix E.

Sometimes a continuous system is modeled using difference equations. In these models, the time axis is decomposed into time periods of length Δt. The dynamics of the state variables are described by specifying an equation which calculates the value of the state variable at period $k+1$ from the value of the state variable at period k. For example, the following difference equation could be employed to describe the dynamics of the state variable s:

$$s_{k+1} = s_k + a * \Delta t$$

Continuous simulation languages for digital computers normally employ either a block or statement orientation. The block oriented languages employ a set of blocks which functionally emulate the circuit components of an analog computer. Thus the modeler familiar with analog block diagrams would find these languages easy to learn. Most of the recently developed continuous simulation languages employ an equation orientation. In these languages, the differential or difference equations are explicitly coded in equation form. An advantage of the equation orientation is the increased flexibility afforded by the algebraic and logical features of these languages. A committee of the Society for Computer Simulation (16) has developed a set of standards for continuous system-simulation languages (CSSL). A discussion of CSSLs is given in Chapter 12.

3.5   COMBINED DISCRETE-CONTINUOUS MODELS

In combined discrete-continuous models, the independent variables may change both discretely and continuously. The world view of a combined model specifies that the system can be described in terms of entities, their associated attributes, and state variables. The behavior of the system model is simulated by computing the values of the state variables at small time steps and by computing the values of attributes of entities at event times.

There are two types of events that can occur in combined simulations. *Time-events* are those events which are scheduled to occur at specified points in time. They are commonly thought of in terms of discrete simulation models. In contrast, *state-events* are not scheduled, but occur when the system reaches a particular state. For example, as illustrated in Figure 3-7, a state-event could be specified to occur whenever state variable SS(1) crosses state variable SS(2) in the positive direction. Note that the notion of a state-event is similar to the concept of activity scanning in that the event is not scheduled but is initiated by the state of the system. The possible occurrence of a state-event must be tested at each time advance in the simulation.

The first fully documented combined language was GASP IV (12). The GASP IV language is FORTRAN based and provides a formalized world view which combines the discrete event orientation for modeling discrete systems with the state variable equation orientation for continuous system modeling. A PL/I version of GASP IV has also been developed (13). In addition, a combined modeling capability based on the features of GASP IV has since been added to SIMSCRIPT (4). Combined languages employing a network orientation have also been developed and include SMOOTH (18) and SAINT (19). A crop growth and harvesting language, CROPS, based on GASP IV has also been developed (11). The analysis of systems using combined simulation models continues to be a fertile area for research, development, and application.

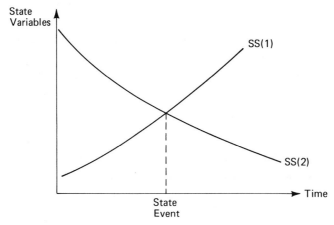

Figure 3-7   Example of a state-event occurrence.

3.6   SLAM: A UNIFIED MODELING FRAMEWORK

In the preceding sections, we described several alternate world views for simulation modeling. Each of these world views presumes a framework within which the system is described. The diversity of world views has persisted because each has certain advantages and disadvantages. For example, in discrete simulation modeling, the process orientation provides a concise and easy to learn modeling framework, but may lack flexibility. On the other hand, the event orientation is normally more difficult to learn but, once mastered, provides a highly flexible modeling framework.

In SLAM, the alternate modeling world views are combined to provide a unified modeling framework. A discrete change system can be modeled within an event orientation, process orientation, or *both*. Continuous change systems can be modeled using either differential or difference equations. Combined discrete-continuous change systems can be modeled by combining the event and/or process orientation with the continuous orientation. In addition, SLAM incorporates a number of features which correspond to the activity scanning orientation.

The process orientation of SLAM employs a *network* structure comprised of specialized symbols called *nodes* and *branches*. These symbols model elements in a process such as queues, servers, and decision points. The modeling task consists of combining these symbols into a network model which pictorially represents the system of interest. In short, a network is a pictorial representation of a process. The entities in the system (such as people and items) flow through the network model. The pictorial representation of the system is transcribed by the modeler into an equivalent statement model for input to the SLAM processor.

In the event orientation of SLAM, the modeler defines the events and the potential changes to the system when an event occurs. The mathematical-logical relationships prescribing the changes associated with each event type are coded by the modeler as FORTRAN subroutines. A set of standard subprograms is provided by SLAM for use by the modeler to perform common discrete event functions such as event scheduling, file manipulations, statistics collection, and random sample generation. The executive control program of SLAM controls the simulation by advancing time and initiating calls to the appropriate event subroutines at the proper points in simulated time. Hence, the modeler is completely relieved of the task of sequencing events to occur chronologically.

A continuous model is coded in SLAM by specifying the differential or difference equations which describe the dynamic behavior of the state variables. These equations are coded by the modeler in FORTRAN by employing a set of special SLAM defined storage arrays. The value of the Ith state variable is maintained as variable SS(I) and the derivative of the Ith state variable, when required, is maintained as the variable DD(I). The immediate past values for state variable I and its derivative are maintained as SSL(I) and DDL(I), respectively. When differential equations are included in the continuous model, they are automatically integrated by SLAM to calculate the values of the state variables within an accuracy prescribed by the modeler.

An important aspect of SLAM is that alternate world views can be combined within the same simulation model. There are six specific interactions which can take place between the network, discrete event, and continuous world views of SLAM:

1. Entities in the network model can initiate the occurrence of discrete events.
2. Events can alter the flow of entities in the network model.
3. Entities in the network model can cause instantaneous changes to values of the state variables.
4. State variables reaching prescribed threshold values can initiate entities in the network model.
5. Events can cause instantaneous changes to the values of state variables.
6. State variables reaching prescribed threshold values can initiate events.

The ability to construct combined network-event-continuous models with interactions between each orientation greatly enhances the modeling power of the systems analyst.

3.7   CHAPTER SUMMARY

In this chapter, we described the alternate world views of simulation modeling and introduced the unified modeling framework of SLAM. In the chapters which follow we describe the network, event, continuous, and combined modeling features of SLAM. As the reader masters each of these orientations within the unified framework of SLAM, the concepts and relationships discussed in this chapter should become clear. The discussion of specific languages presented in Chapter 12 will elaborate on the concepts presented in this chapter.

3.8 EXERCISES

3-1. Consider the operation of a physician's office. Specify the boundaries of the system, and describe its operation in terms of entities, attributes, relationships, and activities.

3-2. Give an example of a situation in which the end of an activity cannot be scheduled in advance but must be based on the status of the system.

3-3. A paint shop employs six workers who prepare jobs to be spray painted. The preparation time is lengthy compared to the spraying operation and, hence, only two spraying machines are available. After a worker completes the preparation of a job, he proceeds to a spraying machine where he waits if necessary for a free spraying machine. Jobs to be prepared and painted are always available to the workmen. Describe this system using the event orientation and the process orientation.

3-4. Describe a residential heating and cooling control system in terms of state variables, time-events, and state-events.

3-5. Model an elevator system to ascertain energy usage. The elevator serves five floors. Assume the arrival of passengers at each floor is a random variable and that the probability associated with the passenger's floor to floor transition are known. Note that energy use is a function of the dynamic characteristics of the elevator's motion.

3-6. Write a simulation model of a single-server queueing system using a general purpose programming language such as FORTRAN, PL/I, or BASIC. Assume that the time between customer arrivals is exponentially distributed with mean of 5 time units and the service time is uniformly distributed between 2 and 6 time units. Estimate the average queue length, server utilization, and time-in-system based on 1000 customers.

Embellishment: Change the model to include two parallel servers and a finite queue capacity of 10 customers.

3.9 REFERENCES

1. Birtwhistle, G. M., O. Dahl, B. Myhrhaug, and K. Nygaard, *SIMULA Begin,* Auerbach, 1973.
2. Buxton, J. N. and J. G. Laski, "Control and Simulation Language," *Computer Journal*, Vol. 5, 1964, pp. 194-199.
3. Carnahan, B., H. A. Luther, and J. O. Wilkes, *Applied Numerical Methods,* John Wiley, 1969.
4. Delfosse, C. M., Continuous Simulation and Combined Simulation in SIMSCRIPT II.5, CACI, Inc., Arlington, Va., 1976.

5. Franta, W. R., *The Process View of Simulation,* North Holland, 1977.

6. Gordon, G., *The Application of GPSS V to Discrete Systems Simulation,* Prentice-Hall, 1975.

7. Kiviat, P. J., *Digital Event Simulation: Modeling Concepts,* The Rand Corporation, RM-5378-PR, Santa Monica, Calif., 1967.

8. Kiviat, P. J., *Digital Computer Simulation: Computer Programming Languages,* The Rand Corporation, RM-5883-PR, Santa Monica, Calif., 1969.

9. Kiviat, P. J., R. Villanueva, and H. Markowitz, *The SIMSCRIPT II Programming Language,* Prentice-Hall, 1969.

10. Markowitz, H. M., H. W. Karr, and B. Hausner, *SIMSCRIPT: A Simulation Programming Language,* Prentice-Hall, 1963.

11. Miles, G. E., R. M. Peart, and A. A. B. Pritsker, "CROPS: A GASP IV Based Crops Simulation Language," *Proceedings, Summer Computer Simulation Conference,* 1976, pp. 921-924.

12. Pritsker, A. A. B., *The GASP IV Simulation Language,* John Wiley, 1974.

13. Pritsker, A. A. B. and R. E. Young, *Simulation with GASP_PL/I,* John Wiley, 1975.

14. Pritsker, A. A. B., *Modeling and Analysis Using Q-GERT Networks,* Halsted Press and Pritsker & Associates, Inc., 1977.

15. Schriber, T., *Simulation Using GPSS,* John Wiley, 1974.

16. SCi Software Committee, "The SCi Continuous-Systems Simulation Language," *Simulation,* Vol. 9, 1967, pp. 281-303.

17. Shampine, L. F. and R. C. Allen, Jr., *Numerical Computing: An Introduction,* W. B. Saunders, 1973.

18. Sigal, C. E. and A. A. B. Pritsker, "SMOOTH: A Combined Continuous-Discrete Network Simulation Language," *Simulation,* Vol. 21, 1974, pp. 65-73.

19. Wortman, D. B., S. D. Duket et al, *Simulation Using SAINT: A User-Oriented Instruction Manual,* AMRL-TR-77-61, Aerospace Medical Research Laboratory, Wright-Patterson AFT, Ohio, 1978.

CHAPTER 4

Network Modeling with SLAM

4.1   INTRODUCTION

In Chapter 3, we introduced SLAM as a simulation language which allows the modeler to select the "world view" that is most applicable to the system under study. As such, the modeler can employ SLAM in any of the following orientations: process, event, continuous, and activity scanning. He also can simultaneously use any combination of these outlooks in his modeling effort. For exposition simplicity, SLAM modeling for these various orientations will be presented separately. This chapter describes the process orientation or network modeling procedures available in SLAM.

As an introduction to SLAM network modeling, let us consider a simple queueing system in which items arrive, wait, are processed by a single resource, and then depart the system. Such a sequence of events, activities, and decisions is referred to as a *process*. *Entities* flow through a process.† Thus, items are considered as entities. An entity can be assigned *attribute* values that enable a modeler to distin-

---

† Entities that flow through processes are sometimes referred to as transactions.

guish between individual entities of the same type or between entities of different types. For example, the time an entity enters the system could be an attribute of the entity. Such attributes are attached to the entity as it flows through the network. The resources of the system could be servers, tools, or the like for which entities compete while flowing through the system. A resource is busy when processing an entity, otherwise it is idle.

SLAM provides a framework for modeling the flow of entities through processes. The framework is a network structure consisting of specialized nodes and branches that are used to model resources, queues for resources, activities, and entity flow decisions. In short, a SLAM network model is a representation of a process and the flow of entities through the process.

4.2   A SLAM NETWORK OF A SINGLE SERVER QUEUEING SYSTEM

To illustrate the basic network concepts and symbols of SLAM, we will construct a model of an inspection process in the manufacturing of transistor radios. In this system, manufactured radios are delivered to an inspector at a central inspection area. The inspector examines each radio. After this inspection, the radio leaves the inspection area. Although we could model the entire manufacturing process, we are only interested in the operations associated with the inspection of radios. Therefore, we concern ourselves with the following three aspects of the system:

1. The arrival of radios to the inspection area;
2. The buildup of radios awaiting inspection; and
3. The activity of inspecting radios by a single inspector.

This is a single resource queueing system, and is similar to the bank teller system described in previous chapters. The radios are the system's entities. The inspector is the resource and will at first be modeled as a *server*. The *service activity* is the actual inspection, and the buildup of radios awaiting services is the *queue*.

A pictorial diagram of this inspection system is shown below.

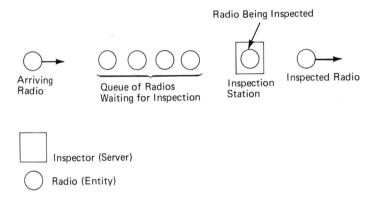

4.2.1   Modeling Queues and Servers

Let us now build a network for this one server system. The passage of time is represented by a *branch*. Branches are the graphical representation of activities. Clearly, the service operation (the inspection of the radios) is an activity and, hence, is modeled by a branch. If the service activity is ongoing, that is, the server (the inspector) is busy, arriving entities (radios) must wait. Waiting occurs at QUEUE nodes. Thus, a one-server, single-queue operation is depicted in SLAM by a QUEUE node and a branch as follows:

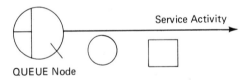

In our example, radios wait for service at the queue. When the inspector is free, he removes a radio from the queue and performs the service activity. The procedure for specifying the time to perform the service operation will be discussed later. A wide variety of service time distributions are available for use in SLAM.

Since there may be many queues and service activities in a network, each can be identified numerically. Entities waiting at queues are maintained in files, and a file number, IFL, is associated with a queue. Service activities are assigned a value to indicate the number, N, of parallel servers described by the branch, that is, the number of possible concurrent processings of entities. Activities can also be given an activity number, A, for identification and statistics collection purposes. The notation shown below is the procedure for labeling these elements of the network.

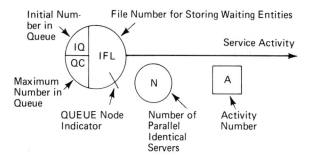

The file number is put on the right-hand side of the node. The procedure for ranking entities in the file is specified separately and is not shown on the graphic model. Also specified for a QUEUE node are the initial number of entities at the QUEUE node, IQ, and the capacity of the queue, QC. This latter quantity is the largest number of entities that can wait for service at the QUEUE node. Arriving entities to a full queue will either balk or be blocked. A QUEUE node has a "hash" mark in the lower right-hand corner to make the symbol resemble the letter Q. For the service activity, the number of parallel servers is put in a circle below the branch, and the activity number is put in a square below the branch.

4.2.2   Modeling the Arrival of Entities

Turning our attention to the entities (the individual radios), we must somehow model the arrival of radios to the system. In SLAM, entities are inserted into a network by CREATE nodes. The symbol for the CREATE node is shown below

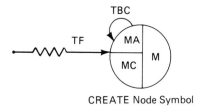

CREATE Node Symbol

where:
TF is the time at which the first entity is to be created and sent into the network;
TBC is the time between creations of entities;
MA is the attribute number in which the creation or mark time is to be maintained;

MC is the maximum number of entities that can be created at this node; and
M is the maximum number of branches along which a created entity can be routed
from this node (referred to as the M-number or "max take" value).

There are several important features to note about the CREATE node. At a prescribed time, TF, a first entity will be created. If desired, the time at which an
entity is created can be assigned to attribute MA of the entity. This time is usually
referred to as the "mark" time. The created entity will be routed over the branches
emanating from the node in accordance with the M-number. If M is equal to one
and there are two branches emanating from the node, the entity will only be routed
over one of the two branches. Procedures for selecting which branch over which
to route the entity will be described later. If all branches are to be taken, M need
not be specified.

The second entity created at the node will occur at time TF + TBC where TBC
is the time between creation of entities. For the radio example, TBC is the time
between the arrivals of radios which can be a constant, a SLAM variable, or a
random variable. This is described in the section on specifying attribute or duration
assignments. The variable MC prescribes a maximum number of entities that can
be created at the node. If no limit is specified, entities will continue to be created
until the end of the simulation of the system under study.

4.2.3   Modeling Departures of Entities

We have now modeled the arrival pattern of entities and the waiting and service
operations. All that remains is the modeling of the departure process for the entity.
For our simple system, we will let the entities leave the system following the completion of service. The modeling of the departure of an entity is accomplished by a
TERMINATE node as shown below.

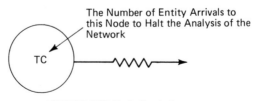

TERMINATE Node Symbol

A squiggly line is used on the output side of a node to indicate that entities are to
be terminated or destroyed at the node. TERMINATE nodes are one way to specify

the stopping procedure to be used when analyzing a SLAM network. Each analysis of a network is referred to as a run. For example, the TERMINATE node could specify that TC entity arrivals at the TERMINATE node are required to complete one run. As we shall see, the stopping condition can also be based on a time period. For example, a run could be made for 1000 hours of operation.

4.2.4   Combining Modeling Concepts

We are now ready to combine the arrival, service, and departure operations to obtain a complete network model of the one server, single queue process. This SLAM model is shown below with data values prescribed for the variables associ-

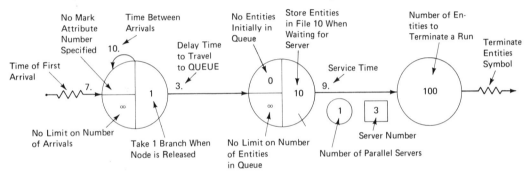

ated with the network symbols. This network depicts the flow of an entity and all the potential processing steps associated with the entity. The first entity arrives to the system at the CREATE node at time 7. The next entity is scheduled to arrive 10 time units later, which would be at time 17. The first entity is routed to the service activity by the branch to the QUEUE node. The branch represents the activity of traveling to the server and is prescribed to be 3 time units in duration. When the entity arrives at the QUEUE node, it will immediately be serviced if server 3 is idle. If this occurs, the entity flows from the QUEUE node to the TER-MINATE node in 9 time units. During this time, server 3 is busy.

Other entities will also follow the pattern described above. However, if server 3 is busy when an entity arrives at the QUEUE node, the entity is placed in file 10 which models the queue of entities waiting for server 3. When an entity joins a queue, a rule is used that specifies the order in which the entities are ranked in the queue. (The ranking rule for the queue is a characteristic of the file and is not specified on the graphical model.) If no ranking rule is specified, a first-in, first-out (FIFO) procedure is used, that is, entities are taken from the queue in the order in which they arrived to the queue. After entities are served by server 3, they reach the TERMINATE node where the entity is removed from the system since its routing through the process is completed.

4.3   SLAM NETWORK MODELING

A SLAM network model consists of a set of interconnected symbols that depict the operation of the system under study. The symbols can be converted into a form for input to a program that analyzes the model using simulation techniques. The input corresponding to a graphic SLAM model has been designed to be in the form of *statements*. Thus, there is a statement model that depicts the flow of entities through a process. It is feasible to build the statement model directly. We do not recommend this approach as it has been found in practice that the pictorial representation assists both in the communication and in the documentation of models. To provide an illustration of a statement model, the network model presented previously is given in statement form below. A semicolon is used to indicate the end of the data on a particular record. Comments can be given following a semicolon. The sequence of statements must correspond to the process an entity encounters as it flows through the network.

```
;EXAMPLE OF A SLAM STATEMENT MODEL
NETWORK;                  START OF NETWORK STATEMENTS
        CREATE,10.,7.;    TIME BETWEEN ARRIVALS = 10
        ACTIVITY,3;       TIME TO REACH QUEUE NODE IS 3
        QUEUE(10);        USE FILE 10 FOR QUEUE
        ACTIVITY(1)/3,9;  SERVICE TIME = 9
        TERMINATE,100;    RUN MODEL FOR 100 ENTITIES
        ENDNETWORK;       END OF NETWORK STATEMENTS
```

This illustration is only to indicate the similarity of the graphic model and the statement model that is acceptable as input for computer analysis. Later in this section, a description of the basic SLAM symbols and statements are presented.

As previously seen, a network consists of an interrelated set of nodes and branches. The nodes and branches can be considered as elements that are combined and integrated into a system description. The task of the modeler is to integrate the elements into a network model for the system of interest.

Before presenting the basic SLAM symbols and statements, several comments on general sequencing and entity flow are in order. Flow of entities normally follows the directed branches indicated on the network. Node labels are used to identify non-standard flows of entities. In statements, node labels are used as statement labels in a fashion similar to statement numbers in a FORTRAN program. Node labels can be appended to any node. On the graphic model, they are placed below the node symbol. On the statement, they precede the node name. The node or statement name is given starting in column seven or later on the input record, whereas the node label if required is given in columns one through five of the input record.

As described previously, branches are used to depict activities. In some situations, it is desired to have entities flow from one node to another node with no intervening activity. Such transfers are depicted on the network by branches with no specifications or by broken (nonsolid) lines, and are referred to as connectors. No statements are required in the statement model to describe connectors.

With this brief background, let us proceed to describe the SLAM network symbols and statements.

4.3.1   Routing Entities from Nodes (Branching)

Entities are routed along the branches emanating from nodes. The maximum number of branches, M, that can be selected is specified on the right-hand side of the node through the value assigned to M. When M equals 1, at most one branch will be taken. Two special cases are identified when $M = 1$. If probabilities are assigned to the branches emanating from a node that has $M = 1$, then the node is said to have *probabilistic branching*. If conditions were assigned to the branches leaving the node that has $M = 1$, then we refer to the node as having *conditional, take-first branching*. When $M = \infty$ then we have the special cases of deterministic and conditional, take-all branching. If no conditions or probabilities are prescribed for the branches, and M equals the number of branches emanating from the node then *deterministic branching* is specified. Deterministic branching causes an entity to be duplicated and routed over every branch emanating from the node. When conditions are prescribed for routing entities over the branches and M is equal to the number of branches, then *conditional, take-all branching* is specified. In this case, any branch whose condition is not satisfied is not taken.

The branching concept prescribed by the value of M is quite general. It allows the routing of entities over a subset of branches for which conditions are prescribed. For example, if M is equal to 2 and there are five branches emanating from the node, then the transaction would be routed over the first two branches for which the condition is met.

An even more complex situation involves a combination of probabilistic and conditional branching. Letting p_i be the probability of routing an entity over branch i and letting c_j be the condition for routing over branch j, consider the following situation:

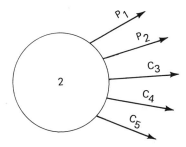

For this example, $M = 2$ which signifies that at most two of the five branches are to be taken. Assuming the branches are evaluated in the order 1, 2, 3, 4, and 5, a random selection between branches 1 and 2 will be made ($p_1 + p_2$ must equal 1) and then branch 3 will be taken if condition 3 (c_3) is satisfied. If not, c_4 is tested and then c_5. If c_3 is satisfied, the other branches would not be taken even though c_4 or c_5 were satisfied. In the statement model, when branches (activities) emanate from a node, a statement describing each activity is placed immediately after the statement describing the node. The order of the activity statements defines the order in which the conditions are evaluated.

4.3.2   CREATE Node

The CREATE node generates entities and routes them into the system over activities that emanate from the CREATE node. A time for the first entity to be created by the CREATE node is specified by the variable TF. The time between creations of entities after the first is specified by the variable TBC. TBC can be specified as a constant, a SLAM variable, or a SLAM random variable. Entities will continue to be created until a limit is reached. This limit is specified as MC, the maximum number of creations allowed at the node. When MC entities have been input to the system, the CREATE node stops creating entities.

The time at which the entity is created can be assigned to an attribute of the entity. This time is referred to as the *mark time* of the entity and it is placed in the MAth attribute of the entity. As will be discussed shortly, the variable

ATRIB(MA) stores this value. The symbol and statement for the CREATE node are shown below.

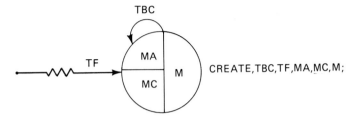

CREATE,TBC,TF,MA,MC,M;

The following are examples of the CREATE node.

1. Create entities starting at time zero and every 10 time units thereafter. Put the mark time into attribute 2 of the entity. Take all branches emanating from the CREATE node.

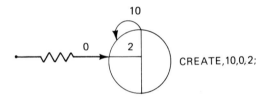

CREATE,10,0,2;

The default values taken are: MC = ∞ and M = ∞.

2. Create fifty entities starting at time 100.0. The time between creations should be 30. Take 2 branches emanating from the node.

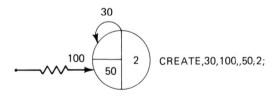

CREATE,30,100,,50;2;

The default value for MA is not to mark the entities.

3. Create 1 entity at time 75 and take all branches emanating from the node.

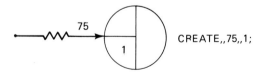

CREATE,,75,,1;

The default values are: no marking; TBC = ∞; and M = ∞.

4.3.3   QUEUE Node

A QUEUE node is a location in the network where entities wait for service. When an entity arrives at a QUEUE node, its disposition depends on the status of the server that follows the QUEUE node. If the server is idle, the entity passes through the QUEUE node and goes immediately into the service activity. If no server is available, the entity waits at the QUEUE node until a server can process it. When a server does become available, the entity will automatically be taken out of the queue and service will be initiated. SLAM assumes that no delay is involved from the time a server becomes available and the time service is started on an entity that was waiting in the QUEUE node.

When an entity waits at a QUEUE node, it is stored in a file which maintains the entity's attributes and the relative position of the entity with respect to other entities waiting at the same QUEUE node. The order in which the entities wait in the QUEUE is specified outside the network on a priority card which defines the ranking rule for the file associated with the QUEUE. Files can be ranked on: first-in, first-out (FIFO); last-in, first-out (LIFO); low-value first based on an attribute K (LOW(K)); and high-value first based on attribute K (HIGH(K)). FIFO is the default priority for files.

Entities can initially reside at queues, as the initial number of entities at a QUEUE node, IQ, is part of the description of the QUEUE node. These entities all start with attribute values equal to zero. When $IQ > 0$, all service activities emanating from the Q-node are assumed to be busy initially working on entities with all attribute values equal to zero. QUEUE nodes can have a capacity which limits the number of entities that can reside at the queue at a given time. The basic symbol and statement for the QUEUE node are shown below.

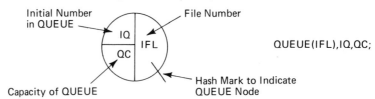

When an entity arrives at a QUEUE node which is at its capacity, its disposition must be determined. This decision is based on a specification at the QUEUE node as to whether the entity should balk or be blocked. In the case of balking, the entity can be routed to another node of the network. This node is specified by providing the label of the node. If no balking node label is specified, the entity is deleted from the system. The symbol for balking is shown below in a network segment involving balking from one QUEUE node to another QUEUE node labeled QUE2. There is no restriction on the type of node to which entities can balk.

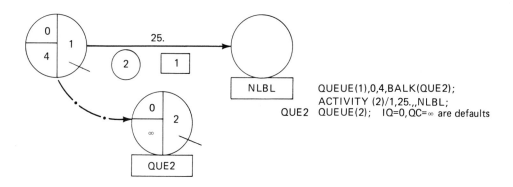

When an entity is blocked by a QUEUE node, it waits until a free space is available in the queue. The activity which just served the entity that is blocked is also considered as blocked. A blocked entity will join the queue when a space is available. At that time, the blocked activity becomes free to process other entities waiting for it. No time delay is associated with these deblocking operations. The symbol and statement for blocking at a QUEUE node are shown below.

QUEUE nodes may only block service activities.

When more than one service activity follows a queue and the service activities are not identical, a selection of the server to process an entity must be made. This selection is not made at the QUEUE node but at a SELECT node that is associated with the QUEUE node. The label of the SELECT node associated with a QUEUE node is entered on the QUEUE statement. When an entity arrives at a QUEUE node, its associated SELECT node is interrogated. When a SELECT node finds a free server, the entity arriving at the QUEUE node is transferred to the SELECT node and is immediately put into service. Direct transfers of this type are shown in SLAM through the use of dashed lines. An illustration of a QUEUE node-SELECT node combination is shown below.

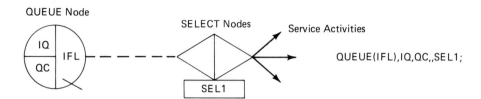

QUEUE(IFL),IQ,QC,,SEL1;

Additional information on SELECT nodes is given in Section 4.9.

The following are examples of QUEUE nodes:

1. Cause arriving entities to wait in file 7 if the number of waiting entities is less than 6 and the following server is busy.

QUEUE(7),,6;

The default values are: IQ = 0 implying no initial entities are at the QUEUE node; no balking node is specified, implying that entities arriving to the queue when it is full are lost to the system; no SELECT nodes are specified, implying a single type of service activity is represented by the branch that follows the QUEUE node.

2. Cause arriving entities to be blocked if two entities are waiting in the QUEUE node called QUE1. Entities at QUE1 wait in file 3. Two servers can process entities arriving to the QUE1. Initially there is one entity waiting at QUE1.

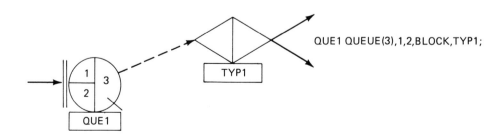

QUE1 QUEUE(3),1,2,BLOCK,TYP1;

In this example, the branch incident to QUE1 represents a server who will be blocked if he finishes processing an entity when two entities are already waiting at QUE1 (in file 3). The service activities that process entities waiting in QUE1 are represented by the branches following SELECT node TYP1.

4.3.4   TERMINATE Node

The TERMINATE node is used to destroy or delete entities from the network. It can be used to specify the number of entities to be processed on a simulation run. This number of entities is referred to as the termination count or TC value. When multiple TERMINATE nodes are employed, the first termination count reached ends the simulation run. If a TERMINATE node does not have a termination count, the entity is destroyed and no further action is taken. The symbol and statement for the TERMINATE node are shown below.

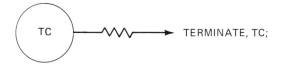

As an example, consider the ending of a simulation run after 25 entities arrive to node HELP. This would be modeled as shown below.

Every entity routed to a TERMINATE node is destroyed. To facilitate the graphic modeling, the TERMINATE operation can also be displayed as follows:

$$TC$$

This symbol allows an entity to be destroyed after it is processed at any node of the network from which branching occurs. A separate TERMINATE statement would still be used but would follow the node statement directly.

4.3.5   ASSIGN Node

The ASSIGN node is used to prescribe values to the attributes of an entity passing through the ASSIGN node or to prescribe values to system variables that pertain to the network in general. The ASSIGN node can also change values pertaining to discrete and continuous models that can be a part of SLAM. Table 4-1 presents the definitions of variables to which assignments can be made.

Table 4-1   Variables to which assignments can be made.

Variable Name[†]	Definition
II	An integer global variable. II is frequently used as an index or argument.
ATRIB(I)	Attribute I of a current entity
SS(I)	State variable I
DD(I)	Derivative of SS(I)
XX(I)	System or global variable I

[†]The argument I can be an integer constant or the variable II.

A value assigned to a variable can be used as an activity duration, as a routing condition, and in program inserts. In combined simulations, assignments can be used to change the values of variables that are part of the discrete or continuous model. This latter concept will be described in more detail in later chapters where combined discrete and continuous modeling concepts are presented.

The vector $ATRIB(\cdot)$ defines the attributes of entities as they flow through the network. Each entity has its own attribute vector which is attached to the entity as it moves through nodes and across branches. The variable $XX(I)$ can be used in a network model as a global variable that is set in one portion of the network and can be used at any other portion of the network. Procedures are available to obtain time-integrated statistics on $XX(I)$, $SS(I)$, or $DD(I)$.

The values assigned to variables at an ASSIGN node can take on a wide variety of forms. The value can be a constant, one of the variables described above, a network status variable, the current time, a sample from a probability distribution, or a value set in a user-written function (a program insert). Table 4-2 defines the values from which variables can be assigned numeric quantities. The parameters used in the probability functions are those described in the equations presented in Section 2.9. In network assignments, the stream number, IS, can be omitted and a default stream number (stream number 9), is used.

The symbol and statement for the ASSIGN node are shown below.

Basically, each line in the ASSIGN node can be considered as a FORTRAN replacement statement with a left-hand side variable being restricted to those presented in Table 4-1. The right-hand side expression can involve one arithmetic operation using the constants and variables defined in Table 4-2. Specifically, the replacement statement must be in the form: A = B $\otimes$ C where A is from Table 4-1; B and C are from Table 4-2; and $\otimes$ is one of [+,−,*,/]. The expression is further restricted in that if $\otimes$ is employed B may not be a constant and parentheses are not permitted. An example of the ASSIGN node is shown below.

In this example, the value of attribute 2 of the entity passing through the node is changed to seven. The value of attribute 3 is replaced by its current value divided by XX(2). The third assignment specifies that XX(1) be given a value that is a sample from a normal distribution whose mean is 4 and whose standard deviation is 2. The value of M is set to one to indicate that the entity is to be routed through only one branch. Since the statement is long, it can be divided and placed on separate lines (the details associated with statement continuation and input procedures are described in Chapter 5). For example, the statement could have been written as

ASSIGN,ATRIB(2) = 7.0,
          ATRIB(3) = ATRIB(3)/XX(2),
          XX(1) = RNORM(4.,2.),   1;

To allow indirect addressing of subscripts or arguments, the variable II is made available. Illustrations of its uses are shown below.

ASSIGN,II = ATRIB(2),ATRIB(3) = XX(II);
ASSIGN,II = UNFRM(0.,10.),ATRIB(4) = II;

Table 4-2   List of variables/functions from which assignment values can be obtained.

Variable/Function[†]	Definition
Constant	A constant real value
TNOW	Current time
ATRIB(I)	Attribute I of current entity
SS(I)	Value of state variable I
DD(I)	Value of the derivative of state variable I
XX(I)	Value of global variable I
NNACT(I)	Number of active entities in activity I at current time
NNCNT(I)	The number of entities that have completed activity I
NNGAT(GLBL)	Status of gate GLBL at current time : 0→ open; 1→ closed
NNRSC(RLBL)	Current number of units of resource type RLBL available
NNQ(I)	Number of entities in file I at the current time (Recall entities in QUEUE nodes are stored in files)
II	An integer global variable. II is frequently used as an index or argument
DRAND(IS)	A pseudo-random number obtained from random number stream IS
EXPON (XMEAN,IS)	A sample from an exponential distribution with mean XMEAN using random number stream IS
UNFRM (ULO,UHI,IS)	A sample from a uniform distribution in the interval ULO to UHI using random number stream IS
WEIBL (BETA,ALPHA,IS)	A sample from a Weibull distribution with scale parameter BETA and shape parameter ALPHA using random number stream IS

Table 4-2 (Continued).

Variable/Function[†]	Definition
TRIAG (XLO,XMODE,XHI,IS)	A sample from a triangular distribution in the interval XLO to XHI with mode XMODE using random number stream IS
RNORM (XMN,STD,IS)	A sample from a normal distribution with mean XMN and standard deviation STD using random number stream IS
RLOGN (XMN, STD,IS)	A sample from a lognormal distribution with mean XMN and standard deviation STD using random number stream IS
ERLNG (EMN,XK,IS)	A sample from a Erlang distribution which is the sum of XK exponential samples each with mean EMN using random number stream IS
GAMA (BETA,ALPHA,IS)	A sample from a gamma distribution with parameters BETA and ALPHA using random number stream IS
BETA (THETA,PHI,IS)	A sample from a beta distribution with parameters THETA and PHI using random number stream IS
NPSSN (XMN,IS)	A sample from a Poisson distribution with mean XMN using random number stream IS
USERF (I)	A sample obtained from the user-written function USERF with user function number 1

† The variable I can be an integer constant or the variable II. Each parameter for a distribution can be specified as a constant, ATRIB(I), or XX(I). If one parameter is specified as a constant, then the other parameters must be constants.

See Section 2.9 for the equations of the distribution functions associated with the random variables including the definitions of the function arguments.

In network models, the argument for NNGAT and NNRSC can be either a label or a number. In discrete or continuous models, it must be a numeric value. GATES and RESOURCES are assigned numeric values based on their position in the statement model.

In the first illustration, II is set equal to attribute 2 and attribute 3 is set equal the global variable XX with an index that is obtained from attribute 2.

In the second example, II is set equal to a sample from a uniform distribution in the range (0,10). Since II is integer, the real values will be truncated, and II will take on the values 0 through 9 with an equal probability of 0.10. ATRIB(4) can then be set equal to II as a sample from a discrete uniform distribution.

As another example of the flexibility of the ASSIGN node, consider the setting of XX(1) equal to a sample from an exponential distribution whose mean is taken as ATRIB(1) using stream 2. This is accomplished with the following statement:

ASSIGN,XX(1) = EXPON(ATRIB(1),2);

The variables to which attributes are assigned can be used for many purposes. The primary uses involve the routing of entities and the duration of activities based on assigned values. Specific examples of the use of assignments will be deferred until these concepts are presented.

In summary, attribute I of the entity passing through the ASSIGN node is changed if any of the assignments involve the variable ATRIB(I) on the left-hand side of the replacement statement. Global system variables are not associated with entities but are changed by the passage of an entity through an ASSIGN node. A global variable retains its value until another entity passes an ASSIGN node at which the global variable is recomputed. Following the assignments, the entity is routed from the ASSIGN node in accordance with the M-number prescribed for the node.

4.4 ACTIVITIES

Branches are used to model activities. Only at branches are explicit time delays prescribed for entities flowing through the network. Activities emanating from QUEUE or SELECT nodes are referred to as service activities. Service activities restrict the number of concurrent entities flowing through them to be equal to the number of servers represented by the activity. Activities represented by branches emanating from other node types have no restriction on the number of entities that can simultaneously flow through them. The duration of an activity is the time delay that an entity encounters as it flows through the branch representing the activity.

Each branch has a start node and an end node. When an entity is to be routed from the start node, the branch may be selected as one through which the entity should be routed. The selection can be probabilistic in which case a probability is part of the activity description. The selection can be conditional in which case a condition is specified as part of the activity description. Service activities cannot have prescribed conditions, as their availability is limited and they must be allocated when free. If no probability or condition is specified (a common situation), the activity will be selected unless the M-number associated with its start node has been satisfied.

Activities can be given activity numbers. If the number I is prescribed for an activity then statistics are maintained and reported on the number of entities that are currently being processed through the activity, NNACT(I), and the number of entities that have completed the activity, NNCNT(I).

For service activities, the number of parallel identical servers represented by the activity needs to be specified if different from one. (For non-service activities, the number of parallel processes is assumed as infinite.) For service activities, SLAM automatically provides utilization statistics.

The symbol for a branch representing an activity is shown below.

where

N is the number of parallel servers if the activity represents a set of identical servers;

A is an activity number (an integer);

DUR is the duration specified for the activity;

PROB is the probability of selecting the activity;

COND is a condition for selecting the activity if the activity is a non-server; and

NLBL is the end node label and is only required if the end node is not specified by the next statement (input record).

4.4.1 Activity Durations

Activity durations (DUR) can be specified by any expression containing the variables described in Table 4-2. Thus, a duration can be assigned a value in the same way as an attribute or system variable is assigned a value. For example, a duration can be taken as the value of attribute 3 by specifying DUR to be ATRIB(3) or as a sample from an exponential distribution whose mean is ATRIB(3), that is, EXPON(ATRIB(3)). If a sample from a probability distribution is negative, and the sample is used for an activity duration, SLAM assumes a zero value for the activity's duration.

The duration can be made to depend on the release time of a node of the network by specifying that the activity continue until the next release of a node.† This is accomplished using the REL(NLBL) specification. When the duration is specified in this manner, the activity will continue in operation, holding the entity being processed until the next release of the node with the prescribed label. The REL specification corresponds to an activity scanning orientation as described in Section 3.3.2.

4.4.2   Probability Specification for Branches

Probabilities are specified for branches as real values between 0.0 and 1.0. The sum of the probabilities of those branches with probabilities emanating from the same node must be one. Probabilities may be assigned to branches emanating from QUEUE nodes. In this case, the activities emanating from the QUEUE node are assumed to be the same server(s) and the probabilities can be used to obtain different duration specifications or different routings for entities processed by the same server(s).

4.4.3   Condition Specification for Branches

As stated above, the condition specification only applies to non-service activities. Conditions are prescribed in the form: VALUE. OPERATOR. VALUE. VALUE can be a constant, a SLAM variable, or a SLAM random variable (see Table 4-2). OPERATOR is one of the standard FORTRAN relational codes defined below.

Relational Code	Definition
LT	Less than
LE	Less than or equal to
EQ	Equal to
NE	Not equal to
GT	Greater than
GE	Greater than or equal to

---

† By release of a node is meant the act of an entity arriving at the node and the attempt to route it from the node. In the section 4.6, the ACCUMULATE node is described where entities arrive but may not release (pass through) the node.

Examples of condition codes are:

Condition	Take branch if
TNOW. GE. 100.0	Current time greater than or equal to 100.
ATRIB(1).LT.DRAND(2)	Attribute 1 of the current entity is less than a random number obtained from stream 2.
NNQ(7).EQ.10	The number of entities in file 7 is equal to 10.

The union and intersection of two or more conditions can be prescribed for an activity using .AND. and .OR. specifications. Thus, a possible conditional expression for a branch could be

TNOW. GE. 100.0 .AND. ATRIB(2).LT.5.0

An example of the use of the union of two conditions is

NNQ(7).EQ.10 .OR. II.NE.4

If more than two conditions are combined using the .AND. and .OR. specifications, then the .AND. conditions are tested prior to the .OR. conditions as is done in FORTRAN. The use of parentheses is not permitted. Complicated logic testing requiring parentheses can be done by using the user-written function USERF.

4.5   ILLUSTRATIVE EXAMPLES

In this section, we present examples that illustrate the node and activity concepts presented previously. Both network and statement models are presented.

4.5.1   Illustration 1. Two Parallel Servers

Consider a situation involving the processing of customers at a bank with two tellers and a single waiting line. A network that models this situation is shown below.

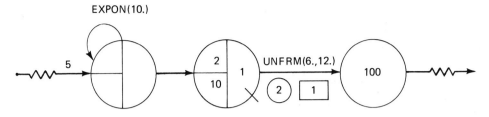

```
NETWORK;
        CREATE,EXPON(10.),5;
        QUEUE(1),2,10;
                ACTIVITY(2)/1,UNFRM(6.,12.);
        TERM,100;
        ENDNETWORK;
```

In this example, two parallel servers (tellers) are associated with activity 1. The service time of each server is uniformly distributed between 6 and 12 time units. Entities (customers) that arrive at the QUEUE node when both servers are busy wait in file 1. Initially, there are two entities in the QUEUE which causes both servers to be busy initially. Thus, there are four in the system initially; two in service and two waiting at the QUEUE node. A capacity of ten entities has been assigned to the QUEUE.

The TERMINATE node indicates that the model is to be analyzed until 100 entities have completed processing. The time between arrivals is prescribed at the CREATE node as samples from an exponential distribution with a mean of 10. The first entity is scheduled to arrive at time 5.

4.5.2   Illustration 2. Two Types of Entities

Consider a situation involving two types of jobs that require processing by the same server. The job types are assumed to form a single queue before the server. The network model of this situation is shown below.

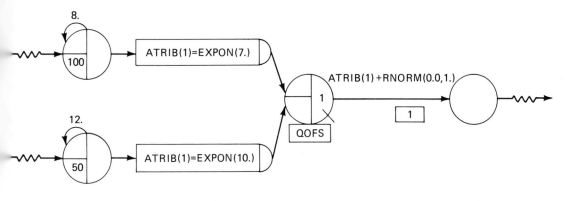

```
NETWORK;
        CREATE,8,,,100;
        ASSIGN,ATRIB(1)=EXPON(7.);
            ACTIVITY,,,QOFS;
        CREATE,12,,,50;
        ASSIGN,ATRIB(1)=EXPON(10.);
QOFS    QUEUE(1);
            ACTIVITY/1,ATRIB(1)+RNORM(0.0,1.0);
        TERM;
        ENDNETWORK;
```

In this model, one type of entity is scheduled to arrive every 8 time units and only 100 of them are to be created. These entities have a service time estimated to be a sample from an exponential distribution with a mean time of 7. This service time is assigned to attribute 1 at an ASSIGN node. For the other type of entity the time between arrivals is 12 time units and 50 of these entities are to be created. The estimated service time for each of these entities is exponentially distributed with a mean time of 10. Both types of entities are routed to a QUEUE node whose label is QOFS. Entities at QOFS wait in file 1 and are ranked on small values of attribute one. This priority specification is made through a PRIORITY statement that will be described in Chapter 5. The server is modeled as activity 1 where the service time is specified as attribute 1 plus a sample from a normal distribution. Thus, the actual processing time is equal to the estimated processing time plus an error term that is assumed to be normally distributed. This model might be used to represent a job shop in which jobs are performed in the order of the smallest estimated service time.

Many default values were assumed in the above model. Both entity types have their first arrival at time zero and neither are marked. The M-number for all the CREATE and ASSIGN nodes are defaulted which causes an infinite M-number to be used, that is, take all branches. The default value for the initial number in the QUEUE node is zero and the capacity of the QUEUE node is assumed to be infinite. No specification for the termination count is made at the TERMINATE node and, hence, the run is completed when all entities created have passed through the system, which in this case is 150. (Note: this termination condition cannot be determined absolutely from the model description, as a completion time for the network could have been prescribed. The procedure for specifying a completion time is discussed in Chapter 5.)

4.5.3   Illustration 3. Blocking and Balking from QUEUE Nodes

Consider a company with a maintenance shop that involves two operations in series. When maintenance is required on a machine and four machines are waiting for operation 1, the maintenance operations are subcontracted to an external vendor. This situation is modeled below.

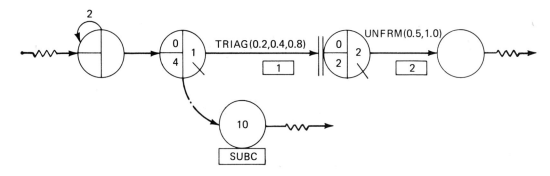

```
NETWORK;
        CREATE,2;
        QUEUE(1),0,4,BALK(SUBC);
            ACT/1,TRIAG (0.2,0.4,0.8);
        QUEUE(2),0,2,BLOCK;
            ACT/2,UNFRM(0.5,1.0);
        TERM;
SUBC    TERM,10;
        ENDNET;
```

In this model, entities are created every two time units and routed directly to a QUEUE node that has a capacity of four. At this node, entities are stored in file 1 and, if an entity arrives when there are four other entities in file 1, it balks to the TERMINATE node SUBC. When ten entities balk to node SUBC, the run is to be ended. The service time for activity 1 is triangularly distributed with a mode of 0.4 and minimum and maximum values of 0.2 and 0.8, respectively. When service activity 1 is completed, entities are routed directly to a second QUEUE node. File 2 is used to store waiting entities if less than two entities are waiting for server 2. If two entities are already waiting for server 2, the entity is blocked along with service activity 1. No further service activities can be started for server 1 even though entities are waiting in file 1. When the number of entities in file 2 decreases below 2, the blocked entity is routed to file 2 and another service activity for server 1 can be started. The processing time for server 2 is uniformly distributed between 0.5 and 1. This illustration is used in Chapter 6 to demonstrate the complete inputs and outputs from the SLAM processor.

4.5.4   Illustration 4. Conditional and Probabilistic Branching

Consider a situation involving an inspector and an adjustor. Presume that seventy percent of the items inspected are routed directly to packing and thirty percent of the items require adjustment. Following adjustment, the items are returned for reinspection. We will let the inspection time be a function of the number of items waiting for inspection (NNQ(1)) and the number waiting for adjustment (NNQ(2)). The model corresponding to this description is shown below.

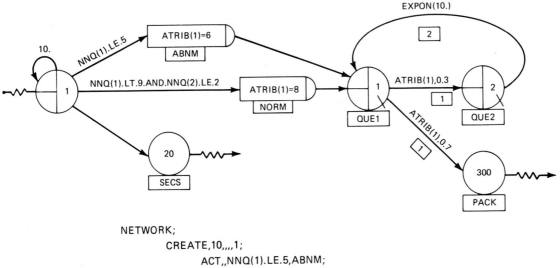

```
            NETWORK;
                    CREATE,10,,,,1;
                            ACT,,NNQ(1).LE.5,ABNM;
                            ACT,,NNQ(1).LT.9.AND.NNQ(2).LE.2,NORM;
                            ACT;
            SECS    TERM,20;
            ABNM    ASSIGN,ATRIB(1)=6;
                            ACT,,,QUE1;
            NORM    ASSIGN,ATRIB(1)=8;
            QUE1    QUEUE(1);
                            ACT/1,ATRIB(1), 0.3,QUE2;
                            ACT/1,ATRIB(1),0.7,PACK;
            QUE2    QUEUE(2);
                            ACT/2,EXPON(10.),,QUE1;
            PACK    TERM,300;
                    ENDNET;
```

In this model, conditional branching is specified from the CREATE node where the M-number is one. That is, a maximum of one of the three branches emanating from the CREATE node is to be taken. The entity is routed to node ABNM if the number of entities in file 1 is less than or equal to 5. At ASSIGN node ABNM, ATRIB(1) is set equal to 6 time units. ATRIB(1) will be used in this illustration to represent the processing time for an entity. The branch from the CREATE node to the ASSIGN node NORM is taken if the number of entities in file 1 is less than 9 and the number of entities in file 2 is less than or equal to 2. When this occurs, a processing time of 8 time units is stored in ATRIB(1) at the ASSIGN node NORM.

No condition is specified on the branch from the **CREATE** node to the **TERM** node SECS. Since the conditions are evaluated in the order prescribed by the statement model, this branch will only be taken if the preceding two branches are not taken. This branch represents a non-processing of an entity through the server process. If 20 such occurrences materialize, the run is to be completed.

QUE1 is the QUEUE node for server 1. With probability 0.3, the entity is routed to QUE2. With probability 0.7, it is routed to the TERM node PACK. Both of these activities represent service activity 1. Service time is prescribed to be set equal to attribute 1 previously defined at the ASSIGN nodes. At QUE2, the entity goes through a second service activity whose service time is exponentially distributed with a mean time of 10. Entities are then routed back to QUE1 for additional processing by server 1. At TERMINATE node PACK, a requirement of 300 transaction arrivals is indicated in order to complete one run of the network. Thus, a run can be terminated by an entity arrival to either node PACK or node SECS.

4.5.5   Illustration 5. Service Time Dependent on Node Release

Consider an assembly line that is paced so that units can only be completed at the end of ten-minute intervals. This situation is modeled below.

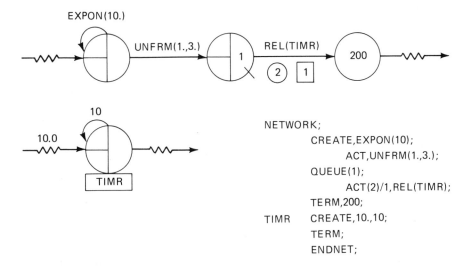

```
                              NETWORK;
                                     CREATE,EXPON(10);
                                             ACT,UNFRM(1.,3.);
                                     QUEUE(1);
                                             ACT(2)/1,REL(TIMR);
                                     TERM,200;
                              TIMR    CREATE,10.,10;
                                      TERM;
                                      ENDNET;
```

This model depicts two identical servers with a single queue and is similar to the model presented in Illustration 1. However, for this model the service time duration is specified as the next release time of CREATE node TIMR. CREATE node TIMR is released for the first time at time 10 and every 10 time units thereafter. This specifies that the duration for service activity 1 will end at a multiple of 10. If the service activity 1 starts at time 13 then the end time will be 20. Thus, the service duration will be 7. If an entity is put into service at time 49, it will complete service at time 50 and its duration will be 1. Other aspects of this illustration were described previously.

This completes the discussion and illustration of the basic concepts associated with CREATE, QUEUE, TERMINATE, and ASSIGN nodes and ACTIVITIES.

4.6   ACCUMULATE NODE

The ACCUMULATE node or ACCUM node is only released when a prescribed number of entities have arrived to it. The release of an ACCUMULATE node causes branching from the node to be initiated. At the ACCUMULATE node, a release specification is required. This specification involves the number of incoming entities needed to release the node for the first time (FR), the number required for subsequent releases (SR), and a rule for deciding which entity's attributes to save when more than one incoming entity is required to release the node (SAVE). The possible rule specifications are:

1. Save the attributes of the first entity arriving to the node (FIRST);
2. Save the attributes of the entity that causes the release of the node (LAST);
3. Save the attributes of the incoming entity that has the highest value of attribute I (HIGH(I));
4. Save the attributes of the incoming entity which has the lowest value of attribute I (LOW(I));
5. Create a new entity whose attributes are equal to the sum of the attributes of all incoming entities (SUM);
6. Create a new entity whose attributes are equal to the product of the incoming attributes of all incoming entities (MULT).

As an example of the release mechanism specification, consider that two incoming entities are required to release the node for the first time and only one incoming entity is required to release the node on subsequent times. On the first release, it is desired to save the attributes of the second arriving entity. The specification of the release mechanism for this situation is: 2,1,LAST. The specification of the release mechanism is given by FR,SR, and SAVE where:

FR = First release requirement;
SR = Subsequent release requirement; and
SAVE = Rule for saving attributes when entities are accumulated.

The symbol and statement for the ACCUMULATE rule are:

 ACCUMULATE,FR,SR,SAVE,M;

The above example would be coded as:

 ACC,2,1,LAST;

where the default value of M = ∞ is used. If the SAVE criterion was specified as SUM, then the sum of the attributes of the first two entities arriving would be maintained as the attributes of the entity routed from the node. By using this criterion and by specifying zero attribute values for selected attributes for each entity, a mixture of attribute values can be obtained.

The ACCUMULATE node is used extensively in project planning networks (PERT,CPM) where multiple activities must be completed prior to the start of additional activities. The SAVE criterion can be used to maintain information about entities that cause the ACCUMULATE node to be released.

4.7 GOON NODE

The GO ON or GOON node is included as a CONTINUE type node.† It is a special case of the ACCUMULATE node that has FR = 1, SR = 1 and no SAVE rule associated with it. The symbol and statement for the GOON node are:

 GOON,M;

---

† The name CONTINUE was not used to avoid confusion with a CONTINUOUS statement that is used to define information for continuous simulation models.

The GOON node is used in the modeling of sequential activities since the start of one activity must be separated from the end of a preceding activity by a node.

4.8   COLCT NODE

Statistics can be collected on five types of variables at a COLCT node. Four of the variables refer to the time or times at which an entity arrives at the COLCT node. The fifth statistic type allows the collection of system variables at specified nodes. The five types of variables are:

1. Time-of-first arrival (FIRST). At most one value is recorded during a run, independent of the number of entities that arrive to the node during the run.
2. Time-of-all arrivals (ALL). Every time an entity arrives to the node, the arrival time is added to all previous arrival times. At the end of a run, an average time of arrival is computed.
3. Time between arrivals (BETWEEN). The time of first arrival is used as a reference point. On subsequent arrivals, the time between arrivals is collected as an observation of the statistic of interest.
4. Interval statistics (INT(NATR)). This statistic relates to the arrival time of an entity minus an attribute value of the entity. Statistics are maintained on the time interval between the entity's arrival time at the node and the mark time value stored in attribute NATR of the entity.
5. SLAM variable. The value of a SLAM variable is recorded as an observation every time an entity arrives to the node.

For each of the above five types of variables, estimates for the mean and standard deviation of the variables are obtained. In addition, a histogram of the values collected at a COLCT node can be obtained. This is accomplished by specifying on input the number of cells; the upper limit of the first cell, HLOW; and a cell width, HWID, for the histogram.

The number of cells specified, NCEL, is the number of interior cells, each of which will have a width of HWID. Two additional cells will be added that contain the interval $(-\infty, \text{HLOW}]$ and $(\text{HLOW} + \text{NCEL*HWID}, \infty)$. The cells are closed at the high value. Thus, if HLOW = 0, the value 0 will be included in the first cell. For the specification: NCEL = 5; HLOW = 0; and HWID = 10; the number of times the variable on which statistics are being maintained is in the following intervals would be presented as part of the standard SLAM summary report:

$(-\infty,0]$, $(0,10]$, $(10,20]$, $(20,30]$, $(30,40]$, $(40,50]$, and $(50,\infty)$.

If the number of cells is specified as zero, no histogram will be prepared. A 16 character identifier can be associated with a COLCT node. This identifier (denoted ID) will be printed on the SLAM summary report to identify the output associated with the COLCT node.

The symbol and statement for the COLCT node are:

Since histograms are not always requested, a single field identified as 'H' is used on the symbol where it is implied that H represents NCEL/HLOW/HWID. Examples of the COLCT node are given below.

1. Collect statistics on the completion time of a project with no histogram required:

2. Collect statistics on the time in the system of an entity whose time of entering the system is maintained in ATRIB(3). No histogram is requested for this COLCT node and the entity is to be routed over one branch.

3. Collect statistics on the value of global variable, XX(2), every time an entity passes through the COLCT node. Identify the statistical output with the identifier SAFETY STOCK. Prepare a histogram consisting of 20 cells for which the first cell interval is $(-\infty,10]$ and the width of the next 20 cells is 5. Set the maximum number of branches to be taken to 2.

In this illustration, XX(2) can be considered as an inventory level and the entity arriving to the COLCT node represents a replenishment of the units in inventory.

4.9   SELECT NODE

SELECT nodes are points in the network where a decision regarding the routing of an entity is to be made and the decision concerns either QUEUE nodes or servers or both. To accomplish the routing at the SELECT node, the modeler chooses a *queue selection rule* (*QSR*) and/or a *server selection rule* (*SSR*). The selection of a rule establishes the decision process by which SLAM will route entities when a decision point is reached. The decision points in the SLAM network occur at the following times:

1. An entity is to be routed to one of a set of parallel queues;
2. A service activity has been completed and parallel queues exist that have entities waiting for the service activity. In this situation, a SELECT node is used to decide from which QUEUE node the entity should be taken; and
3. An entity is to be routed to one of a set of non-identical idle servers.

The SELECT symbol is more complex than other SLAM symbols in that the decision at the node can involve both a "looking ahead" and a "looking behind" capability. A look ahead capability is necessary to route entities to one of a set of parallel queues and to select from a set of parallel servers. These are decision types

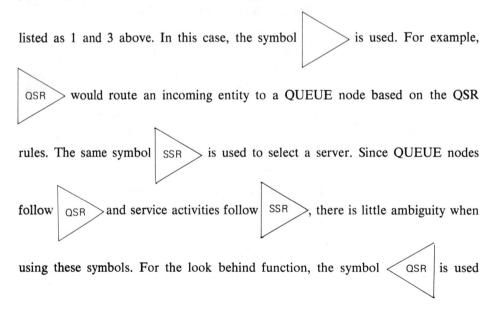

listed as 1 and 3 above. In this case, the symbol ▷ is used. For example, QSR ▷ would route an incoming entity to a QUEUE node based on the QSR rules. The same symbol SSR ▷ is used to select a server. Since QUEUE nodes follow QSR ▷ and service activities follow SSR ▷, there is little ambiguity when using these symbols. For the look behind function, the symbol ◁ QSR is used where QUEUE nodes would precede the symbol and the SELECT node would perform the function listed as 2 above. A single SELECT node can perform both the look-behind and look-ahead functions in which case we use the symbol

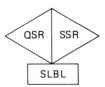

where the SELECT node label, SLBL, has been attached. In all cases, we employ the same statement type which is

SLBL SELECT,QSR,SSR,BLOCK or BALK(NLBL),QLBLs;

When QSR or SSR are not required, default values should be requested. In the above statement, the QLBLs are the QUEUE node labels associated with the QSR rule. The QUEUE nodes could be before or after the SELECT node.

Four observations regarding the SELECT node are:

1. QUEUE nodes can not be on both sides of a given SELECT node.
2. If service activities follow a SELECT node then QUEUE nodes must precede the SELECT node to hold entities when all the service activities are ongoing.
3. Balking and blocking occur at a SELECT node when all following QUEUE nodes are at their capacity and the BALK or BLOCK option is prescribed. The symbolism for this is shown below.

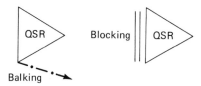

4. Whenever the look-behind capability is required, a SELECT node label SLBL will be required as the preceding QUEUE nodes must refer to the SELECT node.

A list of queue selection rules (QSR) available for specification at the SELECT node is given in Table 4-3, page 115. The list of server selection rules (SSR) is given in Table 4-4, page 116. Illustrations of the use of SELECT nodes follow.

1. Route entities to QUE1 or QUE2 based on the rule: smallest number in queue (SNQ)

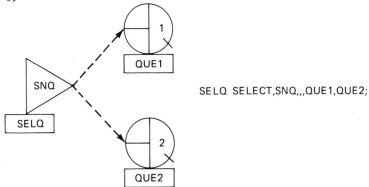

SELQ SELECT,SNQ,,,QUE1,QUE2;

This network segment could model the routing of customer entities to parallel queues before two airline ticket sellers.

2. Select a server from servers 1, 2, and 3 to process entities waiting in queue, WAIT. It is preferred to use server 1 to server 2 to server 3, that is, a preferred order for selecting servers is to be used.

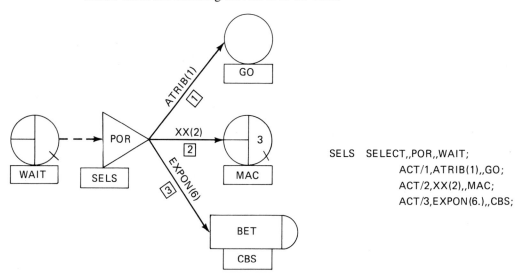

SELS   SELECT,,POR,,WAIT;
       ACT/1,ATRIB(1),,GO;
       ACT/2,XX(2),,MAC;
       ACT/3,EXPON(6.),,CBS;

This network segment could represent three machines that can be used to process jobs waiting in QUEUE node WAIT. The processing time and the routing after processing is modeled as being machine dependent.

3. Illustrations 1 and 2 are combined below so that SELECT node SELS takes entities from QUEUE nodes QUE1 and QUE2 (rather than QUEUE node WAIT). A cyclic queue selection rule is used at SELECT node SELS.

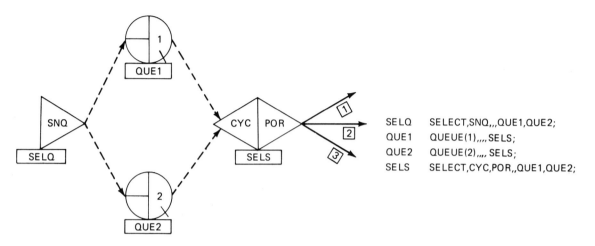

```
SELQ    SELECT,SNQ,,,QUE1,QUE2;
QUE1    QUEUE(1),,,,SELS;
QUE2    QUEUE(2),,,,SELS;
SELS    SELECT,CYC,POR,,QUE1,QUE2;
```

In this network model, entities are routed by SELECT node SELQ to either QUE1 or QUE2 depending on which QUEUE node has fewer entities in it at the time of routing. If the queues have an equal number of entities in them, then QUE1 is selected as it is listed first. When an entity arrives to either QUEUE node and a server (activity 1, 2 or 3) is not busy, the entity is routed to the free server. If more than one server is free, the POR server selection rule associated with SELECT node SELS will select the first free server activity listed after the SELS SELECT node statement. Thus, the POR server selection rule gives priority to servers in the order they are listed in the statement model.

When a server becomes free and entities are waiting in both QUE1 and QUE2, SELECT node SELS uses the CYCLIC rule and takes an entity from the QUEUE node that was not selected when the last entity was routed to a server.

4.9.1 ASSEMBLY Queue Selection Rule

One of the queue selection rules listed in Table 4-3 is the ASM or assembly rule. This rule differs from the other rules in that it involves the combining of two or more entities into an assembled entity. In this case the selection process requires that at least one entity be in each QUEUE node before any entity will be routed to a service activity. An air freight example of this assembly procedure is the requirement for both an aircraft entity and a cargo entity to be available before aircraft loading can begin. A network segment is shown for this situation where aircraft entities wait at QUEUE node ACFT, cargo entities wait at QUEUE node CARG, and aircraft loading is modeled as activity 3.

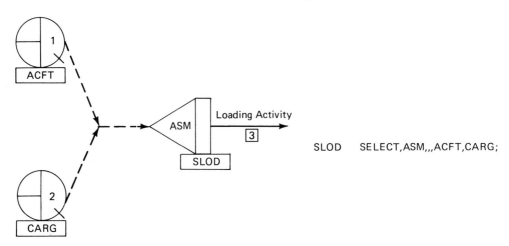

SLOD   SELECT,ASM,,,ACFT,CARG;

SELECT node SLOD does not route an entity to service activity 3 until there is one entity in each QUEUE node. At the SELECT node, ASM is prescribed as the QSR procedure. In addition, the dashed lines preceding the SELECT node have been joined prior to the SELECT node to indicate that an entity is required at each QUEUE node before any entity is sent to the server. A SELECT node that employs the ASM queue selection rule can assemble entities from two or more queues.

When entities are assembled by a SELECT node, it is permissible to specify a save attribute criterion, SAVE, by which the appropriate attributes of one of the entities to be assembled can be maintained. The concept is similar to that presented earlier for ACCUMULATE nodes. The SAVE criterion is specified in the same manner as was done for the ACCUMULATE node and the SELECT node symbol is expanded to accommodate this specification. The SAVE criterion can be based on HIGH(I), LOW(I), SUM or MULT as defined on page 106.

If no SAVE criterion is specified, then the attributes of the entity in the first queue node listed in the SELECT statement will be assigned to the assembled entity. The symbolism and statement for the ASSEMBLY queue selection rule are

Table 4-3   Priority rules associated with SELECT nodes for selecting from a set of parallel queues.

Code	Definition
POR	Priority given in a preferred order.
CYC	Cyclic Priority—transfer to first available QUEUE node starting from the last QUEUE node that was selected
RAN	Random Priority—assign an equal probability to each QUEUE node that has an entity in it.
LAV	Priority given to the QUEUE node which has had the largest average number of entities in it to date
SAV	Priority is given to the QUEUE node which has had the smallest average number of entities in it to date.
LWF	Priority is given to the QUEUE node for which the waiting time of its first entity is the longest.
SWF	Priority is given to the QUEUE node for which the waiting time of its first entity is the shortest.
LNQ	Priority is given to the QUEUE node which has the current largest number of entities in it.
SNQ	Priority is given to the QUEUE node which has the current smallest number of entities in it.
LRC	Priority is given to the QUEUE node which has the largest remaining unused capacity.
SRC	Priority is given to the QUEUE node which has the smallest remaining unused capacity.
ASM	Assembly mode option—all incoming queues must contribute one entity before a processor may begin service (this can be used to provide an "AND" logic operation).

shown below. Note that the SAVE criterion is specified after ASM in the statement and that the delimiter is a slash.

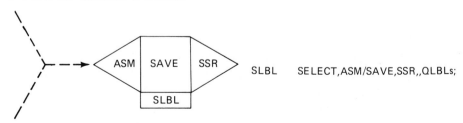

Table 4-4   Priority rules associated with SELECT nodes for selecting from a set of parallel service activities.

Code	Definition
POR	Select from free servers in a preferred order.
CYC	Select servers in a cyclic manner. That is, select the next free server starting with the last server selected.
LBT	Select the server that has the largest amount of usage (busy time) to date.
SBT	Select the server which has the smallest amount of usage (busy time) to date.
LIT	Select the server who has been idle for the longest period of time.
SIT	Select the server who has been idle for the shortest period of time.
RAN	Select randomly from free servers according to preassigned probabilities.

As an example, consider the aircraft and cargo example presented previously. Suppose we desired to save the attributes of the aircraft. If aircraft entities are identified by a value of 1 in attribute 3 and cargo entities have a value of 2 in attribute 3, then specifying that the attributes of entities having a low value of attribute 3 will cause the aircraft entity's attributes to be saved. The statement for this case would be:

```
SLOD    SELECT,ASM/LOW(3),,,ACFT,CARG;
```

4.10   MATCH NODE

MATCH nodes in SLAM are nodes that match entities residing in specified QUEUE nodes that have equal values of a specified attribute. When each QUEUE node preceding a MATCH node has an entity with the specified common attribute value, the MATCH node removes each entity from the corresponding QUEUE node and routes it to a node associated with the QUEUE node. Thus, each entity is routed individually. The symbol and statement for the MATCH node are shown on page 117.

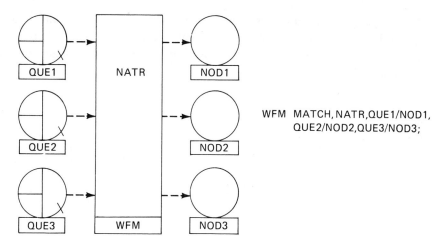

WFM MATCH,NATR,QUE1/NOD1,
        QUE2/NOD2,QUE3/NOD3;

Note that for the MATCH node, there are nodes on both sides of the symbol and a node-to-node transfer is made when a match occurs. If there is no route node specified for one of the QUEUE nodes, the entity in that QUEUE node is destroyed after a match is made. The attribute number on which the match is based is specified within the MATCH node symbol. Only QUEUE nodes can precede MATCH nodes and the initial number in the QUEUE node must be zero. Illustrations of the use of MATCH nodes are shown below.

1. Hold entities in files 1 and 2 at QUEUE nodes TYP1 and TYP2 until there is an entity in each QUEUE node that has an attribute 3 value that is the same. Route both entities to ACCUMULATE node MAA and save the attribute set of the entity whose attribute 2 value is the largest.

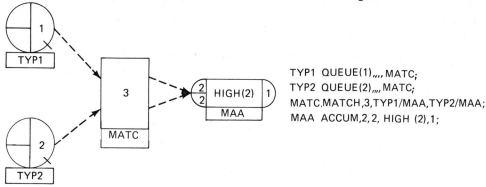

TYP1 QUEUE(1),,,, MATC;
TYP2 QUEUE(2),,,, MATC;
MATC,MATCH,3,TYP1/MAA,TYP2/MAA;
MAA ACCUM,2,2, HIGH (2),1;

This model segment could be used to represent an aircraft and crew where only a particular crew can be used with a given aircraft.

2. Hold a patient entity until his health records arrive. Route the patient to the queue before the doctor's office when both the patient and his records are available. Destroy the record entity. Patient identification is maintained as attribute 1.

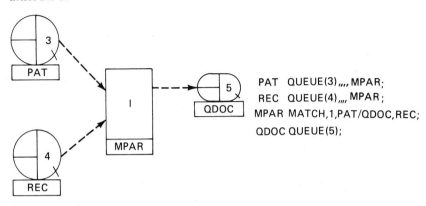

```
PAT   QUEUE(3),,,,MPAR;
REC   QUEUE(4),,,,MPAR;
MPAR  MATCH,1,PAT/QDOC,REC;
QDOC  QUEUE(5);
```

4.11   RESOURCES AND GATES

In previous discussions, the flow of entities depended on node types and server status. When service activities were encountered, entities waited in queues for servers to become idle. Servers are a particular type of resource that remain stationary, that is, a service activity is only associated with the entity while the entity is flowing through the branch that represents the service activity. Situations arise where an entity requires a resource during a set of activities. SLAM provides a capability to model this situation through the definition of resource types. For each resource type, the number of units available to be allocated to entities is defined.

An entity that requires a resource waits for it at an AWAIT node where the number of units of the resource required is specified. When an entity arrives to an AWAIT node, it proceeds through it to the activity emanating from the node if sufficient units of the resource are available. Otherwise, its flow is halted. A file is associated with the AWAIT node to maintain entities waiting for resources. The AWAIT node differs from the QUEUE node in that no service activities follow the AWAIT node. An entity is removed from the AWAIT node when the units of resource required have been freed up by other entities and have been assigned to the awaiting entity.

To allow an entity to acquire a resource currently allocated to an entity that has a lower priority, a PREEMPT node is employed. If a resource cannot be preempted, then the entity waits in a file prescribed at the PREEMPT node in a fashion similar to that for the AWAIT node. PREEMPT nodes can only be used for entities requiring a single unit of a resource.

Resources are allocated to entities waiting in AWAIT and PREEMPT nodes in a prescribed order. This order is established through the use of a RESOURCE block. Also defined at the RESOURCE block is the initial number of available units of the resource type.

When an entity no longer requires the use of a resource, it is routed to a FREE node where a specified number of units of the resource are freed (made available for reallocation). The PREEMPT and AWAIT nodes associated with the resource type are then interrogated to determine if the freed units can be allocated to waiting entities.

The number of units available for a resource type can be changed by routing entities through an ALTER node. ALTER nodes are used to increase or decrease the level of resource availability and can be used to model resource level changes such as machine failures, employee breaks, and daily shifts.

In Section 4.6, it was shown that entities can be held at an ACCUMULATE node until other entities arrive and release the node according to a specified release mechanism. In this section, this concept is generalized so that models can be built that halt the flow of entities in one part of the network until entities arrive at nodes in another portion of the network. The vehicle for accomplishing the stopping and starting of entity flow is the GATE node. Entities can be routed to AWAIT nodes which require that a specified GATE be open before the entity can proceed through the AWAIT node. If the GATE associated with the AWAIT node is closed, the entity waits in a file until the GATE is opened. A GATE is opened when an entity flows through an OPEN node. It can be closed by an entity passing through a CLOSE node. The files in which entities may be waiting for a GATE to be opened are defined at a GATE block. When a gate is opened, all entities waiting at AWAIT nodes for the gate are permitted to pass through the AWAIT node and are routed to the branches emanating from the AWAIT node.

For example, a gate can be used to stop the flow of passenger entities in a bus system until a bus entity arrives to an OPEN node. When the passenger entities are loaded on the bus, the bus entity would be routed through a CLOSE node to restrict again the flow of passenger entities onto a bus.

After a brief illustration of network modeling using resources, descriptions of resource and gate related nodes are given.

4.12   ILLUSTRATION OF THE USE OF RESOURCES

As an illustration of the use of resources, consider the situation in which the radio inspector described in Section 4.2 performs an inspection operation and, if the radio requires adjustment, the inspector also performs that operation. Assume that fifteen percent of the radios manufactured require adjustment. In this situation, the inspector can be thought of as a resource that is allocated or assigned to the processing (inspection and adjustment) of the radio. Thus the inspector is not always available to perform another inspection because he may be required to perform the adjustment operation. One way of modeling this situation is shown below in both the network and statement models.

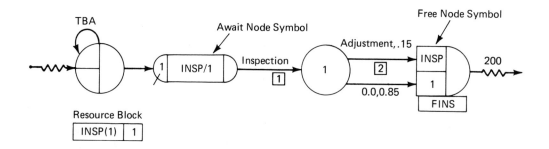

```
NETWORK;
        RESOURCE/INSP(1),1;
        CREATE,TBA;
        AWAIT(1),INSP/1;
            ACT/1,inspection time;
        GOON,1;
            ACT/2,adjustment time,0.15,FINS;
            ACT,0.0,0.85;
FINS    FREE,INSP/1;
        TERM,200;
        ENDNET;
```

In this model, the RESOURCE block indicates that one unit of the resource INSP is available and that it is allocated at an AWAIT node where file 1 is used to maintain waiting entities. After an entity is created, it is routed to the AWAIT node and, if the inspector resource is available, it is processed through ACTIVITY 1. At the GOON node, it is routed either through the adjustment activity (ACTIVITY 2) with probability 0.15 or to an activity that requires zero time with probability 0.85. In either case, the entity flows through the FREE node to make the inspector available to process the next radio waiting in file 1. After freeing the inspector, the radio entity that was inspected and possibly adjusted is terminated at the TERM node. When 200 radios depart the network, one run is completed. This completes the illustration of the use of resources.

4.13 RESOURCE BLOCK

The RESOURCE block is used to identify: the resource name or label, RLBL; the initial resource capacity, that is, number of resource units available, IRC; and the order in which files associated with AWAIT and PREEMPT nodes are to be polled to allocate freed units of the resource to entities. The word "block" is employed instead of "node" because the RESOURCE block has no inputs or outputs as entities do not flow through it. The RESOURCE block is a definitional vehicle to specify a resource type (name), the available number of units for the resource type, and an allocation procedure for entities waiting for units of the resource. On the network diagram, blocks can be placed together to form a legend.

The RESOURCE name, generically referred to as RLBL, is used in AWAIT, PREEMPT, FREE, and ALTER nodes to identify the resource type associated with the nodes. The name can be any string of characters beginning with an alphanumeric and excluding the special characters [,/( )+−*';]. However, only the first eight characters are significant. The initial level of resource availability, IRC, is the number of units of the resource that can be allocated at the beginning of a run. During a run, the level of resource availability can be increased or decreased by entities passing through ALTER nodes. The number of units of a particular resource in use is the number that have been assigned to entities at AWAIT and PREEMPT nodes and which have not been released at FREE nodes. Statistics are automatically collected on resource utilization and are printed as part of the SLAM summary report.

At the RESOURCE block, the file numbers are listed in the order in which the PREEMPT and AWAIT nodes for this resource type are to be polled. The RESOURCES block symbol and statement are shown below.

| RLBL(IRC) | IFL1 | IFL2 | ... |

RESOURCE/RLBL(IRC),IFLs;

4.14   AWAIT NODE

AWAIT nodes are used to store entities waiting for UR units of resource RLBL or waiting for gate GLBL to open. When an entity arrives to an AWAIT node and the units of resource required are available or the GATE is opened, the entity passes directly through the node and is routed according to the M-number prescribed for the node. If the entity has to wait at the node, it is placed in file IFL in accordance with the priority assigned to that file. Regular activities emanate from the AWAIT node.

The symbolism and statement for the AWAIT node are shown below.

```
AWAIT(IFL),RLBL/UR,M;
or
AWAIT(IFL),GLBL,M;
```

No capacity restrictions are placed on the number of entities waiting at an AWAIT node. Thus, blocking and balking are not permitted. Such decisions must be made prior to the entities encountering an AWAIT node. For example, conditions could be placed on the branches leading to the AWAIT node which restrict entity flow if insufficient resource units are available.

4.15   PREEMPT NODE

The PREEMPT node is a special type of AWAIT node in which an entity can preempt one unit of a resource that has been allocated to some other entity. If the entity using the resource came from an AWAIT node, preemption will always be attempted. The preemption will also be attempted if the priority assigned to the PREEMPT node is greater than the priority of the preempt node from which the entity currently using the resource type came. The symbolism and statement for the PREEMPT node are shown below.

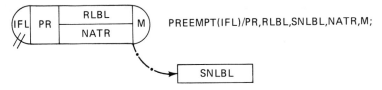

```
PREEMPT(IFL)/PR,RLBL,SNLBL,NATR,M;
```

The priority, PR, is specified as LOW(K) or HIGH(K) where K is an attribute number. The incoming entity will attempt to preempt another entity if its Kth attribute gives it a higher priority. A preemption attempt is not satisfied if the resource is currently in use by an entity that: 1) is being processed in a service activity; 2) is in a file; or 3) has other resources allocated to it. Entities that do not cause a preemption to occur wait for the resource in file IFL.

An entity that is preempted is routed to a node as specified by the SEND node label; SNLBL. The time remaining to process the entity when it is preempted is stored in ATRIB(NATR). If no SEND node label is specified then the preempted entity is routed to the AWAIT or PREEMPT node at which it was allocated the resource. At that node, it is established as the first entity waiting for the resource. When the resource is reassigned to the preempted entity, its remaining processing time will be used.

As described above, several restrictions are associated with the PREEMPT node. First, preemptions are only allowed for resources having a capacity of 1 unit. Second, an entity holding a resource that currently is in a QUEUE or AWAIT node will not be preempted. Also, if other resources have been allocated to the entity, it will not be preempted. This includes a service activity.

PREEMPT nodes only apply to resources, as the concept of preempting a GATE is not meaningful.

4.16   FREE NODE

FREE nodes are used to release units of a resource type when an entity arrives to the node. Every entity arriving to a FREE node releases UF units of resource type RLBL where UF and RLBL are specified values for the FREE node. UF can be a constant or a SLAM variable. The freed units are then allocated to entities waiting in PREEMPT and AWAIT nodes in the order prescribed by the RESOURCE block. The entity arriving to the FREE node is then routed in accordance with the M-number associated with the FREE node. The symbol and statement for the FREE node are shown below.

4.17   ALTER NODE

The ALTER node is used to change the available number of units (the capacity) of resource type RLBL by CC units. CC can be a constant or a SLAM variable. If CC is positive, the number of available units is increased. If CC is negative, the availability is decreased. The symbol and statement for the ALTER node are shown below.

When the ALTER node is used to decrease availability (CC is negative), the change is only invoked if a sufficient number of units of the resource are not in use. If this is not the case, the availability is reduced to the current number in use. Further reductions then occur when resources are freed at FREE nodes. In no case will the available number of units of a resource be reduced below zero. Any additional reductions requested when the availability has been reduced to zero are ignored.

4.18   GATE BLOCK

A GATE block is used to define the GATE named GLBL, the initial status of the GATE, and the file numbers associated with entities waiting for a gate to be opened at AWAIT nodes. The naming convention for gates is the same as for resources. GATE blocks are not connected to other nodes and are used only to provide the above definitional information. The symbol and statement for the GATE block are shown below:

GLBL	OPEN or CLOSE	IFL1	IFL2

GATE/GLBL,OPEN or CLOSE,IFLS;

4.19 OPEN NODE

An OPEN node is used to open a GATE with name GLBL. Each entity arriving to an OPEN node causes gate GLBL to be opened. When this occurs, all entities waiting for GLBL are removed from the files associated with the AWAIT nodes for GLBL and are routed in accordance with the M-number of the AWAIT node. The entity that caused GLBL to be opened is then routed from the OPEN node. The symbol and statement for the OPEN node are shown below.

4.20 CLOSE NODE

A CLOSE node is used to close a GATE with name GLBL. An entity arriving to a CLOSE node causes all gates with name GLBL to be closed. Any entity arriving to an AWAIT node after GLBL is closed will wait for GLBL to be opened. The entity that causes GLBL to be closed at the CLOSE node is routed in accordance with the M-number associated with the CLOSE node. The symbol and statement for the CLOSE node are shown below.

4.21 ILLUSTRATIONS OF MODELS INVOLVING RESOURCES AND GATES

4.21.1 Illustration 6. Day Shifts

Consider the situation in which packages arrive to a post office over a 24-hour period; however, they are only weighed, stamped, and loaded into trucks during the day shift. This can be modeled by having the packages, as represented by entities, created and then routed to an AWAIT node that is associated with a gate called DSFT. In a disjoint network, an entity is created that closes the gate after eight hours then opens it sixteen hours later. The network and statement models for this illustration are shown below. The model involving the processing of the packages through the operations on the day shift has not been detailed.

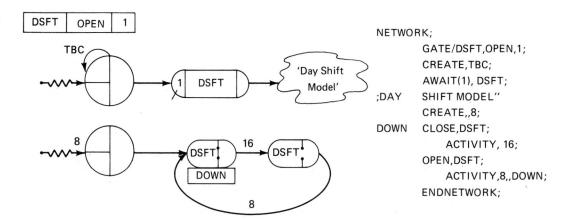

```
NETWORK;
        GATE/DSFT,OPEN,1;
        CREATE,TBC;
        AWAIT(1), DSFT;
;DAY    SHIFT MODEL"
        CREATE,,8;
DOWN    CLOSE,DSFT;
        ACTIVITY, 16;
        OPEN,DSFT;
        ACTIVITY,8,,DOWN;
        ENDNETWORK;
```

4.21.2 Illustration 7. Machine Breakdowns

Consider the situation in which packages are to be processed through a scale. The scale encounters failures which stop the processing of packages until the scale is repaired. In this situation, the scale is modeled as a resource and the packages as entities that require one unit of the resource. An entity representing scale status is modeled in a disjoint network. Following the appropriate failure time, the scale-status entity encounters a PREEMPT node which stops the weighing of a package by the scale. A repair time for the scale is then scheduled. Following the repair time, the scale is freed and the preempted package, if there was one, can be continued. The next failure of the scale is scheduled by routing the status-of-scale entity back through an activity representing the failure time. The network and statement models for this illustration are shown below.

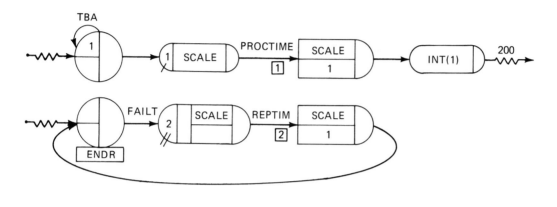

```
NETWORK;
        RESOURCE/SCALE(1),2,1;
        CREATE,TBA,,1;
        AWAIT(1), SCALE;
            ACT/1,PROCTIME;
        FREE,SCALE;
        COLCT,INT(1);
        TERM,200;
ENDR    CREATE;
            ACT,FAILT;
        PREEMPT(2), SCALE;
            ACT/2,REPTIME;
        FREE SCALE;
            ACT,,,ENDR;
        ENDNETWORK;
```

4.21.3   Illustration 8. Machine Breakdowns on the Day Shift

This illustration combines Illustrations 6 and 7 above by making a repairman available only eight hours a day while the weighing process works on a 24-hour basis. Any failure occurring while the repairman is not on duty waits until the day shift. A gate called repairman availability, RAVL, is used to prohibit the starting of repair when the repairman is not available. The network and statement models for this illustration that are in addition to those given for Illustration 7 are shown below.

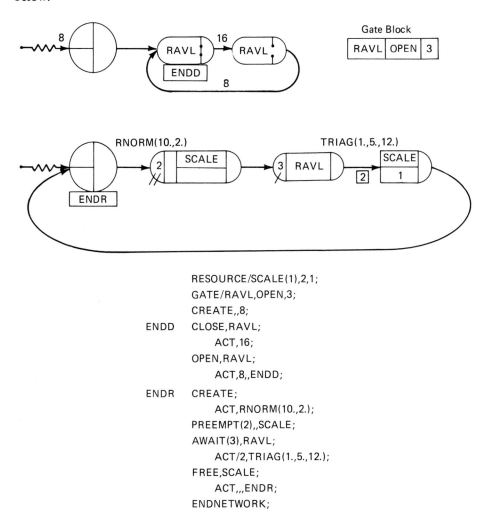

RESOURCE/SCALE(1),2,1;
GATE/RAVL,OPEN,3;
CREATE,,8;
ENDD   CLOSE,RAVL;
        ACT,16;
OPEN,RAVL;
        ACT,8,,ENDD;
ENDR   CREATE;
        ACT,RNORM(10.,2.);
PREEMPT(2),,SCALE;
AWAIT(3),RAVL;
        ACT/2,TRIAG(1.,5.,12.);
FREE,SCALE;
        ACT,,,ENDR;
ENDNETWORK;

An alternative formulation for Illustration 8 can be built by considering the repairman as a resource. Rather than use a gate to prohibit the start of repair, the available capacity of the repairman resource can be altered to be 1 during the day shift and 0 otherwise. This is accomplished using ALTER nodes. The changes required in the network model for this alternative formulation are shown below.

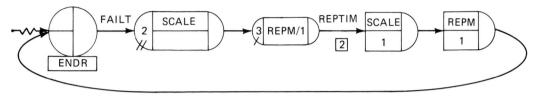

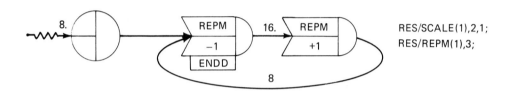

RES/SCALE(1),2,1;
RES/REPM(1),3;

4.22   SUMMARY OF SYMBOLS AND STATEMENTS

Table 4-5 presents the basic symbols and statements of SLAM network modeling. There is only one activity symbol and it is used to represent both servers and non-service activities. An explicit delay in the processing of an entity can only be modeled by using an activity. Excluding resources and gates, there are nine different node types in SLAM. Thus, we believe that SLAM presents a concise network language that will be easy to learn. The examples in Chapter 6 will illustrate the flexibility available in modeling with these basic symbols.

The symbols and statements associated with resources and gates are summarized in Table 4-6. Five node types are used for modeling with resources and three node types are associated with gates. Resources and gates greatly increase the modeling flexibility available with SLAM. The default values associated with SLAM network statements will be presented in Chapter 5, Table 5-1. A complete description of each network element is provided in Appendix B.

Table 4-5 Basic symbols and statements for SLAM networks.†

Name	Symbol	Statement
ACCUMULATE		ACCUMULATE, FR, SR, SAVE, M;
ACTIVITY		ACTIVITY (N)/A, DUR, PROB or COND, NLBL;
ASSIGN		ASSIGN, VAR=VALUE, VAR=VALUE, M;
COLCT		COLCT, TYPE or VAR, ID, NCEL/HLOW/HWID, M;
CREATE		CREATE, TBC, TF, MA, MC, M;
GOON		GOON, M;
MATCH		MLBL MATCH, NATR, QLBL/NLBL, repeats . . . ;
QUEUE		QUEUE (IFL), IQ, QC, BLOCK or BALK (NLBL), SLBLs;
SELECT		SELECT, QSR, SSR, BLOCK or BALK (NLBL), QLBLs;
SELECT VARIATIONS		
TERMINATE		TERMINATE, TC;

Table 4-5   (Continued).

Special Node and Routing Symbols

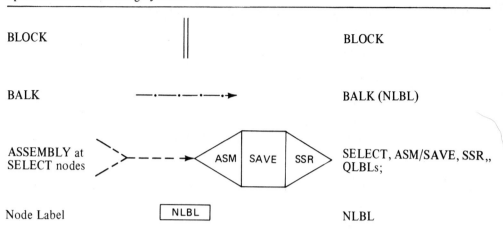

BLOCK	BLOCK
BALK	BALK (NLBL)
ASSEMBLY at SELECT nodes	SELECT, ASM/SAVE, SSR,, QLBLs;
Node Label	NLBL

† Definition of Codes

TBC	Time Between Creations
TF	Time of First creation
MA	Mark Attribute for creation time
MC	Maximum Creations to be made
M	Maximum branches that an entity can be routed from a node
IFL	File number
IQ	Initial number of entities in QUEUE
QC	Queue Capacity to hold entities
BLOCK	Queue BLOCKS incoming entities and servers
BALK	Entities BALK from QUEUE mode
NLBL	Node LaBeL
SLBL	SELECT node LaBeL
TC	Termination Count to stop simulation
VAR	SLAM VARiable (see Table 4-1)
VALUE	SLAM expression for VALUE (see Table 4-2)

Table 4-5   (Continued).

FR	First Release requirement to release node
SR	Subsequent Release requirement to release node
SAVE	Criterion for determining which entities attributes to SAVE
TYPE	Statistics TYPE to be collected
ID	IDentifier
H	NCEL/HLOW/HWID
NCEL	Number of interior CELls of a histogram
HLOW	Upper limit of first cell of a histogram
HWID	Cell WIDth for a histogram
QSR	Queue Selection Rule (see Table 4-3)
SSR	Server Selection Rule (see Table 4-4)
QLBL	QUEUE node LaBeL
NATR	Number of an ATtRibute
N	Number of parallel servers
A	Activity number
DUR	DURation of an activity (see Table 4.2)
PROB	PROBability value for selecting an activity
COND	CONDition for selecting an activity

References to nodes are made through node labels (NLBLs). When a node label is required, it is placed in a rectangle and appended to the base of the symbol.

Only the first three characters of the name are significant and these can be used to define the statement type.

4.23   EXERCISES

4-1.   Entities are generated at a node whose label is START. The first entity is to be generated at time 5. Thereafter the time between entity arrivals is exponentially distributed with a mean of 2 time units. An unlimited number of entities can be generated at node START. Entities are routed to QUEUE node Q1 if gate G1

Table 4-6 Symbols and statements for resources and gates.†

Name	Symbol	Statement
ALTER	RLBL / CC — M	ALTER, RLBL/CC,M;
AWAIT	IFL — RLBL/UR or GLBL — M	AWAIT(IFL), RLBL/UR or GLBL, M;
CLOSE	GLBL M	CLOSE, GLBL, M;
FREE	RLBL / UF — M	FREE, RLBL/UF, M;
GATE	GLBL | OPEN or CLOSE | IFL1 | IFL2	GATE/GLBL, OPEN or CLOSE, IFLs;
OPEN	GLBL M	OPEN, GLBL, M;
PREEMPT	IFL | PR | RLBL / NATR — M → SNLBL	PREEMPT (IFL)/PR, RLBL, SNLBL, NATR, M;
RESOURCE	RLBL(IRC) | IFL1 | IFL2	RESOURCE/RLBL (IRC), IFLs;

†Definition of codes:

IFL	File number
RLBL	Resource LaBeL as defined at a RESOURCE block
UR	Units Requested
UF	Units to Free
CC	Change Capacity by CC
PR	Priority specification for preempting
SNLBL	Node to send preempted entity
NATR	ATtRibute number to store processing time remaining for preempted entity
IRC	Initial Resource Capacity (units available)
GLBL	Gate LaBeL as defined at a GATE block

133

is open. The time to reach mode Q1 is equal to the capacity of the queue which is 5 minus the current number of entities in Q1. Entities that balk from Q1 leave the system. Initially, there are no entities at Q1 and file 1 is used to store entities waiting at Q1. Two servers process entities waiting at Q1. Processing time of these servers is normally distributed with a mean of 3 and a standard deviation of 1. After service, an entity leaves the system. If an entity's time in the system was greater than 10, gate G1 is closed. Gate G1 is open when an entity spends less than 2 time units in the system or when an arrival does not wait for service at queue node Q1. It is desired to collect the time between departures for all entities that have arrived to the system.

Draw the SLAM network of the processing of entities as described above.

Develop a SLAM portion of a network in which the time to traverse an activity is normally distributed with a mean of 10, a standard deviation of 2, a minimum value of 7 and a maximum value of 15. State your assumptions regarding the type of truncation used.

4-3.   There are three stations on the assembly line and the service time at each station is exponentially distributed with a means of 10. Items flow down the assembly line from server 1 to server 2 to server 3. A new unit is provided to server 1 every 15 time units. If any server has not completed processing its current unit within 15 minutes, the unit is diverted to one of two off-line servers who complete the remaining operations on the job diverted from the assembly line. One time unit is added to the remaining time of the operation that was not completed. Any following operations not performed are done so by the off-line servers in an exponentially distributed time with a mean of 16. Draw the SLAM network to obtain statistics on the utilization of all servers, and the fraction of items diverted from each operation.

Embellishments: (a) Assume the assembly line is paced and that the movement of units can only occur at multiples of 15 minutes.

(b) Allow one unit to be stored between each assembly line server.

(c) If a server is available, route units back to the assembly line from the off-line servers.

4-4.   In SLAM, there are many ways to halt the flow of an entity through a network. Describe the node type or procedures you would use to stop and start the flow of an entity in each of the following situations:

(a) An entity called dinner cannot be served until the steak, potatoes, and salad are complete.

(b) An entity called steak cannot be inserted into the oven until five minutes after the oven is turned-on.

(c) The dessert, apple pie and ice cream, cannot be served until four people have completed eating.

(d) One of the dinners requires that the steak be medium rare and that the salad dressing be bleu cheese.

(e) The eating of dinner activity is not started until wine is poured for all diners.

4-5.   Perform a manual simulation of the following network for 28 time units by preparing tables similar to those given in Tables 1-3 and 1-4.

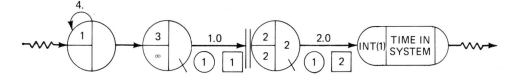

(Note: Since entities are initially in the QUEUE nodes, the servers are busy and all entities initially in the system have an attribute 1 value equal to zero.) Compute the utilization of each server, the fraction of time server 1 is blocked, the average number in each queue, and the average time spent in the system by an entity.

4-6.   At a drive-in bank where there is only one teller, there is space for five waiting cars. If a customer arrives when the waiting line is full, the customer drives around the block and tries to join the waiting line again. The interarrival time between customer arrivals is exponentially distributed with a mean of 10. The time to drive around the block is normally distributed with a mean of 2 and a standard deviation of 0.5. The teller service time is uniformly distributed between 6 and 12. When a customer arrives and can join the queue, it takes a negligible amount of time to become a member of the queue. Initially, no customers are waiting to be served and the teller is idle. Draw the SLAM network associated with this situation which collects statistics on the customer's time in the queue, time in the system, and time between balks.

Embellishment: For this banking situation, cars depart from the teller into a street. The amount of time for a car to find a gap large enough to depart into the street is exponentially distributed with a mean of 3. The design of the drive-in bank parking lot only allows five cars to be waiting to enter the street. Modify your network to include this new feature.

4-7.   A barber has categorized his customers according to the type of haircut desired. He has determined that the time for a regular haircut is uniformly distributed between 15 and 20 minutes whereas the time for customers who desired a stylized haircut is exponentially distributed with a mean of 20 minutes. The barber has determined that 60 percent of his customers request a hair styling. Assuming that the time between customer arrivals is triangularly distributed with a mode of 20, a minimum of 15 and a maximum of 40, draw a SLAM network to represent this situation. Include in the network the collection of statistics on the time spent in the system by each type of customer and by both types of customers collectively.

4-8.   A server is stationed by a conveyor belt and the server can only take items off the conveyor belt if he is idle. Items arrive to the conveyor belt with the time between arrivals a constant 10 time units. Once the item is placed on the conveyor belt, it takes three time units for it to reach the service station. If the server is busy, the item continues on the conveyor belt and returns to the server in 9 time units. Service for the item is exponentially distributed with a mean of 2.5. When the server finishes working on an item, he places it on a second conveyor belt to be processed by a second server. The item spends five time units on the second conveyor belt before arriving at the second server. If the second server is busy, the item stays on the second conveyor belt for 12 time units before it is returned to the second server. The service time of the second server is normally distributed with a mean of 2.0 and a standard deviation of 1. After being served by the second server, the item departs the system. Draw a SLAM network of this situation that collects information on the amount of time an item spends in the system and the number of items on each conveyor belt.

4-9.   Convert a PERT network with which you are familiar into a SLAM network representation. For this SLAM network, presume that there is a probability that some activities in the network will fail which would cause project failure. Redraw the SLAM network to represent this situation.

4-10.   Describe how an ACCUMULATE node of a SLAM network can be used to represent the following logic operations: all preceding activities must be completed before successor activities can be started; any one of the preceding activities must be completed before the activity can be started; and three out of five of the preceding activities must be completed before the activity can be started (or, in general, a majority voting type of logic).

4-11.   At an airline terminal, five ticket agents are employed and current practice is to allow queues to form before each agent. Time between arrivals to the agents is exponentially distributed with a mean of 5 minutes. Customers join the shortest queue at the time of their arrival. The service time for the ticket agents is uniformly distributed between 0.5 and 1.5 minutes. The queues of the ticket agents are not allowed to exceed two customers each. If the queues of all ticket agents are full, the customer goes directly to his gate to be served by a stewardess. Develop the SLAM network from which the total time a customer spends at the ticket agent windows, the utilization of the ticket agents, and the number of customers per minute that cannot gain service from the ticket agents can be determined.

Embellishments: (a) The airline company has decided to change the procedures involved in processing customers by the ticket agents. A single line is formed and the customers are routed to the ticket agent that becomes free next. A tenth of a minute service time is added to the processing time of each ticket agent. Space available in the single line for waiting customers is ten. Develop the SLAM network for this revised situation.

(b) It has been found that a subset of the customers purchasing tickets are taking a long period of time. By segregating ticket holders from non-ticket holders, improvements can be made in the processing of customers. To accomplish this segregation, four ticket agents are used for checking in customers and one agent is used for purchases. The time to check in a person is uniformly distributed between 0.2 and 1 minute and the time to purchase a ticket is exponentially distributed with a mean of 5 minutes. Assuming that 15 percent of the customers will be purchasing tickets, develop the SLAM network for this situation. The time between all customer arrivals is exponentially distributed with a mean of 5 minutes.

CHAPTER 5

Network Simulation: Inputs and Outputs

5.1   INTRODUCTION

In Chapter 4, SLAM was presented as both a graphical framework for concep-
tualizing network models and as a language for describing network models in statement form. SLAM is also a computer program which interprets and executes the
statement equivalent of a network to act out or simulate a model of the real system.
In this chapter, we discuss the use of the SLAM simulation program to simulate
network models. We begin by presenting an overview of the network simulation
procedure employed by the SLAM processor. This is followed by a detailed description of the input statements used in constructing network models.

5.2   NETWORK ANALYSIS THROUGH SIMULATION

We showed in Chapter 4 that the network modeling approach consists of modeling a system as a set of entities which flow through a network of nodes and activities. As entities flow through a network, they occupy servers; advance time; await,
seize and free resources; open and close gates; queue up in files; change variable
values; and, in general, cause changes in the state of the system. A fundamental
observation, which forms the basis for the network simulation approach employed
by SLAM, is that these changes in state can only occur at the time of arrival of an
entity to a node. The SLAM processor generates a complete portrayal of the
changes in state of a network model by processing in a time-ordered sequence the
events representing the arrival of an entity to a node.

The mechanism employed for maintaining the time-ordered sequence of entity
arrival events is the event calendar. The event calendar consists of a list of entity
arrival events, each characterized by an "event time" and an "end node". The event
time specifies the time at which the entity arrival is to occur. The end node specifies
the node to which the entity is to arrive. The events on the event calendar are
ranked low-value-first (LVF) based on their event time.

The next event processing logic employed by SLAM for simulating networks is
depicted in Figure 5-1. The processor begins by interpreting the SLAM statements.
This is followed by an initialization phase which is completed prior to the start of
the simulation. During this initialization phase, the processor places on the event

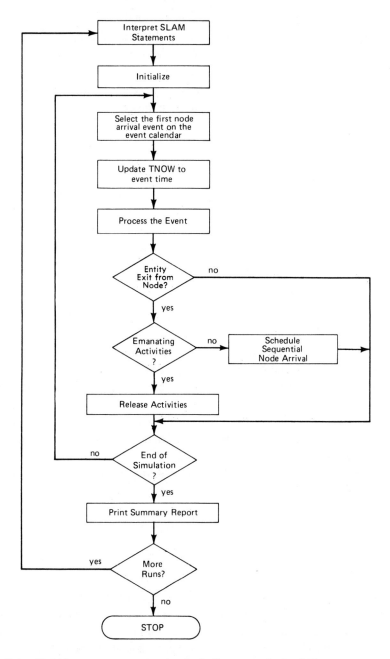

Figure 5-1   SLAM next event processing logic for network simulations.

calendar an entity arrival event to occur at each CREATE node at the time of the first release of the node. Also entities initially in QUEUE nodes are created and end-of-service activity events are scheduled where appropriate. Therefore, the event calendar will initially contain one arrival event corresponding to each CREATE node and one end-of-service event for each busy server in the network.

The execution phase of a simulation begins by selecting the first event on the calendar. The processor advances the current simulated time, TNOW, to the event time corresponding to this event. It processes the event by performing all appropriate actions based on the decision logic associated with the node type to which the entity is arriving. For example, if the entity is arriving to an AWAIT node, the decision logic involved with realizing the event consists of testing to determine if the required level of resource is available; if yes, the entity seizes the desired units of resource and exits the node; otherwise, the entity is placed in the specified file and awaits the required resource. Although the decision logic is different for each node, the logic will result in one of three possible outcomes for the arriving entity:

1. The entity will be routed to another node;
2. The entity will be destroyed at the node; or
3. The entity will be delayed at the node based on the state of the system.

The routing of an entity from a node involves a test for activities emanating from the node. If there are no emanating activities, then the entity is scheduled to arrive at the sequential node at the current time, TNOW. If there is no sequential node, the entity is destroyed. When there are emanating activities, as many as M activities are selected in accordance with the probability or conditions associated with each activity where M is the M-number associated with the node. If an activity is selected, the entity or its duplicate is routed to the end node of the activity at the current time, TNOW, plus the duration of the activity.

After all events have been scheduled, the SLAM processor tests for one of the following end-of-simulation conditions:

1. TNOW is greater than or equal to the user specified ending time of the simulation;
2. There are no events on the event calendar; or
3. A TERMINATE node has been released.

If none of the end of simulation conditions are satisfied, the SLAM processor selects the next arrival event on the event calendar and continues. When a simulation run is ended, statistics are calculated, and the SLAM Summary Report is printed. A test is then made to determine if additional simulation runs are to be executed. If more runs remain, the next run is initiated. If all simulation runs have been completed, execution by the SLAM processor is stopped and control is returned to the operating system.

The next event logic described above is well defined except when two or more arrival events are scheduled to occur at the same instant in time. To illustrate the problem, consider the case where we have a gate named DOOR which is currently open, and entities are scheduled to arrive at precisely the same time to the following statements:

Statement 1	*Statement 2*
AWAIT, DOOR;	CLOSE, DOOR;

If statement 1 is processed before statement 2, the gate DOOR will be open and the entity will exit the AWAIT node. However, if statement 2 is processed before statement 1, the transaction arriving at statement 1 will be delayed at the AWAIT node because the gate DOOR was just closed. Therefore, the order in which simultaneous events are processed can affect the results of the simulation.†

In describing the node arrival tie-breaking rules employed by SLAM, it is convenient to classify all events on the event calendar as either "current events" or "future events". Current events are those events which are scheduled to occur at the current simulation time (TNOW), whereas future events are those events which are scheduled to occur at some simulated time in the future (not at TNOW). The reason for conceptually distinguishing between current and future events is that different tie-breaking procedures are employed depending upon whether the event is initially scheduled as a current event or as a future event.

The scheduling of an arrival event as a current event results from scheduling either a sequential node arrival or an end of activity node arrival where the activity has a duration of zero. In either case, the time at which the event is to occur is the current simulated time (TNOW). The scheduling procedure employed by SLAM is to always place current events at the top of the event calendar, regardless of other events on the calendar. Therefore, current events are scheduled onto the calendar on a last-in, first-out (LIFO) basis. In the case where several zero duration activities emanate from a single node, the arrival events corresponding to the end of the activities are placed at the front of the calendar in the order that the activities appear in the statement model; that is, the first event would correspond to the first zero duration activity, the second event would correspond to the second zero duration activity, and so on.

---

† This difficulty is not as severe as in some simulation languages where an integer-valued clock time is used.

Since the only mechanism for advancing time in a SLAM network model is the activity, the scheduling of a future event necessarily corresponds to the arrival event resulting from an end of activity of nonzero duration. The tie-breaking procedure for scheduling future events employs a secondary ranking procedure which is defaulted to first-in, first-out (FIFO). The secondary ranking can be specified by the modeler (see Section 5.6.3) to be FIFO; LIFO; LVF(NATR), low-value-first based on attribute NATR; or HVF(NATR), high-value-first based on attribute NATR. In the case of the LVF or HVF secondary ranking, ties can still exist and they are broken using the FIFO rule.

At this point, the reader may be questioning the rationale of scheduling current events using LIFO as the tie-breaking rule while scheduling future events using a user specified tie-breaking rule. Why not just use one rule and avoid distinguishing between current and future events? The reason is that the LIFO rule is not only considerably more efficient in terms of computer execution time for scheduling current events, but it moves one entity at a time as far through the network as possible until it is either destroyed, delayed by the status of the system, or encounters a time delay. A FIFO rule would advance one entity one node, then advance the next entity one node, and so on, round robin. The advantage of the LIFO flow pattern will become apparent when the reader encounters traces of entity flow (the TRACE option is discussed in Section 5.6.9).

5.3   SLAM INPUT STATEMENTS

Although the network statements for nodes and activities presented in Chapter 4 are sufficient for describing a network model, the network description by itself does not comprise a simulation program. Additional input statements are required to specify such quantities as run length, initial conditions, output options, and file rankings. In the following sections, we summarize the format conventions applicable to the SLAM input statements required for network simulation programs.

5.4   GENERAL FORMAT CONVENTIONS

Input statements are read by the SLAM processor from punched cards or their equivalent. Each input statement is uniquely defined by the first three letters of the statement name. Each field in the statement is separated by a comma [,], slash [/], or offset in parentheses [( )]. The appropriate field separator is dependent upon the specific statement type and field entry and is specified in the description of each statement type. Basically, slashes and parentheses are used for optional specifications and are optional also. Commas separate fields that are not optional. The special characters [+ − * /] are used to denote arithmetic operations and the semi-colon character [;] is used to denote the end of a statement. *These characters should not be employed within network statement labels or within user defined alphanumeric names.*

A field in a statement can be defaulted by simply omitting the entry while including the terminator. For example, an activity, with zero duration that has no condition, and an end node labeled EXIT can be specified by defaulting the duration and condition fields as follows:

    ACTIVITY,,,EXIT;

Also, if a statement is terminated with remaining fields unspecified, the remaining fields take on their default values. For example, an ACTIVITY of duration 1, unconditionally taken, with an end node as the sequential node can be specified by defaulting the last two fields as follows:

    ACTIVITY, 1;

The end node for this activity is assumed to be the next node statement encountered.

Input statements are read using a free format which permits a statement to be spaced across a line or over several lines. One restriction is that a field may not be split between lines. A continuation of a statement to the next line is assumed if the last non-blank character of the statement is a [,/(+−*)] or the last period of a logical operator such as [.AND.]. If the last non-blank character is any other character, an end of statement is assumed. However, the preferred method for ending a statement is the explicit use of the statement terminator [;] which permits the inclusion of comments following the terminator. All blanks are ignored, except within alphanumeric fields, and therefore can be freely employed to improve the readability of statements. For example, the following ACTIVITY statement:

    ACTIVITY,10,ATRIB(1).EQ.1.AND.TNOW.LT.100,LOOP;

can be spaced over three lines as follows:

    ACTIVITY,10,
        ATRIB(1).EQ.1.AND.
        TNOW.LT.100,   LOOP;

However, it should be noted that the three lines would require a longer processing time than that required for the single line.

Numeric data can be entered as whole numbers (integers) or numbers with a fractional part (decimal numbers), and may be signed or unsigned. In addition, extremely large or extremely small numbers can be entered in scientific notation using an E format. For example, the number ten can be entered as 10 or 10. or +10. or 1.E+1 or 1E1 or 100E−1. If a decimal number is entered in a field specified to be integer, the fractional part is dropped. Likewise if an integer is entered in a field specified to be decimal, its decimal equivalent is used. Therefore, the SLAM input processor does not distinguish between 1. and 1 regardless of the field type specified.

Alphanumeric fields can be inputted as any string of characters (including numerals) which begins with an alphabetic character *but does not contain the special characters* [,/() + − * ;]. Blank characters are significant within alphanumeric fields; hence L 1 is not considered the same as L1. Since fields cannot be split between lines, an alphanumeric field is limited to a maximum of 80 characters. However, depending upon the field being entered, only the first 3, 4, 8, 16, or 20 characters are read. Examples of valid alphanumeric fields are BARBER or CRANE or S927 or K?1. or J. DOE.

5.5   NETWORK STATEMENT FORMATS

The network statements described in Chapter 4 are prepared beginning in column 7 or after, with columns 1 through 5 reserved for node labels. Although node labels can appear anywhere in the first five spaces, *only the first four characters of a label are significant*. This means that the label LANE1 would not be distinguished from the label LANE2.

The network statements must be preceded by a NETWORK statement and followed by an ENDNETWORK statement. The NETWORK statement consists of the characters NET entered anywhere on a line and denotes to the SLAM processor that the lines to follow are network statements. The ENDNETWORK statement consists of the characters END punched on a line beginning in or after column 7 and denotes an end to all network statements. A list of network statements is presented in Table 5-1. Included in Table 5-1 are the default values for each field.

Some of the features of the network input statements require further explanation. The overall design is intended to increase the readability of the statements without

Table 5-1   SLAM network statement types.

Statement Form	Statement Defaults(ND=no default)
Nodes	
ACCUM,FR,SR,SAVE,M;	ACCUM,1,1,LAST,∞;
ALTER,RLBL/CC,M;	ALTER,ND/ND,∞;
ASSIGN,VAR=value,VAR=value,...,M;	ASSIGN,ND=ND,ND=ND,...,∞;
AWAIT(IFL),RLBL/UR or GLBL,M;	AWAIT(first IFL in RLBL's or GLBL's list), ND/1,∞;
CLOSE,GLBL,M;	CLOSE,ND,∞;
COLCT,TYPE or VARIABLE,ID,NCEL/ HLOW/HWID,M;	COLCT,ND,blanks,no histogram/0./1.0,∞;
CREATE,TBC,TF,MA,MC,M;	CREATE,∞,0,no marking,∞,∞;
DETECT,XVAR,XDIR,VALUE,TOL,M;	DETECT,ND,ND,ND,0,∞;
ENTER,NUM,M;	ENTER,ND,∞;
EVENT,JEVNT,M;	EVENT,ND,∞;
FREE,RLBL/UF,M;	FREE,ND/1,∞;
GOON,M;	GOON,∞;
MATCH,NATR,QLBL/NLBL,...,M;	MATCH,ND,ND/no routing,ND/no routing,...,∞;
OPEN,GLBL,M;	OPEN,ND,∞;
PREEMPT(IFL)/PR,RLBL,SNLBL,NATR,M;	PREEMPT(first IFL in RLBL's last)/no priority, ND,AWAIT node where transaction seized resource,none,∞;
QUEUE(IFL),IQ,QC,BLOCK or BALK (NLBL),SLBL;	QUEUE(ND)/0,∞,none,none;
SELECT,QSR/SAVE,SSR,BLOCK or BALK (NLBL),QLBLs;	SELECT,POR/none,POR,none,ND;
TERMINATE,TC;	TERMINATE,∞;
Blocks	
GATE/GLBL,OPEN or CLOSE,IFLs/repeats;	GATE/ND,OPEN,ND/repeats;
RESOURCE/RLBL(IRC),IFLs/repeats;	RESOURCE/ND(1),ND/repeats;
Regular Activity	
ACTIVITY/A,duration,PROB or COND,NLBL;	ACTIVITY/no ACT number,0.0,take ACT,ND;
Service Activity	
ACTIVITY(N)/A, duration,PROB,NLBL;	ACTIVITY(1)/no ACT number,0.0,1.0,ND;

145

encumbering the user with extraneous information requirements. This goal led to the use of four delimiters to separate values:

1. Commas are used to separate fields.
2. Slashes (virgules) are used to allow an optional or normally defaulted value to be contained as a second value in a field. Slashes may also be used to indicate that a set of fields is to be repeated.
3. Parentheses are used to indicate a capacity or associated file.
4. A semicolon is used to end a statement.

With these delimiters, efficient input statement preparation has been obtained. The examples in Chapter 6 demonstrate this point. As with any simulation language, it does require using the language to feel comfortable with the wide range of alternatives.

Another aspect of the input statements is that all node types have been given verbs as names. This corresponds to the modeling approach which requires decisions and logical functions to be performed at the nodes of the network.

5.6   SIMULATION CONTROL STATEMENTS

In this section, we describe additional statement types which are used in writing SLAM simulation programs. In contrast to network input statements which begin in or after column 7, the control statements can start in any column. Typically, they are started in Column 1. A list of the statement types is presented in Table 5-2. Each statement type is described individually below.

5.6.1   GEN Statement

The GEN statement provides general information about a simulation in the format shown below.

GEN,NAME,PROJECT,MONTH/DAY/YEAR,NNRNS,ILIST,IECHO,
    IXQT,IPIRH,ISMRY/FSN;

The GEN statement must be the first statement in any SLAM simulation program. Included on the GEN statement are: the analyst's name, a project identifier, date, number of simulation runs, and report options. The NAME and PROJECT are both alphanumeric fields with 20 characters of significance and are used for output reports to identify the analyst and the project. Recall that blanks are significant within alphanumeric fields. The MONTH, DAY, and YEAR are entered as an integers separated by slashes. The SLAM variable NNRNS is entered as an integer, has a default value of 1, and denotes the number of simulation runs to be made. The last five fields are specified as *YES* or *NO* and correspond to the following options:

ILIST	If yes, a numbered listing of all input statements is printed including error messages if any; otherwise the listing is omitted.
IECHO	If yes, an echo summary report is printed; otherwise the report is omitted.
IXQT	If yes, execution is attempted if no input errors are detected. If specified as no, execution is not attempted.
IPIRH	If yes, the heading INTERMEDIATE RESULTS is printed prior to execution of each simulation run; otherwise the printing is omitted.
ISMRY/FSN	If yes, the SLAM Summary Report is printed following each simulation run; otherwise the report is suppressed. The value of FSN specifies to print a summary report: after the first run only (F); after the first and last runs (S); or after the first and every Nth run (N).

Table 5-2 SLAM control statements.

Statement Form

GEN, NAME, PROJECT, MON/DAY/YEAR, NNRNS, ILIST, IECHO, IXQT, IPIRH, ISMRY/FSN;
LIMITS, MFIL, MATR, MNTRY;
PRIORITY/IFL, ranking/repeats;
TIMST, VAR, ID;
SEEDS, ISEED(IS)/R, repeats;
INTLC, VAR=value, repeats;
INITIALIZE, TTBEG, TTFIN, JJCLR/NCCLR/JCNET, JJVAR, JJFIL;
ENTRY/IFL, ATRIB(1), ATRIB(2), . . . , ATRIB (MATR)/repeats;
MONTR, option, TFRST, TBTWN;
SIMULATE;
FIN;

For most network simulation programs, the YES option is used for these fields and that is the default condition.

5.6.2 LIMITS Statement

The format of the LIMITS statement is shown below.

LIMITS,MFIL,MATR,MNTRY;

The second statement in any SLAM simulation program is the LIMITS statement. The LIMITS statement is used to specify integer limits on the largest file number used (MFIL), the largest number of attributes per entity (MATR), and the maximum number of concurrent entries in all files (MNTRY). Normally an estimate of MNTRY must be made, as it is the total number of entities that can exist in the model at one time. We recommend the judicious use of a safety factor when estimating MNTRY.

5.6.3   PRIORITY Statement

The format of the PRIORITY statement is shown below.

PRIORITY/IFILE, ranking/repeats;

The PRIORITY statement is used to specify the criterion for ranking entities within a file. There are four possible specifications for the criterion:

FIFO   Entries are ranked based on their order of insertion in the file with early insertion given priority. This is a *first-in, first-out* ranking criterion.

LIFO   Entries are ranked based on their time of insertion with late insertions given priority. This is a *last-in, first-out* ranking criterion.

HVF(N)   The entries are ranked *high-value-first* based on the value of the Nth attribute.

LVF(N)   The entries are ranked *low-value-first* based on the value of the Nth attribute.

The default value for the criterion for all files is FIFO, therefore a PRIORITY statement for a file need be included only if the file is ranked LIFO, HVF(N), or LVF(N). A file ranking is specified by entering the file number IFILE followed by a comma and the file ranking. The rankings for different files can be specified on a single PRIORITY statement by separating the inputs with slashes.

The PRIORITY statement can also be used to specify the secondary ranking procedure for breaking ties between simultaneous node arrivals which are scheduled as future events by specifying the file value, IFILE, with the alphanumeric characters NCLNR denoting the event calendar. The event code can be used as the attribute specification by inserting the characters JEVNT for the attribute number. The following statement specifies that file 3 is to be ranked on a LIFO basis and the tie-breaking rule for events is high-value-first based on attribute 4:

PRIORITY/3,LIFO/NCLNR,HVF(4);

If the secondary ranking for the event calendar is to be low-value-first based on the event code, the statement would be:

PRIORITY/3,LIFO/NCLNR,LVF(JEVNT);

5.6.4 TIMST Statement

The format for the TIMST statement is shown below.

TIMST,VAR,ID;

The TIMST statement is employed to initiate the automatic collection of time-persistent statistics on the global variable $XX(N)$, or on the state or derivative variables $SS(N)$ and $DD(N)$. To employ the TIMST statement to initiate statistics on the indexed variable $XX(N)$ where N is an integer, the user simply enters $XX(N)$ in the variable field followed by a comma and an alphanumeric identifier (ID) which is to be used in displaying the statistics in the SLAM Summary Report. The first 16 characters of the identifier are significant. An example of the TIMST statement to collect statistics on the global variable $XX(1)$ defined to be the number of entities currently in the network is shown below.

TIMST,XX(1),NUMBER IN SYSTEM;

5.6.5 SEEDS Statement

The format for the SEEDS statement is shown below.

SEEDS,ISEED(IS)/R, repeats;

The purpose of the SEEDS statement is to permit the user to specify the starting unnormalized random number seed for any of the 10 random number streams available within SLAM and to control the reinitialization of streams for multiple simulation runs. The seeds are entered as integers with the stream number of the seed given in parentheses. If the stream number is not specified, then stream numbers are assigned based on the position of the seed. The first seed is for stream 1, the second for stream 2 and so on. The reinitialization of each stream is controlled by specifying *YES* or *NO* as a subfield following a slash immediately after the seed value and stream number. If the subfield is not included, the default case is assumed and the seed values are not reinitialization. If the SEEDS input statement is not included, the SLAM processor uses default seed values. An example of the SEEDS input statement is shown below:

SEEDS,9375295(1)/YES,0(2)/YES,6315779(9),2734681;

This statement initializes the seed for stream 1 to 9375295 and specifies that this value be used as the first value for each run. The zero specifies that the default value should be used for stream 2 and that it should be the first value for each run. The seed value for stream 9 is 6315779 and it is not to be reinitialized on subsequent runs. The seed value for stream 10 is 2734681 and is not to be reinitialized. Seed values for stream 3 through 8 will take default values and are not to be reinitialized. If antithetic random numbers are desired for a run (see Chapter 13) then a negative seed value is used. The sequence of random numbers generated will then be the complement of the numbers generated from the use of a positive value of the seed.

5.6.6   INTLC Statement

The format for the INTLC statement is: INTLC,VAR=value, repeats;

The INTLC statement is used to assign initial values to the SLAM variables $XX(N)$, $SS(N)$, or $DD(N)$ where N is an integer. The initial value can be specified on the statement by simply separating each assignment by a comma. An example is: INTLC,XX(1)=0, XX(2)=3.0;

5.6.7   INITIALIZE Statement

The format for the INITIALIZE statement is shown below.

INITIALIZE,TTBEG,TTFIN,JJCLR/NCCLR/JCNET,JJVAR,JJFIL;

The INITIALIZE statement is used to specify the beginning time (TTBEG) and ending time (TTFIN) for a simulation, and initialization options for clearing statistics, initializing variables, and initializing files. The last three fields are specified as *YES* or *NO* and are normally defaulted to YES. If JJCLR is specified as YES, NCCLR specifies the number of the collect variable up to which clearing is to be performed. If JJCLR is specified as NO, NCCLR specifies the collect variable number up to which clearing is not to be performed. JCNET is specified as YES or NO and indicates whether statistics collected at COLCT nodes in the network are to be cleared. The default value for NCCLR is all collect variables and for JCNET is YES. If JJVAR is specified as YES, TNOW is initialized to time TTBEG, and the variables XX(N), SS(N), and DD(N) are initialized to their starting values before each simulation run. If the field is specified as *NO*, the initializations are not performed. If JJFIL is specified as YES, the filing system is initialized before beginning each simulation run, otherwise it is not. The initialization of the filing system causes all file statistics to be cleared, removes all entries from the files, and places any initial QUEUE node entities into their appropriate files.

5.6.8   ENTRY Statement

The format for the ENTRY statement is shown below.

ENTRY/IFILE,ATRIB(1),ATRIB(2),...,ATRIB(MATR)/repeats;

The ENTRY statement is used to place initial entries into files. An entry is specified by entering the file number (IFILE) followed by the attributes of the entry separated by commas. The slash is used to denote the beginning specification of a new entry and causes any unspecified attribute values for the last entry to default to zero. If file IFILE is associated with a QUEUE or AWAIT node, the entry is processed as an entity arrival to the node at time TTBEG (beginning time of the simulation). In the case where multiple AWAIT nodes employ the same file, the arrival is processed at the first AWAIT node listed in the network model. An example of an ENTRY statement is shown below.

ENTRY/1,7.0,3.2/3,10.,5.5;

The ENTRY statement applies only to a single run and must be repeated when used with multiple runs. This statements inserts an entity into file 1 with attribute 1 equal to 7 and attribute 2 equal to 3.2, and an entity into file 3 with attributes 10. and 5.5.

5.6.9   MONTR Statement

The format for the MONTR statement is shown below.

MONTR,Option,TFRST,TBTWN;

The MONTR statement is used to monitor selected intermediate simulation results. The MONTR statement can also be used to clear statistical arrays after a "warm up" period in order to reduce any bias that is due to initial starting conditions. The values on the MONTR statement consist of the MONTR option, the time for the first execution of the option (TFRST), and the time between successive executions of the option (TBTWN). The times TFRST and TBTWN default to TTBEG and infinity, respectively. If TBTWN is defaulted, the MONTR option is executed only at time TFRST. However, if TBTWN is specified, the MONTR option is executed at time TFRST and every TBTWN time units thereafter. There are five MONTR options available and they are listed below:

SUMRY   Causes a SLAM Summary Report to be printed.

FILES   Causes a listing of all entries in the files to be printed.

STATES   Causes the continuous variables SS(N) and DD(N) to be printed.

CLEAR   Causes all statistical arrays, including the file statistics, to be cleared.

TRACE   Causes the starting and stopping of detailed tracing of each entity as it moves through the network. The trace will start at time TFRST. TBTWN is used in a different mode with the TRACE option and specifies the stopping time. Following the stopping time, the user can specify up to 5 attributes to be printed for each event traced. The output report generated by the trace option is described in Section 5.8.3.

Below are input examples:

Statement	*Description*
MONTR,SUMRY,200.,100.;	Summary report at TNOW=200 and every 100 time units thereafter
MONTR,CLEAR,500;	Clear STATISTICS at TNOW=500
MONTR,TRACE,0,150,2,3,7;	Start TRACE at TNOW=0, stop TRACE at TNOW=150. Print attributes 2, 3 and 7 on TRACE output

MONTR statements apply only to a single run and must be restated for each new run.

5.6.10   SIMULATE Statement

The SIMULATE statement consists of a single field as shown below.

SIMULATE;

The SIMULATE statement is used when making multiple simulation runs. One simulation run is executed for the statement cards preceding the SIMULATE statement. Following each SIMULATE statement, the user can insert any updates such as new random number seeds using the SEEDS statement, new ENTRY statements, or new initial values for the XX(N) variables using the INTLC statement. These new conditions apply to all subsequent simulation runs. In particular, the conditions for the first run apply unless altered by new statements. Thus, if only one simulation run is being made (NNRNS=1), or multiple runs are being made (NNRNS > 1) with the same starting conditions, the SIMULATE statement is not required. Recall, however, that ENTRY and MONTR statements only apply for one run.

5.6.11 FIN Statement

The FIN statement consists of a single field as shown below.

FIN;

The FIN statement denotes the end to all SLAM input statements. The FIN statement causes the execution of all remaining simulation runs.

This completes the description of network input statements and statements for executing network models. The description of other input statements that relate to discrete, continuous, and combined models is given in later chapters.

5.7 PROGRAM SETUP FOR NETWORK MODELS

The statements in a simulation program other than the network statements can be input in any order with the following exceptions:

1. The GEN statement must be the first statement in the deck, the LIMITS statement must be the second statement in the deck, and the FIN statement must be the last SLAM statement.
2. The network description statements must be immediately preceded by the NETWORK statement and immediately followed by the ENDNETWORK statement.
3. The INITIALIZE statement (if used) must precede ENTRY and MONTR statements (if any).

To illustrate the typical input setup for network simulations, consider the network model for the radio inspection problem presented in Chapter 4. Consider that two runs are to be made with the inspection time being uniformly distributed between 15 and 25 on the first run and uniformly distributed between 20 and 30 on the second run.

Since two runs are required and the lower and upper values for the uniformly distributed inspection time differ between the runs, the duration for the activity representing the inspection is specified as UNFRM(XX(1),XX(2)). The values for XX(1) and XX(2) will be assigned using the INTLC statement prior to the execution of each run.

The complete SLAM simulation program for a three inspector, radio model is depicted in Figure 5-2. The first statement is the GEN statement and specifies the analyst's name, project title, date, and number of runs. The second statement is the LIMITS statement and specifies that the simulation employs 1 file, 0 attributes, and a maximum of 30 entities in the system at any one time. The next statement is the NETWORK statement and denotes that a network model follows immediately. The network model consists of the next six statements and is ended by the END-NET statement which follows. Recall that all network statements and the ENDNET statement begin in or after column 7, with columns 1-5 reserved for node labels (not used here). The next statement is the INIT statement and specifies that the beginning time of the simulation (TTBEG) is time 0 and that the ending time (TTFIN) is time 480. Since all three initialization options are defaulted to YES, the statistical arrays are cleared, all variables are initialized, and the filing system is initialized before each simulation. The INTLC statement which follows specifies

```
GEN,C.D.PEGDEN,RADIO INSPECTION, 3/15/77,2;
LIMITS,1,0,30;
NETWORK;
        RESOURCE/INSPECT(3),1;
        CREATE,EXPON(10);              CREATE RADIO
        AWAIT,INSPECT;                 WAIT FOR INSPECTOR
        ACT,UNFRM(XX(1),XX(2));        INSPECTION ACTIVITY
        FREE, INSPECT;                 FREE INSPECTOR
        TERM;                          RADIO INSPECTION COMPLETED
        ENDNETWORK;
INIT,0,480;
INTLC,XX(1)=15.0,XX(2)=25.0;
SIMULATE;
INTLC,XX(1)=20.0,XX(2)=30.0;
FIN;
```

Figure 5-2 Illustration of SLAM input statement sequence.

initial conditions for XX(1) and XX(2) as 15 and 25, respectively. The next statement is the SIMULATE statement and causes execution of the first simulation run. Following the first simulation run, the values of XX(1) and XX(2) are reset by the second INTLC statement. The last statement is the FIN statement, which denotes the end of all SLAM input statements and causes all remaining simulation runs to be executed. This small example illustrates the basic program setup for network simulation programs. Although it does not illustrate all the statements presented in this section, it provides the information necessary to prepare the input for the SLAM processor. The other input statements will be illustrated in the examples presented in later chapters.

5.8 SLAM OUTPUT REPORTS

The purpose of this section is to describe the output reports which are generated by the SLAM processor. The output reports include the input listing, echo report, trace report, and SLAM Summary Report. A description of each report follows.

5.8.1 Statement Listing and Input Error Messages

The SLAM processor interprets each input statement and performs extensive checks for possible input errors. If the variable ILIST on the GEN statement is specified as YES or defaulted, the processor prints out a listing of the input statements. Each statement is assigned a line number and if an input error is detected an error message is printed immediately following the statement where the error occurred. The following types of input errors are detected by the SLAM processor.

Redundant Label: This error is caused by assigning the same node label to two or more nodes. Recall that only the first four characters are significant in node labels.

Unresolved Label: This error is caused by a reference to a node label which does not exist. A list of all unresolved labels is printed following the listing of input statements.

Incorrect Statement Sequence: This error is caused by an illogical or incorrect statement sequence. For example, an ACTIVITY following a TERM node would cause this error.

Multiple Defined File Number: This error is caused by illegally assigning the same wait file number to more than one node. The only case where the same wait file can be legally assigned to more than one node is in the case of AWAIT and PREEMPT nodes with the same resource or gate.

Invalid Numeric Field: This error is caused by an uninterpretable numeric field. For example, the entry 1.2.3 would cause this error.

Invalid Alphanumeric Field: This error is caused by an unrecognizable alphanumeric field. For example, misspelling the QUEUE statement as QEUE would cause this error.

Incorrect Field Type: This error is caused by entering a numeric field where an alphanumeric field is required or vice versa. For example, a numeric node label (or one whose first character was numeric) would cause this error.

Value Out of Range: This error is caused by specifying a numeric value which is out of the allowable range. For example, this error would be caused if ATRIB(6) was referenced in a network model where the maximum number of attributes was specified on the LIMITS statement as 5.

All input errors are treated as fatal errors in SLAM; that is, no execution is attempted if there is one or more input errors detected.

5.8.2   Echo Report

The SLAM Echo Report provides a summary of the simulation model as interpreted by the SLAM processor. This report is particularly useful during the debugging and verification phases of the simulation model development process.

5.8.3   Trace Report

The Trace Report is initiated by the MONTR statements using the TRACE option and causes a report summarizing each entity arrival event to be printed during execution of the simulation. The Trace Report generates a detailed account of the progress of a simulation by printing for each entity arrival event, the event time, the node label and type to which the entity is arriving, and the attributes of the arriving entity. In addition, a summary of all regular activities which emanate from the node is printed denoting if the activity was scheduled, the duration of the activity, and the end node of the activity.

5.8.4 SLAM Summary Report

The SLAM Summary Report displays the statistical results for the simulation and is automatically printed at the end of each simulation run. The report consists of a general section followed by the statistical results for the simulation categorized by type. The output statistics provided by the report are defined in Figure 5-3 and Table 5-3. The first category of statistics is for variables based on discrete observations and includes the statistics collected within network models by the COLCT statement. The second category of statistics is for time-persistent variables and corresponds to the statistics for the $XX(\cdot)$ variables over time. This is followed

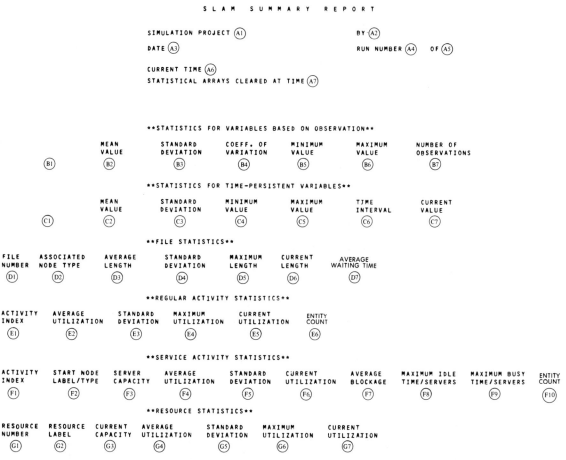

Figure 5-3 Definition of SLAM output statistics corresponding to Table 5-3.

Table 5-3 Definition of output statistics corresponding to Figure 5-3.

General Section

(A1)   The first 20 characters of project title entered on GEN statement

(A2)   The first 20 characters of analyst name entered on GEN statement

(A3)   The MONTH/DAY/YEAR entered in GEN statement

(A4)   The number of the simulation run

(A5)   The number of simulation runs to be made

(A6)   The current value of TNOW

(A7)   Time at which all statistical arrays were last cleared

Statistics for Variables Based on Observation

(B1)   The first 16 characters of the statistics label

(B2)   The arithmetic mean of the observations

(B3)   The standard deviation of the observations

(B4)   The coefficient of variation (standard deviation/mean)

(B5)   The minimum value over all observations

(B6)   The maximum value over all observations

(B7)   The number of observations

Statistics for Time-Persistent Variables

(C1)   The first 16 characters of the statistics label

(C2)   The average value of the variable over time

(C3)   The standard deviation over time

Table 5-3 (Continued)

C4 The minimum value of the variable over time

C5 The maximum value of the variable over time

C6 The time interval over which the statistics are accumulated

C7 The current value of the variable

File Statistics

D1 The file number

D2 The node type (if any) associated with the file

D3 The average number of entities in the file over time

D4 The standard deviation of the number of entities in the file over time

D5 The maximum number of entities in the file at any one time

D6 The current number of entities in the file

D7 **The average waiting time of all entities that arrived to the file including those that did not wait**

Regular Activity Statistics

E1 The activity index number for the activity

E2 The average number of entities undertaking the activity

E3 The standard deviation of the number of entities undertaking the activity over time

E4 The maximum number of entities undertaking the activity at any one time

E5 The number of entities currently undertaking the activity

E6 The number of entities which have completed the activity

159

Table 5-3 (Continued)

Service Activity Statistics
_____

(F1)   The activity number for the activity; A zero if a number is not assigned. Statistics are listed in the same order as the input statements.

(F2)   The label and type (QUEUE or SELECT) of the start node of the activity.

(F3)   The number of parallel identical servers represented by the activity.

(F4)   The average number of entities in service over time. If the capacity of the server is 1, this corresponds to the fraction of time the server is busy.

(F5)   The standard deviation of the number of entities in service over time.

(F6)   The current number of entities in service

(F7)   The average number of servers blocked over time. If the capacity of the server is 1, this corresponds to the fraction of time blocked.

(F8)   If the capacity of the server is 1, this value specifies the maximum idle time of the server. If the capacity of the server is greater than 1, this value specifies the maximum number of idle servers.

(F9)   Corresponding values for busy time.

(F10)   If the service activity is assigned an activity index number, the value printed corresponds to the number of entities completing service; otherwise no value is printed.

Resource Statistics
_____

(G1)   The resource number assigned by the processor

(G2)   The first 8 characters of the resource label as specified on the RESOURCE statement

160

Table 5-3   (Continued)

(G3)   The current capacity of the resource

(G4)   The average utilization of the resource over time

(G5)   The standard deviation of the resource utilization over
             time

(G6)   The maximum number of units of resource utilized at any
             one time

(G7)   The current number of units of resource utilized

by statistics on all user files. The next two categories correspond to statistics collected on regular and service activities, respectively. The last category of statistics is for resource statistics and is followed by the printout of histograms corresponding to variables based on observations. A SLAM Summary Report includes only those categories of statistics which are applicable to the particular simulation, and therefore may include none or all of the above categories.

5.9   CHAPTER SUMMARY

This chapter summarizes the input statements and output reports associated with SLAM network models. Over 80 percent of all inputs and outputs related to SLAM are presented in this chapter. The overall processing logic for simulating SLAM networks is also described in this chapter.

5.10   EXERCISES

5-1.   Prepare the SLAM input statements for the following network.

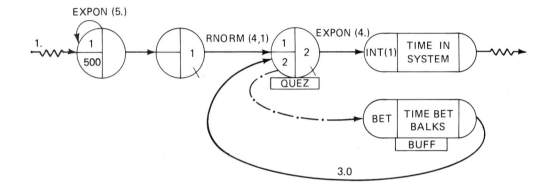

Set up the input data to make 10 independent replications with each run processing the 500 entities completely through the network.

5-2.   Redo the input data for Exercise 5-1 to stop each simulation run at time 2500 or following processing of 500 entities, whichever occurs first. Clear the statistical arrays at time 200. on each run using the MONTR statement.

5-3.   Given the following input statements, draw the equivalent SLAM network and describe the system.

```
GEN,C.D.PEGDEN, INVERT, 6/23/78,2;
LIMITS,1,2,20;
PRIORITY/1,LVF(2);
NETWORK;
        CREATE,EXPON(4.0),,1;
        ASSIGN,ATRIB(2)=1.0;
        ACT,,,WAIT;
        CREATE,EXPON(2.0),,1;
        ASSIGN,ATRIB(2)=2.0;
WAIT  QUEUE(1);
        ACT,EXPON(1.0);
        COLCT,INT(1),TIME IN SYSTEM;
        TERM;
        END NETWORK;
    INIT,0,1000;
    FIN;
```

5-4.   Redo the data statement in Exercise 5-3 to begin each simulation with an entity in service with ATRIB(1)=0.0 and ATRIB(2)=2.0.

5-5.   In the following input statements, detect at least nine errors.
GEN, PRITSKER-PEGDEN,ERRORS, JULY/23/1978,2;
LIMITS,2,1,0;
PRIORITY / 3,HVF(2);
INTLC,XX(1)= 2.0;
NETWORK;
       CREATE,UNIFORM(XX(1), 10.);
       AWAIT(1),TELLER;
       ACT,EXPON (4.0);
       FREE, TELLER;
       TERM;
INIT,0,100;
SIMULATE;
INTLC,XX(1)=4.0;
FIN;

5-6.   Prepare the input data for Illustration 2 in Section 4.5.2 to make 5 runs with each run lasting 1000 time units. On the second run, the mean and standard deviation for the normal distribution should be changed to 0.0 and 2.0. No additional changes are required on the third run. On the fourth run, the ranking at QUEUE node QOFS should be changed to last-in, first-out. No additional changes are required for run number 5.

5-7.   For the thief of Baghdad problem given in Exercise 2-7 draw the network and prepare the data input for 1000 runs using the following information: $p_F=0.3$, $p_S=0.2$, $p_L =0.5$ and the time in the short tunnel is exponentially distributed with a mean of 3, and the time in the long tunnel is lognormally distributed with a mean of 6 and a standard deviation of 2.

Suppose the thief's remaining time to live is normally distributed with a mean of 10 and a standard deviation of 2. Redraw the network and redo the data input in order to ascertain the probability that the thief reaches freedom before he dies based on 1000 simulations of the network.

5-8.   For the following network, describe the chronological sequence of node arrival events if the secondary ranking for future events is FIFO.

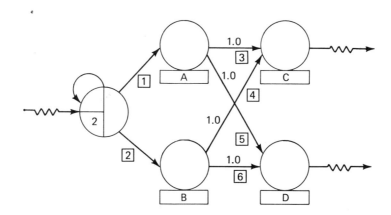

Embellishment: Repeat the exercise if secondary ranking for future events is LIFO.

5-9. Prepare the SLAM input statements for Exercise 5-8 to make two runs. The secondary ranking for future events should be FIFO on the first run and LIFO on the second run. Obtain a TRACE report on both runs.

5-10. Perform a simulation of a queueing situation using SLAM and discuss the meaning of each output statistic that is given on the SLAM Summary Report.

CHAPTER 6

Problem Solving Using SLAM Networks

6.1   Approaching Network Modeling Using SLAM

The network concepts presented in Chapter 4, combined with the SLAM processor description and input procedures presented in Chapter 5, provide the reader with the necessary tools to model a large class of systems as networks. The task facing the analyst is one of utilizing the network concepts to formulate a network model which reflects the important characteristics of the system. In approaching network modeling using SLAM, the analyst confronts two related problems: 1) deciding what detail to include in the model and 2) deciding how to represent that detail within the SLAM network framework.

In modeling and simulation, the level of detail to include in a model is relative to the purpose of the model. By knowing the purpose of the model, the relative worth of including specific details can be assessed. Only those elements that could cause significant differences in decision making resulting from the outputs from the simulation need be considered. In addition, for larger models it is often advantageous to decompose the models into stages of development. The decomposition could consist of initially developing an aggregate model which crudely approximates the system under study, and then improving the model through embellishments in subsequent stages, or it could consist of segmenting the total system into subsystems each of which are modeled separately and then combined. In any case, the prerequisite step in developing a network model of a system is to construct a problem statement which defines the purpose so that the specific detail level to be included in the simulation model can be decided.

Once the problem statement is complete, the system can be represented as entities which flow through a network of nodes and activities. The first step in this modeling process is to define the elements which are to be represented as entities. Recall that an entity is any object, being, unit of information, or combination thereof which defines or can alter the state of the system. Therefore the entities to be modeled can be identified by defining the variables that represent the system state and determining the changes in state that can occur. For example, in the radio inspection problem, the status of the system could be represented by the number of busy inspectors and the number of radios waiting for inspection. Status changes are due entirely to the movement of a radio through the system; therefore the entity to be modeled is the radio. For more complicated problems, the entities may be more abstract and there may be more than one entity type within the simulation.

The next and most challenging step in developing a network model is the synthesis of a network of nodes and activities which represents the process through which the entities flow. Although the synthesis can be done using either the graphic or statement form of the network elements, the initial development most often takes place using the graphic symbols. The advantage of using the graphic symbols is that they provide a pictorial medium for both conceptualization and communication. The graphic symbols of SLAM play a role for the simulation analyst similar to that of the free body diagram for mechanical engineers or the circuit diagram for electrical engineers. Once the graphic model is complete, the transcribing of the graphic model into the equivalent statement representation is straightforward.

Perhaps the most critical decision which the analyst must make in developing the network model is the choice between modeling resources as service activities or as explicit resources defined in a RESOURCE statement. For some problems, there is little advantage of one approach over the other. For example, the inspection problem could have just as easily been modeled by representing the inspectors as a resource. However in many problems there are distinct advantages in one approach over the other. It is difficult to state categorically which approach is best for specific types of applications and there is considerable overlap between applications of each approach. However, it can be noted that the service activity approach seems best suited in cases where the resource is utilized in one location in the system, particularly in cases involving queue and/or server selection rules, or where balking or blocking is involved. In contrast, the use of explicit resources is usually advantageous when the use of the resource is not restricted to one location in the system, when the capacity of a resource changes during a simulation, or when the resource can be preempted. The combination of both resource modeling approaches within SLAM provides the analyst with considerable flexibility, and can greatly simplify the network modeling task.

The final step in developing a network simulation is to combine the network description statements with the necessary control statements described in Section 5.6. These statements must include the GEN, LIMITS, and FIN statements plus any additional statements as determined by the requirements of the simulation runs.

In the following sections, we present nine examples of network modeling using SLAM. The examples are necessarily small, however, they are informative since they illustrate numerous network modeling concepts. The emphasis in the examples is on the construction of SLAM network simulation programs rather than on the solving of specific problems. Therefore the reader is encouraged to imagine other situations which could be modeled in the same or similar way. In general, we have found that network model building is performed iteratively with small models being embellished and expanded into larger models. Thus, the presentation of a diverse set of small models is preferred to the presentation of one large model that has many features.

In all the examples, a standard format is employed. First, the problem statement is presented which describes in detail the system to be modeled including the objective of the analysis. The *Concepts Illustrated* are then given which describes the major concepts which the example is intended to illustrate. The *SLAM Model* is then presented and described in detail including the network model and a listing of the statement model. Finally, a *Summary of Results* is presented including a reproduction of the SLAM Summary Report where appropriate.

6.2   Example 6-1.   WORK STATIONS IN SERIES

The maintenance facility of a large manufacturer performs two operations. These operations must be performed in series; operation 2 always follows operation 1. The units that are maintained are bulky, and space is available for only eight units including the units being worked on. A proposed design leaves space for two units between the work stations, and space for four units before work station 1. The proposed design is illustrated in Figure 6-1. Current company policy is to subcontract the maintenance of a unit if it cannot gain access to the in-house facility (7,9).

Historical data indicates that the time interval between requests for maintenance is exponentially distributed with a mean of 0.4 time units. Service times are also exponentially distributed with the first station requiring on the average 0.25 time units and the second station, 0.5 time units. Units are transported automatically from work station 1 to work station 2 in a negligible amount of time. If the queue of work station 2 is full, that is, if there are two units waiting for work station 2, the first work station is blocked and a unit cannot leave that station. A blocked work station cannot serve other units.

To evaluate the proposed design, statistics on the following variables are to be obtained over a period of 300 time units:

1. work station utilization;
2. time to process a unit through the two work stations;
3. number of units/time unit that are subcontracted;
4. number of units waiting for each work station; and
5. fraction of time that work station 1 is blocked.

Concepts Illustrated. This example will illustrate the general SLAM network modeling procedure which consists of: (1) identifying the entities to be modeled; (2) constructing a graphical model of the entity flow process through the system; and (3) transcribing the graphical model into the SLAM statement representation of the system. Specific network modeling concepts illustrated by this example include the creation of entities by a CREATE node, the modeling of a service system

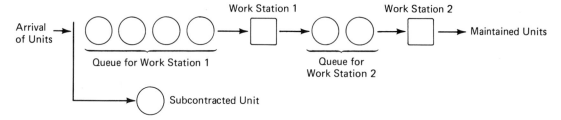

Figure 6-1 Schematic diagram of work stations in series.

with a QUEUE node and ACTIVITY, balking and blocking at QUEUE nodes, and statistics collection at a COLCT node.

SLAM Model.   The maintenance facility described in this example is representative of a large class of queueing-type systems in which units can be represented by entities that flow through the work stations. In this example, the entity flow process can be conveniently modeled by representing the storage area preceding each work station by a QUEUE node. The QUEUE node for work station 2 will be prescribed to have a blocking capability to stop the processing of units by work station 1 when work station 1 has completed processing a unit and the queue before work station 2 is at its capacity. Each work station is represented by a service ACTIVITY with one server associated with each work station.

The SLAM graphical model for this system is depicted in Figure 6-2. Entities representing the units are created at the CREATE node with the time between entities specified to be exponentially distributed with mean of 0.4 time units. Each entity's first attribute (ATRIB(1)) is marked with its time of creation at the CREATE node. Marking is specified to permit interval statistics to be collected on the

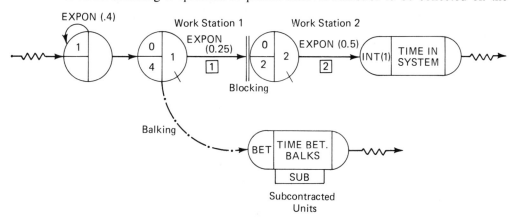

Figure 6-2 SLAM network model of maintenance facility.

time in the system for each entity. The entity is sent to the first QUEUE node which is used to represent the waiting area for work station 1. The parameters for this QUEUE node specify that the queue is initially empty, has a capacity of four, and that entities waiting in the queue are placed in file 1. The subcontracting for the maintenance of units is modeled by the balking option for this QUEUE node. Entities which arrive to the system when the queue is full are denied access to the queue and are routed to the COLCT node labeled SUB. The COLCT node collects values on the time between entity arrivals which corresponds to the time between the subcontracting of units. The first work station is represented by activity 1 emanating from the QUEUE node with the service time specified as exponentially distributed with a mean of 0.25 time units.

Following completion of service at work station 1, the entity attempts to enter the second QUEUE node which is used to model the storage area for work station 2. The parameters for this node specify that the QUEUE node is initially empty, has a capacity of two, and that entities waiting in the queue are placed in file 2. In addition, the blocking option is specified as indicated by the two parallel lines preceding the QUEUE node. Thus, if an entity completes service activity 1 when there are two entities waiting in file 2, work station 1 will be blocked from further processing until work station 2 completes service on an entity. Work station 2 is represented by activity 2 and has a service time specified as exponentially distributed with mean of 0.5 time units.

Following completion of service by work station 2, the entity proceeds to a COLCT node where INT(1) statistics are collected on the interval of time between the time recorded in attribute 1 of the entity and the current simulated time. Since the entity was marked at the CREATE node, attribute 1 is the time of arrival of the entity to the system. Thus, the interval of time represents the total processing time of the entity in the system. Following the COLCT node, the entity is terminated.

Once the graphical representation of the system is completed, the next step in the modeling process is to transcribe the graphical representation of the system into the equivalent SLAM statement representation according to the format specifications described in Chapter 5. The statement representation for this example is shown in Figure 6-3. Note that the sequence numbers along the left side of the figure are included to simplify statement referencing and are not part of the input data. Note also that the comments appearing on the right of the statement listing occur after the line terminator character (the semicolon) and are therefore ignored by the SLAM processor.

The first statement in the simulation program listing has the code GEN in field 1 and is used to provide general project information including the simulation author's name, project title, date, and number of simulation runs. This card is followed by the LIMITS card which specifies that the maximum number of files used in the simulation is 2, the maximum number of user attributes is 1, and the maximum number of concurrent entities in the system is 50. (In this example there can be 2 entities in service, 6 in files for QUEUE nodes, 1 in creation, and 2 in the departure process. Thus, a value of 9 could have been used.) This is followed by the NETWORK card which specifies that the simulation includes a network model with the network statement representation beginning with the next card.

```
1    GEN,C. D. PEGDEN,SERIAL WORK STATIONS,7/14/77,1;
2    LIMITS,2,1,50;
3    NETWORK;
4          CREATE,EXPON(.4),,1;                     CREATE ARRIVALS
5          QUEUE(1),0,4,BALK(SUB);                  STATION 1 QUEUE
6          ACT/1,EXPON(.25);                        STATION 1 SERVER TIME
7          QUEUE(2),0,2,BLOCK;                      STATION 2 QUEUE
8          ACT/2,EXPON(.50);                        STATION 2 SERVER TIME
9          COLCT,INT(1),TIME IN SYSTEM,20/0/.25;    COLLECT STATISTICS
10         TERM;
11   SUB   COLCT,BET,TIME BET. BALKS;               COLLECT STATISTICS
12         TERM;
13         END
14   INIT,0,300;
15   FIN;
```

Figure 6-3   Input statements for maintenance facility model.

The network statement representation of the system parallels closely the graphical network representation of the system. The CREATE statement (line 4) specifies that entities are marked in ATRIB(1). The time between entity arrivals is specified to be exponentially distributed with a mean of 0.4 time units. Since the time of first creation is not specified, a zero value is used. Also, there is no limit to the number of entities generated at this node. Each entity proceeds to the QUEUE statement (line 5). The parameters for the QUEUE statement specify that entities residing in the queue waiting for service are stored in file 1, that initially there are no entities in the queue, the queue has a capacity of four, and entities arriving to the queue when the queue is at capacity balk to the node labeled SUB. The ACT statement (line 6) following the queue statement is a service activity representing work station 1 with a service time exponentially distributed with a mean of 0.25 time units.

Following completion of service at work station 1, the entities continue to the second QUEUE node (line 7). The parameters for this QUEUE statement specify that entities waiting in the queue for service are stored in file 2, the queue is initially empty, has a capacity of two, and incoming entities (and service activities) are blocked when the queue is at capacity. The ACT statement (line 8) following the

QUEUE statement is a service activity representing work station 2 with a service time that is exponentially distributed with a mean of 0.5 time units.

Following completion of service at work station 2, the entities arrive at the COLCT node (line 9) which causes interval statistics to be collected using the mark time in attribute 1 as a reference time, with the output statistics labeled TIME IN SYSTEM. A histogram is requested with 20 cells, with the upper limit of the first cell set equal to 0, and with a cell width equal to 0.25 units. Entities are then terminated as specified by the TERM statement (line 10).

The subcontracting of units which cannot gain access to the in-house facility is modeled by the balking of entities from the QUEUE statement (line 5) to the COLCT node labeled SUB (line 11). The options listed for the COLCT statement specify that statistics are to be collected on the time BETWEEN entity arrivals to SUB, and that the output statistics are to be labeled TIME BET. BALKS. No histogram is requested. The entities representing the subcontracted units are then destroyed by the TERM statement (line 12). The ENDNETWORK statement (line 13) denotes an end to the network description portion of the simulation program.

The simulation is initialized by the INIT statement (line 14) which sets the beginning time of the simulation (TTBEG) to 0 and the ending time of the simu-

```
                    S L A M   S U M M A R Y   R E P O R T

        SIMULATION PROJECT SERIAL WORK STATIONS      BY C. D. PEGDEN

        DATE  7/14/1977                              RUN NUMBER   1 OF    1


        CURRENT TIME      .3000+03
        STATISTICAL ARRAYS CLEARED AT TIME      .0000
```

STATISTICS FOR VARIABLES BASED ON OBSERVATION

	MEAN VALUE	STANDARD DEVIATION	COEFF. OF VARIATION	MINIMUM VALUE	MAXIMUM VALUE	NUMBER OF OBSERVATIONS
TIME IN SYSTEM	.3122+01	.1431+01	.4583+00	.6006-01	.6775+01	562
TIME BET. BALKS	.1233+01	.2342+01	.1899+01	.3689-02	.2031+02	239

FILE STATISTICS

FILE NUMBER	ASSOCIATED NODE TYPE	AVERAGE LENGTH	STANDARD DEVIATION	MAXIMUM LENGTH	CURRENT LENGTH	AVERAGE WAITING TIME
1	QUEUE	2.4581	1.3973	4	0	1.3052
2	QUEUE	1.5154	.7549	2	1	0.8061

SERVICE ACTIVITY STATISTICS

ACTIVITY INDEX	START NODE LABEL/TYPE	SERVER CAPACITY	AVERAGE UTILIZATION	STANDARD DEVIATION	CURRENT UTILIZATION	AVERAGE BLOCKAGE	MAXIMUM IDLE TIME/SERVERS	MAXIMUM BUSY TIME/SERVERS	ENTITY COUNT
1	QUEUE	1	.5156	.4998	1	.4260	1.1716	4.4140	564
2	QUEUE	1	.9401	.2372	1	.0000	1.0031	25.5549	562

Figure 6-4 SLAM summary for serial work station model.

lation (TTFIN) to 300 time units. The FIN statement (line 15) denotes an end to all SLAM simulation input and causes execution of the simulation to begin.

Summary of Results.   The results for the simulation are summarized by the SLAM Summary Report depicted in Figure 6-4. The first category of statistics is for variables based upon observations. For this example, these statistics were collected by the network model at the COLCT nodes and include the interval statistics for TIME IN SYSTEM and the between statistics for TIME BET. BALKS. During the 300 simulated time units, there were a total of 562 units processed by the in-house facility. The average time in the system for these units was 3.122 time units with a standard deviation of 1.431 time units and times ranged from .06006 to 6.755 time units. The distribution for time in the system is depicted by the histogram generated by SLAM and included as Figure 6-5. There were a total of 239 observations of time between balks, and therefore, there were 240 units that were subcontracted. Recall that the time of first release of the COLCT node is not included as a value for between statistics because it may not be a representative value.

The second category of statistics for this example is the file statistics. The statistics for file 1 and file 2 correspond to the units waiting for service at work stations 1 and 2, respectively. Thus, the average number of units waiting at work station 1

```
                              **HISTOGRAM NUMBER   1**

                                 TIME IN SYSTEM


 OBSV      RELA      CUML       UPPER
 FREQ      FREQ      FREQ     CELL LIMIT     0        20        40        60        80       100
                                            +     +     +     +     +     +     +     +     +     +
    0     .000      .000      .0000         +                                                    +
    1     .002      .002      .2500+00      +                                                    +
    6     .011      .012      .5000+00      ++*                                                  +
   12     .021      .034      .7500+00      ++C                                                  +
   16     .028      .062      .1000+01      ++ *   C                                             +
   14     .025      .087      .1250+01      ++ *    C                                            +
   24     .043      .130      .1500+01      ++**      C                                          +
   39     .069      .199      .1750+01      ++**         C                                       +
   35     .062      .262      .2000+01      ++**            C                                    +
   34     .060      .322      .2250+01      ++**              C                                  +
   25     .044      .367      .2500+01      ++*                 C                                +
   34     .060      .427      .2750+01      ++**                   C                             +
   34     .060      .488      .3000+01      ++**                      C                          +
   31     .055      .543      .3250+01      ++**                         C                       +
   25     .044      .587      .3500+01      ++*                            C                     +
   32     .057      .644      .3750+01      ++**                             C                   +
   36     .064      .708      .4000+01      ++**                               C                 +
   30     .053      .762      .4250+01      ++**                                  C              +
   38     .068      .829      .4500+01      ++**                                    C            +
   25     .044      .874      .4750+01      ++*                                        C         +
   15     .027      .900      .5000+01      ++*                                          C       +
   56     .100     1.000       INF         ++****                                              C
  ---                                       +     +     +     +     +     +     +     +     +     +
  562                                       0        20        40        60        80       100
```

Figure 6-5   SLAM histogram for time in system, serial work station model.

was 2.4581 units, with a standard deviation of 1.3973 units, a maximum of 4 units waited, and at the end of the simulation there were no units in the queue.

The last category of statistics for this example is statistics on service activities. The first row of service activity statistics corresponds to the server at work station 1 who was busy 51.56 percent of the time and blocked 42.60 percent of the time. Since the capacity of the server is one, the values 1.1716 and 4.4140 refer to the maximum length of the server idle period and busy period, respectively.

A number of additional statistics not provided by the SLAM Summary Report can be obtained by straightforward analysis using the statistics provided. For example, the average time that units spent waiting for service (2.372) can be obtained by subtracting the sum of the average service times (0.75), from the average time in the system (3.122). The fraction of time idle (0.0584) for the server at work station 1 can be determined by simply subtracting the sum of the average utilization (0.5156) and average blockage (0.4260) from 1.

In analyzing the proposed work station design with the aid of the simulation results, it appears that the design can be improved by shifting storage space from work station 1 to work station 2. This conclusion is reached by observing the high average blockage of work station 1 and the high percent utilization of the assigned storage space for work station 2 relative to work station 1.

6.3   Example 6-2. INSPECTION AND ADJUSTMENT STATIONS ON A PRODUCTION LINE

The problem statement for this example is taken from Schriber (11), who presents a GPSS model of the problem. A Q-GERT model of this example is presented by Pritsker (9). Assembled television sets move through a series of testing stations in the final stage of their production. At the last of these stations, the vertical control setting on the TV sets is tested. If the setting is found to be functioning improperly, the offending set is routed to an adjustment station where the setting is adjusted. After adjustment, the television set is sent back to the last inspection station where the setting is again inspected. Television sets passing the final inspection phase, whether for the first time or after one or more routings through the adjustment station, are routed to a packing area.

The situation described is pictured in Figure 6-6 where "circles" represent television sets. "Open circles" are sets waiting for final inspection, whereas "circled x's" are sets whose vertical control settings are improper, and which are either being serviced at the adjustment station or are waiting for service there.

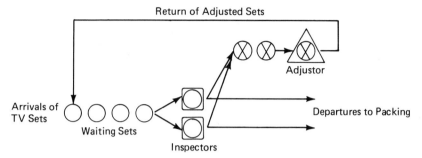

Figure 6-6 Schematic diagram of inspection and adjustment stations.

The time between arrivals of television sets to the final inspection station is uniformly distributed between 3.5 and 7.5 minutes. Two inspectors work side-by-side at the final inspection station. The time required to inspect a set is uniformly distributed between 6 and 12 minutes. On the average, 85 percent of the sets pass inspection and continue on to the packing department. The other 15 percent are routed to the adjustment station which is manned by a single worker. Adjustment of the vertical control setting requires between 20 and 40 minutes, uniformly distributed.

The inspection station and adjustor are to be simulated for 480 minutes to estimate the time to process television sets through this final production stage and to determine the utilization of the inspectors and the adjustor.

Concepts Illustrated. This example illustrates the uses of a service activity to model parallel identical servers. In addition, this example illustrates the use of regular activities for probabilistic branching. The procedure for obtaining a SLAM trace through the use of a MONTR statement is illustrated.

SLAM Model. The entities to be modeled in this system are the television sets. The television sets arrive and are routed to the inspection station. The two inspectors at the inspection station are represented as servers. If both inspectors are busy, a queue of television sets forms. This process can be conveniently modeled in SLAM with a QUEUE node that precedes a service activity that represents two servers. Following the service activity representing the inspectors, 85 percent of the entities are accepted and depart to packing. The remaining 15 percent of the televisions do not pass inspection and are routed to the adjustor. If the adjustor is busy, a queue would form of televisions waiting for the adjustor. The adjustment process can be modeled as a QUEUE node followed by a service activity with a capacity of one. Following the adjustment operation, the entity is routed back to the queue of the inspectors.

The above describes the complete processing and routing of television sets through the inspection and adjustment stations. The SLAM graphical model can be built directly from this discussion and is shown in Figure 6-7. Entities representing the television sets are created by the CREATE node with the time between entities uniformly distributed between 3.5 and 7.5 time units. The entity's arrival time is recorded as attribute 1. Each entity proceeds to the QUEUE node labeled INSP, and will proceed directly into service if an inspector represented by the emanating service activity is free. Recall that the 2 in the circle under the service ACTIVITY denotes two parallel identical servers. The service time for each server is specified as uniformly distributed between 6 and 12. Entities which arrive to the QUEUE node when both servers are busy wait in the QUEUE node which prescribes that they be stored in file 1.

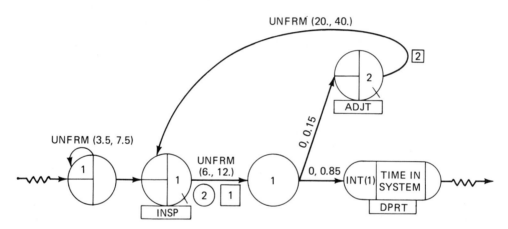

Figure 6-7   SLAM network model of TV inspection and adjustment stations.

Following inspection, the entities arrive at a GOON node where they are probabilistically routed since the M-number of the GOON node is 1 and probabilities are associated with the two activities emanating from the GOON node. One activity leads to the COLCT node labeled DPRT representing departure to the packing area. The other activity leads to the QUEUE node labeled ADJT representing the waiting line for the adjustment operation. Entities in the ADJT QUEUE wait for the adjustor in file 2. The adjustment operation is represented by the emanating service activity whose duration is uniformly distributed between 20 and 40 time units. Following adjustment, television entities are routed back to the QUEUE node labeled INSP. Entities which are routed to the COLCT node DPRT have interval statistics collected based on the time interval from when they were marked at the CREATE node in attribute 1. This interval of time corresponds to the total

```
 1   GEN,C. D. PEGDEN,TV INSP. AND ADJUST.,6/25/77,1;
 2   LIMITS,2,2,50;
 3   NETWORK;
 4         CREATE,UNFRM(3.5,7.5),,1;              CREATE TELEVISIONS
 5   INSP  QUEUE(1);                              INSPECTION QUEUE
 6         ACT(2)/1,UNFRM(6.,12.);                INSPECTION
 7         GOON;
 8         ACT,,.85,DPRT;                         85% DEPART
 9         ACT,,.15,ADJT;                         15% ARE RE-ADJUSTED
10   ADJT  QUEUE(2);                              ADJUST QUEUE
11         ACT/2,UNFRM(20.,40.),,INSP;            ADJUSTMENT
12   DPRT  COLCT,INT(1),TIME IN SYSTEM;           COLLECT STATISTICS
13         TERM;
14         END;
15   INIT,0,480;
16   MONTR,TRACE,0,60,1;
17   FIN;
```

Figure 6-8 Network statement model for television set inspection and adjustment stations.

time that the television set spends in the inspection and adjustment process. The entities are then terminated.

The SLAM statement listing follows directly from the network model and is shown in Figure 6-8. Entities representing televisions are created by the CREATE statement (line 4) with a time between creations that is uniformly distributed in the range (3.5, 7.5) time units. The arrival time is marked as attribute 1 at the CREATE node. The entity is routed to the INSP QUEUE where they wait in file 1 for a free server. The two parallel inspectors are represented by an ACT statement (line 6). The 2 in parentheses indicates two parallel identical servers and the duration for each is specified as uniformly distributed between 6 and 12. Entities completing inspection arrive at the GOON statement (line 7) which has two emanating activities. The first activity (line 8) has a default duration of zero, and is taken with a probability of 0.85 and routes the entity to the statement labeled DPRT. The second activity (line 9) has a default duration of zero, and is taken with a probability of 0.15 and routes the entity to the statement labeled ADJT. Entities which arrive to the ADJT QUEUE wait in file 2 for the adjustor. The adjustor is represented by the emanating service activity (line 11) which has a duration uniformly distributed from 20 to 40 and routes entities to the statement labeled INSP. Entities which arrive to the DPRT statement (line 12) have interval statistics collected from the mark time recorded in attribute 1, and the statistics are labeled TIME IN SYSTEM. The entities then continue to the TERM statement (line 13) where they are destroyed. The END statement (line 14) denotes an end to the network description. The MONTR statement (line 16) initiates the tracing of events at time 0, stops the tracing of events at time 60, and specifies that the value of attribute 1 be printed. The trace output is shown on page 178.

```
                         SLAM TRACE BEGINNING AT TNOW=    .0000

----------------------------------------------------------------------------------
                     NODE  ARRIVAL                      REGULAR ACTIVITY SUMMARY
      TNOW    JEVNT   -------------                     ------------------------
                     LABEL   TYPE                       INDEX   DURATION   END NODE
                                 ATTRIBUTE :    1
----------------------------------------------------------------------------------

     .0000                   CREATE        .0000
     .0000          INSP QUEUE        .0000
     .6220+01                GOON          .0000
                                                          0   NOT RELEASED     DPRT
                                                          0            .0000   ADJT
     .6220+01       ADJT QUEUE        .0000
     .7480+01                CREATE       .7480+01
     .7480+01       INSP QUEUE       .7480+01
     .1308+02                CREATE       .1308+02
     .1308+02       INSP QUEUE       .1308+02
     .1813+02                CREATE       .1813+02
     .1813+02       INSP QUEUE       .1813+02
     .1857+02                GOON         .7480+01
                                                          0            .0000   DPRT
                                                          0   NOT RELEASED     ADJT
     .1857+02       DPRT COLCT       .7480+01
     .1857+02            TERM         .7480+01
     .2222+02            CREATE       .2222+02
     .2222+02       INSP QUEUE       .2222+02
     .2459+02            GOON         .1308+02
                                                          0            .0000   DPRT
                                                          0   NOT RELEASED     ADJT
     .2459+02       DPRT COLCT       .1308+02
     .2459+02            TERM         .1308+02
     .2751+02            CREATE       .2751+02
     .2751+02       INSP QUEUE       .2751+02
     .2808+02            GOON         .1813+02
```

Summary of Results.   The results for this simulation are summarized in the SLAM Summary Report shown in Figure 6-9. The first category of statistics for this example is statistics for variables based on observations. It consists of the interval statistics on the TIME IN SYSTEM collected by the COLCT statement (line 12). During the 480 minutes of simulated operation, a total of 80 television sets completed processing with the sets spending an average of 20.89 minutes in the system. However, there was a high variability in times in the system between television sets as reflected by the minimum and maximum time and the high standard deviation and coefficient of variation. This is to be expected since a fraction of the television sets have much larger times in the system due to their being adjusted. Also, 480 time units is insufficient to reach steady-state values.

The second category of statistics for this example is the file statistics. The results show that there was an average of .4138 television sets waiting for inspection in file 1, and .6666 television sets waiting for adjustment in file 2. Again, the high standard deviations relative to the averages indicate a high degree of variation in queue length over time.

The final category of statistics is the service activity statistics. In this example, there are two service activities corresponding to the inspectors and adjustors, respectively. The first service activity represents the inspectors and they had an average utilization of 1.8225. Note that since this activity has a capacity of 2, the maximum idle and busy values refer to the number of servers. The output indicates that both servers were idle at one point during the simulation and that both servers were busy at one point during the simulation. The second service activity represents the adjustor who had an average utilization of 0.9505. The longest period of time for which the adjustor was idle was 11.9379 minutes and the longest period of time for which the adjustor was busy was 216.6403 minutes. The summary report also indicates that one television is waiting for adjustment and that

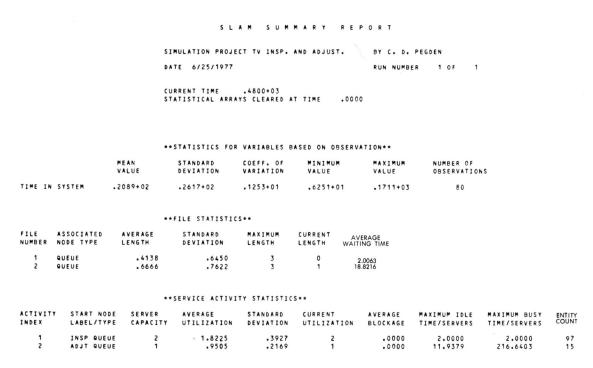

S L A M   S U M M A R Y   R E P O R T

SIMULATION PROJECT TV INSP. AND ADJUST.   BY C. D. PEGDEN

DATE 6/25/1977   RUN NUMBER   1 OF   1

CURRENT TIME   .4800+03
STATISTICAL ARRAYS CLEARED AT TIME   .0000

STATISTICS FOR VARIABLES BASED ON OBSERVATION

	MEAN VALUE	STANDARD DEVIATION	COEFF. OF VARIATION	MINIMUM VALUE	MAXIMUM VALUE	NUMBER OF OBSERVATIONS
TIME IN SYSTEM	.2089+02	.2617+02	.1253+01	.6251+01	.1711+03	80

FILE STATISTICS

FILE NUMBER	ASSOCIATED NODE TYPE	AVERAGE LENGTH	STANDARD DEVIATION	MAXIMUM LENGTH	CURRENT LENGTH	AVERAGE WAITING TIME
1	QUEUE	.4138	.6450	3	0	2.0063
2	QUEUE	.6666	.7622	3	1	18.8216

SERVICE ACTIVITY STATISTICS

ACTIVITY INDEX	START NODE LABEL/TYPE	SERVER CAPACITY	AVERAGE UTILIZATION	STANDARD DEVIATION	CURRENT UTILIZATION	AVERAGE BLOCKAGE	MAXIMUM IDLE TIME/SERVERS	MAXIMUM BUSY TIME/SERVERS	ENTITY COUNT
1	INSP QUEUE	2	1.8225	.3927	2	.0000	2.0000	2.0000	97
2	ADJT QUEUE	1	.9505	.2169	1	.0000	11.9379	216.6403	15

Figure 6-9 Summary report for TV inspection and adjustment stations.

both inspectors and the adjustor are busy at the end of the simulation run. Adding these four television sets to the 80 that were completely processed indicates that 84 television sets were created. This is comparable to the 480/5.5 or approximately 87 arrivals expected.

The information on the SLAM summary report can be used to assess system performance relative to questions such as: Are the queue storage areas large enough? Is the allocation of manpower between the inspection station and adjustor station proper? Is the time to process a television too long? In general, "what if" type questions are readily addressed using SLAM.

**6.4   Example 6-3.   MODELING OF A TRUCK
                        HAULING SITUATION**

The system to be modeled in this example consists of one bulldozer, four trucks and two man-machine loaders (3,9). The bulldozer stockpiles material for the loaders. Two piles of material must be stocked prior to the initiation of any load operation. The time for the bulldozer to stockpile material is Erlang distributed and consists of the sum of two exponential variables each with a mean of 4. (This corresponds to an Erlang variable with a mean of 8 and a variance of 32.) In addition to this material, a loader and an unloaded truck must be available before the loading operation can begin. Loading time is exponentially distributed with a mean time of 14 minutes for server 1 and 12 minutes for server 2.

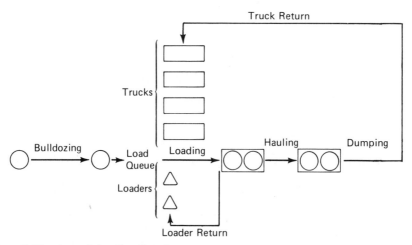

Figure 6-10   A truck hauling situation.

After a truck is loaded, it is hauled, then dumped and must be returned before the truck is available for further loading. Hauling time is normally distributed. When loaded, the average hauling time is 22 minutes. When unloaded, the average time is 18 minutes. In both cases, the standard deviation is 3 minutes. Dumping time is uniformly distributed between 2 and 8 minutes. Following a loading operation, the loader must rest for a 5 minute period before he is available to begin loading again. A schematic diagram of the system is shown in Figure 6-10. The system is to be analyzed for 8 hours and all operations in progress at the end of 8 hours should be completed before terminating the operations for a run.

Concepts Illustrated.   This example illustrates the use of the SELECT node for routing entities from multiple QUEUE nodes to multiple service ACTIVITY's. Additional concepts illustrated by this example include the use of the ACCUM node for combining entities, the use of conditional branching for testing system status, the representation of several entity types by entities within the same model, and the ending of a simulation by completing processing of all entities in the system.

SLAM Model.   In this example, there are four distinct entities to be modeled. The first entity type is the pile of material created by the bulldozing operation. Since two piles must be combined to make one load, the entities representing piles of material must be combined two at a time to create a new entity representing a load. This accumulation of entities can be modeled with an ACCUM node that requires that 2 entities be combined for the first release (FR=2), and 2 entities be combined for subsequent releases (SR=2). No attributes are used in this example, and, hence, no SAVE rule is required at the ACCUM node. Before the loading operation can begin, in addition to a load, there must also be an available truck and loader, each represented by separate entities. The loading operation can be performed by either of two non-identical servers.

This process can be modeled by employing separate QUEUE nodes for the trucks, loads, and loaders, in conjunction with a following SELECT node with two emanating servers. By specifying the ASM (assembly) and LIT (longest idle time) options for the queue and server selection rules, respectively, an entity is required in each queue before a service can be initiated, and available servers are selected based on longest idle time for each server. Following a loading operation, the entity is split and two entities are routed. One represents the truck and the other the loader. The entity representing the loader is delayed 5 minutes before being available to begin loading again. The consecutive activities of hauling, dumping, and return trip can be represented by serial ACTIVITY's with the last ACTIVITY returning the truck entity to the QUEUE node representing available trucks. The SLAM network model of the system is depicted in Figure 6-11.

The SLAM simulation statement listing for this example is shown in Figure 6-12. The network description begins with the CREATE statement (line 4) which creates the first entity at time 0. Thereafter, the time between entities is specified according to the Erlang distribution. The parameters for the Erlang distribution are: each exponential sample has a mean of 4 and there are to be 2 exponential samples. The entity continues through the conditional ACTIVITY (line 5) if TNOW is less than 480; otherwise the activity is not released and the entity is destroyed. This condition stops the creation of piles by the bulldozer after 480 minutes of operation. Since there is no INIT statement, an ending time for the simulation is not specified. In this situation, the run will end when all operations

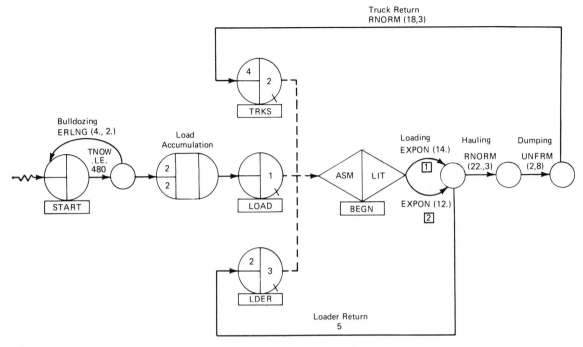

Figure 6-11   SLAM network model of truck hauling system.

```
1   GEN,C. D. PEGDEN,TRUCK HAULING,7/12/77,1;
2   LIMITS,3,1,50;
3   NETWORK;
4   START CREATE;                          CREATE LOAD TRANSACTION
5         ACT,,TNOW.LE.480;                STOP IF AFTER 8 HOURS
6         GOON;                            ELSE
7         ACT,ERLNG(4.,2.),,START;         BRANCH BACK TO START
8         ACT;                             AND CONTINUE
9         ACCUM,2,2;                       ACCUMULATE TWO PILES
10  LOAD  QUEUE(1),,,,BEGN;                QUEUE OF LOADS
11  TRKS  QUEUE(2),4,,,BEGN;               QUEUE OF TRUCKS
12  LDER  QUEUE(3),2,,,BEGN;               QUEUE OF LOADERS
13  BEGN  SELECT,ASM,LIT,,LOAD,TRKS,LDER;  ASM OF LOAD,TRKS, AND LDER
14        ACT/1,EXPON(14.);                LOADER 1 TIME
15        ACT/2,EXPON(12.);                LOADER 2 TIME
16        GOON;
17        ACT,5,,LDER;                     LOADER RESTING TIME
18        ACT,RNORM(22.,3.);               TRUCK HAULING TIME
19        GOON;
20        ACT,UNFRM(2.,8.);                TRUCK DUMPING TIME
21        GOON;
22        ACT,RNORM(18.,3.),,TRKS;         TRUCK RETURN TIME
23        END
24  FIN;
```

Figure 6-12   SLAM statement listing for truck hauling example.

in progress at time 480 are completed since the arrival process was halted. SLAM ends a run when the executive routine attempts to advance time and no events exist on the event calendar.

Entities representing piles arrive at the ACCUM statement (line 9), where they are combined in pairs to form load transactions and continue to the LOAD QUEUE statement (line 10). The LOAD QUEUE is related to the TRKS QUEUE (line 11) and the LDER QUEUE (line 12), all of which have the statement labeled BEGN as a following SELECT node. The TRKS QUEUE represents the queue of waiting trucks which are stored in file 2. There are initially four trucks in the queue. The LDER QUEUE represents the queue of waiting loaders which are stored in file 3. The queue is initialized to have two loaders in the queue at the beginning of the simulation. The SELECT statement labeled BEGN (line 13) employs the ASM queue selection rule, LIT server selection rule, has neither balking nor blocking, and selects from the preceding QUEUE's labeled LOAD, TRKS, and LDER. Following the SELECT statement are two non-identical servers. The first server (line 14) representing loader 1 is assigned an activity number of 1 and has a service time which is exponentially distributed with a mean of 14 minutes. The second server (line 15) representing loader 2 is assigned an activity number of 2 and has a service time which is exponentially distributed with a mean of 12 minutes.

At the end of the loading operation, the entity arrives at the GOON statement (line 16). Following the GOON statement are two regular ACTIVITY's. The first ACTIVITY (line 17) representing the loader resting time has a duration of five minutes and routes the entity to the statement labeled LDER. The entity proceeding through the second ACTIVITY statement (line 18), representing the truck hauling operation, continues to a GOON statement (line 19). Next, the entity continues through the ACTIVITY statement (line 20) representing the dumping operation which ends at a GOON statement (line 21). The last ACTIVITY statement (line 22) models the return trip of the truck and routes the entity to the statement labeled TRKS.

In summarizing the SLAM model for this example, it is interesting to note the representation of loaders as both service ACTIVITY's and entities queueing up at the LDER QUEUE. This dual representation is used to include the resting time for the loader. If the resting time requirement were omitted from the problem statement, the loaders could be modeled by the service ACTIVITY's only, and thus statements 12 and 17 could be deleted from the model.

Summary of Results.   The SLAM Summary Report for this example is shown in Figure 6-13. The first category of statistics is the file statistics for files 1, 2, and 3, and correspond to the queue of loads waiting for service, the queue of idle

```
          S L A M   S U M M A R Y   R E P O R T

     SIMULATION PROJECT TRUCK HAULING          BY C. D. PEGDEN

     DATE  7/12/1977                           RUN NUMBER    1 OF    1


     CURRENT TIME     .5699+03
     STATISTICAL ARRAYS CLEARED AT TIME      .0000
```

FILE STATISTICS

FILE NUMBER	ASSOCIATED NODE TYPE	AVERAGE LENGTH	STANDARD DEVIATION	MAXIMUM LENGTH	CURRENT LENGTH	AVERAGE WAITING TIME
1	QUEUE	.2138	.4588	2	0	4.2015
2	QUEUE	1.0330	.9879	4	4	17.8396
3	QUEUE	1.0469	.7745	2	2	19.2461

SERVICE ACTIVITY STATISTICS

ACTIVITY INDEX	START NODE LABEL/TYPE	SERVER CAPACITY	AVERAGE UTILIZATION	STANDARD DEVIATION	CURRENT UTILIZATION	AVERAGE BLOCKAGE	MAXIMUM IDLE TIME/SERVERS	MAXIMUM BUSY TIME/SERVERS	ENTITY COUNT
1	BEGN SELECT	1	.4185	.4933	0	.0000	43.3261	62.1060	13
2	BEGN SELECT	1	.2801	.4490	0	.0000	56.4137	34.4187	16

Figure 6-13   SLAM summary report for truck hauling example.

trucks, and the queue of available loaders, respectively. The second category of statistics is the service activity statistics representing the two loaders. A count of entities completing the two activities indicates that a total of 29 loads were processed through the system. This small number of observations suggest that considerable variation in both queue lengths and service activity utilizations can be expected between simulation runs employing different seed values.

6.5   Example 6-4.   MODELING OF QUARRY OPERATIONS

In this example, the operations of a quarry are modeled. In the quarry, trucks deliver ore from three shovels to a single, primary crusher. Trucks are assigned to specific shovels, so that a truck will always return to its assigned shovel after dumping a load at the crusher. There are two different truck sizes in use, twenty-ton and fifty-ton. The size of the truck affects its loading time at the shovel, travel time to the crusher, dumping time at the crusher, and return trip time from the crusher back to the appropriate shovel. For the twenty-ton trucks, these loading, travel, dumping, and return trip times are: exponentially distributed with mean 5; a constant 2.5; exponentially distributed with mean 2; and a constant 1.5. The corresponding times for the fifty-ton trucks are: exponentially distributed with mean 10; a constant 3; exponentially distributed with mean 4; and a constant 2. To each shovel is assigned two twenty-ton and one fifty-ton truck. The shovel queues are all ranked on a first-in, first-out basis. The crusher queue is ranked on truck size, largest trucks first. A schematic diagram of the quarry operations is shown in Figure 6-14. It is desired to analyze this system over 480 time units to determine the utilization and queue lengths associated with the shovels and crusher (9).

Concepts Illustrated. In the previous examples, entities have been entered into the network by the CREATE node. In this example, we illustrate an alternate approach of directly inserting entities into the network using the ENTRY statement. Additional concepts illustrated by this example include the specification of activity durations as a function of the attributes of the entities and the ranking of entities at a QUEUE node based upon attribute values.

SLAM Model. The network modeling of the quarry operations involves the routing of two distinct entity types representing the twenty-ton and fifty-ton trucks. Each entity is assigned five attribute values consisting of: 1) truck tonnage (either 20 or 50); 2) shovel number to which the truck is assigned; 3) mean shovel loading duration; 4) mean crusher dumping duration; and 5) return trip time. The SLAM statement model for processing the entities through the quarry operations is depicted in Figure 6-15. Note that entities are neither created nor terminated

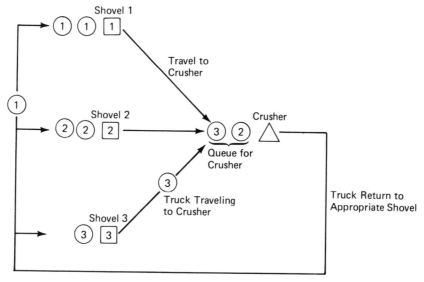

Figure 6-14 Quarry operations description.

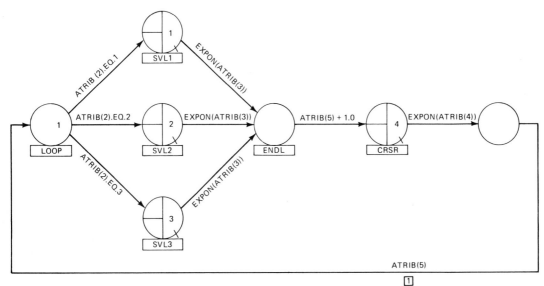

Figure 6-15   Network representation of quarry operations.

within the graphical model. Therefore, to initiate the simulation, we must insert six entities representing the twenty-ton trucks and three entities representing the fifty-ton trucks directly into the network. These entities will continue to cycle through the network until the simulation is terminated. However, before discussing the procedure for inserting the truck entities into the network, we will complete our description of the network model.

We begin our description at the far left GOON node labeled LOOP. Entities arriving to the GOON node represent trucks completing their return trip from the crusher. An arriving entity is routed through one of the emanating ACTIVITY's to the appropriate shovel queue by conditional branching based on the value of ATRIB(2). Recall ATRIB(2) contains the shovel number to which the truck is assigned. Each shovel queue is represented by a QUEUE node with the loading operation represented by an emanating ACTIVITY. The duration of the service ACTIVITY is specified to be exponentially distributed with a mean given by ATRIB(3). ATRIB(3) is equal to 5 or 10 depending upon whether the entity represents a twenty-ton or fifty-ton truck. Therefore the duration of the ACTIVITY is dependent upon the type of entity being processed. After completing the loading operation, the entity then undertakes the ACTIVITY with duration ATRIB(5)+1.0 representing the loaded travel time. The entity continues to the QUEUE node labeled CRSR representing the queue of trucks waiting to dump ore at the crusher. Entities waiting at the QUEUE node wait in file 4 which is ranked on high values of attribute 1 (HVF(1)). Since the first attribute denotes truck tonnage, priority is given to the fifty-ton trucks. The dumping operation is represented by the service ACTIVITY emanating from the CRSR QUEUE node and is exponentially distributed with a mean given by ATRIB(4) of the truck entities. Following completion of the dumping operation, the entity arrives to the GOON node and then continues through the emanating ACTIVITY representing the return trip. The ACTIVITY has a duration given by ATRIB(5), is assigned activity index 1, and routes the entity back to the GOON node labeled LOOP.

The statement model for this example is shown in Figure 6-16. The PRIORITY statement (line 3) specifies that file 4 corresponding to the crusher queue is ranked on HVF(1). The network model consists of statements 9 through 25. Entities arriving to the GOON node labeled LOOP (line 9) are routed by the three ACTIVITY's to the appropriate shovel QUEUE labeled SVL1, SVL2, or SVL3. Each QUEUE is followed by a service ACTIVITY which represents the loading activity and routes the entity to the GOON statement labeled ENDL (line 19).

```
 1   GEN,C. D. PEGDEN,QUARRY OPERATIONS,4/19/77,1;
 2   LIMITS,4,5,75;
 3   PRIORITY/4,HVF(1);
 4   NETWORK;
 5   ;
 6   ;      ATRIB(1)=TONNAGE,ATRIB(2)=SVL NO.,ATRIB(3)=SVL TIME
 7   ;      ATRIB(4)=CRSR TIME,ATRIB(5)=RETURN TRIP TIME
 8   ;
 9   LOOP   GOON,1;
10          ACT,,ATRIB(2).EQ.1,SVL1;
11          ACT,,ATRIB(2).EQ.2,SVL2;
12          ACT,,ATRIB(2).EQ.3,SVL3;
13   SVL1   QUEUE(1);
14          ACT,EXPON(ATRIB(3)),,ENDL;
15   SVL2   QUEUE(2);
16          ACT,EXPON(ATRIB(3)),,ENDL;
17   SVL3   QUEUE(3);
18          ACT,EXPON(ATRIB(3));
19   ENDL   GOON;
20          ACT,ATRIB(5)+1;
21   CRSR   QUEUE(4);
22          ACT,EXPON(ATRIB(4));
23          GOON;
24          ACT/1,ATRIB(5),,LOOP;
25          END;
26   INIT,0,480;
27   ;
28   ;      PLACE TWO 20 TON AND ONE 50 TON TRUCK IN EACH SHOVEL QUEUE
29   ;
30   ENTRY/1,20,1,5,2,1.5/1,20,1,5,2,1.5/1,50,1,10,4,2;
31   ENTRY/2,20,2,5,2,1.5/2,20,2,5,2,1.5/2,50,2,10,4,2;
32   ENTRY/3,20,3,5,2,1.5/3,20,3,5,2,1.5/3,50,3,10,4,2;
33   FIN;
```

Figure 6-16 Statement model of quarry operations.

The travel time from a shovel to the crusher is represented by an ACTIVITY (line 20) with a duration equal to ATRIB(5)+1. Following the QUEUE node CRSR is a service ACTIVITY (line 22) representing the dumping operation which ends at the sequential GOON node (line 23). The last ACTIVITY (line 24) is assigned activity index number 1, has a duration given by ATRIB(5), and routes the entity back to the GOON statement labeled LOOP.

The initial insertion of truck entities into the network is accomplished by the ENTRY statements (lines 30-32). Recall that each ENTRY statement places an entity into the file specified with attribute values as listed. Multiple entities can be inserted by a single ENTRY statement by separating the entities with a slash. For example, the first ENTRY statement places three entities into file 1 with attribute values of (20, 1, 5, 2, 1.5), (20, 1, 5, 2, 1.5), and (50, 1, 10, 4, 2.0). These entities correspond to two twenty-ton trucks and one fifty-ton truck. Since file 1 is the wait file for the SVL1 QUEUE, the filing of an entity into file 1 is processed as an arrival to node SVL1. Likewise, entities filed in file 2 and file 3 are processed as arrivals to SVL2 QUEUE and SVL3 QUEUE, respectively. Therefore the ENTRY statements place two twenty-ton and one fifty-ton truck in each shovel queue.

Summary of Results.   The results for this example are summarized by the SLAM Summary Report shown in Figure 6-17. Note that in addition to statistics on queue lengths and server utilizations, statistics are also provided on the numbered ACTIVITY. Activity 1 represents the return trip from the crusher to the shovels. The results show that 154 trucks completed the return trip during the 480 time units of simulation, and that there was an average of 0.5458 trucks in transit between the crusher and the shovels. The maximum number of trucks on the return road at any one time was five.

6.6   Example 6-5.   INVENTORY SYSTEM WITH
LOST SALES AND BACKORDERS (8)

A large discount house is planning to install a system to control the inventory of a particular radio. The time between demands for a radio is exponentially distributed with mean time of 0.2 weeks. In the case where customers demand the radio when it is not in stock, 80 percent will go to another nearby discount house

```
S L A M   S U M M A R Y   R E P O R T


SIMULATION PROJECT QUARRY OPERATIONS          BY C. D. PEGDEN

DATE  4/19/1977                               RUN NUMBER    1 OF    1


CURRENT TIME     .4800+03
STATISTICAL ARRAYS CLEARED AT TIME     .0000
```

FILE STATISTICS

FILE NUMBER	ASSOCIATED NODE TYPE	AVERAGE LENGTH	STANDARD DEVIATION	MAXIMUM LENGTH	CURRENT LENGTH	AVERAGE WAITING TIME
1	QUEUE	.6269	.7736	2	0	5.5724
2	QUEUE	.5687	.7987	2	0	4.9632
3	QUEUE	.5037	.6982	2	0	4.4773
4	QUEUE	2.8531	2.3034	8	8	8.4018

REGULAR ACTIVITY STATISTICS

ACTIVITY INDEX	AVERAGE UTILIZATION	STANDARD DEVIATION	MAXIMUM UTILIZATION	CURRENT UTILIZATION	ENTITY COUNT
1	.5458	.7471	5	0	154

SERVICE ACTIVITY STATISTICS

ACTIVITY INDEX	START NODE LABEL/TYPE	SERVER CAPACITY	AVERAGE UTILIZATION	STANDARD DEVIATION	CURRENT UTILIZATION	AVERAGE BLOCKAGE	MAXIMUM IDLE TIME/SERVERS	MAXIMUM BUSY TIME/SERVERS	ENTITY COUNT
0	SVL1 QUEUE	1	.7360	.4408	0	.0000	26.6495	89.0040	
0	SVL2 QUEUE	1	.6256	.4840	0	.0000	25.8304	75.5575	
0	SVL3 QUEUE	1	.7554	.4299	0	.0000	14.3618	60.5699	
0	CRSR QUEUE	1	.8682	.3383	1	.0000	7.9933	105.5405	

Figure 6-17   SLAM summary report for quarry operations example.

to find it, thereby representing lost sales, while the other 20 percent will backorder the radio and wait for the next shipment arrival. The store employs a periodic review-reorder point inventory system where the inventory status is reviewed every four weeks to decide if an order should be placed. The company policy is to order up to the stock control level of 72 radios whenever the inventory position, consisting of the radios in stock plus the radios on order minus the radios on backorder, is found to be less than or equal to the reorder point of 18 radios. The procurement lead time (the time from the placement of an order to its receipt) is constant and requires three weeks.

The objective of this example is to simulate the inventory system for a period of six years (312 weeks) to obtain statistics on the following quantities:

1. number of radios in stock;
2. inventory position;
3. safety stock (radios in stock at order receipt times); and
4. time between lost sales.

The initial conditions for the simulation are an inventory position of 72 and no initial backorders. In order to reduce the bias in the statistics due to the initial starting conditions, all the statistics are to be cleared at the end of the first year of the six year simulation period.

Concepts Illustrated.   This example illustrates the use of: a RESOURCE block for modeling an inventory level; an AWAIT node for holding backorders; a FREE node for satisfying backorders; the logical .OR. operator for specifying the condition for selecting an activity; the CLEAR option on the MONTR statement for clearing statistics; and the TIMST statement for obtaining time-persistent statistics on an XX variable.

SLAM Model.   The inventory system for this example can be thought of in terms of two separate processes. The first process is the customer arrival process and consists of arriving customers demanding radios. If a radio is available, the customer buys a radio and departs the system. If a radio is not available, the arriving customer either backorders a radio or balks to a nearby competitor. The second process is the inventory review through which radios are replenished. This process consists of a review, every four weeks, of the inventory position. If the inventory position is less than or equal to the reorder point, an order is placed. The size of the order is equal to the stock control level minus the inventory position, thus increasing the inventory position to the stock control level. Receipt of the order occurs three weeks later. The radios received are first used to satisfy backorders. Any remaining radios are used to increase the number of radios on-hand.

The two processes described above can be modeled within the network framework of SLAM by representing the radios on-hand as a resource named RADIO whose capacity is 72 units. The buying and backordering of radios in the customer arrival process can be modeled as entities representing customers arriving to an AWAIT node. Likewise, the replenishment of radios in the inventory review process can be modeled as an entity representing a radio shipment arriving to a FREE node. Thus, the resource RADIO is depleted in the customer arrival process by entities representing customers and replenished in the inventory review process by entities representing radio shipments.

The SLAM statement model for this example is presented in Figure 6-18. The model employs three XX variables representing: the inventory position $XX(1)$; the reorder point, $XX(2)$; and the stock control level, $XX(3)$. The INTLC statement (line 3) assigns initial values to the XX variables of 72, 18, and 72, respectively. The TIMST statement (line 4) causes time-averaged statistics to be collected

```
1   GEN,C. D. PEGDEN,INVENTORY PROBLEM,9/12/77,1;
2   LIMITS,1,2,30;
3   INTLC,XX(1)=72,XX(2)=18,XX(3)=72;
4   TIMST,XX(1),INV. POSITION;
5   NETWORK;
6   ;
7   ;      XX(1)=INV. POSITION,XX(2)=REORDER POINT,XX(3)=STOCK CONTROL LEVEL.
8   ;      ------------------------------------------------------------
9   ;
10  ;      RESOURCE/RADIO(72),1;
11  ;
12  ;      CUSTOMER ARRIVAL PROCESS
13  ;      ------------------------
14  ;
15         CREATE,EXPON(.2),,,,1;                 CREATE ARRIVAL TRANSACTIONS
16         ACT,,NNRSC(RADIO).GT.0.OR.DRAND.LE..2; CONTINUE IF RADIO AVAIL OR P=.2
17         ACT,,,LOST;                            ELSE BRANCH TO LOST SALE
18         ASSIGN,XX(1)=XX(1)-1;                  DECREMENT INVENTORY POSITION
19         AWAIT,RADIO;                           SEIZE A RADIO
20         TERM;                                  DEPART THE SYSTEM
21  LOST   COLCT,BET,TB LOST SALES;               COLLECT BET STATS ON LOST SALES
22         TERM;                                  DEPART THE SYSTEM
23  ;
24  ;      INVENTORY REVIEW PROCESS
25  ;      ------------------------
26  ;
27         CREATE,4;                              CREATE A REVIEW TRANSACTION
28         ACT,,,XX(1).LE.XX(2);                  IF POSITION IS BELOW REODER PT.
29         ASSIGN,ATRIB(1)=XX(3)-XX(1),XX(1)=XX(3); ORDER UP TO STOCK CONTROL LEVEL
30         ACT,3;                                 DELAY RECEIPT BY 3 WEEKS
31         COLCT,NNRSC(RADIO),SAFETY STOCK;       COLLECT STATS ON SAFETY STOCK
32         FREE,RADIO/ATRIB(1);                   INCREMENT RADIOS ON HAND
33         TERM;                                  END REVIEW
34         END;
35  INIT,0,312;
36  MONTR,CLEAR,52;
37  FIN;
```

Figure 6-18   Statement model of inventory example.

on the XX(1) variable and the results to be printed using the label INV. POSI-
TION. The RESOURCE block (line 10) is used to define the radios on-hand resource and sets the initial level (availability) to 72. It identifies file 1 as the location
of customers awaiting radios. The average number of radios on-hand is equal to the
average availability of this resource.

The customer arrival process is modeled by statements 15 through 22. Entities representing customers are generated by the CREATE node with an interarrival time that is exponentially distributed with mean of 0.2 weeks. A maximum of 1 emanating activity is taken at each release of the CREATE statement. The first emanating ACTIVITY (line 16) is taken by entities that represent the non-balking customers; that is, the customers who purchase an available radio or the 20 percent of the customers who backorder a radio when no radio is available. The duration of this ACTIVITY is zero and it is taken conditionally if the current number of available units of RADIO is greater than zero or if the random variable DRAND is less than or equal to 0.2. The non-balking customers arrive at the ASSIGN node (line 18) where the inventory position is decremented by 1. The entities then continue to the AWAIT node where they either immediately seize (buy) or wait for one unit of RADIO. Each entity exiting the AWAIT node is destroyed at the TERM statement (line 22) corresponding to the departure of the customer from the system.

The second ACTIVITY (line 17) following the CREATE node has a duration of zero, is selected unconditionally, and ends at the COLCT node (line 21) labeled LOST. Since the CREATE node specifies that at most one emanating ACTIVITY is to be taken at each release, the second ACTIVITY will be taken if and only if the first ACTIVITY is not taken. The entities undertaking this ACTIVITY represent balking customers and are therefore lost sales. These entities are routed by the ACTIVITY to the COLCT node where statistics are collected on the time between lost sales. Each entity is then destroyed at the TERM node.

The inventory review process is modeled by statements 27 through 33. The CREATE node (line 27) creates an entity representing a review every four weeks. The emanating ACTIVITY is taken if $XX(1)$, the inventory position, is less than or equal to $XX(2)$, the reorder point; otherwise no activity is selected and the review entity is destroyed. At the ASSIGN node (line 29), the first attribute of the entity, $ATRIB(1)$, is set equal to the stock control level minus the inventory position and then the inventory position is reset to the stock control level. The exiting entity represents a radio shipment with the number of radios in the shipment specified by $ATRIB(1)$. The entity next takes the ACTIVITY of three weeks duration representing the shipment delay time or lead time. At the completion of the ACTIVITY, the entity arrives at the COLCT node (line 31) where statistics are collected on the number of available units of resource RADIO. This value corresponds to the inventory on-hand level at the order receipt time. This quantity is referred to as the safety stock. The entity next moves to the FREE node (line 32) where $ATRIB(1)$ units of resource RADIO are freed. These radios are then available to the entities representing non-balking customers in the

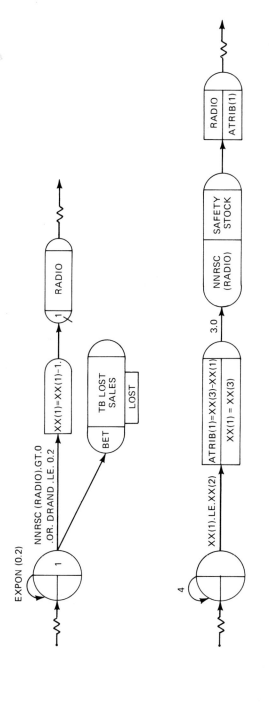

Figure 6-19 Network model for inventory example.

193

arrival segment of the model. The TERM statement (line 33) then destroys the entity.

The clearing of statistics in order to reduce any bias due to the starting conditions is accomplished by the MONTR statement (line 36) with the CLEAR option. This statement causes all statistical arrays including the file statistics to be cleared at time 52. Therefore, the statistical results for the simulation are based upon values recorded during the last 260 weeks of simulated operation.

The network corresponding to the statements presented in Figure 6-18 is shown in Figure 6-19. The network is given after the statements in this example to illustrate that the statement model can be prepared without the accompanying network.

```
          S L A M   S U M M A R Y   R E P O R T

   SIMULATION PROJECT INVENTORY PROBLEM          BY C. D. PEGDEN

   DATE   9/12/1977                              RUN NUMBER   1 OF   1


   CURRENT TIME        .3120+03
   STATISTICAL ARRAYS CLEARED AT TIME    .5200+02
```

STATISTICS FOR VARIABLES BASED ON OBSERVATION

	MEAN VALUE	STANDARD DEVIATION	COEFF. OF VARIATION	MINIMUM VALUE	MAXIMUM VALUE	NUMBER OF OBSERVATIONS
TB LOST SALES	.2652+01	.7528+01	.2839+01	.8865-02	.4886+02	101
SAFETY STOCK	.1000+01	.2000+01	.2000+01	.0000	.7000+01	19

STATISTICS FOR TIME-PERSISTENT VARIABLES

	MEAN VALUE	STANDARD DEVIATION	MINIMUM VALUE	MAXIMUM VALUE	TIME INTERVAL	CURRENT VALUE
INV. POSITION	.4255+02	.1946+02	-.2000+01	.7200+02	.2600+03	.6200+02

FILE STATISTICS

FILE NUMBER	ASSOCIATED NODE TYPE	AVERAGE LENGTH	STANDARD DEVIATION	MAXIMUM LENGTH	CURRENT LENGTH	AVERAGE WAITING TIME
1	AWAIT	.1175	.5604	6	0	0.0253

RESOURCE STATISTICS

RESOURCE NUMBER	RESOURCE LABEL	CURRENT CAPACITY	AVERAGE UTILIZATION	STANDARD DEVIATION	MAXIMUM UTILIZATION	CURRENT UTILIZATION
1	RADIO	72	43.0141	19.7950	72	10

Figure 6-20   SLAM summary report for inventory example.

Even when this is done, the network model is useful for checking and communication purposes.

Summary of Results.   The SLAM Summary Report for this example is given in Figure 6-20. The report provides statistics on time between lost sales, safety stock, and inventory position which were requested by the user. Automatically obtained are file 1 statistics corresponding to backordered radios and resource statistics corresponding to the average resource utilization or the average number of radios seized. The average number of radios on-hand is found by subtracting the average utilization (43.0141) from the resource capacity (72) and is 28.9859. The values given above could be used to compute the average profit for the inventory decision policy employed in the model. An investigation of different parameter settings for this policy can be made by changing the input values of the reorder point, the stock control level, and the time between reviews.

6.7   Example 6-6.   PORT OPERATIONS

This problem statement is taken from Schriber (11). A Q-GERT model has also been presented (9). "A port in Africa is used to load tankers with crude oil for overwater shipment. The port has facilities for loading as many as three tankers simultaneously. The tankers, which arrive at the port every 11±7 hours†, are of three different types. The relative frequency of the various types, and their loading time requirements, are as follows:

Type	Relative Frequency	Loading Time, Hours
1	.25	18±2
2	.55	24±3
3	.20	36±4

There is one tug at the port. Tankers of all types require the services of this tug to move into a berth, and later to move out of a berth. When the tug is available, any berthing or deberthing activity takes about one hour. Top priority is given to the berthing activity.

---

† All durations given as ranges are uniformly distributed.

"A shipper is considering bidding on a contract to transport oil from the port to the United Kingdom. He has determined that 5 tankers of a particular type would have to be committed to this task to meet contract specifications. These tankers would require 21±3 hours to load oil at the port. After loading and de-berthing, they would travel to the United Kingdom, offload the oil, and return to the port for reloading. Their round-trip travel time, including offloading, is esti-mated to be 240±24 hours.

"A complicating factor is that the port experiences storms. The time between the onset of storms is exponentially distributed with a mean of 48 hours and a storm lasts 4±2 hours. No tug can start an operation until a storm is over.

"Before the port authorities can commit themselves to accommodating the pro-posed 5 tankers, the effect of the additional port traffic on the in-port residence time of the current port users must be determined. It is desired to simulate the operation of the port for a one-year period (8640 hours) under the proposed new commitment to measure in-port residence time of the proposed additional tankers, as well as the three types of tankers which already use the port."

Concepts Illustrated.   This example illustrates the use of the AWAIT and FREE nodes to model constrained resources. The ALTER node is used to reduce and increase the capacity of a resource during the simulation.

SLAM Model.   In this example, entities representing tankers flow through a net-work model of the port facilities. The port facilities are constrained by the three berths and one tug. In the previous examples, resources have been modeled as service activities. However, in this example, the tug is required for both the berth-ing and the deberthing operation and its availability can be altered by storms. In addition, a tanker requires both a berth and a tug before berthing can be under-taken. Therefore, a network model of the port operations can most easily be con-structed by using explicit resources to model both the tug and the berths.

The network model for this example is presented in Figure 6-21 and the state-ment listing is given in Figure 6-22. The explanation of the model will be given in terms of the statement model. The first statement in the network section is the RESOURCE block (line 4) which defines the resource BERTH. The resource BERTH is assigned a capacity of 3 and entities waiting for a BERTH reside in file 1. The resource TUG is defined in statement 5 and is not assigned a capacity and, therefore, has the default capacity of one. Entities waiting for the TUG reside in either file 2 or file 3. Recall that the priority for allocating free resources to waiting entities is determined by the order in which these files are listed in the

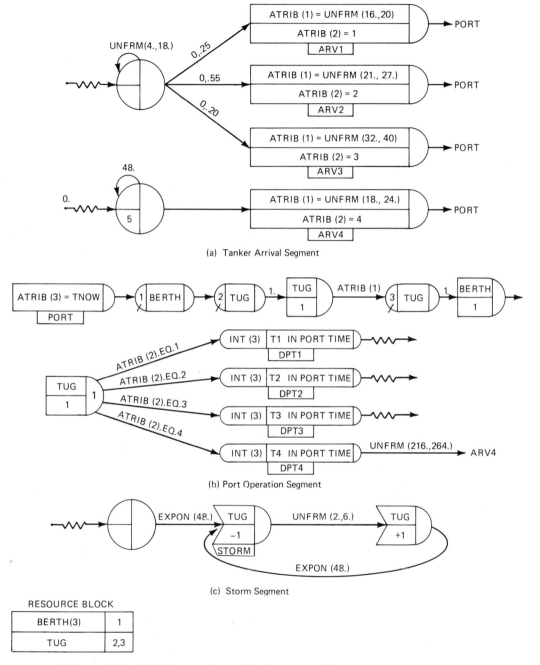

(a) Tanker Arrival Segment

(b) Port Operation Segment

(c) Storm Segment

RESOURCE BLOCK

BERTH(3)	1
TUG	2,3

Figure 6-21   SLAM network model of port operations.

```
 1  GEN,C. D. PEGDEN,AFRICA PORT,5/21/77,1;
 2  LIMITS,3,3,30;
 3  NETWORK;
 4          RESOURCE/BERTH(3),1;
 5          RESOURCE/TUG,2,3;
 6  ;
 7  ; TANKER ARRIVAL SEGMENT
 8  ;----------------------
 9          CREATE,UNFRM(4.,18.);
10          ACT,,.25,ARV1;
11          ACT,,.55,ARV2;
12          ACT,,,20,ARV3;
13  ARV1    ASSIGN,ATRIB(1)=UNFRM(16.,20.),ATRIB(2)=1;
14          ACT,,,PORT;
15  ARV2    ASSIGN,ATRIB(1)=UNFRM(21.,27.),ATRIB(2)=2;
16          ACT,,,PORT;
17  ARV3    ASSIGN,ATRIB(1)=UNFRM(32.,40.),ATRIB(2)=3;
18          ACT,,,PORT;
19          CREATE,48,0,,5;
20  ARV4    ASSIGN,ATRIB(1)=UNFRM(18.,24.),ATRIB(2)=4;
21  ;
22  ; PORT OPERATION SEGMENT
23  ;----------------------
24  PORT    ASSIGN,ATRIB(3)=TNOW;
25          AWAIT,BERTH;
26          AWAIT,TUG;
27          ACT,1;
28          FREE,TUG;
29          ACT,ATRIB(1);
30          AWAIT(3),TUG;
31          ACT,1;
32          FREE,BERTH;
33          FREE,TUG;
34          ACT,,ATRIB(2).EQ.1,DPT1;
35          ACT,,ATRIB(2).EQ.2,DPT2;
36          ACT,,ATRIB(2).EQ.3,DPT3;
37          ACT,,ATRIB(2).EQ.4,DPT4;
38  DPT1    COLCT,INT(3),T1 IN PORT TIME;
39          TERM;
40  DPT2    COLCT,INT(3),T2 IN PORT TIME;
41          TERM;
42  DPT3    COLCT,INT(3),T3 IN PORT TIME;
43          TERM;
44  DPT4    COLCT,INT(3),T4 IN PORT TIME;
45          ACT,UNFRM(216.,264.),,ARV4;
46  ;
47  ; STORM SEGMENT
48  ;--------------
49          CREATE;
50          ACT,EXPON(48.);
51  STORM   ALTER,TUG,-1;
52          ACT,UNFRM(2.,6.);
53          ALTER,TUG,+1;
54          ACT,EXPON(48.),,STORM;
55          END;
56  INIT,0,8640;
57  FIN;
```

Figure 6-22 Statement model for port operations example.

RESOURCE block. Therefore entities waiting in file 2 for a TUG have priority over entities waiting in file 3 for a TUG.

The statement model for this example can be divided into three major segments. The first segment represents the arrival process for the system and consists of statements 9 through 20. The second major segment models the port operations and consists of statements 24 through 45. The last segment models the storm process and includes statements 49 through 54.

The arrival process for this problem is composed of two classes of arrivals. The first arrival class represents the existing tanker traffic consisting of tanker types 1, 2, and 3. These entities are generated by the CREATE node (line 9) and are routed probabilistically by the three emanating ACTIVITY's to either ARV1, ARV2, or ARV3 ASSIGN nodes. At these ASSIGN nodes, ATRIB(1) is set equal to the appropriate loading time and ATRIB(2) is set equal to the appropriate tanker type. Following any of these ASSIGN nodes, the entity is routed to the ASSIGN node labeled PORT.

The second arrival class involves inserting five entities representing the proposed type 4 tankers into the network. The entities are created by the CREATE node (line 19) which generates an entity every 48 time units, with the first entity at time 0, and a maximum of five entities created. At an ASSIGN node (line 20) labeled ARV4, ATRIB(1) is set equal to the loading time and ATRIB(2) is set equal to the tanker type. The entities then continue to the PORT ASSIGN node (line 24).

The second major segment in the model represents the port operations and begins with the ASSIGN statement labeled PORT. Entities arriving to this statement represent tankers arriving to the port. The PORT ASSIGN node records the time of arrival to the port as ATRIB(3) of the entity. The entity then proceeds to the AWAIT node (line 25) where it waits for a BERTH. Since no wait file is specified at the AWAIT statement, the wait file number defaults to the first wait file listed for BERTH in the RESOURCE block, which in this case is file 1. Thus, entities which arrive to the AWAIT node when no BERTH's are available reside in file 1. When a BERTH is available, the entity continues to the next AWAIT node (line 26) where it waits in file 2 for the TUG. The ACTIVITY (line 27) following this AWAIT node represents the berthing operation and has a duration of one hour. Following berthing, the entity arrives at a FREE node (line 28) which frees one unit of the resource TUG. The ACTIVITY (line 29) that follows represents the tanker loading activity which has a duration of ATRIB(1). Recall that the appropriate loading time for the tanker entity was previously assigned to ATRIB(1) in the arrival segment of the model. Following the loading operation, a tanker requires a tug before the deberthing operation can begin. The next AWAIT node (line 30) models this requirement by causing the entity to wait in file 3 for a TUG. Since file 3 is listed after file 2 in the RESOURCE block for the TUG, the TUG will be allocated to the deberthing operation only if the TUG is not required for a berthing operation. The ACTIVITY (line 31) with a duration of one hour represents the deberthing operation. When a TUG is finished deberthing, the BERTH (line 32) and the TUG (line 33) are freed.

Statements 34 through 45 represent the tanker departure process from the port. After freeing the TUG, the tanker entity is conditionally branched based on tanker type by the four ACTIVITY's (lines 34-37) to the appropriate departure COLCT node where interval statistics on port residence time is recorded. The entities corresponding to the existing tanker traffic of types 1, 2, and 3 are terminated. The round trip travel time to the United Kingdom and back for tankers of type 4 is represented by the ACTIVITY (line 45) which routes the entity back to the ARV4 ASSIGN node. Therefore the five type 4 tankers continue to cycle through the model until the simulation is terminated after 8640 hours of operation.

The storm segment of the model starts with the creation of a storm entity at a CREATE node (line 49). The first storm is delayed by an exponentially distributed time with a mean of 48 by an ACTIVITY (line 50). The TF option of the CREATE node cannot be used in this case since TF is restricted to be a constant by the SLAM processor. At the node with label STORM (line 51), the TUG resource is requested to be altered by −1 units. This decrease in capacity will occur immediately if the tug is not in use or at the end of the tug's current operation. Thus, the tug does not abandon a tanker in stormy waters. The storm duration is uniformly distributed between 2 and 6. This ACTIVITY starts immediately and does not depend on the status of the resource TUG. Following the storm, the TUG resource capacity is increased by 1 at an ALTER node (line 53). The next storm is then scheduled by an ACTIVITY (line 54) and the storm entity is routed back to node STORM. This completes the description of the model.

Summary of Results.   The SLAM Summary Report for this example is shown in Figure 6-23. The first category of statistics is for variables based on observations and consists of the in-port times collected on each tanker type at the COLCT nodes. This is followed by the file statistics for files 1, 2, and 3 which correspond to tankers awaiting a berth, tankers with a berth awaiting a tug for berthing, and loaded tankers awaiting a tug for deberthing, respectively. The last category of statistics for this example is the resource statistics. The results show that on the average 2.8285 of the 3 BERTH's were utilized and that the TUG was busy 21.35 percent of the time.

```
S L A M    S U M M A R Y    R E P O R T


SIMULATION PROJECT AFRICA PORT                    BY C. D. PEGDEN

DATE  5/21/1977                                   RUN NUMBER    1 OF    1


CURRENT TIME     .8640+04
STATISTICAL ARRAYS CLEARED AT TIME      .0000
```

STATISTICS FOR VARIABLES BASED ON OBSERVATION

	MEAN VALUE	STANDARD DEVIATION	COEFF. OF VARIATION	MINIMUM VALUE	MAXIMUM VALUE	NUMBER OF OBSERVATIONS
T1 IN PORT TIME	.3068+02	.1149+02	.3744+00	.1804+02	.6944+02	202
T2 IN PORT TIME	.3689+02	.1155+02	.3132+00	.2302+02	.7562+02	413
T3 IN PORT TIME	.4917+02	.1131+02	.2299+00	.3402+02	.8526+02	149
T4 IN PORT TIME	.3454+02	.1116+02	.3232+00	.2106+02	.6994+02	157

FILE STATISTICS

FILE NUMBER	ASSOCIATED NODE TYPE	AVERAGE LENGTH	STANDARD DEVIATION	MAXIMUM LENGTH	CURRENT LENGTH	AVERAGE WAITING TIME
1	AWAIT	1.1349	1.2914	6	0	10.5549
2	AWAIT	.0233	.1537	2	0	0.2167
3	AWAIT	.0268	.1729	3	0	0.2501

RESOURCE STATISTICS

RESOURCE NUMBER	RESOURCE LABEL	CURRENT CAPACITY	AVERAGE UTILIZATION	STANDARD DEVIATION	MAXIMUM UTILIZATION	CURRENT UTILIZATION
1	BERTH	3	2.8285	.4166	3	3
2	TUG	1	.2135	.4098	1	0

Figure 6-23   SLAM summary report for port operations model.

The outputs indicate a high utilization of berths and the potential for a large queue of tankers waiting for berths. At one time during the year as many as six tankers were waiting for a berth. Based on this information, port management should not accept the proposed five new tankers unless an additional berth is constructed or loading times are reduced. The model should be rerun to ascertain the effects of such changes.

6.8   Example 6-7.   A MACHINE TOOL WITH BREAKDOWNS (9)

A schematic diagram of job processing and machine breakdown for a machine tool is given in Figure 6-24. Jobs arrive to a machine tool on the average of one

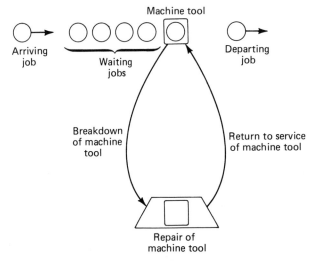

Figure 6-24   Schematic diagram of the processing of jobs by a machine tool that has breakdowns.

per hour. The distribution of these interarrival times is exponential. During normal operation, the jobs are processed on a first-in, first-out basis. The time to process a job in hours is normally distributed with a mean of 0.5 and a standard deviation of 0.1. In addition to the processing time, there is a set-up time that is uniformly distributed between 0.2 and 0.5 of an hour. Jobs that have been processed by the machine tool are routed to a different section of the shop and are considered to have left the machine tool area.

The machine tool experiences breakdowns during which time it can no longer process jobs. The time between breakdowns is normally distributed with a mean of 20 hours and a standard deviation of 2 hours. When a breakdown occurs, the job being processed is removed from the machine tool and is placed at the head of the queue of jobs waiting to be processed. Jobs preempted restart from the point at which they were interrupted.

When the machine tool breaks down, a repair process is initiated which is accomplished in three phases. Each phase is exponentially distributed with a mean of ¾ of an hour. Since the repair time is the sum of independent and identically distributed exponential random variables, the repair time is Erlang distributed.

The machine tool is to be analyzed for 500 hours to obtain information on the utilization of the machine tool and the time required to process a job. Statistics are to be collected for five simulation runs.

Concepts Illustrated.   This example illustrates the concept of preemption of a resource through the use of a PREEMPT node.

SLAM Model. The machine tool can be considered as a single server. Service involves two operations: job setup and job processing. Since two operations are involved, a resource will be used to model the machine tool. Entities representing jobs will arrive and await the availability of the machine tool if necessary. The jobs will be set up and processed when the machine tool is available and following processing will depart the system.

The breakdown of the machine tool will be modeled using a breakdown entity which preempts the machine tool and holds it while a repair operation is performed. The breakdown entity is processed through a disjoint network.

The SLAM network model of the machine tool processing with breakdowns is shown in Figure 6-25. The corresponding statement model is given in Figure 6-26. Consider first the flow of job entities through the first network segment. Jobs are created at the CREATE node with an exponential time between arrivals having a mean of one hour. The job entities are routed to the AWAIT node. If a TOOL is available they proceed to activity 1. If a TOOL is not available, they wait in file 1. Activity 1 represents the setup time and is uniformly distributed between 0.2 and 0.5 hours. Following setup, the job entity proceeds to activity 2 which represents the machine tool processing operation which is normally distributed with a mean of 0.5 and a standard deviation of 0.1 hours. Following processing, the machine tool is made available by having the job entity pass through a FREE node. The machine tool resource would then be used to process another job if one was waiting in file 1. The job entity proceeds to the COLCT node where time-in-system statistics are computed for the job entity. The job entity is then terminated.

```
 1    GEN,C. D. PEGDEN,MACHINE BREAKDOWN,7/5/77,5;
 2    LIMITS,2,1,50;
 3    NETWORK;
 4          RESOURCE/TOOL,2,1;
 5          CREATE,EXPON(1.),,1;                   CREATE ARRIVALS
 6          AWAIT(1),TOOL;                         AWAIT THE TOOL
 7          ACT/1,UNFRM(.2,.5);                    SET UP
 8          GOON;
 9          ACT/2,RNORM(.5,.1);                    PROCESSING
10          FREE,TOOL;                             FREE THE TOOL
11          COLCT,INT(1),TIME IN SYSTEM;           COLLECT STATISTICS
12          TERM;
13    ;
14          CREATE,,20,,1;                         CREATE 1ST BREAKDOWN
15    DOWN  PREEMPT(2),TOOL;                       PREEMPT THE TOOL
16          ACT/3,ERLNG(.75,3.);                   DOWN TIME
17          FREE,TOOL;                             FREE THE TOOL
18          ACT,RNORM(20.,2.),,DOWN;               TIME BETWEEN FAILURES
19          END;
20    INIT,0,500;
21    FIN;
```

Figure 6-26 SLAM statement model of machine tool with breakdowns.

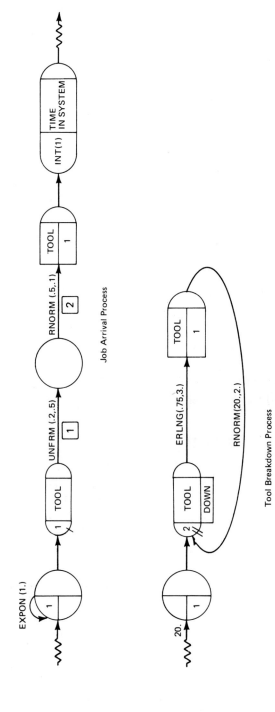

Figure 6-25 SLAM network model of machine tool with breakdowns.

The second network segment illustrates the processing of breakdown entities. The first breakdown is generated at time 20 hours. The CREATE node indicates that only one machine breakdown entity is to be generated. This machine breakdown entity will be recycled in the network segment as machine breakdown times are conditioned upon the time that the machine tool completes repair. Following the creation of the machine breakdown entity it is routed to a PREEMPT node where the resource TOOL is captured. If TOOL was processing a job entity, the entity is interrupted. We will discuss what happens to the interrupted job following the description of this network segment. The machine breakdown entity is then processed by activity 3 which represents the repair time which is Erlang distributed as prescribed. Following repair, the machine tool resource is made available by routing the entity through a FREE node. The next machine breakdown is then scheduled by routing the entity back to the PREEMPT node DOWN following an activity that represents the time between breakdowns which is normally distributed with a mean of 20 and a standard deviation of 2 hours.

Consider now the disposition of the job entity that was preempted. At the PREEMPT node the remaining processing time attribute and the SEND node label were defaulted. The default values for these quantities are to route the entity back to the AWAIT node where it captured the resource and to save the remaining processing time. In this case, the job that was preempted is replaced in file 1 since that is the file number associated with the AWAIT node where the job entity captured the resource TOOL. The job entity is made the first entry in file 1. When the resource TOOL is made available, following the completion of the repair activity (activity 3), the job entity that was preempted will be removed from file 1 and it will be placed in the activity from which it was preempted. The time to perform the activity will be the remaining service time for the activity. In this case, the job entity can be preempted from either activity 1 or activity 2 and, hence, following repair, it will be reinserted in either activity 1 or activity 2 with the time to perform the activity, as the remaining processing time when the job was interrupted.

The control statements shown in Figure 6-26 indicate that five runs are to be made with each run lasting for 500 hours.

Summary of Results.   A summary of the output reports from SLAM is shown in Table 6-1. The results show a high variability in the average time in the system for jobs. This can be attributed to the high variability in both the interarrival times and the service times. A different job arrival sequence was used on each run so that an entirely different 500 hour simulation was performed on each run. The variability of the service times is due to service being the sum of the setup time

Table 6-1   Summary of 5 runs for machine breakdown example.

Run Number	Average Time in System	Average Number of Jobs Waiting	Average Tool Use	Average Tool Idleness	Average Tool Repair Time
1	6.93	6.09	0.85	0.04	0.11
2	12.37	11.86	0.87	0.02	0.11
3	16.57	16.54	0.88	0.01	0.11
4	3.75	2.75	0.80	0.09	0.11
5	8.35	7.27	0.82	0.07	0.11

and the processing time and then sometimes including a machine tool repair time. In 500 hours, 22 machine tool breakdowns are expected, that is, (500-20)/(2.25 +20).

When a breakdown occurs, all jobs in the system are delayed by the repair time. Based on the results, a large buffer area for holding jobs waiting for processing will be required. Furthermore, if tight due dates are set on jobs, many jobs will be late. Methods should be investigated for better scheduling of job arrivals and for reducing the number of breakdowns.

6.9   Example 6-8.   ANALYSIS OF A PERT-TYPE NETWORK

PERT is a technique for evaluating and reviewing a project consisting of interdependent activities (5). A number of books have been written that describe PERT modeling and analysis procedures (1, 6, 12). A PERT network is a graphical illustration of the relations between the activities of a program.

A PERT network model of a repair and retrofit project (9) is shown in Figure 6-27 and activity descriptions are given in Table 6-2. All activity times will be assumed to be triangularly distributed. For ease of description, activities have been aggregated. The activities relate to power units, instrumentation, and a new assembly and involve standard types of operations.

In the following description of the project, activity numbers are given in parentheses. At the beginning of the project, three parallel activities can be performed that involve: the disassembly of power units and instrumentation (1); the installation of a new assembly (2); and the preparation for a retrofit check (3). Cleaning,

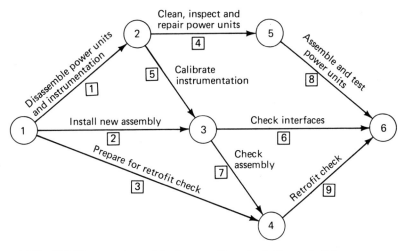

Figure 6-27 PERT network model of a retrofit project, Example 6-8.

inspecting, and repairing the power units (4) and calibrating the instrumentation (5) can be done only after the power units and instrumentation have been disassembled. Thus, activities 4 and 5 must follow activity 1 in the network. Following the installation of the new assembly (2) and after the instruments have been calibrated (5), a check of interfaces (6) and a check of the new assembly (7) can be made. The retrofit check (9) can be made after the assembly is checked (7) and the preparation for the retrofit check (3) have been completed. The assembly and test of power units (8) can be performed following the cleaning and maintenance of power units (4). The project is considered completed when all nine ac-

Table 6-2 Description of activities, example 6-8.

Activity Number	Description	Mode	Minimum	Maximum	Average
1	Disassemble power units and instrumentation	3	1	5	3
2	Install new assembly	6	3	9	6
3	Prepare for retrofit check	13	10	19	14
4	Clean, inspect and repair power units	9	3	12	8
5	Calibrate instrumentation	3	1	8	4
6	Check interfaces	9	8	16	11
7	Check assembly	7	4	13	8
8	Assemble and test power units	6	3	9	6
9	Retrofit check	3	1	8	4

tivities are completed. Since activities 6, 8, and 9 require the other activities to precede them, their completion signifies the end of the project. This is indicated on the network by having activities 6, 8, and 9 incident to node 6, the sink node for the project. The objective of this example is to illustrate the procedures for using SLAM to model and simulate project planning networks.

Concepts Illustrated.   No new concepts are illustrated by this example. The AC-CUMULATE node is used to model activity precedent relations. Four hundred simulations of the network are achieved by routing an entity back to node 1 of the network and requiring four hundred entity arrivals at a TERMINATE node.

SLAM Model.   The SLAM network model corresponding to the PERT network is shown in Figure 6-28. The SLAM network is similar to the PERT network with the addition of: 1) the number of first and subsequent releases (equal to the number of incoming branches); and 2) a specification that INT(1) statistics are to be collected after a node is released. When a single incoming activity releases the node, a COLCT node can be used directly. When more than one activity is required, an ACCUM node is also required.

In this SLAM model, the CREATE node is only used to generate a single entity and, hence, no further specification is required (all default values are appropriate). Following the collection of statistics at the COLCT node after node N6, an entity is routed to the TERM node to decrease the termination count by 1, and an entity is routed back to node N1 to restart the simulation. At node N1, attribute 1 is reset to TNOW to provide a reference value for statistics collection at the COLCT nodes where INT(1) statistics are collected.

The SLAM statement model for this example is given in Figure 6-29. The coding of the statement model follows directly from the network model.

Summary of Results.   The final summary report for 400 independent simulations of the network is shown in Figure 6-30. The average time to complete the project is 20.87 time units with a standard deviation of 2.18 time units. The estimate of the standard deviation of the average time to complete the project is the standard deviation divided by 20 or approximately 0.10 time units. By the central limit theorem, the average project duration is approximately normally distributed and we estimate with 99.7% confidence that if we performed an independent run involving 400 simulations, the average project duration would be between 20.57 and 21.17 time units by using three standard deviation confidence limits.

The average values for nodes 2, 3, 4, and 5 provide estimates of the average starting times for activities emanating from these nodes. Additional information

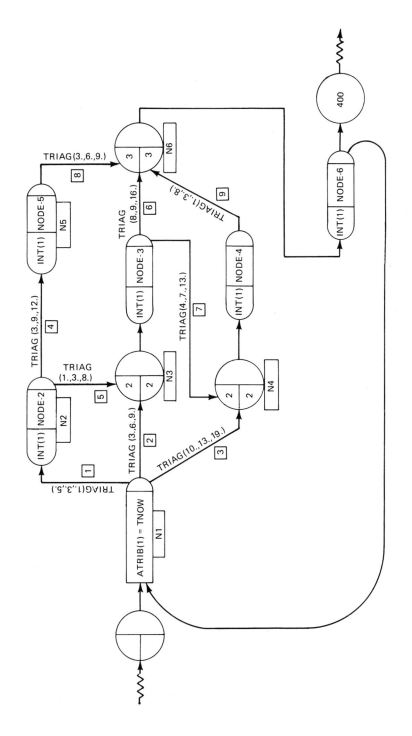

Figure 6-28 SLAM network model of a PERT network.

```
1   GEN,PRITSKER,PERT NETWORK,3/15/1978,1;
2   LIM,,1,700;
3   NETWORK;
4          CREATE;
5   N1     ASSIGN,ATRIB(1)=TNOW;
6          ACT,TRIAG(1.,3.,5.),,N2;
7          ACT,TRIAG(3.,6.,9.),,N3;
8          ACT,TRIAG(10.,13.,19.),,N4;
9   N2     COLCT,INT(1),NODE 2,10,0.0,0.5;
10         ACT,TRIAG(3.,9.,12.),,N5;
11         ACT,TRIAG(1.,3.,8.),,N3;
12  N3     ACCUM,2,2;
13         COLCT,INT(1),NODE 3,20,3,0.5;
14         ACT,TRIAG(8.,9.,16.),,N6;
15         ACT,TRIAG(4.,7.,13.),,N4;
16  N4     ACCUM,2,2;
17         COLCT,INT(1),NODE 4,20,10.,0.5;
18         ACT,TRIAG(1.,3.,8.),,N6;
19  N5     COLCT,INT(1),NODE 5,20,12.,0.5;
20         ACT,TRIAG(3.,6.,9.),,N6;
21  N6     ACCUM,3,3;
22         COLCT,INT(1),PROJ. COMPLETION,20,15.,0.5;
23         ACT;
24         ACT,,,N1;
25         TERM,400;
26         ENDNETWORK;
27  FIN;
```

Figure 6-29   SLAM statement model for PERT network example.

concerning all nodes is available on the histograms obtained. The histogram for project completion is shown in Figure 6-31. From Figure 6-31, estimates of the probability that the project will be completed by a certain time can be made. Thus, it is estimated that the probability of the project being completed by 19 time units is 0.210; hence, the probability of the project taking more than 19 time units is 0.790. This provides an indication of the gross nature of PERT assumptions since the expected completion time as estimated using PERT techniques is 19 time units (4).

S L A M   S U M M A R Y   R E P O R T

SIMULATION PROJECT PERT NETWORK   BY PRITSKER

DATE 3/15/1978   RUN NUMBER   1 OF   1

CURRENT TIME   .8349+04
STATISTICAL ARRAYS CLEARED AT TIME .   .0000

STATISTICS FOR VARIABLES BASED ON OBSERVATION

	MEAN VALUE	STANDARD DEVIATION	COEFF. OF VARIATION	MINIMUM VALUE	MAXIMUM VALUE	NUMBER OF OBSERVATIONS
NODE 2	.3015+01	.8238+00	.2732+00	.1125+01	.4856+01	400
NODE 3	.7394+01	.1457+01	.1971+00	.3396+01	.1194+02	400
NODE 4	.1606+02	.2074+01	.1291+00	.1103+02	.2251+02	400
NODE 5	.1103+02	.2004+01	.1817+00	.5535+01	.1599+02	400
PROJ. COMPLETION	.2087+02	.2183+01	.1046+00	.1543+02	.2744+02	400

Figure 6-30   SLAM summary report for 400 simulations of retrofit project.

HISTOGRAM NUMBER   5

PROJ. COMPLETION

OBSV FREQ	RELA FREQ	CUML FREQ	UPPER CELL LIMIT	0 20 40 60 80 100
0	.000	.000	.1500+02	+
1	.002	.002	.1550+02	+
2	.005	.007	.1600+02	+
4	.010	.017	.1650+02	+C
3	.007	.025	.1700+02	+C
9	.022	.047	.1750+02	++C
16	.040	.087	.1800+02	+++ C
23	.057	.145	.1850+02	+++* C
26	.065	.210	.1900+02	+++* C
27	.067	.277	.1950+02	++++ C
29	.072	.350	.2000+02	+++++ C
35	.087	.437	.2050+02	+++++ C
38	.095	.532	.2100+02	++++++ C
35	.087	.620	.2150+02	+++++ C
33	.082	.702	.2200+02	++++ C
31	.077	.780	.2250+02	+++++ C
25	.063	.842	.2300+02	++++ C
20	.050	.892	.2350+02	+++ C +
13	.032	.925	.2400+02	+++ C +
9	.022	.947	.2450+02	++ C +
4	.010	.957	.2500+02	+ C +
17	.042	1.000	INF	+++ C
---				+ + + + + + + + + + +
400				0 20 40 60 80 100

Interpretive statements

1. Probability of project completion by 19 time units = 0.210
2. Probability of project taking more than 19 time units = 1 − 0.210 = 0.790
3. Probability of project taking more than 24 time units = 1 − 0.925 = 0.075

Figure 6-31   Histogram of retrofit project completion time.

6.10   Example 6-9.   SINGLE LANE TRAFFIC ANALYSIS

The system to be modeled in this example consists of the traffic flow from two directions along a two lane road, one lane of which has been closed for 500 meters for repairs (2). Traffic lights have been placed at each end of the closed lane to control the flow of traffic through the repair section. The lights allow traffic to flow for a specified time interval from only one direction. This arrangement is depicted in Figure 6-32. When a light turns green, the waiting cars start and pass the light every two seconds. If a car arrives to a green light when there are no waiting cars, the car passes through the light without delay. The car arrival pattern is exponentially distributed, with an average of 12 seconds between cars from direction 1 and 9 seconds between cars from direction 2. A light cycle consists of green in direction 1, both red, green in direction 2, both red, and then the cycle is repeated. Both lights remain red for 55 seconds to allow the cars in transit to leave the repair section before traffic from the other direction can be initiated.

The objective is to simulate the above system to determine values for the green time for direction 1 and the green time for direction 2 which yield a low average waiting time for all cars.

Concepts Illustrated.   This example illustrates the use of the OPEN and CLOSE nodes in conjunction with a gate to control entity flow through a system. Multiple

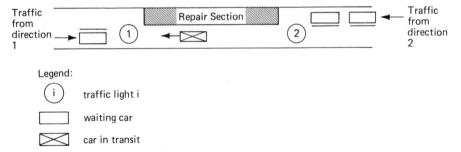

Figure 6-32   Schematic diagram of traffic lights.

simulation runs are made and activity durations are specified as $XX(\cdot)$ values to facilitate the changing of durations between runs.

SLAM Model. There are three separate processes in this system consisting of: traffic flow from direction 1; traffic flow from direction 2; and information flow representing the traffic light cycle. Each of these processes is modeled by the movement of an entity through a subnetwork. We will model the traffic lights by the gates LIGHT1 and LIGHT2 where an open gate represents a green light and a closed gate represents a red light. To insure that only one car passes through the light at a time, a resource with a capacity of one is employed in conjunction with each gate. These resources are named START1 and START2 corresponding to LIGHT1 and LIGHT2 and represent the starting location before each light. The starting location is seized by each car entity before passing through the light and then freed immediately after it passes the light. In this way only one car can pass through the starting location at a time.

The network model for this example is depicted in Figure 6-33. First, consider the traffic flow from direction 1. Entities representing cars are created at the CREATE node with the time between cars exponentially distributed with a mean of 9 seconds. The time of creation of each car entity is recorded as ATRIB(1). Each entity then awaits the resource START1. In the RESOURCE block, the capacity of this resource is set to 1 so that only one car passes through the node at a time. The entity then proceeds to the AWAIT node where it continues if LIGHT1 is open; otherwise it is delayed. The following COLCT node records values of the waiting time of the car at the light and the entity is then routed through one of the two emanating ACTIVITY's since an M-number of 1 is specified. A car that stopped has an arrival time different from the current time, TNOW. The condition specified on the first activity is for those cars that stopped and causes a two second delay for the car to pass the light. Since the M-value of the COLCT node is 1, the second ACTIVITY is taken if and only if the first is not taken. This ACTIVITY models the passage of moving cars that do not incur a delay. The resource START1 is then freed and the entity is terminated. The traffic flow for direction 2 is modeled in an analogous manner with LIGHT2 replacing LIGHT1 and START2 replacing START1.

The traffic light segment of the model controls the changes in the traffic lights and consists of a series of OPEN and CLOSE nodes separated by ACTIVITY's. A single entity is entered into the subnetwork by a CREATE node. It is delayed 55 seconds (both lights are red) before opening GATE LIGHT1. The information entity is then delayed by $XX(1)$ seconds before closing GATE LIGHT1. Next, it is delayed by 55 seconds, opens LIGHT2, is delayed $XX(2)$ seconds,

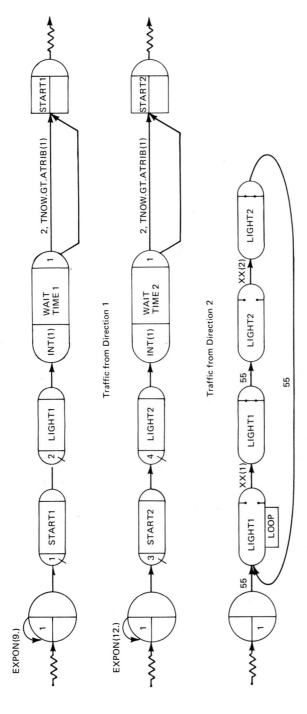

Figure 6-33 SLAM network model of a traffic light situation.

214

closes LIGHT2, and then loops back after a delay of 55 seconds. By specifying the green time for LIGHT1 and LIGHT2 as XX(1) and XX(2) respectively, we can experiment with different values by prescribing new values for XX(1) and XX(2) in INTLC statements.

```
1   GEN,C. D. PEGDEN,TRAFFIC LIGHTS,7/12/77,3;
2   LIMITS,4,1,100;
3   INTLC,XX(1)=60,XX(2)=45;
4   NETWORK;
5           RESOURCE/START1,1/START2,3;              DEFINE STARTING PLACES
6           GATES/LIGHT1,CLOSE,2/LIGHT2,CLOSE,4;     DEFINE TRAFFIC LIGHTS
7   ;TRAFFIC FROM DIRECTION 1
8   ;--------------------------
9           CREATE,EXPON(9.),,1;                     CREATE ARRIVALS
10          AWAIT,START1;                            AWAIT STARTING PLACE
11          AWAIT,LIGHT1;                            AWAIT GREEN LIGHT
12          COLCT,INT(1),WAIT TIME 1,,1;             COLLECT WAIT STATISTICS
13          ACT,2,TNOW.GT.ATRIB(1);                  CAR BEGAN STOPPED
14          ACT;                                     CAR BEGAN MOVING
15          FREE,START1;                             FREE THE STARTING PLACE
16          TERM;
17  ;TRAFFIC FROM DIRECTION 2
18  ;-----------------------
19          CREATE,EXPON(12.),,1;                    SIMILAR TO ABOVE
20          AWAIT,START2;
21          AWAIT,LIGHT2;
22          COLCT,INT(1),WAIT TIME 2,,1;
23          ACT,2,TNOW.GT.ATRIB(1);
24          ACT;
25          FREE,START2;
26          TERM;
27  ;TRAFFIC LIGHTS
28  ;--------------
29          CREATE,,,,1;
30          ACT,55;                                  BOTH LIGHTS RED
31  LOOP    OPEN,LIGHT1;                             LIGHT 1 TURNS GREEN
32          ACT,XX(1);                               GREEN TIME 1
33          CLOSE,LIGHT1;                            LIGHT 1 TURNS RED
34          ACT,55;                                  BOTH LIGHTS RED
35          OPEN,LIGHT2;                             LIGHT 2 TURNS GREEN
36          ACT,XX(2);                               GREEN TIME 2
37          CLOSE,LIGHT2;                            LIGHT 2 TURNS RED
38          ACT,55,,LOOP;                            BEGIN NEW CYCLE
39          END;
40  INIT,0,3600;
41  SIMULATE;
42  INTLC,XX(1)=80,XX(2)=60;
43  SIMULATE;
44  INTLC,XX(1)=40,XX(2)=30;
45  FIN;
```

Figure 6-34 SLAM statement model of traffic light system.

The SLAM statement model for this example is given in Figure 6-34 and follows directly from the network model. As specified on the input, three separate runs were made with the following values for XX(1) and XX(2).

Run Number	XX(1)	XX(2)
1	60	45
2	80	60
3	40	30

Summary of Results. The results of primary interest for this problem are the average waiting times for cars in direction 1 and direction 2. The results for the three runs are summarized in the following table. Note that the statistics include the cars that waited for zero time units.

Run	Green Times		Average Waiting Time	
Number	Direction 1	Direction 2	Direction 1	Direction 2
1	60	45	66.28	79.17
2	80	60	72.17	89.71
3	40	30	132.00	213.50

These results indicate that the best combination of green times was obtained from run 1 and suggest additional simulations should be performed with green times in the range of 60 seconds for direction 1 and 45 seconds for direction 2. After further exploration, we should check the statistical stability of the results by making several runs (replications) with different random number seed values for the values of XX(1) and XX(2) that resulted in the smallest average waiting times.

6.11 CHAPTER SUMMARY

This chapter presented an extensive set of examples to illustrate SLAM network concepts, inputs, and outputs. Listed below are the specific concepts presented in each example.

Example Number	Example Title	Concepts Illustrated
6-1	Work Stations in Series	CREATE node; QUEUE node; COLCT node; regular activity, service activity; and balking and blocking at QUEUE nodes.

6.12 EXERCISES

6-1. For the maintenance facility situation involving work stations in series, Example 6-1, analyze the results and redistribute the six storage spaces to work station 1 and work station 2. Test your alternative design using SLAM. If you were to begin a research and development program for improving the production line, on what quantity would you place your initial efforts?

6-2. Modify the SLAM model of the inspection and adjustment stations, Example 6-2, to accommodate the following changes:

(a) an arrival of television sets to the inspection station involves two television sets to be inspected;

(b) the adjustor routes 40% of the adjusted sets directly to packing and 60% back to the inspectors;

(c) by adding a step to the inspection process, it is felt that the probability of sending a set to the adjustor can be decreased to 0.10; the added step takes 5 minutes.

Redraw the network to indicate these changes. For one of the above situations, run the model and analyze the results.

6-3.   A new design has been proposed for the television inspection and adjustment situation presented in Example 6-2 so that television sets requiring a third adjustment are sent to a rebuild operation. The rebuild operation is not modeled. For this proposal develop the network. Assume the adjustor spends more time on a television set on the second time it is adjusted. (Increase both limits on the uniform distribution by 2.) Because of this added time, the probability of requiring a third adjustment is reduced to 0.10.

6-4.   A certain machine repair shop consists of a work station where incoming units are repaired and an inspection station where the repaired units are either released from the shop or recycled. The work station has three parallel servers, and the inspection station has one inspector. Units entering this system have interarrival times which are exponentially distributed with a mean of 10.25 time units. The repair time for a unit is Erlang distributed with mean 22 and variance 242. The "shortest processing time" priority dispatching rule is used at the work station: the unit with the smallest repair time is served first. Repaired units queue up for inspection on a FIFO basis. The inspection of a unit requires 6 time units; the unit is then rejected with probability p^n, where $p=.15$ and $n=$ the number of times the unit has already been repaired. Rejected units queue up at the work station to be repaired again.

The initial conditions are:

1. Two servers are busy with service completions scheduled for times 1.0 and 1.5, respectively.
2. The first new arrival will occur at time 0.
3. The inspector is idle.

Simulate the operation of this shop for 2000 time units to obtain estimates of the following quantities:

1. Server utilization;
2. Mean, standard deviation, and histogram of total waiting time for each repaired unit;
3. Mean, standard deviation, and histogram of total time spent in the system by each unit;
4. Average number of units in the system;
5. Mean, standard deviation, and histogram of number of repair cycles required of a unit before it leaves the shop.

Embellishments: (a) Modify the priority dispatching rule used at the work station so that recycled items are processed ahead of new arrivals. Among recycled units priority is based on time spent in the system.

(b) Let the repair time be uniformly distributed in the range 0-48.

(c) Modify the original problem so that all units arriving before time 2000 are processed, and statistics concerning these items should be included in the overall statistics for the simulation.

(d) Evaluate the effect of a lognormally distributed inspection time with mean 6 and standard deviation 1.5.

6-5. A conveyor system involves five servers stationed along a conveyor belt. Items to be processed by the servers arrive at the first server at a constant rate of four per minute. Service time for each server is 1 minute, and is exponentially distributed. No storage is provided before each server; therefore, the server must be idle if he is to remove the item from the conveyor belt. If the first server is idle, the item is processed by that server. At the end-of-service time, the item is removed from the system. If the first server is busy when the item arrives, it continues down the conveyor belt until it arrives at the second server. The delay time between servers is 1 minute. If an item encounters a situation in which all servers are busy, it is recycled to the first server with a time delay of 5 minutes. Simulate the above conveyor system for 100 time units to determine statistics concerning the time spent in the system by an item, the percentage of time each server is busy, and the number of items in the conveyor system.

Embellishments: (a) Repeat the simulation with a time delay of 2 minutes between servers. Is there an effect on the utilization of the servers because of a change in the time delay between servers, that is, the speed of the conveyor?

(b) Evaluate the situation in which the last server has sufficient space for storage so that all items passing servers 1, 2, 3, and 4 are processed by server 5. Simulate this situation.

(c) Assess the increased performance obtained by allowing a one item buffer before each server. Based on the results of this study, specify how you would allocate ten buffer spaces to the five servers.

(d) Discuss how you would evaluate the tradeoffs involved between reducing the number of servers in the conveyor system versus increasing the buffer size associated with each server.

6-6. Simulate the activities of the PERT network described on page 220 400 times. Compute statistics and prepare a histogram on the time to reach each node of the network. Compare the results with the PERT calculations for the network.

Embellishment: (a) Based on the SLAM simulation of a PERT network, develop a schedule of early start times and late start times for the activities in the network.

6-7. Simulate the network of Example 6-8 assuming each activity time is Beta distributed with the same mode, minimum and maximum.

6-8. Cargo arrives at an air terminal in unit loads at the rate of two unit loads per minute. At the freight terminal there is no fixed schedule, and planes take off as soon as they can be loaded to capacity. Two types of planes are available for transporting cargo. There are three planes with a capacity of 80 unit loads and two planes that have a capacity of 140 unit loads. The round trip time for any plane is normally distributed with a mean of 3 hours, a standard deviation of 1 hour, and minimum and maximum times of 2 and 4 hours, respectively. The loading policy of the terminal manager is to employ smaller planes whenever possible. Only when 140 unit loads are available will a plane of type 2 be em-

Activity Number	Start Node	End Node	Distribution Type	Mean	Variance
1	1	2	Lognormal	10	4.00
2	1	3	Exponential	6	36.00
3	2	4	Uniform	7	3.00
4	2	9	Gamma	14	21.00
5	3	2	Beta	8	4.71
6	3	4	Uniform	13	5.33
7	3	6	Normal	5	1.00
8	4	9	Erlang	8	32.00
9	6	5	Constant	7	0.00
10	6	7	Normal	4	2.16
11	6	7	Normal	4	3.00
12	5	4	Normal	2	1.20
13	5	8	Normal	6	10.40
14	7	8	Normal	8	26.40
15	8	9	Normal	5	2.00

ployed. Develop a SLAM network to model this system to estimate the number of unit loads waiting and the utilization of the two types of planes over a 100 hour period. Assume at first that the loading time of planes is negligible. Embellish the model to include a one minute per unit loading time.

6-9.   Consider a banking system involving two inside tellers and two drive-in tellers. Arrivals to the banking system are either for the drive-in tellers or for the in-house tellers. The time between arrivals to the drive-in tellers is exponentially distributed with a mean of 0.75 minutes. The drive-in tellers have limited waiting space. Queueing space is available for only three cars waiting for the first teller and four cars waiting for the second teller. The first drive-in teller service time is normally distributed with a mean of 0.5 minutes and standard deviation of 0.25 minutes. The second drive-in teller service time is uniformly distributed between 0.2 and 1.0 minutes. If a car arrives when the queues of both drive-in tellers are full, the customer balks and seeks service from one of the inside bank tellers. However, the inside bank system opens one hour after the drive-in bank.

Customers who directly seek the services of the inside tellers arrive through a different arrival process with the time between arrivals exponentially distributed with a mean of 0.5 minutes. However, they join the same queue as the balkers from the drive-in portion. A single queue is used for both inside tellers. A maximum of seven customers can wait in this single queue. Customers who arrive when there are seven in the inside queue balk and do not seek banking service. The service times for the two inside tellers are triangularly distributed between 0.1 and 1.2 minutes with a mode of 0.4 minutes. Simulate the operation of the bank for an 8 hour period.

6-10.   Modify the bank teller operations described in Exercise 6-9 to model a credit inquiry on selected non-drive-in bank customers. A credit inquiry is performed by the bank manager on new customers. Ten percent of the non-drive-in customers are in this category. The bank manager obtains the necessary information on the customer and initiates the inquiry which takes between 2 and 5 minutes, uniformly distributed. The time for a credit inquiry is exponentially distributed with a mean of 5 minutes during which time the customer waits in a separate room. The manager processes other customers during the time the credit inquiry is being performed, and there is no limit to the number of simultaneous credit inquiries that can be done. When the credit inquiry is completed, the customer for which the credit inquiry was made is served again by the manager and is given preference over customers who have not seen the manager. The manager completes any information gathering task before he issues the credit inquiry which takes 1 minute. Five percent of the credit inquiries result in a negative response and the customer is not routed to the tellers. The time to give a negative response is exponential with a mean of 10 minutes.

Embellishment: Model the manager in the case where the rule is that two inquiries are made for each customer requiring an inquiry. Each inquiry has a 0.05 negative response probability.

6.13 REFERENCES

1. Archibald, R. D. and R. L. Villoria, *Network-Based Management Systems (PERT/ CPM)*, John Wiley, 1968.
2. Bobillier, P. A., B. C. Kahan, and A. R. Probst, *Simulation with GPSS and GPSS V*, Prentice-Hall, 1976.
3. Halpin, D. W. and W. W. Happ, "Digital Simulation of Equipment Allocation for Corps of Engineering Construction Planning", U. S. Army, CERL, Champaign, Illinois, 1971.
4. MacCrimmon, K. R. and C. A. Ryavec, "An Analytical Study of the PERT Assumptions," *Operations Research*, Vol. 12, 1964, pp. 16-38.
5. Malcolm, D. G., J. H. Rosenbloom, C. E. Clark and W. Frazer, "Application of a Technique for Research and Development Program Evaluation," *Operations Research*, Vol. 7, 1959, pp. 616-669.
6. Moder, J. J. and C. R. Phillips, *Project Management with CPM and PERT (Second Edition)*, Van Nostrand-Reinhold, 1970.
7. Pritsker, A. A. B. and P. J. Kiviat, *Simulation with GASP II*, Prentice-Hall, 1969.
8. Pritsker, A. A. B., The GASP IV Simulation Language, John Wiley, 1974.
9. Pritsker, A. A. B., *Modeling and Analysis Using Q-GERT Networks*, Halsted Press and Pritsker & Associates, Inc., 1977.
10. Pritsker, A. A. B., "Resources in Q-GERT: The Next Chapter," Pritsker & Associates, Inc., P. O. Box 2413, West Lafayette, IN, 1977.
11. Schriber, T., *Simulation Using GPSS*, John Wiley, 1974.
12. Weist, J. and F. Levy, *Management Guide to PERT-CPM*, Prentice-Hall, 1969.

CHAPTER 7

Discrete Event Simulation Using SLAM

7.1   INTRODUCTION

The network orientation presented in the previous chapters is a valuable approach to modeling a large class of systems. However, for some systems the network orientation lacks the flexibility needed to model the system under study. For systems requiring flexibility beyond that afforded by the network orientation, the discrete event orientation provides a useful approach to simulation modeling. In this chapter, we describe and illustrate the basic concepts and procedures employed in constructing discrete event simulation models using SLAM. The discussion of advanced discrete event concepts is deferred until Chapter 8.

7.2   DISCRETE EVENT ORIENTATION

In this section, we review the concepts of discrete event modeling described in Chapter 3. The world view embodied in a discrete event orientation consists of modeling a system by describing the changes that occur in the system at discrete points in time. An isolated point in time where the state of the system may change is called an "event time" and the associated logic for processing the changes in state is called an "event." A discrete event model of a system is constructed by defining the events where changes in system states can occur and then modeling the logic associated with each event type. A dynamic portrayal of the system is produced by causing the changes in states according to the logic of each event in a time-ordered sequence.

The state of a system in a discrete event model is similar to that of a network model and is represented by variables and by entities which have attributes and which belong to files. The state of the system is initialized by specifying initial values for the variables employed in the simulation, by creating the initial entities, if any, in the system, and by the initial scheduling of events in the model. During execution of the simulation, the system moves from state to state as its entities engage in activities that change the state of the system. In discrete event simulation, system status changes only occur at the beginning of an activity when something is started or at the end of the activity when something is terminated. Events are used to model the start and completion of activities.

The concept of an event which takes place instantaneously at a point in time and either starts or ends an activity is a crucial one. This relationship is depicted in Figure 7-1. Time does not advance within an event and changes in the state of the system occur only at event times. The system behavior is simulated by state changes that occur as events happen.

When an event occurs, the state of the system can change in four ways: by altering the value of one or more variables associated with the simulation; by altering the number of entities present in the system; by altering the values assigned to one or more attributes of an entity; or by altering the relationships that exist among entities through file manipulations. Methods are available within SLAM for accomplishing each of these changes. Note that an event can occur in which a decision is made not to change the state of the system.

Events are scheduled to occur at a prescribed time during the simulation. Events have attributes and are maintained in chronological order in a file. For example, when scheduling an end-of-service event, the attributes of the customer undertaking service are part of the event and are then made available at the time of the end-of-service event processing. Thus, if an entity undertakes a series of activities with the end of each activity represented by an event, the attributes of the entity will be carried along through the system as each event is processed.

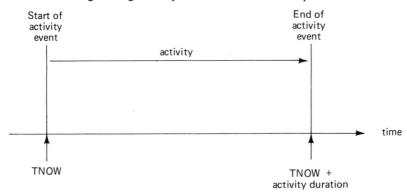

Figure 7-1 Relationship between activities and events.

7.2.1 Event Model of a Queueing Situation

To illustrate the concepts involved in discrete event modeling, consider a bank with one teller where it is desired to obtain statistics on the time each customer spends in the system. Customers arrive to the system, wait for the teller, undergo service, and depart the system. For simplicity, it will be assumed that there is no time delay between the time the service ends for one customer and begins for the next waiting customer, if any. The states of the system will be measured by the number of customers in the system and the status of the teller. Two event types can be used to model the changes in system state: a customer arrival event, and an end-of-service event. As a modeler, one must decide on the events that model the system. Here we assume all significant changes in system status can occur only at the arrival time of a customer or at the time that a service ends.† In our model, it is assumed that the state of the system does not change between these event times.

There is one activity associated with this system consisting of the service activity. The service activity for a customer begins at either the time of arrival of the customer to the system or at the time that the teller completes service for another customer. Therefore, the starting event for the service activity can be either the customer arrival event or the end-of-service event. The ending event for the service activity is the end-of-service event.

In constructing the event logic for this example, we will employ the variable BUSY to describe the status of the teller where a value of 1 denotes busy and a value of 0 denotes idle. Customers in the system will be represented as entities with one attribute denoting the arrival time of the customer to the system. This attribute will be used in the model for collecting statistics on the time in the system for each customer in a fashion similar to the mark time employed in network modeling. The model will employ a file ranked first-in, first-out (FIFO) for storing entities representing customers waiting for service when the teller is busy. The state of the system at any instant in time is defined by the value of the variable BUSY and the entities and associated attribute values in the system.

The initialization logic for this example is depicted in Figure 7-2. The variable BUSY is set equal to zero to indicate that the teller is initially idle. The arrival event corresponding to the first customer is scheduled to occur at time 0. Thus, the initial status of the system is empty and idle with the first customer arrival scheduled at time 0.

The logic for the customer arrival event is depicted in Figure 7-3. The first action which is performed is the scheduling of the next arrival to occur at the current time plus the time between arrivals. Thus, each arrival will cause another arrival to occur at some later time during the simulation. In this way only one arrival event is scheduled to occur at any one time; however, a complete sequence

---

† There are other events that could be defined such as a death of a teller, a fire in the bank, etc. It is the modeler's task to decide on the significant events to include in his model.

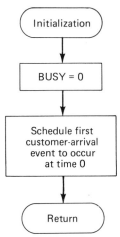

Figure 7-2 Initialization logic for bank teller problem.

of arrivals is generated.† The first attribute of the arrival entity associated with the event is then set equal to TNOW to mark the arrival time of the customer to the system. A test is then made on the status of the teller to determine if the service activity can begin or if the entity representing the customer must be placed in a file to wait for the teller. If service can begin, the variable BUSY is set equal to one and the end-of-service event for the current customer is scheduled and the event processing is completed. Otherwise, the entity and its attributes are placed in the file representing waiting customers and the event processing is completed.

At each end-of-service event, statistics are collected on the time in the system for the customer completing service. The first waiting customer, if any, is removed from the wait file and placed into service. The logic for the end-of-service event is depicted in Figure 7-4. The variable TSYS, corresponding to the time in the system for this customer, is computed as $TNOW - ATRIB(1)$. Since $ATRIB(1)$ was previously assigned the arrival time of the customer to the system, TSYS is the elapsed time between the arrival and departure of the customer on which service was completed. A test is then made to determine if there are customers waiting for service. If not, the status of the teller is made idle by setting BUSY equal to 0 and the event processing is completed. Otherwise, the first customer entity is removed from the wait file. Processing of the customer is modeled by scheduling an end-of-service event to occur at the current time plus the service time.

---

† The next arrival event could also be read from an input device which contained an "historical" sequence of events. In this case, we refer to the simulation model as being "trace driven." Of course, the historical sequence could have been generated by a separate simulation model.

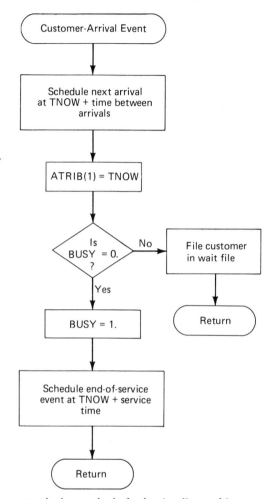

Figure 7-3 Customer arrival event logic for bank teller problem.

This simple example illustrates the basic concepts of discrete event simulation modeling. Variables and entities with their attributes and file memberships make up the static structure of a simulation model. They describe the state of the system but not how the system operates. The events specify the logic which controls the changes that occur at specific instants of time. The dynamic behavior is then obtained by sequentially processing events and recording status values at event times. Since status is constant between events, the complete dynamic system behavior is obtained in this manner.

This example illustrates several important types of functions which must be performed in simulating discrete event models. The primary functional requirement in

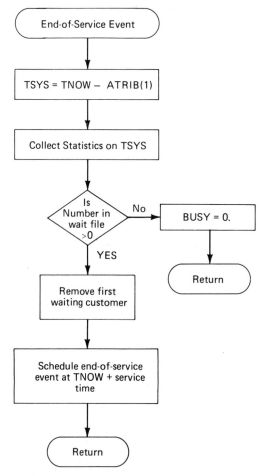

Figure 7-4   End-of-service event logic for the bank teller problem.

discrete event simulation involves scheduling events, placing events in chronological order, and advancing time. Other functional requirements which are illustrated by this example include mechanisms for file manipulations, statistics collecting and reporting, and random sample generation. In Section 7.3 we describe the use of SLAM for performing these and other functions in discrete event simulation modeling. First, we discuss how SLAM can be used to study inventory systems.

7.2.2 Event Modeling of Inventory Systems

To illustrate the generality of the event modeling approach, we now consider the analysis of inventory systems and indicate the event modeling procedures.

All inventory systems involve the storage of particular items for future sale or use. Demands are imposed on an inventory by customers seeking supplies of an individual item. A company must establish an inventory policy that specifies: (1) when an order for additional items should be placed (or manufactured); and (2) how many of the items should be ordered at each order time. When the items stored in inventory are discrete units, simulation of the inventory system using the next event philosophy is quite natural. The primary system variables are the number of units in storage, called the *inventory-on-hand,* and the number of units that are theoretically on the books of the company, called the *inventory position.* The inventory position is equal to the inventory-on-hand, plus the number of units on order (the number due-in), minus the number of units that have been backordered by customers (the number due-out). The inventory-on-hand represents the number of units available to be sold to customers. The inventory position represents the number of units that is or will be available to the company for potential sale. Inventory decisions regarding when to place an order and how much to order are normally based on the inventory position. Other attributes associated with inventory situations are: the number of units sold, the number of orders placed, the number of lost sales and/or the number of backorders, and the number of times the inventory position is reviewed to make a decision whether to place an order.

The events associated with an inventory situation at which these attributes could change their value are: a demand by a customer for the items in inventory, a review of the status of the inventory position to determine if an order should be placed, the receipt of goods from the distributor to be placed in inventory, and the satisfying of the customers' demands for the item. Each of these events could be modeled as a distinct event. However, several of the above will occur at the same point in time. When this happens, it is efficient to combine the events into a single event. For example, the satisfying of a customer demand would normally take place either when the customer demand is placed or when a shipment of units is received from the distributor. When this is done, the modeler assumes that the time delay in delivering a unit to a customer has an insignificant effect on the expected cost or profit associated with the inventory situation.

Customer demand events are normally modeled by specifying the time between customer demands. In this way, each demand event can be used to specify the time of the next demand. Then only the first demand event, which starts the demand process, and the time between demands would need to be specified.

Two types of review procedures to determine if an order should be placed are common in industry. A *periodic review procedure* specifies that a review should be performed at equally spaced points in time, for example, every month. The other review procedure involves the examination of the inventory position every time it decreases. This type of review is called *transaction reporting* and involves keeping a running log of the inventory position. When a transaction reporting review procedure is being studied, no separate review event is required since the inventory position can only be decreased when a customer demand occurs. Thus, the review procedure can be incorporated into the customer demand event.

The event involving the receipt of units from the distributor does not change the inventory position since the inventory position was increased when the units were ordered. However, the inventory-on-hand and the number of backorders could change when the receipt event occurs. The time at which the receipt event occurs is based on the time at which it was decided to place an order (at a review time) plus the time for processing the order and shipping the units. The time from the placing of the order to the receipt of the units is called the *lead time*.

The above general discussion of events that can occur in an inventory situation provides a general framework for simulating any inventory system. To obtain a simulation using SLAM, it would only be necessary to write subroutines for each of the events required by the specific inventory situation. The point in time at which the individual events occur would automatically be handled by SLAM using the time between events as specified by the user in the appropriate event routines. The user would schedule the next demand event (in his subroutine representing the demand event) and the receipt of units to occur, at the review time plus the lead time, if it was decided that an order was to be placed. Of significant importance in the simulation of inventory systems is the absence of the need to specify the interdemand time distribution, the lead time distribution, the number of units requested by a customer at a demand point, and so forth, when discussing the overall procedure for simulating an inventory system. This information is only important when simulating a specific system. The SLAM organizational structure for discrete event simulation allows the modeling of systems prior to data collection and, in fact, can be used to help specify the data required to analyze a system. In the next section, the SLAM subroutines to support discrete event modeling are described.

7.3   THE DISCRETE EVENT FRAMEWORK OF SLAM

To simulate a discrete event model of a system using SLAM, the analyst codes each discrete event as a FORTRAN subroutine. To assist the analyst in this task, SLAM provides a set of FORTRAN subprograms for performing all commonly encountered functions such as event scheduling, statistics collection, and random sample generation. The advancing of simulated time (TNOW) and the order in which the event routines are processed are controlled by the SLAM executive program. Thus, SLAM relieves the simulation programmer of the task of sequencing events in their proper chronological order.

Each event subroutine is assigned a positive integer numeric code called the *event code*. The event code is mapped onto a call to the appropriate event subroutine by subroutine EVENT(I) where the argument I is the event code. This subroutine is written by the user and consists of a computed GO TO statement indexed on I causing a transfer to the appropriate event subroutine call followed by a return. An example of the EVENT(I) subroutine for a simulation model with two events consisting of an arrival event coded in subroutine ARVL and assigned event code 1, and an end-of-service event coded in subroutine ENDSV and assigned event code 2 is depicted in Figure 7-5.

The executive control for a discrete event simulation is provided by subroutine SLAM which is called from a user-written *main* program. The reason for making SLAM a subroutine and not the main program is to allow the user to dimension the SLAM storage arrays NSET and QSET in the main program without the need to recompile the SLAM executive control program. The array QSET is in unlabeled COMMON and is equivalenced to the array NSET which is prescribed to have the same dimension. This allows both integer and real data to be stored within a single contiguous array storage area. These arrays are employed by SLAM for storing both events with their associated attributes and entities in files with their associated attributes. The term entry is used to refer to both events and entities which are stored in the arrays NSET/QSET. Thus, the dimension of the arrays NSET/QSET determines the maximum number of entries which can be in the system at any one time. The maximum number of entries (MNTRY) that can exist in the system at any one instant in time is limited by the following relationship:

$$MNTRY \le NNSET/(MATR + 4)$$

where

NNSET is the dimension of NSET/QSET, and

MATR is the maximum number of attributes per entry employed in the simulation model.

```
SUBROUTINE EVENT(I)
  GO TO (1,2),I
1 CALL ARVL
  RETURN
2 CALL ENDSV
  RETURN
  END
```

Figure 7-5   Sample subroutine EVENT(I).

A discussion of the arrays NSET/QSET and the way in which entries are stored is deferred until Chapter 8. For now the reader should simply note that SLAM utilizes the arrays NSET/QSET for storing entries, network elements, and plot data points. NSET/QSET must be dimensioned by the user in the main program to provide space for all three uses.

The main program is also used to specify values for the SLAM variables NNSET, NCRDR, NPRNT, and NTAPE which are in the labeled COMMON block named SCOM1. As discussed above, NNSET is the dimension assigned to the arrays NSET/QSET and must be set accordingly. The variable NCRDR denotes the unit number from which SLAM input statements are read and would normally be set equal to 5 to denote the card reader unit. Likewise, the variable NPRNT denotes the unit number to which all SLAM output is to be written and would normally be set to 6 to denote the line printer unit. The variable NTAPE is the number of a temporary scratch file which must be assigned by the user for use by the SLAM processor for interpreting the free form SLAM input statements and data. A sample main program is depicted in Figure 7-6.

Two additional user-written subroutines which are commonly employed in discrete event simulation models are subroutines INTLC and OTPUT. Subroutine INTLC is called by SLAM before each simulation run and is used to set initial conditions and to schedule initial events. Subroutine OTPUT is called at the end of each simulation and is used for end-of-simulation processing such as printing problem specific results for the simulation.

The SLAM next-event logic for simulating discrete event models is depicted in Figure 7-7. The SLAM processor begins by reading the SLAM input statements, if any, and initializing SLAM variables. A call is then made to subroutine INTLC which specifies additional initial conditions for the simulation. SLAM contains a version of subroutine INTLC which contains only a RETURN statement so that the user need not include subroutine INTLC if no additional initialization is required. The processor then begins execution of the simulation by removing the first event from the event calendar. Events are ordered on the calendar based on low

```
      DIMENSION NSET(1000)
      COMMON/SCOM1/ ATRIB(100),DD(100),DDL(100),DTNOW,II,MFA,MSTOP,NCLNR
     1,NCRDR,NPRNT,NNRUN,NNSET,NTAPE,SS(100),SSL(100),TNEXT,TNOW,XX(100)
      COMMON QSET(1000)
      EQUIVALENCE (NSET(1),QSET(1))
      NNSET=1000
      NCRDR=5
      NPRNT=6
      NTAPE=7
      CALL SLAM
      STOP
      END
```

Figure 7-6 Sample main program.

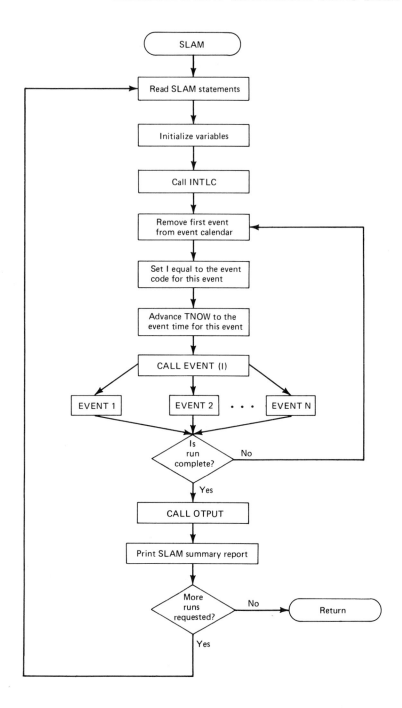

Figure 7-7   SLAM next event logic for simulating discrete event models.

values of event times. The variable I is set equal to the event code and TNOW is advanced to the event time for the next event. SLAM then calls the user-written subroutine EVENT(I) which in turn calls the appropriate event routine. Following execution of the user-written event routine, a test is made to determine if the simulation run is complete. A discrete event simulation is ended if any of the following conditions are satisfied:

1. TNOW is greater than or equal to TTFIN, the ending time of the simulation;
2. no events remain on the event calendar for processing; or
3. the SLAM variable MSTOP has been set in a user-written event routine to −1.

If the run is not complete, the new first event is removed from the event calendar and processing continues. Otherwise, a call is made to subroutine OTPUT. (As with INTLC, a version of OTPUT is included in SLAM.) After the return from OTPUT, the SLAM Summary Report is printed. A test is then made on the number of runs remaining. If more runs remain, control branches back to the beginning and the next simulation run is executed. Otherwise, a return is made from the SLAM processor back to the user-written main program.

The description above provides an overview of the SLAM framework for simulating discrete event models. To write a discrete event simulation program, the user writes program main, subroutine EVENT(I) to decipher the event code I and to call the appropriate event subroutine, and event routines to specify the changes that occur at event times. Subroutines INTLC and OTPUT are written if special initial conditions or end-of-simulation processing is required. Based on this overview of the SLAM discrete event framework, we next describe the functional capabilities provided by SLAM for assisting the analyst in developing the user-written subroutines.

7.4   SAMPLING FROM PROBABILITY DISTRIBUTIONS

An important aspect of many systems of interest is the stochastic nature of one or more elements in the system. For example, in queueing systems the arrival times and service times are usually not known with certainty but are depicted as random variables. Therefore, in order to build models of such systems, the simulation programmer needs to be able to sample from commonly encountered distributions such as the exponential, normal, and beta as well as from user-defined distributions. SLAM provides FORTRAN function statements for this purpose. A list of such functions is summarized in Table 7-1. Note that the functional names are the same

Table 7-1   Function statements to obtain random samples.†

Function	Description †
DRAND (IS)	A pseudo-random number obtained from random number stream IS
EXPON (XMEAN, IS)	A sample from an exponential distribution with mean XMEAN using random number stream IS
UNFRM (ULO, UHI, IS)	A sample from a uniform distribution in the interval ULO to UHI using random number stream IS
WEIBL (BETA, ALPHA, IS)	A sample from a Weibull distribution with shape parameter ALPHA and scale parameter BETA using random number stream IS
TRIAG (XLO, XMODE, XHI, IS)	A sample from a triangular distribution in the interval XLO to XHI with mode XMODE using random number stream IS
RNORM (XMN, STD, IS)	A sample from a normal distribution with mean XMN and standard deviation STD using random number stream IS
RLOGN (XMN, STD, IS)	A sample from a lognormal distribution with mean XMN and standard deviation STD using random number stream IS
ERLNG (EMN, XK, IS)	A sample from an Erlang distribution which is the sum of XK exponential samples each with mean EMN using random number stream IS
GAMA (BETA, ALPHA, IS)	A sample from a gamma distribution with parameters BETA and ALPHA using random number stream IS
BETA (THETA, PHI, IS)	A sample from a beta distribution with parameters THETA and PHI using random number stream IS
NPSSN (XMN, IS)	A sample from a Poisson distribution with mean XMN using random number stream IS
DPROB (CPROB, VALUE, NVAL, IS)	A sample from a user-defined discrete probability function with cumulative probabilities and associated values specified in arrays CPROB and VALUE, with NVAL values using random stream IS

†See Section 2.9 for the equations of the distribution functions associated with the random variables including the definitions of the function arguments.

as those employed in network models and the parameter specifications are identical to those specified in Chapter 4. The reader should note that these are FORTRAN function subprograms, and the stream parameter cannot be defaulted as in the case of network statements.

FUNCTION DPROB allows the user to obtain a sample from a user-defined discrete distribution (a probability mass function). The user must convert the probability mass function into a cumulative distribution. Two user arrays are required to describe this distribution: the first for the potential values of the random variable and the second for the associated cumulative probabilities. The arguments of FUNCTION DPROB are: the user array name for the cumulative probabilities (CPROB), the user array name for the associated values (VALUE), the number of values (NVAL) contained in CPROB and VALUE, and the random stream number (IS).

As an example of the use of FUNCTION DPROB, consider the following probability mass function for the random variable X:

X	$f(X)$
3	.1
4	.4
5	.5

First, the probability mass function is converted to a cumulative distribution. We define the cumulative distribution using arrays XVAL(I) and FX(I) as follows:

I	XVAL(I)	FX(I)
1	3	.1
2	4	.5
3	5	1.0

These values can be conveniently assigned to the arrays by a FORTRAN DATA statement in the subroutine calling FUNCTION DPROB or can be read from input records. The following statement draws a sample, X, from the desired probability mass function using random stream number 1.

X = DPROB(FX,XVAL,3,1)

7.5   SCHEDULING EVENTS

The SLAM processor completely relieves the user of the responsibility for chronologically ordering the events on an event calendar. The user simply schedules events to occur, and SLAM causes each event to be processed at the appropriate time in the simulation. Events are scheduled by calling subroutine SCHDL (KEVNT, DTIME, A) where KEVNT denotes the event code of the event being scheduled and DTIME denotes the number of time units from the current time, TNOW, that the event is to occur. Attributes associated with an event are specified by passing the buffer array A as the third argument of SCHDL. The buffer array A can be a user-defined vector or the ATRIB array as was used in network models. The values of the attributes in the buffer array A at the time the event is scheduled are stored on the event calendar with the event. These values are then removed from the event calendar by SLAM and copied back into the ATRIB buffer array at the time the event is executed. Thus, the ATRIB array at the time of event processing will always contain the values that were in the buffer array A at the time that the event was scheduled.

To illustrate the use of subroutine SCHDL(KEVNT, DTIME, A), consider the scheduling of a customer arrival event with event code 1 to occur at the current time plus a sample from an exponential distribution with mean of 5 and using random stream number 1. In addition, the entity representing the customer has its first attribute value equal to 2. The coding to accomplish this is as follows:

```
A(1)=2
TIMINC=EXPON(5.,1)
CALL SCHDL (1,TIMINC,A)
```

These statements cause SLAM to call subroutine EVENT(I) with I equal to 1 at time TNOW + EXPON(5.,1) and to set ATRIB(1) equal to 2, prior to the call to EVENT(I).

7.6   FILE MANIPULATIONS

Entities which are grouped together because of a relationship between the entities are maintained in files. Files are used extensively in discrete event simulation models. For example, in the bank teller problem discussed earlier in this chapter, a file is used to store customer entities which must wait for the teller. A file provides the mechanism for storing the attributes of an entity in a prescribed ranking with respect to other entities in the file. In network models, files were used to maintain entities waiting at QUEUE, AWAIT, and PREEMPT nodes.

Associated with a file is a ranking criterion which specifies the procedure for ordering entities within the file. Thus, each entity in a file has a rank which specifies its position in the file relative to the other members in the file. A rank of one denotes that the entity is the first entry in the file. Possible ranking criterion for files are: first-in, first-out (FIFO); last-in, first-out (LIFO); high-value-first (HVF) based on an attribute value; and low-value-first (LVF) based on an attribute value. The ranking criterion for entries in a file is assumed to be FIFO unless otherwise specified using the PRIORITY statement described in Chapter 5.

In SLAM, files are distinguished by integer numbers assigned to the files by the user. SLAM automatically collects statistics on each file and provides the function NNQ(IFILE) which returns the number of entries in file IFILE. For example, NNQ(2) denotes the number of entries in file 2.

SLAM provides the user with a set of subroutines for performing all file manipulations which are commonly encountered in discrete event simulations. We will now describe the use of these subroutines for file manipulations where entries are referenced by their rank in the file. In Chapter 8, we will describe the SLAM filing system in more detail and describe the use of the subroutines for file manipulations using the more flexible approach of referencing entities by their location in the storage array NSET/QSET.

7.6.1   Subroutine FILEM(IFILE,A)

Subroutine FILEM(IFILE,A) files an entry with attributes specified in the buffer array A into file IFILE. The entry's rank in the file is determined by SLAM based upon the ranking criterion specified by the user. As noted earlier, if no ranking criterion is specified then a first-in, first-out ranking is assumed. The attributes of the entry are stored with the entry and are returned when the entry is removed from the file. As an example of the use of subroutine FILEM(IFILE,A), the following statements cause an entry with its first attribute set equal to the current simulation time to be inserted into file 1:

        A(1) = TNOW
        CALL FILEM(1,A)

On input, the user defines the value of MNTRY, the maximum number of entries permitted in all files. If an attempt is made to file more than MNTRY entries in the file storage area, a SLAM execution error results.

7.6.2   Subroutine RMOVE(NRANK,IFILE,A)

Subroutine RMOVE(NRANK,IFILE,A) removes an entry with rank NRANK from file IFILE and places its attributes into the attribute buffer array A. As an example of the use of subroutine RMOVE, the following statement causes the second entry in file 3 to be removed and its attributes to be placed in the array ATRIB:

    CALL RMOVE(2,3,ATRIB)

As a second example, the following statement removes the last entry in file 1 and places its attributes in an array called A:

    CALL RMOVE(NNQ(1),1,A)

The dimension of the user-defined array A should be set greater than or equal to the maximum number of attributes per entry, MATR, plus 2. If the user attempts to remove an entry from file IFILE with rank greater than NNQ(IFILE), a SLAM execution error results.

7.6.3   Subroutine COPY(NRANK,IFILE,A)

Sometimes it is desirable to copy the attributes of an entity belonging to a file without removing it from the file. Subroutine COPY(NRANK,IFILE,A) provides this capability by copying the attributes into the array A of the entry with rank NRANK in file IFILE without removing the entry from the file. For example, the following statement causes the attributes of the first entry in file 4 to be copied into the ATRIB array:

    CALL COPY(1,4,ATRIB)

As in the case of subroutine RMOVE, if the user attempts to copy an entry in file IFILE with rank greater than NNQ(IFILE), a SLAM execution error results.

7.6.4   Function NFIND(NRANK,IFILE,NATR,MCODE,X,TOL)

In some cases the rank of a specific entry of interest may not be known. Function NFIND(NRANK,IFILE,NATR,MCODE,X,TOL) can be used to determine the rank of an entry in file IFILE which contains a value for attribute NATR that bears a relationship designated by the user to a specified value, X. Definitions of the arguments to NFIND for determining the rank of an entry are:

    NRANK   The rank of the entry where the search is to begin.
    IFILE   The number of the file being searched.

NATR   The attribute number specified to find the entry meeting the conditions specified by MCODE.

MCODE A code specifying the relationship between X and the attribute value. The following five options are available.

MCODE =   2: maximum value but greater than X
MCODE =   1: minimum value but greater than X
MCODE =   0: first value within X ± TOL
MCODE = −1: minimum value but less than X
MCODE = −2: maximum value but less than X

X   A specified value used to search for an entry in file IFILE.

TOL   A tolerance value for equality comparisons when MCODE = 0 is specified. (FORTRAN requires that the argument be included for MCODE values of 1, 2, −1, or −2 even though the value is not used.)

If no entry is found in the file which meets the condition, NFIND returns a zero value. Otherwise, NFIND is returned as the rank of the first entry in the file which meets the condition which has a rank of at least NRANK. As an example of the use of NFIND, the following coding is used to search file 3 beginning with the sixth entry to determine the rank of the entry which has its fourth attribute exactly equal to 10.:

NRANK = NFIND(6, 3, 4, 0, 10.0, 0.0)

In Chapter 8, we describe procedures by which the user can search for an entry in a file which satisfies two or more conditions simultaneously.

7.6.5   File Manipulations Involving the Event Calendar

The filing system subroutines can also be used for manipulations of entries on the event calendar by specifying the file number as the SLAM variable NCLNR. For example, the following coding would cause the attributes of the next event to be copied into the ATRIB array.

CALL COPY(1,NCLNR,ATRIB)

As in the case of other files, if the user specifies a rank greater than NNQ(NCLNR), a SLAM execution error results.

When using this feature, the user may want to test and/or change the event code or event time of the event calendar entry. These values are automatically maintained by the SLAM processor as attributes of the entry with the event code being attribute number MATR + 1 and the event time being attribute number MATR + 2 where MATR is the maximum number of user attributes specified on the LIMITS card. For example, if the user specified MATR as 5 on the LIMITS card, then ATRIB(6) and ATRIB(7) would contain the event code and event time, respectively.

As a second example of the use of the filing system subroutines involving the event calendar, consider a simulation model with MATR equal to 5. The following statements would remove the first event from the event calendar, add 10.0 to its event time, and then place it back onto the calendar.

    CALL RMOVE(1,NCLNR,ATRIB)
    ATRIB(7) = ATRIB(7) + 10.
    CALL FILEM(NCLNR, ATRIB)

7.7   STATISTICS COLLECTION

In discrete event simulations, there are two distinct types of statistics which are of interest to the analyst. These are: (1) statistics based on observations; and (2) statistics on time-persistent variables. In this section, we describe the procedures employed in SLAM discrete event simulations for collecting and estimating values associated with both types of statistics.

7.7.1   Statistics Based on Observations

Statistics based on observations are statistics computed from a finite number of samples. Each sample value is considered as an observation. For example, in the bank teller problem, statistics on the random variable TSYS representing the time in the system for each customer are based on observations where each customer processed through the system is considered as one observation. The statistics on the variable TSYS depend only upon the value of each observation and not upon the time at which each observation is collected.

Each variable for which observation statistics are collected must be defined by the user with a STAT statement following the general format conventions described in Section 5.4. The format for the STAT statement is as follows:

STAT, ICLCT, ID, NCEL/HLOW/HWID;

where ICLCT is an integer code associated with the variable used to distinguish variable types;

ID is an alphanumeric identifier with 16 significant characters which is printed on the SLAM Summary Report to identify the output associated with the variable; and

NCEL/HLOW/HWID are histogram parameters specifying the number of interior cells, the upper limit for the first cell, and the width of each cell, respectively. If histogram parameters are not specified, then no histogram is prepared.

As an example, the following statement specifies that observation statistics are to be collected on variable type 1, the results are to be displayed as TIME IN SYSTEM, and a histogram is to be generated with 10 interior cells with the upper limit for the first cell equal to 0 and with interior cell widths of 1:

STAT, 1, TIME IN SYSTEM, 10/0/1;

Observations for each variable type defined by the STAT statement are collected within the event subroutines by a call to subroutine COLCT(XVAL,ICLCT) where the variable XVAL contains the value of the observation and ICLCT is the integer code associated with the variable type. For example, the following statement would cause one observation to be collected on the variable TSYS which is coded as COLCT variable type number 1:

CALL COLCT(TSYS,1)

If a call is executed to subroutine COLCT with an ICLCT code not defined by a STAT input statement, a SLAM execution error results.

7.7.2   Statistics on Time-Persistent Variables

Statistics on time-persistent variables refer to statistics maintained on variables which have a value defined over a period of time. For example, the variable BUSY in the bank teller example is used to denote the status of the teller over time. The fraction of time that BUSY equals 1 is the teller utilization. Therefore the utilization of the teller would be a time-persistent statistic.

Statistics on time-persistent variables are obtained in SLAM discrete event simulations by the use of the SLAM dimensioned variable XX. By including the TIMST input statement described in Section 5.6.4, time persistent statistics are automatically accumulated by the SLAM processor on any XX variable of interest. This relieves the user of the burden of calling a subroutine within the event routines to obtain time-persistent statistics. For example, to invoke time-persistent statistics on the variable XX(1), with the output identified as TELLER BUSY TIME, the user simply includes the following statement as part of the SLAM input:

TIMST, XX(1), TELLER BUSY TIME;

To improve the mnemonics within the coding of the event routines, the FORTRAN EQUIVALENCE statement can be employed. For example, time-persistent statistics could be obtained on the FORTRAN variable BUSY by using the TIMST statement described above in conjunction with the following equivalence statement:

EQUIVALENCE(BUSY,XX(1))

This EQUIVALENCE statement must be included in each event subroutine in which the value of BUSY can change.

7.8 VARIABLES AND COMMON BLOCKS

Variables which are employed in a SLAM discrete event simulation model can be of two types: SLAM variables; and user-defined variables. SLAM variables are those defined by the SLAM language. Table 7-2 summarizes some of the important SLAM variables which are used in discrete event simulation models. As we present additional concepts in later chapters, the number of SLAM variables will increase slightly.

The values of SLAM variables are transferred between the SLAM processor and user-written subroutines through the SCOM1 named (labeled) COMMON block. Therefore any user-written subroutine which references a SLAM variable must contain the SCOM1 COMMON block. The variable list for the SCOM1 COMMON block is shown below.

COMMON/SCOM1/ATRIB(100),DD(100),DDL(100),DTNOW,II,MFA,MSTOP,NCLNR
1, NCRDR,NPRNT,NNRUN,NNSET,NTAPE,SS(100),SSL(100),TNEXT,TNOW,XX(100)

The array sizes selected for the dimensions of COMMON variables are those that have been found to satisfy most SLAM users without requiring an excessive amount of core storage.

Table 7-2 Definitions of some important discrete event variables.

Variable	Definition
ATRIB(I)	Buffer for the Ith attribute value of an entry to be inserted or removed from the file storage area
MSTOP	Set by the user to –1 to stop a simulation run before time TTFIN
NCLNR	The file number of the event calendar
NCRDR	The unit number from which SLAM input statements are read. Normally set to 5 to denote the cardreader
NNRUN	The number of the current simulation run
NNSET	The dimension of the arrays NSET/QSET
NPRNT	The unit number to which SLAM output is to be written Normally set to 6 to denote the lineprinter
NSET/QSET	Equivalenced arrays employed by SLAM for storing file entries
NTAPE	The unit number of a scratch tape
TNOW	The value of current simulated time
TNEXT	The time of the next scheduled discrete event
XX(I)	The Ith global variable. Time persistent statistics will be collected if XX(I) is specified on the TIMST input statement.

In addition to SLAM variables, the user may also employ user-defined variables in describing the state of a system. For example, the user variable BUSY was employed in the bank teller problem to denote the status of the teller. The values of user-defined variables are transferred between user-written subroutines by user-defined named COMMON blocks. *The user must not employ unnamed (blank) COMMON for user-defined variables.* As noted earlier in this chapter, all entries in files are stored in the equivalenced arrays NSET and QSET where the array QSET is in unnamed COMMON. The use of additional unnamed COMMON by the user will cause the values stored in the arrays NSET/QSET to be overwritten and will result in an error.

7.9 INPUT STATEMENTS

In discrete event simulation models, input statements are required for specifying a project title, run length, file rankings, monitor events and the like. The input statements employed in discrete event models are identical to those described for network models in Chapter 5. One addition is the STAT input statement described in Section 7.7.1. Thus, a discrete event model must include a GEN card, LIMITS card, and FIN card, plus any additional input statements required by the simulation model.

7.10   DISCRETE EVENT OUTPUT REPORTS

The results for each simulation run are summarized by the SLAM Summary Report which is automatically printed by the SLAM processor at the end of each simulation run. The SLAM Summary Report for discrete event models is identical to that produced for network models with the network statistics omitted, and includes statistics on variables based on observations, statistics on time-persistent variables, file statistics, and histograms. Definitions for the statistical quantities provided by the summary report are provided in Section 5.8.4.

The SLAM processor also prints a trace report if the TRACE option has been specified using the MONTR statement. The SLAM Trace Report for discrete-event models includes the event time, the event code, and up to 5 attributes of each event processed during the tracing period. The use of the TRACE option and the SLAM trace report for discrete event models is illustrated by the example simulation model presented in Section 7.13. In Chapter 8, we describe subprograms for obtaining additional intermediate results during a simulation run.

7.11   COMBINING FUNCTIONAL CAPABILITIES

In the preceding sections, we described the FORTRAN based framework of SLAM and a set of subprograms which allows the user to perform the commonly encountered functions in discrete event simulation models. In this section, we illustrate how these SLAM functional capabilities are used in constructing discrete event simulation models by describing the coding of the SLAM discrete event model of the bank teller example. In the coding which follows, we assume that customers arrive to the bank with the time between arrivals given by the exponential distribution with a mean of 20 minutes and that the teller service time is uniformly distributed between 10 and 25 minutes. The operation of the bank teller system is to be simulated for a period of 480 minutes.

To construct a discrete event simulation model of the bank teller problem, the user must do the following:

1. Write the main program to dimension NSET/QSET, specify values for NNSET, NCRDR, NPRNT, and NTAPE, and call SLAM.
2. Write subroutine EVENT(I) to map the user assigned event codes onto a call to the appropriate event subroutine.
3. Write subroutine INTLC to initialize the model in accordance with the logic depicted in Figure 7-2.
4. Write event subroutines to model the logic for the customer arrival event depicted in Figure 7-3 and the end-of-service event depicted in Figure 7-4.
5. Prepare the input statements required by the problem.

The event model of the bank teller problem contains two events: the customer arrival event and the end-of-service event. We will code the logic for the customer arrival event in subroutine ARVL and assign it event code number 1. The code for the logic for the end-of-service event will be written in subroutine ENDSV and it will be referenced as event code number 2. Thus, subroutine EVENT(I) is as depicted previously in Figure 7-5.

The entities in the system representing customers have only a single attribute. Assuming that there will not be more than 20 customers in the system at any one time, that is, MNTRY = 20, the minimum dimension of NSET/QSET is given by $20*(1 + 4) = 100$. Thus, the main program depicted in Figure 7-6 (page 232) assigns more than a sufficient amount of file storage area to simulate this problem.

The initialization logic for the bank teller problem is coded in subroutine INTLC as depicted in Figure 7-8. The user-defined variable BUSY is equivalenced to the SLAM variable XX(1) which is contained in the SLAM named COMMON block SCOM1 included in the subroutine. The variable BUSY is set to zero to denote that the teller is initially idle. Next, the customer arrival event which has an event code of 1 is scheduled onto the event calendar to occur after 0.0 time units. No attribute values are associated with this scheduled arrival event. However, FORTRAN convention requires that all arguments for a subroutine be included when the subroutine is called. Thus, ATRIB is used as the third argument in the call to SCHDL.

The logic for the customer arrival event is coded in subroutine ARVL and is presented in Figure 7-9. The values of the SLAM discrete event variables are passed to the event routine through COMMON block SCOM1 and the SLAM variable

```
SUBROUTINE INTLC
COMMON/SCOM1/ ATRIB(100),DD(100),DDL(100),DTNOW,II,MFA,MSTOP,NCLNR
1,NCRDR,NPRNT,NNRUN,NNSET,NTAPE,SS(100),SSL(100),TNEXT,TNOW,XX(100)
EQUIVALENCE (XX(1),BUSY)
BUSY=0.
CALL SCHDL(1,0.,ATRIB)
RETURN
END
```

Figure 7-8 Subroutine INTLC for bank teller problem.

XX(1) is equivalenced to the user defined variable BUSY. The first function performed by the event is the rescheduling of the next arrival event to occur at the
current time plus a sample from an exponential distribution with mean of 20. and
using random stream number 1. The first attribute of the current customer is then
set equal to the arrival time, TNOW, of the customer to the system. A test is then
made on the variable BUSY to determine the current status of the teller. If BUSY
is equal to 0.0, then the teller is idle and a branch is made to statement 10 where
BUSY is set to 1. to indicate that the teller is busy and the end-of-service event is
scheduled to occur at time TNOW plus a sample from a uniform distribution between 10. and 25. using random stream number 1. Otherwise, the customer is
placed in file 1 to wait for the teller. In either case, the customer is identified by
his arrival time which is stored as attribute 1 in the entry placed in file 1 or on the
event calendar (file NCLNR).

The logic for the end-of-service event is coded as event code 2 in subroutine
ENDSV depicted in Figure 7-10. The variable TSYS is set equal to the current
time, TNOW, minus the first attribute of the current customer being processed.
When an event is removed from the event calendar, the ATRIB buffer array is
assigned the attribute values that were associated with the event when it was
scheduled. Since the value of ATRIB(1) for this customer was set to TNOW in
the arrival event, the value of TSYS represents the elapsed time between the arrival and end-of-service event for this customer. A call is then made to subroutine

```
    SUBROUTINE ARVL
    COMMON/SCOM1/ ATRIB(100),DD(100),DDL(100),DTNOW,II,MFA,MSTOP,NCLNR
   1,NCRDR,NPRNT,NNRUN,NNSET,NTAPE,SS(100),SSL(100),TNEXT,TNOW,XX(100)
    EQUIVALENCE (XX(1),BUSY)
    CALL SCHDL(1,EXPON(20.,1),ATRIB)
    ATRIB(1)=TNOW
    IF(BUSY.EQ.0.) GO TO 10
    CALL FILEM(1,ATRIB)
    RETURN
 10 BUSY=1.
    CALL SCHDL(2,UNFRM(10.,25.,1),ATRIB)
    RETURN
    END
```

Figure 7-9 Subroutine ARVL for bank teller problem.

```
      SUBROUTINE ENDSV
      COMMON/SCOM1/ ATRIB(100),DD(100),DDL(100),DTNOW,II,MFA,MSTOP,NCLNR
     1,NCRDR,NPRNT,NNRUN,NNSET,NTAPE,SS(100),SSL(100),TNEXT,TNOW,XX(100)
      EQUIVALENCE (XX(1),BUSY)
      TSYS=TNOW-ATRIB(1)
      CALL COLCT(TSYS,1)
      IF(NNQ(1).GT.0) GO TO 10
      BUSY=0.
      RETURN
   10 CALL RMOVE(1,1,ATRIB)
      CALL SCHDL(2,UNFRM(10.,25.,1),ATRIB)
      RETURN
      END
```

Figure 7-10   Subroutine ENDSV for bank teller problem.

COLCT to collect statistics on the value of TSYS as collect variable number 1. A test is made on the SLAM function NNQ(1) representing the number of customers waiting for service in file 1. If the number of customers waiting is greater than zero, a transfer is made to statement 10 where the first customer waiting is removed from file 1 and placed onto the event calendar. The end-of-service event is scheduled to occur at time TNOW plus the service time. If no customer is waiting, the status of the teller is changed to idle by setting the variable BUSY to 0.

The input statements for this example are shown in Figure 7-11. The GEN statement specifies the analyst's name, project title, date, and number of runs. The LIMITS statement specifies that the model employs 1 file (not including the event calendar), the maximum number of attributes is 1, and the maximum number of simultaneous entries in the system is 20. The STAT statement specifies that collect variable number 1 is to be displayed with the label TIME IN SYSTEM and that a histogram is to be generated with 10 interior cells, the upper limit of the first cell is to be 0, and the cell width of each interior cell is to be 4. The TIMST statement causes time-persistent statistics to be automatically maintained on the SLAM variable XX(1) and the results to be displayed using the label UTILIZATION. The INIT statement specifies that the beginning time of the simulation is time 0 and that the ending time is time 480. The FIN statement denotes the end to all SLAM input statements. This completes the description of the discrete event model of the bank teller system.

Although the coding of the bank teller problem is relatively simple, it illustrates the general approach of combining SLAM functional capabilities to code discrete

```
            GEN,C. D. PEGDEN,BANK TELLER,11/20/77,1;
            LIMITS,1,1,20;
            STAT,1,TIME IN SYSTEM,10/0/4;
            TIMST,XX(1),UTILIZATION;
            INIT,0,480;
            FIN;
```

Figure 7-11   Data statements for bank teller problem.

event simulation models. Larger and more complicated models are developed in the same way and differ only in the number and complexity of the event subroutines. In the next sections, we present two additional discrete event examples which are slightly more complicated and further illustrate discrete event modeling using SLAM.

7.12 EXAMPLES OF DISCRETE EVENT MODELS

In the introduction to this chapter, we noted that in some cases the network approach lacks the flexibility needed to model a system of interest. In such cases, the discrete event orientation of SLAM provides the user with the needed flexibility by providing a framework where the user has access to the complete programming power of FORTRAN in combination with the SLAM subprograms for performing the commonly encountered simulation functions. The two example problems presented in this chapter illustrate the flexibility afforded by the discrete event modeling framework. The first example is a simulation of a two lane drive-in bank where cars can jockey between lanes. The second example is a simulation of the operation of a discount store.

7.13 Example 7-1. DRIVE-IN BANK WITH JOCKEYING

A drive-in bank has two windows, each manned by a teller and each has a separate drive-in lane. The drive-in lanes are adjacent. From previous observations, it has been determined that the time interval between customer arrivals during rush hours is exponentially distributed with a mean time between arrivals of 0.5 time units. Congestion occurs only during rush hours, and only this period is to be analyzed. The service time is normally distributed for each teller with a mean service time of one time unit and a standard deviation of 0.3 time units. It has also been shown that customers have a preference for lane 1 if neither teller is busy or if the waiting lines are equal. At all other times, however, a customer chooses the shortest line. After a customer has entered the system, he may not leave until he is serviced. However, he may change lanes if he is the last customer in his lane and a difference of two customers exists between the two lanes. Because of parking space limitations, only three cars can wait in each lane. These cars, plus the car of the customer being serviced by each teller, allow a maximum of eight cars in the system. If the system is full when a customer arrives, he balks and is lost to the system.

The initial conditions are as follows:

1. Both drive-in tellers are busy. The initial service time for each teller is normally distributed with mean of one time unit and standard deivation of 0.3 time units.
2. The first customer is scheduled to arrive at 0.1 time units.
3. Two customers are waiting in each queue.

The objective is to develop a simulation model that can be used to analyze the banking situation in terms of the following statistics:

1. Teller utilization $= \dfrac{\text{total time performing service}}{\text{total simulation time}}$
2. Time-integrated average number of customers in the system.
3. Time between departures from the drive-in windows.
4. Average time a customer is in the system.
5. Average number of customers in each queue.
6. Percent of arriving customers who balk.
7. Number of times cars jockey.

The system is to be simulated for 1000 time units and an event trace is to be obtained for the first 10 time units.

Concepts Illustrated. This example illustrates the facility with which complex queueing problems can be analyzed by discrete event simulation using SLAM. Difficult aspects of a queueing situation, such as balking or jockeying, are simulated with little additional effort. This example also illustrates the use of the trace option for discrete event simulation models.

SLAM Model. The events used to model the banking system are: (1) customer arrival to the system (ARVL); and (2) end of service (ENDSV). Customers are modeled as entities with two attributes. The first attribute is used to record the arrival time of the customer to the system and is used to compute the time in the system for the customer. The second attribute is used when scheduling the end-of-service event and denotes the teller number from which the customer is obtaining service. A customer entity waiting for teller I is stored in file I where I = 1 or 2.

The following variables are employed in the simulation:

Variable	Definition	Initial Value
XX(I)	0 if teller I is idle	(1.,1.)
	1 if teller I is busy	
NBALK	Number of customers that balk	0
NCUST	Number of customers that arrive	6
NJOCK	Number of customers that jockey	0
TLAST	Time of last customer departure from the system	0.

```
        ┌─────────────────────┐
        │  Subroutine ARVL    )
        └─────────────────────┘
                  │
                  ▼
        ┌─────────────────────┐
        │ Cause next arrival  │
        │ Mark arrival time   │
        │ Increment NCUST     │
        └─────────────────────┘
                  │
                  ▼
              ╱ Is  ╲       Yes      ┌─────────────────────┐
             ╱ system ╲──────────────▶│  NBALK = NBALK + 1  │
             ╲  full  ╱               └─────────────────────┘
              ╲  ?  ╱                           │
                  │ No                          ▼
                  │                     (    Return    )
                  ▼
              ╱ Is  ╲        No      ┌─────────────────────┐
             ╱ a teller ╲────────────▶│ Set IFILE to index  │
             ╲  free   ╱              │ of shortest queue   │
              ╲  ?  ╱                 └─────────────────────┘
                  │ Yes                         │
                  ▼                             ▼
        ┌─────────────────────┐      ┌─────────────────────┐
        │ Set ITLR to idle    │      │ Place customer in   │
        │ teller number       │      │ file IFILE          │
        └─────────────────────┘      └─────────────────────┘
                  │                             │
                  ▼                             ▼
        ┌─────────────────────┐         (    Return    )
        │ ATRIB(2) = ITLR     │
        │ XX(ITLR) = 1        │
        │ Schedule end of     │
        │ service event       │
        └─────────────────────┘
                  │
                  ▼
          (    Return    )
```

Figure 7-12   Flowchart of arrival to bank event.

The main program and subroutine EVENT(I) are straightforward and are identical to the bank teller problem discussed in the previous section. Event code 1 signifies the customer arrival event and event code 2 signifies the end-of-service event.

Consider first the event "arrival at the bank" which is flow charted in Figure 7-12. The first function performed is to schedule the next arrival to occur at the current time plus the time between arrivals. The arrival time of the current customer is marked as the first attribute of the customer and the variable NCUST, denoting the number of customers arriving to the system, is incremented by 1. A test is then made on the number of waiting customers. If the system is full (6 customers waiting), the number of balking customers (NBALK) is increased by 1, and a return is made to the SLAM processor. Otherwise, a test is made to determine if a teller is free. If a teller is free, ITLR is set to the teller number of the first free teller, ATRIB(2) of the customer is set to ITLR, teller ITLR is set to busy, and an end-of-service event for the customer is scheduled. If neither teller is idle, the customer is placed in file 1 or file 2 based on which file has the smaller number in it.

The coding for subroutine ARVL is depicted in Figure 7-13 and follows directly from the flowchart. Note that separate random number streams have been employed

```
      SUBROUTINE ARVL
      COMMON/SCOM1/ ATRIB(100),DD(100),DDL(100),DTNOW,II,MFA,MSTOP,NCLNR
     1,NCRDR,NPRNT,NNRUN,NNSET,NTAPE,SS(100),SSL(100),TNEXT,TNOW,XX(100)
      COMMON/UCOM1/ NBALK,NCUST,NJOCK,TLAST
C*****CAUSE NEXT ARRIVAL,MARK ARRIVAL TIME, AND INCREMENT NCUST
      CALL SCHDL(1,EXPON(.5,1),ATRIB)
      ATRIB(1)=TNOW
      NCUST=NCUST+1
C*****IF THE SYSTEM IS FULL
      IF(NNQ(1)+NNQ(2).LT.6) GO TO 10
C*****THEN BALK
      NBALK=NBALK+1
      RETURN
C*****OTHERWISE IF A TELLER IS FREE
   10 IF(XX(1)+XX(2).GT.1.0) GO TO 20
C*****THEN SET ITLR TO FIRST FREE TELLER
      ITLR=1
      IF(XX(1).EQ.1.) ITLR=2
C*****AND SET TELLER TO BUSY,SCHEDULE END OF SERVICE, AND RETURN
      XX(ITLR)=1.
      ATRIB(2)=ITLR
      CALL SCHDL(2,RNORM(1.,0.3,2),ATRIB)
      RETURN
C*****ELSE PLACE CUSTOMER IN SHORTEST LINE
   20 IFILE=1
      IF(NNQ(1).GT.NNQ(2)) IFILE=2
      CALL FILEM(IFILE,ATRIB)
      RETURN
      END
```

Figure 7-13 Subroutine ARVL for 2 lane drive-in bank.

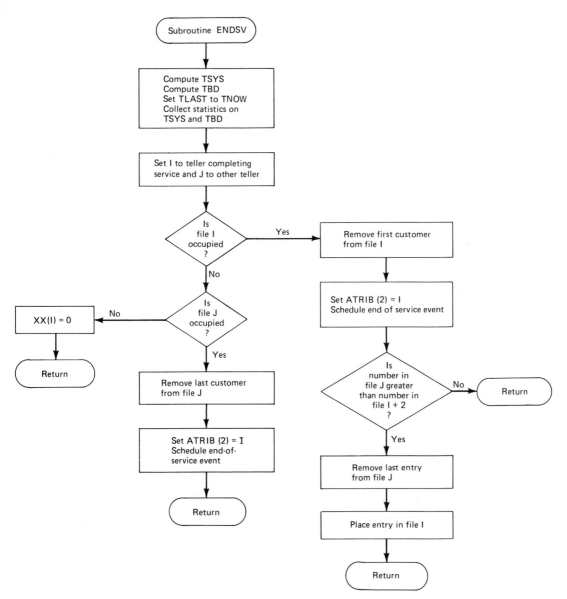

Figure 7-14 Flowchart of end-of-service event.

for obtaining interarrival times and service times. This is normally a good practice since it allows the arrival time sequence to be kept fixed and different service time sequences to be evaluated or vice versa.

The flowchart for the end-of-service event is given in Figure 7-14. The time in the system, TSYS, for the current customer is calculated as TNOW − ATRIB(1)

```
      SUBROUTINE ENDSV
      COMMON/SCOM1/ ATRIB(100),DD(100),DDL(100),DTNOW,II,MFA,MSTOP,NCLNR
     1,NCRDR,NPRNT,NNRUN,NNSET,NTAPE,SS(100),SSL(100),TNEXT,TNOW,XX(100)
      COMMON/UCOM1/ NBALK,NCUST,NJOCK,TLAST
C****COLLECT STATISTICS ON DEPARTING CUSTOMERS
      TSYS=TNOW-ATRIB(1)
      TBD =TNOW-TLAST
      TLAST=TNOW
      CALL COLCT(TSYS,1)
      CALL COLCT(TBD,2)
C****SET I TO TELLER ENDING SERVICE, J TO OTHER TELLER
      I=ATRIB(2)
      J=1
      IF(I.EQ.1) J=2
C****TEST NUMBER OF WAITING CUSTOMERS
      IF(NNQ(I).GT.0) GO TO 20
      IF(NNQ(J).GT.0) GO TO 10
C****BOTH LANES ARE EMPTY,THEREFORE SET TELLER I TO IDLE AND RETURN
      XX(I)=0.
      RETURN
C****LANE I IS EMPTY AND LANE J IS OCCUPIED, THEREFORE JOCKEY J TO I
   10 CALL RMOVE(NNQ(J),J,ATRIB)
      ATRIB(2)=I
      CALL SCHDL(2,RNORM(1.,0.3,2),ATRIB)
      NJOCK=NJOCK+1
      RETURN
C****LANE I IS OCCUPIED, THEREFORE PROCESS THE FIRST CUSTOMER IN LANE I
   20 CALL RMOVE(1,I,ATRIB)
      ATRIB(2)=I
      CALL SCHDL(2,RNORM(1.,0.3,2),ATRIB)
C****IF THE NUMBER IN LANE J EXCEEDS THE NUMBER IN LANE I BY TWO
      IF(NNQ(J).LT.NNQ(I)+2) RETURN
C****THEN JOCKEY LAST CUSTOMER IN LANE J TO LANE I
      CALL RMOVE(NNQ(J),J,ATRIB)
      CALL FILEM(I,ATRIB)
      NJOCK=NJOCK+1
      RETURN
      END
```

Figure 7-15   Subroutine ENDSV for 2 lane drive-in bank.

and the time between departures, TBD, is calculated as TNOW − TLAST. The variable TLAST is then updated to TNOW and statistics are collected on TSYS and TBD. The variable I is then set equal to ATRIB(2) which contains the teller number completing service. The variable J is set equal to the index of the other teller. A test is made on the number of customers in file I. If the file is occupied, the first waiting customer in file I is removed, ATRIB(2) for that customer is set equal to I, and the end-of-service event is scheduled. Since the number of customers in file I has been reduced by 1, a comparison between file lengths is made to test for a jockey from file J to file I. If a jockey condition exists, the last customer is removed from file J and placed in file I. In either case, control is returned to SLAM.

If file I is empty, a test is made on the number of customers in file J. If file J is also empty then there are no waiting customers in either lane and teller I is set to idle and control is returned to SLAM. If file J is not empty, the last customer

```
      SUBROUTINE INTLC
      COMMON/SCOM1/ ATRIB(100),DD(100),DDL(100),DTNOW,II,MFA,MSTOP,NCLNR
     1,NCRDR,NPRNT,NNRUN,NNSET,NTAPE,SS(100),SSL(100),TNEXT,TNOW,XX(100)
      COMMON/UCOM1/ NBALK,NCUST,NJOCK,TLAST
      ATRIB(1)=0.
      DO 10 K=1,2
      XX(K)=1.
      ATRIB(2)=K
      CALL SCHDL(2,RNORM(1.,0.3,2),ATRIB)
      CALL FILEM(K,ATRIB)
   10 CALL FILEM(K,ATRIB)
      CALL SCHDL(1,.1,ATRIB)
      RETURN
      END
```

Figure 7-16   Subroutine INTLC for 2 lane drive-in bank.

in file J is removed and is placed immediately into service by teller I and control is returned to SLAM.

The coding for the end-of-service event follows directly from the flow chart and is shown in Figure 7-15.

The initial conditions for the simulation are established in subroutine INTLC which is given in Figure 7-16. Both tellers are set to busy and an end-of-service event is scheduled for each teller. Two customers are placed in both file 1 and file 2 and the first arrival event is scheduled to occur at time 0.1.

Subroutine OTPUT is employed in this example to obtain the specialized output required in the problem statement. This subroutine is presented in Figure 7-17. The subroutine prints the number of arriving customers, the percent of customers that balked, and the number of customers that jockeyed during the simulation.

The input statements for this problem are shown in Figure 7-18. The GEN statement specifies the analyst's name, project title, date, and number of runs. This is followed by the LIMITS statement which specifies that two user files are employed, the number of attributes per entry is 2, and at most 10 entries are expected in the file storage area at any one time. The STAT statements are required to define the alphanumeric identifier associated with each variable type for which statistics based on observations are collected by subroutine COLCT. The TIMST statements are used to specify to the SLAM processor that time-persistent statistics are to be

```
      SUBROUTINE OTPUT
      COMMON/SCOM1/ ATRIB(100),DD(100),DDL(100),DTNOW,II,MFA,MSTOP,NCLNR
     1,NCRDR,NPRNT,NNRUN,NNSET,NTAPE,SS(100),SSL(100),TNEXT,TNOW,XX(100)
      COMMON/UCOM1/ NBALK,NCUST,NJOCK,TLAST
      PBALK=100.*FLOAT(NBALK)/FLOAT(NCUST)
      WRITE(NPRNT,10) NCUST,PBALK,NJOCK
   10 FORMAT(//35X,30HNUMBER OF ARRIVING CUSTOMERS =,I8,/35X,30HPERCENT
     1OF CUSTOMERS BALKING =,F8.5,/35X,19HNUMBER OF JOCKEYS =,11X,I8)
      RETURN
      END
```

Figure 7-17   Subroutine OTPUT for 2 lane drive-in bank.

```
GEN,C. D. PEGDEN,TWO LANE BANK,10/25/77,1;
LIMITS,2,2,10;
STAT,1,TIME IN SYSTEM;
STAT,2,TIME BET. DEPART;
TIMST,XX(1),TELLER 1 UTIL;
TIMST,XX(2),TELLER 2 UTIL;
INIT,0,1000;
MONTR,TRACE,0,10,1,2;
FIN;
```

Figure 7-18 Input statements for discrete event model of drive-in bank.

accumulated on variables $XX(1)$ and $XX(2)$ which represent the utilization of teller 1 and teller 2, respectively. The INITIALIZE statement specifies that the simulation is to begin at time 0.0 and to end at time 1000. This is followed by the MONTR statement which causes the trace to begin at time 0. and to end at time 10. The FIN statement denotes an end to all input statements and causes execution of the simulation to begin.

Summary of Results. The results for this example are summarized by the SLAM Summary Report shown in Figure 7-19. Statistics for variables based on observa-

```
                  S L A M   S U M M A R Y   R E P O R T


          SIMULATION PROJECT TWO LANE BANK          BY C. D. PEGDEN

          DATE 10/25/1977                           RUN NUMBER    1 OF    1


          CURRENT TIME        .1000+04
          STATISTICAL ARRAYS CLEARED AT TIME      .0000
```

STATISTICS FOR VARIABLES BASED ON OBSERVATION

	MEAN VALUE	STANDARD DEVIATION	COEFF. OF VARIATION	MINIMUM VALUE	MAXIMUM VALUE	NUMBER OF OBSERVATIONS
TIME IN SYSTEM	.2381+01	.1020+01	.4282+00	.2352+00	.5211+01	1847
TIME BET. DEPART	.5413+00	.3665+00	.6771+00	.0000	.3503+01	1847

STATISTICS FOR TIME-PERSISTENT VARIABLES

	MEAN VALUE	STANDARD DEVIATION	MINIMUM VALUE	MAXIMUM VALUE	TIME INTERVAL	CURRENT VALUE
TELLER 1 UTIL	.9413+00	.2351+00	.0000	.1000+01	.1000+04	.1000+01
TELLER 2 UTIL	.9062+00	.2915+00	.0000	.1000+01	.1000+04	.1000+01

FILE STATISTICS

FILE NUMBER	ASSOCIATED NODE TYPE	AVERAGE LENGTH	STANDARD DEVIATION	MAXIMUM LENGTH	CURRENT LENGTH	AVERAGE WAITING TIME
1		1.3755	1.0641	3	2	1.3433
2		1.1846	.9978	3	1	1.5546

Figure 7-19 SLAM summary report for discrete event model of drive-in bank.

tions are given first with the identifiers specified on the STAT input statements. For this example, observation statistics were collected on the time in the system for each customer and the time between departures of customers. From the summary report, it is seen that 1847 customers were served and the average time in the system was 2.381 minutes. Also customers leave the bank every 0.54 minutes on the average.

The second category of statistics for this example is the statistics for time-persistent variables. The results show that teller 1 was busy 94.13 percent of the time while teller 2 was busy 90.62 percent of the time. The slightly higher utilization of teller 1 results because of the preference by customers for teller 1 if both tellers are idle or if the waiting lines are equal.

The final category of statistics relate to the number of customers waiting in line for teller 1 and teller 2, respectively. The results show that there was an average of 1.3755 customers waiting in file 1 for service by teller 1 and an average of 1.1846 customers waiting in file 2 for service by teller 2. The slightly longer length of the waiting line for teller 1 as compared to teller 2 is because of the preference by customers for teller 1 when both waiting lines are equal. This information could be used by bank management for assigning tellers to windows.

Subroutine OTPUT was employed in this example to provide specialized output not provided by the SLAM Summary Report. Recall that subroutine OTPUT is called by the SLAM processor at the end of each simulation run prior to the printing of the SLAM Summary Report. The information printed by subroutine OTPUT is as follows:

```
NUMBER OF ARRIVING CUSTOMERS = 2007
PERCENT OF CUSTOMERS BALKING  =    8.02
NUMBER OF JOCKEYS             =  260
```

The output shows that 2007 customers sought service from the bank during the 1000 simulated time units of operation of which 8.02 percent or 165 balked because the system was full when they arrived. Since 1847 were processed, and 2 are in service and 3 are waiting, this accounts for all 2007 arrivals. There was a total of 260 lane changes during the simulation. Since over 10 percent of the customers are changing lanes, it may be desirable to install dividers or distractions (such as television sets) to eliminate jockeying. This assumes jockeying may be anxiety producing and possibly dangerous.

The SLAM trace report as requested for this simulation by use of the MONTR card with the TRACE option is shown in Figure 7-20. The trace report details the event time, the event code, and the attributes of the event for each event that is executed during the trace period. It depicts the operation of the model and should be used for verifying program operation and for communicating model and system characteristics.

```
                    SLAM TRACE BEGINNING AT TNOW=    .0000

-----------------------------------------------------------------------------
                      NODE ARRIVAL
       TNOW    JEVNT  -----------                 CURRENT ATTRIBUTE BUFFER
                      LABEL   TYPE                 -----------------------
                                    ATTRIBUTE :   1               2
-----------------------------------------------------------------------------

      .1000+00    1                      .0000      .2000+01
      .1024+00    1                      .0000      .2000+01
      .1385+01    2                      .0000      .1000+01
      .1464+01    2                      .0000      .2000+01
      .1756+01    1                      .0000      .2000+01
      .1896+01    1                      .0000      .2000+01
      .2102+01    2                      .0000      .2000+01
      .2218+01    1                      .0000      .2000+01
      .2300+01    1                      .0000      .2000+01
      .2702+01    2                      .0000      .1000+01
      .2775+01    1                      .0000      .2000+01
      .2818+01    1                      .0000      .2000+01
      .3056+01    2                      .0000      .2000+01
      .3540+01    2                      .0000      .1000+01
      .3773+01    1                      .0000      .2000+01
      .4041+01    1                      .0000      .2000+01
      .4445+01    1                      .0000      .2000+01
      .4490+01    1                      .0000      .2000+01
      .4499+01    2                    .1000+00     .1000+01
      .4648+01    2                    .1024+00     .2000+01
      .4651+01    1                      .0000      .2000+01
      .4691+01    1                      .0000      .2000+01
      .4927+01    1                      .0000      .2000+01
      .5115+01    1                      .0000      .2000+01
      .5120+01    2                    .1756+01     .1000+01
      .5426+01    1                      .0000      .2000+01
      .5656+01    2                    .2775+01     .1000+01
      .5803+01    1                      .0000      .2000+01
      .5867+01    1                      .0000      .2000+01
      .6043+01    2                    .1896+01     .2000+01
      .6268+01    1                      .0000      .2000+01
      .6585+01    1                      .0000      .2000+01
      .6696+01    2                    .3773+01     .1000+01
      .6875+01    2                    .2218+01     .2000+01
      .6956+01    1                      .0000      .2000+01
      .6973+01    1                      .0000      .2000+01
      .7281+01    2                    .4651+01     .1000+01
      .7401+01    1                      .0000      .2000+01
      .7673+01    1                      .0000      .2000+01
      .7878+01    2                    .4041+01     .2000+01
      .7945+01    1                      .0000      .2000+01
      .8131+01    1                      .0000      .2000+01
      .8382+01    1                      .0000      .2000+01
      .8540+01    1                      .0000      .2000+01
      .8609+01    2                    .5426+01     .1000+01
      .8827+01    1                      .0000      .2000+01
      .9269+01    2                    .5803+01     .1000+01
      .9319+01    2                    .4691+01     .2000+01
      .9801+01    1                      .0000      .2000+01
      .1000+02          END OF TRACE
```

Figure 7-20   Trace report for discrete event model of drive-in bank.

7.14   Example 7-2.   SIMULATION OF A DISCOUNT STORE OPERATION

A discount store has developed a new procedure for serving customers. Customers enter the store and determine the item they wish to purchase by examining display items. After selecting an item, the customer proceeds to a centralized area where he is served by a clerk who must travel to an adjacent warehouse to pick up the item. Clerks will service as many as six customers at a time. The time for the clerk to travel to the warehouse is uniformly distributed between 0.5 and 1.5 minutes. The time to find an item depends on the number of items the clerk must locate in the warehouse. This time is normally distributed with a mean equal to three times the number of items to be picked up. The standard deviation is equal to 0.2 of the mean. Thus, if one item is to be obtained from the warehouse, the time to locate the item is normally distributed with a mean of 3 and a standard deviation of 0.6 minutes. The time to return from the warehouse is uniformly distributed within the range of 0.5 and 1.5 minutes. When the clerk returns from the warehouse, he completes the sale for each customer that he is serving. The time to complete the sale is uniformly distributed between 1 and 3 minutes. The completion of sales for the customers is performed sequentially in the same order that requests for items were made of the clerk. The time between customer requests for items is assumed to be exponentially distributed with the mean of 2 minutes. Three clerks are available to serve the customers. A schematic diagram of the store operation is shown in Figure 7-21.

The objective of this simulation is to determine the utilization of the clerks, the time required to serve a customer from the point at which he requests an item until the completion of a sale, and the number of requests handled by a clerk for each trip to the warehouse. The simulation is to be run for 1000 minutes.

Concepts Illustrated.   This example illustrates the use of a user-defined array for filing and removing the attributes of an entity.

SLAM Model.   The discrete event model for this example consists of a customer arrival event and an end-of-service event. At first glance, it may also appear that

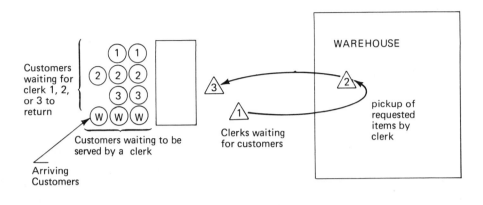

Legend:

$\triangle i$ clerk i, i = 1, 2, 3

$\bigcirc i$ customer being served
by clerk i, i = 1, 2, 3 or
waiting for a clerk, i = w

Figure 7-21 Schematic diagram of discount store operation.

events are required to explicitly model the clerk arrival and departure from the warehouse. However, no specific interactions occur during the time that the clerk is filling a request, and therefore the explicit modeling of these intermediate points by event routines is not necessary. If competition for resources were involved in filling the requests, then a more detailed model of the procedure for locating items would be required. Such a situation would exist if resources were required in the warehouse, say for example, a forklift.

There are five files employed in this example. The first four files are employed for storing the attributes of entities representing customers. Customers which arrive to the system when all clerks are busy are stored in file 4. Customers which have placed their orders and are waiting for clerk number 1, 2, or 3 to return reside in files 1, 2, and 3, respectively. File 5 is employed for storing the attributes of entities representing free clerks waiting for customers to arrive. The ATRIB buffer array is utilized for filing and removing customers from the first four files and the user-defined array CLERK is employed for filing and removing clerks from file 5. There is one attribute associated with the customer entities which is used to record the arrival time of the customer to the system. There is also one attribute associated with the clerk entities and it is used to denote the clerk number as 1, 2, or 3. Since a user-defined attribute buffer array must be dimensioned to at least 2 greater than MATR, the variable CLERK is dimensioned to 3.

The customer arrival event is assigned event code 1 and is coded in subroutine ARVL. The end-of-service event is assigned event code 2 and is coded in subroutine ENDSV. Subroutine EVENT(I) for this example is shown in Figure 7-22. It maps the event code onto the appropriate subroutine call.

```
      SUBROUTINE EVENT(I)
      GO TO (1,2),I
    1 CALL ARVL
      RETURN
    2 CALL ENDSV
      RETURN
      END
```

Figure 7-22   Sample subroutine EVENT(I).

First, consider the logic associated with the customer arrival event. A flowchart for this event is depicted in Figure 7-23, and the coding is shown in Figure 7-24. Before processing the current arrival, the next arrival is scheduled to occur after an exponential time delay with a mean of 2 minutes by a call to subroutine SCHDL. The arrival time of the current customer is then recorded as ATRIB(1) of the entity. The disposition of the current customer request is determined based on the status of the clerks. A test is made on the number of free clerks waiting in file 5. If file 5 is empty, the customer must wait until a clerk becomes free. File 4 is used to store customers waiting for clerks. If the customer must wait, no further functions can be performed at the arrival event time and a return is made.

If a clerk is available, the order processing can be initiated. The first free clerk is removed from file 5 which causes the attributes of the clerk to be loaded into the array CLERK. The user variable ICLRK is then set to the first attribute of the clerk which corresponds to the clerk number. The attributes of the current customer which are stored in the array ATRIB are then inserted into file ICLRK to wait for the return and end-of-service processing by clerk number ICLRK. Statistics are collected on the number of customers being served per clerk, which in this case is one. The statistics code for this collect variable is set as 2. The total time spent in traveling to the warehouse, in filing customer requests, returning from the warehouse, and completing the order is then computed as the variable DT. The end-of-service event is then scheduled to occur DT minutes later with the attributes of the clerk associated with the event. A return to SLAM is then made.

Next, consider the logic for the end-of-service event. A flowchart for this event is given in Figure 7-25 and the SLAM coding is shown in Figure 7-26. The attributes associated with the event are passed by SLAM to the event routine in the ATRIB buffer array. Since both clerk and customer attributes will be used in

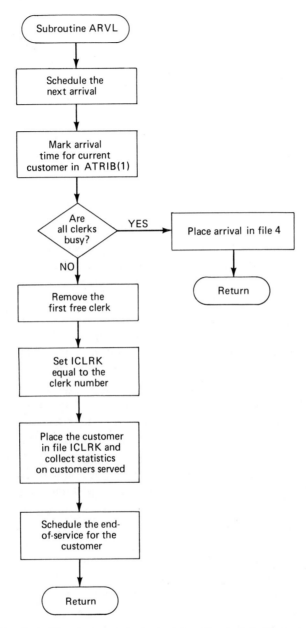

Figure 7-23   Flowchart of customer arrival event for discount store example.

this subroutine, the ATRIB buffer is copied into the user-defined array CLERK. The user variable ICLRK is then set to CLERK(1) and denotes the number of the clerk processing the end-of-service for the customer. The customer completing

```
      SUBROUTINE ARVL
      COMMON/SCOM1/ ATRIB(100),DD(100),DDL(100),DTNOW,II,MFA,MSTOP,NCLNR
     1,NCRDR,NPRNT,NNRUN,NNSET,NTAPE,SS(100),SSL(100),TNEXT,TNOW,XX(100)
      DIMENSION CLERK(3)
C*****SCHEDULE NEXT ARRIVAL
      CALL SCHDL(1,EXPON(2.,1),ATRIB)
C*****MARK ARRIVAL TIME FOR CURRENT CUSTOMER
      ATRIB(1)=TNOW
C*****IF ALL CLERKS ARE BUSY
      IF(NNQ(5).GT.0) GO TO 10
C*****THEN PLACE ARRIVAL IN WAIT FILE AND RETURN
      CALL FILEM(4,ATRIB)
      RETURN
C*****ELSE REMOVE THE FIRST FREE CLERK
   10 CALL RMOVE(1,5,CLERK)
      ICLRK=CLERK(1)
C*****PLACE THE CUSTOMER IN FILE ICLRK AND COLLECT STATS ON NUMBER SERVED
      CALL FILEM(ICLRK,ATRIB)
      CALL COLCT(1.,2)
C*****AND SCHEDULE THE END OF SERVICE FOR THE CUSTOMER AND RETURN
      DT=UNFRM(.5,1.5,1)+RNORM(3.,.6,1)+UNFRM(.5,1.5,1)+UNFRM(1.,3.,1)
      CALL SCHDL(2,DT,CLERK)
      RETURN
      END
```

Figure 7-24 SLAM code for customer arrivals to discount store.

service is then removed from file ICLRK and its attributes are loaded by SLAM into the ATRIB buffer array. The time in the system for the customer is computed and statistics are collected on this value as collect variable number 1. A test is then made on the SLAM function NNQ(ICLRK) to determine if more customers remain. In NNQ(ICLRK) is greater than zero, the end-of-service event for the next customer is scheduled followed by a return. Otherwise, a test is made on NNQ(4) to determine if there are customers waiting to place their orders with a clerk. If customers are waiting, then the user variable NCUST is set to the number of customers to be processed and statistics are collected on this quantity as collect variable number 2. These customers are then removed from file 4 and inserted into file ICLRK to await end-of-service processing. The total time spent in traveling to the warehouse, in filling customer requests, returning from the warehouse, and completing the order for the first customer is then computed as variable DT. Note that the time to fill requests is obtained as a sample from a normal distribution with a mean XMN equal to the number of customers, NCUST, times 3. The standard deviation, STD, is two-tenths of the mean, that is, $STD = 0.2*XMN$. The end-of-service event for the first customer to be processed is then scheduled to occur DT minutes later, followed by a return. In the case where there are no customers waiting to place their orders, the attributes of the clerk are placed in file 5 which is the file used for storing free clerks.

Subroutine INTLC is used to put the three clerks into file 5 as it is assumed that all clerks are idle at the beginning of the simulation run. The first customer arrival event is scheduled to occur at time 0.0 by calling SCHDL with an event code of 1.

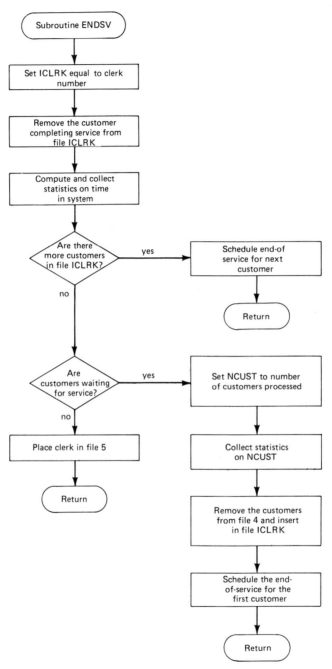

Figure 7-25 Flowchart of end-of-service event for discount store example.

```
      SUBROUTINE ENDSV
      COMMON/SCOM1/ ATRIB(100),DD(100),DDL(100),DTNOW,II,MFA,MSTOP,NCLNR
     1,NCRDR,NPRNT,NNRUN,NNSET,NTAPE,SS(100),SSL(100),TNEXT,TNOW,XX(100)
      DIMENSION CLERK(3)
      CLERK(1)=ATRIB(1)
C****REMOVE THE CUSTOMER COMPLETING SERVICE FROM THE WAIT FILE
      ICLRK=CLERK(1)
      CALL RMOVE(1,ICLRK,ATRIB)
C****COLLECT STATISTICS ON TIME IN SYSTEM
      TSYS=TNOW-ATRIB(1)
      CALL COLCT(TSYS,1)
C****IF MORE CUSTOMERS REMAIN IN THE WAIT FILE
      IF(NNQ(ICLRK).EQ.0) GO TO 10
C****THEN SCHEDULE THE END OF SERVICE FOR THE NEXT CUSTOMER AND RETURN
      CALL SCHDL(2,UNFRM(1.,3.,1),CLERK)
      RETURN
C****ELSE
   10 CONTINUE
C****IF CUSTOMERS ARE WAITING FOR SERVICE
      IF(NNQ(4).EQ.0) GO TO 30
C****THEN SERVICE UP TO SIX CUSTOMERS
      NCUST=NNQ(4)
      IF(NCUST.GT.6) NCUST=6
      XCUST=NCUST
      CALL COLCT(XCUST,2)
      DO 20 J=1,NCUST
      CALL RMOVE(1,4,ATRIB)
   20 CALL FILEM(ICLRK,ATRIB)
C****AND SCHEDULE THE END OF SERVICE FOR THE FIRST CUSTOMER AND RETURN
      XMN=NCUST*3
      STD=.2*XMN
      DT=UNFRM(.5,1.5,1)+RNORM(XMN,STD,1)+UNFRM(.5,1.5,1)+UNFRM(1.,3.,1)
      CALL SCHDL(2,DT,CLERK)
      RETURN
C****ELSE PLACE THE CLERK IN THE FILE OF FREE CLERKS AND RETURN
   30 CALL FILEM(5,CLERK)
      RETURN
      END
```

Figure 7-26 SLAM code for customer end-of-service event at discount store.

The listing of subroutine INTLC is given in Figure 7-27. The input statements for this example are shown in Figure 7-28.

Summary of Results. The SLAM Summary Report for this example is given in Figure 7-29. The report reveals that during the 1000 minutes of simulated operation, 494 customers were processed through the system with customers spending an average of 21.45 minutes in the system. The average number of requests handled by each clerk was 2.483 with a total of 205 trips completed by the clerks. These results indicate that management should investigate the hiring of additional clerks or change the policy regarding the minimum or maximum number of customers a clerk should serve at one time.

Although the average utilization of the clerks is not directly provided by the report, this statistic can be estimated using the average length of file 5. Since idle

```
      SUBROUTINE INTLC
      COMMON/SCOM1/ ATRIB(100),DD(100),DDL(100),DTNOW,II,MFA,MSTOP,NCLNR
     1,NCRDR,NPRNT,NNRUN,NNSET,NTAPE,SS(100),SSL(100),TNEXT,TNOW,XX(100)
      DIMENSION CLERK(3)
C*****ESTABLISH THREE CLERKS IN FILE 5
      DO 10 J=1,3
      CLERK(1)=J
   10 CALL FILEM(5,CLERK)
C*****SCHEDULE ARRIVAL EVENT AT TNOW AND RETURN
      CALL SCHDL(1,0.,ATRIB)
      RETURN
      END
```

Figure 7-27   Subroutine INTLC for discount store example.

```
      GEN,C. D. PEGDEN,DISCOUNT STORE,1/25/78,1;
      LIMITS,5,1,50;
      STAT,1,TIME IN SYSTEM
      STAT,2,NUM OF REQUEST;
      INIT,0,1000;
      FIN;
```

Figure 7-28   Input statements for discount store example.

clerks reside in file 5, the average number of busy clerks is the number of clerks minus the average number in file 5, that is, 2.912.

```
                    S L A M     S U M M A R Y     R E P O R T


       SIMULATION PROJECT DISCOUNT STORE              BY C. D. PEGDEN

       DATE   1/25/1978                               RUN NUMBER    1 OF    1


       CURRENT TIME      .1000+04
       STATISTICAL ARRAYS CLEARED AT TIME     .0000
```

STATISTICS FOR VARIABLES BASED ON OBSERVATION

	MEAN VALUE	STANDARD DEVIATION	COEFF. OF VARIATION	MINIMUM VALUE	MAXIMUM VALUE	NUMBER OF OBSERVATIONS
TIME IN SYSTEM	.2145+02	.1119+02	.5219+00	.4133+01	.5880+02	494
NUM OF REQUEST	.2483+01	.1725+01	.6948+00	.1000+01	.6000+01	205

FILE STATISTICS

FILE NUMBER	ASSOCIATED NODE TYPE	AVERAGE LENGTH	STANDARD DEVIATION	MAXIMUM LENGTH	CURRENT LENGTH	AVERAGE WAITING TIME
1		2.9761	1.8116	6	6	19.2007
2		2.9919	1.9633	6	3	18.8107
3		2.9214	1.8379	6	6	19.0943
4		2.1799	2.8007	16	13	5.8757
5		.0880	.3041	3	0	0.9074

Figure 7-29   SLAM summary report for discount store example.

7.15   CHAPTER SUMMARY

This chapter presents the SLAM discrete event simulation modeling procedures. The procedures for sampling from probability distributions, scheduling events, file manipulations, and statistical collection routines are described. A list of important discrete event variables is presented in Table 7-2. Only one additional input statement, STAT, is required. Two examples of discrete event modeling using SLAM are presented. The first deals with a two-server drive-in bank which has two queues, jockeying between queues, and balking from the system when it is full. The second example involves a discount store where clerks must go through multiple operations before completing service on customers.

The organization of a SLAM program for discrete event modeling is illustrated in Figure 7-30.

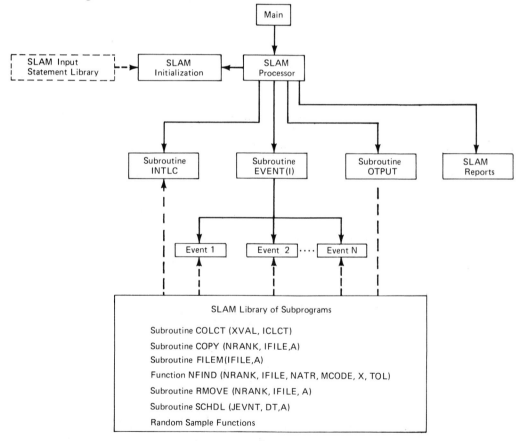

Figure 7-30   SLAM organization for discrete event modeling.

7.16   EXERCISES

7-1.   Simulate a single server queueing system where service is exponentially distributed with a mean service time of one hour and there are two types of arrivals. Arrival type 1 is an item of high priority and waits only for the processing of other high priority items. The time intervals between arrivals of high priority items is exponentially distributed with a mean time between arrivals of four hours. The time between arrivals of low priority items is also exponentially distributed, but has a mean time between arrivals of two hours. Obtain statistics regarding server utilization and information concerning the time in the system and in the queue for high and low priority items. Assume that service on low priority items is not interrupted to process high priority items.

Embellishment: Repeat the simulation with the assumption that high priority items interrupt the servicing of low priority items. Interrupted items are inserted at the beginning of the queue of low priority items. Show that the time remaining for those items interrupted is exponentially distributed with a mean time equal to the mean service time.

7-2.   Jobs arrive at a job shop so that the interarrival time is exponentially distributed with a mean time between arrivals of 1.25 hours. The time to process a job is uniformly distributed in the interval 0.75 to 1.25 hours. The time to process the jobs is estimated prior to the time the job is performed. Simulate the processing of jobs in the order of shortest processing time first. Obtain statistics describing the average time jobs are in the shop, the variation of the time the jobs are in the shop, and the utilization of the server. Assume that the *actual* processing times for the jobs are equal to the *estimates* of the processing times. Repeat the simulation with jobs with the longest processing time performed first. Then carry out the simulation with the jobs processed in order of their arrival time. Compare the results.

Embellishment: Repeat the simulation for a situation in which the actual processing time is equal to the estimated processing time plus a sample drawn from a normal distribution with a mean of zero and a standard deviation of 0.2.

7-3.   Build a discrete event model for the two work stations in series described in Example 6-1.

Embellishment: (a) Before subcontracting a unit, check the end-of-service times for the work stations. If the next end-of-service is within 0.1 hours of the current time, the unit is not subcontracted but returns to the work station in 0.2 hour.

(b) Redevelop the work station model under the assumption that the manufacturer only maintains 100 units. The time to failure for each unit is exponentially distributed with a mean of 40 hours. The time to repair a unit if subcontracted is triangularly distributed with a mode of 4, a minimum of 3, and a maximum of 6.

7-4.   Develop a discrete event simulation of the PERT network given in Example 6-8. Hint: The simulation of PERT networks involves a single event representing the end of an activity. Perform a simulation of the PERT network for 400 runs.

Embellishment: Estimate the probability that an activity is on the critical path in a run. This probability is referred to as a criticality index.

7-5.   Develop a discrete event model of the inventory situation presented in Example 6-5.

Embellishments: (a) Make the lead time for the receipt of orders lognormally distributed with a mean of 3 and standard deviation of 1.

(b) Include in the model information that each customer may demand more than one radio. The number of radios demanded per customer is Poisson distributed with a mean of 3. The minimum number of radios demanded is 1. Presume if there are insufficient radios to meet the total number of radios demanded by a customer, the entire order is backordered with probability 0.2.

(c) Convert the periodic review system to a transaction reporting system where the inventory position is reviewed after every sale or backorder.

(d) Make the mean time between customer demands a function of the number of lost sales and backorders. If the average number of lost sales and backorders per week is less than 1, the mean time between demands is 0.18 week. If the average number of lost sales and backorders is greater than 2, the mean time between demands is 0.22. Otherwise, the mean time between demands is 0.20.

(e) Add the following income and cost structure to the inventory situation. Radios sell for $65 and cost the store $40. An inventory carrying charge of $0.004 per dollar/week is used. The cost of placing an order for radios from the supplier is estimated to be $50. Each review of inventory costs $30. A lost sale results in a loss of goodwill and is estimated to cost $20. The cost for maintaining a backorder is $10. Run a simulation of this inventory situation for 312 weeks.

(f) Evaluate the effect of alternative inventory policies on average profit using the cost and income data provided in embellishment (e).

7-6.   Build a discrete event model for the conveyor situation described in Exercise 6-5.

7-7.   Embellish Example 7-1 by including a model of the departure process of cars into the street next to the bank. Cars departing from the bank tellers can enter the street when a large enough gap exists between cars traveling on the street. The time between such gaps is uniformly distributed between 0.3 and 0.5 minutes. The space following the tellers is only sufficient to allow 3 cars to wait for a gap in the street traffic.

7-8.   Embellishment to Example 7-2. Alter the discount store operation so that clerks wait for 1 minute before traveling to the warehouse to serve a single customer. Determine the effect of this new policy on customer waiting time and clerk utilization. Evaluate alternative time intervals for waiting for additional customers before traveling to the warehouse.

7-9.   Embellishment to Example 7-2. In a simulation of the discount store operation, it has been determined that there is a probability that the clerk will return from the warehouse with an incorrect item. When this occurs the clerk immediately returns to the warehouse to obtain the correct item. The probability of retrieving an incorrect item is 0.15. In addition, there is a probability of 0.1 that the item requested was not in inventory. When this occurs, there is a probability of 0.25 that the customer will request a new item. Evaluate the effect of this new information on clerk utilization and customer waiting time.

7-10.   For the network simulation of Exercise 7-4, determine the number of simulation runs that would be required to obtain a 95% probability that: (a) the estimate of the project duration is within 0.1 of a standard deviation of the theoretical project duration; (b) the estimate of the variance of the project duration is within 10% of the theoretical variance of the project duration; and (c) the difference between the observed and theoretical criticality indices is less than or equal to 0.005.

CHAPTER 8

Advanced Discrete Concepts
and Subprograms

271

8.1   INTRODUCTION

The procedures presented in Chapter 7 provide sufficient information to model complex systems using a discrete event approach. Many support routines can be added to SLAM to perform functions common to a variety of simulation models. In this chapter, we present those subprograms which we feel are of sufficient generality to be included in the standard version of SLAM. By including these functions in SLAM, standard names will be employed within simulation models and, thus, program readability will be enhanced. The addition of subprograms, of course, tends to increase the perceived complexity of the language. Herein lies the language developers' design tradeoff. Since SLAM is FORTRAN based, it is a relatively simple matter to add new functions to the language. We encourage such additions as they will keep the language growing and evolving. We also believe in a natural evolution and expect the survival of only those functions which make significant contributions to simulation modeling.

In this chapter, we present information on: additional file manipulation routines; auxiliary attribute subroutines; report writing subroutines; functions for accessing statistical quantities; and miscellaneous support routines. An example that uses some of these routines is presented at the end of this chapter.

8.2   ADDITIONAL FILE MANIPULATION ROUTINES

The primary function of the SLAM file storage array is to store entries, events and entities, with their associated attributes. Entries are stored in a single, one-dimensional array. By the use of an equivalence statement, EQUIVALENCE (NSET(1),QSET(1)), it is possible to use the same storage array for either real or integer type data. This technique permits entry pointers to be stored as integers, and entry attributes to be stored as reals. To simplify reference to the storage array in this text, the name NSET is used to denote the array when either name applies. Normally the array is not referenced directly by the SLAM user. However, if the user does reference an attribute value, the QSET variable must be used. If a pointer is referenced, the NSET variable must be used.

NSET is one dimensional and resides in unnamed (blank) COMMON. Because NSET resides in COMMON storage, it is accessible to the SLAM subroutines without having to be included as an argument in their calling sequence. Since NSET is in unnamed COMMON, the user can dimension NSET in the main program, and all subprograms can be precompiled with NSET dimensioned to one.

8.2.1   Functions for Accessing File and Entry Pointers: FUNCTIONS MMFE, MMLE, NPRED, and NSUCR

Entries in a file can be thought of as items on a list, customers in a queue, days on a calendar, and so forth. The entries stored in a file are considered by SLAM in a logical order, not a physical order. The first and second entries in a file are not necessarily stored next to one another. Their order in the file is maintained by a pointing system. Each entry potentially has a predecessor and successor entry in the file. Pointers are used to keep track of each entry's predecessor and successor. The pointers establish the location in NSET where the entries are stored. A zero value for a pointer indicates that either no predecessor or no successor exists.

Pointers in SLAM reference a location in the array NSET where the first word of an entry is stored. The number of words associated with an entry is known; hence all information about an entry can be obtained given the pointer to the starting location of the entry. The pointer to the first entry in file IFILE is obtained by using the function MMFE(IFILE). The function MMLE(IFILE) returns the pointer to the last entry in file IFILE. Thus, the statement NTRY=MMLE(3) defines NTRY as the location in NSET where the first piece of information concerning the last entry in file 3 is stored.

By knowing the pointer to the first entry and by accessing the successor of the first entry, we can obtain the pointer to the second entry. The function NSUCR (NTRY) is used to obtain the pointer to the location of the successor of NTRY. With this function it is possible to proceed in a forward direction from a particular entry in a file until the last entry is encountered. The last entry in a file has no successor and, hence, the function NSUCR would return a zero value when the successor of the last entry is requested. To search through a file from the last entry, MMLE(IFILE), to the first, the function NPRED(NTRY) is provided.

As an example of the use of these functions, consider the problem of locating an entry in file 4 whose second attribute is equal to seven. We desire to locate the entry that is closest to the beginning of the file. The code for accomplishing this search is shown below.

```
C****    SEARCH FILE 4 FROM THE BEGINNING FOR AN ENTRY
         NEXT = MMFE(4)
C****    IF NEXT .EQ. 0, THE SEARCH ENDS
   10    IF (NEXT .EQ. 0) RETURN
         CALL COPY (-NEXT,4,ATRIB)
         IF (ATRIB(2) .EQ. 7.0) GO TO 20
         NEXT = NSUCR(NEXT)
         GO TO 10
C****    AT STATEMENT 20, NEXT IS THE DESIRED ENTRY
   20    CONTINUE
```

In this code, the variable NEXT is used to indicate the next entry to be tested for the desired condition. We start with the first entry in file 4 because the search is to start from the beginning of the file. If NEXT = 0 then there are no entries in the file, as function MMFE returns a zero value when the file is empty.

The statement CALL COPY (−NEXT,4,ATRIB) causes the attributes of the entry whose pointer is NEXT to be copied into the ATRIB buffer. In this statement, the negative of the pointer to the location of the entry is used to notify subroutine COPY that a specific location is being passed to it rather than the rank of the entry in the file. As will be discussed later, if the variable used to indicate the rank of an entry has a negative value, the SLAM subprograms assume that it is a pointer to a location rather than the value of the rank in the file. Subroutine COPY loads the array given as the second argument with the attributes of the entry. In the next statement, the particular attribute number is tested against 7.0 to determine if the prescribed condition is met. If it is, a transfer to statement 20 is made as NEXT has been established as the pointer to the desired entry. If the condition was not met, the successor entry is obtained through the use of function NSUCR. A transfer to statement 10 is made to determine if a successor entry exists.

If it is desired to search file 4 from the end of the file then only minor changes are required in the code. The first entry to be tested is established as the last entry in the file, that is, NEXT = MMLE(4). In addition, it is necessary to obtain the next entry to be tested by using function NPRED, that is, NEXT = NPRED(NEXT).

8.2.2   The Availability File

The space in the file structure that is not used for storing entries can be considered as available locations for storing new entries. This, in essence, is an availability file which is maintained in SLAM as a linked list. The pointer to the first available space for storing an entry is maintained as the SLAM variable MFA. The second available space for storing an entry can be accessed by using the function NSUCR, that is, NMFA = NSUCR(MFA) where NMFA is the pointer to the location in NSET where the second entry to be filed will be stored. When subroutine FILEM is called, the entry to be filed is stored in NSET starting at location MFA. The value of MFA is then updated to its successor value. Through knowledge of MFA and its successor, the SLAM user can ascertain where entries are filed within the file structure. Thus, if two calls to subroutine FILEM are made in succession, the user can obtain the information as to where the second entry associated with the second call to FILEM will be stored. Whenever subroutine RMOVE is called, the value of MFA is updated to be equal to the entry that is removed from the file. The successor of this entry is the value of MFA prior to the call to subroutine RMOVE. In this way, the list of available locations for storing entries in the file is linked.

8.2.3   File Rank to Pointer Translation: FUNCTION LOCAT

Since SLAM allows the referencing of entries in files both by the pointer to the entry and by the rank of the entry, function LOCAT has been included for translating the rank of an entry to the pointer to the location of the entry. The arguments to LOCAT are an entry's rank and file number and, hence, we have: FUNCTION LOCAT(IRANK,IFILE). Thus to obtain the pointer for the entry that is ranked third in file 7, the following statement would be used

NTRY = LOCAT(3,7)

8.2.4   Using SLAM Routines With Pointer Values

As noted above, whenever a negative value is placed in a subroutine call where SLAM expects the rank of the entry in a file to be given, SLAM interprets the value as the negative of the pointer to the location of the entry. This feature pertains to the following subprograms: COPY, FILEM, NFIND, and RMOVE. With this convention either of the following two statements will remove the last entry in file 6 and place the attributes of the entry in the array A:

CALL RMOVE(NNQ(6),6,A)

or

CALL RMOVE(−MMLE(6),6,A)

8.2.5 Direct Accessing of Attributes

If the pointer to an entry in the array NSET/QSET is known, then a specified attribute can be accessed directly. The value of the Ith attribute of the entry with a pointer of NTRY is stored in the QSET array in location NTRY+I. Thus the second attribute of the first entry in file 1 can be directly accessed by using the statements NTRY = MMFE(1) and A2 = QSET(NTRY+2). In this way an attribute value can be examined or changed without the use of the SLAM filing subroutines. However, the ranking attribute of an entry should not be changed in this manner.

8.2.6 Entry Removal and Filing Without Attribute Copying: SUBROUTINES ULINK and LINK

An entry can be unlinked from other entries in a file without its attribute values being copied or deleted from NSET. The subroutine that provides this capability is subroutine ULINK(NRANK,IFILE). When subroutine ULINK is called, the value of MFA is updated but the attributes of the entry remain at the same location. The entry is no longer considered as a member of file IFILE. If the next file operation is a call to subroutine LINK(IFILE) then SLAM presumes that the attributes of the entry to be inserted into file IFILE are already located in NSET with a pointer value of MFA. As an example, consider the removal of the first entry in file 3 and the filing of this entry into file 2. The following statement accomplishes this without removing the attribute values from QSET:

CALL ULINK(1,3)
CALL LINK(2)

Since ULINK and LINK do not copy the attributes out of and into NSET/QSET, they execute faster than RMOVE and FILEM.

8.2.7   Two Standard Functions for File Attribute Computation

SLAM provides functions for obtaining the sum or product of one attribute value for each entry in a file. These functions are described below.

Function SUMQ(NATR,IFILE).   Occasionally it is desired to find the sum of all values of an attribute for each entry in a file. For example, if entries in a file represent jobs in a queue waiting for a machine with ATRIB(1) of each entry denoting the processing time for that job, it might be desired to find the total processing time for all jobs waiting in the queue. Function SUMQ(NATR,IFILE) provides this capability by returning SUMQ as the sum of all values of attribute number NATR currently in file IFILE. As an example of the use of function SUMQ, the following statement sets the variable TOTAL equal to the sum of all values of attribute 1 corresponding to the entries currently in file 4.

TOTAL = SUMQ(1,4)

Function PRODQ(NATR,IFILE).   Sometimes it is desired to find the product of all values of an attribute for each entry in a file. For example, if entries in a file represent parallel components in a system with the probability of failure of each entry given by ATRIB(3), then the probability that all components would fail would be the product of all values of ATRIB(3) in the file. Function PRODQ (NATR,IFILE) provides the capability for computing this product by returning PRODQ as the product of all values of attribute NATR currently in file IFILE. For example, the following statement would set the variable PFAIL to the product of all values of ATRIB(3) corresponding to the entries currently in file 2.

PFAIL = PRODQ(3,2)

8.2.8   Summary of File Manipulation Routines

A list of file manipulation functions is given in Table 8-1. It should be noted that a zero value is used as an indicator that no first or last entry exists and that an entry has no predecessor or successor. Also note that the following functional equivalents exist:

MMFE(IFILE) = LOCAT(1,IFILE)

and

MMLE(IFILE) = LOCAT(NNQ(IFILE),IFILE)

For the file processing routines, a positive argument is used to signify a rank value and a negative argument signifies a pointer.

Table 8-1   List of file manipulation subprograms.

FUNCTION	DESCRIPTION [†]
LOCAT (IRANK, IFILE)	Returns pointer to location of entry with rank IRANK in file IFILE
MMFE (IFILE)	Returns pointer to first entry (rank 1) in file IFILE
MMLE (IFILE)	Returns pointer to last entry (rank NNQ(IFILE)) in file IFILE
NNQ (IFILE)	Returns number of entries in file IFILE
NPRED (NTRY)	Returns pointer to the predecessor entry of the entry whose pointer is NTRY
NSUCR (NTRY)	Returns pointer to the successor entry of the entry whose pointer is NTRY
PRODQ (NATR, IFILE)	Returns the product of the values of attribute NATR for each current entry in file IFILE
SUMQ (NATR, IFILE)	Returns the sum of the values of attribute NATR for each current entry in file IFILE
SUBROUTINES	DESCRIPTION
LINK (IFILE)	Files entry whose attributes are stored in MFA in file IFILE
ULINK (NRANK, IFILE)	Removes entry with rank NRANK from file IFILE without copying its attribute values. If NRANK < 0, it is a pointer

[†] A pointer value of zero indicates that no entry exists that satisfies the desired function.

8.3   AUXILIARY ATTRIBUTES

It is sometimes desirable to augment the SLAM filing system with user-defined arrays that maintain attribute values associated with events and entities that are members of SLAM files.

Attributes associated with file entries that are not stored in the file array NSET are referred to as auxiliary attributes. Auxiliary attributes are used when one file has many more attributes than the other files or when entities flow through different files and it is convenient not to carry all the attributes along with the entity. For these situations, we provide subroutines to store and retrieve attributes in user-defined arrays and to identify the location where the auxiliary attributes are maintained in the user-defined array. The location is used as an attribute of the entity stored in NSET.

The subroutines for processing auxiliary attributes allow the user to employ different arrays for different sets of auxiliary attributes. In addition, the user can point to the same set of auxiliary attributes from different entries. In the next section, the definition of the subroutines are given. Following the definitions, examples of the use of the subroutines are presented.

8.3.1   Subroutines for Auxiliary Attributes

Four subroutines are available for storing and retrieving auxiliary attributes. These subroutines are:

SETAA: Sets up an array (defined by the user) that will maintain auxiliary attributes

PUTAA: Puts (files) a set of values of auxiliary attributes in an array

GETAA: Gets (removes) a set of auxiliary attributes and establishes a vector of the values of the auxiliary attributes

COPAA: Copies the values of a set of auxiliary attributes without removing the attribute values from the user's auxiliary storage array

Each of the above routines requires a set of arguments, and the definition of these arguments is given below. When calling a subroutine, the user substitutes his own variables for the ones defined below.

AUXF: A one-dimensional array defined by the user to store auxiliary attributes

MFAA: A pointer from which the location of the auxiliary attributes stored in AUXF can be determined. Specifically, AUXF(MFAA+I) will contain the value of the Ith auxiliary attribute

NAUXA: The number of auxiliary attributes associated with each entry in AUXF

NDAUX: The dimension of the auxiliary filing array AUXF

NTRYA: A pointer to an entry to be removed (GET) or copied

VALUE: A vector containing the values of the auxiliary attributes to be put into the auxiliary filing array AUXF or to be obtained from the auxiliary file AUXF

The subroutines described above can now be explicitly presented.

8.3.2   Subroutine SETAA(NAUXA,AUXF,MFAA,NDAUX)

This subroutine is used to establish a pointing structure in the array AUXF which has dimension NDAUX and for which each entry has NAUXA elements. MFAA is a pointer to a location in AUXF where the next group of auxiliary attributes will be stored.

8.3.3   Subroutine PUTAA(NAUXA,AUXF,MFAA,VALUE)

This subroutine puts the values stored in VALUE(I),I=1,NAUXA into the filing array AUXF(J) with J=MFAA+1,MFAA+2,...,MFAA+NAUXA. Prior to the call to subroutine PUTAA, the user should establish a pointer to the auxiliary attributes by storing the value of MFAA as an attribute of the entity to be filed in NSET. *PUTAA updates the value of MFAA automatically.*

8.3.4   Subroutine GETAA(NTRYA,NAUXA,AUXF,MFAA,VALUE)

This subroutine gets the values of the auxiliary attributes whose pointer is NTRYA and stores them in the vector VALUE(.) where VALUE(I)=AUXF (NTRYA+I) for I=1,NAUXA. The value of MFAA is then updated to be equal to NTRYA so that the storage space that was used in AUXF is available for storing a new set of auxiliary attributes.

8.3.5   Subroutine COPAA(NTRYA,NAUXA,AUXF,VALUE)

This subroutine copies the values of auxiliary attributes whose pointer is NTRYA into the vector VALUE(.) where VALUE(I)=AUXF(NTRYA+I),I=1,NAUXA. Subroutine COPAA does not change MFAA or the values stored in AUXF.

8.3.6   Example of the Use of Subroutines for Filing Auxiliary Attributes

Consider the situation where a SLAM file represents a queue for a machine group. If a job cannot gain access to a machine in a machine group, it is stored in the file of the machine group. If the job can be processed by the machine group, it is associated with an event representing an end of service for the machine group. Associated with each job is a routing which sends the job from machine group to machine group. Suppose there is a possibility that the routing consists of up to 10 machine group specifications and there can be as many as 100 jobs being processed simultaneously.

For this setup, it is desirable to store the routing for each job as auxiliary attributes where there can be as many as 10 auxiliary attributes associated with each job as it flows through the system. Since there can be 100 jobs in the system, we will need an auxiliary filing array that is dimensioned to 1,000. For this auxiliary filing array, we will make the following definitions: ROUTS(1000) is the filing array for storing routings of jobs; NROUTA is the number of auxiliary attributes associated with a routing and is set equal to 10; NDROUT is the dimension of the array ROUTS; MROUT is the pointer to the next available set of cells for storing a routing; NTRY is the pointer to the location where the routing for a job is stored.

In subroutine INTLC, the array ROUTS is established to store as many as 100 jobs, each of which has 10 auxiliary attributes, by a call to subroutine SETAA as shown below:

NROUTA = 10
NDROUT = 1000
CALL SETAA(NROUTA,ROUTS,MROUT,NDROUT)

This call sets up the array ROUTS for use in storing auxiliary attributes and establishes MROUT as equal to zero.

When a job arrives it is necessary to store its routing in the array ROUTS. Assume that the ten machine group numbers have been defined in the vector

ROUTE. Further assume that jobs are queued in files corresponding to the auxiliary attributes defining the routing of a job. When the job arrives, it will be sent to the first machine group number as defined by ROUTE(1). Let attribute 2 be the number of machine groups that the job has visited. Further presume that the job must wait at the machine group that is first in its routing. The following statement will accomplish the above.

```
ATRIB(1) = MROUT
ATRIB(2) = 1
MG = ROUTE(1)
CALL FILEM(MG,ATRIB)
CALL PUTAA(NROUTA,ROUTS,MROUT,ROUTE)
```

At a future time, this job is removed from file MG and an end-of-service event is established for it. The values of attributes 1 and 2 described in the above code will be identified with the end-of-service event. In other words, the job will be removed from the queue and the pointer to the auxiliary attributes will be maintained with the event that is scheduled. When the end-of-service event occurs, SLAM will remove the event from the event file. One of the functions of the end-of-service event will be to route the job to its next machine group, if there is one. The next machine group in the routing of a job can be obtained by using the following code:

```
NTRY = ATRIB(1)
CALL COPAA(NTRY,NROUTA,ROUTS,ROUTE)
I = ATRIB(2)
NEXTMG = ROUTE(I+1)
```

In the above code ATRIB(2) represents the number of machine groups that the job has visited and I represents the position in the routing for the next machine group. Of course, the value of NEXTMG could also be obtained by the following code:

```
NTRY = ATRIB(1)
I = ATRIB(2)
IC = NTRY+I+1
NEXTMG = ROUTS(IC)
```

In this code, the Ith auxiliary attribute is obtained. The pointer to auxiliary attributes points to the location preceding the first attribute, hence, the Ith auxiliary attribute is stored in cell location NTRY+I.

When a job has finished its routing, a call to subroutine GETAA would be made to remove the auxiliary attributes from the system. In this example, the auxiliary attribute subroutines were only used to store attributes in conjunction with one set of user-defined arrays. The subroutines are written in general form to allow the user to employ multiple auxiliary attribute files in a simulation program.

8.4 REPORT WRITING SUBROUTINES

A set of subroutines is contained within SLAM to enable the user to obtain summary reports or sections of a summary report. These subroutines can be used to obtain summary information of a specific type. The output from a subroutine corresponds to a specific section of the SLAM summary report (see Section 5.8.4).

Table 8-2 SLAM report writing subroutines.

Subroutine	Description
SUMRY	Prints the SLAM Summary Report.
PRNTF (IFILE)	If IFILE > 0, prints statistics and the contents of file IFILE. If IFILE = 0, prints summary statistics for all files. If IFILE < 0, prints summary statistics and contents of all files.
PRNTC (ICLCT)	If ICLCT > 0, prints statistics for COLCT variable number ICLCT. If ICLCT ≤ 0, prints statistics for all COLCT variables.
PRNTH (ICLCT)	If ICLCT > 0, prints a histogram for COLCT variable number ICLCT. If ICLCT ≤ 0, prints all histograms.
PRNTP (IPLOT)	If IPLOT > 0, prints a plot and/or table for plot/table number IPLOT. If IPLOT ≤ 0, prints all plots/tables.
PRNTT (ISTAT)	If ISTAT > 0, prints statistics for time-persistent variable ISTAT. If ISTAT ≤ 0, prints statistics for all time-persistent variables.
PRNTR (IRSC)	If IRSC > 0, prints statistics for resource number IRSC. If IRSC ≤ 0, prints statistics for all resources.
PRNTS	Prints the contents of the state storage vectors SS(I) and DD(I).
PRNTA	Prints statistics for activities.

The list of subroutines along with the definitions of their arguments is presented in Table 8-2.

The terminology used in naming the subroutines is to append a specific letter onto the letters PRNT. Thus, PRNTF is used as the name of a subroutine to print files and PRNTH is used as the name of the subroutine to print histograms. The arguments to these subroutines have been standardized so that an argument value greater than zero requests a specific item to be printed. If the argument is given as a zero value then all items associated with the subroutine are printed. In the case of subroutine PRNTF(IFILE), the contents of all files can be obtained by specifying a negative value for the argument IFILE. When a negative argument is specified for any of the other subprograms, the output obtained is the same as if a zero value is specified.

Listed below are examples of the use of the report writing routines.

Statement	*Description*
CALL SUMRY	Prints a complete summary report at time of calling (TNOW)
CALL PRNTF(3)	Prints statistics on file 3 and gives a listing of all entries in the file.
CALL PRNTT(0)	Prints statistics on all time-persistent variables
CALL PRNTA	Prints statistics on all network activities that were given activity numbers

8.5 FUNCTIONS FOR OBTAINING VALUES ASSOCIATED WITH STATISTICAL ESTIMATES

Functions have been included in SLAM to allow the user to access information related to statistical estimates during the execution of a simulation model. The names of the functions are all five letters in length with the first two letters being identical and representing one of the four types of variables for which statistics are desired. The last three letters of the function name prescribes the statistic of interest. The four types of variables are: variables based on observation (CC); time-persistent variables (TT); file variables (FF); and resource utilization variables (RR). The statistical quantities associated with these variables and their three letter codes are: average value (AVG); standard deviation (STD); maximum observed value (MAX); minimum observed value (MIN); number of observations

(NUM); time period over which the time-persistent variable was observed (PRD); and time of last change to a time-persistent variable (TLC).

The twenty-one functions included within SLAM to obtain values associated with the variables and statistical quantities are presented in Table 8-3. These func-

Table 8-3   SLAM statistical calculation functions.

Statistics for Variables Based on Observations (COLCT)

Function	Description
CCAVG(ICLCT)	Average value of variable ICLCT
CCSTD(ICLCT)	Standard deviation of variable ICLCT
CCMAX(ICLCT)	Maximum value of variable ICLCT
CCMIN(ICLCT)	Minimum value of variable ICLCT
CCNUM(ICLCT)	Number of observations of variable ICLCT

Statistics for Time-Persistent Variables (TIMST)

Function	Description
TTAVG(ISTAT)	Time integrated average of variable ISTAT
TTSTD(ISTAT)	Standard deviation of variable ISTAT
TTMAX(ISTAT)	Maximum value of variable ISTAT
TTMIN(ISTAT)	Minimum value of variable ISTAT
TTPRD(ISTAT)	Time period for statistics on variable ISTAT
TTTLC(ISTAT)	Time at which variable ISTAT was last changed

Queue Statistics

Function	Description
FFAVG(IFILE)	**Average number of entities in file IFILE**
FFAWT(IFILE)	**Average waiting time in file IFILE**
FFSTD(IFILE)	Standard deviation for file IFILE
FFMAX(IFILE)	Maximum number of entities in file IFILE
FFPRD(IFILE)	Time period for statistics in file IFILE
FFTLC(IFILE)	Time at which number in file IFILE last changed

Resource Statistics

Function	Description
RRAVG(IRSC)	Average utilization of resource IRSC
RRSTD(IRSC)	Standard deviation of utilization of resource IRSC
RRMAX(IRSC)	Maximum utilization of resource IRSC
RRPRD(IRSC)	Time period for statistics in resource IRSC
RRTLC(IRSC)	Time at which resource IRSC utilization was last changed

tions can be called from any SLAM subprogram and the values can be used for decision making within SLAM models.

The arguments to the SLAM statistical calculation functions are always a numeric value. File numbers are prescribed for both discrete event and network models and there should be no ambiguity regarding the arguments for the file related functions. For resources, SLAM assigns a resource number in sequence to each resource statement in a network statement model. It is this resource sequence number that must be used as the argument to functions RRAVG, RRSTD, RRMAX, RRPRD, and RRTLC. For collect variables, numeric values are assigned by the user in discrete event models and by SLAM in network models (for each COLCT node). SLAM assigns a sequential numeric code for each COLCT statement starting with the first number above the highest user-assigned number of variables listed on STAT statements. Thus, if there are three STAT variables assigned codes 1, 2, and 3 and two COLCT nodes, the average associated with the first COLCT node in the network description would be accessed by the statement.

AVE=CCAVG(4)

For time persistent statistics, the order in which the TIMST input statements appear in the input determines the number to be used in the functions beginning with the letters TT.

8.6   MISCELLANEOUS INPUT STATEMENTS AND SUPPORT SUBPROGRAMS

There are many concepts associated with discrete simulation that are supported by SLAM indirectly through input statement types or by support subprograms that are described in either the network or continuous modeling chapters of this book. In this section, we discuss subroutines UMONT, CLEAR, ERROR, UERR, and GTABL.

8.6.1   Subroutine UMONT(IT)

To obtain statistics after time TFRST on a simulation run, the input statement

MONTR,CLEAR,TFRST;

is used as described in Section 5.6.9. The MONTR input statement is also used to obtain a trace of events as they occur. The standard SLAM trace can be suppressed or augmented by writing subroutine UMONT(IT). If the user sets IT to 1 in subroutine UMONT, the standard SLAM trace is suppressed. If IT is not reset to 1, both user written information and SLAM generated trace information are generated. The information can be segregated if desired by using different output device numbers. An example of the output from a version of subroutine UMONT written for an analysis of hot metal carriers (submarines) in a steel plant (2) is presented in Figure 8-1. We strongly encourage the use of tailor-made traces like the one presented in Figure 8-1. They assist in program debugging and verification and

10:57 AM	DEPARTURE FROM DESULFURIZATION WITH 3 SUBS FIRST SUB NO. = 14.
10:57 AM	SUB 9. ARRIVES AT BF AREA
10:57 AM	HML 2. UNLOADS INTO BOF 1.
10:58 AM	BOF 2. ENDS CYCLE
10:59 AM	END UNLOAD OF SUB 23. INTO HML 2.
11: 0 AM	SCRAP MELTER COMPLETED A CYCLE
11: 1 AM	END CAST ON FURNACE G WITH SUBS 12 5
	HAVING LOADS OF 219. 28.
	NO. OF FULL SUBS = 9 NO. OF SUBS IN Q OF BF = 0
11: 3 AM	HML 1. UNLOADS INTO BOF 2.
11: 3 AM	END UNLOAD OF SUB 17. INTO HML 2.
11: 6 AM	END UNLOAD OF SUB 18. INTO HML 2.
11: 9 AM	ARRIVAL AT DESULFURIZATION WITH 2 SUBS FIRST SUBS NO. = 2.
11:10 AM	END UNLOAD OF SUB 18. INTO HML 1.
11:11 AM	SUB 11. ARRIVES AT BF AREA
11:13 AM	SUB 15. ARRIVED AT SCRAP MELTER
11:13 AM	START CAST ON FURNACE J WITH SUBS 8 9 5
	HAVING INITIAL LOADS OF 19. 0 28.
11:15 AM	END UNLOAD OF SUB 3. INTO HML 1.
11:16 AM	ARRIVAL AT BOF WITH 3 SUBS FIRST SUB NO. = 14. BOF Q = 1
11:31 AM	END CAST ON FURNACE H WITH SUBS 7 6 16
	HAVING LOADS OF 219. 41. 0
	NO. OF FULL SUBS = 9 NO. OF SUBS IN Q OF BF = 0
11:33 AM	ARRIVAL AT DESULFURIZATION WITH 1 SUBS FIRST SUBS NO. = 12.
11:35 AM	SUB 23. ARRIVES AT BF AREA
11:46 AM	BOF 2. ENDS CYCLE
11:49 AM	DEPARTURE FROM DESULFURIZATION WITH 2 SUBS FIRST SUB NO. = 2.
11:49 AM	SUB 18. ARRIVES AT BF AREA
11:51 AM	HML 2. UNLOADS INTO BOF 2.
11:52 AM	END UNLOAD OF SUB 3. INTO HML 2.
11:56 AM	SUB 17. ARRIVES AT BF AREA
11:59 AM	END UNLOAD OF SUB 21. INTO HML 2.
12. 0 PM	START CAST ON FURNACE C WITH SUBS 11 16 23
	HAVING INITIAL LOADS OF 0 0 0
12. 0 PM	END UNLOAD OF SUB 14. INTO HML 2.

Figure 8-1 Example of user-trace output produced from UMONT.

they support communication about the model. The importance of this communication was discussed in Chapter 1 with regard to implementing results. Additionally, traces support external model validation.

8.6.2   Subroutine CLEAR

This subroutine initializes the statistical storage arrays associated with a simulation model. The user invokes this subroutine by the statement

CALL CLEAR

or, by the input statement,

MONTR,CLEAR,TFRST;

When the MONTR input statement is employed, SLAM calls subroutine CLEAR at the time specified by the variable TFRST. The user may desire to call subroutine CLEAR based on system status and a MONTR statement would not be applicable.

When subroutine CLEAR is employed in a simulation model, all statistical estimates presented on the SLAM summary report are based on data collected from the time subroutine CLEAR was called to the time at which the summary report was prepared. Recall that SLAM summary reports can be prepared periodically through the use of a MONTR input statement which employs the SUMRY option and specifies a time between reports value.

The function TTCLR(T) is included in SLAM to obtain the last time subroutine CLEAR was called if it was before or equal to time T. If the clearing time is greater than T, function TTCLR returns a zero value. Function TTCLR is commonly called with an argument of TNOW.

8.6.3   Subroutine ERROR(KODE) and UERR(KODE)

ERROR is called when an error is detected in a SLAM subprogram. It provides useful diagnostic information by listing the error code, TNOW, and current values in ATRIB. A call is made to subroutine UERR(KODE) which permits the user to print out user-specific information when an error is detected. An attempt is then made to print a complete SLAM summary report. Finally, subroutine ERROR has a deliberate FORTRAN error to cause the standard FORTRAN diagnostic and trace-back information to be printed.

8.6.4   Function GTABL(TAB,X,XLOW,XHIGH,XINCR)

GTABL is the SLAM table look-up function. The definition of the arguments are given below.

Argument	Definition
TAB	The array containing the values of the dependent variable
X	The independent variable
XLOW	The lowest value of the independent variable for which TAB contains a value for the dependent variable
XHIGH	The highest value of the independent variable for which TAB contains a value for the dependent variable
XINCR	The increment of the independent variable between corresponding values for the dependent variable

To use GTABL the user must provide an array and store the appropriate values for the dependent variable in the array. The values must correspond to the equally spaced values of the independent variable between XLOW and XHIGH in increments of XINCR.

The value of the dependent variable returned by GTABL is computed by linear interpolation within the defined range of the independent variable. If the independent variable is outside the range given, the appropriate end point value of the dependent variable is returned. The use of function GTABL is illustrated in Section 9.8 and in Example 10-2.

8.7   Example 8-1.   A JOB SHOP SCHEDULING MODEL†

This example illustrates how SLAM can be used for simulating job shops which employ dynamic scheduling practices. The example is based on the article "Experiments with the SI^x Rule in Job Shop Scheduling" by Eilon, Chowdhury and Serghiou (1). The job shop consists of six machines with each machine performing a different operation. The estimated processing time for each machine is 20 minutes on the average with an exponential distribution (processing times are

---

† We wish to thank Ms. Kathy Stecke for suggesting the use of this example.

rounded off to integer values with no value being less than 1). Actual processing time is equal to the estimated processing time plus a random component which is normally distributed with a mean of zero and a standard deviation equal to three-tenths of the estimated processing time (the random component is white noise). Note that the job shop has been balanced so that each machine has the same average processing time.

Jobs arrive to the shop with interarrival times being exponentially distributed with a mean of 25 minutes. The interarrival times are integerized and must be greater than or equal to 1. Each job consists of a set of operations to be performed on the machines in the job shop. The number of operations per job is normally distributed with a mean of 4 and a standard deviation of 1. However, no job can require less than 3 operations nor more than 6 operations. The routing of a job through the machines is determined by random assignment. An illustration of the job shop and the routing of two jobs is given in Figure 8-2.

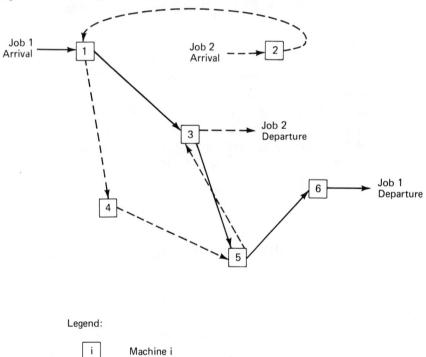

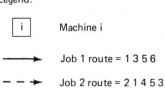

Figure 8-2   Pictorial sketch of job shop and job routings.

As Eilon et al. point out, "If the arrival of jobs, their processing requirements, and the operating facilities are all given, the only control parameter at the disposal of the scheduler is . . . the order in which the job should be processed." The dispatching rule included in this example is the SI^x rule which processes jobs at a machine in the order of the shortest estimated processing time for the job that is in a high priority class. Priority jobs are defined as those jobs whose float is negative. Float is defined for a job as the due date minus the current time minus the estimated time remaining to perform operations on the job minus a safety factor. The SI^x rule divides jobs in front of a given machine into two classes and within each class the jobs are ordered based on shortest estimated processing time. This example will illustrate how SLAM can be used to evaluate a dispatching rule in a job shop environment.

Concepts Illustrated.   This example illustrates the use of advanced file manipulation subprograms for changing the ranking of file members. The accessing of attribute values directly is illustrated. An auxiliary attribute array is used to maintain fixed and dynamic information associated with an entity. Also illustrated is a procedure for sampling from a distribution without replacement. Another procedure illustrated in this example is the use of a derived attribute to obtain complex ranking rules in a SLAM file.

SLAM Model.   The job shop system is essentially a queueing situation in which jobs arrive, are routed to machines in a prescribed order, and then leave the shop. Basically, there are two events required to model this situation: the arrival of a job to the shop; and end of processing by a machine. When a job arrives, the number of operations to be performed on the job is determined. The order in which the operations are to be performed as well as the estimated time required on each machine is calculated. From this information, a due date is established from which the float associated with the job can be computed. The machine routing, estimated processing times, the number of operations to be performed, the job arrival time, and the job due date will be stored as auxiliary attributes in the job information array XJINF. The job entity will have attribute 1 as a pointer to the location in XJINF of these auxiliary attributes. In the arrival event, the job will be routed to the first machine in its routing. The job will be processed if the machine is idle or will be placed in the queue of the machine if the machine is busy. The variable XX(MACH) will be used to represent the status of machine MACH with a zero indicating an idle machine and a 1 indicating a busy machine. Attribute 2 of the job will be used to rank jobs in the machine queues with a low-value-first ranking rule. Ranking will be based on the estimated processing time at the machine if float is negative. If float is positive, then a large constant will be added to the estimated processing time so that a categorization of jobs waiting for the machine can be made. By ranking the jobs in the queue based on low value of attribute 2, the jobs at the front of the queue will be those whose float is negative and they will be ordered by the smallest value of estimated processing time. By adding the large constant to attribute 2 for those jobs whose float is positive, the jobs at the back of the queue will be "non-priority" jobs which will also be ranked by their shortest estimated processing time.

A third attribute will be associated with the job entity which is a modified due date. The modified due date, attribute 3, will be set equal to the due date minus the estimated remaining processing time for the job minus the safety factor. Whenever attribute 3 is greater than the current time, the job is classified as a non-priority job. However, if attribute 3 is less than the current time, the float is negative and the job classification must be changed. This involves changing the value of attribute 2 for the job. Since decisions regarding which job to process are only made when there is an end-of-service at the machine, it is only necessary to update the classification of the jobs waiting in the queue of the machine at these times. This is accomplished by scanning the file containing the jobs waiting for the machine and updating attribute 2 in accordance with the value of attribute 3 as related to current time as described above. Other details of the SLAM model for the job shop situation are similar to the queueing example presented in Chptaer 7. The detailed description of the variables and subprograms included in this model will now be given.

In this example, six files and the event calendar will be used. For the arrival event, no attributes are required. For the end-of-service event, the following three attributes are used:

1. Pointer to the location in the auxiliary attribute array, $XJINF(\cdot)$, where job attributes are stored;
2. Machine number for which the end-of-service event is occurring;
3. Modified due date for the job on which service is ending.

The modified due date is computed by subtracting from the due date both a safety factor, SAFET, and the remaining processing time for operations to be performed for the job. By comparing the current time to the modified due date, the priority class for a job can be ascertained.

File I, for I=1,6, is used as the queue of jobs for machine I. Attributes 1 and 3 of a job entity in these files are the same as the ones described for the event calendar. Attribute 2 will be the estimated processing time for machine I if the job has priority status; otherwise, it will be the estimating processing time for machine I plus 1000.

The definitions of the variables used in this SLAM model are presented below.

Variable	Definition	Initial Value
AAJOB(I)	Auxiliary attribute buffer array	—
JBPTR	Pointer to location in XJINF where a job's auxiliary attributes are maintained	—
JOBF	Pointer to next set of locations for storing auxiliary attributes	—
NATT	Dimension of AAJOB($\cdot$)	15
NLATE	Number of jobs that exceeded their due date	0
NMG	Number of machines in the job shop	6
NUMJOB	Number of jobs that have been processed through job shop	0
PT	Mean processing time for an operation	20.0
SAFET	Safety factor in computation of float	50.0
TBA	Mean time between job arrivals	25.0
XJINF	Auxiliary attribute array	—
XX(MACH)	$\begin{cases} 0 \text{ if machine MACH is idle} \\ 1 \text{ if machine MACH is busy} \end{cases}$	0.0

The auxiliary attribute array for job information, XJINF, has NATT=15 values associated with each job. The values are defined below where the left column specifies the value to be added to the job pointer, JBPTR.

Auxiliary Attribute Number	Definition
I=1,NMG	Ith machine in routing: if none, 0
I=NMG+1,2*NMG	Processing time on (I-NMG)th machine in routing
NATT-2	Current operation number for job
NATT-1	Arrival time of job
NATT=2*NMG+3	Due date for job

The coding of this example follows the standard SLAM discrete modeling approach presented in Chapter 7. The main program and subroutine EVENT are in standard form and are shown in Figure 8-3. Subroutine INTLC is used to perform the following: establish constants for the model; initialize to zero the number of jobs processed, NUMJOB, and number of jobs that are late, NLATE; initialize the auxiliary attribute array XJINF and first pointer for extra job information, JOBF; and to schedule the first job arrival at time zero. The coding for subroutine INTLC is also shown in Figure 8-3.

```
      DIMENSION NSET(1000)
      COMMON/SCOM1/ ATRIB(100),DD(100),DDL(100),DTNOW,II,MFA,MSTOP,NCLNR
     1,NCRDR,NPRNT,NNRUN,NNSET,NTAPE,SS(100),SSL(100),TNEXT,TNOW,XX(100)
      COMMON QSET(1000)
      EQUIVALENCE (NSET(1),QSET(1))
      NNSET=1000
      NCRDR=5
      NPRNT=6
      NTAPE=7
      CALL SLAM
      STOP
      END
      SUBROUTINE EVENT(I)
      GO TO (1,2),I
    1 CALL ARRIV
      RETURN
    2 CALL ENDSV
      RETURN
      END

      SUBROUTINE INTLC
      COMMON/SCOM1/ ATRIB(100),DD(100),DDL(100),DTNOW,II,MFA,MSTOP,NCLNR
     1,NCRDR,NPRNT,NNRUN,NNSET,NTAPE,SS(100),SSL(100),TNEXT,TNOW,XX(100)
      COMMON/UCOM1/ XJINF(3000),AAJOB(15),JOBF,NMG,NATT,SAFET,NLATE,
     1NUMJOB
C
C******XX(MACH) IS BUSY STATUS OF MACHINE MACH
C
      NMG=6
      NATT=2*NMG+3
      SAFET=50.
      DO 10 MACH=1,NMG
   10 XX(MACH) = 0.0
      CALL SETAA(NATT,XJINF,JOBF,3000)
      CALL SCHDL(1,0.0,ATRIB)
      NUMJOB=0
      NLATE=0
      RETURN
      END
```

Figure 8-3   Main program, subroutine EVENT, and subroutine INTLC for job shop model.

The coding of the arrival event, ARRIV, is shown in Figure 8-4. The first three statements in subroutine ARRIV determine the time until the next job arrival, DT, and schedule the next arrival event to occur. Note that the arrival time is a sample from an exponential distribution which is rounded down to the next lowest integer. The interarrival time is then required to be at least one.

Subroutine DESJOB(AAJOB) is used to establish the routing of the job, the processing time for each machine on the routing, and the due date for the job.

These values are returned to subroutine ARRIV through the vector AAJOB. By using a separate subroutine for describing the job, job descriptions can be altered without altering the arrival event routine. The description of subroutine DESJOB will be deferred until after the arrival event has been described.

```
      SUBROUTINE ARRIV
      COMMON/SCOM1/ ATRIB(100),DD(100),DDL(100),DTNOW,II,MFA,MSTOP,NCLNR
     1,NCRDR,NPRNT,NNRUN,NNSET,NTAPE,SS(100),SSL(100),TNEXT,TNOW,XX(100)
      COMMON/UCOM1/ XJINF(3000),AAJOB(15),JOBF,NMG,NATT,SAFET,NLATE,
     1NUMJOB
      DATA TBA/25.0/
C
C*****SCHEDULE NEXT JOB ARRIVAL
C
      IDT=EXPON(TBA,1)
      DT= MAXO(IDT,1)
      CALL SCHDL(1,DT,ATRIB)
C
C*****SET UP ATTRIBUTES AND CHARACTERISTICS OF THIS JOB
C
      CALL DESJOB(AAJOB)
      ATRIB(1) = JOBF
      CALL PUTAA(NATT,XJINF,JOBF,AAJOB)
      ATRIB(3) = DDM(AAJOB)
      ATRIB(2) = AAJOB(NMG+1) +1000.
      IF(ATRIB(3).LE.TNOW) ATRIB(2) = AAJOB(NMG+1)
C
C*****DETERMINE DISPOSITION OF JOB
C
      MACH = AAJOB(1)
      IF(XX(MACH).GT.0.0) GO TO 10
C
C*****SET MACHINE BUSY.  SCHEDULE END OF SERVICE
C
      XX(MACH) =1.0
      ETIME = AAJOB(NMG+1)
      CALL SCHES(MACH,ETIME)
      RETURN
C
C*****PUT JOB IN QUE FOR MACHINE
C
   10 CALL FILEM(MACH,ATRIB)
      RETURN
      END
```

Figure 8-4 Subroutine ARRIV for job shop model.

Attribute 1 for the job entity is set equal to the pointer, JOBF, to the auxiliary attribute array. The auxiliary attributes as described in the vector AAJOB are then inserted into XJINF by a call to subroutine PUTAA. Attribute 3 of the job is set equal to the modified due date as computed in function DDM. Function DDM will also be described later. Attribute 2 of the job is then set equal to the estimated processing time for the first machine in the routing of the job plus 1000. If the modified due date is less than or equal to TNOW then attribute 2 is reset to the estimated processing time. We are now ready to determine the disposition of the arriving job. The first machine on which the job is to be processed is established as the variable MACH as obtained from AAJOB(1). If machine MACH is busy, a transfer is made to statement 10 where the job is placed in the queue for the machine by a call to subroutine FILEM.

If the machine is idle, it is made busy by setting XX(MACH) equal to 1. The estimated processing time is established as the variable ETIME and subroutine SCHES is called to schedule an end-of-service for machine MACH for a job whose estimated processing time on MACH is ETIME. A return is then made from subroutine ARRIV.

To describe a job in terms of its routing, operation processing times, and due date, a call was made to subroutine DESJOB(A) where A is a vector in which the auxiliary attributes associated with a job are to be defined. Subroutine DES-JOB(A) is shown in Figure 8-5. The first statement in subroutine DESJOB establishes the number of operations NOPS to be performed on the job as a sample from a normal distribution whose mean is 4, standard deviation is 1, and stream number is 3. A value of 0.5 is added to the sample from the normal distribution so that the number of operations is rounded to the nearest integer. If NOPS is less than 3, it is set equal to 3. Similarly if it is greater than 6, it is set equal to 6 as the problem statement establishes that the number of operations must be between 3 and 6. This procedure for setting NOPS corresponds to obtaining a sample from a mixed distribution where the probability in the tails of the distribution are lumped at the minimum and maximum points specified. As explained in Chapter 2, this type of sample is different than one obtained from a truncated distribution. Next, the vector A is initialized to zero as is the variable SUM. SUM is used to obtain a sum of the processing times for all operations for this job.

The next section of the code is used to set the route for the arriving job. First, the vector MA(I) is set to I to indicate that any machine can be the first in routing for the job. A random sampling of the value MA(I) is to be made. The variable TOP is set equal to the number of machines plus 1, which for this illustration will set TOP = 7. Next, a DO loop is employed with a running index I set equal to the operation number for the arriving job. BOT is established as the real equivalent of the operation number. INDEX is established as an integer from the operation number to the number of machines. By sampling between the values of BOT and TOP, an integer is selected between I and NMG with each integer being equally likely. Thus, when BOT = 1.0 and TOP = 7.0 each integer from 1 to 6 will have a one-sixth probability of being selected. The machine number selected is stored in MA(INDEX) and this is inserted into the vector A in the Ith position to specify MA(INDEX) as the Ith machine to be visited by the arriving job. The value MA(INDEX) is then redefined to be equal to MA(I). This statement interchanges

```
      SUBROUTINE DESJOB(A)
      COMMON/SCOM1/ ATRIB(100),DD(100),DDL(100),DTNOW,II,MFA,MSTOP,NCLNR
     1,NCRDR,NPRNT,NNRUN,NNSET,NTAPE,SS(100),SSL(100),TNEXT,TNOW,XX(100)
      COMMON/UCOM1/ XJINF(3000),AAJOB(15),JOBF,NMG,NATT,SAFET,NLATE,
     1NUMJOB
      DIMENSION A(15),MA(6)
      DATA PT/20.0/
      NOPS =RNORM(4.0,1.0,3) +.5
      IF(NOPS.LT.3)NOPS=3
      IF(NOPS.GT.6) NOPS = 6
      DO 30 I = 1,NATT
   30 A(I) = 0.0
C
C*****SAMPLE TO SET MACHINE ROUTE WITHOUT REPLACEMENT
C
      DO 35 I=1,NMG
   35 MA(I) = I
      TOP = NMG + 1
      SUM = 0.0
      DO 40 I =1,NOPS
      BOT = I
      INDEX= UNFRM(BOT,TOP,4)
      A(I) = MA(INDEX)
      MA(INDEX) = MA(I)
      IETIM = EXPON(PT,4)
      A(I+NMG) = MAXO(IETIM,1)
   40 SUM= SUM + A(I+NMG)
C
C*****SET CURRENT OPERATOR NUMBER TO 1
C
      A(NATT-2) = 1.0
C
C*****SET ARRIVAL TIME OF JOB TO TNOW
C
      A(NATT-1) = TNOW
C
C*****SET DUE DATE TO TWICE THE ESTIMATED PROCESSING TIME
C
      A(NATT) = 2.*SUM+TNOW
      RETURN
      END
```

Figure 8-5 Subroutine DESJOB for describing a job in the job shop model.

the machine selected with one that was not selected. By this process, a routing is established which does not include a machine on the routing more than once. This code illustrates the procedure for sampling without replacement from a set of integers. Note that INDEX will be a sample from a uniform distribution where the low value is continually increased by 1 since BOT is reset to I for each passage through the DO loop. Thus, when I = 2 there can be five values for INDEX and the five machines still to be selected are stored in MA(2) through MA(6).

An integer value for the processing time is obtained as a sample from an exponential distribution. The estimated processing time is stored in A(I+NMG). Processing times smaller than 1 are not permitted. At statement 40, the end of the DO loop, the sum of the processing times is recorded in the variable SUM.

```
      FUNCTION DDM(A)
      COMMON/SCOM1/ ATRIB(100),DD(100),DDL(100),DTNOW,II,MFA,MSTOP,NCLNR
     1,NCRDR,NPRNT,NNRUN,NNSET,NTAPE,SS(100),SSL(100),TNEXT,TNOW,XX(100)
      COMMON/UCOM1/ XJINF(3000),AAJOB(15),JOBF,NMG,NATT,SAFET,NLATE,
     1NUMJOB
      DIMENSION A(15)
      DMM = A(NATT)-.5*(A(NATT)-TNOW)-SAFET
      RETURN
      END
```

Figure 8-6   Function DDM for computing a modified due date in the job shop model.

The last three statements of subroutine DESJOB are used to set the current operation number to 1, the arrival time of the job to TNOW, and the due date to be twice the estimated processing time for the job. These values are stored in the last three cells of the A vector. The establishment of the due date as twice the sum of the estimated processing times is taken from the statement of the problem as presented by Eilon.

The function for computing the modified due date DDM is shown in Figure 8-6. The modified due date is the value of the due date minus the estimated processing time minus a safety factor. This involves one statement as shown in Figure 8-6.

The subroutine to schedule end of service, SCHES, is presented in Figure 8-7. The arguments for this subroutine are the machine number, MG, and the estimated processing time, ET. The actual processing time is equal to the estimated processing time plus a sample from a normal distribution which has a mean of 0 and a standard deviation equal to 0.3 times the estimated processing time. The service time, SERVT, is then set equal to the estimated processing time plus the sample from the normal distribution. A check is then made to insure that the service time is positive (since a negative value greater than the estimated processing time can be obtained from the normal distribution). Attribute 2 is then established as the current machine number MG. The modified due date is then altered to no longer include the estimated operation time of the machine being scheduled. (Alternatively,

```
      SUBROUTINE SCHES(MG,ET)
      COMMON/SCOM1/ ATRIB(100),DD(100),DDL(100),DTNOW,II,MFA,MSTOP,NCLNR
     1,NCRDR,NPRNT,NNRUN,NNSET,NTAPE,SS(100),SSL(100),TNEXT,TNOW,XX(100)
      SIGMA = 0.3*ET
      SERVT = ET + RNORM(0.0,SIGMA,2)
      IF(SERVT.LT.0.0) SERVT = 0.0
      ATRIB(2) = MG
C
C*****UPDATE THE MODIFIED DUE DATE TO NOT INCLUDE ESTIMATED SERVICE
C*****TIME OF THE CURRENT OPERATION
C
      ATRIB(3) = ATRIB(3) + ET
C
C*****SCHEDULE END OF SERVICE EVENT
C
      CALL SCHDL(2,SERVT,ATRIB)
      RETURN
      END
```

Figure 8-7   Subroutine SCHES for scheduling an end of service for job shop model.

this updating of the modified due date could be done after the job is processed on this machine.) The end-of-service event is then scheduled by a call to subroutine SCHDL with event code 2, service time SERVT, and attribute buffer ATRIB. Note that ATRIB(1) need not be reset as the pointer to the auxiliary attribute array is established prior to the call to subroutine SCHES. This completes the description of what occurs when a job arrives including the establishment of the job description, the due date, and the scheduling of an end-of-service event if the machine required for the first operation is available for processing the job. Next we consider the second event, an end of service, ENDSV, for a job at a particular machine.

When ENDSV is called, the SLAM processor has loaded the attribute buffer, ATRIB, with the following attributes:

ATRIB(1) = pointer to the position in the auxiliary attribute array XJINF for information concerning the job on which service was just completed;

ATRIB(2) = machine on which service ended; and

ATRIB(3) = modified due date for job completing service.

In subroutine ENDSV shown in Figure 8-8, JBPTR is set equal to the job pointer (ATRIB(1)) and MACHE is set equal to the machine on which service is ended (ATRIB(2)). Next, the number of operations completed for the job is accessed directly from XJINF(ICOPN) where ICOPN is the thirteenth (NATT-2) auxiliary attribute associated with the job. The next operation number is defined as IOPN which is one more than the current operation number. Since there can be at most 6 operations for a job, an IOPN value of 7 indicates that no further machines in the job shop are to be visited. When this occurs, a transfer to statement 50 is made to delete the job from the job shop.

If IOPN is not 7, the auxiliary attribute array is updated to the new current operation number and the new machine number, NEWM, is accessed. If the new machine number is 0, the job has also completed its tour through the job shop and a transfer is made to statement 50. If the job is to go to another machine, the estimated processing time is obtained from the appropriate cell of XJINF and stored as the variable ET. The code described above obtains the next machine and estimated processing time for the job that just completed service; we are now ready to route the job.

First, a check is made to see if the new machine is busy. If it is, a transfer is made to statement 20 where the value of ATRIB(2) is established. The job is then filed in the queue of the new machine, NEWM. If NEWM was idle, its status is changed to busy by setting XX(NEWM) to 1.0. An end of service for the job

```
      SUBROUTINE ENDSV
      COMMON/SCOM1/ ATRIB(100),DD(100),DDL(100),DTNOW,II,MFA,MSTOP,NCLNR
     1,NCRDR,NPRNT,NNRUN,NNSET,NTAPE,SS(100),SSL(100),TNEXT,TNOW,XX(100)
      COMMON/UCOM1/ XJINF(3000),AAJOB(15),JOBF,NMG,NATT,SAFET,NLATE,
     1NUMJOB
      JBPTR = ATRIB(1)
C
C*****SAVE MACHINE NUMBER ON WHICH SERVICE ENDED
C
      MACHE= ATRIB(2)
C
C*****DETERMINE DISPOSITION OF JOB ON WHICH SERVICE ENDED
C
      ICOPN = JBPTR + NATT - 2
      IOPN=IFIX(XJINF(ICOPN))+1
      IF(IOPN.EQ.7) GO TO 50
      XJINF(ICOPN) = IOPN
      NEWM = XJINF(JBPTR+IOPN)
      IF(NEWM.EQ.0) GO TO 50
      ET = XJINF(JBPTR + IOPN +NMG)
      IF(XX(NEWM).GT.0.0) GO TO 20
      XX(NEWM) = 1.0
      CALL SCHES(NEWM,ET)
      GO TO 100
   20 ATRIB(2) = ET + 1000.
      IF(ATRIB(3).LE.TNOW) ATRIB(2) = ET
      CALL FILEM(NEWM,ATRIB)
      GO TO 100
   50 NUMJOB = NUMJOB + 1
      CALL GETAA(JBPTR,NATT,XJINF,JOBF,AAJOB)
      TISYS= TNOW-AAJOB(NATT-1)
      CALL COLCT(TISYS,1)
      TLATE = AAJOB(NATT) - TNOW
      CALL COLCT(TLATE,3)
      IF(TNOW.LE.AAJOB(NATT)) GO TO 100
      NLATE = NLATE +1
      CALL COLCT(TLATE,2)
C
C*****DETERMINE DISPOSITION OF MACHE
C
  100 IF(NNQ(MACHE).GT.0) GO TO 110
      XX(MACHE) = 0.0
      RETURN
C
C*****UPDATE PRIORITY OF JOBS WAITING IN QUEUE OF MACHINE
C
  110 CALL UPDAT(MACHE)
      CALL RMOVE(1,MACHE,ATRIB)
      ETIME=ATRIB(2)-1000.
      IF(ETIME.LE.0.0) ETIME = ATRIB(2)
      CALL SCHES(MACHE,ETIME)
      RETURN
      END
```

Figure 8-8   Subroutine ENDSV for job shop model.

on NEWM is then scheduled by calling subroutine SCHES. After determining the disposition of the job that just completed service, a transfer is made to statement 100 where the disposition of the machine that just completed service is determined.

Before going to statement 100, we will describe what happens when a job has been completely processed. The number of jobs completed by the job shop is increased by 1. The attributes of the job are removed from the system by a call to subroutine GETAA which loads the auxiliary attributes into the vector AAJOB and frees up the space that was used for the auxiliary attributes of the job on which service was completed. Statistics are then collected on time in the system by subtracting the job's arrival time (the 14th auxiliary attribute) from TNOW and calling subroutine COLCT with code 1. Next, a check is made to see if the current time is less than or equal to the assigned due date. If not, the number of late jobs is increased by one and statistics are computed on the amount of time the job was late by calling subroutine COLCT with code 2. This completes the description of a job that has completed its routine through the machine shop.

The disposition of machine MACHE is determined starting at statement 100. First, a check is made to see if any jobs are waiting to be processed. If none is waiting, XX(MACHE) is set to 0 to indicate that MACHE is idle, and a return is then made to the SLAM processor. If a job is waiting, a transfer is made to statement 110. At statement 110, subroutine UPDAT(MACHE) is called to update the priority class of those jobs waiting for machine MACHE. This updating is required since a job's priority could change while it was waiting in the queue and, hence, its position in the queue could change. For example, if the first job in the queue had an estimated processing time of 15.0 and was in the priority class, and the seventh job in the queue of the machine had a processing time of 12 but was in the non-priority class when the machine last started processing a job, then if the priority of the job that is seventh in the queue changed, it should be processed prior to the job that is first in the queue since it has a smaller estimated processing time. Subroutine UPDAT performs the necessary rearrangement of the jobs in the queue. When the rearrangement is completed, subroutine RMOVE is called to remove the first job in the queue of MACHE and to load the job's attributes into ATRIB. The estimated processing time, ETIME, is set equal to ATRIB(2) − 1000. If ETIME is less than or equal to 0 then ETIME is reset to ATRIB(2). Throughout the code, it is presumed that no estimated processing time is greater than 1000. If this was not the case, a larger constant would have to be used to distinguish between jobs of different priority. Throughout the code, it was also assumed that non-priority jobs were more frequently encountered than priority jobs and, hence, attribute 2 was more frequently greater than 1000 than not. An end-of-service event is scheduled for MACHE and the job by calling subroutine SCHES. This completes the description of the code for the end-of-service subroutine.

Subroutine UPDAT(MACH) is shown in Figure 8-9 and is used to update the priority class of jobs waiting in the queue for machine MACH. The procedure for updating jobs will be to start at the last job in the file and to proceed toward the

```
      SUBROUTINE UPDAT(MACH)
      COMMON/SCOM1/ ATRIB(100),DD(100),DDL(100),DTNOW,II,MFA,MSTOP,NCLNR
     1,NCRDR,NPRNT,NNRUN,NNSET,NTAPE,SS(100),SSL(100),TNEXT,TNOW,XX(100)
      DIMENSION NSET(1)
      COMMON QSET(1)
      EQUIVALENCE (NSET(1),QSET(1))
      NTRY = MMLE(MACH)
   11 IF(NTRY.EQ.0) RETURN
      IF(QSET(NTRY+2).LT.1000.) RETURN
      IF(QSET(NTRY+3).GT.TNOW) GO TO 15
      NEXT = NPRED(NTRY)
      QSET(NTRY+2) = QSET(NTRY+2) -1000.
      CALL ULINK(-NTRY,MACH)
      CALL LINK(MACH)
      NTRY = NEXT
      GO TO 11
   15 NTRY = NPRED(NTRY)
      GO TO 11
      END
```

Figure 8-9   Subroutine UPDAT for updating job priority class in the job shop model.

first job in the file. As soon as a job is encountered which is in the priority class, that is, its second attribute is less than 1000, we know that no further jobs need be considered for updating. If the second attribute of a job is greater than 1000 then the modified due date is compared to the current time to determine if the priority class should be updated. If it should, the second attribute is reduced by 1000, the job is taken out of its current position in the file, and then refiled in order that its correct position will be determined based on its new value of attribute 2. The removing and refiling of the job is done by calls to subroutine ULINK and LINK. The scanning of the file is accomplished by accessing the pointers to entries. The pointer to the last entry in the file is obtained by using function MMLE. Predecessor entries are obtained by using function NPRED. We will now describe the code explicitly.

The first statement in subroutine UPDAT establishes NTRY as the pointer to the last entry in file MACH. If NTRY is zero, no further entries exist in the file and a return from subroutine UPDAT is made. The second attribute of the entry is stored in QSET(NTRY+2). Rather than employ subroutine COPY to access the second attribute, we will access it directly. If the second attribute is less than 1000 then no further changes in priority for jobs in the queue need be considered and a return from UPDAT is made. If the second attribute is greater than or equal to 1000, the third attribute is tested to determine if the float is negative. If it is not, a transfer to statement 15 is made where NTRY is set equal to the predecessor of NTRY and the process is started again by a return to statement 11. If the float is negative, the priority class for the job whose pointer is NTRY must be changed. First the pointer NEXT is established as the predecessor of NTRY. It is necessary

```
     SUBROUTINE OTPUT
     COMMON/SCOM1/ ATRIB(100),DD(100),DDL(100),DTNOW,II,MFA,MSTOP,NCLNR
    1,NCRDR,NPRNT,NNRUN,NNSET,NTAPE,SS(100),SSL(100),TNEXT,TNOW,XX(100)
     COMMON/UCOM1/ XJINF(3000),AAJOB(15),JOBF,NMG,NATT,SAFET,NLATE,
    1NUMJOB
     AVE= FLOAT(NLATE)/FLOAT(NUMJOB)
     WRITE(NPRNT,10) TNOW,NUMJOB,NLATE,AVE
  10 FORMAT(F10.2,2I10,F10.5)
     RETURN
     END
```

Figure 8-10   Subroutine OTPUT for job shop model.

to save this predecessor pointer since the entry under consideration is going to be unlinked from the other entries and, hence, its predecessor pointer will change. The second attribute is reduced by 1000 which is the procedure used in this example to increase the priority of the job. A call is then made to subroutine ULINK with a negative first argument to indicate that a pointer rather than a rank is being used. The entry is then reinserted into the file by a call to subroutine LINK. ULINK and LINK were employed to illustrate their use. For this example, since the second attribute was changed the code could have employed subroutine RMOVE, then updated the second attribute and refiled the entry with a call to subroutine FILEM. After linking the entry back into file MACH, the next entry to be considered, NTRY, is set equal to NEXT and a transfer to statement 11 is made to continue the scanning of the file. This completes the description of subroutine UPDAT.

The code for subroutine OTPUT is shown in Figure 8-10. In subroutine OTPUT, the number of jobs processed and the amount of time required to process the jobs is shown. Also printed are the number of jobs late and the fraction of jobs that were late.

The input statements for the job shop model are shown in Figure 8-11. The GEN statement indicates that only one run is to be made. The LIMITS statement specifies

```
     GEN,PRITSKER,ADVANCED JOBSHOP,2/19/1978,1;
     LIMITS,6,3,200;
     PRIORITY/1,LVF(2)/2,LVF(2)/3,LVF(2)/4,LVF(2)/5,LVF(2)/6,LVF(2);
     PRIORITY/NCLNR,HVF(JEVNT);
     TIMST,XX(1),MACHINE 1 UTIL;
     TIMST,XX(2),MACHINE 2 UTIL;
     TIMST,XX(3),MACHINE 3 UTIL;
     TIMST,XX(4),MACHINE 4 UTIL;
     TIMST,XX(5),MACHINE 5 UTIL;
     TIMST,XX(6),MACHINE 6 UTIL;
     STAT,1,JOB PROC TIME,20/100./20.0;
     STAT,2,JOB TARDINESS,20/-100./5.0;
     STAT,3,JOB LATENESS;
     INI,0,20000;
     FIN;
```

Figure 8-11   Input statements for job shop model.

that six files are to be used, that there are three attributes per entry, and at most there will be 200 entries. The 200 entries is our best estimate of the maximum possible number of concurrent jobs. The priority statement establishes that each file is to be ranked on low-value-first using attribute 2. A priority statement for the event calendar is also given which specifies that secondary ranking for the event calendar should be based on high-value-first based on the event code. In this way if an arrival event and end-of-service event occur at the same time, the end-of-service event will be processed first since it has the higher event code. The remaining input statements prescribe the statistics to be collected during the simulation run.

Summary of Results. The SLAM Summary Report for this example is shown in Figure 8-12 for a simulation length of 20000 minutes. The estimate of the mean job processing time is approximately 148 minutes based on 808 jobs. The standard deviation estimate is approximately 87 minutes and indicates an extremely high variability in the time to process a job through the shop. This can be attributed to the variability in the number of operations required per job (normally distributed with mean of 4) and the variability of each operation time (exponentially distributed with mean 20). Thus, the job processing time is a random sum of random variables†. The variance of the sample mean is not estimated so we do not have a reliability value for the estimate of the mean processing time. However, the machine utilization statistics indicate a relatively low usage of machines (from 0.51 to 0.62) and the file statistics indicate a small amount of queueing on the average (from 0.35 to 0.63). Thus, the jobs although not independent have less interaction than expected. In such a situation, the standard deviation of the sample mean can be hypothesized based on independent job times. This value is $148/\sqrt{808}$ or approximately 5.3. By the central limit theorem, we expect the average processing time to be normally distributed and, hence, 95 percent of the values to be within 2 standard deviations of the mean. This can be interpreted for this example as expecting an average processing time on a replication of the simulation to be in the range 142 to 153 in 95 out of 100 replications. Because we assumed independence of the jobs, the range is likely to be smaller than expected.

Let us investigate other outputs of the model to see if they agree with our expectations. The number of job arrivals in 20000 time units is 810. This includes 808

---

† The variance of a random sum of independent random variables, σ_J^2, is given by

$$\sigma_J^2 = E[N]\sigma_S^2 + E^2[S]\sigma_N^2$$

where N is the number of operations and S is the service time random variable (see Appendix to Chapter 13).

jobs processed, plus 2 jobs currently on machines. The mean job interarrival time is given as 25 minutes which corresponds to a rate of 0.04 jobs/minute. Thus in 20000 minutes, we expect 800 jobs. Since the interarrival times are exponential†, the number of arrivals is Poisson distributed and the variance of the number of job arrivals in 20000 minutes is also 800. The standard deviation of number of job arrivals is approximately 28, and the observed number of 810 is within 1 standard deviation of the mean value of 800. From this discussion, the estimates derived from this simulation run for utilization should be higher than average since the number of job arrivals is higher than average. This point is explored further below.

The utilization of a shop is usually estimated as the arrival rate divided by the service rate. The average arrival rate was given above as 0.04 jobs/minute. The average service rate for the shop is 0.05 operations/minute/machine. Since there are six machines, we have an average capacity of 0.30 operations/minute. To convert the average arrival rate from jobs/minute to operations/minute, we must estimate the expected number of operations/job. The number of operations/job was described as normally distributed with mean of 4 but with the tails of the distribution clipped at 3 and 6. As described in Chapter 2, this is referred to as a mixed distribution. The probability of requiring 3, 4, 5, or 6 operations/job can be obtained from normal probability tables as given below.

Number of Operations/Job	Probability
3	0.3085
4	0.3830
5	0.2417
6	0.0668

Using this table, the expected number of operations/job is computed as 4.0668. Using the above estimates, we compute a hypothesized utilization of 0.542. The average of the six average machine utilization values given in Figure 8-12 is slightly higher than the theoretical value computed as anticipated. The observed average utilization is close to an adjusted theoretical average where an adjustment factor based on the number of jobs completed (808) divided by the expected number of jobs (800) is applied to the expected utilization. This agreement between theoretical and simulation results based on average and linearity assumptions is better than usual due to the low utilization factor employed. As explained

---

† If interarrival time were not exponential, then the central limit theorem could be used to estimate the variance (see Appendix to Chapter 13).

previously, a low utilization factor reduces job interference and, hence, statistical dependence. The above analysis does, however, provide guidelines that assist in comprehending the outputs from a simulation.

```
                    S L A M    S U M M A R Y    R E P O R T

        SIMULATION PROJECT ADVANCED JOBSHOP          BY PRITSKER

        DATE  2/19/1978                              RUN NUMBER    1 OF    1


        CURRENT TIME      .2000+05
        STATISTICAL ARRAYS CLEARED AT TIME      .0000
```

```
              **STATISTICS FOR VARIABLES BASED ON OBSERVATION**
```

	MEAN VALUE	STANDARD DEVIATION	COEFF. OF VARIATION	MINIMUM VALUE	MAXIMUM VALUE	NUMBER OF OBSERVATIONS
JOB PROC TIME	.1475+03	.8692+02	.5892+00	.8241+01	.6922+03	808
JOB TARDINESS	-.5547+02	.5521+02	-.9954+00	-.3775+03	-.5828+00	303
JOB LATENESS	.1372+02	.7226+02	.5268+01	-.3775+03	.2355+03	808

```
              **STATISTICS FOR TIME-PERSISTENT VARIABLES**
```

	MEAN VALUE	STANDARD DEVIATION	MINIMUM VALUE	MAXIMUM VALUE	TIME INTERVAL	CURRENT VALUE
MACHINE 1 UTIL	.6203+00	.4853+00	.0000	.1000+01	.2000+05	.0000
MACHINE 2 UTIL	.5051+00	.5000+00	.0000	.1000+01	.2000+05	.0000
MACHINE 3 UTIL	.5519+00	.4973+00	.0000	.1000+01	.2000+05	.1000+01
MACHINE 4 UTIL	.5236+00	.4994+00	.0000	.1000+01	.2000+05	.0000
MACHINE 5 UTIL	.5137+00	.4998+00	.0000	.1000+01	.2000+05	.1000+01
MACHINE 6 UTIL	.5693+00	.4952+00	.0000	.1000+01	.2000+05	.0000

```
                    **FILE STATISTICS**
```

FILE NUMBER	ASSOCIATED NODE TYPE	AVERAGE LENGTH	STANDARD DEVIATION	MAXIMUM LENGTH	CURRENT LENGTH	AVERAGE WAITING TIME
1		.6258	1.0677	8	0	38.8707
2		.3584	.8163	8	0	21.9887
3		.5328	1.0763	7	0	34.8257
4		.3465	.7421	8	0	23.6504
5		.3473	.7550	4	0	21.1767
6		.4758	1.0089	11	0	33.6220

Figure 8-12 SLAM summary report for job shop model.

Returning now to the SLAM Summary Report, we see that job lateness has an average value of 13.72. If we desire a zero average lateness then the due-date setting procedure should be adjusted by decreasing the safety factor by 13.72. This adjustment affects the priority assignments of jobs and we should not expect the average to be precisely zero. From the summary report, it is seen that 303 of the 808 jobs processed were tardy, that is, they were completed after their assigned due day, and the average tardiness was 55.47 Since the shop has a low utilization, the inability to meet due dates is primarily due to the due date setting procedure.

This example illustrates how job shop dispatching rules can be analyzed using SLAM. Extensions to more complex siuations are easily incorporated. The basic structure of the model need not be changed in order to study advanced job shop procedures.

8.8   CHAPTER SUMMARY

In this chapter, advanced file manipulation subprograms are discussed and their use illustrated. Procedures for accessing and using file entry pointers are presented. Four subprograms for associating auxiliary attributes with an entry in the SLAM filing system are described. SLAM subprograms for directly obtaining statistical estimates for variables on which data is collected, and for presenting and preparing specialized output reports, are detailed. An example of outputs obtained from a user-developed trace of events by coding subroutine UMONT is provided. Subprograms CLEAR, ERROR, and GTABL are described. An example involving a job shop model is presented which illustrates the use of auxiliary attributes and the advanced SLAM file manipulation subprograms.

8.9   EXERCISES

8-1.   Write the statements required to determine the location of the entry that satisfies the following conditions:
   (*a*)   The entry in file 2 that has attribute 3 equal to 10 .
   (*b*)   The entry with the largest value of attribute 4 greater than 0 in file 1. What subroutine should be used to remove this entry from file 1?
   (*c*)   The entry whose third attribute is closest to 10 but does not exceed 10 in file 3.
   (*d*)   In file 3, the entry whose third attribute is closest to 10 but is not less than 10.
   (*e*)   The entry in file 4 whose second attribute is the largest. Entries with the value of attribute 2 less than 3 cannot be used.

8-2.   Write the statements necessary to obtain the attribute values associated with the second event in the event file. Specify the values of the variables that would be obtained.

8-3.   Specify whether you would use subroutine COLCT or a TIMST input statement to collect statistics on each of the following variables. Give an explanation for your decision.

(a)   The age of individuals going to a barber shop.

(b)   The time it takes a secretary to type a letter.

(c)   The amount of time devoted by employees to breaks.

(d)   The amount of water in a reservoir.

(e)   The price of a stock during a given day.

(f)   The price of a stock over the last 100 days.

(g)   The dollars in your bank account.

8-4.   Given that a histogram has 10 cells, the lower limit is specified as 5, and the width of each cell is specified as 1, determine the cell number into which each of the following values would be inserted: 7.2, 9.1, 5.0, 4.1, 22.7, and 3.3

8-5.   Write a program to compute 400 samples from a normal distribution with a mean of 50, a standard deviation of 10, a minimum value of 0, and a maximum value of 100. In this program, compute the average and standard deviation of the samples, the minimum and maximum value obtained from the samples, and a histogram of the sample values between 30 and 70 with a cell width equal to 4.

8-6.   Develop a function subprogram that determines the total number of entries in all files. Define the function name as NTOTE.

8-7.   Write a subroutine called FIND3 that locates an entry NTRY in file J such that the value of ATRIB(1) is less than X(1), the value of ATRIB(2) is less than X(2), and the value of ATRIB(3) is greater than or equal to X(3). If no entry in file J satisfies the above conditions, return a negative value to the calling routine. Write a statement using FIND3 that locates an entry in file 4 whose first two attributes are less than three and whose third attribute is greater than five.

8-8.   Write a subprogram that will compute the sum of the product of two attributes of a given file.

8-9.   Develop a function subprogram for inclusion in SLAM that performs a table look-up function for a table whose independent variable is not specified in equal increments.

8-10.   Develop a subroutine for SLAM called RGRES that will generate samples from any desired regression equation involving terms in x with the exponents ½, 1, 2, and 3, and terms of the form e^x and $1n(X)$. Assume that the random portion of the regression sample is normally distributed and the coefficients are arguments to the subroutine.

8-11.   Write the code to schedule an event into file 1 and to file an entry into file 3. The event and entry have the following attributes:

Attributes of event:

Event time   Current time plus a sample from a uniform distribution between 10. and 20.

Event code   7

Attribute 1   Location of the entry to be placed in file 3

Attributes of entry in file 3:

1	127.
2	TNOW
3	Location of the *event* described above

8-12. (From Schriber (2)) A production shop is comprised of six different groups of machines. Each group consists of a number of identical machines of a given kind as indicated below.

Machine Group Number	Kind of Machines in Group	Number of Machines in Group
1	Casting units	14
2	Lathes	5
3	Planers	4
4	Drill presses	8
5	Shapers	16
6	Polishing machines	4

Three different types of jobs move through the production shop. These job-types are designated as Type 1, Type 2, and Type 3. Each job-type requires that operations be performed at specified kinds of machines in a specified sequence. All operation times are exponentially distributed. The visitation sequences and average operation times are shown below.

Visitation Sequences and Mean Operation Times for the Three Types of Jobs

Job Type	Total Number of Machines to be Visited	Machine Visitation Sequence	Mean Operation Time (Minutes)
1	4	Casting Unit	125
		Planer	35
		Lathe	20
		Polishing machine	60
2	3	Shaper	105
		Drill press	90
		Lathe	65
3	5	Casting unit	235
		Shaper	250
		Drill press	50
		Planer	30
		Polishing machine	25

Jobs arrive at the shop with exponential interarrival times with a mean of 9.6 minutes. Twenty-four percent of the jobs in this stream are of Type 1, 44 percent are of Type 2, and the rest are of Type 3. The type of arriving job is independent of the job type of the preceding arrival. Build a SLAM model which simulates the operation of the production shop for five separate 40-hour weeks to obtain: 1) the distribution of job residence time in the shop, as a function of job-type; 2) the utilization of the machines; and 3) queue statistics for each machine group.

Embellishments: (a) Employ a shortest processing time rule for ordering jobs waiting before each machine group. Compare output values.

(b) Give priority to jobs on the basis of type. Job type 3 is to have the highest priority then Type 2 and then Type 1 jobs.

(c) Change the average job interarrival time to 9 minutes and evaluate system performance.

(d) Develop a cost structure for this problem that would enable you to specify how to spend $100,000 for new machines.

8-13. Generate the job sequences and processing times for the production shop of Exercise 8-12 so that they can be used to test different operating rules and machine configurations.

8-14. Consider a job shop in which there can be as many as 10 machine groups. The number of machines/machine group is an input. The types of jobs processed in the job shop have not been categorized. The number of operations per job, the processing time/job and the routing of a job is established as input. Develop a general SLAM program to simulate the job shop.

Embellishment: Use this general purpose job shop model to study the production shop described in Exercise 8-12.

8.10   REFERENCES

1. Eilon, S., I. G. Chowdhury, and S. S. Serghiou, "Experiments with the SI^x Rule in Job Shop Scheduling," *Simulation*, Vol. 24, 1975, pp. 45-48.
2. Schriber, T., *Simulation Using GPSS*, John Wiley, 1974.
3. Wineberger, A. et al., "Use of Simulation to Evaluate Capital Investment Alternatives in the Steel Industry: A Case Study," Bethlehem Steel Corporation. Presented at the Winter Simulation Conference, December 1977.

8.11   APPENDIX: THE SLAM FILING SYSTEM

The SLAM filing system employs a double link list pointing system for storing entities in files and future events on the event calendar. Each entry consists of a set of real-valued attributes and is linked to other entries in the file by a predecessor and successor pointer. The attribute values and associated pointers are stored as a group in the companion arrays NSET and QSET. By use of the equivalence statement, EQUIVALENCE(NSET(1),QSET(1)), it is possible to use a single contiguous storage area for storing both integer pointers and real-valued attributes. Integer pointers must be referenced using the array NSET and real attribute values must be referenced using the array QSET. However, as noted earlier, the name NSET is used in this text to denote the storage area when either name applies.

The entries stored in a file are considered by SLAM in a logical order, not a physical order. Their order in the file is maintained by the pointing system. Pointers are used to keep track of each entry's predecessor and successor. The pointers establish the location in NSET where the entries are stored. A zero value for a pointer indicates that either no predecessor or no successor exists.

As an example let NSET be a 16 cell storage array and let the entries in NSET have only two attributes. Four cells would be required to store the entry: the first cell stores the entry's predecessor pointer, the next two cells are for the attribute values, and the last cell stores the entry's successor pointer. Since there are only 16 cells and it takes four cells per entry, four entries, at most, could be stored in the 16 cells of NSET. This is shown below.

```
1  2  3  4  5  6  7  8  9 10 11 12 13 14 15 16   Cell number
┌──┬──┬──┬──┬──┬──┬──┬──┬──┬──┬──┬──┬──┬──┬──┬──┐
│  │  │  │  │  │  │  │  │  │  │  │  │  │  │  │  │   NSET
└──┴──┴──┴──┴──┴──┴──┴──┴──┴──┴──┴──┴──┴──┴──┴──┘
```

The pointer to an entry is the first cell number of the group of cells in which the entry is stored. Thus in the example above, the pointer to an entry stored in cells 1−4 is 1, cells 5−8 is 5, and so forth. At initialization, each group of cells is linked to a successor group using the pointers, as shown below.

```
1  2  3  4  5  6  7  8  9 10 11 12 13 14 15 16   Cell number
┌──┬──┬──┬──┬──┬──┬──┬──┬──┬──┬──┬──┬──┬──┬──┬──┐
│-1│  │  │ 5│-1│  │  │ 9│-1│  │  │13│-1│  │  │ 0│   NSET
└──┴──┴──┴──┴──┴──┴──┴──┴──┴──┴──┴──┴──┴──┴──┴──┘
```

For a given group, the pointer to its successor group is stored in the last cell of the given group. Its first cell is used to store the pointer to the entry's predecessor. As previously noted, zeros indicate that either no predecessor or no successor exists. On initialization a −1 is put in each cell normally used for the predecessor pointer. In the example above, if we name each group by its first cell number, group 1 has as its successor group 5. The successor of group 5 is group 9. After initialization, all groups of cells are available for storing attributes of entries. The way NSET is initialized, group 1 is the first available group. The variable MFA is used to point to this first available group and, at initialization, MFA = 1. The second available group is the successor to the first available group. The successor pointer stored in cell 4 shows that this is the group whose first cell number is five. The SLAM variable NNATR defines the total number of attributes per entry and is equal to MATR + 2. The variables NNAPO and NNAPT are equal to NNATR

+ 1 and NNATR + 2, respectively. For the example being considered, NNATR = 2. In general terms, the pointer to the successor group of the first available group (MFA) is stored in NSET(LC) where LC = MFA + NNAPO. By continuing in this manner, all groups that are available for storing entries can be determined.

Thus far only the available groups of cells for storing entries have been discussed. Suppose that an entry must be inserted into file 1. The user first defines the attribute values by using a buffer array A. These would be inserted into file 1, using the SLAM subprogram FILEM, and the statement would be CALL FILEM(1,A). This entry, which consists of the above two attributes, would be stored in the first available group of NSET. Thus the two attribute values would be stored in cells 2 and 3 of QSET and the predecessor and successor pointers for group 1 would be changed to show that group 1 is in file 1 and is no longer a member of the file of groups available for storing entries. In this case, the pointers for the new entry would both be zero since there are no other entries in file 1. In SLAM, the function MMFE(I) and MMLE(I) are the values of the pointers to the first entry in file I and the last entry in file I, respectively. Whenever MMFE(I) or MMLE(I) is zero, there are no entries in file I. SLAM automatically updates these pointers and keeps track of statistics on the number of entries in each file. Thus the functions MMFE(1) and MMLE(1) would assign the value 1 if invoked to indicate that group 1 is the only entry in file 1.

Since an entry has been put into available group 1, group 1 is no longer the first available group for storing an entry. The new first available group is the successor of the old first available group. As a result, MFA is updated and given a value of five to indicate that cell 5 is the starting location of the new first available group. Note that by this procedure a consistent list of available groups is maintained and only the first one on the list has been deleted. As entries are removed from files, their storage cells become available for storing new entries, and the group of cells is placed at the top of the list by updating MFA and the successor pointer of the new group. If the value for MFA is zero, there is no longer a group of cells available for storing an entry. If the user attempts to store an entry when MFA is zero, an error will result. (All SLAM error codes are listed in Appendix D).

Multiple files are maintained in NSET by use of pointers to the first and last entry in each file. Since each entry in a file has both a predecessor and successor pointer, all entries in a file can be traced from either the first or last entry. The following diagram illustrates two files in NSET (expanded to 32 cells) where each entry has two attributes.

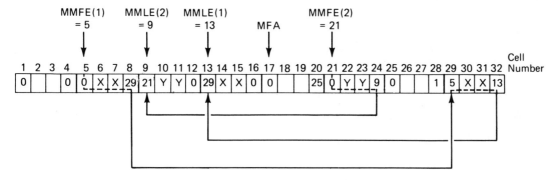

Entries are inserted and removed by use of the file processing routines described in Chapters 7 and 8. These routines automatically update the entry pointers as required. In the case of insertion of an entry into a file, the relative rank of the entry within the file is determined based on the ranking procedure prescribed for that file.

CHAPTER 9

Combined Network-Discrete
Event Modeling with SLAM

9.1   INTRODUCTION

In the previous chapters, we described two distinct world views of simulation modeling. The network orientation has the advantage that a working simulation model can be developed with relative ease. The disadvantage of the network orientation is that not all systems can be accurately represented by the available network elements. In contrast, the discrete event world view provides the analyst with the capability to model any level of complexity of a system. However, this flexibility is obtained by an increase in the modeling effort. Thus, both world views are of importance to the simulation analyst.

Given a system to be simulated, the SLAM modeler may be faced with the choice of which world view to employ. If the system can be represented by the network world view, then the time and effort required to develop the simulation will normally be less than that required by the discrete event world view. Thus, the choice between the world views is generally made by employing the network orientation if possible. As with most decisions of this type, it is not a clear-cut one. The main judgmental factor to consider here is the extent to which the model will have to be embellished in future problem-solving efforts. Fortunately, SLAM allows for both network and discrete event additions.

Thus in SLAM, the advantages of both world views are combined into a single modeling framework which permits a simulation model to be represented using a combined network-discrete event approach. With this unified framework, an analyst can model the portion of a system which can be accommodated by the network approach as a network with the discrete event viewpoint employed only for those selected portions of the system which demand the increased flexibility afforded by the discrete event orientation. Since large complex systems normally contain major portions which can be conveniently modeled using network concepts, a reduction in modeling effort can be anticipated.

In this chapter, we describe the procedures for constructing combined network-discrete event models. We begin by describing the EVENT and ENTER nodes which provide the key interface points between the network portion and discrete event portion of a combined model. We next describe a set of SLAM provided subprograms which allow the modeler to change the status of the network elements by freeing units of resources, altering resource capacities, opening and closing gates, stopping activities, and specifying attribute values and activity durations from discrete event subprograms. This is followed by a description of the SLAM processing logic for simulating combined network-discrete event models and a summary of the data input procedures for combined models. Two combined network-discrete event examples are used to illustrate the procedures.

9.2 THE EVENT NODE

The symbol and the input statement for the EVENT node are shown below.

EVENT, JEVNT, M;

The EVENT node is included in the network model to interface the network portion of a model with a discrete event. The EVENT node causes subroutine EVENT(JEVNT) to be called every time an entity arrives to the EVENT node. The value of JEVNT specifies the event code of the discrete event to be executed, and M specifies the maximum number of emanating activities to be taken following the processing of the EVENT node. Since the logic associated with the EVENT node is coded by the modeler as a discrete event, its operational logic provides complete modeling flexibility. Thus, if the modeler is faced with an operation for which a standard network node is not provided, the modeler can employ the event node to perform the specialized logic required.

The statement format for the EVENT node consists of the node name EVENT beginning in or after column seven, followed by the event code JEVNT and the M value separated by commas. A node label may be specified anywhere in the first five columns; however, as with other node types only the first four characters of the label are significant.

The procedure for coding an event created by an EVENT node is identical to the procedure for coding an event in a discrete event simulation model. Subroutine EVENT maps the event code JEVNT onto the appropriate event subroutine containing the coding for the event logic. In coding the event logic, the modeler has access to the SLAM provided subprograms for performing commonly encountered functions such as random sampling, file manipulation, and event scheduling.

When an entity arrives to an EVENT node, the SLAM processor loads the attributes of the arriving entity into the ATRIB array prior to the call to subroutine EVENT(JEVNT). Following the return from subroutine EVENT(JEVNT), the SLAM processor assigns the values in the ATRIB array as the attributes of the entities exiting from the EVENT node. Thus, the modeler can make assignments to attributes of network entities which pass through the EVENT node from within the associated discrete event. The use of the ATRIB buffer should be reserved for this purpose when processing an event from an EVENT node.

The logic associated with a discrete event in a combined model may involve testing the status or changing the value of variables associated with the network portion of the model. Values of network related variables can be obtained using the SLAM functions listed in Table 9-1. These correspond to the functions that can be used in a network to assign values to attributes (see Table 4-2).

Table 9-1   Functions for accessing the status of an activity, gate, or resource.

Function	Definition
NNACT(I)	Number of active entities in activity I at current time
NNCNT(I)	The number of entities that have completed activity I
NNGAT(I)	Status of gate number I at current time: 0 → open, 1 → closed
NNRSC(I)	Current number of resource type I available

The combined network-discrete event framework of SLAM permits the modeler to reference a file number in a discrete event which is employed in the network portion of the model. This is an important feature in many combined models. For example, entities which are waiting in file 1 at a QUEUE node in the network model may be removed within a discrete event by referencing file number 1 in the call to subroutine RMOVE. Thus, the following statement would remove the first entity waiting at the QUEUE node in file 1 and place its attributes in the array A.

    CALL RMOVE(1,1,A)

When this statement is invoked, the entity removed from file 1 is no longer in the network.

The modeler can also reference a file associated with a network node from a discrete event when using subroutine FILEM(IFILE,A). If IFILE is associated with a network node, the SLAM processor does not directly insert the entity into the file, but processes the entity as an arrival to the node immediately following the return from the discrete event routine to the SLAM processor. For example, assume that file 1 is associated with a QUEUE node in the network model, the following statement would schedule an entity arrival to occur at the QUEUE node with the first attribute of the entity equal to 10.

    A(1)=10.
    CALL FILEM(1,A)

This arrival event will be the next event processed unless other calls to subroutine FILEM or SCHDL are made in the event routine.

   Following the return from the discrete event to the SLAM processor, the entity arrival to the QUEUE node with file 1 would be processed with the arriving entity either going directly into service if a server is idle, balking if the queue is full, or being inserted into file 1 to wait for a server. Note, however, that the value of the number of entries in file 1, obtained from NNQ(1), would not change until after the return to the SLAM processor.

   The modeler can, when referencing files associated with network nodes, employ any of the file manipulation routines which are available in discrete event simulations. For example, the modeler can employ function NFIND to search for a specific entity waiting at an AWAIT node.

9.3   THE ENTER NODE

   The symbol and the input statement for the ENTER node are shown below.

ENTER, NUM, M;

   A second interface point between the network and discrete portions of a combined model is the ENTER node. The ENTER node is provided to permit the modeler to insert selectively an entity into the network from a user-written discrete event subroutine. Each ENTER node has a unique user-assigned integer code NUM and a M value which specifies the maximum number of emanating activities to be taken at each release of the node. The ENTER node is released from within a discrete event at each call to subroutine ENTER(NUM,A) where NUM is the numeric code of the ENTER node being released and A is the name of the array containing the attributes of the entity to be inserted into the network at the ENTER node NUM. The ENTER node can also be released by entity arrivals to the node.

The statement format for the ENTER node consists of the node name ENTER beginning in or after column seven followed by the numeric code NUM and the M value separated by commas. A node label may be specified anywhere in the first five columns with the first four letters of the label significant.

9.4 SUBPROGRAMS FOR COMBINED MODELING

Within the discrete event portion of a combined network-discrete event simulation model, the user has complete access to all the discrete event subprograms described in Chapters 7 and 8. These include the subprograms for event scheduling, file manipulations, and report writing. In addition to these functional capabilities, SLAM provides the modeler with a set of subprograms which allow the user to effect changes in the network portion of a combined model from within a discrete event. These subprograms permit the modeler to change the status of resources, change the status of gates, cause an end of activity to occur for a specified entity or a specified group of entities, and to define attribute values and activity durations. In the following sections, we describe the subprograms and procedures for performing these functions.

9.5 CHANGING THE STATUS OF A RESOURCE

SLAM provides the modeler with subroutines which free a specified number of units of a resource or alter the capacity of a resource by a specified amount. Before describing these routines, the method for referencing a resource needs to be established.

In network statements, resources are referenced by either the resource name or number. In the resource subroutines, a resource must be referenced by its number. Recall from Chapter 4 that the SLAM processor automatically numbers the resources in the order in which the RESOURCE blocks are inputted to the SLAM processor. The first resource is assigned number 1, the second resource is assigned number 2, and so on. For example, consider the following set of RE-SOURCE blocks included in the network portion of a model:

RESOURCE/TUG(2), 1, 2/BERTH(3), 3;
RESOURCE/CREW, 4;

The processor would assign the TUGs as resource number 1, the BERTHs as resource number 2, and the CREW as resource number 3. When changing the status of a resource from within a discrete event, the resource number is included as an argument to the appropriate subroutine to distinguish between resource types.

9.5.1   Freeing Resources

Subroutine FREE(IR,N) releases N units of resource number IR. The freed units of the resource are made available to waiting entities according to the order of the file numbers specified in the RESOURCE statement included in the network model. For the RESOURCE blocks depicted above, the statement

CALL FREE(1,2)

would release 2 units of the resource TUG. These tugs are made available to entities waiting in file 1. If both tugs are not used, then file 2 would be interrogated to determine if an entity was waiting for the use of a tug. The execution of the statement CALL FREE(1,2) is identical to the execution of the following network statement:

FREE, TUG/2;

9.5.2   Altering Resource Capacities

Subroutine ALTER(IR,N) changes the capacity of resource number IR by N units. In the case where the capacity of the resource is decreased below current utilization, the excess capacity is destroyed as it becomes freed. The capacity can be reduced to a minimum of zero with additional reduction requests having no effect. Assuming the RESOURCE blocks depicted earlier, the following statement would reduce the number of tugs by 1 unit:

CALL ALTER(1,−1)

This statement produces the same effect as the execution of the following network statement:

ALTER,TUG/−1;

9.6 CHANGING THE STATUS OF A GATE

SLAM provides the capability to open and close gates from within a discrete event. A gate must be referenced by its gate number from within a discrete event. The gate number is automatically assigned by SLAM to each gate in the order that the GATE blocks are inputted to the SLAM processor. For example, consider the following set of GATE blocks included in the network portion of a model:

GATE/DOOR1,OPEN,4;
GATE/DOOR2,CLOSED,5;

The processor would assign DOOR1 as gate number 1 and DOOR2 as gate number 2.

9.6.1 Opening a Gate

Subroutine OPEN(IG) opens gate number IG and releases all waiting entities in the AWAIT files specified in the GATE block. For the GATE blocks depicted above, the following statement would open DOOR2:

CALL OPEN(2)

This statement is equivalent to the network statement

OPEN,DOOR2;

9.6.2 Closing a Gate

Subroutine CLOSX(IG) closes gate number IG†. For the GATE blocks depicted above, the following statement would close DOOR1:

CALL CLOSX(1)

This statement is equivalent to the network statement

CLOSE, DOOR1;

---

† The subroutine name CLOSE was not used because of a conflict with a system routine on the UNIVAC 1100 Series Computers.

9.7   STOPPING AN ACTIVITY

In complex systems, the length of a specific activity may not be known a priori but may depend upon the dynamics of the system. For example, in a queueing system the service rate may be a function of the number of entities waiting for the server and thus may change over time. Therefore the duration of the activity is unknown at the start time of the activity and is affected by future arrivals. One way of modeling an indefinite activity duration using network concepts is to specify the activity duration as keyed to the release of a labeled node in the network. When the labeled node to which the duration is keyed is released, all entities undergoing the activity are completed. The combined network-discrete event framework of SLAM also permits the modeler to specify that a specific on-going activity is to be stopped from within a discrete event. This allows the user to selectively stop a specific entity undergoing an activity without stopping the other entities undergoing the same activity.

To stop an activity for a network entity from within a discrete event, the modeler must specify the duration of the activity in the network model as STOPA (NTC) where NTC is a positive integer which is user-assigned as an entity code to distinguish the entity from other entities in the same activity or elsewhere in the network. If NTC is specified as a real value it is truncated to the nearest integer. The value of NTC can be specified as a number, a SLAM variable, or a SLAM random variable. By specifying the entity code as an attribute of the entity or as a random variable, the modeler can assign different entity codes to entities within the same activity. Examples of valid network specifications for the STOPA activity duration are as follows:

```
ACT,STOPA(1);
ACT,STOPA(ATRIB(3));
```

The first example specifies that all entities in the activity are to be assigned entity code 1. The second example specifies that the third attribute of each entity is to be assigned as the entity code.

The mechanism for stopping the activity for a network entity from within the discrete event is to call subroutine STOPA(NTC). A call to subroutine STOPA (NTC) causes an end of activity to occur for every entity with entity code NTC that is being processed by an activity whose duration is specified as STOPA. For example, execution of the following statement causes all activities to be completed whose duration was specified as STOPA(NTC) if the entity in the activity has entity code 1:

CALL STOPA(1)

Since the execution of the call STOPA(NTC) statement causes the end of an activity to occur for each entity with entity code NTC, there may be none, one, or several activities ended by a call to STOPA(NTC). For each activity that is ended, the end-of-activity event for the entity in the activity is placed at the top of the event calendar to be processed immediately following the return from the discrete event back to the SLAM processor. If more than one activity is stopped in this manner, then the end-of-activity event for each entity is processed following the return to SLAM in the order in which the activities were started. If no entities are currently keyed to STOPA(NTC), then execution of a call to STOPA(NTC) has no effect.

9.8 USER-CODED ATTRIBUTE ASSIGNMENTS AND ACTIVITY DURATIONS

To permit the network modeler to make his own assignment of a value to an attribute or to establish a duration for an activity, SLAM includes the option of specifying the function USERF(IFN) to be prescribed. The argument IFN is a code established by the user and is referred to as a user function number. Function USERF is user-written and is called in two situations:

1. An entity passes through an ASSIGN node and one of the assignments is to be made in USERF; and
2. A duration for an activity is specified as USERF.

The function USERF allows a modeler to make programming inserts into the network model in the two locations described above. In the programming insert, the user can employ all FORTRAN coding procedures and the SLAM subprograms described in Chapters 7 and 8 with the restriction that file operations associated with the event calendar are not permitted. When it is desired to manipulate files, an EVENT node must be employed.

As an example of the uses of function USERF, consider the following single-server, single-queue network.

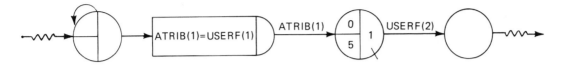

In this network, user function 1 is used to assign a value to attribute 1 at the ASSIGN node, and user function 2 is used to specify the duration of the service time of activity 1. ATRIB(1) is the duration of the activity representing the entity's travel to the QUEUE node. In this example, we will make this time a function of the number of remaining spaces in the QUEUE node, that is, 5-NNQ(1). If ATRIB(1) was used only as the duration of the activity then user function 1 could have been specified for the activity. Here we illustrate a concept and demonstrate the use of function USERF to assign an attribute value. If future decisions were made based on the value of ATRIB(1) then the model as depicted would be required.

The service time for activity 1 will also be made a function of the number of entities waiting for service. The general form for writing function USERF(IFN) is shown below.

```
    FUNCTION  USERF(IFN)
    GO  TO  (1,2),IFN
1 Set USERF as the time to travel to QUEUE node
    RETURN
2 Set USERF as service time as a function of number in queue
    RETURN
    END
```

This example illustrates how IFN, the user function number, is decoded to allow different user functions to be employed throughout the network model.

For this example, user function 1 only requires USERF to be set equal to 5-NNQ(1). When a return is made, SLAM assigns the value of USERF to ATRIB(1). For user function 2, we require knowledge of how service time varies as a function of the number of entities in the QUEUE node. For illustrative purposes, we will assume an exponential service time whose mean decreases as the number in the queue is increased to a value of 3. When there are more than 3 in the queue, the mean service time increases. A table of mean service time as a function of the number in the queue is shown below.

Number in Queue	Mean Service Time
0	10.
1	9.
2	8.
3	7.
4	9.
5	10.

The specific coding for function USERF(IFN) for this situation would be:

```
      FUNCTION  USERF(IFN)
      DIMENSION  ST(6)
      DATA  ST/10.,9.,8.,7.,9.,10./
      GO  TO  (1,2),IFN
    1 USERF = 5 − NNQ(1)
      RETURN
    2 XNINQ=NNQ(1)
      AVEST=GTABL(ST,XNINQ,0.0,5.0,1.0)
      USERF=EXPON(AVEST,1)
      RETURN
      END
```

The first two statements of the function dimension the array ST and establish values for ST through a DATA statement. Next, the function number is decoded. At statement 1, USERF is established as the value to be assigned when user function 1 is invoked. At statement 2, XNINQ is established as the current number in file 1. The average service time is determined through the use of function GTABL which is the SLAM table look-up function described in Chapter 8, Section 8.6.4. The arguments to function GTABL are the dependent variable values, the independent variable for which the table look-up is being performed, the value of the independent variable corresponding to the first value in the ST array, the value of the independent variable corresponding to the last value of the ST array, and the increment between the values of the independent variables corresponding to the values of the dependent variables given in the array ST. The value of USERF is then set equal to a sample from an exponential distribution using AVEST as the average service time and employing stream number 1. Note that the stream number must be given in function EXPON since direct coding is being employed. Also note that the arguments to function GTABL must all be real values to correspond to the arguments used when coding function GTABL.

Although the above example is straightforward, it does illustrate the potential flexibility employed by allowing program inserts to be made in network models. Function USERF can be made as complex as necessary to meet the modeling requirements of the user.

9.9 THE SLAM PROCESSING LOGIC FOR COMBINED NETWORK-DISCRETE EVENT MODELS

The next event processing logic employed by SLAM for simulating combined network-discrete event models is depicted in Figure 9-1. The processor begins by interpreting the SLAM input statements. This is followed by an initialization phase and a call to the user-written subroutine INTLC for establishing user-defined initial conditions for the simulation. During the initialization phase, the processor places on the event calendar an entity arrival event to occur at each CREATE node in the network portion of the model at the time of the first release of the node. In addition, entities initially in QUEUE nodes are created and end-of-service events are scheduled for the service activities following the QUEUE nodes.

The execution phase of the combined network-discrete event simulation begins by selecting the first event on the event calendar. This event may be either a user-coded event corresponding to the discrete event portion of the model or a node arrival event corresponding to the network portion of the model. In either case, the processor advances the current simulated time, TNOW, to the event time of this event. A test is then made to determine if the event is associated with the network or discrete event portion of the model. If the event is associated with the discrete event portion of the model, then the attributes of the event are loaded into the ATRIB buffer array, JEVNT is set to the event code for this event, and a call is made to the user-written subroutine EVENT(JEVNT) which maps the event code onto the appropriate event subroutine call. If the event is associated with the network portion of the model, then the node arrival event is processed. If the node type is an EVENT node, then the logic for processing the node is coded by the user as a discrete event. Otherwise, the logic for processing the node arrival event is provided by the SLAM processor. Following the realization of the node arrival event, the emanating activities are tested and possibly released or the sequential node arrival event is scheduled as appropriate.

After the processing of the event as either a user-coded discrete event or a node arrival event, a test is made for one of the following end of simulation conditions:

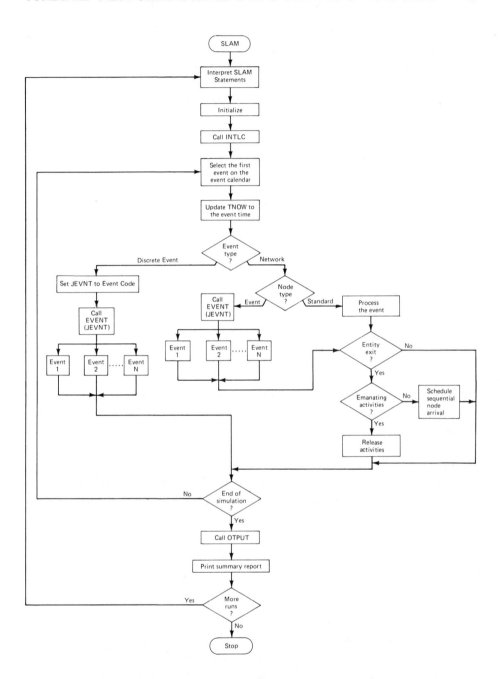

Figure 9-1 SLAM processing logic for combined network-discrete event models.

1. TNOW is greater than or equal to the ending time of the simulation.
2. There are no events on the event calendar.
3. The value of MSTOP has been set to -1 in the discrete event portion of the model.
4. A TERMINATE node has reached its specified terminate count in the network portion of the model.

If none of the end of simulation conditions is satisfied, the processor selects the next event on the event calendar and continues. If the simulation run is ended, statistics are calculated, a call is made to subroutine OTPUT, and the SLAM Summary Report is printed. Finally, a test is made to determine if additional runs are to be executed. If more runs remain, the next run is initiated. If all simulation runs have been completed, SLAM returns control to the user-written main program.

9.10   INPUT STATEMENTS FOR COMBINED NETWORK-DISCRETE EVENT MODELS

The SLAM input statements for combined network-discrete event models follow the same conventions as outlined separately for network and discrete event models with one additional restriction. This restriction is that the STAT statements (if any) associated with the discrete event portion of the model must precede the network statements. The reason for this restriction is that the internal processing by SLAM for COLCT nodes in the network portion of the model utilizes subroutine COLCT(Z,ICLCT), where the value of ICLCT is sequentially assigned by SLAM to each COLCT node beginning at a value of one above the largest ICLCT value specified by the modeler on a STAT statement. For example, if the largest ICLCT entered on a STAT statement for the discrete event portion of the model was 5 and the network portion of the model employed two COLCT nodes, then statistics for the first COLCT node read by SLAM would be collected using subroutine COLCT with ICLCT equal to 6, and statistics for the second COLCT node would be collected using subroutine COLCT with ICLCT equal to 7. If the user attempts to enter a STAT statement following the network statement model, a fatal input error results specifying an incorrect statement sequence.

To summarize, the SLAM input statements for combined network-discrete event models must be prepared in accordance with the following rules:

1. The GEN statement must be the first statement in the program, the LIMITS statement must be the second statement in the program, and the FIN statement must be the last SLAM input statement.
2. The STAT statements (if any) must precede the network statements.
3. The network description statements must be immediately preceded by the NETWORK statement and immediately followed by the ENDNETWORK statement and must precede all ENTRY statements.
4. The INITIALIZE statement (if used) must precede ENTRY and MONTR statements (if any).

9.11 EXAMPLES OF COMBINED NETWORK-DISCRETE EVENT MODELS

In this section we present two examples of combined network-discrete event simulation models. The first example is the drive-in bank problem with jockeying of cars between lanes which was modeled in Chapter 7 using the discrete event world view. The second example is a simulation of the operation of a psychiatric ward. In both cases, the combined network-discrete event world view of SLAM simplifies the modeling task.

9.12 Example 9-1. DRIVE-IN BANK WITH JOCKEYING (1)

Consider the drive-in bank example which was modeled as Example 7-1 using the discrete event world view. The drive-in bank modeled has two windows and each is manned by a teller. Cars wait for service in separate drive-in lanes. Arriving customers have a preference for lane 1 if there is an equal number of cars in the lanes. At all other times, a customer chooses the shortest lane. Customers will jockey if there is a difference of two between lanes. A maximum of eight cars can be in the drive-in bank system concurrently and an arriving customer balks if he encounters a full system. Interarrival times, service times, initial conditions, and modeling objectives are the same as described in the example in Chapter 7. The problem is to model this system using the combined network-discrete event world view of SLAM.

Concepts Illustrated. This example illustrates the combined network-discrete event modeling approach using SLAM. Two key concepts which are specifically illustrated by this example are: 1) the use of the EVENT node to interface the network portion of a model with a discrete event; and 2) the referencing of a common file number between the network and discrete event portions of a model. In addition, this example illustrates balking from a SELECT node.

SLAM Model.   The drive-in bank example is amenable to modeling with network concepts with the exception of the jockeying of cars between lanes when the lanes differ by two cars or more. Therefore, we will represent the drive-in bank system as a combined network-discrete event model where the jockeying of cars is modeled using a discrete event and all other processes in the system are modeled using network concepts. Since jockeying can occur only when a teller completes service on a customer, the discrete event for processing the jockeying of cars between lanes will be executed following the end-of-service for each entity in the system.

The network model for this example is depicted in Figure 9-2. Arriving cars are created by the CREATE node which marks current time as ATRIB(1). The first entity is created at time 0.1, and the time between car arrivals is exponentially distributed with mean of 0.5 time units. The SELECT node routes each entity to either the LEFT or RIGHT QUEUE node based on the smallest number in the queue rule (SNQ). The LEFT QUEUE node initially contains two entities and permits a maximum of three waiting entities which are stored in file 1. The LEFT QUEUE is followed by an ACTIVITY representing teller 1 which is prescribed as activity number 1. The duration of the activity is normally distributed with a mean of 1.0 and a standard deviation of 0.2. The ACTIVITY routes the entity to an EVENT node whose event code is 1. The RIGHT QUEUE node also initially contains two entities and permits a maximum of three waiting entities which are stored in file 2. The ACTIVITY following the RIGHT QUEUE node is assigned activity number 2, is normally distributed, and routes the entities to the EVENT node with event code 2. This ACTIVITY represents the service by teller 2.

At the EVENT nodes, SLAM calls the user-coded subroutine EVENT(JEVNT) with JEVNT set equal to 1 or 2 to process the discrete event logic associated with the node. The jockeying event logic is coded directly in subroutine EVENT (JEVNT) as depicted in Figure 9-3.

In subroutine EVENT(JEVNT), the variables NL1 and NL2 are computed as the number of cars in lane 1 (LEFT) and lane 2 (RIGHT), respectively. Note that the number in each lane is calculated to include the customer in service, if any. At statement 1, jockeying from the RIGHT lane to the LEFT lane is investigated. If the number of cars in the RIGHT lane exceeds the number in the LEFT

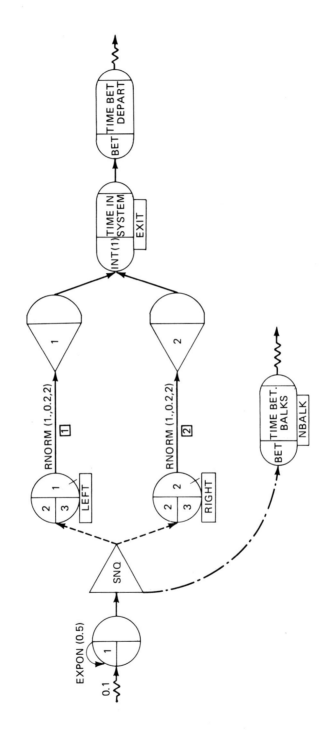

Figure 9-2 Network for combined network-discrete event model of drive-in bank.

331

```
      SUBROUTINE EVENT(I)
      COMMON/SCOM1/ ATRIB(100),DD(100),DDL(100),DTNOW,II,MFA,MSTOP,NCLNR
     1,NCRDR,NPRNT,NNRUN,NNSET,NTAPE,SS(100),SSL(100),TNEXT,TNOW,XX(100)
      NL1=NNQ(1)+NNACT(1)
      NL2=NNQ(2)+NNACT(2)
      GO TO (1,2),I
C*****IF THE NUMBER IN LANE 2 EXCEEDS LANE 1 BY 2
    1 IF(NL2.LT.NL1+2) RETURN
C*****THEN JOCKEY FROM 2 TO 1
      CALL ULINK(NNQ(2),2)
      CALL LINK(1)
      RETURN
C*****IF THE NUMBER IN LANE 1 EXCEEDS LANE 2 BY 2
    2 IF(NL1.LT.NL2+2) RETURN
C*****THEN JOCKEY FROM 1 TO 2
      CALL ULINK(NNQ(1),1)
      CALL LINK(2)
      RETURN
      END
```

Figure 9-3 Subroutine EVENT for combined network-discrete event model of the drive-in bank.

lane by two, then the last entity in file 2 (whose rank is NNQ(2)) is removed from the RIGHT QUEUE node by a call to ULINK with IFILE=2 and is scheduled to arrive at the LEFT QUEUE node at the current simulated time by a call to subroutine LINK with IFILE=1. This completes the code for jockeying and is followed by a RETURN statement.

At statement 2, if the number of cars in the LEFT lane exceeds the number in the RIGHT lane by two, the reverse jockeying procedure is executed. If the lanes do not differ by two cars, then a return from subroutine EVENT is made without a car jockeying.

Following execution of the EVENT node, each entity (car) continues to the COLCT node EXIT where interval (INT) statistics are collected using the mark time in ATRIB(1) as a reference. The results are displayed using the identifier TIME IN SYSTEM. A second COLCT node collects statistics on the time between departures and displays the results using the identifier TIME BET. DEPART. The entities are then terminated. The input statements for the model are shown in Figure 9-4.

The reader should note the simplicity of the combined network-discrete event model for the drive-in bank problem as compared to the discrete event model presented in Chapter 7 for the same problem. The advantages of the combined modeling framework of SLAM become even more important for larger and more complex problems.

Summary of Results. The results for this example are provided by the SLAM Summary Report shown in Figure 9-5 and are comparable to the results for the discrete event model of the system described in Chapter 7.

```
 1  GEN,C D PEGDEN,DRIVE IN BANK,4/12/77,1;
 2  LIMITS,2,1,75;
 3  NETWORK;
 4        CREATE,EXPON(.5,1),,1,1;
 5        SELECT,SNQ,,BALK(NBALK),LEFT,RIGHT;
 6  LEFT  QUEUE(1),2,3;
 7        ACT/1,RNORM(1.,,2,2);
 8        EVENT,1;
 9        ACT,,,EXIT;
10  RIGHT QUEUE(2),2,3;
11        ACT/2,RNORM(1.,,2,2);
12        EVENT,2;
13  EXIT  COLCT,INT(1),TIME IN SYSTEM;
14        COLCT,BET,TIME BET. DEPART;
15        TERM;
16  NBALK COLCT,BET,TIME BET. BALKS;
17        TERM;
18        END
19  INIT,0,1000;
20  FIN;
```

Figure 9-4   Input statements for combined network-discrete event model of the drive-in bank.

```
          S L A M   S U M M A R Y   R E P O R T


     SIMULATION PROJECT DRIVE IN BANK          BY C D PEGDEN

     DATE  4/12/1977                           RUN NUMBER    1 OF    1


     CURRENT TIME       .1000+04
     STATISTICAL ARRAYS CLEARED AT TIME      .0000
```

STATISTICS FOR VARIABLES BASED ON OBSERVATION

	MEAN VALUE	STANDARD DEVIATION	COEFF. OF VARIATION	MINIMUM VALUE	MAXIMUM VALUE	NUMBER OF OBSERVATIONS
TIME IN SYSTEM	.2401+01	.9472+00	.3944+00	.4901+00	.4783+01	1856
TIME BET. DEPART	.5389+00	.3548+00	.6585+00	.4120-03	.4229+01	1855
TIME BET. BALKS	.6531+01	.1557+02	.2384+01	.6701-02	.9573+02	150

FILE STATISTICS

FILE NUMBER	ASSOCIATED NODE TYPE	AVERAGE LENGTH	STANDARD DEVIATION	MAXIMUM LENGTH	CURRENT LENGTH	AVERAGE WAITING TIME
1	QUEUE	1.3974	1.0397	3	2	1.2280
2	QUEUE	1.2145	.9880	3	2	1.3244

SERVICE ACTIVITY STATISTICS

ACTIVITY INDEX	START NODE LABEL/TYPE	SERVER CAPACITY	AVERAGE UTILIZATION	STANDARD DEVIATION	CURRENT UTILIZATION	AVERAGE BLOCKAGE	MAXIMUM IDLE TIME/SERVERS	MAXIMUM BUSY TIME/SERVERS	ENTITY COUNT
1	LEFT QUEUE	1	.9424	.2330	1	.0000	2.9729	72.4425	937
2	RIGH QUEUE	1	.9142	.2801	1	.0000	6.4972	67.9237	919

Figure 9-5   SLAM summary report for the combined network-discrete model of the drive-in bank.

9.13   Example 9-2.   PSYCHIATRIC WARD

Clients to a psychiatric ward arrive at the rate of two per day. Each client is given a test and the test scores are uniformly distributed between 30 and 44. When the ward is full, clients are not admitted if their score is greater than 41. The ward has space for 25 clients. A patient is discharged from the ward when his test score exceeds 48. A patient's test score is estimated to change daily in a uniform manner in the range from −0.2 to 1.2. When a potential patient arrives to the ward and the ward is full, a current patient will be bumped from the ward if he (she) has achieved a test score of 47 or higher. Initially there are 18 patients in the ward and their test scores range from 30 to 40. The objective is to simulate the operation of the ward for 1000 days to determine the average time in the system for each patient, the ward utilization, the number of clients balking, and number of patients bumped.

Concepts Illustrated.   This example illustrates the use of the ENTER node, subroutine ENTER, the STOPA duration specification, and subroutine STOPA. This example also illustrates the use of the function USERF.

SLAM Model.   In this problem, the discharge from the system for each patient in the ward cannot be scheduled in advance. The test scores for each patient and the ranking of patients based on test scores change daily. This process can be modeled using the combined network-discrete event framework of SLAM by representing patients in the ward as entities in an ACTIVITY with duration specified as STOPA(II) where II denotes the space or bed number in the ward. The test scores for patients in each of the twenty-five spaces is maintained in the SLAM variable XX(II). If space number II is not occupied, then XX(II) is set equal to 0.

The network portion of the combined network-discrete model is depicted in Figure 9-6. Entities which represent clients seeking admittance to the ward are created at the CREATE node with the current time marked as ATRIB(1) and the time between entities exponentially distributed with mean of 0.5 day. The entities proceed to the ASSIGN node where the initial test score is assigned as ATRIB(2) of the entity. The M value for the ASSIGN node is specified as 1, thus a maximum of one of the three emanating ACTIVITY's will be taken. If the ward is full (the number of active entities in the ACTIVITY with index number 1 is 25) and the test score for this client (ATRIB(2)) is greater than 41, then the entity is routed

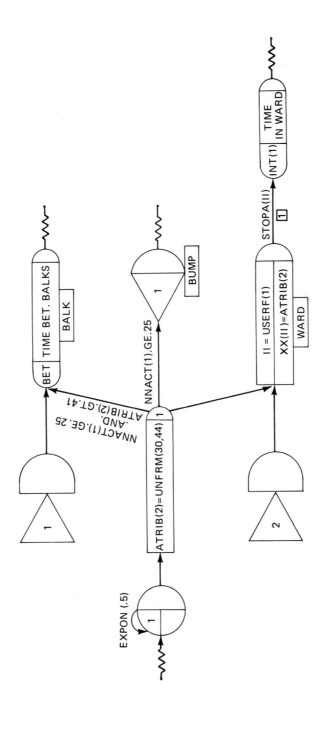

Figure 9-6 Network for combined network-discrete event model of psychiatric ward.

to the COLCT node labeled BALK. If this ACTIVITY is not taken and the ward is full, then the entity is routed to the EVENT node labeled BUMP. If neither of these ACTIVITY's is taken, then the entity is routed to the ASSIGN node labeled WARD.

Consider the entities which arrive to the COLCT node BALK. At each entity arrival to the node, statistics are collected on the time between entity arrivals with the results displayed using the identifier TIME BET. BALKS. The entities are then terminated from the system. No terminate count is used so that the entity is destroyed, but no end of run will occur because of it.

Next, consider the entities which are routed to the EVENT node BUMP, which represents a client attempting to bump one of the patients currently on the ward. Determining if a patient can be bumped is a complex decision and the logic for processing this node is coded as a discrete event with an event code of 1. Based on the current test scores of the patients in the ward, the discrete event logic either does not admit the new client or discharges a bumped patient. In the former case, the client entity is sent into the network through ENTER node 1 to arrive at node BALK. In the latter case, the client entity enters into the network through ENTER node 2 to arrive at the ASSIGN node WARD. Before describing the code for event 1, we will complete our description of the network portion of the model.

```
      FUNCTION USERF(I)
      COMMON/SCOM1/ ATRIB(100),DD(100),DDL(100),DTNOW,II,MFA,MSTOP,NCLNR
     1,NCRDR,NPRNT,NNRUN,NNSET,NTAPE,SS(100),SSL(100),TNEXT,TNOW,XX(100)
      DO 10 J=1,25
      IF(XX(J).GT.0.) GO TO 10
      USERF=J
      GO TO 20
  10  CONTINUE
      CALL ERROR(1)
  20  RETURN
      END
```

Figure 9-7 Function USERF(I) for psychiatric ward example.

The entities which are routed to the ASSIGN node WARD, represent clients who are to become patients and assigned to an available space in the ward. At the ASSIGN node, the index variable II is set equal to the value computed in the user-coded function USERF(I) with I=1. The coding for function USERF is shown in Figure 9-7 and it returns the value of USERF as the smallest index J for which XX(J) is equal to zero. An XX(J)=0 indicates that space J is available. Since entities should only arrive to the ASSIGN node WARD when at least one space is available, a call is made to subroutine ERROR to cause an error exit from SLAM if all spaces are full. Following the assignment of the first available space number to II, we set XX(II) to the initial test score for this patient.

The ACTIVITY following the ASSIGN node WARD represents the duration for which the patient remains in the ward. The duration for the ACTIVITY is specified to be STOPA(II) denoting that the duration is to be terminated from within a discrete event by a call to subroutine STOPA(NTC) with NTC equal to space number II of the patient who is to leave the ward. In this manner, each patient can be selectively discharged from the ward by specifying NTC as the space number for the patient. Following discharge from the ward, interval statistics on the time in system are collected at the COLCT node using the mark time in ATRIB(1) as a reference time. The identifier is TIME IN SYSTEM. The entity is then terminated. The input statements for this example are shown in Figure 9-8.

```
 1   GEN,C. D. PEGDEN,PSYCHIATRIC WARD,12/20/77,1;
 2   LIMITS,0,2,50;
 3   NETWORK;
 4        CREATE,EXPON(.5),,1;
 5        ASSIGN,ATRIB(2)=UNFRM(30.,44.),1;
 6        ACT,,NNACT(1).GE.25.AND.ATRIB(2).GT.41,BALK;
 7        ACT,,NNACT(1).GE.25,BUMP
 8        ACT,,,WARD;
 9   ;
10        ENTER,1;
11   BALK COLCT,BET,TIME BET. BALKS;
12        TERM;
13   ;
14   BUMP EVENT,1;
15        TERM;
16   ;
17        ENTER,2;
18   WARD ASSIGN,II=USERF(1),XX(II)=ATRIB(2);
19        ACT/1,STOPA(II);
20        COLCT,INT(1),TIME IN WARD;
21        TERM;
22        ENDNETWORK;
23   INITIALIZE,0,500;
24   FIN;
```

Figure 9-8 Statement model for psychiatric ward example.

There are two events in the discrete event portion of the model. The first event is initiated by an entity arrival to the EVENT node BUMP and is coded in subroutine BUMP. The second event processes the daily changes in the patients' test scores and discharges patients as necessary. The logic for this event is coded in subroutine TEST. Subroutine EVENT(I) which maps the event code onto the appropriate event subroutine is shown in Figure 9-9.

Subroutine BUMP contains the processing logic for the EVENT node BUMP and is depicted in Figure 9-10. Recall subroutine BUMP will only be called when a new client arrives. Initially, the variable SCORE is set to 47, and the variable JJ is set to 0. The DO loop then searches the current test scores of patients and sets JJ equal to the index of the patient with the largest test score greater than 47.

```
            SUBROUTINE EVENT(I)
            GO TO (1,2),I
          1 CALL BUMP
            RETURN
          2 CALL TEST
            RETURN
            END
```

Figure 9-9 Subroutine EVENT(I) for psychiatric ward example.

If no patient has a score greater than 47., a branch is made to statement 20 where an entity is entered into the network at ENTER node 1 to represent the departure of the new client. A return from subroutine BUMP is then made. If a patient can be bumped, an entity is entered into the network at ENTER node 2 and the bumped patient is discharged from the ward by setting the test score for space JJ to 0, that is, XX(JJ)=0.0, and calling subroutine STOPA(JJ). A return from subroutine BUMP is then made. Note that in the latter case, the order in which the subroutine calls are executed is important. The call to subroutine ENTER(2,ATRIB) is executed first and causes an entity arrival to the ENTER node to be scheduled at the top of the calendar. This is followed by the call to subroutine STOPA(JJ) which causes the end-of-activity event for the patient with entity code JJ to be scheduled at the top of the event calendar. Therefore upon the return to SLAM, the end-of-activity event will be processed prior to the entity arrival to ENTER node 2.

The coding for subroutine TEST which processes the daily changes in each patient's test score is depicted in Figure 9-11. The processing is performed in the DO loop which changes each patient's score by adding a uniform sample between −0.2 and 1.2 using stream 1 to their current score. Those patients with test scores exceeding 48.0 are discharged from the ward by calling STOPA(J) and setting

```
            SUBROUTINE BUMP
            COMMON/SCOM1/ ATRIB(100),DD(100),DDL(100),DTNOW,II,MFA,MSTOP,NCLNR
           1,NCRDR,NPRNT,NNRUN,NNSET,NTAPE,SS(100),SSL(100),TNEXT,TNOW,XX(100)
            SCORE=47.
            JJ=0
            DO 10 J=1,25
            IF(XX(J).LE.SCORE) GO TO 10
            SCORE=XX(J)
            JJ=J
         10 CONTINUE
            IF(JJ.EQ.0) GO TO 20
            CALL ENTER(2,ATRIB)
            XX(JJ)=0.
            CALL STOPA(JJ)
            RETURN
         20 CALL ENTER(1,ATRIB)
            RETURN
            END
```

Figure 9-10 Subroutine BUMP for psychiatric ward example.

```
      SUBROUTINE TEST
      COMMON/SCOM1/ ATRIB(100),DD(100),DDL(100),DTNOW,II,MFA,MSTOP,NCLNR
     1,NCRDR,NPRNT,NNRUN,NNSET,NTAPE,SS(100),SSL(100),TNEXT,TNOW,XX(100)
      DO 10 J=1,25
      IF(XX(J).EQ.0.) GO TO 10
      XX(J)=XX(J)+UNFRM(-.2,1.2,1)
      IF(XX(J).LT.48.) GO TO 10
      CALL STOPA(J)
      XX(J)=0.
   10 CONTINUE
      CALL SCHDL(2,1.,ATRIB)
      RETURN
      END
```

Figure 9-11   Subroutine TEST for psychiatric ward example.

XX(J)=0.0 where J is the space number occupied by a discharged patient. Following the processing of test scores, the TEST event is rescheduled for processing the next day by calling subroutine SCHDL with an event code equal to 2 and the time interval equal to 1.

The initial conditions for the simulation are established in subroutine INTLC which is shown in Figure 9-12. This subroutine inserts the initial 18 patients into the network through ENTER node 2 and schedules the first TEST event to occur in 1.0 time unit.

Summary of Results.   The SLAM Summary Report shown in Figure 9-13 displays statistics for the time in the ward for each patient, the time between balks from the system, and the utilization of the twenty-five spaces in the ward. The results show that on the average 24.6 of the 25 available spaces in the ward are utilized and that nearly half of the patients seeking admittance to the ward balked from the system as the result of the lack of space on the ward. These results clearly indicate the need for additional space for patients. Additional runs should be made with increased spaces available to determine the number of spaces that should be added. Cost information should also be added to the model to assess the worth of proposed new additions. If space cannot be added then research on new patient-improvement procedures and on the criterion for discharge should be initiated.

```
      SUBROUTINE INTLC
      COMMON/SCOM1/ ATRIB(100),DD(100),DDL(100),DTNOW,II,MFA,MSTOP,NCLNR
     1,NCRDR,NPRNT,NNRUN,NNSET,NTAPE,SS(100),SSL(100),TNEXT,TNOW,XX(100)
      ATRIB(1)=TNOW
      DO 10 J=1,18
      ATRIB(2)=UNFRM(30.,44.,1)
   10 CALL ENTER(2,ATRIB)
      CALL SCHDL(2,1.,ATRIB)
      RETURN
      END
```

Figure 9-12   Subroutine INTLC for psychiatric ward example.

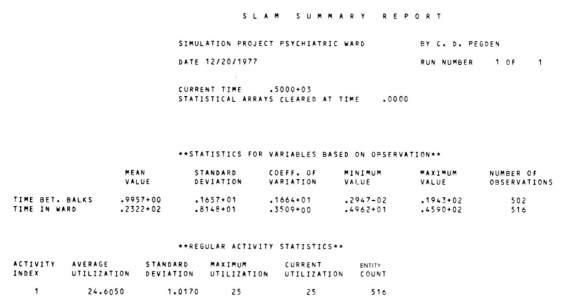

Figure 9-13   SLAM summary report for psychiatric ward example.

9.14   CHAPTER SUMMARY

   This chapter presents the interfaces between network and discrete event models. To transfer from the network into the discrete event model, the EVENT node is employed. A function subprogram can also be used to compute the value to be assigned to an attribute of an entity or the duration of an activity through the use of function USERF. From a discrete event model, an entity can be entered into the network model through the use of subroutine ENTER. The entity defined in subroutine ENTER is inserted into the network model at the corresponding ENTER node.

   Functions are described in this chapter which make available status variables associated with a network to the discrete event modeler. In addition, subroutines are available for freeing resources, altering resource capacities and changing the status of a gate. The capability for specifying that the duration of an activity is to be ended by the user in a discrete event is described. Subroutine STOPA is made available for this purpose. The organization employed by SLAM in processing combined network-discrete event models is shown in Figure 9-1. A combined network-discrete event model for the drive-in bank example with jockeying is presented. A second example models the processing of patients through a psychiatric ward.

9.15   EXERCISES

9-1.   For a one server, single queue situation, develop the SLAM network model when the service time is a sample from the probability mass function as shown below.

Probability	Service Time (*min.*)
.2	4
.3	6
.1	7
.4	10

The interarrival times are exponentially distributed with a mean of 7.75 minutes.

9-2.   In Example 6-7, add the feature that if there are more than three jobs to be processed by the machine tool when it breaks down, all jobs except the last three to arrive are routed to a subcontractor. The job in progress is also routed to the subcontractor.

9-3.   For Example 6-7, redevelop the model to include the possibility that the repairman process breaks down and a delay of three hours is incurred in order to get a spare part for the repair process. The time between repair process breakdowns is exponentially distributed with a mean of 100 hours. If the repair breakdown occurs when the repair process is not active, no action is taken.

9-4.   Build a network-discrete event SLAM model of the production shop described in Example 8-1. Discuss the development of a general production shop simulator that uses SLAM elements as its basis.

9-5.   Model and analyze the admitting process of a hospital as described below. The following three types of patients are processed by the admitting function:

Type 1.   Those patients who are admitted and have previously completed their pre-admission forms and tests;

Type 2.   Those patients who seek admission but have not completed pre-admission; and

Type 3.   Those who are only coming in for pre-admission testing and information gathering.

Service times in the admitting office vary according to patient type as given below.

Patient Types and Service Times

Patient Type	Relative Frequency	Mean Time to Admit
1	0.90 before 10:00 A.M. 0.50 after 10:00 A.M.	15 minutes
2	0.10 always	40 minutes
3	0 before 10:00 A.M. 0.40 after 10:00 A.M.	30 minutes

Note: All of the above times are normally distributed with $\sigma = 0.1\mu$ (min. = 0.0).

On arrival to admitting, a person waits in line if the two admitting officers are busy. When idle, an admitting officer always selects a patient who is to be admitted before those who are only to be pre-admitted. In addition, Type 1 patients are given highest priority. After filling out various forms in the admitting office, Type 1 patients are taken to their floors by an orderly while Type 2 and 3 patients walk to the laboratory for blood and urine tests. Three orderlies are available to escort patients to the nursing units. Patients are *not* allowed to go to their floor by themselves as a matter of policy. If all orderlies are busy, patients wait in the lobby. Once a patient has been escorted to a floor, they are considered beyond the admitting process. It takes the orderly 3 time units to return to the admitting room. Those patients who must go to the lab are always ambulatory, and as a result require no escorts. After arriving in the lab, they wait in line at the registration desk. After registration, they go to the lab waiting room until they are called on by one of two lab technicians. After the samples are drawn, they walk back to the admitting office if they are to be admitted or leave if only pre-admission has been scheduled. Upon return to admitting, they are processed as normal Type 1 patients. The admitting office is open from 7:00 A.M. until 5:00 P.M. However, no pre-admissions (Type 3) are scheduled until 10:00 A.M. because of the heavy morning workload in the lab. At 4:00 P.M., incoming admissions are sent to the outpatient desk for processing. However, Type 2 patients returning from the lab are accepted until 5:00 P.M. which is the time both admitting officers go home and the office is closed. Analyze the above system for 10 days. It is of interest to determine the time in the system, that is, the time from arrival until on a floor (Type 1 and 2) or exit from the lab (Type 3). Also, determine the time between arrivals to the laboratory. Assume all patient queues are infinite and FIFO ranked except where noted. Activity times are specified below.

Activity Times (all times in minutes)

Explanation	Distribution: Parameters
time between arrivals to admitting office, t_1	exponential: mean = 15
travel time between admitting and floor, t_2	uniform: min = 3, max = 8
travel time between admitting and lab or lab and admitting, t_3	uniform: min = 2, max = 5
service time at lab registration desk, t_4	Erlang-3: mean = 4.5, k = 3
time spent drawing lab specimen, t_5	Erlang-2: mean = 5, k = 2
time for orderly to return from floor to admitting desk, t_6	constant: 3

9-6.   Simulate the airline ticket agent system described in Exercise 4-11.

9-7.   In a private branch exchange telephone switching system, two types of telephone lines must be available to make an outgoing call: 1) a line for talking (voice communication) which is referred to as a G1 line; and 2) a line for dialing (for digit transmission) which will be referred to as a G2 line. Since the dialing operation takes much less time than a conversation, the company has installed 10 G1 lines and one G2 line. From past data, it has been determined that the time between outgoing calls is exponentially distributed with a mean of 1 minute (minimum of 0 and maximum of 60 minutes). If all G1 lines are busy at the time of a call, the caller hangs up and tries to call again in T minutes where T is normally distributed with a mean of 15, standard deviation of 2, minimum of 0 and maximum of 60. If a G1 line is available, the caller waits for a G2 line if necessary. The G1 line is held while waiting for a G2 line. When a line of each type is available, the customer dials and the dialing time is exponentially distributed with a mean of 0.2 minute, minimum 0.1 and maximum 0.5. After dialing, the G2 line is released and the G1 line is held for the duration of the conversation. Conversation time is exponentially distributed with a mean of 10 minutes, minimum of 3 minutes and a maximum of 30 minutes. Develop a SLAM model of this situation to obtain statistics on the following quantities: time to complete dialing; time to complete conversation; total time to complete a call; utilization of G1 and G2 lines; rate at which callers were not able to complete their call.

9-8. A company has six retail outlets in a given city. The distribution of demand for a particular item at these outlets is Poisson-distributed with a mean of 10 units per day. These retail outlets are serviced by a distribution warehouse. It takes 1 day for an order to be received at the distribution warehouse from a retail outlet. Orders can be delivered from the distribution warehouse to each retail outlet in 5 days on the average. The distribution of this time is lognormal with variance of 1. The distribution warehouse places orders on the factory every 14 days. The time for the distribution warehouse to obtain a shipment from the factory is normally distributed with a mean of 90 days and a standard deviation of 10 days; however, orders never are received in either less than 60 days or more than 120 days. Simulate the problem to determine the variation in inventory levels for a given inventory policy at the retail outlets and the distribution warehouse for 3-years, assuming 240 days per year. Print yearly summary reports.

The initial conditions for the simulation are as follows: first demand at time 0; stock at each outlet, 70 units; inventory position at each outlet, 70 units; stock at warehouse, 1,920 units; three procurements from factory are in process, each for 1,800 units, one due to be received at day 30, one at day 60, and one at day 90; and first review of warehouse inventory position will be at day 30.

9-9. Let the storage space before each server for the conveyor system described in Exercise 6-5 be two units. When storage exists before each server of a conveyor system, decisions regarding the removal of items must be established. Propose decision rules for determining whether items should be removed from the conveyor belt and placed in storage before a particular server. Simulate the decision rules to obtain the statistics requested in Exercise 6-5.

9-10. Simulate the following resource constrained PERT network (1) to evaluate a set of dispatching rules for determining the order in which to perform activities when the resources available are insufficient to perform all the activities that have been released.

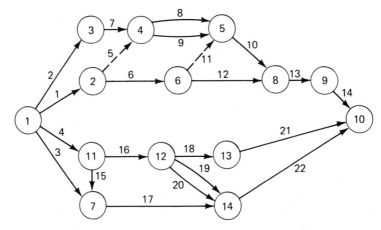

Parameters of Activities of the Network

Activity Number	Distribution	Mean Time	Variance	Requirement for Resource Type			
				1	2	3	4
1	Lognormal	7	2	2	0	1	3
2	Constant	3	0	2	0	1	1
3	Constant	10	0	0	2	0	0
4	Constant	5	0	1	1	1	1
5	Dummy	0	0	0	0	0	0
6	Constant	5	0	2	0	3	2
7	Uniform	3	1/3	1	0	2	3
8	Gamma	8	6	3	0	0	1
9	Constant	3	0	1	0	0	0
10	Constant	5	0	2	0	1	3
11	Dummy	0	0	0	0	0	0
12	Constant	2	0	2	1	2	2
13	Constant	6	0	1	1	0	0
14	Constant	10	0	0	0	0	0
15	Exponential	10	0	1	1	1	0
16	Constant	3	0	1	1	2	0
17	Constant	5	0	0	1	1	1
18	Constant	2	0	0	1	0	3
19	Normal	5	4	1	0	0	2
20	Constant	1	0	1	1	0	0
21	Constant	15	0	0	1	2	0
22	Constant	5	0	0	1	0	0

Resource Availability and Types

Type	Description	Availability
1	Systems analyst	3
2	Marketing personnel	2
3	Mantenance personnel	3
4	Engineering personnel	3

The following statistics are to be recorded based on 100 simulations of the network for each dispatching rule.

1. Average time at which each node is realized.
2. Minimum time at which each node is realized.
3. Maximum time at which each node is realized.
4. Standard deviation of the time each node is realized.
5. Histograms of the time to realize nodes.
6. Percentage of the simulation runs in which an activity was on a critical path (a criticality index).
7. Network completion time distribution.
8. Utilization of each resource type.

9-11. A multiprocessor computing system is composed of two processors (CPUs) sharing a common memory (CM) of 131 pages, four disk drives, each of which can be accessed by either processor, and a single data channel. A schematic diagram of the system is shown below.

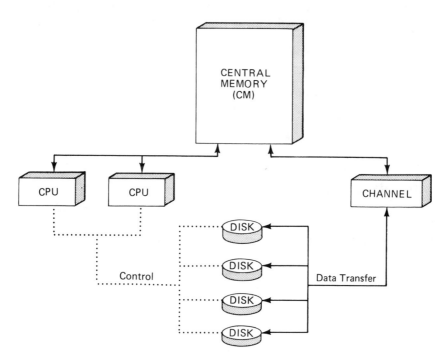

Schematic Diagram of a Multiprocessor Computing System

Jobs arrive at the system at an average rate of 12 jobs per minute in accordance with a Poisson distribution. Total CPU time for a job follows a normal distribution with a mean of 10 seconds and a standard deviation of 3 seconds. The CPU processing time consists of bursts each of which is followed by an I/O requirement. Each burst follows a negative exponential distribution whose mean is equal to the reciprocal of the average I/O rate of a job. The average I/O rate per job varies uniformly from 2 to 10. I/O operations are assigned to a specific disk upon arrival.

Jobs arriving to the system are assigned a priority which is inversely related to their memory requirements. The CM requirements for a job are distributed equiprobably between 20 and 60 pages. Once memory has been allocated to a job it begins execution on any available CPU. Upon issuing an I/O request, the job can continue using the CPU as long as only one I/O request is outstanding. Thus, if an I/O request is made and the job has an I/O request pending, the CPU is relinquished and the I/O request is queued. Following completion of a non-pending I/O request, CPU operations on the job can be reinitiated if a CPU is available.

After a CPU burst, an I/O request is automatically made on the disk assigned to the job, that is, direct access to the disks from the CPUs is made. The seek time to locate the proper position on any disk is assumed to be uniformly distributed between 0. and .075 seconds. Only one seek operation per disk can be performed at a time. Following the seek operation, a data transfer through the data channel is made. The transfer time is equal to $.001*(2.5 + U)$ where U is uniformly distributed between 0 and 25. After the transfer, the I/O request is considered satisfied.

Simulate the computing system to determine the residence time of jobs processed by the system, and the utilization statistics for the four disks, the input/output channel, and the two processors (CPUs). Also, the average use of memory is to be obtained. Statistics on the number of jobs waiting for a resource and the waiting time of jobs are also desired. The simulation is to be run for 12,000 seconds.

9.16   REFERENCE

1. Pritsker, A. A. B., *The GASP IV Simulation Language,* John Wiley, 1974.

CHAPTER 10

Continuous Models

10.1   INTRODUCTION

Continuous modeling involves the characterization of the behavior of a system by a set of equations. The time-dependent portrayal of the variables described by the equations is one of the desired outputs from such models. The models can consist of sets of algebraic, difference, or differential equations and can contain stochastic components. The status of a system defined in this manner is changing continuously with time. Events may occur, however, and instantaneously effect the status of the system.

The continuous systems modeler has two basic tasks: 1) the development of the equation set and events that describe the time-dependent, stochastic behavior of the system; and 2) the evaluation of the equation set and events to obtain specific values of system behavior for different operating policies. A simulation language for continuous models assists in the first task by defining the format for the equation set. However, it is in task 2 that the simulation language has its greatest impact. The language provides the mechanisms for obtaining the values of the variables described by the equations. It does this by solving the equation set at a single point in time and by recording the values for future reporting. Time is then advanced in a step-wise fashion and the equations are again solved for the values of the variables at this new time, assuming knowledge of the variables at previous times. When events occur, the effect of the event is incorporated into the model and in the evaluation of the variable values. In this manner, the entire time history of the model variables are obtained. The procedures employed by SLAM in supporting continuous system modeling are described in this chapter.

10.2   SLAM ORGANIZATION FOR CONTINUOUS MODELING

Models of continuous systems involve the definition of state variables by equations and the definition of state-events based on the values of state variables. The development of a SLAM continuous simulation program requires the user to write subroutine STATE for defining state equations, SEVNT input statements to prescribe the conditions that define state-events, and subroutine EVENT(I) for modeling the consequences of the occurrence of state-event I. In addition, the user must write a main program that calls the SLAM executive. Initial conditions are established by writing subroutine INTLC or through INTLC input statements as described in Chapter 5. Specialized outputs of the system variables can be obtained by writing subroutine OTPUT or through the RECORD and VAR input statements which will be described in this chapter. A block diagram of the SLAM organization for continuous models is shown in Figure 10-1.

The function of the main program is to call the SLAM processor which controls the running of the simulation. The SLAM processor first calls upon the standardized initialization routine to initialize SLAM variables and to read SLAM input statements that define the characteristics of the model. Non-SLAM variables can be initialized in subroutine INTLC which is called after the SLAM input statements are read (including the INTLC cards). The user can perform additional initialization functions in subroutine INTLC.

After initialization, the executive routine calls subroutine STATE in order to obtain new values for the state variables. The function of subroutine STATE is to

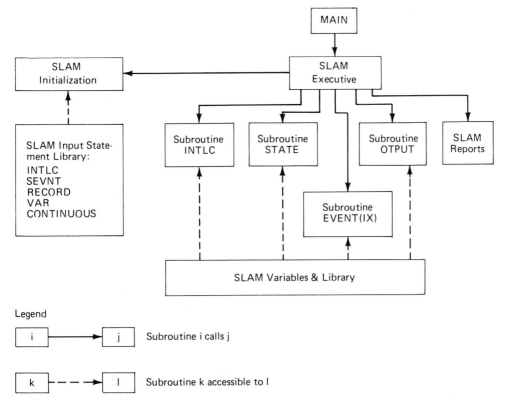

Figure 10-1 SLAM organization for continuous modeling.

define the dynamic equations for the state variables. If only difference equations are used in subroutine STATE, the executive routine will call STATE at periodic intervals called steps unless an intervening event or information request is encountered. In subroutine STATE, the state variable values at the end of the step are computed from the user-written equations. If differential equations are included in subroutine STATE, then the executive routine calls subroutine STATE many times within a step. In either case, values for the state variables at the end of a step are computed. The executive routine then tests if conditions defining state-events are included in the model. These conditions are specified in terms of state variables crossing prescribed thresholds. The user specifies such conditions on SEVNT input statements. One input statement is required for each state condition definition. If a state-event is detected, the executive routine calls subroutine EVENT(I) with the state-event code that was specified on the SEVNT input statement. It is the user's responsibility to code the changes to be made to the system when a particular state-event occurs. In SLAM, the following types of changes are allowed:

1. Changes in the defining equations for the state variables;
2. Discrete changes in the values of the state variables;
3. Changes in the state variables and/or thresholds involved in state condition specifications;
4. Changes to SLAM or non-SLAM variables.

To record the performance of the system over time, the executive routine collects system status information throughout a simulation run. The information to be collected is specified by the user on TIMST and RECORD input statements. The frequency with which the information is recorded is user specified during the standardized initialization. The options are to record: at periodic intervals, at the end of each step, and at each event time.

The ending of the simulation can be specified either by a state-event condition or by a total simulation time. When the executive routine determines that the simulation is ended, subroutine OTPUT is called. In OTPUT, the user can write a specialized output report and perform any end-of-simulation processing that is required. Following the call to subroutine OTPUT, standardized summary reports are printed. These standardized summary reports include any tables and plots of data requested through RECORD statements, along with any statistical computations of values recorded during the simulation.

As can be seen from the above description and from Figure 10-1, the SLAM organization has decomposed a problem by specifying the subprograms within which the user must define the state variables and the potential changes to the state variables when state-events occur. Superimposed on these functional elements are information processing statements and routines for detecting state variable crossings (SEVNT), recording state variable values (RECORD), initializing variables (INTLC), and reporting specialized output (OTPUT).

10.3 EXECUTIVE FUNCTION FOR CONTINUOUS SIMULATION MODELS

The executive function in SLAM establishes the current simulation time, TNOW, and calls an appropriate user-written routine in accordance with the defined SLAM organizational structure. If state variables are to be updated, the executive function defines the step size, DTNOW, and calls subroutine STATE where the user has written equations that update state variables to time TNOW.

As was the case in discrete models, the executive function is performed by subroutine SLAM which is called by the user from the MAIN program. Subroutine SLAM calls subroutine STATE to update the values of the state variables. Subroutine SLAM then determines if a state-event has occurred, and, if it has, calls subroutine EVENT(JEVNT) to communicate to the user that an event with code JEVNT has occurred. The executive routine also determines if the newly computed values are to be recorded as specified by a RECORD input statement. The next step size is then computed and the above procedure repeated.

10.4 STATE VARIABLES

The SLAM variable SS(I) is used to represent state variable I. The derivative of state variable I is defined by the SLAM variable DD(I), that is,

DD(I) = dSS(I)/dt

SLAM solves for the values of state variables over time by taking steps in simulated time. The state variable values at each immediately preceding step are maintained as the SLAM variables SSL(I). With these SLAM variables, it is possible to write a difference equation for state variable I in subroutine STATE in the following fashion:

$$SS(I) = SSL(I) + DTNOW*RATE(I)$$

where DTNOW is the step size and RATE(I) is a user variable that specifies the rate of change of state variable I during DTNOW. This equation states that the value of state variable I at time TNOW is equal to the last value of state variable I plus the amount of change that would occur over time DTNOW. The value of RATE(I) could be determined as a function of other system variables. The executive function calls subroutine STATE every time a step is to be made so that the updating of time is implicit in the equation given above for SS(I).

An alternative method for defining SS(I) would be to define its derivative in subroutine STATE. In this case the derivative is integrated by SLAM to obtain the value of SS(I) at each step. Hence, an equivalent formulation for the above difference equation would be the following statement in subroutine STATE:

$$DD(I) = RATE(I)$$

The user may define SS(I) by either an algebraic expression, a difference equation, or a DD(I) equation. However only one method for each variable is allowed.

More formally, the SLAM variables SS(I), SSL(I), DD(I), and DDL(I) are used to define the state variables and their derivatives at time TNOW and TTLAS, where

TNOW = time at which values of the state variables are being computed.
TTLAS = time at the beginning of the current step (the time at which the values for the state variables were last accepted).
DTNOW = TNOW − TTLAS
SS(I) = value of state variable I at time TNOW.
SSL(I) = value of state variable I at time TTLAS.
DD(I) = value of the derivative of state variable I at time TNOW.
DDL(I) = value of the derivative of state variable I at time TTLAS.

As mentioned above, to define a state variable by a differential equation, the user would write a defining equation in terms of $DD(\cdot)$. For example, if the differential equation for state variable j is given by

$$dy_j/dt = Ay_j + B$$

the corresponding SLAM statement is

$$DD(J) = A*SS(J) + B$$

where SS(J) represents y_j.

In this situation, the SLAM processor calls subroutine STATE many times within a step in order to obtain estimates of the derivatives (DD(J)) within the step. These estimates are used to compute SS(J) at TNOW from the equation

$$SS(J) = SSL(J) + \int_{TTLAS}^{TNOW} DD(J) \, dt$$

where TTLAS is the time at the beginning of the step and corresponds to the time at which SSL(J) was computed. The integration involved in the above equation is performed by a Runge-Kutta-Fehlberg (RKF) numerical integration algorithm in which a user-prescribed single-step accuracy specification is maintained (4,12, 13). If the accuracy is not maintained, the step size is reduced and the integration recalculated as described in Appendix E. This process is repeated if necessary until a user-specified minimum step size, DTMIN, is encountered.

10.5 SPECIFYING VALUES TO RECORD AT SAVE TIMES

Variables to be tabled and/or plotted are specified on RECORD input statements. Through the specification of DTSAV, the recording frequency for these variables is established. DTSAV is specified on the CONTINUOUS input statement which is described in Section 10.12.

The use of a RECORD statement communicates to the SLAM processor that a specified table or plot is to be prepared in accordance with the recording frequency DTSAV. A flexible recording frequency can be obtained by identifying a plot number, IPLOT, with the RECORD statement which specifies that the user desires to record information by calling subroutine GPLOT(IPLOT). The variable IPLOT is referred to as a plot number.

10.5.1 Subroutine GPLOT(IPLOT)

Subroutine GPLOT collects values of up to ten dependent variables specified on a VAR input statement for one independent variable specified on a RECORD input statement. It provides a table or plot or both of the collected data. The plot number IPLOT can be user specified on the RECORD input statement. If no plot number is specified, the SLAM processor automatically assigns a plot number and all calls to GPLOT are made internally. RECORD statements without plot numbers must follow RECORD statements with plot numbers in the input statement sequence. Subroutine GPLOT stores the collected data either in core (in the array QSET) or on a peripheral storage device. When the data is stored in QSET, only one plot and/or associated table with up to ten variables can be prepared. If a peripheral device is used, up to ten plots and/or tables with as many as ten variables per plot may be prepared. When the storage medium is core, a check is made to see if sufficient space has been allocated to the array QSET. If there is not sufficient space, the simulation continues but a message indicating that the complete plot could not be obtained due to insufficient space is printed at the end of the plot.

The output of a plot or table is part of the SLAM Summary Report. It can also be obtained using calls to subroutine PRNTP as described in Section 8.4. For a table, all values recorded are printed with the independent variable given in the first column. The output of a plot progresses line by line with each line consisting of three components. The first is the value of the independent variable associated with that line. The second component contains 101 print positions corresponding to the plot points. The third component of a plotted line is a duplicates column that indicates any instances in which two different plot symbols occupy the same plot position. If this happens, the first symbol processed is plotted and the duplicates column contains a symbol pair showing the plotted symbol followed by the symbol that should occupy the same plot position. As many as five duplicates may be printed per plot line. If there are more, the first five are printed followed by an asterisk. The symbols that can be used on a plot are prescribed on a VAR input statement and are described in Section 10.5.3.

10.5.2   RECORD Input Statement

The RECORD input statement provides general information concerning the values to be recorded at save times. This includes an explicit specification for a plot number, IPLOT, or an implicit value determined by the order in which the RECORD statement appears. Also provided on the RECORD statement are definitions for the independent variable, the storage medium, and detailed specifications concerning the type and time interval for the output reports.

The fields of the RECORD statement are:

RECORD(IPLOT),INDVAR,ID,ITAPE,P or T or B,DTPLT,TTSRT,TTEND,KKEVT;

with the definitions of the variables listed below.

Variable	Definition	Default
IPLOT	PLOT number for user calls to subroutine GPLOT (IPLOT)	Optional
INDVAR	The name of the variable which is to serve as the independent variable for the table or plot corresponding to this RECORD statement. Possible variables are: TNOW, SS($\cdot$), DD($\cdot$), and XX($\cdot$).	Required
ID	An alphanumeric identifier for the independent variable. The first 16 characters of the identifier are significant.	Blanks
ITAPE	Peripheral device number on which the recorded variables are to be stored. If ITAPE is set to 0, the recorded variables are stored in NSET/QSET.	0
P, T, or B	A description of the output format for the recorded information. A P indicates a plot is to be printed, a T indicates that a table is to be printed, and a B indicates that both a plot and table are to be printed.	P
DTPLT	The printing increment of the independent variable between successive plot points. For tables, DTPLT is not employed and all recorded values are printed in the table.	5.0
TTSRT	The time at which the recording of values is to be initiated.	TTBEG
TTEND	The time at which the recording of values is to be halted.	TTFIN
KKEVT	A YES or NO field to indicate if values of variables at event times are to be recorded: YES → recording at event times; NO → do not record at event times.	YES

For each RECORD statement included, there is one independent variable and a set of dependent variables. The specification of the dependent variables is given immediately following the RECORD statement in a manner to be illustrated below. The independent variable defined on the RECORD statement is used to specify the first column of a table or the abscissa for a plot. Examples of tables and plots are given as part of the example in Section 10.13. When the value of the variable ITAPE is set to zero, space must be allocated in the NSET/QSET array for storing the independent variable and each dependent variable. Thus, the number of values to be stored is equal to the number of recordings times the number of dependent variables plus one.

When no CONTINUOUS statement is used, the variable DTPLT is used to define the recording frequency, DTSAV. In such a case, DTSAV is set to the largest DTPLT value.

If KKEVT = YES, values are recorded before and after each event of the simulation. This double recording is to insure that any changes made in event routines are recorded. To suppress recordings at event times, the value of KKEVT should be set to NO.

When ITAPE is set greater than zero, peripheral device numbers must be specified for storing the values to be recorded. This should be done through the job control language or program cards as required.

10.5.3   VAR Input Statement

The VAR statement is used in conjunction with the RECORD statement to define the dependent variables that are to be recorded for each value of the independent variable. The form for the VAR statement is:

VAR,DEPVAR,SYMBL,ID,LOORD,HIORD;

The definitions of the fields for the VAR statement are shown below.

Variable	Definition	Default
DEPVAR	The name of the dependent variable defined by the statement. The dependent variable can be TNOW, SS($\cdot$), DD($\cdot$), or XX($\cdot$).	Required
SYMBL	The symbol used on the plot to identify the dependent variable. If only a table is requested, this field can be defaulted.	Blank
ID	An alphanumeric label of up to 16 characters to identify the dependent variable.	Blanks

Variable	*Definition*	*Default*
LOORD	The low ordinate specification that defines the left-hand scale for plots. This can be a value; the minimum observed, MIN; or MIN rounded down to a nearest multiple of IVAL, MIN (IVAL).	MIN
HIORD	The high ordinate value that defines the right-hand scale for plots. This can be a value; the maximum observed, MAX; or MAX rounded up to a nearest multiple of IVAL, MAX(IVAL).	MAX

The specification of the low and high ordinate values has been made flexible to enable the obtaining of properly scaled plot information. Specific values can be assigned for the low and the high ordinate fields. In the low ordinate field, MIN can be specified to indicate that the minimum value obtained during a simulation run should be prescribed for the left-hand scale. If MIN(IVAL) is specified, the minimum value observed during the simulation run is rounded down to the nearest multiple of IVAL and this value is used as the left-hand scale. For example, if the lowest value observed was 547 and the specification MIN(100) was made, the low ordinate would be set to 500.

For the high ordinate value, the specification MAX would cause the maximum value observed to be used for the right-hand scale. The specification MAX(IVAL) would cause the right-hand scale to be set to the nearest multiple of IVAL above the maximum value observed. Thus, if the maximum value observed was 2317 and the specification for the high ordinate was MAX(1000), the right-hand scale would be set at 3000.

The number of VAR statements following a RECORD statement specifies the number of dependent variables associated with each recording of values. *The dependent variables associated with a recording must be specified immediately after the RECORD statement.* The symbol character used for the dependent variable may be any character in the FORTRAN character set; however, three are treated in a special manner. The symbols plus [+], period [.] and blank [ ] can be replaced in the plot vector by any plot symbol and no duplicates information will be maintained. Normally, the plus and blank are used only by SLAM. The symbol period may be used by the programmer for cursors or in any other situation in which it is desired that the symbol appear only if no other symbol occurs at the same point.

10.6 AN ILLUSTRATION OF CONTINUOUS MODELING

To illustrate the ease with which models of continuous systems can be analyzed using SLAM, we present a model of Cedar Bog Lake that was developed by Williams (15).

The model includes three species, a solar energy supply (x_s), and the organic matter that forms a sediment on the lake bottom (x_o). These lake variables are modeled in terms of their energy content (calories/centimeter^2) and the energy transfers between the various lake variables and losses to the environment (x_e). The three species are plants (x_p), herbivores (x_h), and carnivores (x_c). The differential equations relating these species to the sediment and the solar energy source are shown below.

$$\frac{dx_p}{dt} = x_s - 4.03x_p.$$

$$\frac{dx_h}{dt} = 0.48x_p - 17.87x_h.$$

$$\frac{dx_c}{dt} = 4.85x_h - 4.65x_c.$$

$$\frac{dx_o}{dt} = 2.55x_p + 6.12x_h + 1.95x_c.$$

$$\frac{dx_e}{dt} = 1.00x_p + 6.90x_h + 2.70x_c.$$

The values of the variables at time zero are: $x_p(0) = 0.83$, $x_h(0) = 0.003$, $x_c(0) = 0.0001$, $x_o(0) = 0.0$ and $x_e(0) = 0.0$.

The annual cycle in solar radiation is simulated using the following equation:

$$x_s = 95.9 \ (1 + 0.635 \sin 2\pi t)$$

where t is time in years. These equations represent such processes as the predation of one species by another, plant photosynthesis, and the decaying of dead species. Energy transfers between lake entities and their environment are due to respiration and migration.

We will use SLAM to illustrate the procedure for obtaining the values of the variables x_p, x_h, x_c, x_o, x_e, x_s over time. First, we make an equivalence between the model variables and the SLAM state vector SS($\cdot$) as shown below.

$$SS(1) = x_p \rightarrow DD(1) = \frac{dx_p}{dt}$$

$$SS(2) = x_h \rightarrow DD(2) = \frac{dx_h}{dt}$$

$$SS(3) = x_c \rightarrow DD(3) = \frac{dx_c}{dt}$$

$$SS(4) = x_o \rightarrow DD(4) = \frac{dx_o}{dt}$$

$$SS(5) = x_e \rightarrow DD(5) = \frac{dx_e}{dt}$$

and

$$SS(6) = x_g.$$

The entire SLAM program consists of writing the main program, subroutine STATE, and the input statements. These are shown in Figure 10-2. As can be seen, the main program is in standard form. NSET/QSET is dimensioned to 1000

```
DIMENSION NSET(1000)
COMMON QSET(1000)
COMMON/SCOM1/ ATRIB(100),DD(100),DDL(100),DTNOW,II,MFA,MSTOP,NCLNR
1,NCRDR,NPRNT,NNRUN,NNSET,NTAPE,SS(100),SSL(100),TNEXT,TNOW,XX(100)
EQUIVALENCE (NSET(1),QSET(1))
NCRDR=5
NPRNT=6
NTAPE=7
NNSET=1000
CALL SLAM
STOP
END


SUBROUTINE STATE
COMMON/SCOM1/ ATRIB(100),DD(100),DDL(100),DTNOW,II,MFA,MSTOP,NCLNR
1,NCRDR,NPRNT,NNRUN,NNSET,NTAPE,SS(100),SSL(100),TNEXT,TNOW,XX(100)
DATA PI/3.14159/
SS(6)=95.9*(1.+0.635*SIN(2.*PI*TNOW))
DD(1)=SS(6)-4.03*SS(1)
DD(2)=0.48*SS(1)-17.87*SS(2)
DD(3)=4.85*SS(2)-4.65*SS(3)
DD(4)=2.55*SS(1)+6.12*SS(2)+1.95*SS(3)
DD(5)=SS(1)+6.9*SS(2)+2.7*SS(3)
RETURN
END


GEN,PRITSKER,CEDAR BOG LAKE,3/5/1978,1;
CONTINUOUS,5,1,.00025,.025,.025;
INTLC,SS(1)=.83,SS(2)=.003,SS(3)=.0001,SS(4)=0.0,SS(5)=0.0;
RECORD,TNOW,TIME,0,P,.025;
VAR,SS(1),P,PLANTS;
VAR,SS(2),H,HERBIVORES;
VAR,SS(3),C,CARNIVORES;
VAR,SS(4),O,ORGANIC;
VAR,SS(5),E,ENVIRONMENT;
VAR,SS(6),S,SOLAR ENERGY;
INITIALIZE,0,2.0;
FIN;
```

Figure 10-2 SLAM program of Cedar Bog Lake.

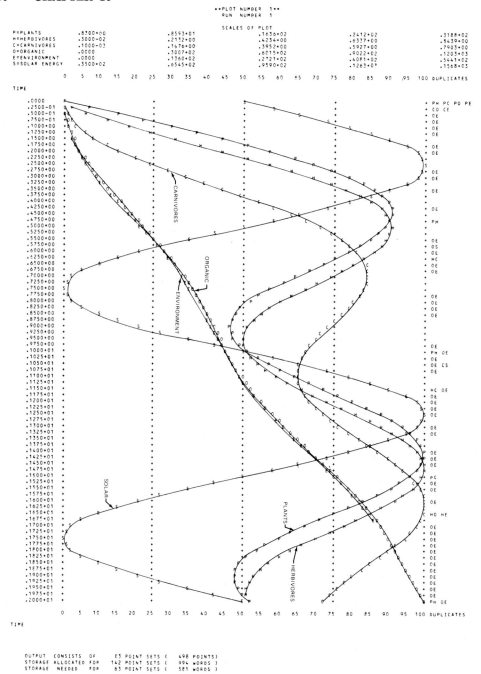

Figure 10-3 Plot of variables for Cedar Bog Lake illustration.

as the plot of the state variables will be maintained in core storage in NSET/QSET. In subroutine STATE, the set of differential equations is coded. The translation of the equations from the model to the SLAM code is direct and normally does not require an excessive amount of work. The input statements for the model involve mainly the definitions of the variables to record on RECORD and VAR input statements. The CONTINUOUS statement is defined later in this chapter in Section 10.12.1 after a detailed description of the SLAM time advance procedure is given. For this example, the CONTINUOUS statement specifies five differential equations (NNEQD), one state variable equation (NNEQS), a minimum step size (DTMIN) of 0.00025, a maximum step size (DTMAX) of 0.025, and a recording interval (DTSAV) of 0.025. The INTLC statement initializes the SS($\cdot$) values as prescribed by the problem statement, and the INITIALIZE statement specifies that the simulation should start at time zero and end at time 2. A segment of the plot requested through the RECORD statement is shown in Figure 10-3. This example illustrates the ease of coding continuous models in SLAM.

10.7 COLLECTING TIME-PERSISTENT STATISTICS ON STATE VARIABLES

State variables and their derivatives are recomputed at the end of each step; hence, their values can be considered to be changing continuously over time. An average value for the variable can be computed by integrating the state variable and dividing by the time period of the integration. This could be accomplished by the SLAM user through the definition of a new state variable. For example, if it is desired to obtain the average value of state variable 3, we could define state variable 10 to be the integral of state variable 3. The following statement coded in subroutine STATE would achieve the desired integration:

DD(10) = SS(3)

In subroutine OTPUT, the average of SS(3) could be computed as SS(10)/TNOW.

To avoid the definition of new state variables to compute averages and to obtain second moments about the mean for state variables, SLAM allows the use of the input statement TIMST to be used with state variables and their derivatives. The format for the TIMST input statement is

TIMST,VAR,ID;

When VAR is defined as an SS($\cdot$) or DD($\cdot$) variable, SLAM assumes a linear function between the state variable values at the ends of steps and computes an average and standard deviation based on this linear approximation. The statistical estimates are included in the portion of the SLAM Summary Report that presents information on time-persistent variables.

10.8   STATE-EVENTS: THE SEVNT INPUT STATEMENT

When acceptable values of the state variables, SS(J), are obtained, SLAM determines if any state variables crossed specified thresholds within allowable tolerances. State-events are defined as points in time at which such crossings occur. Figure 10-4 illustrates positive and negative crossings. A state-event can cause status changes to the system model in the same manner as time-events.

To assist the user in specifying state-events, the SLAM input statement SEVNT is provided. SEVNT causes the detection of the crossings of one state variable against a threshold. A tolerance is specified for detecting the crossing. The crossing can be in the positive, the negative, or in both directions. The tolerance and direction of crossing are specified as fields in the SEVNT input statement. The format for the SEVNT input statement is

SEVNT,JEVNT,XVAR,XDIR,VALUE,TOL;

where
 JEVNT is a user supplied state-event code;
 XVAR is a variable and can be SS(J) or DD(J) with J specified;
 XDIR specifies the direction of crossing: X$\rightarrow$ either direction; XP$\rightarrow$ positive direction; XN$\rightarrow$ negative direction;
 VALUE is the crossing threshold and can be a constant, SS(I) or DD(I) variable.

Below are three examples of the SEVNT statement:

1. Define state-event 1 to occur when SS(3) crosses 100 in the positive direction with a tolerance of 2.0 (See Fig. 10-4(a))
    SEVNT,1,SS(3),XP,100.,2.0;
2. Define state-event 2 to occur when SS(2) crosses SS(1) in the negative direction with a tolerance 0.01. (See Fig. 10-4(b))
    SEVNT,2,SS(2),XN,SS(1),0.01;

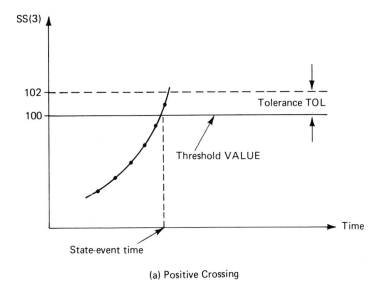

(a) Positive Crossing

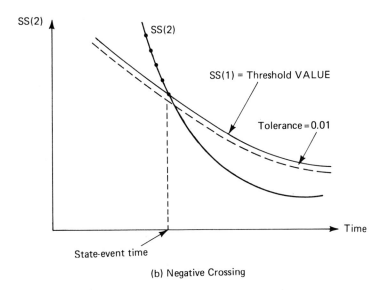

(b) Negative Crossing

Figure 10-4 Illustrations of positive and negative crossings defining state-events.

3. Define state-event 4 to occur when DD(1) crosses 0.0 in either direction with a tolerance of 0.0.

SEVNT,4,DD(1),X,0.0,0.0;

In this case, state-event 4 detects minimums, maximums, or points of inflection of state variable 1. A tolerance of 0.0 insures that the minimum step size DTMIN will be used to detect the crossing if necessary.

When a crossing within tolerance is determined, the executive function calls subroutine EVENT(JEVNT) to indicate that state-event JEVNT has occurred. If a crossing occurs that is not within tolerance, the step size is automatically reduced and the above process is repeated until a crossing within tolerance is obtained or the minimum step size is used. The user would then code in subroutine EVENT the logic involved and system status changes required when such an event is detected.

In event routines, discrete changes to state variables can be made by changing the value of SS(J). For example, the statement SS(3) = SS(3)+5.0 changes the value of state variable 3 by 5 units. In addition, parameters of equations and system status indicators used in STATE equations can be changed at event times. Thus, the values of coefficients and in effect the entire STATE equation structure could be changed at an event occurrence.

10.9   CODING SUBROUTINE STATE

Subroutine STATE is written to compute the current value of each state variable or its derivative. SLAM permits state variables to be defined by state equations or derivative equations in subroutine STATE. Subroutine STATE is frequently called, especially if there are active derivative equations, and therefore should contain only essential code. It is most efficient if the state variables are numbered sequentially.

As described in Section 10.4, the state storage array consists of four one-dimensional arrays. The vectors SS($\cdot$) and DD($\cdot$) contain values associated with time TNOW. The vectors SSL($\cdot$) and DDL($\cdot$) contain values associated with time TTLAS, the most current value of simulated time for which model status has been completely updated. When the model status has been updated to TNOW, TTLAS is reset to TNOW.

The problem-specific definition of the state storage array is determined by the user. There are several policies regarding the writing of state equations that must be followed. The user inputs the variable NNEQD which is defined as the largest subscript used in a derivative equation. Therefore, equations defining the rate of change of state variables, that is, equations for DD(I), must satisfy the expression I ≤ NNEQD. Equations defining SS(I) must satisfy the expression NNEQD + 1 ≤ I ≤ NNEQT where NNEQT is the largest subscript I in the defining equations for SS(I). Thus, if there is an equation defining DD(M) and another defining SS(N), then M≤NNEQD; M<N; and NNEQD + 1 ≤ N ≤ NNEQT. NNEQS = NNEQT − NNEQD is the largest possible number of equations written in terms of SS(I). Since it is most efficient to have the DD(·) numbered sequentially, NNEQD is often referred to as the number of defining equations written for DD(·) variables. Similarly, NNEQS is often referred to as the number of defining equations written for SS(·) variables. NNEQD, NNEQS, or both can be zero.

The above numbering policy can be summarized by the following four cases:

Case 1. NNEQD = 0; NNEQS = 0. No continuous variables are included in the simulation, that is, a discrete or network simulation is to be performed.

Case 2. NNEQD > 0; NNEQS = 0. All state variables are defined by differential equations written for DD(I). SLAM uses an integration algorithm to compute SS(I). Multiple calls to subroutine STATE are made to evaluate DD(I) for use in the numerical integration algorithm.

Case 3. NNEQD = 0; NNEQS > 0. All state variables are defined by algebraic or difference equations written for SS(I). The user must compute SS(I) in subroutine STATE. For example,

SS(I)=SSL(I)+DTNOW*RATE

could be coded in subroutine STATE. In this case, the variable DD(I) is not used by SLAM.

Case 4. NNEQD > 0; NNEQS > 0. The first NNEQD state variables are defined by differential equations, and the next NNEQS variables are defined by algebraic or difference equations. The evaluation procedure is a combination of cases (2) and (3) above.

In subroutine STATE, the order in which the equations are written is left to the user, that is, a statement defining SS(5) can precede one defining DD(3). Because SLAM does not change the execution sequence of state equations, correct sequencing of state and derivative equations is the responsibility of the user. If the defining equations for DD(·) do not involve other DD(·) variables, any order is permitted and the integration procedure simultaneously solves for all DD(·) and corresponding SS(·) variables. Thus DD(1) = A * SS(1) + B * SS(2) and DD(2) = C * SS(1) + F * SS(2) can be written in either order, and the values obtained for DD(1), DD(2), SS(1), and SS(2) will be the same.

If the defining equations for DD(·) do involve other DD(·) variables, ordering becomes important. For example, if DD(3) = f(DD(5)), the equation for DD(5) must precede the equation for DD(3) according to standard FORTRAN conventions. If there are simultaneous equations involving DD($\cdot$) variables, the user must develop an algorithm for solving the set of equations. This is also the case when a set of simultaneous algebraic state equations is written.

In subroutine STATE, the equations for DD($\cdot$) and SS($\cdot$) can be written in a variety of forms. The equations†

DD(M)=RATE

and

SS(M)=SSL(M)+DTNOW*RATE

are essentially equivalent (SLAM sets DTNOW = TNOW − TTLAS). When an equation for DD(M) is written, values of SS(M) are obtained through the integration routine contained within SLAM. Values of DDL(M) and SSL(M) are automatically maintained. The step size is automatically determined to meet specified accuracy requirements on the computation of SS(M) and tolerances on state-event occurrences. When the equation is written for SS(M), only SSL(M) and not DD(M) or DDL(M) is maintained by SLAM. Accuracy requirements are not specified on SS(M), and the step size DTNOW for updating SS(M) is maintained at the maximum value specified by the user unless there is an intervening event. DTNOW is automatically reduced if there are intervening time-events, state-events, or a need to record a value of SS(M) for eventual communication (output).

The form of the equations for DD($\cdot$) and SS($\cdot$) is limited only by FORTRAN statement types. Thus, the user has a great deal of flexibility in defining the state variables for the model. In fact, the user can make the description conditional on time or on any model variable. For example, if a rate changes after TC time units have elapsed, it could be written as

DD(M) = RATE1
IF(TNOW.GE.TC) DD(M) = RATE2

State- or time-events could be used to trigger the change by resetting the rate values or by setting an indicator, possibly IND, equal to 1 at the time of the event. In the former case, DD(M) = RATE, where RATE is set equal to RATE1 or RATE2 in subroutine EVENT or in an event routine. In the latter case, we could write the following in subroutine STATE:

DD(M) = RATE1
IF(IND.EQ.1) DD(M) = RATE2

---

† Equations that define both DD(M) and SS(M) are permitted only if M > NNEQD. In this case, DD(M) is *not* related to SS(M) by SLAM and is processed as if it were an SS($\cdot$) variable.

10.10   MODELING USING DERIVATIVES OF STATE VARIABLES

SLAM uses a Runge-Kutta-Fehlberg (RKF) algorithm (see Appendix E) to integrate the equations of subroutine STATE written in terms of the DD($\cdot$) variables. The RKF algorithm is used to obtain a solution to a set of simultaneous first-order ordinary differential equations of the form

$$y_j'(t) = f_j(y_1, y_2, \ldots, y_m, t), \qquad j = 1, 2, \ldots, m$$

where

$$y_j'(t) = \frac{dy_j(t)}{dt}.$$

In SLAM, these equations would be expressed in the following form;

DD(J)=f$_j$(SS(1),SS(2), . . . , SS(M), TNOW), J=1, 2, . . . , M.

For example, if

$$y_1'(t) = a_1 y_1 + b_1 y_2$$

and

$$y_2'(t) = a_2 y_1 + b_2 y_2,$$

the corresponding SLAM coding would be

DD(1)=A1*SS(1)+B1*SS(2)

and

DD(2)=A2*SS(1)+B2*SS(2)

Higher order differential equations can be modeled by putting the equations in canonical form. Thus, if an nth order differential equation of the form

$$x^{(n)}(t) = f(x, x', x^{(2)}, \ldots, x^{(n-1)}, t)$$

is to be modeled using SLAM, N variables SS(J), J = 1, 2, . . . ,N, must be defined as follows:

$$SS(1) = x$$
$$SS(2) = x' = DD(1)$$
$$SS(3) = x^{(2)} = DD(2)$$

$$\cdot$$
$$\cdot$$
$$\cdot$$

$$SS(N) = x^{(n-1)} = DD(N-1)$$

By substitution, $DD(N) = f(SS(1), SS(2),\ldots,SS(N),t)$. With these equations, $SS(1)$ is the solution to the nth order differential equation. As an example, consider the second order equation

$$x^{(2)}(t) = Ax'(t) + Bx(t) + C.$$

Let $SS(1) = x(t)$
and $DD(1) = x'(t) = SS(2)$
then $DD(2) = x^{(2)}(t)$

In SLAM, this would be coded in subroutine STATE as

$DD(1) = SS(2)$
$DD(2) = A * SS(2) + B * SS(1) + C$

10.11   MODELING USING STATE VARIABLES

Subroutine STATE can be used to model the state variables, employing any combination of $DD(\cdot)$ and $SS(\cdot)$ variables. The use of $SS(\cdot)$ to model difference equations is a straight translation of the difference equations, that is,

$$y_n = A * y_{n-1} + B$$

is equivalent to the SLAM statement

$SS(1) = A * SSL(1) + B$

where $SS(1)$ is used to represent the value of y at time n, that is, y_n, and $SSL(1)$ represents the value of y at time $n-1$, that is, y_{n-1}. Generalization to allow A and B to be functions of time is also direct. Higher order difference equations can be modeled in a manner similar to that given for higher order differential equations. The translation of

$$y_n = A * y_{n-1} + B * y_{n-2} + C$$

is made by defining $SS(1)$ to be y_n, then $SSL(1)$ corresponds to y_{n-1}. Letting $SS(2) = SSL(1)$ then $SSL(2)$ corresponds to y_{n-2}. The value of y_n can be obtained as $SS(1)$ using the following two state equations:

$SS(1) = A * SSL(1) + B * SSL(2) + C$
$SS(2) = SSL(1)$

State variables can also be used to model differential equations by means of an Euler integration method (1). In this case, the user must provide the integration method to solve the equations for the $SS(\cdot)$ variables. Consider the differential equation

$$\frac{dy}{dt} + A * y = B$$

or

$$y' = B - A * y.$$

Suppose that we know y at the point n−1, and we call this value y_{n-1}^{o}. Then

$$y_{n-1}' = B - A * y_{n-1}^{o}.$$

If we assume that y_{n-1}' is a good approximation of y' between n−1 and n, then

$$y_n = y_{n-1}^{o} + h * y_{n-1}'$$

where h is the interval of time between points n−1 and n.

Substituting yields

$$y_n = y_{n-1}^{o} + h * (B - A * y_{n-1}^{o})$$

and

$$y_n = y_{n-1}^{o} * (1 - h * A) + h * B.$$

In terms of SLAM variables, this becomes

SS(1)=SSL(1)*(1.−DTNOW*A)+DTNOW*B

since DTNOW is the time interval between calculations of state variables. The SLAM user can employ more advanced Euler type integrators by coding such integrators in subroutine STATE.

If the equations involving the $SS(\cdot)$ variables cannot be written sequentially due to an interdependence of the variables, the user must provide the means for solving them. For example, the Gauss-Seidel procedure (2,11) could be used.

10.12   TIME ADVANCE PROCEDURES

In SLAM, the amount by which simulated time is advanced depends on the type of simulation (network, continuous, discrete) being performed and the values of specific variables at the current point in simulated time.

In a network or discrete simulation, time is advanced from one event to the next event. In this case, the time interval between events is TNEXT-TNOW where TNEXT is the time of the next event. Time is advanced from TNOW to TNEXT by resetting TNOW equal to TNEXT and assuming that the system status has remained constant between events. Since status at TNOW is always accepted, there is no need to maintain system status values at TTLAS, and TNOW can be used as both the last update point and then as the new event time, that is, TTLAS is neither required nor used.

For a continuous simulation, the variable DTFUL is the value for a full step size. If all the equations for state variables are written in terms of SS($\cdot$), the variable representing the time advance increment, DTNOW, will normally be set equal to DTFUL. The time at the beginning of the step is TTLAS, and the time at the end of the proposed step is TNOW, that is, TNOW = TTLAS + DTNOW. DTFUL remains constant at the maximum step size prescribed by the user, DTMAX, unless an event occurs within the step.

The increment in time between the recording of the status of the system is specified through the variable DTSAV. For DTSAV > 0, SLAM will record values as specified on RECORD statements every DTSAV time unit. The variable TTSAV is used to define the next time at which the system status is to be recorded. These time points are called record or save times. If a save time occurs within an interval, that is, TTLAS + DTNOW is greater than TTSAV, the step size is reduced to TTSAV − TTLAS. In this way, the status of the system is updated to TNOW = TTSAV. TTLAS is then updated and TTSAV is reset to TNOW + DTSAV.

The size of a step is also reset (decreased) if SLAM determines that the step would cause a state-event to be passed. Thus, if the value of a state variable at time TTLAS + DTNOW results in the crossing of a threshold beyond allowable tolerances, the step size is reduced. If the tolerance is still not met, the step size continues to be reduced until the value of DTFUL is set equal to a user-prescribed minimum step size, DTMIN. Note that DTFUL can be less than DTMIN if either TNEXT − TTLAS < DTMIN or TTSAV − TTLAS < DTMIN. Further note that a fixed step size can be specified for a simulation involving only SS($\cdot$) variables in which there are no time-events by specifying DTMIN = DTMAX.

The most complex time advance procedure occurs when variables defined by DD($\cdot$) equations are included in a SLAM simulation program. In this case, all the considerations described above pertain; in addition, the full step size, DTFUL, is divided into fractions so that the time advance increment, DTNOW, proceeds as required by the RKF algorithm. The SS($\cdot$) variables are evaluated at these intermediate points within the step and used by SLAM in the integration of the equations for DD($\cdot$). These intermediate values for SS($\cdot$) and DD($\cdot$) allow error estimates to be made and simultaneous differential equations to be evaluated.

The variable DTACC is defined as the next step size to be used, based on allowable error specifications. Initially, DTACC is set equal to DTMAX. Whenever the accuracy of the integration algorithm does not meet the user's prescribed accuracy, as defined by an absolute error value AAERR and a relative error value RRERR, the value of DTACC is recomputed. At the start of each step, DTFUL is set equal to DTACC. The decreasing of DTACC when accuracy is not met is permitted only until DTACC becomes less than DTMIN, at which time DTACC is set equal to DTMIN. If the specified accuracy cannot be achieved using DTMIN, the following conditions specified in the CONTINUOUS statement define the appropriate action:

N → Proceed without printing a warning message;
W → Proceed after printing a warning message;
F → Terminate the simulation after printing a fatal error message.

When all state variables are within the accuracy specifications to a significant extent, DTACC is increased by a factor that is dependent on the ratio of the estimated error to the allowed error. In this way, the step size is increased when good estimates for the state variables are obtained by the integration algorithm. In no case will SLAM allow DTACC to become greater than DTMAX.

It is obvious that the time advance procedures included within SLAM involve many variables with many interactions between these variables. SLAM automatically advances time for the user on the basis of the input values prescribed for DTMIN, DTMAX, DTSAV, and the accuracy requirements (AAERR and RRERR) when DD($\cdot$) equations are specified. The calculation of DTFUL, DTNOW, and DTACC, as well as the next discrete event time, TNEXT, and the next save time, TTSAV, are internally computed in SLAM.

10.12.1 CONTINUOUS Input Statement

The SLAM input statement to specify values for continuous models is

CONTINUOUS,NNEQD,NNEQS,DTMIN,DTMAX,DTSAV,W or F or N,AAERR,RRERR;

The definitions of the variables on the CONTINUOUS statement are presented below along with their default values.

Variable	Definition	Default
NNEQD	Largest subscript for DD(·) when defined by a derivative equation. (For efficiency, NNEQD should be the number of derivative equations.)	0
NNEQS	Number of state variables that can be defined by state equations.	0
DTMIN	Minimum allowable step size; not used if NNEQD+NNEQS=0.	0.01*DTMAX
DTMAX	Maximum allowable step size; not used if NNEQD+NNEQS=0.	DTSAV
DTSAV	The frequency at which data values are recorded for RECORD statements. If DTSAV<0, recording done at event times only. If DTSAV=0, recording done at the end of each step. If DTSAV >0, recording done every DTSAV time units and at each event time. When user plots are specified on a RECORD statement, the calls to GPLOT control the frequency at which data values are recorded.	High Value†
W or F or N	Indicates type of error check in Runge-Kutta integration or in state-event crossing detection when a step size smaller that DTMIN is required. If F is specified, then a *fatal* error occurs. If W is specified, then a *w*arning message is printed before proceeding. If N is specified, then execution proceeds with *n*o warning message given.	W
AAERR	Absolute local truncation error allowed in Runge-Kutta integration. Used with RRERR to control accuracy; not used when NNEQD=0.	0.00001
RRERR	Relative local truncation error allowed in Runge-Kutta integration; used with AAERR to control accuracy.	0.00001

† High value is prescribed by the SLAM variable HIVAL. The default for DTSAV if no CONTINUOUS statement is used is the largest DTPLT value on any RECORD statement.

The numerical integration accuracy is controlled by the specification of AAERR and RRERR. The RKF algorithm estimates the single-step error for each variable defined by a differential equation. The Ith error estimate is compared to TERR where

$$TERR(I) = AAERR + ABS(SS(I)) * RRERR$$

If the error estimate is less than or equal to TERR(I) for each I, the values of SS(I) are accepted. If not, the step size is reduced and the integration algorithm is reapplied. The default values of AAERR and RRERR are stringent and a significant reduction in running times can be achieved by liberalizing these values subject, of course, to the accuracy requirements of the simulation model.

10.12.2   Use of DTNOW

A note of caution is in order regarding the use of DTNOW in subroutine STATE. DTNOW is the value of the time increment through which SLAM updates the state variables over a full step of size DTFUL. In many cases, DTNOW = DTFUL. In other cases, this is not so. In fact, if two events occur at the same time, DTNOW will assume a value of zero for the second event processed. Thus, DTNOW should not be used in the denominator of any equation in subroutine STATE. However, DTNOW should be used in any equation in subroutine STATE in which the state variable is updated by a rate multiplied by the increment in time for which the update is being performed.

10.12.3   Summary of Time Advance Procedure

A summary of the time advance procedures used in SLAM are given below. If derivative equations are included (NNEQD > 0), then

DTFUL=min[DTACC; TTSAV−TTLAS; TNEXT−TTLAS; time to next
    state-event],
DTNOW=f(DTFUL),
TNOW=TTLAS+DTNOW,
max DTACC=DTMAX,
min DTACC=DTMIN,
min (full step size to next state-event)=DTMIN.

If derivative equations are not included (NNEQD = 0), but state equations are (NNEQS > 0), then

DTFUL=min [DTMAX; TTSAV−TTLAS; TNEXT−TTLAS; time to
   next state-event],
DTNOW=DTFUL,
TNOW=TTLAS+DTNOW,
min (full step size to next state-event)=DTMIN,
and DTACC is not used.

If NNEQD = 0 and NNEQS = 0, then DTFUL, DTNOW, DTACC, and TTLAS
are not used and TNOW is the time of the current event being processed. In this case
only time-events are possible.

10.13   Example 10-1.   PILOT EJECTION

The pilot ejection system of an aircraft that is flying level and at a constant velocity is to be simulated. This example is frequently cited in the literature and is
referred to as the pilot ejection model. The specific version described here is ex-
tracted from Reference 3.

The pilot ejection system, when activated, causes the pilot and his seat to travel
along rails at a specified exit velocity V_E at an angle θ_E backward from vertical.
After traveling a vertical distance Y_1, the seat becomes disengaged from its mount-
ing rails and at this point the pilot is considered out of the cockpit. When this
occurs, a second phase of operation begins during which the pilot's trajectory is
influenced by the force of gravity and atmospheric drag. A critical aspect of this
phase is whether the pilot will clear the tail of the aircraft. The tail is 60 feet behind and 12 feet above the cockpit. Graphical and mathematical descriptions of
the two phases are shown in Figure 10-5 along with a legend for the variables
of the model.

The objective of this simulation is to determine the trajectory of a pilot ejected
from an aircraft to assess whether he would hit the tail of the aircraft. This information is desired for a fixed ejection velocity and angle for the two aircraft veloci-
ties: 900 feet/second and 500 feet/second.

Concepts Illustrated.   The purpose of this example is to introduce the use of
SLAM for the preparation of a continuous simulation model. The coding of subroutine STATE is illustrated. The procedures for programming different run termination conditions within a run and for making multiple runs are demonstrated.

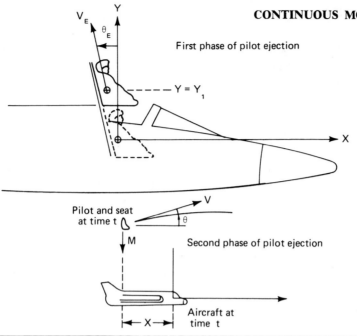

First phase of pilot ejection

$Y = Y_1$

Second phase of pilot ejection

Pilot and seat at time t

Aircraft at time t

Variable	Definition	Equations
X	Horizontal distance from point of ejection	$\dfrac{dX}{dt} = V \cos \theta - V_A$
Y	Vertical distance from point of ejection	$\dfrac{dY}{dt} = V \sin \theta$
Y_1	Vertical distance above point of ejection where first phase ends	$\dfrac{dV}{dt} = 0, \quad 0 \le Y < Y_1$
V_A	Velocity of aircraft	$\dfrac{d\theta}{dt} = 0, \quad 0 \le Y < Y_1$
V	Pilot and seat velocity	
θ	Angle for pilot and seat movement	
V_E	Ejection velocity	
θ_E	Angle of ejection	$D = \dfrac{1}{2} \rho c_d S V^2$
M	Mass of pilot and seat	$\dfrac{dV}{dt} = -\dfrac{D}{M} - g \sin \theta \qquad Y \ge Y_1$
ρ, c_d, S	Parameters of the model	$\dfrac{d\theta}{dt} = -\dfrac{g \cos \theta}{V}, \qquad Y \ge Y_1$

Figure 10-5 Graphical and mathematical description of a pilot ejection model.

On each run, two plots are prepared and printed. On one of the plots, altitude versus distance is graphed to illustrate the plotting of a state variable against an independent variable other than time.

SLAM Model. The pilot ejection model is simulated using continuous variables. The equations describing the state variables and their derivatives are programmed in subroutine STATE. The conditions for state-events are defined on SEVNT input statements. Since this is a continuous model, no time-events are involved. Since multiple runs will be made, the main program will initialize only the non-SLAM variables that are constant for all runs. Other non-SLAM variables and the initial conditions for the simulation will be set in subroutine INTLC. A RECORD statement is used to specify the outputs desired to portray the trajectory of the pilot as he leaves the aircraft. A RECORD statement will also be used to obtain the data to plot the pilot's relative position from the aircraft over time, and his speed and direction over time.

The main program is used only to initialize input/output device numbers, the dimension of the filing array, and the non-SLAM variables that remain constant over all runs. After this is done, subroutine SLAM is called to control the running of the simulation. The FORTRAN listing for the main program is shown in Figure 10-6. The device numbers are set to their standard values and NNSET is set to 1 since the file structure is not employed in this example. Next, SLAM variables are initialized through a READ statement.

The major programming effort for this example is expended in writing subroutine STATE where the equations describing the pilot ejection model are coded. Table 10-1 presents a listing of the SLAM variables that are equivalent to the variables presented in Figure 10-5 and discussed in the problem statement. As can be seen from Table 10-2, there is a direct mnemonic relationship between the SLAM vari-

```
      COMMON/SCOM1/ ATRIB(100),DD(100),DDL(100),DTNOW,II,MFA,MSTOP,NCLNR
     1,NCRDR,NPRNT,NNRUN,NNSET,NTAPE,SS(100),SSL(100),TNEXT,TNOW,XX(100)
      COMMON /UCOM1/ CD,G,RHO,THED,VA,VE,XM,XS,Y1
      NCRDR=5
      NPRNT=6
      NTAPE=7
      NNSET=1
      READ (NCRDR,101) XM,G,CD,XS,Y1,VE,THED,RHO
      CALL SLAM
      STOP
C
  101 FORMAT (7F5.0,E10.4)
C
      END
```

Figure 10-6 Main program for pilot ejection model.

Table 10-1 Variables for pilot ejection model.

Problem Statement	SLAM	Initial Value
X	SS(1)	0.0
dX/dt	DD(1)	Computed
Y	SS(2)	0.0
dY/dt	DD(2)	Computed
V	SS(3)	Computed
dV/dt	DD(3)	0.0
θ	SS(4)	Computed
$d\theta/dt$	DD(4)	0.0
C_d	CD	1.0
g	G	32.2 ft/sec^2
ρ	RHO	2.3769x 10^{-3} slug/ft^3
θ_E (rad)	THE	15./57.3
θ_E (deg)	THED	15.0
V_A	VA	Input
V_E	VE	40.0 ft/sec
M	XM	7 slugs
S	XS	10.0 ft^2
Y_1	Y1	4.0 ft

ables and the variables included in the model. The coding of the equations presented in Fig. 10-5 using SLAM variables is shown below.

```
DD(1)=SS(3)*COS(SS(4))−VA
DD(2)=SS(3)*SIN(SS(4))
DD(3)=0.0                        SS(2)<Y1
DD(4)=0.0                        SS(2)<Y1
DD(3)= −XD/XM−G*SIN(SS(4))       SS(2)≧Y1
DD(4)= −G*COS(SS(4))/SS(3)       SS(2)≧Y1
where
XD=0.5*RHO*CD*XS*SS(3)*SS(3)
```

When $SS(2) \geq Y1$, the pilot is released from the cockpit and the second set of equations for DD(3) and DD(4) is used. Since the relative position of the pilot

```
      SUBROUTINE STATE
      COMMON/SCOM1/ ATRIB(100),DD(100),DDL(100),DTNOW,II,MFA,MSTOP,NCLNR
     1,NCRDR,NPRNT,NNRUN,NNSET,NTAPE,SS(100),SSL(100),TNEXT,TNOW,XX(100)
      COMMON /UCOM1/ CD,G,RHO,THED,VA,VE,XM,XS,Y1
      DD(1)=SS(3)*COS(SS(4))-VA
      DD(2)=SS(3)*SIN(SS(4))
      IF(XX(1).LT.1.) RETURN
  101 XD=.5*RHO*CD*XS*SS(3)*SS(3)
      DD(3)=-XD/XM-G*SIN(SS(4))
      DD(4)=-G*COS(SS(4))/SS(3)
  102 RETURN
C
      END
```

Figure 10-7   Subroutine STATE for pilot ejection model.

during the simulated period of interest will always exceed Y1 after he is released, the test of whether SS(2) is greater than Y1 can serve for specifying when the equations for DD(3) and DD(4) are to be used.

In the coding to follow, the global variable XX(1) will be set to 1.0 to indicate this condition. The listing for subroutine STATE is shown in Figure 10-7. It should be noted that DD(1), DD(2), DD(3), and DD(4) are functions of both SS(3) and SS(4). The RKF integration algorithm of SLAM simultaneously solves for the desired SS($\cdot$) values, and the multiple dependence is taken into account. The order of coding the DD($\cdot$) equations will not affect the results obtained in this example.

In subroutine STATE, DD(3) and DD(4) are not set to zero since this is done in the initialization routines. When SS(2) $\geq$ Y1, a state-event will be coded to change the value of XX(1) to 1. Initially XX(1) = 0. When XX(1) = 1, the values of DD(3) and DD(4) will be recomputed for each call to subroutine STATE. Three conditions define state-events. A state-event occurs when the pilot achieves a relative height of Y1 with respect to the aircraft. When this occurs, the equations governing the pilot's movement are altered as described above. The other two state-events are for stopping the simulation. When the pilot is 60 feet behind the cockpit, he will be beyond the tail. When the pilot is 30 feet above the airplane, he is well above the 12 foot high tail. In either case, the simulation is halted. In terms of the SLAM variables, these conditions are SS(1) $\leq$ -60 and SS(2) $\geq$ 30. The other condition for stopping involves time exceeding four seconds. This is accomplished through the INITIALIZE input statement by setting TTFIN = 4.

The establishment of the conditions for state-events is made using statement type SEVNT. The input statements for the three conditions are shown below:

SEVNT,1,SS(1),XN,−60.,0.0;
SEVNT,1,SS(2),XP,30,0.0;
SEVNT,2,SS(2),XP,4,0.0;

The first SEVNT statement specifies that state-event 1 occurs when SS(1) crosses the value −60 in the negative direction with zero tolerance. This corresponds to the pilot passing the tail in the X-direction. A tolerance of zero is used to force SLAM to use the minimum step size when SS(1) exceeds the value of −60. In this way, a precise determination of when the state-event occurs can be obtained. State-event 1 represents one of the conditions by which the simulation run will be terminated. The second statement specifies that state-event 1 will also occur when SS(2) crosses the value 30 in the positive direction with a tolerance of zero. This statement corresponds to the run termination condition that the pilot exceeds a vertical distance of 30 feet above the cockpit.

The third state-event input statement corresponds to the pilot achieving a vertical distance, SS(2), of four feet. The crossing is prescribed to be in a positive direction and again a zero tolerance is specified to force SLAM to detect the point at which the pilot leaves the aircraft with as much precision as possible. In this manner, the switching from one equation set to another will be accomplished with the precision specified by the input value for DTMIN. This third SEVNT statement prescribes state-event 2 to be the event code associated with the pilot leaving the cockpit.

The effects associated with the occurrence of state-events are modeled in subroutine EVENT(IX). When an event with code one occurs (IX=1), we request a stopping of the simulation by setting MSTOP negative. When IX=2, we desire to change the equations for DD(3) and DD(4). This latter change was prescribed in subroutine STATE to occur when the value of XX(1) was set to 1. The coding for subroutine EVENT is shown in Figure 10-8. Since the code required to model the state-events associated with this problem is extremely short, both state-events are programmed directly in subroutine EVENT. A computed GO TO statement is used to decode state-event codes. When a termination condition is reached, the SLAM variable MSTOP is set to −1 to indicate to the SLAM executive that the run should be terminated. When state-event 2 occurs (IX=2), a transfer is made to statement 2 where XX(1) is set equal to 1 to cause the desired change to be

```
      SUBROUTINE EVENT(IX)
      COMMON/SCOM1/ ATRIB(100),DD(100),DDL(100),DTNOW,II,MFA,MSTOP,NCLNR
     1,NCRDR,NPRNT,NNRUN,NNSET,NTAPE,SS(100),SSL(100),TNEXT,TNOW,XX(100)
      GO TO (1,2) ,IX
    1 MSTOP=-1
      RETURN
    2 XX(1)=1.
      RETURN
      END
```

Figure 10-8 Subroutine EVENT for pilot ejection model.

```
SUBROUTINE INTLC
COMMON/SCOM1/ ATRIB(100),DD(100),DDL(100),DTNOW,II,MFA,MSTOP,NCLNR
1,NCRDR,NPRNT,NNRUN,NNSET,NTAPE,SS(100),SSL(100),TNEXT,TNOW,XX(100)
COMMON /UCOM1/ CD,G,RHO,THED,VA,VE,XM,XS,Y1
READ (NCRDR,101) VA
THE=THED/57.3
VX=VA-VE*SIN(THE)
VY=VE*COS(THE)
SS(3)=SQRT(VX*VX+VY*VY)
SS(4)=ATAN(VY/VX)
XX(1)=0.
RETURN
C
  101 FORMAT (1F10.0)
C
END
```

Figure 10-9   Subroutine INTLC for pilot ejection model.

made in the equations written in subroutine STATE. This completes the description of subroutine EVENT for the pilot ejection model.

Subroutine INTLC is used to initialize the state variables and non-SLAM variables that require initialization before each run. For this example, INTLC is written to allow the aircraft velocity to be initialized through data input before each run. In the listing of INTLC given in Figure 10-9, the first statement performs this reading operation. Initial values of the state variables are then established for a run. The initial position of the pilot relative to the aircraft cockpit is at the origin, that is, $SS(1) = 0.0$ and $SS(2) = 0.0$. These values are automatically established in the SLAM initialization process. The pilot's initial velocity vector, caused by pushing the ejection button, is given by the following equations:

$$V_{\text{initial}} = \sqrt{(V_A - V_E \sin \theta_E)^2 + (V_E \cos \theta_E)^2}$$

and

$$\theta_{\text{initial}} = \tan^{-1} \left(\frac{V_E \cos \theta_E}{V_A - V_E \sin \theta_E} \right).$$

These initial values are set equal to $SS(3)$ and $SS(4)$ at the beginning of each simulation run since ejection is initiated at time zero. The initial values of the derivatives of the state variables are obtained when the SLAM executive calls subroutine STATE at time zero. The last statement in subroutine INTLC sets the value of $XX(1)$ to 0.0 to indicate that the pilot has not left the cockpit at the beginning of each run.

A listing of the input for this example is shown in Figure 10-10. The first input record is for the variables that were initialized through the READ statement in the main program. The second input record describes the general information (GEN statement type) and indicates that two runs are to be made. The INITIALIZE statement specifies that the beginning time for a run (TTBEG) is to be zero and that the ending time (TTFIN) is to be four. Default values for other variables on the INITIALIZE card are to be used. Information regarding the number of equations, step size, recording interval, and accuracy of the RKF algorithm are provided on the CONTINUOUS input statement. Specifically, the following values are prescribed: NNEQD = 4; NNEQS = 0; DTMIN = 0.0001; DTMAX = 0.01; DTSAV = 0.01; W = Warning; AAERR = 0; and RRERR = 0.000005.

With these values for the variables, there are four differential equations and no difference or state equations. The minimum step size is 0.0001 seconds and the maximum step size is 0.01 seconds. The recording or communication interval is also 0.01 seconds. When a state-event cannot be detected within specified tolerances or when the RKF numerical integration algorithm cannot meet accuracy specifications, warning messages are to be printed. The simulation is to be continued even when these conditions are detected. The accuracy requirement for the numerical integration algorithm has a zero value for the absolute error (AAERR) and a five millionth value for the relative error (RRERR).

```
      7. 32.2   1.   10.    4. 40.  15.   .0023769
GEN,PRITSKER,PILOT EJECTION,11/10/1977,2;
INITIALIZE,0,4;
CONTINUOUS,4,,.0001,.01,.01,W,0.,,000005;
RECORD,SS(1),X POS,8,P,-1.0;
VAR,SS(2),Y,Y POS.,0.0,20.;
RECORD,TNOW,TIME,9,B,0.02;
VAR,SS(1),X,X POS.,-70.,30.;
VAR,SS(2),Y,Y POS.,0.0,20.0;
VAR,SS(3),V,SPEED,MIN(100),MAX(100);
VAR,SS(4),T,THETA,MIN,MAX;
SEVNT,1,SS(1),XN,-60.0,0.0;
SEVNT,1,SS(2),XP,30.0,0.0;
SEVNT,2,SS(2),XP,4.0,0.0;
SIMULATE;
        900.
FIN;
        500.
```

Figure 10-10 Data input and statements for pilot ejection model.

The next seven input statements refer to the recording of values for eventual tabling and plotting. The first RECORD statement specifies that the state variable SS(1) is to be the independent variable and it is to be labeled as X POS. The values are to be stored on peripheral device 8 and only a plot of the dependent variable versus the independent variable is desired. The plotting interval is to be −1, that is, successive lines on the plot are to be −1 units apart. A negative interval is used as the X-position of the pilot with respect to the cockpit will be decreasing during the entire simulation. Default values are prescribed for the last three fields of the RECORD card since the card is terminated prior to the specification of these fields. With default values, the plot will be started at TTSRT = TTBEG = 0 and completed at TTEND = TTFIN = 4. KKEVT is defaulted to YES so that variable values at events will be recorded.

There is only one VAR input statement following the RECORD statement which implies that only one dependent variable is to be recorded for each value of the independent variable. The dependent variable is SS(2) which is to have a plot symbol of Y and a label of Y POS. The scale for the dependent variable is specified to have a low ordinate value of 0.0 (the left-hand axis) and a high ordinate value of 20.0 (the right-hand axis).

A second RECORD statement prescribes that a plot and table is desired with the independent variable being current time, TNOW. The label for TNOW is to be TIME. The values associated with this RECORD statement are to be stored on peripheral device 9. A plot interval of .02 is specified. The dependent variables for the plot are prescribed on the next four cards to be SS(1) through SS(4). The plot symbols and labels are easily identified from the input statements. A full range of options is given to define the scale limits for these four dependent variables. The left- and right-hand scales for the X and Y variables are prescribed to be (−70.,30.) and (0.0,20.0), respectively. For SS(3), the speed of the pilot, the low ordinate value is to be taken as the minimum value observed from the simulation rounded down to the nearest multiple of 100. The high ordinate value is to be taken as the maximum value from the simulation rounded up to the next higher multiple of 100. For SS(4), THETA, the minimum and maximum observed values from the simulation run are to be used as the low and high ordinate values, respectively.

The next three input statements describe the state-event conditions; these were described in detail previously. The SIMULATE statement indicates that the execution of the first run is to be initiated. Following the reading of the SIMULATE statement, a call to subroutine INTLC is made. The next input record is read by the READ statement in subroutine INTLC, and it specifies the aircraft velocity, VA, to be 900 feet per second. The next input statement is FIN which specifies that this is the last SLAM statement of the program. After the first run is completed, SLAM attempts to read additional input statements to alter the conditions for the next simulation run. The FIN statement indicates that no changes are to be made in the SLAM data values. The input line with the value 500. on it specifies the aircraft velocity for the second run.

The SLAM echo report for the input presented in Fig. 10-10 is presented in Fig. 10-11. Before examining SLAM outputs for this example, we will describe the sequence in which the subprograms are invoked. Subroutine SLAM is called by the main program and reads in the input statements, initializes SLAM variables, and calls subroutines INTLC and STATE. Subroutine SLAM then controls the simulation by advancing time in steps. During each step advance, the RKF algorithm integrates the $DD(\cdot)$ equations coded in subroutine STATE to evaluate $SS(\cdot)$ values at select time points within the step and at the end of the step.

When accuracy is acceptable, SLAM tests if any state-events occurred because of the updating of the state variables. The state-events are those that were defined on SEVNT input statements. If a state-event was passed, the step size is reduced and the above process is repeated with a new but smaller step size. If a state-event ends the step, subroutine EVENT is called. If the state-event is one that ends the simulation, MSTOP is set to -1 in subroutine EVENT and subroutine SLAM ends the run by calling OTPUT and SUMRY. Subroutine SLAM also checks TNOW against TTFIN and if $TNOW \geq TTFIN$, the simulation run is ended.

Summary of Results. Intermediate results for the first simulation, in which the aircraft velocity was 900 feet/second, are shown in Figure 10-12. Because a zero tolerance was specified on the SEVNT input statements for detecting crossings, warning messages that tolerances could not be met are expected. The messages

```
                         S L A M    E C H O    R E P O R T

              SIMULATION PROJECT PILOT EJECTION          BY PRITSKER

              DATE 11/10/1977                     RUN NUMBER    1 OF    2

                         SLAM VERSION JANUARY 1978

        GENERAL OPTIONS

              PRINT INPUT STATEMENTS (ILIST):            YES
              PRINT ECHO REPORT (IECHO):                 YES
              EXECUTE SIMULATIONS (IXQT):                YES
              PRINT INTERMEDIATE RESULTS HEADING (IPIRH): YES
              PRINT SUMMARY REPORT (ISMRY):              YES


        CONTINUOUS VARIABLES

              NUMBER OF DD EQUQTIONS (NNEQD):               4
              NUMBER OF SS EQUATIONS (NNEQS):               0
              MINIMUM STEP SIZE (DTMIN):            .1000-03
              MAXIMUM STEP SIZE (DTMAX):            .1000-01
              TIME BETWEEN SAVE POINTS (DTSAV):     .1000-01
              ACCURACY ERROR SPECIFICATION (LLERR):  WARNING
              ABSOLUTE ERROR LIMIT (AAERR):         .0000
              RELATIVE ERROR LIMIT (RRERR):         .5000-05

        STATE EVENTS

         NUMBER     MODE/JEVNT        CROSSING      DIRECTION      THRESHOLD       TOLERANCE
                                      VARIABLE      OF CROSSING    VALUE           OF CROSSING

            1       EVENT      1       SS(  1)       NEGATIVE       -.6000+02        .0000
            2       EVENT      1       SS(  2)       POSITIVE        .3000+02        .0000
            3       EVENT      2       SS(  2)       POSITIVE        .4000+01        .0000

        RECORDING OF PLOTS/TABLES

              PLOT/TABLE NUMBER    1

                 INDEPENDENT VARIABLE:             SS(  1)
                 IDENTIFIER:                       X POS
                 DATA STORAGE UNIT:                TAPE/DISC  8
                 DATA OUTPUT FORMAT:               PLOT
                 TIME BETWEEN PLOT POINTS (DTPLT): -.1000+01
                 STARTING TIME OF PLOT (TTSRT):     .0000
                 ENDING TIME OF PLOT (TTEND):       .4000+01
                 DATA POINTS AT EVENTS (KKEVT):    YES
              DEPENDENT VARIABLES

                 VARIABLE   SYMBOL   IDENTIFIER       LOW ORDINATE VALUE           HIGH ORDINATE VALUE
```

Figure 10-11 SLAM echo for pilot ejection model.

```
        SS( 2)      Y     Y POS.        VALUE EQUALS      .0000    VALUE EQUALS      .2000+02

    PLOT/TABLE NUMBER   2

        INDEPENDENT VARIABLE:            TNOW
        IDENTIFIER:                      TIME
        DATA STORAGE UNIT:               TAPE/DISC  9
        DATA OUTPUT FORMAT:              PLOT AND TABLE
        TIME BETWEEN PLOT POINTS (DTPLT):  .2000-01
        STARTING TIME OF PLOT (TTSRT):     .0000
        ENDING TIME OF PLOT (TTEND):       .4000+01
        DATA POINTS AT EVENTS (KKEVT):   YES

    DEPENDENT VARIABLES

        VARIABLE   SYMBOL   IDENTIFIER       LOW ORDINATE VALUE             HIGH ORDINATE VALUE

        SS( 1)      X     X POS.        VALUE EQUALS     -.7000+02    VALUE EQUALS      .3000+02
        SS( 2)      Y     Y POS.        VALUE EQUALS      .0000       VALUE EQUALS      .2000+02
        SS( 3)      V     SPEED         MIN TO NEAREST    .1000+03    MAX TO NEAREST    .1000+03
        SS( 4)      T     THETA         MIN TO NEAREST    .0000       MAX TO NEAREST    .0000

    RANDOM NUMBER STREAMS

        STREAM       SEED      REINITIALIZATION
        NUMBER       VALUE     OF STREAM

           1          0        NO
           2          0        NO
           3          0        NO
           4          0        NO
           5          0        NO
           6          0        NO
           7          0        NO
           8          0        NO
           9          0        NO
          10          0        NO


    INITIALIZATION OPTIONS

        BEGINNING TIME OF SIMULATION (TTBEG):   .0000
        ENDING TIME OF SIMULATION (TTFIN):      .4000+01
        STATISTICAL ARRAYS CLEARED (JJCLR):     YES
        VARIABLES INITIALIZED (JJVAR):          YES
        FILES INITIALIZED (JJFIL):              YES


    NSET/QSET STORAGE ALLOCATION

        DIMENSION OF NSET/QSET (NNSET):            1
        WORDS ALLOCATED TO FILING SYSTEM:         0
        WORDS ALLOCATED TO NETWORK:               0
        WORDS AVAILABLE FOR PLOTS/TABLES:         1

    INPUT ERRORS DETECTED:    0

    EXECUTION WILL BE ATTEMPTED
```

Figure 10-11 (continued).

could have been suppressed by specifying an N in the field for warning messages on the CONTINUOUS input statement. It was decided to retain the diagnostics to indicate the time of occurrence of the specified state conditions. The messages indicate that the pilot left the cockpit at time 0.1035 and that the simulation ended at time 0.4339. Since DTMIN was set at 0.0001, these results indicate that the pilot left the cockpit in the time interval from 0.1034 to 0.1035, and that the conditions for ending the simulation occurred in the interval from 0.4338 to 0.4339.

```
                                    **INTERMEDIATE RESULTS**



    SPECIFIED   TOLERANCE   EXCEEDED FOR SS( 2) AT TIME    .1035+00

    SPECIFIED   TOLERANCE   EXCEEDED FOR SS( 1) AT TIME    .4339+00
```
Figure 10-12 Intermediate results showing diagnostic messages for pilot ejection model.

Figure 10-13 is the plot of the pilot's position relative to the aircraft cockpit which is obtained in accordance with the first RECORD input statement. Note that the independent variable on the first plot is not time but distance (X-position) and that it is monotonically nonincreasing. With SLAM, the independent variable must

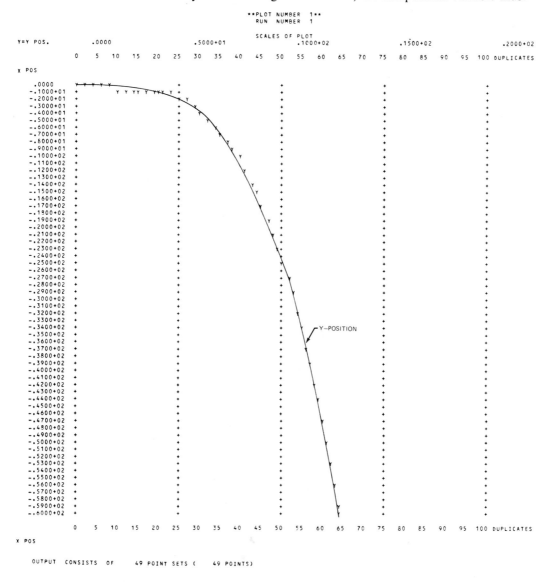

Figure 10-13   Plot of pilot's position relative to aircraft for aircraft velocity of 900 feet/second.

```
                                                **TABLE NUMBER  2**
                                                  RUN  NUMBER    1


TIME          X POS.        Y POS.        SPEED         THETA

 .0000         .0000         .0000        .8905+03      .4340-01
 .0000         .0000         .0000        .8905+03      .4340-01
 .1000-01     -.1035+00      .3864+00     .8905+03      .4340-01
 .2000-01     -.2070+00      .7727+00     .8905+03      .4340-01
 .3000-01     -.3106+00      .1159+01     .8905+03      .4340-01
 .4000-01     -.4141+00      .1545+01     .8905+03      .4340-01
 .5000-01     -.5176+00      .1932+01     .8905+03      .4340-01
 .6000-01     -.6211+00      .2318+01     .8905+03      .4340-01
 .7000-01     -.7246+00      .2705+01     .8905+03      .4340-01
 .8000-01     -.8282+00      .3091+01     .8905+03      .4340-01
 .9000-01     -.9317+00      .3477+01     .8905+03      .4340-01
 .1000+00     -.1035+01      .3864+01     .8905+03      .4340-01
 .1035+00     -.1072+01      .4000+01     .8905+03      .4340-01
 .1035+00     -.1072+01      .4000+01     .8905+03      .4340-01
 .1100+00     -.1167+01      .4248+01     .8819+03      .4317-01
 .1200+00     -.1422+01      .4624+01     .8688+03      .4280-01
 .1300+00     -.1804+01      .4992+01     .8562+03      .4243-01
 .1400+00     -.2312+01      .5351+01     .8439+03      .4205-01
 .1500+00     -.2940+01      .5701+01     .8320+03      .4166-01
 .1600+00     -.3686+01      .6044+01     .8204+03      .4128-01
 .1700+00     -.4545+01      .6378+01     .8091+03      .4088-01
 .1800+00     -.5516+01      .6705+01     .7981+03      .4048-01
 .1900+00     -.6595+01      .7024+01     .7874+03      .4007-01
 .2000+00     -.7779+01      .7336+01     .7770+03      .3966-01
 .2100+00     -.9066+01      .7641+01     .7669+03      .3925-01
 .2200+00     -.1045+02      .7938+01     .7570+03      .3882-01
 .2300+00     -.1194+02      .8228+01     .7474+03      .3840-01
 .2400+00     -.1351+02      .8512+01     .7380+03      .3796-01
 .2500+00     -.1518+02      .8789+01     .7289+03      .3752-01
 .2600+00     -.1695+02      .9059+01     .7200+03      .3708-01
 .2700+00     -.1879+02      .9323+01     .7113+03      .3663-01
 .2800+00     -.2073+02      .9580+01     .7028+03      .3618-01
 .2900+00     -.2275+02      .9831+01     .6945+03      .3571-01
 .3000+00     -.2485+02      .1008+02     .6864+03      .3525-01
 .3100+00     -.2703+02      .1031+02     .6784+03      .3478-01
 .3200+00     -.2929+02      .1055+02     .6707+03      .3430-01
 .3300+00     -.3162+02      .1077+02     .6632+03      .3382-01
 .3400+00     -.3403+02      .1100+02     .6558+03      .3333-01
 .3500+00     -.3651+02      .1121+02     .6485+03      .3284-01
 .3600+00     -.3907+02      .1142+02     .6415+03      .3234-01
 .3700+00     -.4169+02      .1163+02     .6345+03      .3183-01
 .3800+00     -.4438+02      .1183+02     .6278+03      .3132-01
 .3900+00     -.4714+02      .1202+02     .6211+03      .3081-01
 .4000+00     -.4996+02      .1221+02     .6146+03      .3029-01
 .4100+00     -.5285+02      .1239+02     .6083+03      .2976-01
 .4200+00     -.5580+02      .1257+02     .6021+03      .2923-01
 .4300+00     -.5882+02      .1274+02     .5960+03      .2869-01
 .4339+00     -.6001+02      .1281+02     .5936+03      .2848-01
 .4339+00     -.6001+02      .1281+02     .5936+03      .2848-01


MINIMUM       -.6001+02      .0000        .5936+03      .2848-01
MAXIMUM        .0000         .1281+02     .8905+03      .4340-01
```

Figure 10-14   State variables versus time for pilot ejection model with an average velocity of 900 feet/second.

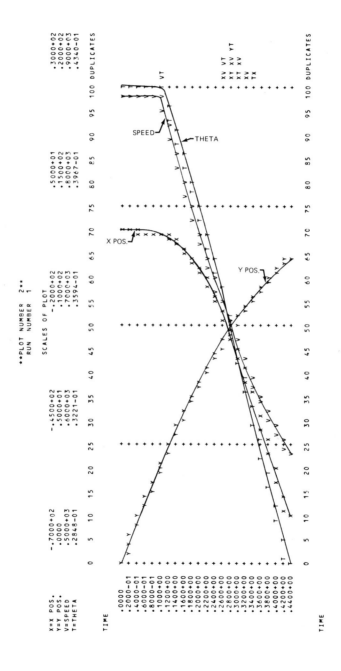

Figure 10-15 Plot of state variables over time for pilot ejection model with an aircraft velocity of 900 feet/second.

387

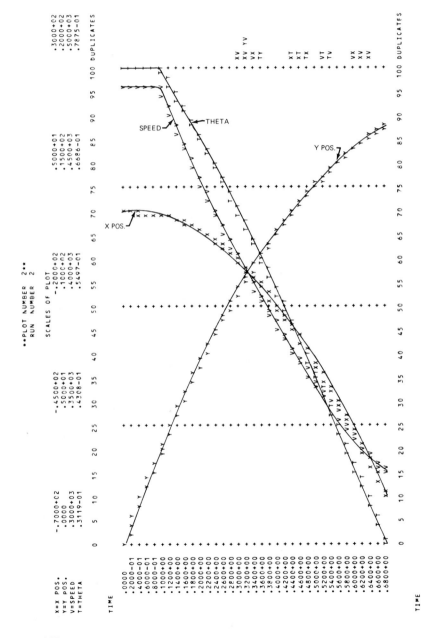

Figure 10-16 Plot of state variables over time for pilot ejection model with an aircraft velocity of 500 feet/second.

be monotonically nonincreasing if DTPLT < 0 and monotonically nondecreasing if DTPLT > 0. From the first plot, it is seen that the pilot clears the cockpit (Y = 4.0) at about X = −1.0. At X = −30.0, Y is approximately 10.6, and at X = −60.0, Y is approximately 12.8. With the tail being 12 feet high, there are design problems with the ejection system when the aircraft velocity is 900 feet/second. If desired, the precise values for X and Y could have been obtained by requesting a table in addition to the plot in the RECORD statement. Since precise values are printed out for plot-table 2, this was not done.

The table from the second RECORD statement is labeled **TABLE NUMBER 2** and is presented in Figure 10-14. In this table, the state variables are given as a function of time. The state-event representing the pilot leaving the cockpit is seen at time 0.1035. At this time, two sets of values are shown in the table since SLAM records the values at the end of the step before the event and immediately after the event occurs. This second set of values is recorded in case the event causes a discrete change in the variables. At the end of the table, minimum and maximum values are printed.

The plot corresponding to Table 2 is presented in Figure 10-15. At the top of the plot, the symbols representing the variables are defined with the scale for each variable. The scales used correspond to the input conditions specified. The plots illustrate how the state variables change with time.

The form of the output of the second run is similar to that for the first run. Figure 10-16 presents the plot of the state variables over time when the aircraft is traveling at 500 feet/second. In this case, the pilot is above 12 feet after 0.36 seconds and he is approximately 15.5 feet behind the cockpit.

10.14   Example 10-2.   A WORLD DYNAMICS MODEL

The world model analyzed in this example was defined by Forrester and has been described by him in detail (7). An extensive analysis of an extended version† of this model has been reported by Meadows (8).

For readers interested in the model development and use, these books are highly recommended. World Dynamics is an aggregate model of world interactions to illustrate the behavior of a set of defined variables depending on whether population growth is eventually suppressed by a shortage of natural resources, pollution,

---

† These extensions are easily coded in SLAM. For explanation purposes, the basic model was selected for presentation.

over-crowding, or an insufficient food supply. The model portrays the world inter-actions by five interrelated state variables: population P; natural resources NR; capital-investment CI; capital investment-in-agriculture fraction CIAF; and pollution POL. Table 10-2 defines the variables that are used in this example. The equations for the model are presented in the discussion of subroutine STATE.

Concepts Illustrated.   The primary objective of this example is to illustrate the coding of the World Dynamics model in SLAM. Systems Dynamics (6) models are easily built using SLAM and extensions to include discrete events are straight-forward (9,14). Difference equations are used to define the state variables. The use of EQUIVALENCE statements for improving the readability of subroutine STATE is also illustrated.

SLAM Model.   The major SLAM coding required for Systems Dynamics prob-lems is for subroutine STATE. State variables are written in terms of rate compo-

Table 10-2   Definition of variables for world dynamics model.

Variable†	Definition
BR	Birth rate
BRCM	Birth-rate-from-crowding multiplier
BRFM	Birth-rate-from-food multiplier
BRMM	Birth-rate-from-material multiplier
BRPM	Birth-rate-from-pollution multiplier
CFIFR	Capital fraction indicated by food ratio
CI	Capital investment
CIAF	Capital-investment-in-agriculture fraction
CID	Capital-investment discard
CIG	Capital-investment generation
CIM	Capital-investment multiplier
CIQR	Capital-investment-from-quality ratio
CIR	Capital-investment ratio
CIRA	Capital-investment ratio in agriculture
CR	Crowding ratio
DR	Death rate
DRCM	Death-rate-from-crowding multiplier
DRFM	Death-rate-from-food multiplier
DRMM	Death-rate-from-material multiplier
DRPM	Death-rate-from-pollution multiplier
ECIR	Effective-capital-investment ratio
F	Food
FC	Food coefficient
FCM	Food-from-crowding multiplier
FPCI	Food potential from capital investment
FPM	Food-from-pollution multiplier

nents and "auxiliary" values that may be required for the computation of the rate components. Using the definitions of Table 10-2, the statements for the rate components as defined by Forrester are:

BR = P*BRN*BRFM*BRMM*BRCM*BRPM
DR = P*DRN*DRMM*DRPM*DRFM*DRCM
NRUR = P*NRMM
CIG = P*CIM*CIGN
CID = CI*CIDN
POLG = P*POLN*POLCM
POLA = POL/POLAT

where all variables on the right-hand side are previous values of state variables or values already obtained in subroutine STATE.

The above equations illustrate that Forrester hypothesized multiplicative relationships in the computation of rate components. For example, birth rate, which is a component rate to be used in the computation of population, is equal to the product of the current population, birth rate normal, birth-rate-from-food multi-

Table 10-2 (*Continued*).

Variable†	Definition
FR	Food ratio
MSL	Material standard of living
NR	Natural Resources
NREM	Natural-resource-extraction multiplier
NRFR	Natural-resources-fraction remaining
NRI	Natural resources, initial
NRMM	Natural-resources-from-material multiplier
NRUR	Natural-resources-usage rate
P	Population
PD	Population density
POL	Pollution
POLA	Pollution absorption
POLCM	Pollution-from-capital multiplier
POLG	Pollution generation
POLR	Pollution ratio
POLS	Pollution standard
QL	Quality of life
QLC	Quality of life from crowding
QLF	Quality of life from food
QLM	Quality of life from material
QLP	Quality of life from pollution
QLS	Quality of life standard

† The letters I, N, and T when added to the variable name respectively denote initial, normal, and table, for example, BRN is birth rate normal.

plier, birth-rate-from-material multiplier, birth-rate-from-crowding multiplier, and birth-rate-from-pollution multiplier. Each of the multipliers are in turn computed from other variables. For example, BRFM, birth-rate-from-food multiplier, is obtained from a table function with the independent variable being the food ratio, FR. FR in turn is equal to a product of terms divided by food normal. Each of these relations is included in subroutine STATE.

With the above rate components, new values for the state variables can be computed using the following statements:

$$P = P+DTNOW*(BR-DR)$$
$$NR = NR+DTNOW*(-NRUR)$$
$$CI = CI+DTNOW*(CIG-CID)$$
$$POL = POL+DTNOW*(POLG-POLA)$$
$$CIAF = CIAF+DTNOW*(CFIFR*CIQR-CIAF)/CIAFT$$
$$QL = QLS*QLM*QLC*QLF*QLP$$

The equation for population P indicates that the population projected to time TNOW is equal to the population at TTLAS, plus the time interval times the rate of change of population. The time interval is DTNOW = TNOW − TTLAS and the rate of change of population is equal to the birth rate, BR, minus the death rate, DR. The above equations are coded directly in subroutine STATE and together with the statements for evaluating the "auxiliaries" comprise the World Dynamics model. The listing of subroutine STATE is given in Figure 10-17. In this example, the state variables are equivalenced to the SS(·) variables.

The listing of the main program for this example is given in Figure 10-18. In the main program, the card reader and printer numbers are set and the table functions are read. Subroutine SLAM is then called to control the simulation.

Subroutine INTLC initializes the non-SLAM variables that specify the starting conditions for the run. The listing for subroutine INTLC is given in Figure 10-19.

A listing of input statements for this example is shown in Figure 10-20.

Summary of Results.   The plotted output for the world model is shown in Figure 10-21. By properly selecting the limits for the plots, five variables can be plotted primarily in the 0-50% range and the other five variables in the 50-100% range. Each plot then consists of a top half and a bottom half and the possible confusion from having ten variables on a plot is decreased. Two plots per run could have been obtained but this would have increased execution time as the core plot option is not available when more than one plot is requested.

In running this simulation, no external excitation of the system is introduced. For stable systems, the dynamic behavior exhibited is due to the transients of the

```
         SUBROUTINE STATE
         REAL MSL,NREM,NRFR,NRMM,NR,NRI,NRUR,NREMT,NRMMT,LA
         COMMON/SCOM1/ ATRIB(100),DD(100),DDL(100),DTNOW,II,MFA,MSTOP,NCLNR
        1,NCRDR,NPRNT,NNRUN,NNSET,NTAPE,SS(100),SSL(100),TNEXT,TNOW,XX(100)
         COMMON /UCOM1/ BR,BRCM,BRFM,BRMM,BRN,BRPM,CFIFR,CIAFI,CIAFN,CIAFT
        1CID,CIDN,CIG,CIGN,CII,CIM,CIQR,CIP,CIRA,CR,DR,DRCM,DRFM,DRMM,DRN,D
        2RPM,ECIR,ECIRN,FC,FCM,FN,FPCI,FPM,LA,NREM,NRFR,NRI,NRMM,NRUR,
        3PDN,PI,POLA,POLAT,POLCM,POLG,POLI,POLN,POLS,QLF,QLM,QLS,XNRUN
         COMMON /UCOM2/ BRCMT(6),BRFMT(5),BRMMT(6),BRPMT(7),CFIFRT(5),CIMT
        1(6),CIQRT(5),DRCMT(6),DRFMT(9),DRMMT(11),DRPMT(7),FCMT(6),FPCIT(7)
        2,FPMT(7),NREMT(5),NRMMT(11),POLATT(7),POLCMT(5),QLCT(11),QLFT(5),Q
        3LMT(6),QLPT(7)
         EQUIVALENCE (P,SS(1)),(NR,SS(2)),(CI,SS(3)),(POL,SS(4)),(CIAF,SS(5
        1)),(POLR,XX(1)),(QL,XX(2)),(FR,XX(3)),(MSL,XX(4)),(QLC,XX(5)),
        2(QLP,XX(6))
C
C*****AUXILIARIES.
C
         NRFR=NR/NRI
         CR=P/(LA*PDN)
         CIR=CI/P
         NREM=GTABL(NREMT,NRFR,0.,1.,,25)
         ECIR=CIR*(1.-CIAF)*NREM/(1.-CIAFN)
         MSL=ECIR/ECIRN
         BRMM=GTABL(BRMMT,MSL,0.,5.,1.)
         DRMM=GTABL(DRMMT,MSL,0.,5.,.5)
         DRCM=GTABL(DRCMT,CR,0.,5.,1.)
         BRCM=GTABL(BRCMT,CR,0.,5.,1.)
         CIRA=CIR*CIAF/CIAFN
         FPCI=GTABL(FPCIT,CIRA,0.,6.,1.)
         FCM=GTABL(FCMT,CR,0.,5.,1.)
         POLR=POL/POLS
         FPM=GTABL(FPMT,POLR,0.,60.,10.)
         FR=FPCI*FCM*FPM*FC/FN
         CIM=GTABL(CIMT,MSL,0.,5.,1.)
         POLCM=GTABL(POLCMT,CIR,0.,5.,1.)
         POLAT=GTABL(POLATT,POLR,0.,60.,10.)
         CFIFR=GTABL(CFIFRT,FR,0.,2.,.5)
         QLM=GTABL(QLMT,MSL,0.,5.,1.)
         QLC=GTABL(QLCT,CR,0.,5.,.5)
         QLF=GTABL(QLFT,FR,0.,4.,1.)
         QLP=GTABL(QLPT,POLR,0.,60.,10.)
         NRMM=GTABL(NRMMT,MSL,0.,10.,1.)
         CIQR=GTABL(CIQRT,QLM/QLF,0.,2.,.5)
         DRPM=GTABL(DRPMT,POLR,0.,60.,10.)
         DRFM=GTABL(DRFMT,FR,0.,2.,.25)
         BRFM=GTABL(BRFMT,FR,0.,4.,1.)
         BRPM=GTABL(BRPMT,POLR,0.,60.,10.)
C
C*****RATE COMPONENTS.
C
         BR=P*BRN*BRFM*BRMM*BRCM*BRPM
         DR=P*DRN*DRMM*DRPM*DRFM*DRCM
         NRUR=P*XNRUN*NRMM
         CIG=P*CIM*CIGN
         CID=CI*CIDN
         POLG=P*POLN*POLCM
         POLA=POL/POLAT
C
C*****LEVELS.
C
         QL=QLS*QLM*QLC*QLF*QLP
         P=P+DTNOW*(BR-DR)
         NR=NR-DTNOW*NRUR
         CI=CI+DTNOW*(CIG-CID)
         POL=POL+DTNOW*(POLG-POLA)
         CIAF=CIAF+DTNOW*(CFIFR*CIQR-CIAF)/CIAFT
         RETURN
C
         END
```

Figure 10-17 Listing of subroutine STATE for world model.

```
      DIMENSION NSET(310)
      COMMON QSET(310)
      COMMON/SCOM1/ ATRIB(100),DD(100),DDL(100),DTNOW,II,MFA,MSTOP,NCLNR
     1,NCRDR,NPRNT,NNRUN,NNSET,NTAPE,SS(100),SSL(100),TNEXT,TNOW,XX(100)
      COMMON /UCOM2/ BRCMT(6),BRFMT(5),BRMMT(6),BRPMT(7),CFIFRT(5),CIMT
     1(6),CIQRT(5),DRCMT(6),DRFMT(9),DRMMT(11),DRPMT(7),FCMT(6),FPCIT(7)
     2,FPMT(7),NREMT(5),NRMMT(11),POLATT(7),POLCMT(6),QLCT(11),QLFT(5),Q
     3LMT(6),QLPT(7)
      EQUIVALENCE(NSET(1),QSET(1))
      NCRDR=5
      NPRNT=6
      NTAPE=7
      NNSET=310
      READ (NCRDR,101) BRCMT
      READ (NCRDR,101) BRFMT
      READ (NCRDR,101) BRMMT
      READ (NCRDR,101) BRPMT
      READ (NCRDR,101) CFIFRT
      READ (NCRDR,101) CIMT
      READ (NCRDR,101) CIQRT
      READ (NCRDR,101) DRCMT
      READ (NCRDR,101) DRFMT
      READ (NCRDR,101) DRMMT
      READ (NCRDR,101) DRPMT
      READ (NCRDR,101) FCMT
      READ (NCRDR,101) FPCIT
      READ (NCRDR,101) FPMT
      READ (NCRDR,101) NREMT
      READ (NCRDR,101) NRMMT
      READ (NCRDR,101) POLATT
      READ (NCRDR,101) POLCMT
      READ (NCRDR,101) QLCT
      READ (NCRDR,101) QLFT
      READ (NCRDR,101) QLMT
      READ (NCRDR,101) QLPT
      CALL SLAM
      STOP
C
  101 FORMAT (7F10.4)
C
      END
```

Figure 10-18   Listing of main program for world model.

model. When the model is simulated for a longer period of time, all levels reach their steady state values.

10.15   CHAPTER SUMMARY

This chapter presents the continuous simulation procedures of SLAM. The defi-nition of state variables is given and the methods for writing differential and differ-

```
      SUBROUTINE INTLC
      REAL MSL,NREM,NRFR,NRMM,NR,NRI,NRUR,NREMT,NRMMT,LA
      COMMON/SCOM1/ ATRIB(100),DD(100),DDL(100),DTNOW,II,MFA,MSTOP,NCLNR
     1,NCRDR,NPRNT,NNRUN,NNSET,NTAPE,SS(100),SSL(100),TNEXT,TNOW,XX(100)
      COMMON /UCOM1/ BR,BRCM,BRFM,BRMM,BRN,BRPM,CFIFR,CIAFI,CIAFN,CIAFT,
     1CID,CIDN,CIG,CIGN,CII,CIQR,CIR,CIRA,CR,DR,DRCM,DRFM,DRMM,DRN,D
     2RPM,ECIR,ECIRN,FC,FCM,FN,FPCI,FPM,LA,NREM,NRFR,NRI,NRMM,NRUR,
     3PDN,PI,POLA,POLAT,POLCM,POLG,POLI,POLN,POLS,QLF,QLM,QLS,XNRUN
      COMMON /UCOM2/ BRCMT(6),BRFMT(5),BRMMT(6),BRPMT(7),CFIFRT(5),CIMT
     1(6),CIQRT(5),DRCMT(6),DRFMT(9),DRMMT(11),DRPMT(7),FCMT(6),FPCIT(7)
     2,FPMT(7),NREMT(5),NRMMT(11),POLATT(7),POLCMT(6),QLCT(11),QLFT(5),Q
     3LMT(6),QLPT(7)
      EQUIVALENCE (P,SS(1)),(NR,SS(2)),(CI,SS(3)),(POL,SS(4)),(CIAF,SS(5
     1)),(POLR,XX(1)),(QL,XX(2)),(FR,XX(3)),(MSL,XX(4)),(QLC,XX(5)),
     2(QLP,XX(6))
C
C*****INITIAL CONDITIONS.
C
      PI=1.65E9
      READ (NCRDR,101) BRN
      ECIRN=1.
      NRI=900.E9
      XNRUN=1.
      DRN=.028
      LA=135.E6
      PDN=26.5
      FC=1.
      FN=1.
      CIAFN=.3
      CII=.4E9
      CIGN=.05
      CIDN=.025
      POLS=3.6E9
      POLI=.2E9
      POLN=1.
      CIAFI=.2
      CIAFT=15.
      QLS=1.
      P=PI
      NR=NRI
      CI=CII
      POL=POLI
      CIAF=CIAFI
      RETURN
C
  101 FORMAT (F5.0)
C
      END
```

Figure 10-19 Listing of subroutine INTLC for world model.

ence equations are prescribed. Four new input statements are introduced: SEVNT, CONTINUOUS, RECORD, and VAR. A detailed description of SLAM's time advance procedure is presented. The use of SLAM to model a pilot ejecting from an aircraft is presented as Example 10-1. As an example of the use of SLAM for building Systems Dynamics models, the coding for Forrester's World Dynamics model is presented as Example 10-2.

```
 1.05       1.          .9        .7        .6        .55
 0.         1.         1.6       1.9       2.
 1.2        1.          .85       .75       .7        .7
 1.02        .9         .7        .4        .25       .15        .1
 1.          .6         .3        .15       .1
  .1        1.         1.8       2.4       2.8       3.
  .7         .8        1.        1.5       2.
  .9        1.         1.2       1.5       1.9       3.
 0.         3.         2.        1.4       1.         .7         .6
  .5         .5
 3.         1.8        1.         .8        .7        .6         .53
  .5         .5         .5        .5
  .92       1.3        2.        3.2       4.8       6.8        9.2
 2.4        1.          .6        .4        .3        .2
  .5        1.         1.4       1.7       1.9       2.05       2.2
 1.02        .9         .65       .35       .2        .1         .05
 0.          .15        .5        .85      1.
 0.         1.         1.8       2.4       2.9       3.3        3.6
 3.8        3.9        3.95      4.
  .6        2.5        5.        8.       11.5      15.5       20.
  .05       1.         3.        5.4       7.4       8.
 2.         1.3        1.         .75       .55       .45        .38
  .3         .25        .22       .2
 0.         1.         1.8       2.4       2.7
  .2        1.         1.7       2.3       2.7       2.9
 1.04        .85        .6        .3        .15       .05        .02
GEN,PRITSKER,WORLD MODEL,3/17/1978,1;
CONT,0,5,.2,.2,8.,W,.00001,.00001;
RECORD,TNOW,TIME,0,P,8.;
VAR,SS(1),P,POP,0.,16E9;
VAR,XX(1),2,POLR,0.0,80.0;
VAR,SS(3),C,CI,0.0,4.0E10;
VAR,XX(2),Q,QL,0.0,4.0;
VAR,SS(2),N,NR,0.0,2.0E12;
VAR,XX(3),F,FR,-2.0,2.0;
VAR,XX(4),M,MSL,-20,2.0;
VAR,XX(5),4,QLC,-2.0,2.0;
VAR,XX(6),5,QLP,-2.0,2.0;
VAR,SS(5),A,CIAF,-.20,0.6;
INITIALIZE,1900.,2100.;
FIN;
  .04
```

Figure 10-20   Listing of input statements for world model.

10.16   EXERCISES

10-1.   Prepare the input statements and experiment with the model of Cedar Bog Lake.

10-2.   Embellishments to Cedar Bog Lake Model:

(a) Superimpose a normally distributed random variation with a mean of 0, and a standard deviation of 9 on the solar energy supplied to the lake ecosystem that occurs every 0.025 years.

(b) Determine the effects of a step increase of 20% in the solar energy input to the lake ecosystem.

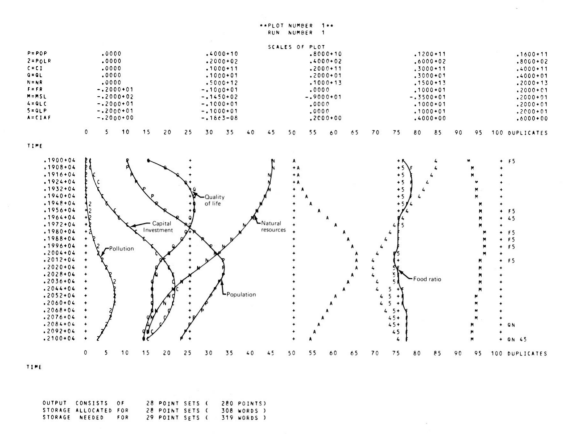

Figure 10-21   Plot of dynamic behavior of world model for a birth rate normal value of 0.04.

(c) Suppose that 20% of the energy losses to the lake sediment are considered as fertilizer and reflected in the rate of change in plant energy. Determine the effect of this change in lake ecosystem structure on the behavior of the model.

(d) Superimpose the following control policies on the natural environment: stock the lake with carnivores by 0.3 cal/cm² every tenth of a year; replenish the lake with 0.2 cal/cm² of herbivores when the population of carnivores increases above 0.6 cal/cm²; and spray the lake to reduce the plant population by 70% every 0.5 year. Simulate Cedar Bog Lake under the above control strategies.

10-3.   Modify the pilot ejection model of Example 10-1 to allow for a two-pilot aircraft. The second pilot ejects from the aircraft 1 sec after the first pilot. The second pilot is located 7 feet behind the first pilot. Simulate the system for an aircraft speed of 500 feet/second to determine if the pilots maintain a separation of 5 feet and if the pilots clear the aircraft. Assume all parameters used in Example 10-1 hold for the two pilot situation.

10-4.   A mass is suspended by a spring and a dashpot. The mass is subjected to a vertical force, $f(t)$, and the vertical movement of the mass is described by

$$m\ddot{y} + k_2\,\dot{y} + k_1\,y = f(t)$$

where

    y is the spring displacement,
    $\dot{y}$ is the derivative of y with respect to time,
    $\ddot{y}$ is the second derivative of y with respect to time,
    m is the mass,
    k_1 is the spring constant, and
    k_2 is the dashpot constant

    Run a 60 second simulation to obtain a plot of the vertical movement of the mass when $m = 1$, $k_1 = 1.0$, and $k_2 = 0.3$, $f(t) = 1.0$ for all t.
    Embellishment: (a) Rerun the simulation when $f(t) = \sin 2\pi t$.
(b) Rerun the simulation when $f(t)$ is sampled every 5 seconds from a uniform distribution whose range is 0.5 to 1.5.

10-5.   A bank has a drive-in teller whose service time is exponentially distributed with a mean time of 0.5 minutes. Customer interarrival time is also exponentially distributed with a mean of 0.4 minutes. Only 1 car can wait for the drive-in teller, that is, customers that arrive when 1 car is waiting balk from the system and do not return. Letting $p_n(t) =$ the probability that n customers are in the system (queue plus service) at time t, the following equations can be derived

$$\frac{dp_0(t)}{dt} = -2.5*p_0(t) + 2.0*p_1(t)$$

$$\frac{dp_1(t)}{dt} = 2.5*p_0(t) - 4.5*p_1(t) + 2.0*p_2(t)$$

and

$$\frac{dp_2(t)}{dt} = 2.5*p_1(t) - 2.0*p_2(t).$$

Assume that at $t=0$ there are no customers in the system and, hence, the teller is idle. Develop a SLAM model to obtain the expected number in the system, $E[N(t)]$, for $t=0,2,4,6,\ldots,100$ where

$$E[N(t)] = \sum_{i=0}^{2} i*p_i(t).$$

    Prepare a table and plot for $p_i(t)$ and $E[N(t)]$ using DTSAV=DTPLT=0.05.

10-6.   Develop a simulation model to portray a single server finite queueing system with exponential interarrival and service times. For a maximum of 20 in the system, plot the transient values for selected probabilities, and the expected value and variance of the number in the system. Also plot the average value of the expected number in the system observed at 5 minute intervals. Let the arrival rate be 4 units/minute and the service rate be 5 units/minute (10).

10-7.   Use SLAM to analyze Forrester's model of industrial dynamics (5).

10-8. For the world model presented as Example 10-2, incorporate the following events (9):

Event	Effect	Event Code
Food shortage, occurs every 20 years and lasts 4 years	Decreases food ratio to 70% of its "normal" value over a 4-year period and population by 10% immediately	1
Discovery of new resources (or equivalent technological development), occurs in 1975	Increases natural resources immediately by 50%	2
Worldwide epidemic, occurs in 1980	Decreases population by 15% and capital investment by 20%	3
Legislative controls go into effect against pollution, occurs 5 years after pollution threshold is reached	Set indicator so that controls are in effect which will decrease POLCM by 75%	4
End of food shortage, occurs 4 years after event 1	Reset indicator to restore food ratio to normal value	5
Initiate zero population growth drive, occurs when population threshold is reached	Decrease birth rate by 15% when population exceeds $2.5*10^9$ (TOL = $1.5*10^8$)	6
Initiate legislation to correct pollution, occurs when pollution threshold is reached	Schedule event 4 to occur in 5 years when pollution exceeds $5*10^8$ (TOL = $5*10^7$)	7
Begin conservation measures to protect supply of natural resources, occurs when natural resources threshold is reached	Set conservation indicator that will cause NRMM to be decreased by 10% when natural resources decrease below $7*10^{12}$ (TOL = $1.05*10^{12}$)	8

10-9. The equation for the current i in a series electrical system is shown below.

$$L\frac{d^2i}{dt^2} + R\frac{di}{dt} + \frac{i}{c} = \omega E \sin \omega t.$$

Develop the equations for simulating the current i in SLAM form. When the current exceeds the value A, a fuse is blown. Develop the statements that would detect the time at which the fuse would be blown. Assume that the tolerance on the current is 0.1 * *A*.

10-10. Prepare a data worksheet for the input to the simulation program for which there are 2 files with a maximum number of 25 entries in all files and a maximum of 4 attributes for any entry. File 1 is a high-value-first file with priority based on attribute 4. Statistics on 5 variables are to be collected in subroutine COLCT and the labels for these variables are HT, WT, TOL, SIZE, and GRADE. Time-persistent statistics are to be recorded on SS(1) and SS(2) and labeled as BAL and POL, respectively. A histogram is to be collected on the variable GRADE, and it is desired to have 15 cells in the histogram, not including the end cells. The lower limit for the histogram is 10 and a cell width of 5 is desired. There are three equations written in terms of the DD(·) variables and two written in terms of the SS(·) variables. If accuracy cannot be met or tolerance on the state-event conditions cannot be satisfied, a warning is to be printed but the simulation is to be continued. The absolute error and relative error for accuracy computation are specified as $1.E - 4$ and $1.E - 5$, respectively. The minimum step size allowed is .001 and the maximum step size permitted is 1.0. The values of the state variables are to be recorded at the end of each step and at event times. One plot is to be obtained using core storage and 5000 words of core are to be allocated for the file. The independent variable of the plot will be TIME and there will be 3 dependent variables for the plot. Plot points should be obtained every 2 time units and both a table and a plot are desired. The minimum and maximum values obtained from the simulation are to be rounded to the nearest integer and used for scaling. The symbols X, Y, and Z are to be plotted for the variables SS(3), SS(4), and SS(5) and the labels for these variables are XPOS, YPOS, and ZPOS, respectively.

The beginning time for the simulation is 10 and the simulation will be completed by an end-of-simulation event. Statistical storage areas are to be cleared. Only one random number stream is to be used and the initial random number seed is 567471923. The filing array is to be initialized and an event of type 2 is to occur at time 11. An end-of-simulation event with event code 3 is to occur at time 225. An entry with ATRIB(1) = 3 and ATRIB(2) = 5 is to be stored in file 2. Events occurring between time 50 and 100 are to be monitored. Summary reports are desired, starting at time 100 and for every 25 time units thereafter, until the end of the simulation. Only one simulation run is to be made.

10.17 REFERENCES

1. Carnahan, B., H. A. Luther, and J. O. Wilkes, *Applied Numerical Methods*, John Wiley, 1969.
2. Conte, S. D. and C. de Boor, *Elementary Numerical Analysis*, McGraw-Hill, 1972.

3. *CONTROL DATA MIMIC—A Digital Simulation Language Reference Manual,* Publication No. 44610400, Revision D, Control Data Corporation, Minneapolis, Minn., 1970.

4. Fehlberg, E., "Low-Order Classical Runge-Kutta Formulas with Step-Size Control and Their Application to Some Heat Transfer Problems," NASA Report TR R-315, Huntsville, Alabama, April 15, 1969.

5. Forrester, J. W., *Industrial Dynamics,* John Wiley, 1961.

6. Forrester, J. W., *Principles of Systems,* Wright-Allen Press, 1971.

7. Forrester, J. W., *World Dynamics,* Wright-Allen Press, 1972.

8. Meadows, D. H., D. L. Meadows, J. Randers, and W. W. Behrens, III, *The Limits to Growth,* Potomac Associates, 1972.

9. Pritsker, A. A. B. and R. E. Young, *Simulation with GASP_PL/I,* John Wiley, 1975.

10. Pritsker, A. A. B., "Three Simulation Approaches to Queueing Studies Using GASP IV," *Computers & Industrial Engineering,* Vol. 1, 1976, pp. 57-65.

11. Ralston, A., *A First Course in Numerical Analysis,* McGraw-Hill, 1965.

12. Shampine, L. F. and R. C. Allen, Jr., *Numerical Computing: An Introduction,* W. B. Saunders, 1973.

13. Shampine, L. F. et al., "Solving Non-Stiff Ordinary Differential Equations—The State of the Art," *SIAM Review,* Vol. 18, 1976, pp. 376-411.

14. Talavage, J. J. and M. Triplett, "GASP IV Urban Model of Cadmium Flow," *Simulation,* Vol. 23, 1974, pp. 101-108.

15. Williams, R. B., "Computer Simulation of Energy Flow in Cedar Bog Lake, Minnesota Based on the Classical Studies of Lindeman," in *Systems Analysis and Simulation in Ecology,* B. C. Patten, Ed., Academic Press, 1971.

CHAPTER 11

Combined Network-Discrete Event-Continuous Models

11.1   INTRODUCTION

Systems are often classified as either discrete change, continuous change, or combined discrete-continuous change, according to the mechanism by which the state space description of the system changes with time. In discrete change systems, the state of the system changes discretely at isolated points in time called event times. As previously described, discrete change systems can be modeled with

402

SLAM using a network, discrete event, or combined network-discrete event orientation. In contrast, continuous change systems are characterized by variables defined through state and derivative equations and the variables are assumed to change continuously with time. Continuous systems are modeled with SLAM by describing the dynamics of the system as a set of differential or difference equations. In combined discrete-continuous change systems, the state of the system may change discretely, continuously, or continuously with discrete jumps superimposed. In this chapter, we describe the procedures for modeling combined discrete-continuous change systems using SLAM.

In combined discrete-continuous change systems, there are three fundamental interactions which can occur between discretely and continuously changing variables. First, a discrete change in value may be made to a continuous variable. Examples of this type of interaction are: the completion of a new power station which instantaneously increases the total energy available within a system; and the chemical spraying of a lake which instantaneously decreases the population of a particular species in the lake. Second, an event involving a continuous state variable achieving a threshold value may cause an event to occur or to be scheduled. As examples consider: a chemical process that is completed when a prescribed concentration level is obtained and the process is shut down for cleaning and maintenance activities; and the shutdown of a refinery when the level of crude oil available for input is below a prescribed value. Third, the functional description of continuous variables may be changed at discrete time instants. Example of this are: the discharge of a pollutant into an ecosystem that immediately alters the growth relationships governing species populations; and the completion of a docking operation of a space vehicle which requires the use of new equations for simulating the space vehicle's motion.

The interaction between the continuous and discrete change state variables in a combined discrete-continuous change system necessitates a broader interpretation of an event than is normally used in discrete change languages. For combined simulation models (3):

> An event occurs at any point in time beyond which the status of the system cannot be projected with certainty.

Note that this definition allows the system status to change continuously without an event occurring, as long as the change has been prescribed in a well-defined manner.

In previous chapters, we have informally distinguished events according to the mechanism through which they occur. We now provide more specific definitions.

Those events that occur at a specified point in time are referred to as *time-events*. They are commonly thought of in terms of next event simulation. Those that occur when the system reaches a particular state are called *state-events*. Unlike time-events, they are not scheduled in the future but occur when continuous state variables meet prescribed conditions. In SLAM state-events can initiate time-events, and time-events can initiate state-events.

11.2   MODELING STATE-EVENTS WITH SLAM

The concept of a state-event is of central importance in modeling combined discrete-continuous change systems. A state-event is the mechanism by which continuous change variables interact with discrete change variables. In SLAM, this interaction can be between the continuous and network portion of the model or between the continuous and discrete event portion of a model. In the following sections, we describe procedures for modeling both types of interaction.

11.3   THE DETECT NODE

The symbol for the DETECT node is given below.

The DETECT node provides the primary interface between the continuous and network portions of a combined model. When a DETECT node is included in the network model, it is released whenever a state variable or its derivative, XVAR, crosses a prescribed VALUE in the direction specified by XDIR. XVAR is referred to as a crossing variable and VALUE as a threshold. The value of TOL specifies an interval beyond the threshold value for which a detection of a crossing is considered within tolerance. If a crossing occurs beyond the allowable tolerance, then as described in Section 10.8, the SLAM processor reduces the step size until the crossing is within tolerance or until the step size is reduced to the user pre-scribed minimum step size, DTMIN.

The DETECT node is released whenever an entity arrives to it. A maximum of M emanating activities are initiated at each release. The statement format for the DETECT node is:

DETECT, XVAR, XDIR, VALUE, TOL, M;

where

XVAR specifies the crossing variable and can be either SS(I) or DD(I) with I given a specific value

XDIR is the crossing direction and can be specified as X, XP, or XN where X → either direction; XP → positive direction and XN → negative direction

VALUE is SS(I), DD(I) or a numeric value

TOL is a numeric value which specifies the tolerance within which the crossing is to be detected.

One common use of the DETECT node in a combined simulation model is to specify or key the duration of an activity to the release of the DETECT node. In this way, the time an entity spends in an activity can be keyed to the time when a continuous state variable achieves a specified condition. This is illustrated by the following queueing system where the ACTIVITY completes service for the entity whenever the value of SS(1) crosses in the negative direction the value of SS(2) with a prescribed tolerance of 0.01. In this situation, the ACTIVITY could be the unloading of a tanker where SS(1) is the amount on the tanker and SS(2) is the amount to be left in the tanker after unloading.

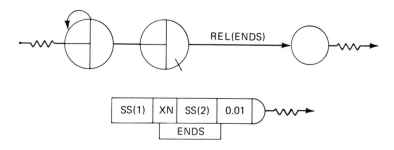

As discussed in Chapter 4, the duration specification REL(ENDS) only applies if an entity is currently engaged in the ACTIVITY. If DETECT node ENDS detects a crossing and no entity is being processed by the ACTIVITY, or any other activity keyed to ENDS, then the crossing has no effect.

11.4   CODING STATE-EVENTS

The interface between the continuous and discrete event portions of a combined model is provided by the SEVNT statement described in Chapter 10. In the SEVNT statement, the event code JEVNT is specified; otherwise the SEVNT statement is identical to the DETECT node statement. In essence, SEVNT and DETECT statements perform similar functions but for different portions of the simulation model. The SEVNT statement causes subroutine EVENT(JEVNT) to be called at each crossing by the crossing variable of the threshold value in the prescribed direction.

In Chapter 10, we limited our discussion of the SEVNT statement to making discrete changes in continuous variables and to changing the equations which define the dynamics of a continuous system. In this chapter, we focus upon the use of the SEVNT statement for modeling changes in the discrete event portion of a combined system which are initiated by state-events occurring in the continuous portion of the system. Examples of this are when either the starting or ending time of an operation in a discrete system is determined by a continuous variable reaching a prescribed threshold.

The coding of the discrete event subroutine associated with a state-event follows exactly the same procedure as for coding discrete event subroutines associated with time-events. In coding the subroutine, the modeler has access to the library of standard SLAM subprograms for file manipulations, statistics collection, report writing, and network status changes. Thus, the logic associated with a state-event can be coded to any level of complexity required.

11.5   SIMULTANEOUS STATE-EVENTS

Sometimes the processing logic associated with a state-event depends upon knowledge concerning the possible occurrence of one or more additional state-events at the same instant in time. Because of this, SLAM provides the modeler with function SSEVT(N) which returns a code defining the status of state-event N at the current time. The state-event number, N, is the value of JEVNT prescribed by the user on SEVNT statements. The status code for state-event N specifies whether the crossing variable crossed the threshold value during the last time advance, and if so, in what direction. In addition, the code denotes whether the minimum step size, DTMIN, permitted the crossing to be isolated within the prescribed tolerance. The codes returned from function SSEVT(N) are listed below.

Code	*Definition*
+2	crossing in the positive direction exceeding tolerance
+1	crossing in the positive direction within tolerance
0	no crossing
−1	crossing in the negative direction within tolerance
−2	crossing in the negative direction exceeding tolerance

As an example, consider that state-event 4 has occurred and subroutine EVENT has been called. If it is necessary to determine if state-event 6 has also occurred then the value obtained from function SSEVT(6) will provide this information. The value of SSEVT(6) is one of the five codes listed above.

11.6   EXAMPLES OF COMBINED DISCRETE-CONTINUOUS MODELS

This section presents two examples of SLAM programs which analyze situations that are modeled using combined discrete-continuous concepts. The first example is a combined network-continuous model of a tanker fleet and illustrates the use of the DETECT node for modeling state-events within a network.

In the simulation, a fleet of tankers that provides crude oil to a refinery is modeled. The unloading of tankers is presumed to be a continuous process. The crude oil is transferred from tankers to a storage tank that serves as the input to a refinery. Continuous state variables are used to represent the amount of crude in the tanker being unloaded and the amount in the storage tank. The input to the storage tank (the output from the tanker) and the output from the storage tank (the input to the refinery) are represented by continuous variables. The level of crude in the storage tank represents an inventory of crude that is used to supply the refinery. The refinery demand is assumed to be constant. When the storage tank cannot supply crude for the refinery, the situation is analogous to the stock-out situation in inventory studies. This example is representative of a wide class of queueing-inventory situations in which the service time is dependent on the status of the system and can vary in a continuous manner.

The second example is a combined network-discrete event-continuous model of a soaking pit furnace and illustrates the use of the SEVNT statement to initiate a discrete event. In this example, the process of heating ingots in a soaking pit furnace is modeled. The ingot temperatures and the furnace temperature are continuous state variables. The end of service for ingots in the furnace is processed as a state-event which occurs when the maximum ingot temperature reaches a prescribed threshold value. If an ingot arrives and the furnace is full, the ingot is put into a queue.

Complete descriptions of the examples are now presented. The discussion emphasizes the interaction between the discrete and continuous aspects of the models and the procedures used to develop a combined simulation program written in SLAM. The examples illustrate the versatility of SLAM in modeling combined problems.

11.7   Example 11-1. TANKER-REFINERY OPERATIONS (3)

A fleet of 15 tankers carries crude oil from Valdez, Alaska to an unloading dock near Seattle, Washington. It is assumed that all tankers can be loaded simultaneously in Valdez, if necessary. In Seattle, there is only one unloading dock, which supplies a storage tank that feeds a refinery through a pipeline. The storage tank receives crude from a tanker at the dock at a constant rate of 300 tb/day†. The storage tank supplies crude to the refinery continuously at a constant rate of 150 tb/day. The unloading dock is open from the hours of 6 a.m. to 12 p.m. Safety considerations require the stopping of unloading of the crude when the dock is shut down. The completion of the tanker unloading occurs when the amount of crude remaining in the tanker is less than 7.5 tb.

The storage tank has a capacity of 2000 tb. When it is full, unloading is halted until the amount in the tank decreases to 80 percent of capacity. When the storage tank is nearly empty (less than 5 tb), supply to the refinery is halted until 50 tb is reached to avoid the possibility of frequent refinery start-ups and shut-downs. The characteristics associated with the tankers are listed below.

---

† tb = thousand barrels

1. Nominal carrying capacity is 150 tb.
2. Travel time loaded is normally distributed with a mean of 5.0 days and standard deviation of 1.5 days.
3. Travel time unloaded is normally distributed with a mean of 4.0 days and a standard deviation of 1 day.
4. Time to load is uniformly distributed in the interval 2.9 to 3.1 days.

The initial conditions for the simulation are that the storage tank is half full and the tankers are to arrive at their loading points at ½ day intervals, starting with the first at time 0.

The objective of this example is to simulate the above systems for 365 days to obtain estimates of the following quantities:

1. Unloading dock utilization.
2. Loading dock utilization.
3. Time refinery has a crude input available.
4. Amount of crude in the storage tank.
5. Tanker round trip time.
6. Tanker waiting time.
7. Number of tankers waiting for unloading.

Concepts Illustrated.   This example illustrates the use of the DETECT node for modeling state-events in combined network-continuous simulation models. The use of a single state variable to represent the amount of crude oil to be unloaded simplifies the system state description. Since all tankers are scheduled to arrive to Valdez, abnormal initial conditions exist. A MONTR statement will be used to CLEAR statistics on day 65.

SLAM Model.   The tanker problem will be simulated using a combined network-continuous model. The continuous variables are used to represent the level of crude oil in the tanker being unloaded and in the storage tank. The network is used to model the movement of tankers through the system and the interactions between the continuous and discrete elements of the system.

Two state variables are used in this simulation: $SS(1)$, the amount of crude in a tanker at the unloading dock; and $SS(2)$, the amount of crude in the storage tank. The state variable $SS(1)$ represents the amount of crude available to be unloaded. $SS(1)$ will be zero when no tanker is in the unloading dock; otherwise it will be equal to the amount of crude in a tanker that is in the unloading dock.

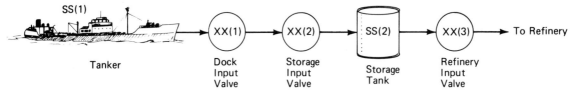

Figure 11-1 Crude oil flow from tanker to refinery.

When a tanker leaves the unloading dock, SS(1) either becomes zero or is set equal to the amount of crude in the next waiting tanker to be unloaded. By defining SS(1) in this manner, a separate state variable for the amount of crude in each tanker need not be defined.

There are three XX variables which are used in the simulation to control the flow of crude between the unloading tanker and the refinery. Each of these variables represent a valve which is open when equal to 1.0 and closed when equal to 0. XX(1) is used to represent the dock input valve and is open between the dock operating hours of 6 a.m. to 12 p.m., and is closed otherwise. XX(2) is used to model the storage tank input valve and is closed whenever the storage tank crude level, SS(2), reaches the tank capacity of 2000 tb. It is reopened when the level of crude decreases to 1600 tb. XX(3) is used to represent the storage tank output valve and is closed whenever the storage tank crude level has decreased to less than 5 tb, thereby halting the flow to the refinery. XX(3) is reset to open when the crude level in the storage tank has increased to 50 tb, thereby restoring the flow of crude to the refinery. A schematic diagram depicting the arrangement of the three valves is provided in Figure 11-1. Note that XX(1) can be opened and closed by scheduling a time-event whereas XX(2) and XX(3) require the concept of a state-event.

The equations describing the state variables SS(1) and SS(2) are coded in subroutine STATE shown in Figure 11-2. The variable RATIN represents the flow rate of crude into the storage tank. It is set to zero if XX(1), XX(2), or

```
      SUBROUTINE STATE
      COMMON/SCOM1/ ATRIB(100),DD(100),DDL(100),DTNOW,II,MFA,MSTOP,NCLNR
     1,NCRDR,NPRNT,NNRUN,NNSET,NTAPE,SS(100),SSL(100),TNEXT,TNOW,XX(100)
C****RATIN = 0 IF DOCK OR STORAGE INPUT CLOSED OR NO WAITING TANKER - ELSE 300
      RATIN=300.
      IF(XX(1)*XX(2)*SS(1).EQ.0) RATIN=0.
C****RATOUT=0 IF REFINERY INPUT OFF - ELSE 150
      RATOUT=150.*XX(3)
      SS(1)=SSL(1)-DTNOW*RATIN
      SS(2)=SSL(2)+DTNOW*(RATIN-RATOUT)
      RETURN
      END
```

Figure 11-2 Subroutine state for tanker example.

SS(1) is zero, and is set equal to 300 otherwise. The variable RATOUT, representing the flow rate of crude from the storage tank to the refinery, equals 150 if XX(3) = 1. and equals 0 if XX(3) = 0. Equations for state variables SS(1) and SS(2) are written as difference equations in terms of RATIN and RATOUT. In this case, we are integrating the state equations explicitly in subroutine STATE. An alternative would be to code subroutine STATE in terms of the derivatives of the state variables as follows:

$$DD(1) = - RATIN$$
$$DD(2) = RATIN - RATOUT$$

In this case, the equations would be integrated by SLAM using the Runge-Kutta-Fehlberg integration algorithm to determine SS(1) and SS(2).

The state equations for this example appear relatively simple but are deceptive since RATIN and RATOUT have different values during the simulation because of the status of the system. These equations could be made more complex if RATIN or RATOUT were functions of the type of crude or the level of crude in the storage tank and tanker. Since these aspects of the system do not add to the organizational aspects of the model, they are not included.

The network model for this example can be viewed as three subprocesses consisting of the tanker flow through the system, the start-up and shut-down of dock operations, and the state-events. Each of these subprocesses is modeled as a separate disjoint network.

The network for the tanker flow subprocess is depicted in Figure 11-3. The initial 15 tankers are created by the CREATE node at 0.50 day intervals, beginning with the first at time 0. The tankers proceed to the ASSIGN node labeled VLDZ where their arrival time to Valdez is marked as ATRIB(1). The tankers then undertake the loading activity which is represented by ACTIVITY 1. The trip from Valdez to Seattle is modeled by ACTIVITY 2. Upon completion of ACTIVITY 2, the tankers arrive to the ASSIGN node where their arrival time to Seattle is placed in ATRIB(2). The tankers then wait in file 1 at the AWAIT node for the resource DOCK. A single unit of resource DOCK is available as specified by the resource block. When the DOCK becomes available, statistics are collected at the COLCT node on the waiting time for the DOCK, and the state variable SS(1) is set to 150 at the ASSIGN node indicating that there is 150 tb of crude available for unloading. The tanker then undergoes ACTIVITY 3 which represents the unloading activity. This ACTIVITY is completed at the next release of the node labeled ENDU. The node labeled ENDU is a DETECT node which is released when SS(1) crosses, in the negative direction, the threshold value of 7.5 which indicates that the state-event "end-of-unloading" has occurred.

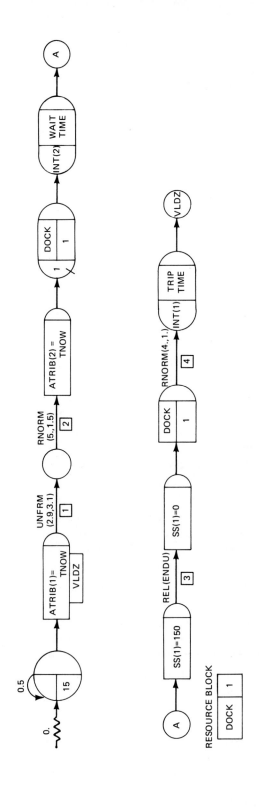

412

Figure 11-3 Tanker flow subprocess for tanker example.

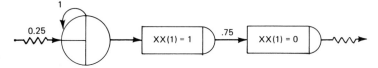

Figure 11-4 Shift start-up/shut-down subprocess for tanker example.

At the completion of unloading, the tanker entity is routed to the ASSIGN node where SS(1) is set to 0, and then releases the DOCK at the FREE node. The return trip to Valdez is modeled by ACTIVITY number 4. At the COLCT node, statistics are collected on the round trip time for the tanker which is then routed to the ASSIGN node labeled VLDZ to repeat the cycle through the network.

The network for the shift start-up and shut-down subprocess is depicted in Figure 11-4. The CREATE node inserts an entity into the network beginning at time 0.25 days (6 a.m.), and then daily thereafter. At the ASSIGN node, the dock input valve is opened by setting XX(1) equal to 1. The dock status remains open during the 0.75 days required for the entity to transverse the ACTIVITY before being closed at the ASSIGN node where XX(1) is reset to 0. The dock status remains closed until the next entity is inserted into the network at 6 a.m. the next day.

There are five possible conditions that could result in a state-event and these are listed below.

Condition	*State-Event*
The level of crude in the unloading tanker, SS(1), has decreased to 7.5.	Tanker unloading is completed
The level of crude in the storage tank, SS(2), has decreased to 5 tb.	Stop supply to refinery by setting $XX(3) = 0$
The level of crude in the storage tank has increased to 50 tb.	Start supplying refinery by setting $XX(3) = 1$
The level of crude in the storage tank has reached its capacity of 2000 tb.	Close input to the storage tank by setting $XX(2) = 0$
The level of crude in the storage tank has decreased to 1600 tb.	Open input to the storage tank by setting $XX(2) = 1$

These five state-events are modeled by the five subnetworks depicted in Figure 11-5. The first subnetwork is used to detect the end of unloading state-event and causes the completion of ACTIVITY 3 whose duration is keyed to the release of the node labeled ENDU. The other four subnetworks are used to detect and

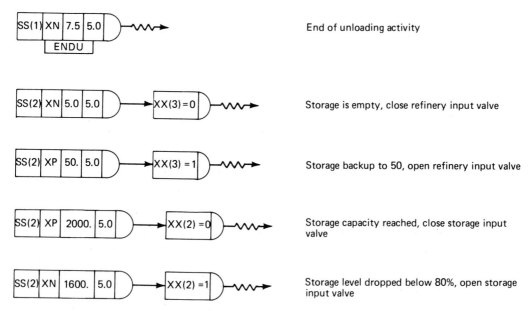

Figure 11-5   State event subprocesses for tanker example.

process state-events which cause the opening and closing of the storage tank and refinery input valves. The tolerance for each state-event is set at 5. The value prescribed for a tolerance is set according to the accuracy with which a state-event should be detected. The value of the tolerance should also consider the value given to DTMIN and the maximum rate of change of the state variable. In this example, DTMIN $= 0.0025$ days and the maximum rate is 300 tb/day, hence tolerances of 0.75 tb or greater should enable detection of state-events within tolerance.

The input statements for this example are depicted in Figure 11-6. In addition to the network statements, the necessary control cards are included to obtain: a plot of the crude level in an unloading tanker and the level in the storage tank; and time-persistent statistics on the refinery input availability and the average crude level in the storage tank. The INITIALIZE card specifies that the model is to be simulated for 365 days. A MONTR statement with the CLEAR option is used to clear statistics at time 65.

Summary of Results.   The SLAM Summary Report for this example is given in Figure 11-7. As can be seen from the output statistics, the refinery is operated 100 percent of the time from day 65 to day 365. This high percentage of refinery utilization occurs at the expense of the tankers which wait on the average 1.37 days for the unloading dock. This is further illustrated by the file statistics

```
1   GEN,C. D. PEGDEN,TANKER FLEET,5/7/77,1;
2   LIMITS,1,2,100;
3   TIMST,XX(3),REFN INPUT AVAIL;
4   CONT,0,2,.0025,.25,.25;
5   RECORD,TNOW,DAYS,0,P,.25;
6   VAR,SS(1),T,TANKER   LEVEL,0,300;
7   VAR,SS(2),S,STORAGE LEVEL,0,2000;
8   TIMST,SS(2),STORAGE LEVEL;
9   INTLC,SS(2)=1000,XX(2)=1,XX(3)=1,XX(1)=0;
10  NETWORK;
11  ;
12  ;TANKER FLOW SUBPROCESS
13  ;--------------------
14        RESOURCE/DOCK,1;
15        CREATE,.5,0,,15;                  CREATE INITIAL ARRIVALS
16  VLDZ  ASSIGN,ATRIB(1)=TNOW;             MARK ARRIVAL TIME TO VALDEZ
17        ACT/1,UNFRM(2.9,3.1);             LOADING ACTIVITY
18        GOON;                             END OF LOADING
19        ACT/2,RNORM(5.,1.5);              TRIP TO SEATTLE
20        ASSIGN,ATRIB(2)=TNOW;             MARK ARRIVAL TIME TO SEATTLE
21        AWAIT,DOCK;                       AWAIT THE DOCK
22        COLCT,INT(2),WAITING TIME;        COLLECT STATISTICS
23        ASSIGN,SS(1)=150;                 RESET TANKER CRUDE LEVEL
24        ACT/3,REL(ENDU);                  UNLOADING ACTIVITY
25        ASSIGN,SS(1)=0;                   SET TANKER CRUDE LEVEL TO 0
26        FREE,DOCK;                        FREE THE DOCK
27        ACT/4,RNORM(4.,1.);               RETURN TRIP TO VALDEZ
28        COLCT,INT(1),TRIP TIME;           COLLECT STATISTICS
29        ACT,,,VLDZ;                       BRANCH TO VLDZ
30  ;
31  ;SHIFT START UP/SHUT DOWN SUBPROCESS
32  ;-----------------------------------
33        CREATE,1.,,.25;
34        ASSIGN,XX(1)=1;                   BEGIN SHIFT AT 6 A.M.
35        ACT,.75;                          CONTINUE FOR 3/4 DAYS
36        ASSIGN,XX(1)=0;                   CLOSE SHIFT AT 6 P.M.
37        TERM;
38  ;`
39  ;STATE EVENT SUBPROCESSES
40  ;-----------------------
41  ENDU  DETECT,SS(1),XN,7.5,5;            END OF UNLOADING ACTIVITY
42        TERM;
43        DETECT,SS(2),XN,5,5;              STORAGE IS EMPTY
44        ASSIGN,XX(3)=0;                   CLOSE REFINERY INPUT SWITCH
45        TERM;
46        DETECT,SS(2),XP,50,5;             STORAGE BACK UP TO 50
47        ASSIGN,XX(3)=1;                   OPEN REFINERY INPUT SWITCH
48        TERM;
49        DETECT,SS(2),XP,2000,5;           STORAGE CAPACITY REACHED
50        ASSIGN,XX(2)=0;                   CLOSE STORAGE INPUT SWITCH
51        TERM;
52        DETECT,SS(2),XN,1600,5;           STORAGE DROPPED BELOW 80%
53        ASSIGN,XX(2)=1;                   OPEN STORAGE INPUT SWITCH
54        TERM;
55        ENDNETWORK;
56  ;
57  INITIALIZE,0,365;
58  MONTR,CLEAR,65;
59  FIN;
```

Figure 11-6 SLAM input statements for tanker fleet model.

```
                    S L A M   S U M M A R Y   R E P O R T

          SIMULATION PROJECT TANKER FLEET              BY C. D. PEGDEN

          DATE  5/ 7/1977                              RUN NUMBER   1 OF   1


          CURRENT TIME    .3650+03
          STATISTICAL ARRAYS CLEARED AT TIME    .6500+02




                   **STATISTICS FOR VARIABLES BASED ON OBSERVATION**

                    MEAN        STANDARD      COEFF. OF     MINIMUM      MAXIMUM       NUMBER OF
                    VALUE       DEVIATION     VARIATION     VALUE        VALUE         OBSERVATIONS

    WAITING TIME    .1366+01    .1239+01      .9070+00      .0000        .5227+01      317
    TRIP TIME       .1427+02    .2158+01      .1513+00      .7744+01     .2020+02      312


                   **STATISTICS FOR TIME-PERSISTENT VARIABLES**

                    MEAN        STANDARD      MINIMUM       MAXIMUM      TIME          CURRENT
                    VALUE       DEVIATION     VALUE         VALUE        INTERVAL      VALUE

    REFN INPUT AVAIL .1000+01   .0000         .1000+01      .1000+01     .3000+03      .1000+01
    STORAGE LEVEL    .1766+04   .1763+03      .9864+03      .2005+04     .3000+03      .1986+04


                   **FILE STATISTICS**

    FILE      ASSOCIATED     AVERAGE        STANDARD      MAXIMUM      CURRENT       AVERAGE
    NUMBER    NODE TYPE      LENGTH         DEVIATION     LENGTH       LENGTH        WAITING TIME

     1        AWAIT          1.4429         1.2642         5            0            1.3655


                   **REGULAR ACTIVITY STATISTICS**

    ACTIVITY   AVERAGE        STANDARD      MAXIMUM       CURRENT        ENTITY
    INDEX      UTILIZATION    DEVIATION     UTILIZATION   UTILIZATION    COUNT

      1        3.1253         1.5115         7             2             313
      2        5.4190         1.6232         11            5             317
      3         .9071          .2902         1             1             316
      4        4.1056         1.4229         8             7             312


                   **RESOURCE STATISTICS**

    RESOURCE   RESOURCE    CURRENT    AVERAGE        STANDARD      MAXIMUM       CURRENT
    NUMBER     LABEL       CAPACITY   UTILIZATION    DEVIATION     UTILIZATION   UTILIZATION

     1         DOCK         1          .9071          .2902         1             1


                   **STATE AND DERIVATIVE VARIABLES**

                   (I)        SS(I)          DD(I)
                    1         .1213+03       .0000
                    2         .1986+04       .0000
```

Figure 11-7   SLAM summary report for tanker fleet model.

which indicate that the average number waiting for the unloading dock is 1.44, and that as many as 5 tankers were waiting at one time. The resource statistics indicate that there was a tanker in the unloading dock 91 percent of the time. This statistic can also be obtained from the statistics for ACTIVITY 3. Also available from the activity statistics is the average number of tankers being unloaded as this quantity is the average utilization of activity 1. From the output, it is seen that approximately 3.13 tankers are being loaded and the maximum number of tankers loaded concurrently is 7.

A plot of the state variables during the initial and middle portions of the simulation is depicted in Figure 11-8. At the start of the simulation, all the tankers were scheduled to arrive at the loading dock at 0.50 day intervals. Thus, there were no tankers to be unloaded. This is represented on the plot by the letter T which is at the zero point. Note that the scales for each variable are different and that T is plotted from 0 to 300 whereas S, the level in the storage tank, is plotted from 0 to 2000. Cursors are provided at the 0, 25, 50, 75, and 100 percent levels.

Since there are no tankers in the unloading dock initially, the amount in the storage tank is depleted by the amount being sent to the refinery. From the plot, this depletion continues until the first tanker arrives and begins unloading its crude. Since the input rate for the storage tank is greater than its output rate, the amount of crude in the storage tank increases momentarily as the tanker is being unloaded. Other tankers arrive and provide sufficient crude to replenish the storage tank after the initial depletion period.

As can be seen, the plot illustrates the combined discrete-continuous nature of the simulation. The second part of the plot illustrates the steady-state behavior of the system. The amount of crude in the storage tank oscillates between 1600 and 2000, and tankers are in the unloading dock waiting for storage space to become available to unload their crude.

11.8   Example 11-2.   SOAKING PIT FURNACE† (1, 2, 4)

Steel ingots arrive at a soaking pit furnace in a steel plant with an interarrival time that is exponentially distributed with mean of 2.25 hours. The soaking

---

† This example describes a hypothetical situation which illustrates combined modeling concepts using SLAM. See Exercise 11-6 for a representative description of the operation of soaking pits.

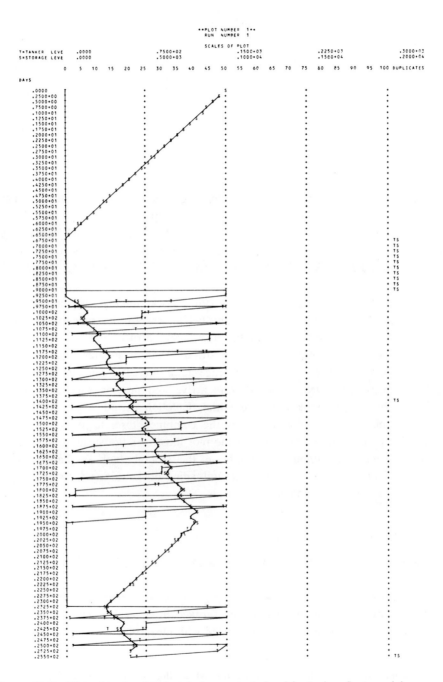

Figure 11-8 Plot of tanker level and storage tank level in tanker fleet model.

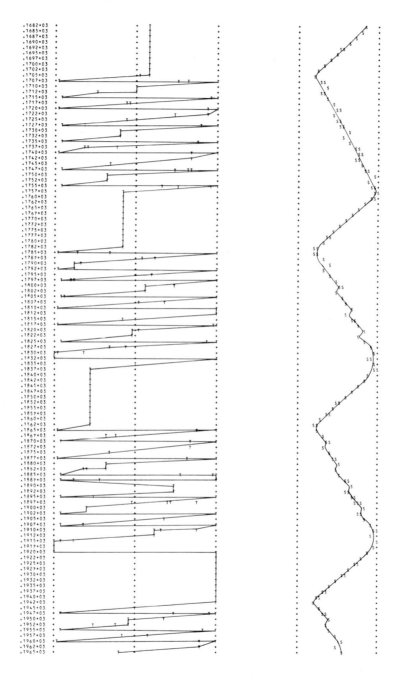

Figure 11-8 (continued).

pit furnace heats an ingot so that it can be economically rolled in the next stage of the process. The temperature change of an ingot in the soaking pit furnace is described by the following differential equation:

$$\frac{dh_i}{dt} = (H - h_i) * C_i$$

where h_i is the temperature of the ith ingot in the soaking pit; C_i is the heating time coefficient of an ingot and is equal to $X + .1$ where X is normally distributed with mean of .05 and standard deviation of 0.01; and H is the furnace temperature which is heated toward 2600°F with a heating rate constant of 0.2, that is,

$$\frac{dH}{dt} = (2600. - H) * 0.2.$$

The ingots interact with one another in that adding a "cold" ingot to the furnace reduces the temperature of the furnace and thus changes the heating time for all ingots in the furnace. The temperature reduction is equal to the difference between furnace and ingot temperatures, divided by the number of ingots in the furnace. There are 10 soaking pits in the furnace. When a cold ingot arrives and the furnace is full, it is stored in a cold ingot bank. It is assumed that the initial temperature of an arriving ingot is uniformly distributed in the interval from 400 to 500°F. All ingots put in the cold ingot bank are assumed to have a temperature of 400°F upon insertion into the soaking pit.

The operating policy of the company is to continue heating the ingots in the furnace until one or more ingots reach 2200°F. At such a time all ingots with a temperature greater than 2000°F are removed. The initial conditions are that there are six ingots in the furnace with initial temperatures of 550, 600, 650, . . ., 800°F. Initially, the temperature of the furnace is 1650°F, and the next ingot is due to arrive at time 0.

The objective is to simulate the above system for 500 hours to obtain estimates of the following quantities:

1. Heating time of the ingots;
2. Final temperature distribution of the ingots;
3. Waiting time of the ingots in the cold storage bank; and
4. Utilization of the soaking pit furnace.

Concepts Illustrated. This example illustrates the stopping of an ACTIVITY in a network model from within a discrete event which is initiated as a state-event, that is, the STOPA activity duration and subroutine are employed in conjunction with an EVENT node. A RESOURCE is used to model the soaking pits.

SLAM Model.   We will simulate the furnace problem using a combined network-discrete event-continuous model. The network will be employed to model the ingot arrival process, the cold bank storage, the soaking activity, and the exit from the system. A time-event which is initiated by an EVENT node will be employed to process the insertion of ingots into the furnace. A state-event will be employed to end the soaking activity and process the removal of the ingots from the furnace. Continuous state variables will be employed to model the temperature of the ingots in the furnace and the temperature of the furnace.

The status of the pits in the furnace will be maintained as occupied or empty by employing the SLAM array XX. If pit number I is occupied by an ingot, $XX(I)$ will be set to 1; otherwise $XX(I)$ will be equal to 0 which indicates that the pit is empty.

The continuous portion of the model employs twelve state variables. The first ten state variables are used to model the temperature of the ingot in each of the ten soaking pits. If soaking pit number I is occupied, $SS(I)$ equals the temperature of the ingot in pit I, otherwise $SS(I)$ is set equal to 0. The temperature of the furnace is modeled as state variable $SS(11)$. State variable $SS(12)$ is set equal to the maximum temperature of all ingots in the furnace.

The equations of state for the temperatures of each ingot and the furnace are coded in subroutine STATE in terms of their derivatives as shown in Figure 11-9. The value of $SS(12)$, representing the maximum ingot temperature, is initially set to 0. In a DO loop, each ingot temperature is compared to the value of $SS(12)$, resetting $SS(12)$ to the temperature of the ingot as appropriate. Also each value of $DD(I)$ is calculated as the rate of change of the temperature for the ingot in the Ith pit. Note that if the Ith pit is empty, then $XX(I)$ equals 0., and therefore $DD(I)$ is set to 0.   The variable $C(I)$ is the normally distributed

```
      SUBROUTINE STATE
      COMMON/SCOM1/ ATRIB(100),DD(100),DDL(100),DTNOW,II,MFA,MSTOP,NCLNR
     1,NCRDR,NPRNT,NNRUN,NNSET,NTAPE,SS(100),SSL(100),TNEXT,TNOW,XX(100)
      COMMON/USER/ C(10)
      SS(12)=0.
      DO 100 I=1,10
      IF(SS(I).GT.SS(12)) SS(12)=SS(I)
100   DD(I)=(SS(11)-SS(I))*XX(I)*C(I)
      DD(11)=(2600.-SS(11))*.2
      RETURN
      END
```

Figure 11-9   Subroutine state for furnace example.

heating coefficient for the ingot in pit I which is set in the discrete event portion of the model and is passed to subroutine STATE through user labeled COMMON. It is assumed that the ingot has material properties that affect its heating rate. Following the exit from the DO loop, DD(11) is set equal to the rate of change of the temperature in the furnace.

The network model for this example is depicted in Figure 11-10. The ingot arrivals are created at the CREATE node with the arrival time marked as ATRIB(1). The time between arrivals of the ingot entities is exponentially distributed with a mean of 2.25 hours. The ingots continue to the ASSIGN node where ATRIB(2) is set equal to a sample from a uniform distribution between 400 and 500 which represents the initial temperature of the ingot. The ingots then wait, if necessary, in file 1 for one unit of resource PIT. Once the ingot has seized a PIT, it proceeds to the EVENT node labeled LOAD where the discrete event with code 1 is executed. This event determines the pit number of the available pit, sets the status of the pit to occupied, sets the initial temperature and heating coefficient for the ingot, and sets ATRIB(3) of the entity equal to the pit number. If the ingot has waited in the cold ingot bank, statistics are collected on the waiting time and ATRIB(1) is remarked as TNOW. In addition, the temperature of the furnace is reduced appropriately as the result of adding a cold ingot to the furnace. The logic for this event is coded in subroutine LOAD and is described following the discussion of the network model.

Following processing by the EVENT node, the ingot undertakes ACTIVITY 1 representing the soaking activity. The duration of this ACTIVITY is indefinite and is terminated from within a discrete event by a call to subroutine STOPA (NTC) where NTC is equal to the PIT number which was assigned to ATRIB(3) in the LOAD event. The execution of subroutine STOPA(I) causes the ingot in pit I to complete the ACTIVITY. The ACTIVITY is terminated by a call to STOPA(I) for each ingot I with SS(I) greater than or equal to 2000° from within a second discrete event assigned event code 2 and coded in subroutine EXITP. This event is initiated as a state-event whenever the temperature of one of the ingots, SS(12), exceeds 2200° within a tolerance of 2° as prescribed on the SEVNT card depicted below.

SEVNT, 2, SS(12), XP,2200.,2.;

Again, we will defer the description of the coding of subroutine EXITP for the processing logic associated with event code 2 until we complete the discussion of the network model.

Following the completion of the soaking ACTIVITY, the ingots proceed to the COLCT node where interval statistics are collected on the heating time for

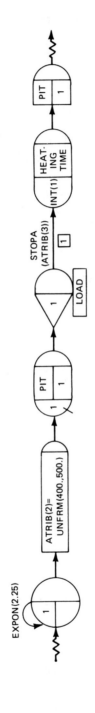

Figure 11-10 Network for furnace example.

```
        SUBROUTINE EVENT(I)
        GO TO (1,2),I
      1 CALL LOAD
        RETURN
      2 CALL EXITP
        RETURN
        END
```

Figure 11-11   Subroutine EVENT(I) for furnace example.

the ingot using the time reference contained in ATRIB(1). The ingots then continue to the FREE node where a PIT is released. The entity representing the ingot is then terminated from the system.

The discrete events for this example are coded in subroutines LOAD and EXITP. Subroutine EVENT(I) maps the event code, I, onto the appropriate subroutine call and is shown in Figure 11-11. Recall that the LOAD event is initiated from within the network model by ingots arriving to the EVENT node with code 1, and the EXITP event is initiated as a state-event from within the continuous model by the maximum ingot temperature reaching 2200°F.

The coding for subroutine LOAD is shown in Figure 11-12. The pit number, JJ, in which the ingot is to be inserted is set equal to the first J such that XX(J) equals 0. The variables associated with pit JJ are then initialized and ATRIB(3)

```
        SUBROUTINE LOAD
        COMMON/SCOM1/ ATRIB(100),DD(100),DDL(100),DTNOW,II,MFA,MSTOP,NCLNR
       1,NCRDR,NPRNT,NNRUN,NNSET,NTAPE,SS(100),SSL(100),TNEXT,TNOW,XX(100)
        COMMON/USER/ C(10)
C*****DETERMINE PIT NUMBER OF AVAILABLE PIT
        DO 10 J=1,10
        JJ=J
        IF(XX(J).EQ.0.) GO TO 20
     10 CONTINUE
        CALL ERROR(1)
C*****TURN PIT ON,SET INITIAL TEMP. AND HEATING COEFF., SET ATRIB(3)=PIT NUMBER
     20 XX(JJ)=1.
        SS(JJ)=ATRIB(2)
        C(JJ)=RNORM(.05,.01,1)+.1
        ATRIB(3)=JJ
C*****IF COLD INGOT - COLLECT STATISTICS, RESET TEMP., AND RE-MARK ATRIB(1)
        WAIT=TNOW-ATRIB(1)
        IF(WAIT.LE.0.) GO TO 30
        CALL COLCT(WAIT,2)
        SS(JJ)=400.
        ATRIB(1)=TNOW
     30 XNUM=NNACT(1)
C*****REDUCE FURNACE TEMP. BY TEMP. DIFFERENCE/ NUMBER OF INGOTS
        REDUCT=(SS(11)-SS(JJ))/XNUM
        SS(11)=SS(11)-REDUCT
        RETURN
        END
```

Figure 11-12   Subroutine LOAD for furnace example.

is set equal to the pit number. If the ingot waited in the cold ingot bank, then statistics are collected on the wait time as COLCT variable number 2, the temperature of the ingot is reset to 400°, and ATRIB(1) is re-marked at TNOW. In either case, the temperature of the furnace is reduced by the difference in temperature between the ingot and the furnace divided by the number of ingots in the furnace.

```
      SUBROUTINE EXITP
      COMMON/SCOM1/ ATRIB(100),DD(100),DDL(100),DTNOW,II,MFA,MSTOP,NCLNR
     1,NCRDR,NPRNT,NNRUN,NNSET,NTAPE,SS(100),SSL(100),TNEXT,TNOW,XX(100)
      DO 10 J=1,10
      IF(SS(J).LT.2000.) GO TO 10
      XX(J)=0.
      CALL COLCT(SS(J),1)
      SS(J)=0.
      CALL STOPA(J)
   10 CONTINUE
      RETURN
      END
```

Figure 11-13 Subroutine EXITP for furnace example.

The coding for subroutine EXITP is shown in Figure 11-13. The temperature of each pit, J, is tested against the desired temperature of 2000°F. If the ingot in pit J has reached 2000°, the variable $XX(J)$ is set to zero to denote the pit is empty, statistics are collected on the temperature of the ingot exiting the pit as COLCT variable number 2, and the temperature of the pit is set equal to 0. In addition, a call is made to subroutine STOPA(J) which causes the entity representing the ingot in pit J to complete the soaking ACTIVITY in the network model. Note that the ingots which have a temperature of less than 2000° remain in the furnace.

The initial conditions for the simulation are established in subroutine INTLC depicted in Figure 11-14. The temperature of the furnace is initialized to 1650° and six ingots having initial temperature of 550, 600, 650, . . ., 800° are in-

```
      SUBROUTINE  INTLC
      COMMON/SCOM1/ ATRIB(100),DD(100),DDL(100),DTNOW,II,MFA,MSTOP,NCLNR
     1,NCRDR,NPRNT,NNRUN,NNSET,NTAPE,SS(100),SSL(100),TNEXT,TNOW,XX(100)
      TEMP=550.
      SS(11)=1650.
      DO 100 I=1,6
      ATRIB(1)=TNOW
      ATRIB(2)=TEMP
      CALL FILEM(1,ATRIB)
  100 TEMP=TEMP+50.
      RETURN
      END
```

Figure 11-14 Subroutine INTLC for furnace example.

```
 1    GEN,C.D.PEGDEN,INGOT PROBLEM,7/1/77,1;
 2    LIMITS,1,4,40;
 3    STAT,1,HEATING TEMP,20/2000/10;
 4    STAT,2,WAITING TIME;
 5    CONT,11,1,.1,10,10;
 6    TIMST,SS(11),FURNACE TEMP.;
 7    SEVNT,2,SS(12),XP,2200.,2.;
 8    NETWORK;
 9    ;
10            RESOURCE/PIT(10),1;
11            CREATE,EXPON(2.25),,1;                    CREATE INGOT ARRIVALS
12            ASSIGN,ATRIB(2)=UNFRM(400.,500.);         ASSIGN INGOT TEMPERATURE
13            AWAIT,PIT;                                AWAIT A PIT
14    LOAD  EVENT,1;                                    LOAD INGOT INTO PIT
15            ACT/1,STOPA(ATRIB(3));                    SOAKING ACTIVITY
16            COLCT,INT(1),HEATING TIME;                COLLECT STATISTICS
17            FREE,PIT;                                 FREE THE PIT
18            TERM;                                     EXIT THE SYSTEM
19            ENDNETWORK;
20    INIT,0,500;
21    FIN;
```

Figure 11-15   Input statements for furnace example.

serted into the network at the AWAIT node by a CALL FILEM(1,ATRIB). These six ingots will be inserted into the furnace at the beginning of the simulation.

The input statements for this example are shown in Figure 11-15. Note that the STAT card for COLCT variable number 1 specifies that a histogram be generated with 20 interior cells, with the upper limit of the first cell equal to 2000°, and a cell width of 10. In addition, time-persistent statistics are specified for state variable SS(11). This specification causes a linear representation to be used for statistics gathering purposes for the values of SS(11) between the ends of steps.

Summary of Results.   The SLAM Summary Report for this example is included as Figure 11-16. The report reveals that during the 500 hours of simulated time, 225 ingots were processed and the average heating time was 20.62 hours. The heating time for ingots varied between 11.71 and 33.83 hours. The variation in the heating time is due to the coupling of the equations of the system through the furnace temperature and to the random component of the equation that was associated with the ingot, that is, the normal sample used to define the heating coefficient, $C(I)$. The average waiting time for ingots in the cold ingot bank was 8.2 hours. Note that waiting time statistics were collected only for 180 ingots that waited. The determination of whether to include the zero waiting time of the ingots that went directly into the furnace is a modeling question that must be decided by the analyst. If waiting times with and without zero values are

```
                    S L A M    S U M M A R Y    R E P O R T

        SIMULATION PROJECT INGOT PROBLEM              BY C.D.PEGDEN

        DATE  7/ 1/1977                               RUN NUMBER    1 OF    1


        CURRENT TIME     .5000+03
        STATISTICAL ARRAYS CLEARED AT TIME     .0000



                  **STATISTICS FOR VARIABLES BASED ON OBSERVATION**

                    MEAN         STANDARD      COEFF. OF     MINIMUM       MAXIMUM       NUMBER OF
                    VALUE        DEVIATION     VARIATION     VALUE         VALUE         OBSERVATIONS

HEATING TEMP        .2162+04     .4142+02      .1916-01      .2001+04      .2202+04      225
WAITING TIME        .8177+01     .4660+01      .5700+00      .5000-01      .2040+02      180
HEATING TIME        .2062+02     .3269+01      .1585+00      .1171+02      .3383+02      225



                  **STATISTICS FOR TIME-PERSISTENT VARIABLES**

                    MEAN         STANDARD      MINIMUM       MAXIMUM       TIME          CURRENT
                    VALUE        DEVIATION     VALUE         VALUE         INTERVAL      VALUE

FURNACE TEMP.       .2127+04     .2670+03      .0000         .2533+04      .5000+03      .2125+04



                        **FILE STATISTICS**

FILE      ASSOCIATED    AVERAGE       STANDARD      MAXIMUM      CURRENT      AVERAGE
NUMBER    NODE TYPE     LENGTH        DEVIATION     LENGTH       LENGTH       WAITING TIME

  1       AWAIT         2.9835        2.7461           13           4         6.2416



                    **REGULAR ACTIVITY STATISTICS**

ACTIVITY    AVERAGE         STANDARD      MAXIMUM       CURRENT       ENTITY
INDEX       UTILIZATION     DEVIATION     UTILIZATION   UTILIZATION   COUNT

  1         9.4647          1.2091           10            10         225



                        **RESOURCE STATISTICS**

RESOURCE   RESOURCE   CURRENT     AVERAGE       STANDARD      MAXIMUM       CURRENT
NUMBER     LABEL      CAPACITY    UTILIZATION   DEVIATION     UTILIZATION   UTILIZATION

  1        PIT        10          9.4647        1.2091           10            10



                    **STATE AND DERIVATIVE VARIABLES**

                    (I)         SS(I)         DD(I)
                     1          .1842+04      .3792+02
                     2          .1053+04      .1540+03
                     3          .1877+04      .3604+02
                     4          .1095+04      .1608+03
                     5          .1928+04      .3285+02
                     6          .1127+04      .1657+03
                     7          .1041+04      .1521+03
                     8          .1101+04      .1617+03
                     9          .1884+04      .3562+02
                    10          .1920+04      .3336+02
                    11          .2125+04      .9491+02
                    12          .1928+04      .0000
```

Figure 11-16 SLAM summary report for furnace example.

```
                        **HISTOGRAM NUMBER  1**

                           HEATING TEMP


OBSV      RELA     CUML       UPPER
FREQ      FREQ     FREQ     CELL LIMIT    0        20       40       60       80      100
                                         +     +     +     +     +     +     +     +     +     +     +
   0      .000     .000      .2000+04     +                                               +
   2      .009     .009      .2010+04     +                                               +
   0      .000     .009      .2020+04     +                                               +
   1      .004     .013      .2030+04     +C                                              +
   3      .013     .027      .2040+04     +*                                              +
   1      .004     .031      .2050+04     + C                                             +
   3      .013     .044      .2060+04     +*C                                             +
   0      .000     .044      .2070+04     + C                                             +
   2      .009     .053      .2080+04     +  C                                            +
   2      .009     .062      .2090+04     +  C                                            +
   3      .013     .076      .2100+04     +* C                                            +
  12      .053     .129      .2110+04     +***  C                                         +
   4      .018     .147      .2120+04     +*    C                                         +
   7      .031     .178      .2130+04     +***    C                                       +
   6      .027     .204      .2140+04     +**      C                                      +
  17      .076     .280      .2150+04     +****       C                                   +
  20      .089     .369      .2160+04     +****          C                                +
  19      .084     .453      .2170+04     +****             C                             +
  31      .138     .591      .2180+04     +*******             C                          +
  23      .102     .693      .2190+04     +*****                  C                       +
  28      .124     .818      .2200+04     +******                     C                   +
  41      .182    1.000       INF         +*********                        C
 ---                                      +     +     +     +     +     +     +     +     +     +     +
 225                                      0        20       40       60       80      100
```

Figure 11-16   (continued).

desired, then two calls to subroutine COLCT can be incorporated into the program.

From both the activity and resource statistics sections of the summary report, it is seen that the average number of pits in use was 9.46. At the end of the simulation, all ten pits were being utilized. These results show that the system is overloaded and that new procedures or additional resources are required.

From the file statistics output, the average number of ingots in the cold storage bank was 2.98 and the maximum number 13. Thus, a storage area for at least 13 ingots is required.

The state and derivative variables portray the final conditions of the simulation. At 500 hours, the furnace temperature was 2125°F and increasing at 95°F/hour. The corresponding value for each ingot in a pit is shown in the summary report. All pits have ingots in them.

The last portion of the summary report displays a histogram of the temperatures of the ingots removed from the pit. The histogram reveals that the ingot temperatures were bunched between 2100°F and 2200°F. This clustering is due to the stopping decision that requires at least one ingot to have a temperature of 2200° before any ingot can be removed from the furnace. Eighteen percent of the ingots reached the 2200°F limit.

11.9   CHAPTER SUMMARY

This chapter combines the modeling approaches of SLAM and demonstrates how SLAM supports alternative modeling approaches. The DETECT node is described for detecting a state-event within a network model. The SLAM function SSEVT(N) which allows the user to access information on simultaneous state-events is described. Two examples of combined modeling are presented. The first example involves tankers supplying oil to a refinery's storage tank. The second example involves the heating of ingots in a soaking pit furnace.

11.10   EXERCISES

11-1.   For the tanker refinery problem, assume that the rate of input to the storage tank decreases exponentially from the nominal value by the factor $1-e^{-x/5}$, where $x=SS(1)/150$. Determine the effects on the system due to this change in flow rate.

11-2.   Develop equations that make the flow rate from tanker to storage tank a function of the level of crude in the tanker, the level of crude in the storage tank, and the viscosity of the crude in the tanker. Develop the code for subroutine STATE to simulate the developed flow equations.

11-3.   It has been proposed that offshore unloading docks be built for unloading tankers at Seattle. Three such docks have been proposed, each of which can process at a rate two-thirds that of the current dock. Compare system operation between the three offshore unloading docks operating on only 1 shift versus the current unloading dock operated on a three-shift basis.

11-4.   For the problem stated in Example 11-1, an elaboration of the refinery is to be made. Consider that the refinery consists of four phases, the first of which is processing. Crude is taken from the initial storage tank and processed in a processing unit at a rate of 150 tb/day. After processing, the material is stored in an intermediate storage tank (phase 2), after which it goes through a filtering unit (phase 3). The rate of filtering is dependent on the condition of the filter. A filter has an expected life of 30 days. Initially, when the filter is new, the filter rate is 200 tb/day. The rate of flow through the filter decreases linearly until it is 100 tb/day after 30 days. The time to replace a filter is exponentially distributed with a mean of 0.5 day. The fourth phase of the refinery is a finished product storage tank. The finished product is removed from the tank according to the demand for the product, which is cyclic over an approximately 90-day period with a mean of 150 tb/day. All other characteristics of the system are identical to those presented in Example 11-1, except that the unloading dock works on a 24-hour schedule. Simulate the above system for 200 days, using different filter replacement policies to obtain the output requested in Example 11-1 and the following quantities: processor utilization, filter utilization, amount in intermediate storage tank, amount in final storage tank, and percentage of time that demand is lost. Initial conditions for the simulation are that the raw material storage tank is 50% full, the intermediate tank is 60% full, and the final storage tank is 40% full. The capacity of each storage tank is 2000 tb.

11-5. In the tanker problem discuss the changes necessary to model the following embellishments:

(a) Introduce a new super tanker into the fleet arriving empty at Valdez, Alaska on day 70. The new tanker has a capacity of 450 tb. The travel times for the super tanker are distributed according to the triangular distribution with a mode equal to the mean of the regular tankers. All other characteristics for the super tanker remain the same. Assume minimum and maximum travel times of 0.9 and 1.2 of the modal value, respectively.

(b) Retire the first three tankers that complete a round trip following the introduction of the new super tanker.

(c) Cause the super tanker to have priority over other tankers waiting for unloading at Seattle.

(d) For the super tanker, unloading rate is a function of the level of crude in the super tanker, that is, $dx/dt = -x$ where x is the amount of crude in the super tanker in thousands of barrels (tb).

11-6. A drag of ingots arrives at the soaking pit on the average every 1.75 hours. The distribution of times between arrivals is exponential. A drag consists of ten ingots. All ten ingots in the drag have the same temperature which is lognormally distributed between 300°F and 600°F with a mean of 400°F and standard deviation of 50°F. Upon arrival, the ingots may be charged directly into an available pit or they may be placed in a waiting-to-be-charged queue. The temperature of the arriving ingots decreases with the square root of the time they must wait, that is, temperature = old temperature − $\sqrt{\text{waiting time}}$ * 157°. When an ingot reaches a temperature of 150°F, it is assumed cold. Charging practice dictates that cold ingots may not be charged into any pit at a temperature of greater than 750°F since this causes surface cracks and, hence, poor quality. Hot ingots (over 150°F) may be charged into any temperature pit. It is assumed that the pit temperature after charging is equal to a weighted average of the pit and ingot temperatures (new pit temperature = 0.7*old pit temperature + 0.3*temperature of ingots in drag), and from then on varies according to the equation $dT/dt = 2600 - T$. When the pit temperature reaches 2200°F, the ingots are ready to soak and the pit temperature remains at this temperature for 2 hours. After the soak time, the ingots are removed and the pit is available to be reloaded. If nothing can be loaded, the pit temperature changes according to the equation $dT/dt = 600 - T$. There are four independent pits and each pit has a capacity of five ingots. (Note: Ingots can be processed in units of 5 which saves on computer storage and processing.)

The initial conditions for the simulation are:

1. Pit temperatures are 1150°F, 800°F, 1500°F, and 1000°F.
2. The pits whose temperatures are 1150°F and 800°F are loaded with 5 ingots. The other pits are not charging.
3. The first drag is scheduled to arrive at time zero.

Simulate the soaking pit system for 400 hours to obtain estimates of the following quantities: heating time for ingots; waiting time for ingots; the number of ingots waiting (total and by temperature class); and the number of loaded pits. Embellishments: (a) Clear statistics at time 100 and obtain summary reports at times 200, 300 and 400 hours.

(b) Give priority to processing the cold ingots at times 200 and 300, that is, if cold ingots are waiting assign pit(s) to process the cold ingots.

(c) Evaluate the policy of making one of the pits a processor of cold ingots.

(d) Simulate the system if the sum of the temperatures of the pits is restricted to 7000°F due to energy considerations.

11-7.   Model and simulate a gas station attendant providing service to arriving customers. The time between arrivals of customers is exponentially distributed with a mean value of 4 minutes. The service station employs one attendant whose service rate is dependent on the number of customers waiting for his service. The relationship between service rate and number in queue is given below

$$S = 1.2\exp(0.173N) \qquad\qquad N < 5$$
$$S = 1.2(0.25\exp(-0.305(N-5))+0.5) \quad N \geqslant 5$$

where N is the number of customers in the queue.

The nominal amount of service time required by each customer is an exponentially distributed random variable with a mean of 3.5 minutes. Analyze this queueing situation for 1000 minutes to obtain statistics on the following quantities: the time a customer spends in the queue, the time a customer spends at the gas station, the fraction of time the attendant is busy, and the number of customers waiting in the queue of the server. A plot is to be made that illustrates the status of the server, the number in the queue, and the remaining service time for a customer (4).

11.8   A hydrogenation reaction is conducted in four reactors operating in parallel. Each reactor may be started, stopped, discharged, or cleaned independently of the others. A compressor with a constant molal flow rate provides a supply of hydrogen gas to the reactors through a surge pressure tank and individual valves for each reactor. The valve connecting each reactor to the surge tank is adjusted by controls that make the effective pressure in each reactor the minimum of surge tank pressure and critical pressure (100 psia).

Initially the surge tank pressure is equal to 500 psia. Each reactor is charged with a fresh batch of reactant, and the four reactors are scheduled to be turned on at half-hour intervals beginning with reactor 1 at time 0. As a reaction proceeds, the concentration of the reactant (and the demand for hydrogen for that reactor) decreases. As long as surge tank pressure remains above the critical pressure of 100 psia, the decrease in concentration is exponential. The concentration of each reactant is monitored until it decreases to 10% of its initial value, at which time the reactor is considered to have completed a batch. At this time the reactor is turned off, discharged, cleaned, and recharged. The time to discharge a reactor is known to be exponentially distributed with a mean time of 1 hour. The time to clean and recharge a reactor is known to be approximately normally distributed with a mean of 1 hour and a standard deviation of 0.5 hour.

The operating policy for the system prescribes that the last reactor started will be immediately turned off whenever surge tank pressure falls below the critical value of 100 psia. All other reactors that are on at that time will continue, but no reactor will be started if surge tank pressure is below a nominal pressure of 150 psia. The parameters and variables of the model are defined in the accompanying table.

Parameters and Variables for Chemical Reaction Model

Model Parameter	Initial Value	Definition
RK(1)	0.03466	Reaction constant for product 1
RK(2)	0.00866	Reaction constant for product 2
RK(3)	0.01155	Reaction constant for product 3
RK(4)	0.00770	Reaction constant for product 4
V(1)	10.0	Volume of reactor 1
V(2)	15.0	Volume of reactor 2
V(3)	20.0	Volume of reactor 3
V(4)	25.0	Volume of reactor 4
VS	50.0	Volume of surge tank
RR	10.73	Gas constant
TEMP	550.0	System operating temperature
FC	0.19	Flow constant of compressor; FC* SUMFO is compressor molal flow rate
PNOM	150.0	Nominal pressure
PCRIT	100.0	Critical pressure
SUMFO	Calculated	Maximum possible molal flow of hydrogen to all reactors
ATDIS	1.0	Average time to discharge a reactor
RTV	RR * TEMP/VS	Composite reaction constant
FCOMP	FC * SUMFO	Compressor molal flow rate
Model Variable		
SS(1)	SO(1) = 0.1	Concentration of reactor 1
SS(2)	SO(2) − 0.4	Concentration of reactor 2
SS(3)	SO(3) = 0.2	Concentration of reactor 3
SS(4)	SO(4) = 0.5	Concentration of reactor 4
SS(5)	SO(5) = 500.0	Surge tank pressure
DD(I), I = 1, 4	0.0	Derivative of SS(I) with respect to time
F(I), I = 1, 4	0.0	Molal flow rate of hydrogen to reactor I
SUMF	0.0	Total molal flow of hydrogen to all reactors

Using the definitions provided, the model's state equations describing the chemical reactor system are:

$$PEFF = \text{Minimum of } (PCRIT, SS(5)); \quad \text{effective surge tank pressure}$$

$$DD(I) = \begin{cases} -RK(I)*SS(I)*PEFF; & \text{if reactor I is on;} \\ 0.0; & \text{if reactor I is off,} \end{cases}$$

$$F(I) = -DD(I)*V(I);$$
$$SUMF = F(1)+F(2)+F(3)+F(4);$$
$$DD(5) = (RR*TEMP/VS)*((FC*SUMFO) - SUMF);$$

Use this model to analyze the chemical reaction process. Obtain a plot of the operation of the process and statistics on the maintenance time, the number of reactors on, and the surge tank pressure (3).

Embellishments: (a) For the chemical reaction process described above, assume that the conditions under which reactors may be started when the surge tank pressure exceeds 150 psi are changed to allow only one reactor to start for each increase of 50 psi above the critical pressure.

(b) Suppose that it is required to have a maintenance man available to clean the reactor. Rewrite the program under the condition that only one maintenance man is available and reactors requiring cleaning and recharging must wait if the maintenance man is busy. Determine the effect on throughput of the requirements to have a maintenance man to perform the cleaning and recharging.

11-9.   For Exercise 11-8, solve the differential equations in terms of the initial conditions and rewrite the simulation program to use the derived solution.

11.11   REFERENCES

1. Ashour, S. and S. G. Bindingnavle, "An Optimal Design of a Soaking Pit Rolling Mill System," *Simulation,* Vol. 18, 1972, pp. 207-214.
2. Golden, D. G. and J. D. Schoeffler, "GSL-A Combined Continuous and Discrete Simulation Language," *Simulation,* Vol. 20, 1973, pp. 1-8.
3. Pritsker, A. A. B., *The GASP IV Simulation Language,* John Wiley, 1974.
4. Pritsker, A. A. B., and R. E. Young, *Simulation with GASP__PL/I,* John Wiley, 1975.

CHAPTER 12

Simulation Languages

12.1   INTRODUCTION

The widespread use of simulation as an analysis tool has led to the development of a number of languages specifically designed for simulation. These languages provide specific concepts and statements for representing the state of a system at a point in time and moving the system from state to state. In this chapter, we describe other simulation languages and discuss their relationship to the modeling framework of SLAM. The intent is not to provide manuals on how to write programs in these languages, but to illustrate the similarities and differences between the various simulation languages.

434

The chapter is organized into sections that describe process-oriented, event-oriented, and continuous simulation languages. Since SLAM builds on GASP IV and Q-GERT concepts, only brief comparisons for these languages will be given. Discussions on GPSS and SIMSCRIPT will be more detailed as these languages have been widely used. Only a brief survey of other discrete languages will be provided. For continuous simulation languages, the discussion will be kept to a minimum as the general orientation of the various continuous languages is similar.

12.2 GPSS/360

GPSS (General Purpose Simulation System) is a process-oriented simulation language for modeling discrete systems. GPSS exists in a number of dialects with GPSS/360 the most widely circulated and used version. The discussion which follows is based on this version. GPSS V is a superset of GPSS/360, and therefore programs written for GPSS/360 are compatible with GPSS V(10). Schriber's book, *Simulation with GPSS* (25), is an excellent text for learning GPSS.

The principal appeal of GPSS is its modeling simplicity. A GPSS model is constructed by combining a set of standard blocks into a block diagram which defines the logical structure of the system. Dynamic entities are represented in GPSS as transactions which move sequentially from block to block as the simulation proceeds. Learning to write a GPSS program consists of learning the functional operation of GPSS blocks and how to logically combine the blocks to represent a system of interest.

The GPSS processor interprets and executes the block diagram description of a system. It is written in assembly language and is specifically designed for discrete simulation. The language is limited in computing power and lacks a capability for floating point or real arithmetic.† As a consequence, the GPSS simulation clock is integer valued. This means that changes in the state of the system can occur only at integer points in time. For example, if we model a single-channel queueing system and we select our unit of time as minutes, then the time between arrivals and the service time for the customers must be an integer number of minutes.‡ Another consequence of an integer valued clock

---

† In GPSS, all real numbers are truncated to their integer parts.
‡ This problem can be reduced by selecting a smaller time unit.

is that simultaneous events frequently occur, and therefore the tie-breaking mechanism takes on added significance. In GPSS, this problem is addressed by assigning each transaction a special attribute called a priority which can be any integer between 0 and 127 with higher values assuming greater priority.

There are over forty different blocks in GPSS. Each block is pictorially represented by a stylized figure which is intended to be suggestive of the operation of the block. Fifteen of the more commonly used blocks are shown in Table 12-1. For each block, there is a corresponding SLAM network element which performs a similar function. The correspondence is not exact, however, and in several cases elements of GPSS and SLAM which have the same names perform different functions.

A GPSS block diagram must be translated by the modeler into an equivalent statement form for interpretation and execution by the GPSS processor. Each block specification is entered on a punchcard and consists of three categories of information. The first is a symbolic location name and is used as a block label similar to the node labels in SLAM. The second category of information is the operation and is a verb suggestive of the function of the block. The third category of information is the block's *operands* which provide specific information concerning the operation of the block. The number and interpretation of the operands depends upon the specific block type and are denoted in general by the letters A, B, C, D, E, F, and G. A fixed format for inputting the three types of information is required. With this brief introduction, we will now describe the operation of the blocks shown in Table 12-1.

Transactions are created in GPSS by use of the GENERATE block with operands A, B, C, D, E, F, and G. The A operand specifies the mean time between creations. If the B operand is specified as a number, then the time between creations is uniformly distributed in the range from A$-$B to A+B. For example, if the A and B operands are specified as 10 and 2, respectively, then the time between creations is uniformly distributed over the integers 8, 9, 10, 11, and 12. We defer until later the discussion of the meaning of a nonnumeric B operand. The C operand specifies the time of the first transaction creation and is referred to as the offset interval. The D operand prescribes a limit on the number of transactions which can enter the model through a given GENERATE block. Each transaction created at the GENERATE block has a priority specified by operand E and has F associated parameters where G specifies the type of parameters. The CREATE node in SLAM is analogous to the GENERATE block.

Transactions are destroyed in GPSS by a TERMINATE block. In addition to destroying each arriving transaction, the TERMINATE block also reduces the termination counter by the value specified as its A operand. The termination

Table 12-1 Basic GPSS blocks and their SLAM equivalents.

Block Symbol	Functional Description of Block	SLAM Network Element Providing Analogous Function
GENERATE A,B,C,D,E,F,G	Creates transactions as prescribed by the operands A, B, C, D, E, F, and G	CREATE node
TERMINATE A	Destroys the arriving transaction and reduces the termination counter by A	TERMINATE node
ADVANCE A,B	Advances simulated time as prescribed by operands A and B	ACTIVITY
SEIZE A	Causes transaction to await and capture facility A	AWAIT node
RELEASE A	Frees facility A	FREE node
ENTER B A	Causes transaction to await and capture B units of storage A	AWAIT node
LEAVE A B	Frees B units of storage A	FREE node

Table 12-1 (continued).

Block Symbol	Functional Description of Block	SLAM Network Element Providing Analogous Function
QUEUE A / B	Increments the number in queue A by B units	†
DEPART A / B	Decrements the number in queue A by B units	†
A, B, C / ASSIGN	Assigns the value specified as B to parameter number A of the transaction	ASSIGN node
MARK A	Assigns the current clock time to parameter number A of the transaction	ASSIGN node
SAVEVALUE / A, B, C	Assigns the value specified as B to save-value location A	ASSIGN node
TRANSFER A (C) (B)	Causes a transfer to location C with probability A, and location B with probability 1-A	ACTIVITY
A X B / TEST (C)	Causes a transfer to location C if A is not related to B according to operator X	ACTIVITY
TABULATE B A	Records and observation for the variable prescribed in table A	COLCT node

438

† Queue statistics are automatically recorded in SLAM

counter is an integer value which is initially specified by the A operand of the GPSS control card START. As transactions arrive to TERMINATE blocks, the counter is decremented accordingly. As soon as the counter is reduced to zero or less, the simulation stops. Note that although there may be many TERMINATE blocks in a model, there is only one termination counter. This differs from the TERMINATE node of SLAM.

Time advance is provided for in GPSS by the ADVANCE block. When a transaction enters the ADVANCE block, its progress is delayed by the time specified by the A and B operands. The A and B operands of the ADVANCE block are defined in the same manner as the A and B operands of the GENERATE blocks. The A operand prescribes the mean delay time and the B operand, when specified as a number, defines the half-width of a uniform distribution.

To generate samples from distributions other than the uniform distribution, a user-written table function must be included in the model. A function is defined by a function header card and one or more function follower cards. The function header card specifies the name of the function, the random number stream, and the number of points specified for the distribution. The function follower cards follow immediately after the function header card and contain the entries $X_1,Y_1/X_2,Y_2/$ . . . $/X_n,Y_n$ where X_i and Y_i are the ith cumulative probability and associated function value, respectively.

A sample from a table function is obtained by specifying the name or number of the function as the A operand and defaulting the B operand of the GENERATE or ADVANCE block. The entry FN1 would be used to reference function number 1 and the entry FN$XPDIS would be used to reference a function named XPDIS. To simplify sampling from an exponential distribution, a special provision is made whereby if the B operand is specified as a function, then the sample is taken as the product of A and B. Thus, if the modeler includes a table function for the exponential distribution[†] with unit mean and prescribes it as the B operand, then a sample from a general exponential distribution can be obtained by specifying the mean of the desired exponential distribution as the A operand. In SLAM, time advance is modeled using an activity.

In GPSS, resources are modeled as either facilities or storages. Facilities have a capacity of one and need not be defined in a declarative statement. Storages may have a capacity greater than one. The capacity of a storage is defined using a STORAGE definition card. There are two distinctions made between facilities and storages in addition to capacity. Facilities may be preempted

---

[†] An approximation of the exponential distribution using a table function is required because there is no logarithm function in GPSS.

using a PREEMPT block whereas storages cannot. Secondly, a facility can only be released by the transaction which seized it. In contrast, any transaction can be used to release one or more units of a storage.

Facilities are seized and released by transactions passing through SEIZE and RELEASE blocks, respectively. The A operand specifies the name of the facility being seized or released. When a transaction arrives to a SEIZE block, it attempts to enter the block and capture the facility. If the facility is busy, the transaction's progress is delayed until the facility becomes free as the result of a transaction passing through a RELEASE block.

The ENTER and LEAVE blocks perform analogous functions for capturing and freeing storages. When a transaction arrives at an ENTER block, it is delayed until B units of storage A are available. The transaction then captures the B units of storage A and continues. Similarly, when a transaction arrives to the LEAVE block, it frees B units of storage A. The correspondence in SLAM for the SEIZE and ENTER blocks is the AWAIT node. The SLAM FREE node is similar to the RELEASE and LEAVE blocks of GPSS.

Statistics on waiting time and queue length for transactions waiting for facilities or storages can be obtained by using the QUEUE and DEPART blocks. An entity arriving to a QUEUE block causes the number of units in queue A to be increased by B. Likewise, an entity arriving to a DEPART block causes the number of units in queue A to be decreased by B. In both cases, the default value for B is 1. Note that the QUEUE block in GPSS and QUEUE node in SLAM perform distinctly different functions. No waiting of transactions occurs at a QUEUE block; its function is simply to record the number of units entering the queue.

During a simulation, the GPSS processor automatically maintains certain variables which describe the status of the system. These variables are collectively referred to as standard numerical attributes (SNA). A partial listing of SNAs is shown in Table 12-2. If a symbolic name is employed for an SNA, it must be preceded by the symbol $. For example, the GPSS variable F$SRVR denotes the status of the facility which has the name SRVR.

Transactions in GPSS can be assigned attributes which are referred to as parameters. The GPSS variable P_j is used to reference parameter number j of a transaction. Hence, the GPSS variable P_j is equivalent to the SLAM variable ATRIB(j). The ASSIGN block is used to assign values to parameters of transactions. The ASSIGN block causes the value specified as the B operand to be assigned to the parameter number specified in the A operand. The B operand can be an integer or any SNA. If a + or − sign is appended to the A operand, then the value specified by the B operand is added to or subtracted

Table 12-2 Selected GPSS standard numerical attributes.

C1	The current value of clock time
Fn	The current status of facility number n.
M1	The transit time of a transaction.
Nn	The total number of transactions that have entered block n.
Pn	Parameter number n of a transaction.
Qn	The length of queue n.
Rn	The space remaining in storage n.
Sn	The current occupany of storage n.
Wn	The number of transactions currently at block n.
Xn	The value of savevalue location n.

from the current value of parameter number A. For example, the statement

ASSIGN   P1+,1

would increment parameter number 1 by 1. A separate block called the MARK block is provided for assigning the value of the current time to a parameter. The A operand of the MARK block specifies the parameter number to which the value of current time is to be assigned.

In some cases, it is desired to record values as global variables rather than as attributes of an entity. In SLAM, this is done by assigning values to the global array XX. In GPSS, this is accomplished by employing the SAVEVALUE block which assigns the value specified by the B operand to savevalue location number A. If a + or − sign is appended to the A operand, then the value specified by the B operand is added to or subtracted from the existing contents of savevalue location A, respectively.

For arithmetic operations beyond the decrementing and incrementing discussed above, the modeler must employ the VARIABLE definition card. This card type can be thought of as defining a user-specified standard numerical attribute. The variable definition card is specified by entering the variable name in the location field, the word VARIABLE in the operation field,† and the arithmetic expression which defines the variable in the operands field. The arithmetic operators available in GPSS are addition (+), subtraction (−), multiplication (*), integer division (/), and modulus division (@).

---

† The use of the word FVARIABLE causes the expression to be calculated and only the result is integerized.

GPSS provides a series of blocks which are used for directing a nonsequential flow of transactions through the block diagram. The TRANSFER block provides a probabilistic branching capability by causing the arriving transaction to be routed to statement location C with probability A and to statement location B with probability 1-A. If A is defaulted, the TRANSFER block causes deterministic branching to statement location B. Transaction routing can also be based on the system status by use of the TEST block. In addition to the normal operands, this block employs an auxiliary operator, X. The TEST block accepts a transaction if operand A is related to operand B according to relationship X; otherwise the transaction is routed to the location specified by the C operand. If the C operand is not specified, the block operates in the refusal mode and the transaction is held until the condition is satisfied. The permissible codes for the auxiliary operator X are:

G	Greater than
GE	Greater than or Equal
E	Equal
NE	Not Equal
LE	Less than or Equal
L	Less than

These GPSS conditional transfer capabilities are a subset of the conditional branching capabilities available in SLAM.

Observation type statistics are recorded in a GPSS model at TABULATE blocks. The purpose of this block is analogous to the function of the COLCT node in SLAM. The A operand of the TABULATE block specifies the name of a TABLE card whose A operand defines the variable for which observation statistics are recorded at each transaction arrival to the TABULATE block. Values corresponding to the SLAM variables HLOW, HWID, and NCEL are specified as the B, C, and D operands of the TABLE card, respectively. The variable for which statistics are to be recorded can be any of the SNA's. The special variable MP_j is provided for collecting interval statistics using the time marked in parameter number j. Hence, by using a MARK block and TABULATE block in conjunction with a TABLE card, the transit time between any two points can be recorded.

To illustrate the modeling features of GPSS, we will present a GPSS model of the following single-server queueing system. Customers arrive with a mean interarrival time of 20 minutes, exponentially distributed. The service time for each customer is uniformly distributed between 10 and 25 minutes. Statistical estimates are desired of the mean queue length, utilization of the server, and time in system.

The GPSS model for this illustration is given in Figure 12-1. The GPSS coding is presented in Figure 12-2. The first segment of the program models the flow of customers through the system. The order in which the blocks appear corresponds to the sequence of steps through which each customer progresses. We

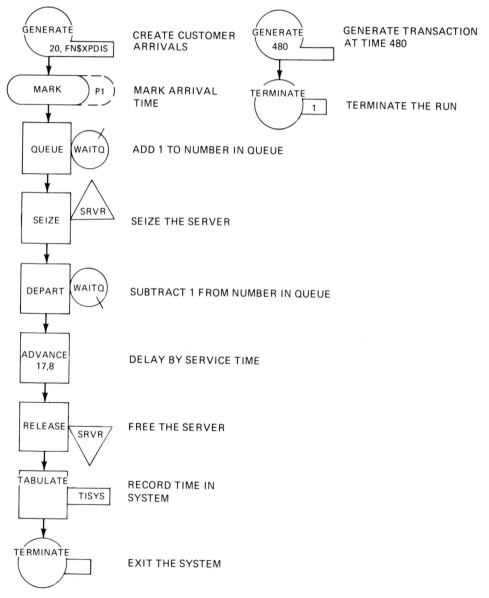

Figure 12-1 GPSS model of a single-server queueing situation.

```
 1     *
 2              SIMULATE
 3     *
 4     XPDIS FUNCTION     RN1,C24
 5     0.0,0.0/0.1,0.104/0.2,0.222/0.3,0.355/0.4,0.509/0.5,0.69
 6     0.6,0.915/0.7,1.2/0.75,1.38/0.8,1.6/0.84,1.83/0.88,2.12
 7     0.9,2.3/0.92,2.52/0.94,2.81/0.95,2.99/0.96,3.2/0.97,3.5
 8     0.98,4.0/0.99,4.6/0.995,5.3/0.998,6.2/0.999,7/0.9997,8
 9     *
10     TISYS TABLE        MP1,0,5,20
11     *
12     *     MODEL SEGMENT
13     *
14           GENERATE     20,FN$XPDIS       CREATE CUSTOMER ARRIVALS
15           MARK         P1               MARK ARRIVAL TIME
16           QUEUE        WAITQ            ENTER THE WAITING LINE
17           SEIZE        SRVR             SEIZE THE SERVER
18           DEPART       WAITQ            EXIT THE WAITING LINE
19           ADVANCE      17,8             DELAY BY SERVICE TIME
20           RELEASE      SRVR             FREE THE SERVER
21           TABULATE     TISYS            RECORD TIME IN SYSTEM
22           TERMINATE                     EXIT THE SYSTEM
23     *
24     *     TIMING SEGMENT
25     *
26           GENERATE     480               CREATE TRANSACTION AT TIME 480
27           TERMINATE    1                 TERMINATE THE RUN
28     *
29     *     CONTROL CARDS
30     *
31           START        1                 START THE RUN
32           END
```

Figure 12-2   GPSS coding of single channel queueing problem.

will describe the model with the coding lines given in parentheses. The transactions representing customers are created at the GENERATE block (line 14) with the time between transactions specified as the product of 20 and function XPDIS. The function XPDIS is entered (lines 4-8) as an approximation to the exponential distribution with unit mean. A transaction proceeds to the MARK block (line 15) where the current clock time is recorded as parameter number 1. The transaction then enters the QUEUE block (line 16) where the number in queue WAITQ is incremented by 1. When the facility SRVR becomes free, it is seized at the SEIZE block (line 17) by the first waiting transaction which then continues to the DEPART block where the number in queue WAITQ is decremented by 1. The service activity is modeled by the ADVANCE block (line 19) which delays the transaction by a sample from a uniform distribution between 9 and 25.† At the completion of service, the transaction is routed to

---

† The (A−B,A+B) range format of GPSS does not allow an even number of points. Therefore, the range from 10 to 25 specified in the problem statement cannot be obtained.

the RELEASE block where the facility SRVR is freed. The transaction then continues to the TABULATE block (line 21) which causes the transaction's transit time to be recorded as prescribed in table TISYS. The transaction is then destroyed at the TERMINATE block (line 22).

The second segment of the model is used to control the duration of the simulation. The GENERATE block (line 26) creates a transaction at time 480. This transaction continues to the TERMINATE block (line 27) where it is destroyed and reduces the termination counter by 1. The termination counter was initially set to 1 on the START card (line 31); hence, the transaction arrival causes the simulation to stop at time 480. The timing segment performs the same function as entering a value for TTFIN on the INITIALIZE statement in SLAM.

Although this example employs only a small subset of the GPSS blocks, it does illustrate the general modeling framework of GPSS. The simplicity of the block orientation of GPSS has made it one of the more popular discrete simulation languages. The commonly cited disadvantages of the language are the lack of a floating point capability, the difficult procedures for sampling from non-uniform distributions, and long computer execution times.

12.3   Q-GERT

Q-GERT is a network oriented simulation language developed by Pritsker (18). GERT is an acronym for Graphical Evaluation and Review Technique. The Q is appended to indicate that queueing systems can be modeled in graphic form. A fundamental contribution of Q-GERT is its method for graphically modeling systems in a manner that permits direct computer analysis with the Q-GERT Analysis Program.

Q-GERT employs an activity-on-branch network philosophy in which a branch represents an activity that models a processing time or delay. Nodes are used to separate branches and are used to model milestones, decision points, and queues. A Q-GERT network consists of nodes and branches. Flowing through the network are entities referred to as transactions. Different types of nodes are included in Q-GERT to allow for the modeling of complex queueing situations and project management systems.

The number of node types in Q-GERT is ten. This small number is possible because the Q-GERT philosophy is to add or combine functions at nodes when they are required. In addition, Q-GERT is designed to facilitate the use of

FORTRAN programming inserts at both nodes and in activities. A list of the node types is given below:

Node Type	Description
SOURCE	Create transactions
REGULAR	Accumulate transactions
STATISTICS	Accumulate transactions and collect statistics
SINK	Accumulate transactions, collect statistics, terminate a run
QUEUE	Determine disposition of transaction: hold or route to a server
SELECT	Determine disposition of transaction and/or server
MATCH	Match transactions in QUEUE nodes with the same attribute value and route transactions when a match occurs
ALLOCATE	Allocate resources to transactions waiting for resources in QUEUE nodes
FREE	Make resources available to be allocated
ALTER	Change capacity of resources

As an example of combining functions, note that QUEUE nodes are used in conjunction with SELECT, MATCH, and ALLOCATE nodes to model specific operations.

As in SLAM, attributes are used to characterize transactions (entities). Attribute values can be assigned at any node. Activity durations are prescribed by a distribution type and a parameter set number. The parameter set includes a specification for a random number stream.

SLAM employs the same activity-on-branch network philosophy as Q-GERT. Hence, the procedures employed for constructing Q-GERT simulation models are essentially the same as those described for constructing SLAM network models. The modeler combines the Q-GERT network elements into a network model that pictorially represents the system of interest. This network model is then transcribed into input records for interpretation and processing by the Q-GERT Analysis Program.

Each node in Q-GERT is assigned a node number. A node is referenced by its node number similar to the use of node labels in SLAM. Except for SELECT, ALLOCATE, and MATCH nodes, node-to-node transfers of transactions in Q-GERT are defined by explicitly including the activity which connects the node pair. The start and end node number of the activity is included in the activity description. For this reason, input statements can be arranged in any order. Note that this procedure differs significantly from that employed in SLAM, where the order in which the network elements are inputted defines the transaction flow sequence. Although the network description cards can be inputted in any order, additional activities are required to define the transaction flow sequence. The node number approach also allows subnetworks to be defined and edited in Q-GERT.

In Q-GERT, the type of branching associated with the activities emanating from a node is specified on the node as opposed to the activities. Hence, all emanating activities must be of the same branching class. Four classes of branching are provided in Q-GERT and include: deterministic; probabilistic; conditional, take-first; and conditional, take-all. SLAM has generalized the branching concepts of Q-GERT by permitting deterministic, probabilistic, and conditional, take-M branching to be associated with activities emanating from the same node.

In addition to the design differences discussed above, there are also functional differences between the nodes in Q-GERT and SLAM. However, the modeler familiar with the network orientation of SLAM should have little difficulty learning and applying the node vocabulary of Q-GERT.

Recent developments associated with Q-GERT involve the use of a graphics terminal for constructing Q-GERT networks. A developmental program has been written that allows Q-GERT networks to be drawn directly on a computer terminal screen. The networks can be edited and the input for the Q-GERT Analysis Program can be automatically prepared based on the network drawn. In addition, a display of a simulation run consisting of transactions flowing through the network can be requested. Such a display is extremely useful for understanding the model of the system. Continued developments involving the use of graphics associated with simulation models are expected.

12.4   OTHER PROCESS-ORIENTED LANGUAGES

In recent years, many process-oriented simulation languages that employ a statement approach have been developed. The best known of these languages is SIMULA which is a superset of ALGOL. SIMULA has many statements that make it attractive for performing discrete event simulation including advanced list processing capabilities. In addition, it has the capability to be extended and has recently been augmented to allow the combined modeling concepts of GASP IV and network techniques of GERT to be used within the SIMULA framework (30). Little use of SIMULA has been made in the United States although it has received considerable attention in Europe. For detailed discussions of SIMULA, we refer the reader to Hills (11), Birtwistle (2, and Franta (9).

A recently developed process-oriented simulation language is SIMPL/I (28,29). SIMPL/I extends the PL/I statement set and includes specific statement types for implementing the simulation of entities flowing through processes. SIMPL/I employs a preprocessor that translates a SIMPL/I program into the corresponding PL/I code. Since little use has been reported of SIMPL/I, we will not describe its statement types in this text.

Other process-oriented languages that have been developed are: SOL (10); ASPOL (1); INS (21); and BOSS (22). In addition, process-oriented features have been added to SIMSCRIPT (23) and GASP (31).

12.5   GASP IV

GASP IV is a FORTRAN based simulation language that provides a conceptual framework and supporting routines for writing discrete event, continuous, and combined discrete event-continuous simulations (19). A historical perspective of GASP developments is given by Pritsker (17). The discrete event and continuous orientations of SLAM are largely based on GASP IV. However, there are a number of specific differences in the event and combined event-continuous features of the languages. In this section, we only describe the event modeling features of GASP IV relative to SLAM.

Discrete event models are written in GASP IV in a fashion similar to event models written in SLAM. The modeler codes a short main program, subroutine EVNTS(I) which is analogous to subroutine EVENT(I) in SLAM, and the event subprograms which define the mathematical-logical relationships for processing the changes in state corresponding to each event type. In addition, the user-coded subroutines INTLC and OTPUT may also be required. Their function is identical to their use in SLAM.

The principal differences between GASP IV and SLAM event models are the procedures and supporting routines used for file manipulations, event scheduling, and statistics collection. We present these differences as a guide to GASP IV users who may wish to use SLAM.

In GASP IV, the attributes of an entity are not included as an argument to the filing routines, but are passed through the ATRIB array in the GASP IV COMMON block. In addition, entities in a file must be referenced by their location in the arrays

NSET/QSET and not by their rank in the file. The variables MFE(I) and MLE(I) point to the location of the first and last entity in file I, respectively. Entities are filed into file IFILE using the statement

CALL FILEM(IFILE)

In a similar fashion, the entity at location NTRY is removed from file IFILE using the statement

CALL RMOVE(NTRY,IFILE)

For example, the following statement would remove the first entry from file 2

CALL RMOVE(MFE(2),2)

In GASP IV, the event calendar is designated as file number 1. Hence, all user files are assigned file numbers 2 or greater. In addition, for entries which are filed onto the event calendar, ATRIB(1) is defined as the event time and ATRIB(2) is defined as the event code of the associated event. User-prescribed attributes for events are assigned to attributes numbered 3 and above. Thus, an event is scheduled by setting ATRIB(1) to the time of the event and ATRIB(2) to the event code and filing the entity in file 1. For example, the following statements would be used to schedule an event of type 2 to occur after a delay of 10 time units:

ATRIB(1) = TNOW + 10.
ATRIB(2) = 2.
CALL FILEM(1)

The analogous operation in SLAM would be performed by the statement CALL SCHDL(2,10.,ATRIB).

There are two subroutines which are employed in GASP IV models for collecting statistics which have been eliminated in the design of SLAM. Subroutine TIMST(X,T,ISTAT) is used in GASP IV to record time-persistent statistics on variable ISTAT. In SLAM, this function is automatically performed by the executive control program. Subroutine HISTO(X,IHIST) is employed in GASP IV models for recording the value X for histogram number IHIST. Again, this function has been automated within SLAM.

There are other specific differences between event models coded in SLAM and GASP IV in addition to those mentioned above. For example, the input formats for the simulation control cards have been changed. Another difference between the languages is the procedure used for specifying parameters for sampling from distributions. In GASP IV, the parameter values are read as data and are stored in the array PPARM. These values are then referenced by an index number included as an argument to the function routine. In SLAM, the parameter values are included directly as arguments to the function routine.

With regard to continuous and combined features, SLAM has eliminated the need for a state-conditions (SCOND) subroutine and a save state variable (SSAVE) subroutine by providing input statements to perform their equivalent functions. Overall, the features of GASP IV and SLAM are sufficiently similar that the modeler familiar with one language should have little difficulty learning to write models in the other. The same is true for GASP_PL/I, the PL/I version of GASP IV.

There have been several recent developments that have enhanced the capabilities of GASP. GASP IV/E is an interactive version of GASP IV that allows simulation data to be displayed during a run upon request of the analyst (24). The analyst can then interrupt the simulation and either change the simulation model or become part of the simulation by acting out the part of a decision-maker. This latter mode of operation corresponds to a nonprogrammed event.

Another development is GASP V (3) which expands the continuous capabilities of GASP IV. The new features in GASP V involve the inclusion of different integration algorithms which can be user-selected; procedures for handling partial differential equations; and logic, memory, and generator functions. Examples of logic functions are input switches, flipflops, and gates. Memory functions included are hysteresis and delays and generator functions for step, ramp, inpulse, and dead spaces are available. These functions can be added to SLAM if the need arises.

12.6   SIMSCRIPT II

SIMSCRIPT II is a computer language developed by Kiviat, Villanueva, and Markowitz (12). A history of SIMSCRIPT developments is given by Markowitz (15). The language is divided into five levels.

Level 1: A simple teaching language designed to introduce programming concepts to nonprogrammers.

Level 2: Statement types that are comparable in power to FORTRAN.

Level 3: Statement types that are comparable in power to ALGOL or PL/I.

Level 4: Statement types that provide a structure for modeling using entity, attribute, and set concepts.

Level 5: Statement types for time advance, event processing, generation of samples, and accumulation and analysis of simulation generated data.

One of the principal appeals of SIMSCRIPT† as a programming and simulation language is its English-like and free-form syntax. Programs written in SIMSCRIPT are easy to read and tend to be self-documenting.

The discrete simulation modeling framework of SIMSCRIPT is primarily event-oriented. The modeling frameworks of SIMSCRIPT and the event portion of SLAM are conceptually similar. In SIMSCRIPT, the state of the system is defined by entities, their associated attributes, and by logical groupings of entities referred to as sets. Thus, the notion of a set in SIMSCRIPT is analogous to a file in SLAM. The dynamic structure of the system is described by defining the changes that occur at event times.

In SIMSCRIPT, two types of entities are considered. An entity which remains throughout a simulation is referred to as a permanent entity. In contrast, the term temporary entity is used to refer to entities which are created and destroyed during execution of the simulation. In the latter case, computer storage space is automatically allocated and freed during execution of the simulation as individual entities are created and destroyed. In a queueing system, each server would be modeled as a permanent entity, and the customers which arrive and depart the system would be modeled as temporary entities. The storage for permanent entities can be considered to correspond to a user-defined array in SLAM and the storage for temporary entities as the SLAM filing array storage.

In SIMSCRIPT, the attributes of entities are separately named, not numbered, thereby enhancing model description. For example, we could define a temporary entity named CUSTOMER which has an attribute named MARK.TIME‡ Sets are also named as opposed to numbered, further enhancing the model description. For example, a set containing customers waiting for service could be named QUEUE.

A SIMSCRIPT simulation model consists of a preamble, a main program, and event subprograms. The preamble is not part of the executable program and is used to define the elements of a model. The preamble also includes declarative statements for defining all variable types and arrays. SLAM COMMON and DIMENSION statements correspond to the SIMSCRIPT preamble.

---

† We will hereafter denote SIMSCRIPT II as simply SIMSCRIPT.
‡ Names in SIMSCRIPT can be of any length, but cannot contain blanks. The period is a valid SIMSCRIPT character and is frequently used in place of blanks in names.

The main program is used for initializing variables, scheduling the initial occurrence of events, and starting the simulation. The event subprograms are used for defining the logic associated with processing each event in the model. The calls to the event subprograms are scheduled by the user but executed by the SIMSCRIPT control program. These SIMSCRIPT subprograms are similar to their SLAM counterparts.

One of the primary functions of the preamble is to define the static structure of the model by prescribing the names of permanent and temporary entities, their associated attributes, and set relationships. These are declared in one or more EVERY statements by using attribute name clauses, set ownership clauses, and membership clauses. These clauses have the following form where capitalized words indicate required terms and lower case words indicate that user-employed variables are to be used.

> EVERY entity name HAS attribute name list
> EVERY entity name OWNS set name list
> EVERY entity name BELONGS TO set name list

Several clauses can be combined within a single EVERY statement by separating each clause by a comma. If desired, a clause can be preceded by the word MAY or CAN. Also, the items in an attribute or set name list must be separated by commas and one of the words A, AN, THE, or SOME. The following is an example of the EVERY statement:

> EVERY CUSTOMER HAS A MARK.TIME AND MAY BELONG TO THE QUEUE

This statement specifies that each entity in the entity class named CUSTOMER has an attribute named MARK.TIME and that these entities may at one time or another during the simulation be a member of the set named QUEUE. Each set employed in a model must be declared as being owned by either an entity or the system. An example of the latter is the following:

> THE SYSTEM OWNS A QUEUE AND HAS A STATUS

This preamble statement defines the existence of a system owned set named QUEUE and a system attribute named STATUS.

A collection of EVERY statements can be used to define either temporary or permanent entities. Temporary entities are defined by preceding the collection of EVERY statements with the statement

> TEMPORARY ENTITIES

Similarly, permanent entities are defined by preceding the collection of EVERY statements with the statement

PERMANENT ENTITIES

EVERY statements are also used to define event names and event attributes by preceding the statements with the statement

EVENT NOTICES

For example, an event named DEPARTURE with an attribute named SERVER could be defined by the following statements

EVENT NOTICES
EVERY DEPARTURE HAS A SERVER

The preamble is also used to define global variables through the use of the DEFINE statement which has the following form:

DEFINE variable name AS A variable type.

Examples of the DEFINE statement are shown below:

DEFINE X AS A REAL VARIABLE
DEFINE Y AS A 2-DIMENSIONAL ARRAY

Another variation of the DEFINE statement is

DEFINE word TO MEAN string of words

In this case whenever the specified word is seen by the SIMSCRIPT compiler, the string of words is automatically substituted for it before the statement is compiled. For example, if the statement

DEFINE BUSY TO MEAN 1

is included in the preamble, then each occurrence of the word BUSY in the program is compiled as the numeral 1. Thus, the DEFINE statement can be used in a fashion similar to the EQUIVALENCE statement in FORTRAN.

Another function of the preamble is to define variables for which statistics are to be collected. This is accomplished using the TALLY and ACCUMULATE statements. The TALLY statement causes observation statistics to be automatically collected on a specified variable. For example, the following statement would cause the variable AVE.TIME to be calculated as the mean of the variable TIME.IN.-SYSTEM:

TALLY AVG.TIME AS THE MEAN OF TIME.IN.SYSTEM

SIMSCRIPT would automatically collect an observation at each assignment of a value to the variable TIME.IN.SYSTEM during the execution of the program. In contrast, SLAM requires the user to explicitly include a call to COLCT for this purpose. Time-persistent statistics are obtained in a similar fashion by use of the ACCUMULATE statement. For example, the following statement would compute the variable AVG.UTIL as the time-persistent average of the variable STATUS

ACCUMULATE AVG.UTIL AS THE MEAN OF STATUS

Hence, the use of the ACCUMULATE statement in the SIMSCRIPT preamble is analogous to the use of the TIMST control card in SLAM. In addition to the MEAN, other statistical quantities such as the VARIANCE, MINIMUM, MAXI-MUM, can also be recorded using the TALLY and ACCUMULATE statements.

Once the description of the static structure is completed by writing the preamble, the next step in writing a SIMSCRIPT program is to code the main program and event subprograms. These are coded by using the general purpose programming statements of SIMSCRIPT in conjunction with special statements for creating and destroying entities, manipulating entities between sets, obtaining random samples, and scheduling events. These statements are similar in function to the SLAM subprograms for event modeling.

Temporary entities are created within the execution portion of a SIMSCRIPT program by the statement (braces are used to indicate options)

CREATE $\begin{Bmatrix} A \\ AN \end{Bmatrix}$ entity name.

For example, we can create a CUSTOMER entity as follows

CREATE A CUSTOMER

When this statement is executed, SIMSCRIPT searches for a block of space large enough to store the entity record that includes the attributes of the entity. Note, however, that the existence of the entity class named CUSTOMER must be defined in the preamble portion of the program. Temporary entities are destroyed in a similar fashion. For example, the statement

DESTROY THE CUSTOMER

causes the record corresponding to the entity CUSTOMER to be deleted and its storage space to be released. Attributes of entities are assigned and referenced by including the name of the entity in parentheses following the name of the attribute. For example, the following statement would assign the current simulated time in days, denoted by the SIMSCRIPT variable TIME.V, to the attribute MARK.TIME of the entity CUSTOMER:

LET MARK.TIME(CUSTOMER) = TIME.V

SIMSCRIPT provides a number of statements for filing, locating, and removing temporary entities from sets. An entity can be filed into a set by using the statement

FILE entity name IN set name

For example, we could file the entity CUSTOMER in the set named QUEUE using the statement

FILE THE CUSTOMER IN THE QUEUE

Entities can be removed in a similar fashion using the statement

REMOVE $\left\{ \begin{array}{l} \text{FIRST} \\ \text{LAST} \end{array} \right\}$ entity name FROM set name

For example, we can remove the first CUSTOMER from the set QUEUE using the statement

REMOVE THE FIRST CUSTOMER FROM THE QUEUE

These set manipulation statements are analogous to subroutine calls to FILEM and RMOVE.

Event scheduling in SIMSCRIPT is accomplished using a statement of the form

SCHEDULE $\left\{ \begin{array}{l} \text{A} \\ \text{AN} \end{array} \right\}$ event name IN variable $\left\{ \begin{array}{l} \text{MINUTES} \\ \text{HOURS} \\ \text{DAYS} \end{array} \right\}$

where variable can be a constant, a variable, or any of the SIMSCRIPT provided random sampling functions. The following is an example.

SCHEDULE AN ARRIVAL IN EXPONENTIAL.F(20.,1) MINUTES

When attributes are associated with an event, the names of the variables specifying the attribute values are included in the SCHEDULE statement as follows:

SCHEDULE $\left\{ \begin{array}{l} \text{A} \\ \text{AN} \end{array} \right\}$ event name GIVEN variables IN variable $\left\{ \begin{array}{l} \text{MINUTES} \\ \text{HOURS} \\ \text{DAYS} \end{array} \right\}$

When passing the attributes of an entity to an event, it is necessary only to pass the name of the entity, which serves as a pointer to the list of attributes associated with the entity. For example, the attributes of the entity CUSTOMER can be passed to the event DEPARTURE as follows:

SCHEDULE A DEPARTURE GIVEN CUSTOMER IN
    UNIFORM.F(10.,25.,1) MINUTES

Within the DEPARTURE event, reference to the attribute MARK.TIME of the entity is made using MARK.TIME(CUSTOMER) where CUSTOMER is a local integer variable containing the pointer to the location of the attributes of the entity CUSTOMER. There is an obvious correspondence between the SCHEDULE statement in SIMSCRIPT and subroutine SCHDL in the event-oriented portion of SLAM.

As an illustration of the simulation features of SIMSCRIPT, we will present a model of the single channel queueing system which was used in Chapter 7 to illustrate the event modeling orientation of SLAM and for which a GPSS model was built. Customers arrive to the system, possibly wait, undergo service, and then exit the system. The interarrival time is exponentially distributed with mean 20. and the service time is uniformly distributed between 10. and 25. Statistics are desired on the mean queue length, utilization of the server, and time in the system.

The SIMSCRIPT coding for this example is shown in Figure 12-3. The model consists of a PREAMBLE, MAIN program, ARRIVAL event, DEPARTURE event, and STOP.SIMULATION event.

```
1       PREAMBLE
2           THE SYSTEM OWNS A QUEUE AND HAS A STATUS
3           TEMPORARY ENTITIES
4               EVERY CUSTOMER HAS A MARK.TIME AND MAY BELONG TO THE QUEUE
5           EVENT NOTICES INCLUDE ARRIVAL AND STOP.SIMULATION
6               EVERY DEPARTURE HAS A SERVER
7           DEFINE BUSY TO MEAN 1
8           DEFINE IDLE TO MEAN 0
9           DEFINE TIME.IN.SYSTEM AS A REAL VARIABLE
10          TALLY NO.CUSTOMERS AS THE NUMBER,AVG.TIME AS THE MEAN, AND
11          VAR.TIME AS THE VARIANCE OF TIME.IN.SYSTEM
12          ACCUMULATE AVG.UTIL AS THE MEAN, AND VAR.UTIL AS THE VARIANCE OF
13          STATUS
14          ACCUMULATE AVE.QUEUE.LENGTH AS THE MEAN, AND VAR.QUEUE.LENGTH AS
15          THE VARIANCE OF N.QUEUE
16      END


1       MAIN
2           LET STATUS=IDLE
3           SCHEDULE AN ARRIVAL NOW
4           SCHEDULE A STOP.SIMULATION IN 8 HOURS
5           START SIMULATION
6       END
```

Figure 12-3 SIMSCRIPT II coding for single-channel queueing problem.

```
1      EVENT ARRIVAL
2          SCHEDULE AN ARRIVAL IN EXPONENTIAL.F(20.,1) MINUTES
3          CREATE A CUSTOMER
4          LET MARK.TIME(CUSTOMER)=TIME.V
5          IF STATUS=BUSY,
6              FILE THE CUSTOMER IN THE QUEUE
7              RETURN
8          ELSE
9              LET STATUS=BUSY
10             SCHEDULE A DEPARTURE GIVEN CUSTOMER IN UNIFORM.F(10.,25.,1)
11             MINUTES
12             RETURN
13     END


1      EVENT DEPARTURE GIVEN CUSTOMER
2          DEFINE CUSTOMER AS AN INTEGER VARIABLE
3          LET TIME.IN.SYSTEM=1440.*(TIME.V-MARK.TIME(CUSTOMER))
4          DESTROY THE CUSTOMER
5          IF THE QUEUE IS EMPTY
6              LET STATUS=IDLE
7              RETURN
8          ELSE
9              REMOVE THE FIRST CUSTOMER FROM THE QUEUE
10             SCHEDULE A DEPARTURE GIVEN CUSTOMER IN UNIFORM.F(10.,25.,1)
11             MINUTES
12             RETURN
13     END


1      EVENT STOP.SIMULATION
2          START NEW PAGE
3          SKIP 5 LINES
4          PRINT 1 LINE THUS
               SINGLE CHANNEL QUEUE EXAMPLE
6          SKIP 4 LINES
7          PRINT 3 LINES WITH NO.CUSTOMERS, AVG.TIME, AND VAR.TIME THUS
       NUMBER OF CUSTOMERS =        ********
       AVERAGE TIME IN SYSTEM =        ****.***
       VARIANCE OF TIME IN SYSTEM = ****.***
11         SKIP 4 LINES
12         PRINT 2 LINES WITH AVG.UTIL AND VAR.UTIL THUS
       AVERAGE SERVER UTILIZATION = ****.***
       VARIANCE OF UTILIZATION =        ****.***
15         SKIP 4 LINES
16         PRINT 2 LINES WITH AVE.QUEUE.LENGTH AND VAR.QUEUE.LENGTH THUS
       AVERAGE QUEUE LENGTH =        ****.***
       VARIANCE OF QUEUE LENGTH =        ****.***
19         STOP
20     END
```

Figure 12-3   (continued).

The PREAMBLE defines a system owned set named QUEUE which represents the waiting area for the server. The status of the server is maintained as the system attribute STATUS where 1 denotes busy and 0 denotes idle. Customers are modeled as temporary entities named CUSTOMER which have an attribute named

MARK.TIME. This attribute is used to record the arrival time of the customer to the system.

The MAIN program initializes the system attribute STATUS to IDLE. The first ARRIVAL event is scheduled to occur at time 0, and the END.OF.SIMULATION event is scheduled to occur in 8 hours. The statement START SIMULATION then causes control to transfer to the SIMSCRIPT timing routine.

The ARRIVAL event program defines the logic associated with processing the arrival of a customer to the system. The first action is to schedule the next arrival to occur at the current time plus the interarrival time (line 2). The entity representing the current arriving customer is then created (line 3), and its MARK.TIME attribute is set (line 4) to the current simulated time, TIME.V. The disposition of the arriving customer is based on the status of the server. If the server is busy, the CUSTOMER is filed in the set named QUEUE (line 6). Otherwise, the status of the server is set to busy (line 9) and the DEPARTURE event is scheduled (line 10-11). Note that the pointer to the CUSTOMER entity is passed as the attribute of the DEPARTURE event.

The DEPARTURE event defines the logic associated with the completion of service and departure of the CUSTOMER from the system. The event declaration statement (line 1) specifies that the attribute of the event is assigned to the local variable CUSTOMER. Since this attribute corresponds to a pointer to the entity CUSTOMER, it is necessary to define the local variable CUSTOMER as an integer variable (line 2). The variable TIME.IN.SYSTEM is set (line 3) to 1440 times the difference between the current simulated time, TIME.V, and the MARK.TIME attribute of the CUSTOMER. The conversion factor 1440 is used to convert the time from days to minutes. Note that the TALLY statement of the preamble (line 10-11) causes statistics on the number of observations, mean, and variance to be automatically recorded each time a value is assigned to TIME.IN.SYSTEM. The current CUSTOMER is then destroyed (line 4), thus freeing the storage space allocated to the entity. A test is then made on the state of the QUEUE. If the QUEUE is empty, the status of the server is set to idle (line 6). Otherwise, the first CUSTOMER is removed from the QUEUE (line 9) and the DEPARTURE event for this customer is scheduled (line 10-11).

The STOP.SIMULATION event displays the results for the simulation and returns control back to the main routine following the STOP statement (line 17). As the reader can observe from the coding, SIMSCRIPT provides flexible statement types for displaying output values.

This example illustrates only a subset of the programming features of SIMSCRIPT II. To make maximum use of the available features, the modeler should master Levels 1 through Level 4 of the language in addition to the simulation features (Level 5). In contrast, since the host language for event models in SLAM is FORTRAN which is usually known, only the simulation features need to be mastered.

As discussed previously, process-oriented capabilities have been added to SIM-SCRIPT (23). In addition, GASP IV combined discrete-continuous features have been incorporated into a recent version of the language that is referred to as C-SIMSCRIPT (7).

12.7   CONTINUOUS SIMULATION LANGUAGES

There are a number of simulation languages which have been specifically developed for continuous system simulation. In this section, we will describe a class of equation-oriented languages referred to as CSSL's which are useful for modeling systems described by differential equations. We will also discuss the DYNAMO language which was developed specifically for use with System Dynamics models.

12.7.1   Continuous System Simulation Languages

The family of languages which have been reasonably standardized by the Society for Computer Simulation's Continuous System Simulation Language Committee (26) are referred to as CSSL's. These languages provide a convenient equation-oriented format which allows the user to enter first order differential equations in a mathematical-like form. In contrast to SLAM continuous models, the user of CSSL's need not know FORTRAN.

Simulation models which are programmed using a CSSL employ a FORTRAN-like symbol convention. However, meaningful symbolic names can be assigned to state and derivative variables without the use of the EQUIVALENCE statement as employed in SLAM. In addition, special operators are provided for integrating derivatives to obtain state values as well as other useful functions. The equations in the model are automatically sorted by the CSSL for execution in the proper procedural order. The languages normally provide the modeler with a choice of an integration algorithm.

Examples of CSSL languages are CSMP III (4), CSSL III (5), CSSL IV, ASCL (16), and DARE-P (14). As a result of the standardization provided by the CSSL Committee, these languages are similar with differences mainly associated with input and output formatting and special library functions. The CSMP III language is available for IBM 360 and 370 series computers and the CSSL III language is available for the CDC 6000 and 7000 series computers. A special continuous language, MIMIC, was also designed specifically for CDC computers (6). Both CSSL IV and ASCL represent improved versions of CSSL III. DARE-P is a relatively new CSSL derived from DARE III-B. An advantage of the DARE-P system is that the processor is written entirely in ANSI FORTRAN IV and is therefore machine independent. Examples of the use of these languages would be similar to the SLAM continuous examples and, hence, we will not illustrate their coding practices.

Table 12-3 Comparison of DYNAMO and SLAM statement forms.

DYNAMO Statement	SLAM Statement
1. PER = 52	1. PER = 52.
2. AID = 6	2. AID = 6.
3. ALF = (1000) (RR1)	3. AIF = 1000.★ RRI
4. TIS.K = IAR.K + IAD.K + IAF.K	4. TIS = IAR + IAD + IAF
5. SNE.K = (SIH)SIN((2PI) (TIME.K)/PER)	5. SNE = SIH ★ SIN(6.28318 ★ TNOW/PER)
6. UOR.K = UOR.J + (DT) (RRR.JK − SSR.JK)	6a. SS(1) = SSL(1) + DTNOW ★ (RR − SSR)
	6b. SS(1) = SS(1) + DTNOW ★ (RRR − SSR) if NNEQD = 0
	6c. DD(1) = RRR − SSR
7. RSR.K = RSR.J + (DT) (1/DRR) (RRR.JK − RSR.J)	7a. DD(3) = (1./DRR) ★ (RRR − RSR)
	7b. SS(3) = SSL(3) + DTNOW ★ (RRR − RSR)/DDR
8. STP.K = STEP(STH,STT)	8. IF(TNOW.GT.STT) STP = STH
9. SSR.KL = CLIP (STR.K,NIR.K, NIR.K,STR.K)	9. SSR = STR IF (NIR.LT.STR)SSR = NIR
10. Y.K = SMOOTH(Q.JK,SMTM)	10a. CALL GDLAY (10,10,Q,SMTM)
	10b. SS(10) = SSL(10) + DTNOW ★(Q − SSL(10))/ SMTM and Y = SS(10)
11. Y.K = DLINF1(X.K,TRX)	11a. CALL GDLAY (11,11,X,TRX)
	11b. DD(11) = (X − S(11))/TRX
	11c. SS(11) = SSL(11) + DTNOW ★(X − SSL(11))/ TRX and Y = SS(11)
12. PSR.KL = DELAY3 (PDR.JK,DCR)	12. CALL GDLAY (18,20,PDR,DCR) and PSR = SS(20)
13. Y.K = DLINF3(X.K,TRX)	13. CALL GDLAY (15,17,X,TRX) and Y = SS(17)

12.7.2   DYNAMO

Systems Dynamics, as developed by Forrester, is a problem solving approach to complex problems which emphasizes the structural aspects of models of systems (8). State variables, called *levels,* are defined in difference equation form and may be nonlinear. Nonlinearities are also included in the model through the use of table functions, delays, and clipping operations. The DYNAMO programming language (20) was developed to provide a language for analyzing Systems Dynamics models. DYNAMO uses a fixed step size, Euler-type integration algorithm to evaluate the level variables over time.

The translation of DYNAMO statements into SLAM or FORTRAN is a straightforward process (3). A comparison of statement forms is shown in Table 12-3. In DYNAMO, variables that are a function of time are indicated by a period following the variable name and subscripts denoting time following the period. Single letters denote points in time and double letters denote that the value holds for an interval. Three points in time are used, which are represented by the letters J, K, and L. The intervals between these points are represented by JK and KL. The length of the interval is fixed and defined by the variable DT. Since Systems Dynamics models can be simulated in SLAM, GASP IV, and the CSSL languages, we recommend using these general languages for this purpose.

12.8   CHAPTER SUMMARY

In this chapter, we have described the basic features of simulation languages in relationship to the modeling framework of SLAM. There are many additional programming details which must be mastered in each language, and only a thorough reading of the latest language manuals and much practice can provide such mastery.

The selection of a simulation language is frequently based on knowledge and availability as opposed to a formal comparison of language features. However, if the frequent use of simulation is anticipated, then a comprehensive evaluation of the available languages and anticipated modeling needs is warranted. Shannon provides a review and diagrams a procedure for making such an evaluation (27). Table 12-4 is a summary of important factors to consider in comparing simulation languages.

Table 12-4 Features on which to evaluate a simulation language.

TRAINING REQUIRED	EASE OF LEARNING THE LANGUAGE
	EASE OF CONCEPTUALIZING SIMULATION PROBLEMS
CODING CONSIDERATION	EASE OF CODING INCLUDING RANDOM SAMPLING AND NUMERICAL INTEGRATION
	DEGREE TO WHICH CODE IS SELF-DOCUMENTING
PORTABILITY	LANGUAGE AVAILABILITY ON OTHER OR NEW COMPUTERS
FLEXIBILITY	DEGREE TO WHICH LANGUAGE SUPPORTS DIFFERENT MODELING CONCEPTS
PROCESSING CONSIDERATIONS	BUILT-IN STATISTICS GATHERING CAPABILITIES
	LIST PROCESSING CAPABILITIES
	ABILITY TO ALLOCATE CORE
	EASE OF PRODUCING STANDARD REPORTS
	EASE OF PRODUCING USER-TAILORED REPORTS
DEBUGGING & RELIABILITY	EASE OF DEBUGGING
	RELIABILITY OF COMPILERS, SUPPORT SYSTEMS, & DOCUMENTATION
RUN-TIME CONSIDERATIONS	COMPILATION SPEED
	EXECUTION SPEED

12.9   EXERCISES

12-1. Build a GPSS block model of the inspection and adjustment stations described in Example 6-2. Embellishment: Build SIMSCRIPT, Q-GERT and SIMULA models for Example 6-2.

12.2. Discuss the similarities and differences between the following: The TERMINATE block of GPSS and the TERMINATE node of SLAM; the CREATE statement in SIMSCRIPT and the CREATE node in SLAM; the SEIZE block of GPSS and the AWAIT node in SLAM; and the ACCUMULATE statement in SIMSCRIPT and the ACCUMULATE node in SLAM.

12-3. Discuss the symbol or statement type that causes simulated time to change in SLAM, GPSS, GASP IV, SIMSCRIPT, Q-GERT, a CSSL, and DYNAMO.

12-4. Grade any six languages on each row of Table 12-4 using the scale: E = Excellent; G = Good; F = Fair; P = Poor; and NA = Not Applicable.

12-5. Discuss the organizational structure of simulation languages and how it supports and/or impedes the development and use of simulation models.

12-6. Modify the SIMSCRIPT II queueing example to include two parallel servers. Assume that the service time for each server is uniformly distributed between 15 and 30 minutes and that the selection of free servers is made randomly.

12.10 REFERENCES

1. *A Simulation Process-Oriented Language (ASPOL)*, Publication No. 17314200, Control Data Corporation, Sunnyvale, CA., 1972.

2. Birtwistle, G., O. J. Dahl, B. Myhrhaug, and K. Nygaard, *SIMULA BEGIN*, Auerbach, 1973.

3. Cellier, F. and A. E. Blitz, "GASP V: A Universal Simulation Package," *Proceedings, IFAC Conference*, 1976.

4. *Continuous System Modeling Program III and Graphic Feature, Program No. 5734-X59 Manual*, IBM Corporation, New York, 1972.

5. *Continuous System Simulation Language, Version 3, User's Guide*, Control Data Corporation, Sunnyvale, California, 1971.

6. *CONTROL DATA MIMIC—A Digital Simulation Language Reference Manual*, Publication No. 44610400, Revision D, Control Data Corporation, Minneapolis, Minn., 1970.

7. Delfosse, C. M., *Continuous Simulation and Combined Simulation in SIMSCRIPT II.5*, CACI, Inc., Arlington, VA., 1976.

8. Forrester, J. W., *Principles of Systems*, Wright-Allen Press, 1971.

9. Franta, W. R., *The Process View of Simulation*, North Holland, 1977.

10. Gordon, G., *The Application of GPSS V to Discrete Systems Simulation*, Prentice-Hall, 1975.

11. Hills, P. R., *An Introduction to Simulation Using SIMULA*, Publication No. S55, Norwegian Computing Center, Oslo, 1973.

12. Kiviat, P. J., R. Villanueva, and H. Markowitz, *The SIMSCRIPT II Programming Language*, Prentice-Hall, 1969.

13. Knuth, D. and J. L. McNeley, "SOL-A Symbolic Language for General Purpose Systems Simulation," *IEEE Transactions on Electronic Computers*, August 1964, pp. 401-408.

14. Korn, G. A. and J. V. Wait, *Digital Continuous-System Simulation*, Prentice-Hall, 1978.

15. Markowitz, H., "SIMSCRIPT", *Encyclopedia of Computer Science and Technology*, J. Belzer, A. G. Holzman, and A. Kent, Editors, Marcel Dekker, Inc., 1978.

16. Mitchell, E. E. L. and J. S. Gauthier, "Advanced Continuous Simulation Language (ACSL)," *Simulation,* Vol. 25, 1976, pp. 72-78.

17. Pritsker, A. A. B., "GASP", *Encyclopedia of Computer Science and Technology,* J. Belzer, A. G. Holzman, and A. Kent, Editors, Vol. 8, Marcel Dekker, Inc., 1977.

18. Pritsker, A. A. B., *Modeling and Analysis Using Q-GERT Networks,* Halsted Press and Pritsker & Associates, Inc., 1977.

19. Pritsker, A. A. B., *The GASP IV Simulation Language,* John Wiley, 1974.

20. Pugh, A. L., III, *DYNAMO II User's Manual,* M.I.T. Press, 1970.

21. Roberts, S. D. and T. E. Sadlowski, "INS: Integrated Network Simulator," *Proceedings, Winter Computer Simulation Conference,* Sacramento, CA., 1975, pp. 575-586.

22. Roth, P. F., "The BOSS Simulator—An Introduction," *Proceedings, Fourth Conference on Applications of Simulation,* New York, 1970, pp. 244-250.

23. Russell, E. C., *Simulating with Processes and Resources in SIMSCRIPT II.5,* CACI, Inc., Arlington, VA., 1974.

24. Sabuda, J., F. H. Grant, III and A. A. B. Pritsker, *The GASP IV/E User's Manual,* Pritsker & Associates, Inc., West Lafayette, IN, 1978.

25. Schriber, T., *Simulation Using GPSS,* John Wiley, 1974.

26. SCi Software Committee, "The SCi Continuous-System Simulation Language," *Simulation,* Vol. 9, 1967, pp. 281-303.

27. Shannon, R. E., *Systems Simulation: The Art and The Science,* Prentice-Hall, 1975.

28. SIMPL/1 Operations Guide, SH 19-5038-0, IBM Corporation, New York: June 1972.

29. SIMPL/1 Program Reference Manual, SH19-5060-0, IBM Corporation, New York: June 1972.

30. Sol, H. G., SIMULA(TION) in the Analysis and Design of Information Systems," *Proceedings, Simulation '77,* ACTA Press, 1977, pp. 67-71.

31. Washam, W., GASPPI: GASP IV With Process Interaction Capabilities, unpublished MS Thesis, Purdue University, West Lafayette, IN, May 1976.

CHAPTER 13

Statistical Aspects of Simulation

13.1   STATISTICAL QUESTIONS FACING SIMULATORS

A simulation model portrays the dynamic behavior of a system over time. A model is built to provide results that resemble the outputs from the real system. Thus, the statistical analysis of the outputs from a simulation is similar to the statistical analysis of the data obtained from an actual system. The main difference is that the simulation analyst has more control over the running of the simulation model. Thus he can design experiments to obtain the specific output data necessary to answer the pertinent questions relating to the system under study.

There are two types of questions that relate to the outputs of simulation models:

1. What is the inherent variability associated with the simulation model?
2. What can be inferred about the performance of the real system from the use of the simulation model?

The first question relates to an understanding of the model and verifying that it performs as designed. The sensitivity of the model outputs to changes in input and model parameters is of interest. The precision of the outputs with respect to the inherent probability distributions employed is a basic part of this type of question.

The second question relates to the validity of the model and to its usefulness. The answer to the second type of question usually involves describing the system performance variables and making statistical computations related to the performance variables. Thus, tables and plots are constructed and viewed as if they were possible outputs from the real system. The computations and statistical analyses made are similar to those performed on data obtained from the real system. If decision-making is based on the probability of occurrence of an outcome or on an average value, such quantities are estimated from the simulation. If the variability of a random variable is important, it is estimated in the same manner as is done in the real system. This mode of simulation analysis is the most common one found in current applications. The fact that a single simulation run represents one sample or time series of a stochastic process is no more bothersome than the fact that an historical record represents only a single time series.

Answering the first type of question involves a detailed statistical analysis to obtain information on the precision and sensitivity of the model. Basically we explore the type of output that would be obtained if the simulation was performed again or run for a longer period of time. In doing this, we recognize that the simulation model is a stochastic one and that the random elements of the model will produce outputs that are probabilistic. This type of analysis can be unfamiliar to the industrial manager since the analysis involves advanced statistical terminology. In addition, more precise responses can be obtained by changing experimental conditions, for example, by performing more runs.

Because the second type of question is system and, hence, model specific, there are no general forms of analysis that can be recommended beyond the standard statistical procedures. The first type of question has been explored extensively, and we provide a description of the techniques that we have found to be useful in this chapter. We would have preferred to present these techniques in a handbook fashion, with detailed examples illustrating each procedure. However, the field has not progressed to such a point, and we can only describe the specific types of problems and current approaches to their resolution.

13.1.1   Definition of Terms

During a simulation, observations of variables of interest are to be recorded. Each potential observation is a time-based sample so that the observations can be considered to be random variables. To provide a standard set of terms, we make the following definitions regarding such random variables:

Let

I = the number of intervals, iterations, or individual observations. The word batch or interval will be used in a generic sense in the remainder of this chapter to mean any of the above.

T_i = ending time of the ith interval, $i=1,2,\ldots,I$ with T_o defined as the start time of the first interval.

N_i = the number of observations in the ith interval, $i = 1,2,\ldots,I$.

$X_i(t)$ = value of X at time t in interval i; $t \epsilon [T_{i-1},T_i]$.

$X_i(n)$ = value of X for nth observation in interval i; $n = 1,2,\ldots,N_i$.

Examples of $X_i(t)$ are the amount of inventory on-hand at time t and the number of customers in a system at time t. These variables were previously referred to as time-persistent variables. Examples of $X_i(n)$ are the time in the queue for the nth customer and the inventory on-hand when the nth receipt of an order arrives. These variables were previously referred to in conjunction with observations. Note that I, T_i, and N_i are usually treated as constants but in some instances may be random variables.

A *stochastic process*† is a set of ordered random variables. Thus $\{X_i(t), t \in [0,\infty)\}$ and $\{X_i(n), n=1,2, \ldots ,\infty\}$ are stochastic processes. A *realization* of a stochastic process is the set of sample paths assumed by the stochastic process. A *time series* is a finite realization of a stochastic process. In simulation terms, each run produces a time series for each stochastic process of interest.

The literature pertaining to stochastic processes and time series is extensive (1,55,9). Here, we only present a brief, informal background to introduce the topic.

A stochastic process is said to be *stationary* if the underlying joint distribution of the random variables in the process remains the same as time progresses, that is, if the random mechanisms producing the process are time invariant. This is referred to as the strictly stationary property (or *strong stationarity*). A special type of stationarity is referred to as *covariance stationarity* which requires all the means, μ_t, and covariances, R_{st}, of the random variables of the process to be finite and covariances separated by h time units to be equal, that is,

$$\mu_t = E[X_i(t)]$$
$$R_{st} = E[(X_i(s)-\mu_s)(X_i(t)-\mu_t)]$$

and

$$R_{st} = R_{rq} \quad \text{if } |t-s| = |q-r| = h$$

A covariance stationary process is also referred to as stationary in the wide sense or as mean square stationarity or as second-order stationarity.

Tests for the stationarity of a sequence are not well developed. The simplest and most frequently used evaluation is to consider the physics or underlying procedures associated with the phenomenon producing the data. If the basic physical factors which generate the phenomenon are time invariant then typically we accept the stationarity of the resulting data. If we believe trends or seasonality factors are involved, then differencing techniques are employed to remove such time-variant behavior.

An *ergodic* process is one from which the properties of the random variables in the process can be estimated from a single time series. A covariance stationary pro-

---

† In this text, we do not differentiate between a stochastic process and a stochastic sequence.

cess is ergodic in the mean and autocovariance if the following two conditions hold (39)

$$\lim_{T\to\infty} \frac{1}{T} \sum_{s=-T+1}^{T-1} R_s = 0$$

and

$$\lim_{T\to\infty} \frac{1}{T} \sum_{s=-T+1}^{T-1} R_s^2 = 0$$

The following important result regarding sequences of sample means is given by Parzen (55). A sequence of sample means, $\{\overline{X}_s, s=1,2,\ldots\infty\}$, may be shown to be ergodic if $Var[\overline{X}_s]\to 0$ as $s\to\infty$.

The significance of this result for simulation analysts is that the sample mean is approximately equal to the process mean if the variance of the sample mean approaches zero as the length of the sample increases.

13.2 IMPORTANCE OF THE VARIANCE OF THE SAMPLE MEAN, VAR[$\overline{X}_I$]

The sample mean is the average of the I random variables X_i as given below.

$$\overline{X}_I = \frac{\sum_{i=1}^{I} X_i}{I}$$

The notation, $\overline{X}_I$, is employed to indicate that the mean is a random variable that is based on the sum of I random variables. Typically, in simulation studies, we are interested in comparing $\overline{X}_I$ values for different alternatives using a test of hypothesis or in setting confidence limits on the value of $\overline{X}_I$ for a single alternative. To accomplish either of these tasks, it is necessary to calculate the variance of the sample mean denoted by $Var[\overline{X}_I]$. Extensive research has been performed on methods for estimating $Var[\overline{X}_I]$ from the time series output associated with a simulation. Procedures have also been suggested for obtaining smaller estimates of $Var[\overline{X}_I]$ which allow more precise statements about $\overline{X}_I$ to be made. These topics are discussed in Sections 13.3 and 13.4 respectively. In this section, we present the background information and formulas that are pertinent to the understanding of the significance of the variance of the sample mean.

13.2.1   Notation

In our exploration of $\overline{X}_I$, we propose the notation that X_i be a random variable associated with interval or batch i. We will use the term batch throughout this chapter where a batch is an undefined quantity that can be a single observation, a set of observations in a subinterval during a run, or an entire run (replication). How a batch is defined is dependent on the procedures employed in the simulation to compute the sample mean which in turn is based on the test of hypothesis to be performed or the confidence interval to be set. Possible definitions for X_i are given below.

A derived observation: $X_i = \begin{cases} 1, \text{success on batch i} \\ 0, \text{failure on batch i} \end{cases}$

A time-averaged value for batch i:

$$X_i = \frac{1}{T_i - T_{i-1}} \int_{t=T_{i-1}}^{T_i} X_i(t)\,dt$$

An observation-averaged value for batch i:

$$X_i = \frac{1}{N_i} \sum_{n=A_i}^{A_{i+1}} X_i(n)$$

$$\text{where} \quad A_i = \sum_{j=1}^{i-1} N_j \text{ and } A_1 = 0$$

Note that the latter two definitions involve the computation of an average within a batch. To simplify the presentation of the formulas to be derived, we will not take advantage of this information during the presentation of formulas. In Section 13.3 where specific calculation methods are proposed, this subject will be discussed.

13.2.2   Formulas for Var [$\overline{X}_I$]

Starting with the definition of the variance, we can derive the following expressions (all summations are from 1 to I and $\mu = E[X_i]$)

$$\text{Var}[\overline{X}_I] = E[(\overline{X}_I - E[\overline{X}_I])^2]$$

$$= E\left[\left(\frac{\sum_i X_i}{I} - E\left[\frac{\sum_i X_i}{I}\right]\right)^2\right]$$

$$= \frac{1}{I^2} E \left[\left(\sum_i X_i - E \left[\sum_i X_i \right] \right) \left(\sum_j X_j - E \left[\sum_j X_j \right] \right) \right]$$

$$= \frac{1}{I^2} E \left[\sum_i (X_i - E[X_i]) \cdot \sum_j (X_j - E[X_j]) \right]$$

$$= \frac{1}{I^2} E \left[\sum_i \sum_j (X_i - \mu)(X_j - \mu) \right]$$

$$= \frac{1}{I^2} \sum_i \sum_j E[(X_i - \mu)(X_j - \mu)]$$

$$= \frac{1}{I^2} \sum_i \sum_j Cov[X_i, X_j] \tag{13-1}$$

$$= \frac{1}{I^2} \left(\sum_i Var[X_i] + \sum_i^I \sum_{\substack{j \\ j \neq i}}^I Cov[X_i, X_j] \right)$$

If X_i and X_j are independent for all i and j and $Var[X_i] = \sigma^2$ for all i then

$$Var[\overline{X}_I] = \frac{1}{I^2} \sum_i^I \sigma^2 = \frac{1}{I} \sigma^2 \tag{13-2}$$

From this equation, we note that when independence applies, $I*Var[\overline{X}_I] = \sigma^2$, a constant, and that $Var[\overline{X}_I]$ decreases in proportion to $1/I$. We will return to this observation shortly.

Under the assumption of independence and mild regularity conditions on X_i, the central limit theorem specifies that for large I the distribution of $\sqrt{I}(\overline{X}_I - \mu)/\sigma$ converges to a normal distribution with mean 0 and variance 1, that is, $N(0,1)$. If the X_i are also normally distributed then $\overline{X}_I$ is in fact normally distributed and $(\overline{X}_I - \mu)/\sqrt{S_X^2/I}$ has a t-distribution with $I-1$ degrees of freedom where S_X^2 is an estimator of σ^2. From this information, an exact confidence interval for $\overline{X}_I$ can be constructed. Note that by making X_i a batch average as discussed above, an assumption of normality for X_i is reasonable. Fishman (23) provides the following equation for the variance of S_X^2:

$$Var[S_X^2] = \sigma^4 \left(\frac{2}{I-1} + \frac{\gamma_2}{I} \right) \tag{13-3}$$

where γ_2 is the excess kurtosis (fourth central moment divided by the square of the second central moment minus three.) Eq. 13-3 indicates the amount of variability that may be expected in the estimate of the underlying process variance.

When $Cov[X_i, X_j]$ cannot be assumed to be zero, but we can assume a covariance stationary process, then $Cov[X_i, X_j] = R_{j-i} = R_h$. Using this notation in Eq. 13-1 and by combining terms, we can obtain

$$\text{Var}[\overline{X}_I] = \frac{1}{I} \sum_{h=1-I}^{I-1} \left(1 - \frac{|h|}{I}\right) R_h \qquad (13\text{-}4)$$

Substituting $\sigma^2 = R_0$ and $R_{-h} = R_h$ into Eq. 13-4 yields

$$\text{Var}[\overline{X}_I] = \frac{1}{I}\left\{ \sigma^2 + 2 \sum_{h=1}^{I-1} \left(1 - \frac{h}{I}\right) R_h \right\} \qquad (13\text{-}5)$$

Procedures for estimating $\text{Var}[\overline{X}_I]$ using this equation are discussed in Section 13.3.5.

If the autocovariance decays exponentially (a common and reasonable assumption is that $R_h = R_0 \alpha^{|h|}$ for $0 < \alpha < 1$) then it can be shown that

$$\lim_{I \to \infty} I\, \text{Var}[\overline{X}_I] = \sum_{h=-\infty}^{\infty} R_h = m \qquad (13\text{-}6)$$

From Eq. 13-6, it is seen that as the number of batches increases the $\text{Var}[\overline{X}_I]$ decreases in proportion to $1/I$. Comparing Eq. 13-6 with Eq. 13-2, we observe that the underlying process variability, σ^2, is related to the sum of all covariances. Throughout this text, we refer to this quantity by the symbol m. Since the value of m is not based on the number of batches I, an estimate of m for a process permits the estimation of $\text{Var}[\overline{X}_I]$ for any I.

13.2.3   Interpreting $\text{Var}[\overline{X}_I]$

As mentioned above, $\text{Var}[\overline{X}_I] \to m/I$ for large I and under appropriate assumptions. Based on this, we can picture the distribution of $\overline{X}_I$ over time as shown in Figure 13-1. There are several observations to be made from Figure 13-1. First, $\overline{X}_I$ is a random variable and, hence, the values estimated are sample values. When making a simulation replication, one should expect a different value of $\overline{X}_I$ to result with the precision based on $f(\overline{X}_I)$ and, hence, $\text{Var}[\overline{X}_I]$. The length of a run or the number of batches can change $f(\overline{X}_I)$, that is, $f(\overline{X}_I)$ depends on I and the distributing of X_i. For the same run length, different estimators may be based on a different number of batches. Furthermore, the three distributions shown in Figure 13-1 all are shown with the same $E[\overline{X}_I]$. This need not be the case as biased estimators can be and are used. Thus, when comparing estimators for $\text{Var}[\overline{X}_I]$ under different experimental conditions, we need a basis to compare the estimates. The criterion used for comparison in most research efforts are m and the mean square error of the sample mean (29) denoted by $\text{MSE}[\overline{X}_I] = E[(\overline{X}_I - \mu_X)^2]$.

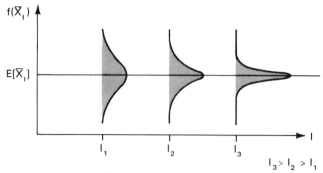

Figure 13-1   Distribution of $\overline{X}_I$.

Unfortunately, equations for the computation of m for non-Markov processes have not been derived. For the number in the system in an M/M/1 queueing situation, Fishman(23) computes m = 6840 for the case in which the arrival rate, λ, equals 4.5 and the service rate, μ, equals 5. Also if $\lambda = 2.0$ and $\mu = 2.25$ then m = 361. For the M|M|∞ situation (55), m = $2\lambda/\mu^2$. A procedure has been developed for obtaining values of m for finite state Markov processes† (35).

The MSE[$\overline{X}_I$] is a criterion that combines the Var[$\overline{X}_I$] and the bias associated with $\overline{X}_I$. This is seen in the following development:

$$
\begin{aligned}
\text{MSE}[\overline{X}_I] &= E[(\overline{X}_I - \mu_X)^2] \\
&= E[(\overline{X}_I - E[X_I] + E[\overline{X}_I] - \mu_X])^2] \\
&\doteq E[(\overline{X}_I - E[\overline{X}_I])^2] + E[(E[\overline{X}_I] - \mu_X])^2] \\
&= \text{Var}[\overline{X}_I] + (\text{Bias}[\overline{X}_I])^2
\end{aligned}
$$

$$(13\text{-}7)$$

When there is bias‡ associated with $\overline{X}_I$, then the probability that the theoretical mean is covered by (contained in) a confidence interval differs from a prescribed value due to the offset caused by the bias. The "coverage" is defined as the probability that the theoretical mean is covered by an interval centered at $E[\overline{X}_I]$ or $\overline{X}_I$. When estimators are employed which are unbiased, then MSE($\overline{X}_I$) reduces to Var[$\overline{X}_I$] and the coverage is the same as the value associated with the confidence interval. We are now ready to examine proposed procedures for estimating Var[$\overline{X}_I$].

---

† For finite state Markov processes, it is also shown that m is a function of both λ and μ and that m($a\lambda,a\mu$)=(1/a)[m(λ,μ)]. It is conjectured that this result holds for countable state Markov processes like the M|M|1 queueing situation. Hence, to compute m for the M|M|1 queue with λ/μ=0.9 but with λ=4, μ=40/9 then a=8/9 and m=9/8(6840)=7695.

‡ A bias could exist if the underlying process was not covariance stationary or if $\overline{X}_I$ was computed using a ratio estimator (see Section 13.3.3).

13.3   PROCEDURES FOR ESTIMATING VAR[$\overline{X}_I$]

As discussed in the previous section, the variance of the sample mean plays a fundamental role in the reliability of simulation output. The estimation of Var[$\overline{X}_I$] from a single simulation run is complicated due to the dependence of the samples that are used in the computation of $\overline{X}_I$. A considerable amount of research has been performed regarding the estimation of Var[$\overline{X}_I$]. This research has resulted in five basic approaches which are listed below:

1. *Replication*—employ separate runs with each run being considered as a batch. From run i, we obtain a value of X_i and the Var[$\overline{X}_I$] is estimated using Eq. 13-2;
2. *Subintervals*—divide a run into equal batches (subintervals) and compute X_i as an average for batch i. Assume each X_i is independent and use Eq. 13-2 for estimating Var[$\overline{X}_I$];
3. *Regenerative cycles*—divide a simulation run into independent cycles by defining states where the model starts anew. Estimate the Var[$\overline{X}_I$] based on observed values in the independent cycles;
4. *Parametric modeling*—fit an equation(s) to the output values or a function of the output values obtained from a run. Derive an estimate of Var[$\overline{X}_I$] from the equations that model the simulation output;
5. *Covariance/spectral estimation*—estimate the autovariance from the sample output and use these in a spectral analysis or directly in Eq. 13-5 to estimate Var[$\overline{X}_I$].

Each of these five procedures will now be presented.

13.3.1   Replications

In this procedure, a value x_i of the random variable X_i is computed on run i. As discussed in Section 13.2.1, the variable X_i could be: the mean number of units in the system on run i; the mean time in the system per customer; or a binomial variable that represents the number of successes in a run. The mean of the X_i values over I runs is used as an estimate of the parameter of interest, that is,

$$\overline{X}_I = \frac{\sum\limits_{i=1}^{I} X_i}{I} \tag{13-8}$$

An estimate of $Var[X_i]$, S_x^2, is then obtained using standard procedures as

$$S_x^2 = \frac{1}{I-1} \sum_{i=1}^{I} (X_i - \overline{X}_I)^2 = \frac{1}{I-1} \sum_{i=1}^{I} X_i^2 - \frac{1}{I(I-1)} \left(\sum_{i=1}^{I} X_i \right)^2 \tag{13-9}$$

Equation 13-9 provides an estimate of the variability associated with a random sample obtained from each run. Since each run is an independent replication, an estimate of the variance of the sample mean can be obtained as shown in Eq. (13-10).

$$S_{\overline{x}}^2 = S_x^2 / I \tag{13-10}$$

Based on $S_{\overline{x}}^2$ and $\overline{X}_I$ and using the central limit theorem, probability statements about the parameter of interest can be made after observations are taken. Tests of hypotheses can also be made based on these theoretic considerations.

The replication procedure has the desirable property that samples are independent. Another advantage is that it can be used for both terminating and steady-state analysis where a terminating analysis is one that is performed for a specific finite time period.† The disadvantages associated with replications are: 1) each replication contains a startup segment which may not be representative of stationary behavior; and 2) only one sample, X_i, is obtained from each replication which could mean that extensive information about the variable of interest is not being gleaned from the data. This is particularly the case when X_i is computed as a mean value for the run.

13.3.2   Subintervals

The approach to estimating the variance of $\overline{X}_I$ using subintervals is to divide a single simulation run into batches. If each batch has b samples of $X_i(n)$ then a batch sample mean, X_i, is computed from

---

† In a recent report (44), Law states "we have concluded from talking with simulation practitioners that a significant proportion of real-world simulations are of the terminating type. This is fortunate because it means classical statistical analysis is applicable . . . ".

$$X_i = \frac{\sum_{n=1}^{b} X_i(n)}{b}$$

If the subintervals are independent then Eq. 13-8, 13-9, and 13-10 are used to estimate $E[\overline{X}_I]$, $Var[X_i]$ and $Var[\overline{X}_I]$, respectively[†]. The assumption of independence is typically made in simulation analyses even though there exists an autocovariance between the values at the end of one subinterval and those at the beginning of the next subinterval. This variance can cause a positive covariance between batch means. By making the batch size b larger, the covariance between the sample batch means should decrease. Procedures for determining the batch size such that the covariance between adjacent batch means is insignificant have been developed by Mechanic and McKay (47), Law (42), and Fishman (24,25). We recommend the use of Fishman's procedure for determining b which is discussed below.

Fishman's proposed procedure involves recomputing the batch values by doubling the batch size b until the null hypothesis that the $X_{i,b}$ for $i=1,2, \ldots, I_b$ are iid is accepted, where the subscript b is appended to X_i to indicate the dependence of it on the batch size. He recommends the use of the test statistic

$$C_b = 1 - \sum_{i=1}^{I_b-1} (X_{i,b} - X_{i+1,b})^2 \Big/ 2 \cdot \sum_{i=1}^{I_b} (X_{i,b} - \overline{X}_{I_b})^2$$

where I_b = number of batches when the batch size is b.
For large b, C_b is approximately the estimated autocorrelation coefficient between consecutive batches.

If the $X_{i,b}$ are independent and normally distributed then C_b has a mean of zero, a variance of $(I_b-2)/(I_b^2-1)$, and a distribution that is close to normal for b as small as 8. Thus, if these conditions hold, a standard test using normal tables can be applied. If $\{X_{i,b}\}$ has a monotone autocovariance function then a one-sided test is appropriate: otherwise a two-sided test is in order.

Several procedural details are necessary when using the above approach to setting the batch size. The observed values $x_i(n)$ must be recorded in order to compute $x_{i,b}$ for different values of b. Any non-representative values of $x_i(n)$ at the beginning of a run should be truncated before applying the test (see Section 13.5.2). An initial batch size needs to be set. Fishman recommends setting b=1 initially. If there is significant correlation in the $X_i(n)$, we recommend a larger starting value for b. One last observation is that successive testing of the hypothesis may increase the probability of accepting the null hypothesis when it is false.

The advantages of using subintervals to estimate the variance of the sample mean are that a single run can be used to obtain an estimate and only one transient

---

[†] It can be shown that if the subintervals are independent, m associated with X_i, denoted $m(X_1)$, is $\frac{1}{b}*m(X_1(n))$ where $m(X_1(n))$ is the m value associated with individual observations.

period is included in the output (or required to be deleted). The disadvantage of the procedure is in establishing the batch size, b, which makes the subintervals independent. Note that for a fixed number of observations, increasing the batch size decreases the number of batches and, hence, could yield larger estimates of $\text{Var}[\overline{X}_I]$. Another disadvantage involves the boundaries of a batch. Care must be taken in computing batch averages when an observation spans more than a single batch, for example, an arrival in batch i that leaves the system during batch i+1.

13.3.3   Regenerative Method

The regenerative method (13, 26, 38) is similar to the subinterval method in that it divides a simulation run into intervals which are referred to as cycles. A cycle starts when a specific state of the system is reached in which future behavior is independent of the past behavior. When a return is made to such a state, the cycle ends and one independent observation of each quantity of interest is obtained. By defining cycles in this manner, independent samples from the model are obtained and the covariance problem encountered when using subintervals is avoided. A different statistical problem arises, however, in that the length of a cycle is not predetermined but is a random variable.

The most commonly used regeneration point in queueing studies is a return to a status where servers are idle and no customers are waiting. If the next customer arrival is processed in a consistent fashion then each time a customer arrives to an empty system is a regeneration point and the start of a regeneration cycle. In inventory models, a possible regeneration point is when the inventory position is equal to a stock control level.

By construction, each cycle of a simulation run will be independent and we can base the estimates of the sample mean on cycle values. Following the development by Crane and Lemoine (14), let

Y_i = the value of interest in the ith cycle, for example, the sum of customer waiting times in the ith cycle†; and

L_i = the length of the ith cycle, for example, the number of customers or the cycle time.

If X_{ik} is the kth sample on the ith cycle and we perform the simulation run until there are I cycles, then the following two equations hold

---

† The value of interest could also be a time-integrated variable, that is, the time-integrated number in the system during the ith cycle.

$$Y_i = \sum_{k=1}^{L_i} X_{ik} \tag{13-12}$$

and

$$\sum_{i=1}^{I} L_i = N \tag{13-13}$$

where N = total number of samples (a random variable).

The average of all the samples for a simulation run, $\overline{X}_I$, would normally be computed as shown in Eq. 13-14

$$\overline{X}_I = \frac{\sum_{i=1}^{I} \sum_{k=1}^{L_i} X_{ik}}{N} \tag{13-14}$$

By substituting in the variables from Eqs. 13-12 and 13-13 into Eq. 13-14, we illustrate that $\overline{X}_I$ can be considered as the ratio of cycle averages.

$$\overline{X}_I = \frac{\sum_{i=1}^{I} \sum_{k=1}^{L_i} X_{ik}}{N} = \frac{\sum_{i=1}^{I} Y_i}{\sum_{i=1}^{I} L_i} = \frac{\sum_{i=1}^{I} Y_i/I}{\sum_{i=1}^{I} L_i/I} = \overline{Y}_I/\overline{L}_I \tag{13-15}$$

Since the number of samples per cycle is a random variable, we cannot specify both the number of cycles and the total number of samples. In such a case, we are using a ratio estimator which can be shown to be biased (23).

An estimate of the variance of $\overline{X}_I$ can be computed using Eq. 13-16

$$S_{\overline{X}}^2 = \frac{S^2}{(\overline{L}_I\sqrt{I})^2} \tag{13-16}$$

where

$$S^2 = S_Y^2 - 2\,\overline{X}_I\,S_{YL} + \overline{X}_I^2\,S_L^2$$

and

$$S_Y^2 = \frac{1}{I-1} \sum_{i=1}^{I} (Y_i - \overline{Y}_I)^2 \ ,$$

$$S_L^2 = \frac{1}{I-1} \sum_{i=1}^{I} (L_i - \overline{L}_I)^2 ,$$

$$S_{YL} = \frac{1}{I-1} \sum_{i=1}^{I} (Y_i - \overline{Y}_I)(L_i - \overline{L}_I) \ .$$

As noted above $\overline{X}_I$ is a biased estimator. To alleviate the problem of bias with ratio estimators, a Jackknife estimator (31,40) can be used which eliminates the bias term of order $1/I$. The equation for the Jackknife estimator of the sample mean is given in Eq. 13-17

$$\overline{J} = \frac{1}{I} \sum_{i=1}^{I} J_i \qquad (13\text{-}17)$$

where J_i is referred to as a psuedo-value computed from

$$J_i = I\,\overline{X}_I - (I-1) \sum_{\substack{j=1 \\ j \neq i}}^{I} Y_j \bigg/ \sum_{\substack{j=1 \\ j \neq i}}^{I} L_j$$

The J_i are considered to be independent and identically distributed so that confidence intervals for $\overline{X}_I$ can be constructed using estimates of $\overline{J}$ and $S_{J_i}/\sqrt{I}$.

The advantages of the regenerative method are that independent and identically distributed random variables for each cycle are obtained. Thus, standard statistical procedures can be used for tests of hypothesis and confidence interval calculations. However, to use the procedure, a regenerative point must be established for which the expected time between returns is finite and for which sufficient cycles are observed to achieve a reasonable confidence interval. As illustrated by the arc sine law presented in an Appendix to this chapter, this may not be an easy determination. An additional advantage is that the problems of determining a start-up procedure are avoided as statistical collection can begin when a regeneration point is reached which, if possible, could be the initial conditions specified. Disadvantages of the procedure are the added computations and the bias associated with the estimator for the sample mean.

13.3.4   Parametric Modeling

Parametric modeling involves the building of a model to describe the outputs from a simulation model. Values of the estimates of quantities of interest are then obtained through computations made on the parametric model. The procedure for employing parametric modeling involves the collection of sample values from a simulation and then fitting an equation(s) to the observed data values. This approach is similar to the one used when attempting to describe real world systems by fitting equations to data obtained from the system.

To provide further rationale for using this approach, consider a single server queueing situation in which customers are processed on a first-come, first-serve basis. If the variable of interest is the waiting time of a customer, we could write an equation that describes the waiting time of the (j+1)st customer in terms of the waiting time of the jth customer, the interarrival time random variable and the service time random variable. Such an equation can be developed based on the pictorial sketch shown below.

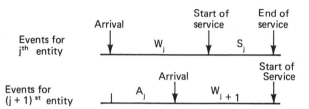

In this sketch, it is assumed that the (j+1)st entity arrives before the end of service for the jth entity. By equating the variables from the two lines given in the sketch, we obtain the following equation

$$W_{j+1} = \begin{cases} W_j + S_j - A_j & \text{if } A_j < W_j + S_j \\ 0 & \text{otherwise} \end{cases}$$

where

W_j is the waiting time of the jth entity,

S_j is the service time of the jth entity, and

A_j is the interarrival time between the jth and (j+1)st entity.

If we had simulated a queueing system and saved the observed values of W_j, S_j, and A_j and were sufficiently astute to derive a model for W_{j+1} such as the one given above, then we could use it to obtain information concerning the waiting time of customers.†

The above model development was presented to provide a rationale for attempting to fit a model to sample data. Past research on parametric modeling of simulation output has primarily been through the use of autoregressive (AR) models. Fishman has done extensive analyses of such models (26). Since the values obtained from the execution of a simulation model can be considered as time series data, we recommend the use of the Box-Jenkins methodology for model identification and estimation (7). An excellent discussion of this methodology is provided by Mabert (46). The Box-Jenkins methodology attempts to derive a parametric model of the sample data using an equation of the following form:

---

† This model is a convenient one for introducing sampling procedures and for performing research on the waiting time associated with a single server queueing situation. Since it is difficult to embellish, it is not a good model for teaching modeling procedures.

$$Y_t = \sum_{k=1}^{p} \phi_k Y_{t-k} - \sum_{l=1}^{q} \theta_l U_{t-l} + U_t \; ; t = 1, 2, \ldots, n \qquad (13\text{-}18)$$

where

$$Y_t = X(t) - E[X(t)]$$

and

U_t is white noise, that is, $E[U_t] = 0$ and

$$E[U_t U_{t-l}] = \begin{cases} \sigma_U^2 & l = 0 \\ 0 & \text{otherwise} \end{cases}$$

The model of Eq. 13-18 is referred to as a combined autoregressive and moving average (ARMA) model. If all the terms which have a coefficient θ_l in Eq. 13-18 are deleted, then an autoregressive model of order p is obtained (AR(p)). An autoregressive model expresses Y_t as a linear combination of previous values of the time series plus a white noise component.

If all the terms with a coefficient of ϕ_k are deleted from Eq. 13-18, then a moving average model is obtained. The moving average model expresses Y_t as a linear combination of the past q error terms. This is referred to as a moving average model of order q and is designated as an MA(q) model.

The Box-Jenkins methodology provides procedures for identifying the order of an autoregressive model, p, and the order of a moving average model, q. In addition, procedures have been computerized for obtaining the best estimates of ϕ_k and θ_l. The program for making such computations can be obtained from The Ohio State University Data Center or The University of Wisconsin. The outputs from this program provide values for θ_l and ϕ_k and an estimate of the variance of the white noise, σ_U^2. With these estimates, an estimate of the variance of the sample mean can be computed as shown in Eq. 13-19

$$s_{\bar{X}}^2 = \frac{\hat{m}}{n} \qquad (13\text{-}19)$$

where

$$\hat{m} = \hat{\sigma}_U^2 \frac{\left(1 - \sum_{l=1}^{q} \theta_l\right)^2}{\left(1 - \sum_{k=1}^{p} \phi_k\right)^2}$$

In our experience, parametric modeling of the time series obtained from a simulation model has not produced reliable estimates of the variance of the sample mean. This could be related to a non-stationary behavior of the time series and a non-normality of the individual observations. Significantly improved results have been obtained by building parametric models using a time series consisting of batch means. By using batch means, assumptions regarding stationarity and normality are alleviated.

The advantage of using parametric modeling is that an equation describing a variable of interest is obtained. Further analyses using the derived model can provide new insights into the system being simulated. The main disadvantage of parametric modeling is the lack of knowledge of the reliability of the model. Building a parametric model of a simulation model takes the analysis one step further away from the real system and requires much care on the part of the analyst.

13.3.5   Estimating Covariances and the Use of Spectral Analysis

In Section 13.2.2, we showed that

$$\text{Var}[\overline{X}_I] = \frac{1}{I}\left[R_0 + 2\sum_{h=1}^{I-1}\left(1 - \frac{h}{I}\right)R_h\right]$$

Thus, if estimates of the autocovariances, R_h, can be obtained, we could compute

$$s_{\overline{X}}^2 = \frac{1}{I}\left[\hat{R}_0 + 2\sum_{h=1}^{I-1}\left(1 - \frac{h}{I}\right)\hat{R}_h\right]$$

In the literature, the following three alternative equations have been proposed for computing $\hat{R}_h$:

$$A_h = \frac{1}{I-h}\sum_{i=1}^{I-h}(X_i - \overline{X}_I)(X_{i+h} - \overline{X}_I)$$

$$B_h = \frac{1}{I}\sum_{i=1}^{I-h}X_i X_{i+h} - \frac{1}{I-h}\left(\sum_{i=1}^{I-h}X_i\right)\left(\sum_{i=1}^{I-h}X_{i+h}\right)$$

$$C_h = \frac{1}{I}\sum_{i=1}^{I-h}(X_i - \overline{X}_I)(X_{i+h} - \overline{X}_I)$$

When a time series is short and the end points differ significantly from $\overline{X}_I$, B_h has been recommended as the estimator. In simulation studies, the time series is normally long and B_h is not employed.

The estimator A_h has intuitive appeal as it averages $(I-h)$ values. However, A_h has a larger mean square error than C_h. C_h has the disadvantage that it is a biased estimator. The current consensus is that for a time series with large I, C_h should be used to estimate R_h.

The past research on estimating the autocovariances dealt primarily with the sample variables, $X_i(t)$ or $X_i(n)$. These variables are highly correlated and estimates of the autocovariances are highly correlated. Thus, if a large value is obtained for the estimator of R_o, we would expect a high value relatively for the estimator of R_h. In simulation experiments, this phenomenon has been observed by Duket (17). The use of batch values, X_i, as recommended previously will alleviate this correlation in the estimates of the autocovariances.

An alternative procedure is to employ spectral analysis. The *spectrum* is defined as

$$g(\lambda) = \frac{1}{2\pi} \sum_{h=-\infty}^{\infty} R_h \, e^{-i\lambda h} \quad -\pi \leq \lambda \leq \pi \tag{13-20}$$

and the *spectral density function* as

$$f(\lambda) = g(\lambda)/R_o$$

The inverse transform of $g(\lambda)$ is given by

$$R_h = \int_{-\pi}^{\pi} g(\lambda) e^{i\lambda h} d\lambda$$

and can be used to obtain values of R_h.
For $h=0$, this yields

$$R_o = \int_{-\pi}^{\pi} g(\lambda) d\lambda$$

Thus, the underlying variance of the process can be thought of as consisting of nonoverlapping contributions at frequency λ. A large value of $g(\lambda)$ indicates variability in the process at frequency λ or periodically at $2\pi/\lambda$.

As discussed in Section 13.2, it can be shown for many systems that

$$\lim_{I \to \infty} I \, \text{Var}[\overline{X}_I] = m = \sum_{h=-\infty}^{\infty} R_h$$

Letting $\lambda=0$ in Eq. 13-20 yields

$$g(0) = \frac{1}{2\pi} \sum_{h=-\infty}^{\infty} R_h$$

and, hence,

$$m = 2\pi \, g(0)$$

Thus, if $g(0)$ can be estimated, an estimate of m can be obtained.

Extensive research has been performed on obtaining estimates of the spectrum for time series. The main difficulties involve the determination of the number of covariances to include in the computation, and the weighting function (lag window) to apply to the estimated autocovariance obtained from finite observations. Weighting functions have been developed by Bartlett, Tukey, and Parzen; others are referred to as the Rectangular and Variance weighting functions (18).

The advantage of the spectral approach is the extensive research that has been performed on spectral methods. The main disadvantage is that point estimates obtained from the spectrum, that is, at $\lambda=0$, are known to be unreliable. Employing data grouped into a single batch observation, as previously suggested, should diminish this reservation (49).

13.4   VARIANCE REDUCTION TECHNIQUES

The variance of the sample mean is a derived measure of the reliability that can be expected if the simulation experiment is repeatedly performed. It has been shown that longer runs should produce smaller estimates of $Var[\overline{X}_I]$. Thus, in some sense, the value of $Var[\overline{X}_I]$ is dependent on experimental procedures and calculations. Variance reduction techniques (VRT) are methods that attempt to reduce the estimated values of $Var[\overline{X}_I]$ through the setting of special experimental conditions or through the use of prior information.

13.4.1   Antithetic Sampling

Eq. 13-1 for $Var[\overline{X}_I]$ contains terms involving the $Cov[X_i,X_j]$. If $Cov[X_i,X_j]$ can be made negative then the $Var[\overline{X}_I]$ will be reduced. Since X_i and X_j are functions of pseudorandom numbers, it has been suggested that if $X_i = f(r_1,r_2, \ldots,r_q)$ then letting $X_j = f(1-r_1,1-r_2, \ldots,1-r_q)$ will induce a negative covariance between X_i and X_j. Obtaining a negative covariance depends on the function f, which reflects a transformation of random numbers into sample values by the simulation model. Clearly, a general result regarding the use of the antithetic values can not be provided. However, in experiments, a variance reduction has been observed when such antithetic sampling is employed. The generation of the antithetic stream of random numbers: $1-r_1$, $1-r_2$, . . . , $1-r_q$, is easily accomplished when using a multiplicative congruence random number generator of the form

$$z_k = az_{k-1} \bmod(c) \quad k=1,2, . . .$$

and

$$r_k = z_k/c$$

It can be shown (40) that if

$$z'_0 = c - z_0$$

is used as a starting value for a sequence of random numbers then[†]

$$z'_k = c - z_k$$

and, hence,

$$r'_k = \frac{z'_k}{c} = 1 - r_k .$$

In SLAM, an antithetic sequence is obtained by specifying a negative initial seed value on the SEEDS control statement, that is, $-z_0$.

The application of antithetic samples within a batch or even within a run is not recommended. The manipulation of batches to produce antithetic samples could cause a distortion of the basic process and seems not to be warranted. Other proposed procedures appear more palatable. For example, perform pairs of independent runs in which antithetic streams are used on the second run of the pair. For a sequence of arrivals, let the kth interarrival time be based on r_k in the first run of a pair and based on $1-r_k$ on the second run of a pair. When doing this, the variance calculation for 2I runs is simplified by combining values across pairs of runs. If X'_i is the antithetic value for X_i, then

$$\mathrm{Var}[\overline{X}_I] = \mathrm{Var}\left(\frac{\sum_{i=1}^{I}(X_i+X'_i)}{2I}\right) = \mathrm{Var}\left(\frac{\sum_{i=1}^{I}U_i}{I}\right)$$

where

$$U_i = \frac{X_i+X'_i}{2} .$$

When combined in this fashion, covariance terms between runs need not be computed.

[†] Care is required when doing this with packaged random number generators that may add 1 to a seed value or that store the initial seed value as a real number.

Another suggestion that is in the spirit of antithetic sampling (25) is to switch the streams employed for interarrival times and service times in alternate runs. To see that this induces antithetic behavior, note that long interarrival times reduce potential congestion whereas long service times increase potential congestion. Results of the application of antithetic sampling are summarized by Kleijnen (40). Typically, the results are for small-scale simulation models. Kleijnen defines a measure of variance reduction as a percentage change, that is, if $\text{Var}_R[\overline{X}_I]$ is obtained using a VRT then

$$\text{Percent Variance Reduction} = \frac{\text{Var}[\overline{X}_I] - \text{Var}_R[\overline{X}_I]}{\text{Var}[\overline{X}_I]} * 100$$

Hammersley and Handscomb (34), Tocher (62), and Fishman (23) define variance reduction as a ratio, that is

$$\text{Variance Reduction} = \frac{\text{Var}[\overline{X}_I]}{\text{Var}_R[\overline{X}_I]}$$

Before ending this discussion of antithetic sampling, two important points should be mentioned. First, although the correlation between antithetic random numbers is $-1.$, the correlation between samples based on such numbers may not be -1. If the samples are from a symmetric distribution, the correlation will be -1. If the samples are from an exponential distribution, Fishman (23) shows the correlation between antithetic samples is -0.645. A similar increase in the negative correlation is obtained for other distributions.

The second point involves the simulation model. If the model involves a square or higher order even relation then the introduction of a negative correlation can result in a positive contribution to the variance of the sample mean.

13.4.2   Common Streams

A typical practice when performing a simulation is to employ historical data as the driving force. As an example, the time of arrivals of jobs to a computer could be maintained and used to define the arrival times and job characteristics for a simulation of the computer center. Simulations involving the use of historical data are sometimes referred to as *trace-driven*. Recognizing that the historical arrival pattern is a single time series, it is apparent that its repeated use reduces the variation of the output from a simulation model. By starting different simulation runs with the same random number seed, that is, employing a common stream, a similar variance reduction can be obtained. Care is required when employing trace-driven or common streams in that the complete variability associated with the system being modeled is not incorporated in the model. The analyst should ensure that the single time series employed by such a practice is representative of the stochastic process being modeled.

A more appealing use of common streams is when comparing alternatives. In this situation, the variance of a difference between sample means is of interest, that is

$$\text{Var}[\overline{X}_I^{(1)} - \overline{X}_I^{(2)}] = \text{Var}[\overline{X}_I^{(1)}] + \text{Var}[\overline{X}_I^{(2)}] - 2\text{Cov}[\overline{X}_I^{(1)}, \overline{X}_I^{(2)}]$$

where $\overline{X}_I^{(k)}$ is the sample mean for the alternative k. By using common streams, the $\text{Cov}[\overline{X}_I^{(1)}, \overline{X}_I^{(2)}]$ should be positive and a reduction in the variance of the difference should be obtained. The use of a common stream here only presumes that the time series generated affects both alternatives in a similar manner. Extreme care must be taken if common streams are employed in conjunction with antithetic sampling techniques as a variance increase has been observed under several situations (40).

13.4.3   Prior Information

The Rao-Blackwell theorem presented in an appendix to this chapter can be interpreted as specifying that a variance reduction can be obtained by estimating the sample mean based on a conditioned random variable. One procedure for implementing this approach is to employ analytic results in the estimation process. We present two illustrations of this procedure.

It is well known that for a wide class of queueing situations, Little's formula (45,61) holds

$$L = \lambda W$$

where

L is the expected number in a system

W is the expected time in the system

λ is the effective arrival rate to the system, that is, the number of arrivals that are eventually served per unit time.

In a run, the average number of entities in a queue, $\overline{N}$, will be equal to the product of the observed arrival rate, λ_0, in the run and the average waiting time of all entities passing through the queue, $\overline{T}$. Notationally, we can write $\overline{N} = \lambda_0 \overline{T}$. This equation can be developed by observing that the time integrated number in the queue is equal to the sum of the waiting times (assuming at the end of the run all entities leave the queue). Based on this information, we could compute

$$\text{Var}[\overline{N}] = \lambda^2 \text{Var}[\overline{T}]$$

assuming λ is a known value. This equation provides the basis for an indirect estimator of the variance of the average number in the system by multiplying the estimate of $Var[\overline{T}]$ obtained from a simulation by the value of λ^2. The rationale for the variance reduction is the use of the theoretical arrival rate λ in the estimation of $Var[\overline{N}]$. In the actual simulation, a sampling process is used and a sample arrival rate would be drawn for the entire simulation. If λ is treated as an independent random variable, the relevant equation would be

$$Var[\overline{N}] = Var[\lambda]Var[\overline{T}] + E^2[\lambda]Var[\overline{T}] + Var[\lambda]E^2[\overline{T}]$$

and, hence, we expect a variance reduction by assuming that λ is a constant, that is, $Var[\lambda] = 0$.

The above establishes that a variance reduction should occur but another question still remains. Should we estimate $Var[\overline{N}]$ directly and use it to obtain an indirect estimate of $Var[\overline{T}]$ or vice versa? Law (43) considered five equations that relate the first moments of number in system, number in queue, time in system, time in queue, and work content in system. Using estimates obtained from regenerative procedures, he showed analytically, assuming steady-state values are of interest, that for the M/G/1 queueing situation, it is more efficient (less variance of the sample means) to use indirect estimators based on the variance of the time in the system.

A second example of the use of prior information is based on the work of Carter and Ignall (8). This study involved the analysis of an inventory situation in which backorders were allowed. For such studies, the expected number of backorders must be estimated. However, backorders may be infrequent and long simulations may be required to obtain low variance estimates of the average number of backorders. The Carter and Ignall approach was to derive an expression for the expected number of backorders given the inventory position at the beginning of a period prior to demands being met. For period t, they showed that

$$E[B_t|A_t] = E[D_t] - A_t + \sum_{d=0}^{A_t} (A_t-d)P[D_t=d]$$

where

B_t is the number of backorders in period t

A_t is the inventory position at beginning of period t

D_t is the demand in period t.

An estimate of the average backorders in the simulation was obtained by observing the values of A_t and solving the above equation for $E[B_t|A_t]$ for $t=1,2, \ldots ,T$. Average values for the T periods could then be obtained.

The above procedure resulted in variance reduction ratios of 3.89 and 8.79 for two different parameter settings. The procedure is a direct application of the Roa-Blackwell theorem in which the prior information concerning the distribution of the demand, D_t, is used in estimating the average number of backorders.

The use of prior information as a variance reduction technique is appealing because it allows the combining of analytical and experimental procedures. Since direct estimation is always possible, a check on the variation reduction is easily made. Since the reliability of results is being considered, the question of why there should be multiple estimates of the variance of the sample mean should not be bothersome. Remember the question raised in the first section of this chapter was related to the variability expected if the simulation experiment is repeated? This implicitly assumes that the same procedures for statistics collection and analysis are used when computing the variance.

The difficulty associated with the use of prior information involves the derivation of equations upon which to base the computations of the sample values.

13.4.4   Control Variates as a VRT

The concept associated with control variates is the identification of a variable, say Y, that has a positive covariance with the variable of interest, say X. If such a control variable exists and if we can derive the theoretical expectations associated with the control variable, then a variance reduction for the variable of interest can be obtained. To see how this is accomplished, consider the following equation that combines the sample means $\overline{X}_I$ and $\overline{Y}_I$ to form a new random variable, $\overline{Z}_I$:

$$\overline{Z}_I = \overline{X}_I + (E[Y] - \overline{Y}_I)$$

clearly, $E[\overline{Z}_I] = E[\overline{X}_I]$ if an unbiased estimator for $E[Y]$ is used. Looking now at variances, we have

$$\text{Var}[\overline{Z}_I] = \text{Var}[\overline{X}_I] + \text{Var}[\overline{Y}_I] - 2\,\text{Cov}[\overline{X}_I, \overline{Y}_I]$$

From this equation, we see that $\text{Var}[\overline{Z}_I] < \text{Var}[\overline{X}_I]$ if $\text{Var}[\overline{Y}_I] < 2\,\text{Cov}[\overline{X}_I, \overline{Y}_I]$.

Extensive research has been performed on the theoretical aspects of control variates (40,51). Generalizations to multiple control variates with weighting coefficients have been explored, that is,

$$\overline{Z}_I = \overline{X}_I + \sum_{k=1}^{K} w_k (E[Y_k] - \overline{Y}_{Ik})$$

However, little practical application of control variates has been reported. Typical control variates suggested are input variables (assuming the output variables are positively correlated with the input variables) and models derived by applying limiting assumptions to the simulation model.

The control variate procedure is easy to comprehend and should be considered further. However, application experience is necessary in order to properly evaluate its signficance.

13.4.5   Other Variance Reduction Techniques

In a section on variance reduction techniques, we feel called upon to mention stratified sampling and importance sampling procedures. These VRT have been used in Monte Carlo studies (34,62) and in standard sampling experiments (11). An excellent review of the procedures and attempts to apply them is contained in Kleijnen (40). Based on a review of the literature, it is our opinion that these techniques require further refinement before they can be applied in advanced simulation applications. Therefore, only a brief review of the techniques is presented.

Stratified Sampling Procedure.   Stratified sampling procedures involve the definition of a variable y from which the stratification classes G_k can be defined. The random samples for X_i are then stratified by examining y_i corresponding to the ith observation and classifying X_i to be in the kth strata if $y_i \epsilon G_k$. It is assumed that $p_k = P(y \epsilon G_k)$ is known and the sample mean based on stratification is computed as

$$\overline{X}_{ST} = \sum_k p_k \overline{X}_k$$

where $\overline{X}_k$ is the sample mean for the kth strata. It can be shown that $\overline{X}_{ST}$ is an unbiased estimator of μ_x. It can also be shown that (11,40)

$$Var[\overline{X}_{ST}] = \sum_k p_k^2 Var[\overline{X}_k] \leq Var[\overline{X}]$$

so that a variance reduction may be obtained through stratification. Greater variance reductions are obtained when the absolute differences between the strata means, μ_k, and population mean, μ_x, are large.

Importance Sampling Procedure.   Importance sampling involves a redefinition of the variable of interest by defining a new density function that gives more weight to the values of X that contribute the most to the expected value. For example, assume we are going to estimate the expected value of g(X) where X is a random variable whose density function is f(x). From the "law of the unconscious statistician" (57), we have

$$E[g(X)] = \int_x g(x)f(x)dx$$

Rewriting the above by defining the density h(x), we have

$$E[g(X)] = \int_x \frac{g(x)f(x)}{h(x)} h(x)dx$$

In importance sampling, this result is used to estimate the sample mean by selecting values of x in accordance with h(x) and then computing a sample value equal to [g(x)f(x)]/[h(x)] for the value of x selected. The estimate of the sample average is obtained by summing these values and dividing by the number of values generated.

13.5   START-UP POLICIES

The initial conditions for a simulation model may cause the values obtained from the model to be different from those obtained after a startup period. If the system being modeled has a natural termination time, then such a transient response is anticipated and the values obtained during the startup period, although different, would be representative of the outputs obtained from the real system. However, when steady-state performance is to be estimated, the initial responses can adversely influence the estimators of steady-state performance. This latter problem is the one discussed in this section.

Startup policies are used for setting the initial conditions for the simulation model and specifying a procedure for establishing a truncation point, d, at which sample values should begin to be included in the estimators being computed. Basically, the initial-condition setting attempts to provide a starting point that requires only a limited amount of data truncation to be performed, that is, one that allows a small value of d to be employed. The truncation point specification involves two considerations. The deletion of initial values tends to reduce the bias of the output estimators. Deletion of values may, however, increase the estimate of the $Var[\overline{X}_I]$ as it would be based on fewer observations. This latter assertion assumes that the deleted values are samples that have a variability similar to the variability associated with steady-state samples. This may not be the case.

From the above discussion, it appears that a trade-off is required in evaluating startup policies between bias reduction and variance reduction. Thus, it seems natural to employ the mean square error and the coverage as evaluation measures for startup policies. A procedure has been developed to make such an evaluation and the reader is referred to Wilson and Pritsker (64,65) for a summary of past research and for further details regarding this trade-off analysis.

In this section, we present various proposed initial condition rules and truncation procedures. Before doing so, several observations are in order. The use of startup policies should be considered in conjunction with the estimation procedure. If estimators are to be obtained using regenerative methods then the startup policy decision is an easy one, that is, start the run in the regenerative state so that the first cycle starts immediately and no truncation is required. If the estimation procedure is based on a single time series then the startup policy is only applied once and it is not too inefficient to truncate. However, if replication is used, the startup policy is used repetitively and great care is needed in establishing it.

Another observation involves past research on startup policies. Theoretical results (6,22) are only available for small, well-behaved models. For such models, the variability associated with sample values during startup is not too different from the steady-state variability. Thus, the theoretical research tends to indicate that no truncation should be performed. Practical applications, however, indicate this is not the case and that truncation is a reasonable policy to follow. This is especially true when dealing with job shops or conveyor systems in which many sequential operations must be performed before the system is "loaded". These points bring the discussion back to initial condition setting.

13.5.1   Initial Condition Setting

The ideal initial condition setting would be to sample from the steady-state distributions that underlie the simulation model and set the initial conditions based on the sample values obtained. Repeated use of this procedure would ensure sound statistical estimates of steady-state performance. This is clearly a "catch 22" situation as knowledge of the steady-state distribution would preclude the need for the simulation model. To avoid such a situation, three basic rules have been proposed for setting the initial state of the system:

1. Start the system "empty and idle";
2. Start the system at the steady-state mode; and
3. Start the system at the steady-state mean.

Rule 1 has the advantage of being easy to implement. It has the disadvantage in application studies of not being a good representative state. For small scale models, such as the M|M|1 queueing situation, it is a good representative state as "empty and idle" is the modal state.

Rule 2 specifies that the most likely state, that is, the state with the highest probability of occurring, should be the starting condition. Through experimental analysis, it was selected as the best initial condition for the models evaluated (64). The main disadvantage is the inability to determine the modal state for a large model.

Rule 3 recommends that the starting state be the expected or average state. The advantage of this rule is that the average state can be approximated through the making of a pilot study or by analyzing a related but analytically tractable model. Intuitively, starting in the expected state should provide initial samples that have a representative variability. However, there have been no published results which indicate that starting a simulation in the "average" state produces better statistical estimators.

13.5.2 Truncation Procedures

The simplest truncation procedure is to specify a time at which the collection of sample data is to be initiated. Actually, in simulation models, such a rule is implemented by discarding all sample values collected up to the truncation point. This is the case in SLAM, and truncation is implemented by either including a MONTR statement in the input with the CLEAR option specified or by directly calling subroutine CLEAR at the time truncation is desired.

The question that arises for setting the truncation point is how to specify the time at which truncation should be made. One approach, which is perhaps the most common in applications, is to make a pilot run and select a time based on the pilot run. Although not normally done on a formal basis, the analyst considers such quantities as the number of consecutive times sample values have increased or decreased, differences between successive batch averages and successive cumulative averages, and crossings of averages by the sample values. Many authors have attempted to formalize these concepts and to provide a truncation rule that can be used in the simulation model for detecting when the conditions for truncation are met by the time series values for a given run.

Papers that survey and evaluate some of these rules are available (28,64,65). A limited summary of these rules is presented in Table 13-1. Most evaluations have been made on small models and indicate that truncation should not be em-

Table 13-1 Truncation rules.†

Proposer	Rule
Conway(39)	Set d so that $x(d+1)$ is neither the maximum nor the minimum of the values $\{x(n) : n=d+1, \cdots, N\}$
Fishman(5)	Set $d=n$ when $\{sgn(x(t) - \overline{x}_n) : t=0,1,2, \cdots n\}$ contains k runs where k is a parameter to be specified. This rule corresponds to setting $d=n$ when the time series $\{x(t) : t=0,1,2, \cdots n\}$ has crossed $\overline{x}_n$ at least $(k-1)$ times.
Schriber(40)	Set $d=n$ when the batch means for the k most recent batches of size b all fall within an interval of length ε.
Fishman(5)	Set d so that the number of observations deleted is "equivalent" to one independent observation where the number of dependent observations to independent observations is given by m/R_o. Thus set $d=m/R_o - 1$.
Gordon(41)	Make k replications to compute $Var[\overline{x}_n], n=1,2, \cdots$. Set $d= n$ for which $Var[\overline{x}_n]$ begins to fall off as $1/n$.
Gafarian(38)	Set d equal to the smallest n for which $x(n)$ is neither the maximum nor minimum of all preceding observations $\{x(t) : t=0,1,2, \cdots, n\}$.

† The notation used in this table suppresses the batch number subscript and employs lower case letters as the rules depend directly on the sample values observed.

ployed. For the reasons cited earlier, these results may not apply for large-scale models.

In the application of the proposed truncation rules, four issues should be kept in mind:

1. The expected value of a sample average lags the expected values of the process variable if the system is initially empty and leads it if the system is loaded to capacity(18);
2. Crossings of averages are not as likely as anticipated;
3. Truncation rules are extremely sensitive to parameter settings. Also, parameter setting procedures are not available for many proposed rules(63); and
4. For a long initial startup period, the application of a truncation rule can be time-consuming and, hence, expensive.

These issues account for the lack of use of truncation procedures in applications and the direct use of a truncation time for clearing statistics.

13.6   STOPPING RULES

Determining the length of a simulation run as specified in terms of the number of batches is a complex problem. If we are willing to assume that $\bar{X}_I$ is unbiased and that $\text{Var}[\bar{X}_I] = \sigma_{\bar{X}}^2/I$ then the number of batches I required to obtain a $(1-\alpha)$ confidence that the mean μ_X is contained in a prescribed interval can be computed using standard statistical formula. Symbolically, suppose we desire

$$P[\bar{X}_I - g \leq \mu_X \leq \bar{X}_I + g] \geq 1 - \alpha$$

where g is a prescribed half-length for the confidence interval. Letting $Z = \sqrt{I}(\bar{X}_I - \mu_X)/\sigma_X$, we have

$$P\left[|Z| \leq \frac{g\sqrt{I}}{\sigma_X}\right] \geq 1 - \alpha$$

with equality holding for the smallest value of I, say I*. Assuming I* is large enough so that the central limit theorem applies, we have

$$I^* = \left(\frac{\sigma_X}{g} Z_{a/2}\right)^2$$

where

$$Z_{a/2} \text{ is such that } \frac{1}{\sqrt{2\pi}} \int_{Z_{a/2}}^{\infty} e^{-y^2/2} \, dy = \alpha/2$$

This equation for I* requires knowledge of σ_X. A common trick is to specify g in relative terms of σ_X, that is, let $g = v\sigma_X$ for v>0. In this case, I* can be computed without knowledge of σ_X. Values of I* for combinations of v and α are given in Table 13-2.

From Table 13-2, we see that it requires almost 400 batches to obtain a 95 percent confidence interval that μ_X is within $(\bar{X}_I - 0.1\,\sigma_X, \bar{X}_I + 0.1\,\sigma_X)$. Similar analyses can be performed for determining the sample size to have a prescribed confidence interval on the variance or on a probability value.

Throughout this chapter, we have proposed the use of a batch mean as the sample value X_I. Because of this, the assumptions required in the above procedure are

Table 13-2   Values of I* for combinations of v and α.

I* v	α 0.02	0.05	0.10
0.01	54093	38416	27060
0.10	541	384	271
0.20	135·	96	68
0.50	22	15	11

tenable. If the independence assumption is not appropriate, then we can use $Var[\bar{X}_I]$ = m/I and replace σ_X^2 in the above equations by m.

Typically, s_X is used in place of σ_X (or $\hat{m}$ for m) in which case $\sqrt{I}(\bar{X}_I - \mu)/s_X$ has a t-distribution. In simulation studies, I is usually large enough to assume that the normal approximation to the t-distribution holds. To set I* before the simulation is started, a value of s_X is required. In some cases, pilot studies are performed to obtain a value for s_X from which I* is estimated. A more general approach is to use a sequential stopping rule.

A sequential stopping rule specifies a condition that when satisfied will yield the desired objective. Starr(60) has shown that if the X_i are iid normal random variables that

$$P\{\bar{X}_{I*} - g \leq \mu \leq \bar{X}_{I*} + g\} \geq \begin{cases} 0.928 \text{ for } 1-\alpha = 0.95 \\ 0.985 \text{ for } 1-\alpha = 0.99 \end{cases} \quad (13\text{-}21)$$

when I* is set according to

$$I* = \min\{I : I \geq 3 \text{ and odd}; s_X^2 \leq Ig^2/t_{a/2,I-1}^2\} \quad (13\text{-}22)$$

where $t_{a/2,I-1}$ corresponds to the $1-\alpha/2$ fractile of the student t-distribution with I−1 degrees of freedom, for example, $t_{.025,10} = 2.228$.

The degradation in the confidence interval occurs because the test is being sequentially applied. Fishman(25) proposes the use of Eq. 13-22 without the requirement for I to be odd, since the requirement for I to be odd is due to the intractability of the analysis when I is even. The use of Eq. 13-22 in a simulation experiment requires a table of t-values, a prescription for g, a batch size specification and then the periodic testing of computed values of s_X until its value is below that required in Eq. 13-22. When this occurs, the confidence interval as specified by Eq. 13-21 holds.

When a relative specification is desired, that is, $-v\mu \leq \overline{X}_I - \mu \leq v\mu$ where $v > 0$, Nadas (52) has shown that the stopping rule

$$I^* = \min \{I : s_{\overline{X}}^2 \leq [(Iv\bar{x}_I/t_{a/2,I-1})^2 - 1]/(I-1)\} \tag{13-23}$$

will result in a limiting confidence interval of

$$\lim_{v \to 0} P[\overline{X}_{I^*}/(1+v) \leq \mu_X \leq \overline{X}_{I^*}/(1-v)] = 1-\alpha$$

Note that for large I and $g = v\bar{x}_I$, the stopping rule given by Eq. 13-23 approximates the rule given by Eq. 13-22.

Since there is a degradation in the coverage associated with the use of the stopping rules specified by Eq. 13-22 and Eq. 13-23, we recommend for important decisions that I^* be established not as the minimum number of batches for which the condition on $s_{\overline{X}}^2$ holds, but as the value of I for which the condition holds a second time. Typically, this should only require one additional batch to be obtained but it may require more. Using this rule should help to compensate for both the degradation expected from Eq. 13-21 and the inherent optimism (smaller variance estimates) associated with the calculation of $s_{\overline{X}}^2$ based on the assumption of iid batch observations.

In addition to determining the sample size to meet desired confidence interval specifications, there are practical issues associated with the stopping of a simulation run. Such questions involve the consideration of what to do about entities in the model at the end of a run. The answers to such questions are problem specific. If such entities are representative of the other entities on which statistics were collected, then the further processing of them should not matter. However, if they are atypical or if some information has been collected on them, then their processing should be considered. For example, in a job shop where a shortest processing time rule was employed, the jobs remaining at the end of a run could be those jobs whose processing times are extremely long. Not processing such jobs would lead to a bias in the statistics on time in system. Care must be taken to avoid such a situation.

A more general procedure for establishing a stopping condition involves the concept of marginal return. It has been proposed that a run should be stopped when the marginal improvement in potential profits based on the run decreases below the marginal costs associated with continuing the run(37,38). Although this is a good general concept, assessing potential profits and calculating marginal costs can be difficult.

13.7   DESIGN OF EXPERIMENTS

A simulation run is an experiment in which an assessment of the performance of a system is estimated for a prescribed set of conditions. In the jargon of design of experiments, the conditions are referred to as factors and treatments where a treatment is a specific level of a factor. The literature in the field of design of experiments is extensive (10,41,53). The purpose of this section is to present the issues relating to the design of experiments, but not to present the details as to how one should design a simulation experiment. The statistical techniques associated with the design of experiments are well documented. Applications of the procedures of analysis of variance (ANOVA); the Shapiro-Wilk test for testing normality assumptions; or the Newman-Keuls test for investigating all pairs of means are not considered to be significantly different in simulation studies from their use in other areas (2).

The major problem involved in simulation experiments is associated with the definition of the inference space associated with the simulation model. Making *a priori* assessments of how widely the results obtained from the simulation model are to be applied, and developing a thorough understanding of the inferences that can be made, are the most neglected aspects of the design of experiments associated with simulation studies. A possible reason for this is the inclusion of factors in the experiment that relate to the multitude of alternatives open to the analyst and the extensive number of experimental controls that must be set when performing the experiment. In previous sections of this chapter we have discussed some of these experimental controls such as: starting conditions; sampling procedures; run length; batch size; and estimation procedures. Documented examples which include all these factors are not available; however, the survey by Kleijnen is extensive and highly recommended(41).

In general, the objectives of simulation experiments are to:
1. obtain knowledge of the effects of controllable factors on experimental outputs;
2. estimate system parameters of interest;
3. make a selection from among a set of alternatives; and
4. determine the treatment levels for all factors which produce an optimum response.

When multiple factors are involved the approach to the first two items listed above is to select one of the many possible experimental designs and to hypothesize a model for the analysis of variance for the experimental design selected. The experimental design specifies the combination of treatment levels along with the number of replications for each combination for which the simulation model must be exercised. Using the data obtained from the experiment, the parameters of the hypothesized model are determined along with the estimation of the error terms. Interaction plots are then drawn to ascertain the joint effects of the various factors. The significance of each factor is then judged based on the derived model, and from this estimates of system parameters of interest can be calculated. This procedure is reminiscent of the parametric modeling approach described earlier in this chapter for a single performance measure of interest.

In the problem of making a choice among alternatives, the statistical procedures of ranking and selection are used. Kleijnen(41) and Dudewicz(16) present state-of-the-art reviews that summarize past research in this area and how it can be used in simulation analysis. Many procedures have been developed for specifying the sample size required in order to select the alternative whose population mean is greater than the next best population mean by a prescribed value with a given probability. The test procedures involve the computation of the sample mean based on the sample size specified and the selection of the largest sample mean observed. Bechhofer developed this approach which is referred to as the indifference zone approach(3,4).

An alternative approach involves grouping the alternatives into statistically equivalent subsets. The procedures involved in making subset selections are given by Gupta who also compares subset selection with the indifference zone approach (32,33).

A final topic relating to the design of experiments is the selection of a best alternative. This problem differs from those previously described in that we are trying to determine the values for the controllable variables which either maximize or minimize an objective function. For example, in the analysis of a periodic review inventory system, we might wish to employ simulation to determine the values for the stock control level, reorder point, and time between reviews which minimize the average monthly cost of the inventory system.

Although the principles of optimization using simulation experiments are essentially the same as for optimization of mathematical expressions, there are some differences which must be considered. Since the response from a simulation typically involves random variables, the objective function or constraint equations written as a function of the simulation response will also be random variables. As a consequence, it is necessary to formulate response constraints as probability statements and to make statistical interpretations of the objective function value.

There have been two basic approaches to optimization using simulation models. The first approach involves a direct evaluation of the independent variables using the simulation model. Farrell(19) divides these techniques into three categories: mathematically naive techniques such as heuristic search, complete enumeration, and random search; methods appropriate to unimodal objective functions such as coordinate search, and pattern search; and methods for multimodal objective functions.

The second approach to optimization using simulation is response surface methodology(48). In this method we fit a surface to experimental observations using a factorial design in the vicinity of an initial search point. We then apply an optimization algorithm such as the gradient method to determine the optimum values of the controllable variables relative to the fitted equation. The optimum values for the fitted surface are then used to define the next search point. Biles has applied this procedure sequentially in a search for optimal decision values(5). A modular FORTRAN program for simulation optimization using first and second order response surfaces has been developed by Smith(59).

The implementation of an optimization procedure within the GASP IV simulation language has been illustrated by Pegden and Gately(56). In SLAM, the determination of the next experimental condition in a search for the optimum can be performed in either subroutine INTLC or OTPUT in a manner similar to the one used by Pegden and Gately in GASP IV.

13.8   CHAPTER SUMMARY

Two distinct aspects of simulation output analysis involve the accuracy and reliability of the sample values obtained. The main emphasis of this chapter is on reliability. The importance of $Var[\overline{X}_I]$ in simulation studies is established. It is recommended that the reliability of simulation outputs be based on observations of batch or cycle averages rather than on individual sample values. Five methods for estimating the variance of sample means, $Var[\overline{X}_I]$, based on I batches are presented. Variance reduction techniques, startup policies, stopping rules, and the design of simulation experiments are described. Overall, this chapter provides both detailed practical results and suggestions for the important statistical problems facing a simulation analyst.

13.9 EXERCISES

13-1.   Define the following terms: Reliable; Batch; Stochastic Process; Ergodic; Stationary; Steady State; Time Series; Sample Mean; Average; Expectation; Mean Square Error; Kurtosis; Spectrum; Regeneration Point; Parametric Modeling; Spectral Density Function; ARMA Model; White Noise; VRT; Stratified Sampling; Catch-22; and Bias.

13-2.   A drive-in bank has two windows, each manned by a teller and each has a separate drive-in lane. The drive-in lanes are adjacent. From previous observations, it has been determined that the time interval between customer arrivals during rush hours is exponentially distributed with a mean time between arrivals of 0.25 time units. Congestion occurs only during rush hours, and only this period is to be analyzed. The service time is exponentially distributed for each teller with a mean service time of 0.4 time unit. It has also been shown that customers have no preference for a teller if the waiting lines are equal. At all other times, a customer chooses the shortest line. After a customer has entered the system, he may not leave until he is serviced. However, he may change lanes if he is the last customer in his lane and a difference of two customers exists between the two lanes. Because of parking space limitations, only nine cars can wait in each lane. These cars, plus the car of the customer being serviced by each teller, allow a maximum of twenty cars in the system. If the system is full when a customer arrives, he balks and is lost to the system.

   The initial conditions are as follows:

1. Both drive-in tellers are busy. The initial service time for each teller is exponentially distributed with mean of 0.4 time unit.
2. The first customer is scheduled to arrive at 0.1 time unit.
3. Two customers are waiting in each queue.

Theoretical Steady-State Results

   Steady-state probabilities: (0.1123, 0.1796, 0.1437, 0.1150, 0.0920, 0.0736, 0.0589, 0.0471, 0.0377, 0.0301, 0.0241, 0.0193, 0.0154, 0.0123, 0.0099, 0.0079, 0.0063, 0.0050, 0.0040, 0.0032, 0.0026)

   Number in system: Mean = 4.232; Variance = 15.83; and m = 177.4.

   Determine the simulation run length required to obtain estimates that are within 10 percent of the theoretical values.

13-3.   Simulate the system described in Exercise 13-2 to obtain estimates of the variance of the sample mean and the value of m for each of the following random variables:

1. The number of customers in the system, and
2. The time a customer spends in the system.

   Develop estimates for $\mathrm{Var}(\bar{X}_I)$ and m using both replication and subinterval sampling procedures. Select a total amount of simulation time on which to base your estimates and give a rationale for your selection. The same amount of simulation time should be used for each procedure.

Embellishments: (a) Perform a spectral analysis of the experimental data. (b) Use regenerative techniques to obtain the requested estimates. (c) Use parametric modeling techniques to build a model of the simulated data. (d) Obtain 95% confidence limits for m using the information that $(k-1)\hat{m}/m$ is Chi-square distributed with $(k-1)$ degrees of freedom.

13-4. Compare the use of the observed data values and batched observations in the embellishments to Exercise 13-3.

13-5. Evaluate the effect of making the initial conditions for the system described in Exercise 13-2 to be the modal state. Evaluate the effect of starting in the expected state.

13-6. Evaluate three truncation rules for the system described in Exercise 13-2.

Embellishment: Develop a truncation rule and evaluate it.

13-7. Perform four experiments each consisting of ten runs of length 200 time units on the bank teller simulation model, Exercise 13-2. In experiment 1, use random number stream 1 for arrival times and stream 2 for service times. In experiment 2, use stream 1 again for arrivals but the antithetic values from stream 2. In experiment 3, employ antithetic values from both streams 1 and 2. In experiment 4, use stream 1 for arrival times and stream 3 for service times.

Define $X_k^{(i)}$ to be the average computed on run k of experiment i where X could be either the average number in the system, $\overline{N}$, or the average time in the system, $\overline{W}$.

(a) Calculate $\text{Var}[\overline{Z}]$ where $\overline{Z}_k = [\overline{X}_k^{(1)} + \overline{X}_k^{(j)}]/2$ using pairs of runs from experiments 1 and 2 and experiments 1 and 3.

(b) Calculate $\text{Var}[\overline{X}_k^{(1)} - \overline{X}_k^{(j)}]$ for $j = 2$ and 4.

(c) For each experiment, use the prior information that $\overline{N} = \lambda_E \overline{W}$ to obtain a variance reduction where λ_E is the effective arrival rate after balking occurs.

13-8. Apply the sequential stopping rule suggested in Section 13.6 to the bank teller model, Exercise 13-2, to obtain a 95 percent confidence interval that has a half length, g, of 0.25. Embellishment: Apply the sequential stopping rate procedure to obtain a 95 percent confidence that the half length is 10 percent of the true mean value.

13-9. Perform Exercises 13-2 through 13-8 for Example 6-2, the inspection and adjustment of television sets model.

13-10. For the single channel queueing situation, evaluate the variance reduction obtained from switching the streams used for generating arrival and service times.

13-11. For the bank teller simulation model, stratify customers based on their service time and then compute the variance of the average time in the system. Compare these results with those obtained without stratification.

13-12. Develop and apply an optimization procedure for setting the reorder point, stock control level and time between reviews for the inventory model and cost values given in embellishment (e) of Exercise 7-5.

13-13. Discuss the issues involved in performing an analysis of variance on experiments that involve the use of common streams and antithetic samples.

13.10   REFERENCES

1. Anderson, T. W., *The Statistical Analysis of Time Series,* John Wiley, 1970.
2. Anderson, V. L. and R. A. McLean, *Design of Experiments: A Realistic Approach,* Marcel Dekker, 1974.
3. Bechhofer, R. E., "A Single-Sample Multiple Decision Procedure for Ranking Means of Normal Populations with Known Variances," *Ann. Math. Stat.,* Vol. 25, 1954, pp. 16-39.
4. Bechhofer, R. E., "Selection in Factorial Experiments," *Proceedings, 1977 Winter Simulation Conference,* 1977, pp. 65-70.
5. Biles, W. E., "Integration-Regression Search Procedure for Simulation Experimentation," *Proceedings, 1974 Winter Simulation Conference,* 1974, pp. 491-497.
6. Blomqvist, N., "On the Transient Behavior of the GI/G/1 Waiting-Times," Skandinavisk Aktuarietidskrift, Vol. 53, 1970, pp. 118-129.
7. Box, G. E. P. and G. M. Jenkins, *Time Series Analysis: Forecasting and Control,* Holden-Day, 1970.
8. Carter, G. and E. J. Ignall, "A Variance Reduction Technique for Simulation," *Management Science,* Vol. 21, 1975, pp. 607-616.
9. Cinlar, E., *Introduction to Stochastic Processes,* Prentice-Hall, 1975.
10. Cochran, W. G. and G. M. Cox, *Experimental Designs,* John Wiley, 1957.
11. Cochran, W. G., *Sampling Techniques,* Third Edition, John Wiley, 1977.
12. Conway, R., "Some Tactical Problems in Digital Simulation," *Management Science,* Vol. 10, 1963, pp. 47-61.
13. Crane, M. A. and D. L. Iglehart, "Simulating Stable Stochastic Systems I: General Multiserver Queues," *J. ACM,* Vol. 21, 1974, pp. 103-113.
14. Crane, M. A. and A. Lemoine, *An Introduction to the Regenerative Method for Simulation Analysis,* Technical Report No. 86-23, California Analysis Corporation, Palo Alto, CA., October 1976.
15. Diananda, P. H., "Some Probability Limit Theorems with Statistical Applications," *Proceedings, Cambridge Phil. Soc.,* Vol. 49, 1953, pp. 239-246.
16. Dudewicz, E. J., "New Procedures for Selection Among (Simulated) Alternatives," *Proceedings, 1977 Winter Simulation Conference,* 1977, pp. 58-62.
17. Duket, S., *Simulation Output Analysis,* unpublished MS Thesis, Purdue University, December 1974.
18. Duket, S. and A. A. B. Pritsker, "Examination of Simulation Output Using Spectral Methods," *Mathematics and Computers in Simulation,* Vol. XX, 1978, pp. 53-60.
19. Farrell, W., "Literature Review and Bibliography of Simulation Optimization," *Proceedings, 1977 Winter Simulation Conference,* 1977, pp. 116-124.
20. Feller, W., *An Introduction to Probability Theory and Its Applications,* Vol. 1, 2nd Edition, John Wiley, 1957.
21. Feller, W., *An Introduction to Probability Theory and Its Applications,* Vol. 2, John Wiley, 1972.

22. Fishman, G. S., "A Study of Bias Considerations in Simulation Experiments," *Operations Research,* Vol. 20, 1972, pp. 785-790.

23. Fishman, G. S., *Concepts and Methods in Discrete Event Digital Simulation,* John Wiley, 1973.

24. Fishman, G. S., "Grouping Observations in Digital Simulation," *Management Science,* Vol. 24, 1978, pp. 510-521.

25. Fishman, G. S., *Principles of Discrete Event Simulation,* John Wiley, 1978.

26. Fishman, G. S., "Statistical Analysis for Queueing Simulation," *Management Science,* Vol. 20, 1973, pp. 363-369.

27. Fishman, G. S., "The Allocation of Computer Time in Company Simulation Experiments," *Operations Research,* Vol. 16, 1968, pp. 280-295.

28. Gafarian, A. V., Ancker, C. J., and Morisaku, T. *The Problem of the Initial Transient with Respect to Mean Value in Digital Computer Simulation and the Evaluation of Some Proposed Solutions,* Technical Report No. 77-1, University of Southern California, 1977.

29. Goldenberger, A. S., *Econometric Theory,* John Wiley, 1964.

30. Gordon, G., *System Simulation,* Prentice-Hall, 1969.

31. Gray, H. L. and W. R. Schucany, *The Generalized Jackknife Statistic,* Marcel Dekker, 1972.

32. Gupta, S. S. and S. Panchapakesan, "On Multiple Decision (Subset Selection) Procedures, *Journal of Math and Physical Sciences,* Vol. 6, 1972, pp. 1-71.

33. Gupta, S. S. and J. C. Hsu, "Subset Selection Procedures with Special Reference to the Analysis of 2-Way Layout: Application to Motor Vehicle Fatality Data," *Proceedings, 1977 Winter Simulation Conference,* 1977, pp. 80-85.

34. Hammersley, J. M. and D. C. Handscomb, *Monte Carlo Methods,* Methuen, 1964.

35. Hazen, G. and A. A. B. Pritsker, "Formulas for the Variance of the Sample Mean in Finite State Markov Processes," *Journal of Statistical Computation and Simulation,* Vol. 12, 1981, pp. 25-40.

36. Hoel, P. G., *Elementary Statistics,* Second Edition, John Wiley, 1966.

37. Hogg, R. V. and A. T. Craig, *Introduction to Mathematical Statistics,* Macmillan, 1970.

38. Kabak, I. W., "Stopping Rules for Queueing Simulations," *Operations Research,* Vol. 16, 1968, pp. 431-437.

39. Karlin, S. and H. Tayler, *A First Course in Stochastic Processes,* Academic Press, 1975.

40. Kleijnen, J. P. C., *Statistical Techniques in Simulation: Part I,* Marcel Dekker, 1974.

41. Kleijnen, J. P. C., *Statistical Techniques in Simulation, Part II,* Marcel Dekker, 1975.

42. Law, A. M., *Confidence Intervals for Steady-State Simulations, I: A Survey of Fixed Sample Size Procedures,* Technical Report 78-5, University of Wisconsin, 1978.

43. Law, A. M., "Efficient Estimators for Simulated Queueing Systems," *Management Science,* Vol. 22, 1975, pp. 30-41.

44. Law, A. M., *Statistical Analysis of the Output Data from Terminating Simulations,* Technical Report 78-4, University of Wisconsin, 1978.

45. Little, J. D. C., "A Proof of the Queueing formula $L=\lambda W$," *Operations Research,* Vol. 9, 1961, pp. 383-387.

46. Mabert, V. A., *An Introduction to Short Term Forecasting Using The Box-Jenkins Methodology,* AIIE Monograph Series, AIIE-PP C-75-1, Atlanta, Georgia, 1975.

47. Mechanic, H. and W. McKay, "Confidence Intervals for Averages of Dependent Data in Simulations II," Technical Report 17-202, IBM Advanced Systems Development Division, August 1966.

48. Meyer, R. H., *Response Surface Methodology,* Allyn & Bacon, 1971.

49. Moeller, T. L. and P. D. Welch, "A Special Based Technique for Generating Confidence Intervals from Simulation Outputs," *Proceedings, 1977 Winter Simulation Conference,* 1977, pp. 176-184.

50. Moran, P. A. P., "Some Theorems on Time Series, I," *Biometrika,* Vol. 34, 1947, pp. 281-291.

51. Moy, W. A., "Practical Variance Reducing Procedures for Monte Carlo Simulations," in *Computer Simulation Experiments with Models of Economic Systems* by T. H. Naylor, John Wiley, 1971.

52. Nadas, A., "An Extension of a Theorem of Chow and Robbins on Sequential Confidence Intervals for the Mean," *Ann. Math. Stat.,* Vol. 40, 1969, pp. 667-671.

53. Naylor, T. H., Editor, *The Design of Computer Simulation Experiments,* Duke University Press, 1969.

54. Page, E. S., "On Monte Carlo Methods in Congestion Problems; II; Simulation of Queueing Systems," *Operations Research,* Vol. 13, 1965, pp. 300-305.

55. Parzen, E., *Stochastic Processes,* Holden-Day, 1962.

56. Pegden, C. D. and M. P. Gately, "Decision Optimization for GASP IV Simulation Models," *Proceedings, 1977 Winter Simulation Conference,* 1977, pp. 127-133.

57. Ross, S., *A First Course in Probability,* Macmillan, 1976.

58. Schriber, T., *Simulation Using GPSS,* John Wiley, 1974.

59. Smith, D. E., *Automated Response Surface Methodology in Digital Computer Simulation (U), Volume I: Program Description and User's Guide (U),* Office of Naval Research, Arlington, VA: September 1975.

60. Starr, N., "The Performance of a Sequential Procedure for the Fixed-Width Interval Estimation of the Mean," *Ann. Math. Stat.,* Vol. 37, 1966, pp. 36-50.

61. Stidham, S., Jr., "L=λW: A Discounted Analog and a New Proof," *Operations Research,* Vol. 20, 1972, pp. 1115-1126.

62. Tocher, K. D., *The Art of Simulation,* Van Nostrand, 1963.

63. Wilson, J. R., *A Procedure for Evaluating Startup Policies in Simulation Experiments,* unpublished M. S. Thesis, Purdue University, December 1977.

64. Wilson, J. R. and A. A. B. Pritsker, "A Survey of Research on the Simulation Startup Problem," *Simulation,* Vol. 31, 1978, pp. 55-58.

65. Wilson, J. R. and A. A. B. Pritsker, "A Procedure for Evaluating Startup Policies in Simulation Experiments," *Simulation,* Vol. 31, 1978, pp. 79-89.

13.11   APPENDIX: THEOREMS OF INTEREST TO SIMULATORS

In this appendix, we present theorems and equations which relate to the analysis of simulation results.

13.11.1   Theorem on Total Probability (57)

The probability of the outcome B is equal to the sum of the conditional probabilities associated with B given the occurrence of mutually exclusive and exhaustive outcomes A_i weighted by the probability of A_i, that is,

$$P[B] = \sum_i P[B|A_i]P[A_i]$$

An analogous result for the expectation of a random variable, Y, is

$$E[Y] = \sum_i E[Y|X=x_i]P[X=x_i]$$

13.11.2   Joint Probabilities (9,55)

The probability of the joint outcome associated with a set of random variables can be expressed as a product of conditional probabilities

$$P[Y_1,Y_2,\ldots,Y_n] = P[Y_1]P[Y_2|Y_1]P[Y_3|Y_1,Y_2] \ldots \quad P[Y_n|Y_1 \ldots Y_{n-1}]$$

If we assume the random variables have the Markovian property that $P[Y_j|Y_1,Y_2, \ldots,Y_{j-1}] = P[Y_j|Y_{j-1}]$, we have

$$P[Y_1,Y_2 \ldots Y_n] = P[Y_1]P[Y_2|Y_1]P[Y_3|Y_2] \ldots \quad P[Y_n|Y_{n-1}]$$

If independence is assumed then

$$P[Y_1,Y_2,\ldots,Y_n] = P[Y_1]P[Y_2]P[Y_3] \ldots \quad P[Y_n]$$

13.11.3   Random Sum of Independent Random Variables (57)

If $X_1, X_2, \ldots, X_K$ are independent and identically distributed random variables and K is a discrete random variable independent of X_i then for the sum

$$Y = \sum_{i=1}^{K} X_i \, ,$$

we have

$$E[Y] = E[X]E[K]$$

and

$$Var[Y] = E[K]Var[X] + Var[K]E^2[X]$$

13.11.4   Change of Variables Formula(36,57)

Given:

$$Y_j = g_j(W_1, W_2, \ldots, W_n) \ , \ j = 1, 2, \ldots, n$$

then the joint density function of the $Y_j, f_Y(\cdot)$, is

$$f_Y(y_1, y_2 \ldots, y_n) = f_W(w_1, w_2 \ldots, w_n) \frac{1}{|J|}$$

where $f_W(\cdot)$ is the joint density function for $W_1, W_2, \ldots, W_n$ and J is the Jacobian defined as the determinant of the matrix

$$\begin{pmatrix} \dfrac{\partial g_1}{\partial w_1} & \dfrac{\partial g_1}{\partial w_2} & \cdots & \dfrac{\partial g_1}{\partial w_n} \\ \cdot & \cdot & & \cdot \\ \cdot & \cdot & & \cdot \\ \cdot & \cdot & & \cdot \\ \dfrac{\partial g_n}{\partial w_1} & \dfrac{\partial g_n}{\partial w_2} & \cdots & \dfrac{\partial g_n}{\partial w_n} \end{pmatrix}$$

and $|J|$ is the absolute value of J. This formula prescribes a procedure for making a transformation of random variables.

13.11.5   Asymptotic Normality of Recurrent Events(20,21)

If a recurrent event is persistent† and the time between events has a finite mean μ and variance σ^2, then T_r and N_t are asymptotically normally distributed where T_r is the time until the rth event occurrence with $E[T_r] = r\mu$ and $Var[T_r] = r\sigma^2$; and N_t is the number of event occurrences in t time units with $E[N_t] = t/\mu$ and $Var[N_t] = t\, \sigma^2/\mu^3$. For example, if in a simulation the time between arrivals has a mean $\mu = 10$ and variance $\sigma^2 = 4$, then the number of the arrivals in $t = 1000$ time units is approximately normal with a mean of 100 and a variance of 4.

The above statement is a central limit theorem for a sequence of dependent variables and can be used to check the reasonableness of input generators for a simulation model.

In addition to the above central limit theorem for recurrent events, there are central limit theorems that establish normality conditions for the sample mean for

---

† Feller's terms recurrent and persistent, although out of fashion, provide understandable descriptions of the concepts involved.

stationary stochastic processes. Moran (50) presents a theorem for moving average (MA) type processes and Dianada (15) for processes in which independence occurs after r lags or time periods.

13.11.6   The First Arc Sine Law   (20)

Consider a binomial random variable Y_n with $P[Y_n=1] = 1/2$ and $P[Y_n=-1] = 1/2$ for $n = 1,2, \ldots, N$. Consider the sequence of partial sums

$$Z_n = \sum_{i=1}^{n} Y_i$$

for all times up to time N. For a fixed α $(0 < \alpha < 1)$, we focus on the experimental outcome in which $Z_n > 0$ for at most $N\alpha$ time units, that is, we look for experiments in which the sequence $\{Z_n : 1 \leq n \leq N\}$ up to time N spends at most α percent of the time above the axis. As $N \to \infty$, the probability of observing such a result tends to

$$\frac{2}{\pi} \sin^{-1}(\sqrt{\alpha})$$

For example, the probability that the fraction of time is less than $\alpha=0.976$ is 0.90. Thus, with probability 0.20, the fraction of time spent on one side of zero or the other is 0.976.

Another result is that, in a time period of length 2N, the probability that the number of partial sums $\{Z_n\}$ equal to zero being at most $\alpha\sqrt{2N}$ tends to

$$\sqrt{\frac{2}{\pi}} \int_0^a e^{-q^2/2} dq \quad \text{as } N \to \infty$$

For example, if we drew 10,000 samples of Y_n then there is a probability of 0.50 that there will be fewer than 68 times when $\sum Y_n = 0$. A related result also given by Feller specifies that the number of changes of sign (crossings) in the sequence of partial sums in N time units increases as the $\sqrt{N}$, that is, in 100N time units we should only expect 10 times as many crossings of 0 as in N time units. These theorems illustrate the conceptual difficulties and nonintuitive behavior associated with even simple stochastic processes. These results indicate potential difficulties associated with the use of returns to a state or the crossing of a state in statistical analysis.

13.11.7   Rao-Blackwell Theorem(37)

Let X and Y denote random variables such that Y has mean μ and variance $\sigma_Y^2 > 0$. Let $E[Y|x] = \phi(x)$. Then $E[\phi(X)] = \mu$ and $\sigma_{\phi(X)}^2 \leq \sigma_Y^2$.

This theorem states that if we are interested in the statistical properties of the random variable Y and can define a related random variable $\phi(X)$ which is the expected value of Y conditioned on X then we can estimate μ from the expected value of $\phi(X)$ and the variance of this estimate will be at least as small as the variance of a direct estimator. This theorem establishes the worth of using prior information in estimating sample means.†

---

† This observation concerning the Rao-Blackwell Theorem as a basis for use of prior information as a variance reduction technique was pointed out to the authors by James R. Wilson.

CHAPTER 14

Applications of Simulation

14.1   AREAS OF APPLICATION

As indicated in Chapter 1 surveys on the use of industrial engineering, management science, and operations research have consistently indicated that simula-

510

tion and statistics are the techniques most widely used in government and industry. The main reason for the widespread use of simulation is the diversity of areas in which simulation can be applied (See Table 1-1 of Chapter 1). In the next sections, capsule summaries of specific simulation projects are given. The summaries show that simulation is a useful technique. They also provide a discussion of problem types for which simulation has been used in actual decision-making situations, and the types of questions that have been answered by using simulation. The procedures employed in building the specific simulation models described are contained in the referenced papers.

The major part of this text has dealt with model development procedures. It is not a difficult task to design and develop models for industrial use. Typically, such models are larger in size, but conceptually not more complex, than those that have been presented. A significant point when developing a simulation model is the understanding that there are alternative approaches to building a model. Thus, as the examples illustrate, it is not necessary to conform to any fixed set of rules when modeling. Using new and novel approaches is encouraged.

Since SLAM is a new language, application experience at the time of the writing of this book is limited. Since SLAM contains networks like Q-GERT, and discrete event and continuous modeling capabilities like GASP IV, past experience in using Q-GERT and GASP IV for solving problems will be the basis for the application summaries presented in the next sections. A good set of applications using other simulation languages for which SLAM models can be built is presented by Reitman(25).

14.2 WORK FLOW ANALYSIS OF A PROPERTY AND CASUALTY INSURANCE COMPANY'S REGIONAL SERVICE OFFICE(17)

The work flow system of a regional service office involves the processing of property and casualty insurance claims through a centralized computer information system. The various types of forms are routed through fourteen distinct operating units or departments within the regional service office which employs over 150 personnel. The system was modeled as a complex queueing situation to identify the bottlenecks of the work flow and to assist in investigating the effects of certain managerial decisions. A Q-GERT model aided in estimating the consequences of specific actions contemplated or anticipated by management. The procedural changes investigated were:

1. Changes in the volume of each type of work handled by the regional service office;
2. Changes in the composition and requirements of the work input;
3. Changes in priority rules for the processing of work in the same operating unit;
4. Changes in the pathways of the work flow system;
5. Reallocation of personnel among the different departments; and
6. Changes in total processing times of customer requests due to training programs in specific areas.

14.3   EVALUATION OF AIR TERMINAL CARGO FACILITIES (2,8)

Managers of the military airlift system need a way of measuring the productive capacity of aerial port cargo processing. Specifically, the managers need to determine the effects of fluctuating demands for airlift cargo on a terminal's ability to meet the demand in a timely manner. Resource utilization is also an important factor.

At a terminal, cargo arrives by truck or by aircraft. The arriving cargo is offloaded and sorted by shipment type, destination, and priority. The sorted cargo is moved to various in-process storage areas where it is held until some form of consolidation is possible. Once consolidated, it is weighed, inspected, and stored. Its status can then be classified as "movement-ready." When movement-ready cargo is selected for a mission, it is transferred to a staging area where it is combined with the other cargo assigned to the mission and defined as a load. The load is then processed by cargo loading equipment and transferred to the aircraft.

A Q-GERT model of this situation was constructed to answer the following procedural questions:

1. Is it worthwhile to introduce automation equipment in ports to improve processing capacity?
2. Where should new equipment be located?
3. How many aircraft can a port load simultaneously?

4. During contingencies, what additional resources will be required to support an increase in the level of air traffic?

14.4 EVALUATION OF A PROPOSED CAPITAL EXPENDITURE IN THE STEEL INDUSTRY(36)

Bethlehem Steel Corporation's Lackawanna Plant was considering a design for new facilities for improving the steel-making process. Included in the design were new operations involving the melting of scrap and the desulfurization of hot metal. The analysis was to determine the need for additional hot metal carriers, called submarines, to support the proposed new operations.

A GASP IV simulation model was developed consistent with the objectives of evaluating a proposed capital expenditure and involved modeling the various operations associated with delivering hot metal from a set of blast furnaces (BF) to a set of basic oxygen furnaces (BOF). A schematic diagram of the operations model is shown in Figure 14-1. The submarines serve as materials handling equipment which transport the hot metal through a series of operations before returning to perform the set of tasks again. The demand for hot metal carriers depends on the casting times of the blast furnaces and the new scrap melter. Casting times are scheduled but actual performance times depend on the hot metal characteristics. Not having submarines available when a cast is ready is a dangerous and expensive situation and could cause a furnace to be shut down.

Scheduling rules were incorporated for routing the submarines through the desulfurization operation, if necessary, and to hot metal ladles which provided inputs to the basic oxygen furnaces. Submarines were also required to transfer hot metal from the scrap melter. A decision rule was also incorporated into the model for determining if an insufficient number of submarines would be available to accommodate the next cast from a blast furnace. When this situation occurs, a submarine dumps its hot metal and returns immediately to serve a blast furnace.

The simulation model showed, in contrast to earlier studies recommending the purchase of three submarines, that by altering the scheduling rules, the current number of submarines could support the new operations. Thus, the simulation analysis resulted in a recommendation which led to an avoidance of a capital expenditure of over one million dollars. In addition, procedures were suggested by which further improvements in the total steelmaking process could be made.

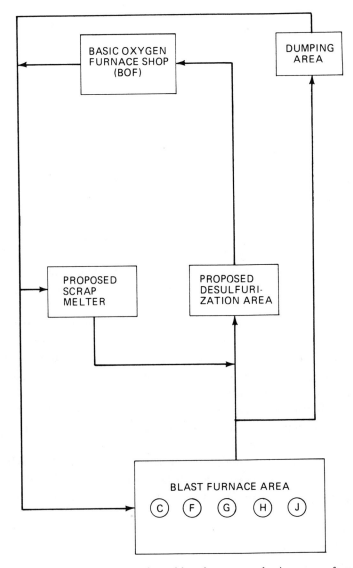

Figure 14-1 Submarine movements from blast furnaces to basic oxygen furnaces.

14.5   DESIGN OF A CORN SYRUP REFINERY

In July 1975, A.E. Staley Manufacturing Company broke ground for a new 85 million dollar corn wetmilling plant in Lafayette, Indiana. The plant was engi-

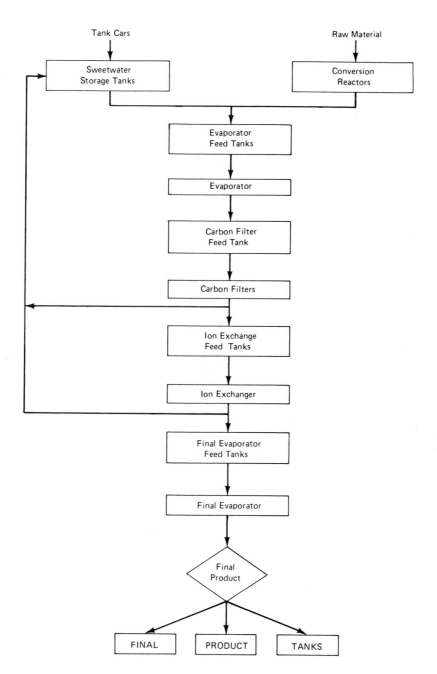

Figure 14-2 Proposed block diagram design of a corn syrup refinery.

neered with a flexible end-product mix capability which would permit Staley to respond to changes in the demand for various types of corn sweeteners. In 1975, a proposed design was developed that is depicted in Figure 14-2. As can be seen from the figure, the process involves two evaporation steps, one carbon refining step, and one ion exchanger step. Also shown are the required material flows from step to step. Water is used extensively in the process. Since it is recycled and contains sweeteners, it is referred to as sweetwater. In addition, storage tanks are required for maintaining balanced operations throughout the process. A discrete continuous GASP IV model of the system was built to determine the size of the storage tanks, evaporators, and ion exchanger(27).

The model was exercised and the most cost effective size of the various units was determined. Since large, special purpose equipment is involved, a lead time of over eighteen months is typical, and simulation was the only feasible way to evaluate the proposed design. In addition to the sizing study, system parameters were investigated for both a manual and a computerized control system. One control system model included the setting of valves to regulate sweetwater-source flows from different tanks, each having a different concentration level. It was presumed that the concentration level in each sweetwater tank could be assessed hourly. With knowledge of the concentration levels, a linear programming blending model was developed and imbedded in the simulation to set valves in order to maximize the profitability associated with the end-product (the end-product is a function of the component saccharide distributions which can change as a function of the concentration in the sweetwater tanks and the process control parameters). Thus, after using the simulation to finalize the design of the plant, it was used to identify the most economical control strategy compatible with production quality and volume requirements. These results have been incorporated into the refinery's process control procedures which are now in operation (28).

14.6   OPTIMUM SYSTEMS ALLOCATION

At Western Electric Company, a general GASP IV simulation model was developed to determine the best man/machine assignment policy consistent with dynamic managerial goals (6). The model has been used to set manpower requirements for several processes. One process involves the twisting of single strand insulated wire to form a twisted conductor. A machine line consisting of sixteen twisting machines, each with two heads, was modeled. Each head on a machine is required to produce the same twist lengths, although in all other aspects heads are independent. Two supply reels feed single strand insulated wire into the machine. The output of the machine is twisted wire which is taken up by reels mounted external to the machine. Ten product twist lengths can be produced on any of the sixteen twisting machines. The machines are shut down for lunch and rest periods, but can be left running unattended for short time intervals.

The simulation model was designed to evaluate system performance given that an operator is assigned to maintain and control a specific number of heads. Events in the simulation model include operator arrival to a head, removal of a full reel, end of installation of an empty take-up reel, and restarting the machine. When a supply reel is empty, the head automatically stops and events associated with the setting up of a full reel are performed. Where operators are assigned to more than two heads, they must travel between machines in order to perform the required functions.

Outputs from the model included the number of twist lengths of each type as a function of the number of heads assigned to each operator. In addition, percent utilization and percent interference as a function of heads assigned to an operator were plotted. From the plots, the optimum allocation of heads to an operator was determined. The simulation model has been used in other situations to optimally assign operators to machines(6).

14.7   RISK ANALYSIS OF PIPELINE CONSTRUCTION

The construction of a pipeline basically involves: 1) preparing a site for laying pipe, 2) laying the pipe, and 3) welding sections of the pipe together. Supporting operations for pipeline construction involve the building, dismantling, and moving of campsites; the construction of roads and other transportation facilities; and relandscaping the site. When pipeline construction is performed in Alaska, the adverse weather conditions must be considered when planning the construction project. A Q-GERT network was developed consisting of the pipeline construction activities, and transportation facility development activities(10). The effects of weather conditions on construction activities were also included in the model. A risk analysis was performed using the Q-GERT Analysis Program to determine the probability of completing pipeline construction by specified due dates. A cost analysis was also performed to determine potential overrun conditions. The analysis indicated that both time and cost overruns could be expected. The effects of changing the activity schedule and construction rates were also evaluated.

14.8   CHEMICAL MANUFACTURING SYSTEMS ANALYSIS

A GASP IV simulation model was developed of a chemical company manufacturing facility(21) consisting of a series of process reactors, pumps, storage tanks, and filtration systems as depicted in Figure 14-3. This manufacturing facility produces batches of different product types to meet customer demands. The model of the process was discrete event oriented with events representing the beginning and ending of each process stage. A discrete event orientation was possible as system status is not altered until a batch is completely processed. Thus, an end of batch processing event can be scheduled from knowledge of when the batch was started and the processing characteristics of a stage. Included in the event routines were complex scheduling procedures to determine the disposition of the batch just completed and the next batch to be started.

The simulation model was used to perform the following types of analyses:

1. Determine the effect of customer demand patterns on the operating requirements of the manufacturing facility.
2. Determine the effect of order lead time requirements on manufacturing costs, inventory levels, and production scheduling.
3. Determine the effect of alternative production scheduling procedures.
4. Determine the effect of alternative system configurations (the number and capacity of storage tanks, filters, reactors, and pipelines).

As an example of the types of results obtained from the model, it was determined that the filtration process was the primary bottleneck. By doubling the capacity of the filtration system, an 80 percent increase in product throughput could be expected. However, additional increases in filtration capacity indicated only marginal gains in throughput. Another analysis indicated that some storage tanks could be eliminated without affecting product throughput. It was also demonstrated how product scheduling procedures impact on product throughput. As is typical of simulation models, the analysis had the added benefit of providing valuable insights into the operation of a complex system.

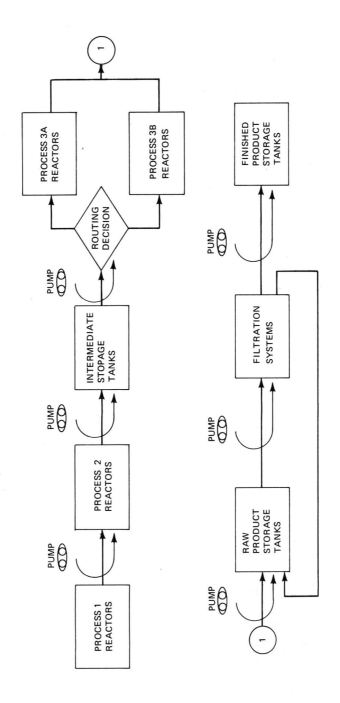

Figure 14-3 General diagram of manufacturing process.

14.9   SIMULATION OF AN AUTOMATED WAREHOUSE

Philip Morris had built a new manufacturing and warehouse facility that contains many computers for controlling product flow. The capacity and potential bottlenecks of the finished goods warehouse were of concern to management since it involved a hierarchical control system using five minicomputers. A GASP IV combined discrete/continuous simulation model of this facility was developed.

Basically, the warehouse receives cases of finished goods from manufacturing and sorts them by brand before they are stored, if necessary, in a high-density stacker storage area for eventual shipment to local customers or distribution warehouses.

Figure 14-4 illustrates the general flow through the "Case Input System." The following discussion is abstracted from Jarvis and Waugh (15). The cases are first received from the manufacturing floor and pass a laser scanner to determine on which tier the product is to be accumulated. Cases then travel on two long conveyors to an input scanner that determines a lane for the case. The case is then tracked by photocells until it arrives at its assigned lane where a computer diverts the case into its assigned lane.

When a sufficient number of cases have been accumulated in a lane (a full pallet load plus five extra cases), the lane is set ready to meter out a load for automatic palletizing. An output belt and a verification scanner are used to verify correct product codes and to build case trains. The case train is routed to a contingency diverter where trains from both tiers can be merged to a single palletizer in the event of a palletizer failure. All cases that were not properly verified at the output scanner are diverted to a manual palletizing area. The verified cases are then fed to the palletizer where they are automatically palletized in a brand-dependent pattern. Considerable logic and a number of conveyor belts between the contingency diverter and the palletizers insure space between cases in several areas where case count is important, and insure the proper merging of case trains when operating in the contingency mode.

An interesting aspect of this simulation involved the modeling of the two generic types of conveyors. The roller conveyors are infrequently turned on and off since case spacing is not too important. Thus, loading and unloading of cases can be modeled as discrete events. Belt conveyors, however, are frequently turned on and off due to downstream conditions and case travel time is not easily projected. These conveyors were modeled using state variables where the belt position is con-

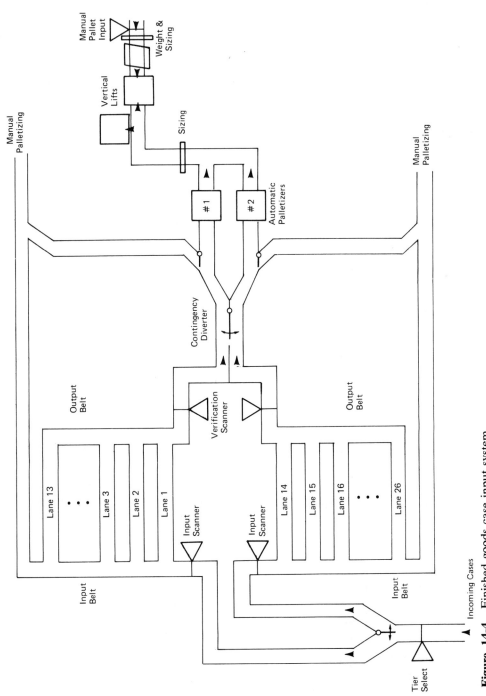

Figure 14-4 Finished goods case input system.

sidered as a state variable and pointers are used to locate the cases on the belt. This modeling approach was incorporated into the GASP IV simulation of the finished goods warehouse.

The results of the study identified that a maximum utilization of 84 percent was obtainable from the palletizers due to conveyor operations. The decrease to be expected in utilization due to down time of specific pieces of equipment was also established. By adding two "zone clear" photocells and changing the location of another photocell, an increase in the maximum utilization was obtained. The results of the study were implemented. The predicted improvement in system performance was observed for the contingency situations involving equipment down time.

The simulation model has been extended and has been used to evaluate a variety of algorithms for surge controlled interleaving, zoning based on turnover, and load leveling (35). Impressive improvements in system operations have been obtained by employing the simulation model for planning purposes.

14.10   INGOT MOULD INVENTORY AND CASTING ANALYSIS

Bethlehem Steel Corporation has a centralized foundry for casting ingot moulds for all Bethlehem plants. The demand for moulds is based on the usage and condemnation of the moulds inventoried at the various plants. A wide variety of mould types and sizes is required since ingot size is a prime determinant of finished product yield per ingot at a steel mill. To obtain increases in yields, larger ingots are being used. However, the ability of the foundry to produce large ingot moulds is constrained by available equipment.

A simulation model of the casting of ingot moulds was written in GASP IV in order to determine capacity expansion requirements for the foundry. The operations involved in casting ingot moulds are shown in Figure 14-5. A discrete event model was developed which included the operation of sand slinging in the moulding pits, baking in the core ovens, pouring of molten metal, cooling, mould removal, sand shakeout, chipping, milling, and shipping. Data collection, scheduling rules, model verification, and output analyses were performed in conjunction with the foundry supervisor and his chief scheduler along with plant industrial engineers.

As part of the study, the demand for ingot moulds was investigated. Data were collected on mould types for a three year period. Specific data values for inventory levels, steel production quantities by mould type, and condemnation rates for moulds were obtained. Based on this information, a procedure was developed for

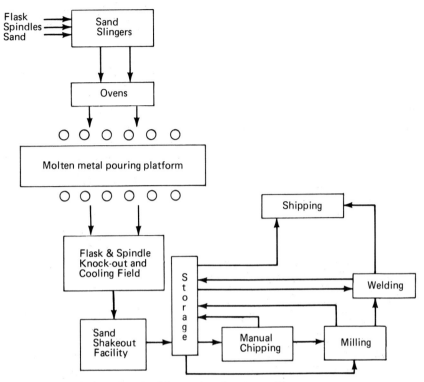

Figure 14-5 Operations involved in casting ingot moulds.

smoothing the demand for ingot moulds. By smoothing the demand for mould types across all Bethlehem plants, the foundry simulation model showed that no increase in foundry capacity was required and, in fact, excess capacity could be obtained which could be used to satisfy special peak demands. In this application, a capital expenditure for new foundry facilities was avoided and, at the same time, corporate inventory levels were reduced.

14.11   Other Application Areas

In the preceding sections, emphasis was placed on simulation models that were used for specific decision-making. There have been many other models used for analyzing a problem situation, for designing a new system, or for projecting future developments. Examples of such areas and references to papers describing these models are listed below:

1. Computer Systems (1,16,37)
2. Communication Systems (13,14)
3. Environmental and Energy Flows (12,19,29,32,33)
4. Crop Management and Ecological Studies (11,20,24,38)
5. Transportation Systems (23,39)
6. Policy Analysis (7,30,34)
7. Project Planning and Control (3,4,5,22)
8. Materials Handling and Computer-Aided Manufacturing (9,18,26,31)

14.12   CHAPTER SUMMARY

In this chapter, an overview of the types of applications in which simulation has been employed is given. Nine illustrations of problem solving using a SLAM-related (GASP or GERT) simulation are described. Our intent is to illustrate that simulation is a practical tool and that SLAM, as a generalization of GASP and GERT, will be a technique of widespread use.

14.13   EXERCISES

14-1.   Select two of the applications presented in this chapter and describe the modeling approach that you would use in resolving the specified problem. Define the necessary entities, attributes, processes, activities and files that you would employ. List the variables on which you would collect statistical information.

14-2.   Categorize the nine applications presented in this chapter by class of sponsor, simulation model type, and simulation modeling approach. Develop other categories for simulation models.

14-3.   Rank the nine applications given in this chapter according to difficulty of the modeling effort; difficulty of obtaining data for the model; difficulty in applying the results; and potential benefit from using the model.

14-4.   Develop specifications for a network simulation language that is based on SLAM but which can be used to build simulation models to evaluate materials-handling equipment.

14-5. Apply SLAM and the simulation methodology presented in this book to a problem with which you are familiar.

14.14 REFERENCES

1. Alexander, E. L., Jr., "SCOPE: A Simulation Approach to Computer Performance Evaluation Using GASP IV," *Proceedings, Summer Computer Simulation Conference,* 1976, pp. 6-10.
2. Auterio, V. J., "Q-GERT Simulation of Air Terminal Cargo Facilities," *Proceedings, Pittsburgh Modeling and Simulation Conference,* Vol. 5, 1974, pp. 1181-1186.
3. Bellas, C. J. and A. C. Samli, "Improving New Product Planning with GERT Simulation," *California Management Review,* Vol. XV, 1973, pp. 14-21.
4. Bird, M., E. R. Clayton, and L. J. Moore, "Sales Negotiation Cost Planning for Corporate Level Sales," *Journal of Marketing,* Vol. 37, 1973, pp. 7-13.
5. Bird, M., E. R. Clayton, and L. J. Moore, "Industrial Buying: A Method of Planning for Contract Negotiations," *Journal of Economics and Business,* 1974, pp. 1-9.
6. Bredenbeck, J. E., M. G. Ogdon, III, and H. W. Tyler, "Optimum Systems Allocation: Applications of Simulation in an Industrial Environment," *Proceedings, Midwest AIDS Conference,* 1975, pp. 28-32.
7. Deporter, E. L., H. A. Kurstedt, Jr., and J. A. Nachlas, "A Combined Simulation Model of the Nuclear Fuel Cycle," *Proceedings, 1977 Winter Simulation Conference,* 1977, pp. 213-216.
8. Duket, S. and D. Wortman, "Q-GERT Model of the Dover Air Force Base Port Cargo Facilities," MACRO Task Force, Military Airlift Command, Scott Air Force Base, Illinois, 1976.
9. Embury, M. C., G. V. Reklaitis, and J. M. Woods, "Simulation of the Operation of a Staged Multi-Product Process with Limited Interstage Storage Buffers," Presented at the Ninth International Conference on Systems, Honolulu, Hawaii, 1976.
10. Federal Power Commission Exhibit EP-237, "Risk Analysis of the Arctic Gas Pipeline Project Construction Schedule," Vol. 167, Federal Power Commission, 1976.
11. Fehr, R. L., J. R. Nuckols et al., "GASP IV Simulation of Flush Water Recycling Systems," *Proceedings, 1977 Winter Simulation Conference,* 1977, pp. 513-519.
12. Gibson, D. F. and E. L. Mooney, "Analyzing Environmental Effects of Improving System Productivity," *Proceedings, AIIE Systems Engineering Conference,* 1975, pp. 76-82.
13. Gracia, J. A. and R. M. Huhn, "Using Simulation to Analyze Pulse Stuffing Network Jitter," *Proceedings, 1977 Winter Simulation Conference,* 1977, pp. 801-810.
14. Green, R. and M. Fox, "AN-TTC-39 Circuit Switch Simulation," *Proceedings, Winter Computer Simulation Conference,* 1975, pp. 211-216.
15. Jarvis, G. L. and R. M. Waugh, "A GASP IV Simulation of an Automated Warehouse," *Proceedings, 1976 Winter Simulation Conference,* 1976, 541-547.

16. Jayakumar, M. S. and T. M. McCalla, Jr., "Simulation of Microprocessor Emulation Using GASP PL/I," *Computer,* April 1977, pp. 20-26.

17. Lawrence, K. D. and C. E. Sigal, "A Work Flow Simulation of a Regional Service Office of a Property and Casualty Insurance Company with Q-GERT," *Proceedings, Pittsburgh Modeling and Simulation Conference,* Vol. 5, 1974, pp. 1187-1192.

18. Lenz, J. E. and J. J. Talavage, *The Optimal Planning of Computerized Manufacturing Systems Simulator (GCMS),* Report No. 7, Purdue University, August 1977.

19. Lyon, R. B., "Radionuclide Pathway Analysis Calculations Using a Set of Computer Programs Interfaced with GASP IV," *Proceedings, 1976 Winter Simulation Conference,* 1976, pp. 549-557.

20. Miles, G. E. et al., "SIMAWEV II: Simulation of the Alfalfa Weevil with GASP IV," *Proceedings, Pittsburgh Conference on Modeling and Simulation,* 1974, pp. 1157-1161.

21. Miner, R. J., D. B. Wortman, and D. Cascio, *An Application of Digital Simulation to a Chemical Manufacturing System,* Pritsker & Associates, Inc., West Lafayette, Indiana, 1977.

22. Moore, L. J. and B. W. Taylor, III, "MultiTeam, Multiproject Research and Development Using GERT," *Management Science,* Vol. 24, 1977, pp. 401-410.

23. Nagy, E. A., "Intermodal Transhipment Facility Simulation: A Case Study," *Proceedings, Winter Computer Simulation Conference,* 1975, pp. 217-223.

24. Peart, R. M., Jr. and J. B. Barrett, Jr., "Simulation in Crop Ecosystem Management," *Proceedings, 1976 Winter Simulation Conference,* 1976, pp. 389-402.

25. Reitman, J., *Computer Simulation Applications,* John Wiley, 1971.

26. Runner, J., *CAMSAM: A Simulation Analysis Model for Computer-Aided Manufacturing Systems,* Unpublished MS Thesis, Purdue University, 1978.

27. Schooley, R. V., "Simulation in the Design of a Corn Syrup Refinery," *Proceedings, Winter Computer Simulation Conference,* 1975, pp. 197-204.

28. Schuman, R. E., E. L. Janzen, and W. H. Dempsey, "Applications of GASP IV Simulation," Presentation to ORSA/TIMS Combined Chicago Chapters, November 16, 1977.

29. Sigal, C. E., "Designing a Production System with Environmental Considerations," *Proceedings, AIIE Systems Engineering Conference,* 1973, pp. 31-39.

30. Standridge, C., C. Macal, A. Pritsker, H. Delcher, and R. Murray, "A Simulation Model of the Primary Health Care System of Indiana," *Proceedings, 1977 Winter Simulation Conference,* 1977, pp. 349-358.

31. Swain, R. W. and J. J. Marsh, III, "A Simulation Analysis of an Automated Hospital Materials Handling System," *AIIE Transactions,* Vol. 10, 1978, pp. 10-18.

32. Sweet, A. L. and S. D. Duket, "A Simulation Study of Energy Consumption by Elevators in Tall Buildings," *Computing and Industrial Engineering,* Vol. 1, 1976, pp. 3-11.

33. Talavage, J. J. and M. Triplett, "GASP IV Urban Model of Cadmium Flow," *Simulation,* Vol. 23, 1974, pp. 101-108.

34. Triplett, M. B., T. L. Willke, and J. D. Waddell, "NUFACTS: A Tool for the Analysis of Nuclear Development Policies," *Proceedings, 1977 Winter Simulation Conference,* 1977, pp. 793-798.

35. Waugh, R. M. and R. A. Ankener, "Simulation of an Automated Stacker Storage System," *Proceedings, 1977 Winter Simulation Conference,* 1977, pp. 769-776.

36. Weinberger, A., A. Odejimi et al., "The Use of Simulation to Evaluate Capital Investment Alternatives in the Steel Industry: A Case Study," Presented at the 1977 Winter Simulation Conference, 1977.

37. Wong, G., "A Computer System Simulation with GASP IV," *Proceedings, Winter Computer Simulation Conference,* 1975, pp. 205-209.

38. Wong, G. A. et al., "A Systematic Approach to Data Reduction Using GASP IV," *Proceedings, 1976 Winter Simulation Conference,* 1976, pp. 403-410.

39. Yu, J., W. E. Wilhelm, and S. A. Akhand, "GASP Simulation of Terminal Air Traffic," *Transp. Eng. J.,* Vol. 100, 1974, pp. 593-609.

APPENDIX A

User Support and
Callable Subprograms of SLAM

SUBROUTINE ALTER(IR,IU)	Changes the capacity of resource type IR by IU units
FUNCTION BETA(THETA,PHI,IS)	Returns a sample from a beta distribution with parameters THETA and PHI using random number stream IS
FUNCTION CCAVG(ICLCT)	Returns average value of variable ICLCT
FUNCTION CCMAX(ICLCT)	Returns maximum value of variable ICLCT
FUNCTION CCMIN(ICLCT)	Returns minimum value of variable ICLCT
FUNCTION CCNUM(ICLCT)	Returns number of observations of variable ICLCT
FUNCTION CCSTD(ICLCT)	Returns standard deviation of variable ICLCT
SUBROUTINE CLEAR	Reinitializes the statistical storage areas when it is called. COLCT, TIMST, histograms, files, resources, and network statistical variables are cleared
SUBROUTINE CLOSX(NGATE)	Closes gate whose number is NGATE
SUBROUTINE COLCT(ZZ,ICLCT)	If ICLCT > 0, records value ZZ as an observation on variable number ICLCT; if ICLCT = 0, computes and reports statistics on all NNCLT variables; if ICLCT < 0, computes and reports statistics on variable −ICLCT

528

SUBROUTINE COPAA(NTRYA,NAUXA, AUXF,VALUE)	Copies the values of a set of auxiliary attributes without removing the attribute values from the user's auxiliary storage array
SUBROUTINE COPY(NRANK,IFILE,A)	Copies the values of the attributes of an entry into the vector A. If NRANK is positive then the NRANK*th* entry is to be copied. If NRANK is negative, then the entry with pointer—NRANK is to be copied
FUNCTION DPROB(CPROB,VALUE, NVAL,IS)	Returns a sample from a user-defined discrete probability function with cumulative probabilities and associated values specified in arrays CPROB and VALUE, with NVAL values using random stream IS
FUNCTION DRAND(IS)	Returns a pseudo-random number obtained from random number stream IS
SUBROUTINE DDUMP(N1,N2)	Prints the storage array NSET/QSET between locations N1 and N2
SUBROUTINE ENTER(IN,A)	Releases ENTER node whose number is IN with an entity whose attribute values are in the vector A
FUNCTION ERLNG(EMN,XK,IS)	Returns a sample from an Erlang distribution which is the sum of XK exponential samples each with mean EMN using random number stream IS
SUBROUTINE ERROR(KODE)	Prints reports and error messages
FUNCTION EXPON(XMEAN,IS)	Returns a sample from an exponential distribution with mean XMEAN using random number stream IS
FUNCTION FFAVG(IFILE)	Returns average number of entities in file IFILE
FUNCTION FFAWT(IFILE)	Returns the average waiting time in file IFILE
FUNCTION FFMAX(IFILE)	Returns maximum number of entities in file IFILE
FUNCTION FFPRD(IFILE)	Returns time period for statistics in file IFILE
FUNCTION FFSTD(IFILE)	Returns standard deviation for file IFILE

FUNCTION FFTLC(IFILE)

Returns time at which number in file IFILE last changed

SUBROUTINE FILEM(IFILE,A)

Files an entry with attributes stored in A into file IFILE

SUBROUTINE FREE(IR,IU)

Frees IU units of resource type IR.

FUNCTION GAMA(BETA,ALPHA,IS)

Returns a sample from a gamma distribution with parameters BETA and ALPHA using random number stream IS

SUBROUTINE GDLAY(IFS,ILS,XIN,DEL)

Variable order exponential delay for Systems Dynamics problems. IFS and ILS are the first and last state variables used to maintain the delay; the order of the delay is ILS − IFS + 1. NNEQD *must be greater than ILS to use GDLAY;* XIN is the input to the delay and DEL is the delay constant

SUBROUTINE GETAA(NTRYA,NAUXA, AUXF,MFAA, VALUE)

Gets (removes) a set of auxiliary attributes and establishes a vector of the values of the auxiliary attributes

SUBROUTINE GPLOT(IPLOT)

If IPLOT > 0, IPLOT is the RECORD statement code and GPLOT stores values of the dependent variables specified on VAR input statements (up to 10 values per plot) for a value of the independent variable specified on a RECORD input statement; if IPLOT = 0, prints table and/or graph for all plots; if IPLOT < 0, prints table and/or graph for code = − IPLOT

FUNCTION GTABL(TAB,X,XLOW, XHIGH,XINCR)

Performs a table look-up to obtain a value of a dependent variable from discrete values stored in the vector TAB for a given value of the independent variable X; XLOW is the value of X corresponding to TAB(1) and XHIGH is the largest value for X; XINCR is the difference in the independent variable for successive values of the dependent variable

FUNCTION INTRN(ISTRM)

Returns the current unnormalized value for random number stream **ISTRM**

SUBROUTINE LINK(IFILE)

Files entry whose attributes are stored in MFA in file IFILE

FUNCTION LOCAT(NRANK,IFILE)

Returns the pointer to the location of the entry whose rank is NRANK in file IFILE

FUNCTION MMFE(IFILE)

Returns pointer to first entry (rank 1) in file IFILE

FUNCTION MMLE(IFILE)

Returns pointer to last entry (rank NNQ(IFILE)) in file IFILE

FUNCTION NFIND(NRANK,IFILE,JATT, MCODE,XVAL,TOL)

Locates an entry with rank $\geqq$ NRANK in file IFILE whose JATT attribute is related to the value XVAL according to the specification given by MCODE as shown below:

MCODE = 2: maximum value but greater than XVAL
MCODE = 1: minimum value but greater than XVAL
MCODE = 0: value within XVAL ± TOL
MCODE =−1: minimum value but less than XVAL
MCODE =−2: maximum value but less than XVAL

FUNCTION NNACT(NACT)

Number of active entities in activity NACT at current time

FUNCTION NNBLK(IACT,IFILE)

Returns the number of entities currently in activity IACT and blocked by the node associated with file IFILE

FUNCTION NNCNT(NACT)

The number of entities that have completed activity NACT

FUNCTION NNGAT(NGATE)

Status of gate number NGATE at current time: $0 \rightarrow$ open, $1 \rightarrow$ closed

FUNCTION NNQ(IFILE)

Returns number of entries in file IFILE

FUNCTION NNRSC(NRES)

Current number of resource type NRES available

FUNCTION NPRED(NTRY)

Returns pointer to the predecessor entry of the entry whose pointer is NTRY

FUNCTION NPSSN(XMN,IS)

Returns a sample from a Poisson distribution with mean XMN using random number stream IS

FUNCTION NSUCR(NTRY)

Returns pointer to the successor entry of the entry whose pointer is NTRY

SUBROUTINE OPEN(NGATE)

Sets the status of gate NGATE to OPEN and empties all files containing entities waiting for the gate to be opened

SUBROUTINE PRNTA

Prints statistics for all activities

SUBROUTINE PRNTC(ICLCT)

If ICLCT > 0, prints statistics for COLCT variable number ICLCT. If ICLCT ≤ 0, prints statistics for all COLCT variables

SUBROUTINE PRNTH(ICLCT)

If ICLCT > 0, prints a histogram for COLCT variable number ICLCT. If ICLCT ≤ 0, prints all histograms

SUBROUTINE PRNTF(IFILE)

If IFILE > 0, prints statistics and the contents of file IFILE. If IFILE $= 0$, prints summary statistics for all files. If IFILE < 0, prints summary statistics and contents of all files

SUBROUTINE PRNTP(IPLOT)

If IPLOT > 0, prints a plot and/or table for plot/table number IPLOT. If IPLOT ≤ 0, prints all plots/tables.

SUBROUTINE PRNTR(NRES)

If NRES > 0, prints statistics for resource number NRES. If NRES ≤ 0, prints statistics for all resources

SUBROUTINE PRNTS

Prints the contents of the state storage vectors SS(I) and DD(I)

SUBROUTINE PRNTT(ISTAT)

If ISTAT > 0, prints statistics for time-persistent variable ISTAT. If ISTAT ≤ 0, prints statistics for all time-persistent variables

FUNCTION PRODQ(NATR,IFILE)

Returns the product of the values of attribute NATR for each current entry in file IFILE

SUBROUTINE PUTAA(NAUXA,AUXF, MFAA,VALUE)

Puts a set of values of auxiliary attributes into an array

FUNCTION RLOGN(XMN,STD,IS)

Returns a sample from a lognormal distribution with mean XMN and standard deviation STD using random number stream IS

SUBROUTINE RMOVE(NRANK, IFILE,A)

Removes an entry defined by the variable NRANK from a file defined by the variable IFILE. If NRANK is positive, it defines the rank of the en-

	try to be removed. If NRANK is negative, it points to the negative of the location where the entry to be removed is stored. RMOVE loads the vector A with the attributes of the entry removed. The value of MFA is reset to the pointer of the entry removed
FUNCTION RNORM(XMN,STD,IS)	Returns a sample from a normal distribution with mean XMN and standard deviation STD using random number stream IS
FUNCTION RRAVG(NRES)	Returns average utilization of resource NRES
FUNCTION RRMAX(NRES)	Returns maximum utilization of resource NRES
FUNCTION RRPRD(NRES)	Returns time period for statistics on resource NRES
FUNCTION RRSTD(NRES)	Returns standard deviation of utilization of resource NRES
FUNCTION RRTLC(NRES)	Returns time at which resource NRES utilization was last changed
SUBROUTINE SCHDL(KEVNT,DTIME,A)	Schedules event type KEVNT to occur at TNOW + DTIME with event attributes as stored in A
SUBROUTINE SET	Initializes file pointers and file statistics arrays
SUBROUTINE SETAA(NAUXA,AUXF, MFAA,NDAUX)	Set up an array (defined by the user) that will maintain auxiliary attributes.
SUBROUTINE SLAM	The SLAM executive
SUBROUTINE STOPA(NTC)	Stops all network activities whose duration is specified by STOPA for which an entity is currently ongoing with an entity code of NTC
FUNCTION SSEVT(JEVNT)	Returns status of state-event JEVNT as follows: $+2$, positive crossing beyond tolerance; $+1$, positive crossing; 0, no crossing; -1, negative crossing; -2, negative crossing beyond tolerance

FUNCTION SUMQ(NATR,IFILE)	Returns the sum of the values of attribute NATR for each current entry in file IFILE
SUBROUTINE SUMRY	Prints the SLAM Summary Report
FUNCTION TRIAG(XLO,XMODE, XHI,IS)	Returns a sample from a triangular distribution in the interval XLO to XHI with mode XMODE using random number stream IS
FUNCTION TTAVG(ISTAT)	Returns time-integrated average of variable ISTAT
FUNCTION TTCLR(T)	Returns last time statistical arrays were cleared. If arrays were not cleared before time T, a zero is returned
FUNCTION TTMAX(ISTAT)	Returns maximum value of variable ISTAT
FUNCTION TTMIN(ISTAT)	Returns minimum value of variable ISTAT
FUNCTION TTPRD(ISTAT)	Returns time period of statistics on variable ISTAT
FUNCTION TTSTD(ISTAT)	Returns standard deviation of variable ISTAT
FUNCTION TTTLC(ISTAT)	Returns time at which variable ISTAT was last changed
FUNCTION ULINK(NRANK,IFILE)	Removes entry with rank NRANK from file IFILE without copying its attribute values. If NRANK < 0, it is a pointer
FUNCTION UNFRM(ULO,UHI,IS)	Returns a sample from a uniform distribution in the interval ULO to UHI using random number stream IS
FUNCTION WEIBL(BETA,ALPHA,IS)	Returns a sample from a Weibull distribution with parameters BETA and ALPHA using random number stream IS
FUNCTION XRN(ISTRM)	Returns the last pseudo random number obtained from stream ISTRM

Network Input Statement Descriptions

This appendix contains a complete description of the network input statements of SLAM. In Table B1, a summary of SLAM input statements and defaults is given. In Tables B2-B23, a detailed description of each network element is provided. A list of tables is given below for ready reference.

Table B1 SLAM network statement types.

Statement Form	Statement Defaults (ND=no default)
Nodes	
ACCUM,FR,SR,SAVE,M;	ACCUM,1,1,LAST,∞;
ALTER,RLBL/CC,M;	ALTER,ND/ND,∞;
ASSIGN,VAR=value,VAR=value,...,M;	ASSIGN,ND=ND,ND=ND,...,∞;
AWAIT(IFL),RLBL/UR or GLBL,M;	AWAIT(first IFL in RLBL's or GLBL's list), ND/1,∞;
CLOSE,GLBL,M;	CLOSE,ND,∞;
COLCT,TYPE or VARIABLE,ID,NCEL/ HLOW/HWID,M;	COLCT,ND,blanks,no histogram/0./1.0,∞;
CREATE,TBC,TF,MA,MC,M;	CREATE,∞,0,no marking,∞,∞;
DETECT,XVAR,XDIR,VALUE,TOL,M;	DETECT,ND,ND,ND,0,∞;
ENTER,NUM,M;	ENTER,ND,∞;
EVENT,JEVNT,M;	EVENT,ND,∞;
FREE,RLBL/UF,M;	FREE,ND/1,∞;
GOON,M;	GOON,∞;
MATCH,NATR,QLBL/NLBL,...,M;	MATCH,ND,ND/no routing,ND/no routing,...,∞;
OPEN,GLBL,M;	OPEN,ND,∞;
PREEMPT(IFL)/PR,RLBL,SNLBL,NATR,M;	PREEMPT(first IFL in RLBL's last)/no priority, ND,AWAIT node where transaction seized resource,none,∞;
QUEUE(IFL),IQ,QC,BLOCK or BALK (NLBL),SLBL;	QUEUE(ND)/0,∞,none,none;
SELECT,QSR/SAVE,SSR,BLOCK or BALK (NLBL),QLBLs;	SELECT,POR/none,POR,none,ND;
TERMINATE,TC;	TERMINATE,∞;
Blocks	
GATE/GLBL,OPEN or CLOSE,IFLs/repeats;	GATE/ND,OPEN,ND/repeats;
RESOURCE/RLBL(IRC),IFLs/repeats;	RESOURCE/ND(1),ND/repeats;
Regular Activity	
ACTIVITY/A,duration,PROB or COND,NLBL;	ACTIVITY/no ACT number,0.0,take ACT,ND;
Service Activity	
ACTIVITY(N)/A, duration,PROB,NLBL;	ACTIVITY(1)/no ACT number,0.0,1.0,ND;

Table B2 ACCUMULATE node description summary.

Node Type: ACCUMULATE   Symbol:

| FR / SR | SAVE | M |

Function: The ACCUMULATE node is used to combine entities. The combining of entities is controlled by the specification of the release mechanism consisting of the number of arrivals required for the first release (FR), the number of arrivals required for subsequent releases (SR), and the attribute holding criterion for entities to be routed (SAVE). A maximum of M emanating activities are initiated.

Input Format: ACCUMULATE,FR,SR,SAVE,M;

Specifications:

Entry	Options	Default
FR	positive integer	1
SR	positive integer	1
SAVE	save criterion specified as: FIRST, LAST, LOW(NATR), HIGH(NATR),SUM,MULT	LAST
M	positive integer	∞

Table B3 ALTER node description summary.

Node Type: ALTER   *Symbol:*

| RLBL | M |
| CC | |

Function: The ALTER node changes the capacity of resource RLBL by CC units. In the case where the capacity is decreascd below current utilization, the excess capacity is destroyed as it becomes freed. The capacity can be reduced to a minimum of zero with additional reductions having no effect. At each release, a maximum of M emanating activities are initiated.

Input Format: ALTER,RLBL/CC,M;

Specifications:

Entry	Options	Default
RLBL	maximum of 8 characters beginning with an alphabetic character†	error
CC	SLAM variable, SLAM random variable, or a constant	error
M	positive integer	∞

---

† The label RLBL must be previously defined with a RESOURCE statement.

Table B4 ASSIGN node description summary.

Node Type: ASSIGN   *Symbol:*

VAR=Value	
•	M
⋮	

Function: The ASSIGN node is used to assign values to SLAM variables (VAR) at each arrival of an entity to the node. A maximum of M emanating activities are initiated.

Input Format: ASSIGN,VAR=value,VAR=value,...,M;

Specifications:

Entry	Options	Default
VAR	ATRIB (INDEX), SS (INDEX), DD (INDEX), XX (INDEX), or II, where INDEX is a positive integer or the SLAM variable II	error
value	an expression containing constants, SLAM variables, or SLAM random variables of the from $A \oplus B$ where the operator $\oplus$ is one of $\{+,-,*,/\}$. If an operator is employed, A cannot be a constant	error
M	positive integer	∞

Table B5 AWAIT node description summary.

Node Type: AWAIT

Symbol:

Function: The AWAIT node operates in two modes. In the resource mode, the AWAIT node delays an entity in file IFL until UR units of resource RLBL are available. The entity then seizes the UR units of RLBL. In the gate mode, the AWAIT node releases the entity if the gate status is open and delays the entity in file IFL if the gate status is closed. At each release of the node a maximum of M activities are initiated.

Input Format: AWAIT(IFL),RLBL/UR or GLBL,M;

Specifications:

Entry	Options	Default
IFL	integer between 1 and MFIL	first IFL in RLBL's list
RLBL or GLBL	maximum of 8 characters beginning with an alphabetic character†	error
UR	positive SLAM variable, SLAM random variable, or constant	1
M	positive integer	∞

† The label RLBL or GLBL must be previously defined with a RESOURCE or GATE statement.

Table B6 CLOSE node description summary.

Node Type: CLOSE

Symbol:

Function: The CLOSE node changes the status of gate GLBL to closed and releases a maximum of M emanating activities.

Input Format: CLOSE,GLBL,M;

Specifications:

Entry	Options	Default
GLBL	maximum of 8 characters beginning with an alphabetic character†	error
M	positive integer	∞

† The label GLBL must be previously defined with a GATE statement.

Table B7   COLCT node description summary.

Node Type: COLCT	*Symbol:*

Function: The COLCT node is used to collect statistics that are related to: either the time an entity arrives at the node (TYPE); or on a VARIABLE at the entity arrival time. ID is an identifier for output purposes and H is a histogram specification for the number of cells (NCEL), the upper limit of the first cell, (HLOW) and the cell width (HWID). A maximum of M emanating activities are initiated

Input Format: COLCT,TYPE or VARIABLE,ID,NCEL/HLOW/HWID,M;

Specifications:

Entry	Options	Default
TYPE or VARIABLE	FIRST,ALL,BETWEEN,INTVL (NATR) or SLAM variable such as ATRIB(NATR), XX(I) or NNQ(I)	none
ID	maximum of 16 characters beginning with an alphabetic character	blanks
NCEL	positive integer	no histograms
HLOW	constant	0.0
HWID	positive constant	1.0
M	positive integer	∞

Table B8 CREATE node description summary.

Node Type: **CREATE**	*Symbol:*

Function: The CREATE node is used to generate entities within the network. The node is released initially at time TF and thereafter according to the specified time between creations TBC up to a maximum of MC releases. At each release, a maximum of M emanating activities are initiated. The time of creation is stored in ATRIB(MA) of the created entity.

Input Format: CREATE,TBC,TF,MA,MC,M;

Specifications:

Entry	Options	Default
TBC	constant, SLAM variable, or SLAM random variable	∞
TF	constant	0.
MA	positive integer	no marking
MC	positive integer	∞
M	positive integer	∞

Table B9   DETECT node description summary.

Node Type: DETECT   *Symbol:*

| XVAR | XDIR | VALUE | XTOL | M |

Function: The DETECT node is used to generate entities whenever the state of system as defined by a crossing variable, XVAR, crosses a prescribed threshold value, VALUE. The node is released whenever a crossing occurs in direction XDIR. The value of XTOL specifies the desired interval beyond the VALUE for which a detection of a crossing is desired. In addition, any entity arriving to a DETECT node causes it to be released. A maximum of M emanating activities are initiated at each release.

Input Format: DETECT,XVAR,XDIR,VALUE,XTOL,M;

Specifications:

Entry	Options	Default
XVAR	SS(I) or DD(I)	error
XDIR	X, XP, or XN	error
VALUE	SS(I), DD(I), or constant	error
XTOL	positive constant	∞
M	positive integer	∞

Table B10   ENTER node description summary.

Node Type: ENTER   *Symbol:*

NUM   M

Function: The ENTER node is provided to permit the user to enter an entity into the network from a user-written event routine. The node is released at each entity arrival and at each user call to subroutine ENTER(NUM). A maximum of M emanating activities are initiated at each release.

Input Format: ENTER,NUM,M;

Specifications:

Entry	Options	Default
NUM	positive integer	error
M	positive integer	∞

Table B11 EVENT node description summary.

Node Type: EVENT *Symbol:*

Function: The EVENT node causes subroutine EVENT to be called with event code JEVNT at each entity arrival. This allows the user to model functions for which a standard node is not provided. A maximum of M emanating activities are initiated.

Input Format: EVENT,JEVNT,M;

Specifications:

Entry	Options	Default
JEVNT	positive integer	error
M	positive integer	∞

Table B12 FREE node description summary.

Node Type: FREE *Symbol:*

Function: The FREE node releases UF units of resource RLBL. The resource is made available to waiting entities according to the order of the wait files specified in the RESOURCE statement. A maximum of M emanating activities are initiated.

Input Format: FREE,RLBL/UF,M;

Specifications:

Entry	Options	Default
RLBL	maximum of 8 characters beginning with an alphabetic character†	error
UF	positive SLAM variable, SLAM random variable or constant	1
M	positive integer	∞

† The label RLBL must be previously defined with a RESOURCE statement.

Table B13 GOON node description summary.

| Node Type: | GOON | Symbol: | M |

Function: The GOON node provides a continuation node where every entering entity passes directly through the node. It is a special case of the ACCUMULATE node with FR and SR set equal to one. A maximum of M emanating activities are initiated.

Input Format: GOON,M;

Specifications:

Entry	Options	Default
M	positive integer	∞

Table B14 MATCH node description summary.

| Node Type: | MATCH | Symbol: | |

Function: The MATCH node is used to delay the movement of entities by keeping them in QUEUE nodes (QLBLs) until entities with the same value of attribute NATR are resident in every QUEUE node preceding the MATCH node. When a match occurs, each entity is routed to a route node NLBL that corresponds to QLBL.

Input Format: MATCH,NATR,QLBL/ NLBL,QLBL/ NLBL,...;

Specifications:

Entry	Options	Default
NATR	positive integer	error
QLBL	a QUEUE node label	error if less than 2 QLBLs specified
NLBL	a node label for any type of node	destroy the entity

Table B15   OPEN node description summary.

Node Type: OPEN	*Symbol:*

$$\text{(GLBL M)}$$

Function: The OPEN node changes the status of gate GLBL to open and releases all waiting entities in the AWAIT files specified in the GATE statement. A maximum of M emanating activities are initiated.

Input Format: OPEN,GLBL,M;

Specifications:

Entry	Options	Default
GLBL	maximum of 8 characters beginning with an alphabetic character†	error
M	positive integer	∞

† The label GLBL must be previously defined in a GATE statement.

Table B16 PREEMPT node description summary.

Node Type: **PREEMPT**   *Symbol:*

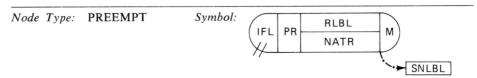

Function: The PREEMPT node is used to preempt a resource specified by RLBL having a capacity of one. Entities attempting to seize a resource at a PREEMPT node have preemptive priority over entities which seized the resource at an AWAIT node. If a priority (PR) is specified at a PREEMPT node, then preempt entities are preempted by preempt entities with higher priorities. A preempted entity is routed to node SNLBL with the remaining processing time placed in ATRIB(NATR). If a send node, SNLBL, is not specified, the preempted entity resides in the await file of the node where the entity originally seized the resource until it can be reactivated at its preempted location in the network. Entities residing in QUEUE nodes, wait files, or which have seized additional resources cannot be preempted. A maximum of M of the emanating activities are released.

Input Format: PREEMPT(IFL)/PR,RLBL,SNLBL,NATR,M;

Specifications:

Entry	Options	Default
IFL	integer between 1 and MFIL	first IFL in RLBL's list
PR	HIGH(ATRIB) or LOW (ATRIB)	non-priority mode
RLBL	maximum of 8 characters beginning with an alphabetic character†	∞
SNLBL	the label of a node to send the preempted entity	AWAIT node where entity seized the resource
NATR	positive integer	none
M	positive integer	∞

† The label RLBL must be previously defined with a RESOURCE statement.

Table B17 QUEUE node description summary.

Node Type: QUEUE	*Symbol:*

Function: The QUEUE node is used to delay entities in file IFL until a server becomes available. The QUEUE node initially contains IQ entities and has a capacity of QC entities. The specification of blocking causes incoming servers to be blocked whenever the queue is at capacity. The specification of balking causes arriving entities to balk whenever the queue is at capacity.

Input Format: QUEUE(IFL),IQ,QC,BLOCK or BALK(NLBL),SLBL;

Specifications:

Entry	Options	Default
IFL	integer between 1 and MFIL	*error*
IQ	non-negative integer	0
QC	integer greater than or equal to IQ	∞
BLOCK or BALK(NLBL)	BLOCK or BALK(NLBL) where NLBL corresponds to the label of a labeled node	none
SLBLs	the labels of SELECT or MATCH nodes separated by commas	none

Table B18   SELECT node description summary.

Node Type: SELECT   *Symbol:*

Function: The SELECT node is used to select among queues and available servers based upon the queue selection rule (QSR) and the server selection rule (SSR). Blocking or balking may be specified similar to the QUEUE node.

Input Format: SELECT,QSR,SSR,BLOCK or BALK(NLBL),QLBLs;

Specifications:

Entry	Options	Default
QSR	CYC,POR,RAN,ASM†,LAV,SWF,LNQ, LRC,SAV,LAF,SNQ,SRC	POR
SSR	CYC,POR,RAN,LBT,SBT,LIT,SIT	POR
BLOCK or BALK(NLBL)	BLOCK or BALK(NLBL) where NLBL corresponds to the label of a labeled node	none
QLBLs	labels of QUEUE nodes separated by commas	error

---

† The attribute holding criterion may be specified following a slash as HIGH(NATR) or LOW(NATR). If the holding criterion is defaulted, the attributes of the entity in the first associated QUEUE node are held.

Table B19   TERMINATE node description summary.

Node Type: TERMINATE   *Symbol:*

Function: The TERMINATE node is used to destroy entities and/or terminate the simulation. All incoming entities to a TERMINATE node are destroyed. The arrival of the TCth entity causes a simulation run to be terminated.

Input Format: TERMINATE,TC;

Specifications:

Entry	Options	Default
TC	positive integer	∞

Table B20   RESOURCE block description summary.

Block Type: RESOURCE	*Symbol:*

RLBL(IRC)	IFL1	IFL2

Function: A RESOURCE block defines a resource by its label RLBL and its initial capacity or availability IRC. The file numbers, IFLs, associated with AWAIT and PREEMPT nodes are where entities requesting units of the resource are queued. The IFLs are listed in the order in which it is desired to allocate the units of the resource when they are made available.

Input Format: RESOURCE/RLBL(IRC), IFLs;

Specifications:

Entry	Options	Default
RLBL	maximum of 8 characters beginning with an alphabetic character	error
IRC	positive integer	1
IFLs	integers between 1 and MFIL	error

Table B21   GATE block description summary.

Block Type: GATE	*Symbol:*

GLBL	OPEN or CLOSE	IFL1	IFL2

Function: A GATE block defines a gate by its label GLBL. The initial status of the gate is set through an OPEN or CLOSE prescription. The file numbers, IFLs, reference the AWAIT nodes where entities waiting for the gate to open are queued.

Input Format: GATE/GLBL, OPEN or CLOSE, IFLs;

Specifications:

Entry	Options	Default
GLBL	maximum of 8 characters beginning with an alphabetic character	error
OPEN or CLOSE	'OPEN' or 'CLOSE'	OPEN
IFLs	integers between 1 and MFIL	error

Table B22 REGULAR activity description summary.

Activity Type: **REGULAR**   *Symbol:* DUR, PROB or COND

Function: A REGULAR activity is any activity emanating from a node other than a QUEUE or SELECT node. The REGULAR activity is used to delay entities by a specified duration, perform conditional/probabilistic testing, and to route entities to non-sequential nodes. If the activity is numbered, statistics are provided on the activity utilization, and the number of active entities and the total entity count are maintained as SLAM variables NNACT(A) and NNCNT(A), respectively.

Input Format: ACTIVITY/A,duration,PROB or COND,NLBL;

Specifications:

Entry	Options	Default
A	positive integer between 1 and 50	no statistics
duration	constant, SLAM variable, SLAM random variable, REL(NLBL) or STOPA(NTC).	0
PROB or COND	probability: constant between 0 and 1 condition: value .OPERATOR. value where value is a constant, SLAM variable, or SLAM random variable, and OPERATOR is LT, LE, EQ, GE, GT, or NE. Two or more conditions can be specified that are separated by .AND. or .OR.	always take activity
NLBL	the label of a labeled node which is at the end of the activity	sequential node

---

Table B23 SERVICE activity description summary.

Activity Type: SERVICE   *Symbol:* DUR, PROB

Function: The service activity is any activity emanating from a QUEUE or SELECT node. The service activity is used in conjunction with the QUEUE node to model single channel queues or queues with N identical servers. The service activity is used in conjunction with the SELECT node to model multiple channel queues with non-identical servers. Statistics are collected on all service activities. If the activity is numbered, the server status (number of busy or blocked servers) and total entity count are maintained as SLAM variables NNACT(A) and NNCNT(A), respectively.

Input Format: ACTIVITY(N)/A,duration,PROB,NLBL;

Specifications:

Entry	Options	Default
N	positive integer	1
A	positive integer between 1 and 50	none
duration	constant, SLAM variable, SLAM random variable, REL(NLBL), or STOPA (NTC)	0.
probability†	constant between 0 and 1	1.
NLBL	label of a labeled node	sequential node

---

† Used only to represent identical servers emanating from a queue node as a set of probabilistic service activities. When used in this way, each activity must have the same N and A values.

SLAM Control Statements

This appendix contains a complete description of the SLAM control statements. In Table C1, a summary of SLAM control statements is given. In Table C2, a detailed description of each statement is provided including a definition of variables, input value options for the variables, and SLAM default values assigned.

Table C1 SLAM control statements.

Statement Form
CONTINUOUS,NNEQD,NNEQS,DTMIN,DTMAX,DTSAV,W or F or N,AAERR,RRERR;
ENTRY/IFL,ATRIB(1),ATRIB(2),...,ATRIB(MATR)/repeats;
FIN;
GEN,NAME,PROJECT,MONTH/DAY/YEAR,NNRNS,ILIST,IECHO,IXQT,IPIRH,ISMRY/FSN
INITIALIZE,TTBEG,TTFIN,JJCLR/NCCLR/JCNET,JJVAR,JJFIL;
INTLC,VAR=value,repeats;
LIMITS,MFIL,MATR,MNTRY;
MONTR,option,TFRST,TBTWN;
PRIORITY/IFL,ranking/repeats;
RECORD(IPLOT),INDVAR,ID,ITAPE,P or T or B,DTPLT,TTSRT,TTEND,KKEVT;
SEEDS,ISEED(IS)/R,repeats;
SEVNT,JEVNT,XVAR,XDIR,VALUE,TOL;
SIMULATE;
STAT,ICLCT,ID,NCEL/HLOW/HWID;
TIMST,VAR,ID;
VAR,DEPVAR,SYMBL,ID,LOORD,HIORD;

Table C2 Definitions and defaults for variables on SLAM control statements.

Statement Type	Variable	Definition	Options	Default
CONTINUOUS	NNEQD	Number of differential equations	Positive integer	0
	NNEQS	Number of state equations	Positive integer	0
	DTMIN	Minimum step size	Positive real	.01*DTMAX
	DTMAX	Maximum step size	Positive real	DTSAV
	DTSAV	Time between recording	$0 \rightarrow$ every step $> 0 \rightarrow$ DTSAV $< 0 \rightarrow$ at event times	∞
	W or F or N	Warning, Fatal, No warning	'W', 'F', 'N'	'W'
	AAERR	Allowed absolute error	Positive real	.00001
	RRERR	Allowed relative error	Positive real	.00001
ENTRY	IFL	File number	Positive integer	none
	ATRIB(I),I=1, MATR	Attribute I	Constant	0
FIN				
GEN	NAME	Analyst's name	20 alphanumeric characters	Blanks
	PROJECT	Project name	20 alphanumeric characters	Blanks
	MONTH	Month number	Positive integer	1
	DAY	Day number	Positive integer	1
	YEAR	Year number	Positive integer	2001
	NNRNS	Number of runs	Positive integer	1
	ILIST	Request for input listing	'Y' or 'N'	'Y'
	IECHO	Request for echo summary report	'Y' or 'N'	'Y'
	IXQT	Request for execution	'Y' or 'N'	'Y'
	IPIRH	Request for intermediate results heading	'Y' or 'N'	'Y'
	ISMRY	Request for SLAM Summary Report	'Y' or 'N'	'Y'
	FSN	Summary report on: first, first and last, every Nth	'F', 'S' or positive integer	1

Table C2 continued.

Statement Type	Variable	Definition	Options	Default
INITIALIZE	TTBEG	Beginning time of run	Constant	0.0
	TTFIN	Finishing time for a run	Constant	∞
	JJCLR	Request to clear statistical arrays	'Y' or 'N'	'Y'
	NCCLR	Value up to which JJCLR pertains	Positive integer	25
	JCNET	Clearing of statistics for COLCT nodes	'Y' or 'N'	'Y'
	JJVAR	Request for SLAM variable initialization	'Y' or 'N'	'Y'
	JJFIL	Request for file structure initialization	'Y' or 'N'	'Y'
INTLC	VAR	'XX(N)', 'SS(N)' or 'DD(N)' where N is an integer	See definition	None
	value	Initial value of VAR	Constant	None
LIMITS	MFIL	Largest file number	Positive integer < 100	1
	MATR	Maximum number of attributes per entity	Positive integer $\leq$ 98	0
	MNTRY	Maximum number of entries in all files	Positive integer	0
MONTR	option	Monitoring option	'SUMRY' 'FILES' 'STATES' 'CLEAR' 'TRACE'	None
	TFRST	Time of first monitoring option	Positive real	0.0
	TBTWN	Time between monitoring option or end of trace	Positive real	∞
PRIORITY	IFL	File number	Positive constant $\leq$ MFIL+1	None
	ranking	File ranking	LVF(NATR) HVF(NATR) FIFO LIFO	FIFO

Statement Type	Variable	Definition	Options	Default
RECORD	IPLOT	Plot number	Positive integer	Next integer
	INDVAR	Independent variable	'TNOW', 'SS(I)', 'DD(I)' or 'XX(I)'	None
	ID	Independent variable identifier	16 alphanumeric characters	Blanks
	ITAPE	RECORD storage medium	0 → NSET/QSET, > 0 peripheral device number	0
	P or T or **B**	Plot, table, or both	'P', 'T', 'B'	'P'
	DTPLT	Interval for independent variable	Constant	5.0
	TTSRT	Time to start recording	Constant	TTBEG
	TTEND	Time to end recording	Constant	TTFIN
	KKEVT	Event record printing	'Y' or 'N'	'Y'
SEEDS	ISEED	Starting random number seed. If negative, use complement of value	Integer	See data statement in DRAND
	IS	Stream number	Positive integer $\leq$ 10	Next sequential stream
	R	Reinitialization of seed value for next run	'Y' or 'N'	'N'
SEVNT	JEVNT	State event code	Positive integer	None
	XVAR	Crossing variable	'SS(N)' or 'DD(N)'	None
	XDIR	Direction of crossing	X→ both directions, XP→ positive crossing, XN→ negative crossing	None
	VALUE	Threshold value for crossing	Constant, 'SS(I)', 'DD(I)'	0.0
	TOL	Tolerance for crossing	Positive constant	∞

Table C2 continued.

SIMULATE

STAT	ICLCT	Statistics code used in calls to subroutine COLCT	Positive integer ≤ 25	None
	ID	Collect variable identifier	16 alphanumeric characters	Blanks
	NCEL	Number of interior cells for histogram	0 → no histogram; positive integer	0
	HLOW	Upper limit of first cell of histogram	Constant	0.0
	HWID	Width of each cell	Positive constant	1.0
TIMST	VAR	Time-persistent variable	'XX(I)', 'SS(I)', or 'DD(I)'	None
	ID	Identifier	16 alphanumeric characters	Blanks
VAR	DEPVAR	Dependent variable for RECORD statement	'SS(I)', 'DD(I)' or 'XX(I)'	None
	SYMBL	Plotting symbol	1 character	Blank
	ID	Identifier	8 alphanumeric characters	Blanks
	LOORD	Low ordinate specification	Constant, 'MIN' or 'MIN(R)'	'MIN'
	HIORD	High ordinate specification	Constant, 'MAX' or 'MAX(R)'	'MAX'

APPENDIX D

SLAM Error Codes and Messages

Error Code	Description
102	Number of state equations incorrectly specified
103	Number of derivative equations incorrectly specified
106	Variable defining number of events on the event calendar is negative
211	Number of collect variables incorrectly specified, or NNCLT value destroyed due to an index of an array out of range
212	Number of time-persistent statistics incorrectly specified, or the variable NNSTA destroyed due to an index out of range
213	Incorrect specification for a histogram number, or value of NNHIS destroyed due to an index out of range
214	Incorrect specification for number of files, or MFIL destroyed due to an index out of range
221	Initialization of file structure requested when maximum number of entries in the file was specified as zero
312	Incorrect pointer to next event
411	File pointer structure has an inconsistency which was detected during a search for an entry
499	Incorrect specification when attempting to make a value assignment or a duration specification
502	Number of observations for a collect variable is negative $(SSOBV(J,3)<0)$.
511	Number of time-persistent variables greater than maximum allowed
521	Histogram number out of range
531	Independent variable of plot is not monotonic
541	Incorrect file values when attempting to print information on a file
551	Incorrect number of equations for state variables when attempting to print state variable values
568	Incorrect network values when attempting to print information on activities
701	Argument out of range or not specified for collect variable, stream number, etc.
811	Request for zero or negative number of resources
901	Pointer to node description incorrect
999	Incorrect index for computing time-persistent statistics on a state variable

Error Code	*Description*
1001	Gate number out of range
1002	Resource number out of range
1003	Stream number out of range
1004	Collect variable number out of range
1005	Activity number out of range
1006	File number out of range
1007	Rank of entry in file out of range
1008	Attribute number out of range
1009	Enter node number out of range
1010	Incorrect specification for MONTR option
1011	Code for stopping activity (STOPA) out of range
1012	TIMST statistics index out of range
1013	State-event code in call to SSEVT out of range
1014	Plot number out of range in call to PRNTP
1020	Entity arrival to MATCH node
1021	Attempt to preempt resource with capacity not equal to 1
1022	Attempt to preempt an entity that is in a service activity
1023	Incorrect specification for cumulative probability distribution
1024	Incorrect parameter specification
1025	Rank of file member referenced is greater than the number of entries in file
1026	Space allocated to files is insufficient
1027	Arguments to subroutine GDLAY incorrectly specified (IFS > ILS)
1028	Attempt to run simulation backwards in time
1029	Specified integration accuracy cannot be met
1030	Number of activities exceeds allowed limit (Redimension array JJVEC)
1031	Number of activities exceeds allowed limit (Redimension array IIACT)
1032	Number of resources increased beyond prescribed capacity
1033	State-event cannot be detected within the prescribed tolerance value
1034	Incorrect specification for auxiliary attributes

APPENDIX E

SLAM Runge-Kutta-Fehlberg Integration

The integration method provided by SLAM is a fourth (fifth) order, variable step size Runge-Kutta routine for integrating systems of first-order ordinary differential equations with initial values. The particular constants and error estimation used are from Fehlberg(2) as further described by Shampine and Allen(3).

Runge-Kutta integration has three advantages that make it an appropriate method for SLAM. First, it is widely used and well-documented. For example, most CSSLs provide Runge-Kutta integration. Second, it is easy to change the step size with a Runge-Kutta routine. This is very important in a combined simulation where events are not normally spaced uniformly in time. The third advantage is closely related to the second. Runge-Kutta integration is self-starting, thus there is no loss of efficiency when restarting from an event. This is of critical importance in a combined simulation.

There are two disadvantages of Runge-Kutta. First, it requires more derivative evaluations per step than some other methods of equivalent accuracy. For example, a fourth (fifth) order Runge-Kutta-Fehlberg (RKF45) method requires six derivative evaluations per step whereas a predictor-corrector method of the same accuracy may require as few as two. A second disadvantage of a Runge-Kutta method is that it is difficult and expensive to find suitable truncation error estimates. Shampine et al provide a good state-of-the-art review of this topic(4).

The RKF algorithm employed in SLAM estimates the local error by simultaneous computation of fourth and fifth order approximations. This method permits the step size to be changed with little additional computation. A derivation and description of Runge-Kutta methods are contained in most books on numerical analysis (1,3)

The Runge-Kutta-Fehlberg method provides the specific capability of numerically integrating a system of first-order ordinary differential equations of the form

$$y'(t) = f(y(t);t)$$

with initial conditions $y(t_o)$ where $y'(t) = dy(t)/dt$. If $y(t)$ is a vector, the above equation represents a system of first-order simultaneous differential equations. It is assumed in the equations given below that $y(t)$ is a vector.

The RKF algorithm is a one step procedure involving six function evaluations over a step of size h. Let $t_1 = t_o + h$. The procedure as implemented in SLAM for computing $y(t_1)$ involves the evaluation of the following equations:

$$a_1 = hf(y(t_o); t_o)$$

$$a_2 = hf(y(t_o) + \frac{1}{4} a_1 \; ; \; t_o + 1/4 \, h)$$

$$a_3 = hf(y(t_o) + \frac{3}{32} a_1 + \frac{9}{32} a_2 \; ; \; t_o + \frac{3}{8} h)$$

$$a_4 = hf(y(t_o) + \frac{1932}{2197} a_1 - \frac{7200}{2197} a_2 + \frac{7296}{2197} a_3 \; ; \; t_o + \frac{12}{13} h)$$

$$a_5 = hf(y(t_o) + \frac{439}{216} a_1 - 8a_2 + \frac{3680}{513} a_3 - \frac{845}{4104} a_4 \; ; \; t_o + h)$$

$$a_6 = hf(y(t_o) - \frac{8}{27} a_1 + 2a_2 - \frac{3544}{2565} a_3 + \frac{1859}{4104} a_4 - \frac{11}{40} a_5 \; ; \; t_o + \frac{1}{2} h)$$

$$EERR = \frac{1}{360} a_1 - \frac{128}{4275} a_3 - \frac{2197}{75240} a_4 + \frac{1}{50} a_5 + \frac{2}{55} a_6$$

$$y(t_o + h) = y(t_o) + \frac{25}{216} a_1 + \frac{1408}{2565} a_3 + \frac{2197}{4104} a_4 - \frac{1}{5} a_5$$

$$TERR = AAERR + RRERR *|y(t_o+h)|$$

where **AAERR** and **RRERR** are the user-specified absolute and relative error values.

In the above procedure a_j is a vector and **EERR** is computed for each state variable. Only if the $EERR \leq TERR$ for all state variables will the $y(t_1)$ be accepted.

The implementation of the above procedure is contained in subroutine GGASP. The function evaluations are obtained through calls to subroutine STATE with the appropriate values for SS($\cdot$) and TNOW representing the two arguments, that is, $f(u;v)$ is evaluated by a call to STATE with $u = SS(\cdot)$ and $v = TNOW$. The value of the function is the value of the derivative of SS($\cdot$) and is stored in DD($\cdot$), which is then available to compute the values of a_j. The procedure is performed over the interval DTFUL so that h is equal to DTFUL. The time interval for specific evaluations is made available as DTNOW.

In the RKF procedure, a variable step size is employed. Let Q be equal to the largest value of |EERR|/TERR for any state variable defined by a differential equation. If Q > 1.0, the values are not accepted and h is reduced. If Q ≤ 1.0, the values are accepted and, depending on the value of Q, the next step size may be increased. If the step is accepted or rejected, the new step size is related to the value of $h/Q^{1/5}$. The new step size is maintained within the user-specified minimum and maximum allowable step sizes, that is,

$$\text{DTMIN} \leq h_{new} \leq \text{DTMAX}$$

The RKF procedure permits the integration of sets of simultaneous differential equations. However, equations of the form y = f(y;t), in which f is not the integration operator, usually require an iterative method of solution. SLAM does not provide such a method since convergence is highly dependent on the set of equations. The user can code such a method directly into subroutine STATE.

REFERENCES

1. Carnahan, B. H., H. A. Luther, and J. O. Wilkes, *Applied Numerical Methods,* John Wiley, 1969.
2. Fehlberg, E., "Low-Order Classical Runge-Kutta Formulas with Step-Size Control and Their Application to Some Heat Transfer Problems," NASA Report TR R-315, Huntsville, Alabama, April 15, 1969.
3. Shampine, L. F. and R. C. Allen, Jr., *Numerical Computing: An Introduction,* W. B. Saunders, 1973.
4. Shampine, L. F. et al., "Solving Non-Stiff Ordinary Differential Equations—The State of the Art," *SIAM Review,* Vol. 18, 1976, pp. 376-411.

Commonly Used FORTRAN Statements

Statement	Use	Example
Arithmetic	Define value for variable	$A = 2. * B + R ** 3$
READ	Define variable through input:	
	Formatted	READ(NCRDR,100)C,D,I
	Unformatted	READ(IUNIT)(B(J),J=1,100)
WRITE	Print values for output:	
	Formatted	WRITE(NPRNT,200)A,B,R,J
	Unformatted	WRITE(IOUT)(ATRIB(I),I=1,NNATR)
FORMAT	Define field lengths for inputs and outputs	200 FORMAT (1X,6HVALUE=,F6.2,E12.4,F10.0,I8)
STOP	End program execution	STOP
END	Last statement of subprogram	END
GO TO	Unconditional transfer	GO TO 7
IF	Conditional transfer (arithmetic)	IF(B**2-4.*A*C)10,20,30
	Conditional transfer (logical)	IF(TNOW.LE.200.0)Q=17.0
DO	Looping through statements	DO 40 I=1,N,2
CONTINUE	Dummy statement	CONTINUE
DIMENSION	Size arrays	DIMENSION AUXF(1000), VECT(10)
Statement Function	One line FUNCTION	VOL(X,Y,Z)=X*Y*Z
FUNCTION	Subprogram to return a value	FUNCTION RNORM(AVE,STD,ISTRM)
SUBROUTINE	Subprogram to perform computations	SUBROUTINE ARRIVE SUBROUTINE COLCT(WAIT,ICLCT)

Statement	Use	Example
RETURN	Return from a subprogram	RETURN
CALL	Invoke a subroutine	CALL COLCT(10.0,1)
COMMON	To make variable and array values the same in different programs	
	Unnamed or Blank†	COMMON A(10),B,IN(100)
	Named or Labeled	COMMON/UCOM1/BUSY(10),TBA,STATUS
DATA	Define variables at compile time	DATA A,B,C/5.0,2.3E+2,−7.2/
Type	Declare variables to be a nonstandard type	INTEGER X, BUSY REAL MSL, NR LOGICAL BINARY, IVAL DOUBLE PRECISION BESS, QUAD COMPLEX INDUCT, CAP
EQUIVALENCE	Define variables to be the same‡	EQUIVALENCE (NSET(1),QSET(1)),(XX(1),BUS)
Computed GO TO	Conditional transfer	GO TO (1,2,3,4), JEVNT

† User Blank COMMON statements are not permitted when coding in SLAM.
‡ Two variables in COMMON cannot be equivalenced.

SLAM Random Sampling Procedures

In this appendix, the methods and equations used in SLAM to obtain random samples from the common distributions are described. In addition, procedures for obtaining random samples from less commonly used distributions are presented. In the discussion, R will be a pseudorandom number. For convenience, the stream number I normally associated with R will be suppressed. Subscripts are used to indicate different random numbers or samples. For definitions of the variables (arguments) and equation forms, see Table 4-2 and Section 2.9.

Uniform Distribution

> Function Name: UNFRM(A, B, I)
> Method: Inverse transformation
> Equation: UNFRM = A + (B − A) * R

Triangular Distribution

> Function Name: TRIAG(A, D, B, I)
> Method: Inverse transformation (10)
> Equations:

$$\text{For } 0 \le R \le \frac{D - A}{B - A}; \text{TRIAG} = A + \text{SQRT}((D - A)*(B - A)*R)$$

$$\text{For } \frac{D - A}{B - A} < R \le 1; \text{TRIAG} = B - \text{SQRT}((B - D)*(B - A)*(1. - R))$$

Normal Distribution

> Function Name: RNORM(U,S,I)
> Method: Transformation of variables used in conjunction with sample rejection
> (1,4)

Procedure: Normal samples are generated in pairs.
Let $A = 2.*R_1 - 1.$ and $B = 2.*R_2 - 1.$
Let $W = A*A + B*B$
If $W > 1.0$, repeat procedure
If $W \leq 1.0$ then
$RNORM_1 = (A*SQRT(-2.*ALOG(W)/W))*S + U$
$RNORM_2 = (B*SQRT(-2.*ALOG(W)/W))*S + U$

Exponential Distribution

Function Name: EXPON(U,I)
Method: Inverse transformation
Equation: $EXPON = -U*ALOG(R)$

Poisson Distribution

Function Name: NPSSN(U,I)
Method: The number of exponential samples in a unit interval (10)
Procedure: Set the sample value, NPSSN, equal to the first value of N such that

$$\prod_{n=1}^{N} R_n \geq e^{-U} > \prod_{n=1}^{N+1} R_n$$

where R_n is the nth pseudorandom number.

Erlang Distribution

Function Name: ERLNG(U,K,I)
Method: Sum K exponential samples each having a mean equal to U
Equation: $ERLNG = -U*ALOG(\prod_{i=1}^{K} R_i)$

Lognormal Distribution

Function Name: RLOGN(U,S,I)
Method: Use a sample, N, from a normal distribution in the equation $L = e^N$.
It can be shown that if N is normally distributed L is lognormally distributed (2).
Equation: $RLOGN = EXP(RNORM(\mu_N, \sigma_N, I)$

where $\sigma_N^2 = \ln(S^2/U^2+1.)$

and $\mu_N = \ln U - \frac{1}{2}\sigma_N^2$

Gamma Distribution

Function Name: GAMA(β,α,I)

Method: The method for obtaining a sample from a gamma distribution is a function of the parameter α. More efficient methods are employed as α is increased. When α is an integer, Function ERLNG should be employed.

For $0 < \alpha < 1$, the method of Jöhnk is employed (3).

For $1 \leqq \alpha < 5$, the method of Fishman (5) as modified by Tadikamalla is employed (12).

For $\alpha \geqq 5$, a weighted selection of Erlang samples is employed.

Procedure: For $0 < \alpha < 1$:

Let $X = R_1{**}(1./\alpha)$ and $Y = R_2{**}(1./(1. - \alpha))$

If $X + Y \leqq 1$, compute $W = X/(X+Y)$. Otherwise recompute X and Y.

Let GAMA $= W{*}(-\text{ALOG}(R_3)){*}\beta$

For $1 \leqq \alpha < 5$:

Let $a = [\alpha]$ and $b = a - [\alpha]$

Compute $X = (\alpha/a){*}(-\text{ALOG}(\overset{a}{\underset{i=1}{\text{II}}} R_i))$

If $R_{a+1} > (X/\alpha)^b \exp(-b{*}\text{INT}(X/\alpha-1.)-1.)$, recompute X.

Otherwise GAMA $= X{*}\beta$

For $\alpha \geqq 5$:

If $R_1 \geqq a - [\alpha]$, GAMA $= \text{ERLNG}(\beta,[\alpha],I)$

If $R_1 < a - [\alpha]$, GAMA $= \text{ERLNG}(\beta,[\alpha] + 1,I)$

Beta Distribution

Function Name: BETA(α,β,I)

Method: Transformation of variables where the beta sample is the ratio of two gamma samples (5)

Equation: BETA $= G1/(G1 + G2)$

where $G1 = \text{GAMA}(1,\alpha,I)$ and $G2 = \text{GAMA}(1,\beta,I)$

Weibull Distribution

Function Name: WEIBL(β,α,I)

Method: Inverse transformation (7)

Equation: WEIBL $= (-\beta{*}\text{ALOG}(R)){**}(1./\alpha)$

where β is a scale parameter and α is a shape parameter.

Probability Mass Function

Function Name: DPROB(CPROB, VALUE, NVAL, I)
Method: Inverse transformation
Procedure: Set DPROB equal to VALUE(N) when
$CPROB(N-1) < R \leq CPROB(N)$ where $CPROB(0) = 0.0$ and $N = 1$ to
NVAL

METHODS FOR OBTAINING SAMPLES FROM OTHER DISTRIBUTIONS

Truncated Distribution

If a sample is desired between the specified limits A and B then generate a sample and if it is within the prescribed limits, accept the sample. If it is outside the limits, reject the sample and repeat the procedure.

Mixed Truncated Distribution

A mixed truncated distribution assumes that samples between A and B are desired and a sample that exceeds either limit is set equal to the limiting value. To obtain samples from a mixed truncated distribution, accept a sample if it is within the limits specified. If the sample is larger than B, set the sample value to B. If the sample is less than A, set the sample value to A.

Truncated Exponential

The inverse transformation equation can be used directly for obtaining a sample from a truncated exponential distribution with the limits (A,B). The cumulative distribution function for a truncated exponential is

$$F_T(x) = \begin{cases} 0 & \text{if } x < A \\ \dfrac{F_X(x) - F_X(A)}{F_X(B) - F_X(A)} & \text{if } A \leq x \leq B \\ 1.0 & \text{if } x > B \end{cases}$$

and

$TEXPON = -U*ALOG((1-R)*EXP(-A*U)+R*EXP(-B*U))$

Cauchy Distribution

Even though a Cauchy random variable is the ratio of two independent standard normal random variables, it is simpler to use the inverse transformation method to generate samples (7).

Chi-Square Distribution

If the degrees of freedom, f, are even, use an Erlang sample that is the sum of f/2 exponential samples each with a mean value of ½. If the degrees of freedom, f, are odd, add the square of a standardized normal ($\mu = 0$, $\sigma = 1$) to a chi-square sample with (f $-$ 1) degrees of freedom. A sample from the F-distribution can be obtained as the ratio of two chi-square samples. A sample from the t-distribution can be obtained as the ratio of a standardized normal sample to a chi-square sample.

Other Discrete Distributions

The inverse transformation method can be used to obtain samples from commonly used discrete distributions. Consider the geometric distribution, for example. If p is the probability of success on a Bernoulli trial then a geometric random variable is the number of trials until the first success is obtained. A geometric random sample is computed as log R/log(1 $-$ p) rounded up if fractional to the next larger integer. Similar procedures are available for the negative binomial and hypergeometric distributions(5,6).

Parameterized Distributions

Pearson (9) and Johnson (6,8) have developed systems of distributions which provide a complete range of shapes. In fact, any first four moments may be obtained by using the appropriate parameter values. However, generation of samples from these systems is complicated since both systems use multiple distribution forms. Schmeiser and Deutsch present a distribution which can assume any first moments (11). Random sampling from this distribution can be performed using the inverse transformation method as shown below:

$$IF(R.LE.XL4) \quad X = XL1 - XL2*(LX4 + R)**XL3$$
$$IF(R.GT.XL4) \quad X = XL1 + XL2*(R - XL4)**XL3$$

The density function and distribution function corresponding to X, the possible distribution shapes, and the procedures for estimating the XLi parameters are detailed by Schmeiser and Deutsch(11).

REFERENCES

1. Ahrens, J. H. and U. Dieter, "Computer Methods for Sampling from the Exponential and Normal Distributions," *Comm. ACM*, Vol. 15, 1972, pp. 873-882.
2. Aitchison, J. and J. A. C. Brown, *The Lognormal Distribution*, Cambridge Press, 1957.
3. Berman, M. B., *Generating Random Variates from Gamma Distributions with Non-Integer Shape Parameters*, The RAND Corporation, R-641-PR, Santa Monica, CA., November 1970.

4. Box, G. E. P. and M. A. Miller, "A Note on the Generation of Random Normal Deviates," *Annals of Math. Stat.,* Vol. 29, 1958, pp. 610-611.

5. Fishman, G. S., *Principles of Discrete Event Simulation,* John Wiley, 1978.

6. Hahn, G. J. and S. S. Shapiro, *Statistical Models in Engineering,* John Wiley, 1967.

7. Hastings, N. A. J. and J. B. Peacock, *Statistical Distributions,* Butterworth, 1975.

8. Johnson, N. L., "Systems of Frequency Curves Generated by Methods of Translation," *Biometrika,* Vol. 36, 1949, pp. 149-176.

9. Pearson, K., "Contributions to the Mathematical Theory of Evolution, II. Skew Variations in Homogeneous Material, *Philosophical Transactions of the Royal Society of London, Series A,* Vol. 186, 1895, pp. 343-414.

10. Pritsker, A. A. B., *The GASP IV Simulation Language,* John Wiley, 1974.

11. Schmeiser, B. W. and S. T. Deutsch, "A Versatile Four Parameter Family of Probability Distributions Suitable for Simulation," *AIIE Transactions,* Vol. 9, 1977, pp. 176-182.

12. Tadikamalla, P. R., "Computer Generation of Gamma Random Variables," *Comm. ACM,* Vol. 21, 1978, pp. 419-421.

Index